D1482076

CURRENT
SOVIET POLICIES
IV

CURRENT
SOVIET POLICIES
IV

THE DOCUMENTARY RECORD OF THE
22nd CONGRESS OF THE COMMUNIST PARTY
OF THE SOVIET UNION

Edited by CHARLOTTE SAIKOWSKI *and* LEO GRULIOW

From the Translations of

THE CURRENT DIGEST OF THE SOVIET PRESS

With a WHO'S WHO OF THE CENTRAL COMMITTEE

Compiled by MARK NEUWELD

COLUMBIA UNIVERSITY PRESS   *New York and London*   1962

ACKNOWLEDGMENTS

This book would be incomplete without credit to the Joint Committee on Slavic Studies appointed by the American Council of Learned Societies and the Social Science Research Council for the patient support which has made possible both the Current Digest and this book. The members of the Joint Committee on Slavic Studies are Abram Bergson, Harvard University, Chairman; Robert F. Byrnes, Indiana University, Secretary; John A. Armstrong, University of Wisconsin; C. E. Black, Princeton University; Deming Brown, University of Michigan; William B. Edgerton, Indiana University; Chauncy D. Harris, University of Chicago; Charles Jelavich, University of California; Henry L. Roberts, Columbia University; Marshall D. Shulman, Harvard University; Donald W. Treadgold, University of Washington, and Sergius Yakobson, Library of Congress.

Acknowledgments are due to the gifted staff of editors and translators whose work has gone into this book, particularly Joseph Wigglesworth, copy editor, and Robert Hankin, translator; Robert Potts, Alex Peskin, Carolyn Rogers, Cerisa Shopkow, and Norman Sloan. Thanks are due to the proofreaders, Ronald Branch and Lucille M. Friesen, and to Agnes Forrest Gruliow, who prepared the index.

CONTENTS

INTRODUCTION

THOSE MILESTONES of Soviet history, the postwar Congresses of the Communist Party of the Soviet Union, have each produced a surprise that overshadowed anything on the formal agenda.

The 19th Congress was held in 1952, ostensibly to approve the directives for the Fifth Five-Year Plan and to amend the Party Statutes. In fact it proved to be the stage setting for a macabre purge that was headed off only by Stalin's death.

The 20th Congress, in 1956, was called to adopt directives for the Sixth Five-Year Plan, but its highlight turned out to be Khrushchev's unscheduled "secret" speech disclosing some of Stalin's crimes.

The 21st was an Extraordinary Congress, convened out of turn in 1959 to adopt a seven-year plan in place of the five-year plan. It focused its attention instead on denunciation of the so-called anti-Party group that had tried to unseat Khrushchev in 1957, and it added new names to the list of known members of this group.

The 22nd Congress, in 1961, had the announced aim of adopting a new Party Program and new Party Statutes to bring them in line with the promised advent of communism. But the spotlight shifted unexpectedly to the removal of Stalin's body from the mausoleum on Red Square and the clash with the Albanian Communists and their Chinese supporters.

THE SURPRISES that marked the successive Party Congresses are matched by another striking feature: the extent to which the work of each Congress has been undone in many major respects within a short time or has been set aside for years before being followed up.

Stalin's death, of course, broke the chain of events which the 19th Congress was preparing in 1952. Khrushchev's sensational speech on Stalin at the 20th Congress was never published in the Soviet Union, and it was several years before it flowered into extensive de-Stalinization; while the Sixth Five-Year Plan adopted at that Congress was abandoned within a year and a half. The fulminations against the "anti-Party group" during the Extraordinary 21st Congress were not followed up until the 22nd, two years later.

Behind these starts, stops and postponements lies a power struggle that comes to light from time to time in flashes of disclosure such as the Kremlin showdown in 1957 and the Albanian schism of 1961.

It is at such times that policy differences become embodied in names—Molotov, Malenkov, Zhukov, Khrushchev—and the pretense of complete unity is temporarily dropped.

Even when the disclosures cast light on the nature of the men and policies involved in the struggle, there is always the nagging puzzle of what really happened and what the defeated men stood for, since in Soviet politics the victor writes the record without challenge or contradiction, and this record is often obscure.

IN THIS CONTINUING POWER STRUGGLE every clue is of value to the analyst and observer; and the Congress documents and Congress proceedings are among the most valuable of our clues.

In perspective the Congresses show, moreover, a continuity of long-range goals and of patterns of political behavior that overrides the surprises, the reversals and the postponements. This continuity, from the 19th Congress decision to revise the Party Program to the adoption of the revised Program nearly a decade later, illumines the whole of Soviet development right up to the present day.

It is because of the lasting importance of this material and the immediate significance of the clues it affords for the interpretation of contemporary Soviet developments that this series of books is published. The introductions to previous volumes in the series have outlined the role played by the Communist Party and its Congresses in Soviet political life and have sketched the background of events leading up to the previous Congresses. The 22nd Congress came so close on the heels of its predecessor and so much has been written about it elsewhere that it has been deemed unnecessary to describe the setting in detail here.

The translations in this book are reprinted from the Current Digest of the Soviet Press, a weekly published at Columbia University by the Joint Committee on Slavic Studies appointed by the American Council of Learned Societies and the Social Science Research Council. Since 1949 the Current Digest has been providing researchers and scholars with week-by-week translations of the documents and current reporting appearing in Soviet newspapers and periodicals. These translations are printed without comment or interpretation. To meet the space limitations of this book, the Current Digest translations of the 22nd Congress proceedings had to be condensed by omitting a number of lesser speeches and the repetitive portions of other speeches at the Congress, as indicated in the text. The record is assembled in book form, with a detailed index and a "Who's Who" of the Central Committee, in the hope that it will be of use to scholars generally.

LEO GRULIOW,
Editor, The Current Digest of the Soviet Press.

New York, June 15, 1962.

I. THE PARTY PROGRAM

The Party Program approved by the 22nd Party Congress (below) is identical with the draft of the Program published July 30, 1961—Current Digest of the Soviet Press, Vol. XIII, Nos. 28, 29 and 30—except for the changes indicated: additions and substitutions by *italics* and deletions by square brackets. Underlining indicates bold face in the Russian text.

THE PROGRAM OF THE COMMUNIST PARTY OF THE SOVIET UNION. (Pravda and Izvestia, Nov. 2, pp. 1-9. Complete text:) INTRODUCTION.—The Great October Socialist Revolution ushered in a new era in the history of mankind, the era of the downfall of capitalism and the establishment of communism. Socialism has triumphed in the Land of Soviets and has achieved decisive victories in the people's democracies; it has become a practical cause to hundreds of millions of people and the banner of the revolutionary movement of the working class of the whole world.

More than 100 years ago Karl Marx and Friedrich Engels, the great teachers of the proletariat, wrote in "The Communist Manifesto": "A specter is haunting Europe—the specter of communism." The courageous and selfless struggle of the proletarians of all countries has brought mankind nearer to communism. First tens and hundreds of people, then thousands and millions, inspired by the ideals of communism, stormed the old world. The Paris Commune, the October Revolution and the socialist revolutions in China and in a number of other countries of Europe and Asia—these are the major historical stages in the heroic battles fought by the international working class for the victory of communism. A very long road, a road drenched in the blood of fighters for the people's happiness, a road of glorious victories and temporary setbacks was traversed before communism, which had once seemed a mere *dream* [specter], became the greatest force of modern times and a society that is being built over vast areas of the globe.

At the beginning of the 20th century the center of the international revolutionary movement shifted to Russia. Russia's heroic working class, led by the party of Bolsheviks headed by Vladimir Ilyich Lenin, became the vanguard of this movement. The Communist Party inspired and led the socialist revolution; it was the organizer and leader of the first workers' and peasants' state in history. The shining genius of Lenin, *the great teacher of the working people of the whole world* whose name will live forever, illumines mankind's road to communism.

The Leninist party of Communists, emerging into the arena of political struggle, raised high over the world the banner of revolutionary Marxism. Marxism-Leninism became the powerful ideological weapon for the revolutionary transformation of society. At each *historical* stage [of historical development] the Party, guided by the teachings of Marx, Engels and Lenin, accomplished the tasks scientifically formulated in its Programs.

In adopting its first Program at its Second Congress, in 1903, the Bolshevist party called on the working class and all the working people of Russia to struggle for the overthrow of the tsarist autocracy and then of the bourgeois system and for the establishment of the dictatorship of the proletariat. In February, 1917, the tsarist regime was swept away. In October, 1917, the proletarian revolution destroyed the capitalist system so hated by the people. A country of socialism came into being for the first time in history. The creation of a new world began.

The first Program of the Party had been carried out.

In adopting the second Program at the Eighth Congress, in 1919, the Party set the task of building a socialist society. Treading unexplored paths and overcoming difficulties and hardships, the Soviet people, under the leadership of the Communist Party, carried out the plan for socialist construction drawn up by Lenin. Socialism triumphed in the Soviet Union completely and finally.

The second Program of the Party has also been carried out.

The very great revolutionary feat accomplished by the Soviet people roused and inspired the masses of the people of all countries and continents. A mighty cleansing thunderstorm is sweeping across the world marking the springtime of mankind. The socialist revolutions in countries of Europe and Asia led to the formation of a world socialist system. A powerful wave of national-liberation revolutions is sweeping away the colonial system of imperialism.

One-third of mankind is building a new life under the banner of scientific communism. The first detachments of the working class to have broken away from the oppression of capitalism are facilitating the victory of new detachments of their class brothers. The world of socialism is expanding, the world of capitalism is shrinking. Socialism will inevitably succeed capitalism everywhere. Such is the objective law of social development. Imperialism is powerless to check the irresistible process of liberation.

The present epoch, the fundamental content of which is the transition from capitalism to socialism, is an epoch of struggle between the two opposing social systems, an epoch of socialist and national-liberation revolutions, an epoch of the downfall of imperialism and the abolition of the colonial system, an epoch of the transition of more and more peoples to the path of socialism, of the triumph of socialism and communism on a worldwide scale. The central factor of the present epoch is the international working class and its chief creation, the world socialist system.

Today the Communist Party of the Soviet Union (C.P.S.U.) is adopting its third Program, a program for the building of a communist society. The new Program creatively generalizes the practice of socialist construction, it takes account of the experience of the revolutionary movement throughout the world, and, expressing the collective thought of the Party, it defines the chief tasks and basic stages of communist construction.

The supreme goal of the Party is to build a communist society on whose banner will be inscribed, "From each according to his abilities, to each according to his needs." The Party's slogan, "Everything in the name of man, for the benefit of man," will be put into effect in full.

The Communist Party of the Soviet Union, true to proletarian internationalism, always follows the militant slogan "Proletarians of all countries, unite!" The Party considers communist construction in the U.S.S.R. as the Soviet people's great internationalist task, in keeping with the interests of the world socialist system as a whole and with the interests of the international proletariat and all mankind.

Communism accomplishes the historic mission of delivering all men from social inequality, from all forms of oppression and exploitation, from the horrors of war, and affirms on earth Peace, Labor, Freedom, Equality, *Brotherhood* and Happiness for all peoples.

PART I. THE TRANSITION FROM CAPITALISM TO COMMUNISM—THE ROAD OF DEVELOPMENT OF MANKIND

I. THE HISTORICAL INEVITABILITY OF THE TRANSITION FROM CAPITALISM TO SOCIALISM.—The world-historic turning of mankind from capitalism to socialism, begun by the October Revolution, is a logical result of the development of society. Marxism-Leninism, having discovered the objective laws of social development, showed the contradictions inherent in capitalism and the inevitability of their revolutionary explosion and of the transition of society to communism.

Capitalism is the last exploiting system. Having developed productive forces enormously, it then turned into a tremendous obstacle to social progress. Capitalism alone is responsible for the fact that the 20th century, a century of colossal growth of productive forces and scientific development, has not yet put an end to the poverty of hundreds of millions of people, has not provided an abundance of material and spiritual benefits for all men on earth. The growing conflict between the productive forces and production relations imperatively confronts mankind with the task of breaking the rotted capitalist framework, unfettering the powerful productive forces created by man and using them for the benefit of all society.

Whatever the particular features of the rise and development of capitalism in this or that country, this system everywhere has common characteristics and objective laws.

The development of world capitalism and of the revolutionary struggle of the working class has fully confirmed the correctness of the Marxist-Leninist analysis of capitalism and its highest stage, imperialism, presented in the first and second Programs of the Party. The basic propositions of this analysis are also given below in the present Program.

Under capitalism, the basic and decisive means of production belong to the numerically small class of capitalists *and landowners*, while the vast majority of the population consists of proletarians and semiproletarians, deprived of means of production and obliged in view of this to sell their labor power and by their labor to create the profits and wealth of the ruling classes of society. The bourgeois state, regardless of its form, is an instrument of the domination of labor by capital.

The development of large-scale capitalist production—production for profit, for the appropriation of surplus value—leads to the elimination of small independent producers, to their onerous dependence on capital. Capitalism exploits woman and child labor extensively. The economic laws of its development inevitably lead to the formation of a huge reserve army of unemployed, which is constantly replenished by ruined peasants and urban petty bourgeoisie. The exploitation of the working class and of all the working people constantly increases, social inequality grows, the gulf between the haves and the have-nots widens and the sufferings and privations of the millions multiply.

Capitalism, by concentrating millions of workers in factories and plants and socializing the labor process, gives production a social character, but the results of the labor are appropriated by the capitalists. This basic contradiction of capitalism—the contradiction between the social character of production and the private-capitalist form of appropriation—manifests itself in production anarchy and in the lag of society's purchasing power behind the expansion of production and leads periodically to destructive economic crises. Crises and periods of industrial stagnation, in turn, still further ruin the small producers, increase even more the dependence of wage labor on capital and lead even more rapidly to the relative, and sometimes absolute, deterioration of the condition of the working class.

As the contradictions inherent in bourgeois society grow and develop, the dissatisfaction of the working people and the exploited masses with the capitalist system also grows, the number and the solidarity of the proletarians increase and their class struggle against the exploiters becomes sharper. At the same time more and more swiftly there arises the material possibility of replacing capitalist production relations with communist production relations—that is, the social revolution that constitutes the goal of the Communist Party, as the conscious exponent of the class movement of the proletariat.

The working class, the most consistent revolutionary class, is the chief motive force of the revolutionary transformation of the world. In the course of class struggles it becomes organized, sets up its trade unions and political parties, and wages an economic, political and theoretical struggle against capitalism. In fulfilling its historic mission as the revolutionary remaker of the old society and creator of a new system, the working class becomes the exponent not only of its own class interests but of the interests of all working people. It is the natural leader of all the forces fighting against capitalism.

The dictatorship of the proletariat and leadership by the Marxist-Leninist party are necessary conditions for the victory of the socialist revolution and the building of socialism. *The highest principle of the dictatorship of the proletariat is the firm alliance between the working class and the toiling peasant masses under the leadership of the working class.*

The process of the concentration and centralization of capital, destroying free competition, led at the beginning of the 20th century to the establishment of powerful capitalist monopoly associations—syndicates, cartels and trusts—which acquired decisive importance in the entire economic life; to the merging of bank capital and immensely concentrated industrial capital; and to the intensified export of capital to other countries. The trusts, encompassing entire groups of capitalist powers, began the economic division of a world already divided territorially among the wealthiest countries. Capitalism entered its final stage, the stage of monopoly capitalism, of imperialism.

The period of a more or less smooth extension of capitalism all over the globe gave way to spasmodic, catastrophic development, causing an unprecedented growth and aggravation of all the contradictions of capitalism—economic, political, class and national. The struggle of the imperialist powers for markets, for spheres of capital investment, for raw materials and manpower—for world domination—became more intense than ever. In an epoch of the undivided rule of imperialism, that struggle inevitably led to devastating wars.

Imperialism is decaying and dying capitalism; it is the eve of the socialist revolution. The world capitalist system as a whole has become ripe for the social revolution of the proletariat.

The extraordinarily high degree of development of world capitalism generally; the replacement of free competition by state-monopoly capitalism; the preparation, by banks as well as by alliances of capitalists, of machinery for the social regulation of the production and the distribution of products; the rising cost of living and the oppression of the working classes by the syndicates, which are due to the growth of capitalist monopolies; the enslavement of the working class by the imperialist state, and the vastly increased difficulty of the economic and political struggle of the proletariat; and the horrors, hardships and ruination caused by imperialist war—all this has made inevitable the collapse of capitalism and the transition to a higher type of social economy.

The revolutionary downfall of imperialism does not take place simultaneously all over the world. The unevenness of the economic and political development of the capitalist countries under imperialism leads to the occurrence of revolutions at different periods in different countries. V. I. Lenin developed the theory of the socialist revolution in the new historical circumstances; he worked out the doctrine of the possibility of the victory of socialism first in a single, separate capitalist country.

Russia was the weakest link in the imperialist system and the focal point of all its contradictions. At the same time, it had all the conditions necessary for the victory of socialism. The working class of Russia was the most revolutionary and best organized in the world and possessed considerable experience of class struggle. At its head stood a Marxist-Leninist party armed with advanced, revolutionary theory and steeled in class battles.

The party of Bolsheviks brought together in one revolutionary stream the struggle of the working class for socialism, the country-wide movement for peace, the peasants' struggle for land and the national-liberation struggle of the oppressed peoples of Russia, and directed these forces toward the overthrow of capitalism.

II. THE WORLD-HISTORIC SIGNIFICANCE OF THE OCTOBER REVOLUTION AND OF THE VICTORY OF SOCIALISM

IN THE U.S.S.R.—Having breached the front of imperialism in Russia, one of the world's largest countries, Great October established the dictatorship of the proletariat and created a new type of state—the Soviet state—and a new type of democracy—democracy for the working people.

The workers' and peasants' rule, born of the revolution, took Russia out of the blood bath of the imperialist war, saved the country from the national catastrophe to which the exploiting classes had doomed it and delivered the peoples of Russia from the menace of enslavement to foreign capital.

The October Revolution undermined the economic foundation on which the system of exploitation and social injustice rested. The Soviet regime nationalized industry, the railroads, banks and the land. It abolished landed proprietorship and fulfilled the peasants' age-old dream of land.

The October Revolution smashed the chains of national oppression; it proclaimed and ensured the right of nations to self-determination, even so far as to secede. The revolution did not leave stone upon stone of the rank and class privileges of the exploiters. For the first time in history, it emancipated woman and granted her equal rights with man.

The socialist revolution in Russia shook the entire structure of world capitalism to its very foundations; the world split into two opposing systems.

For the first time there emerged in the international arena a state that put forward the great slogan of peace and began carrying out new principles in relations among peoples and countries. Mankind acquired a reliable bulwark in its struggle against wars of conquest and for peace and the security of peoples.

The October Revolution led the country onto the road of socialism. The path that faced the Soviet people was an arduous and unexplored one. The reactionary forces of the old world did all they could to strangle Soviet rule in the cradle. The young Soviet Republic had to cope with intervention and civil war, economic blockade and economic devastation, conspiracies, sabotage, subversion, terrorism and many other trials. Socialist construction was rendered incredibly difficult by the socio-economic, technical and cultural backwardness of the country. The victorious workers and peasants lacked knowledge of state administration and the experience necessary for the construction of a new society. The difficulties of socialist construction were multiplied tenfold by the fact that for almost 30 years the U.S.S.R. was the world's only socialist state and was subjected to sharp attacks by the hostile capitalist encirclement. Consequently the class struggle in the period of transition from capitalism to socialism was acute.

The opponents of Leninism maintained that Russia allegedly was not ripe for a socialist revolution, that it was impossible to build socialism in one country. But the opponents of Leninism were put to shame.

A wise, farsighted policy, unshakable stanchness and organization, and a firm faith in their own strength and in the strength of the people were required of the Party and the working class. In a highly complicated international situation, with a relatively weak industrial base and in a country whose economy had been utterly ruined by war and one that had a tremendous preponderance of small-scale commodity production, it was necessary to steer the right course in socialist construction and to ensure the victory of socialism.

The Party proved equal to this historic task. Under Lenin's leadership, it worked out a plan for the radical transformation of the country, for the construction of socialism. Lenin gave the proletarian state a profoundly scientific policy for the entire period of transition from capitalism to socialism. He evolved the New Economic Policy (NEP), designed to bring about the victory of socialism. The main elements of Lenin's plan for the building of a socialist society were industrialization of the country, agricultural cooperation and a cultural revolution.

The Party upheld this plan in a sharp struggle against skeptics and capitulators, against the Trotskyites, Right opportunists, national deviationists and other hostile groups. It rallied the whole of the Soviet people *to the struggle* to carry out Lenin's design.

The question then stood thus: Either perish or forge full steam ahead and overtake the capitalist countries economically.

The Soviet country had first of all to solve the problem of industrialization. In a historically very brief period, without outside help, the Soviet Union built up a large-scale modern industry. By the time it had fulfilled three five-year plans (1929-1941), the Soviet Union had become a mighty industrial power and had achieved complete economic independence from the capitalist countries. The defense capacity of the Soviet state had increased immeasurable. The industrialization of the U.S.S.R. was a great feat performed by the working class and the whole people, who spared neither efforts nor means and consciously accepted deprivations to lift the country out of backwardness.

The fate of socialism in a country such as the U.S.S.R. largely depended on the solution of a most difficult problem, namely, changing from small-scale strip farming to the path of socialist cooperation. Under the leadership of the Party, with the utmost aid and support of the working class, the peasantry took the path of socialism. Millions of small individual farms were voluntarily combined into collective farms. A broad network of Soviet state farms and Machine and Tractor Stations was set up. The Soviet village's change to large-scale socialist farming meant a great revolution in economic relations, in the entire way of life of the peasantry. Collectivization delivered the countryside forever from kulak bondage, from class stratification, ruin and poverty. The eternal peasant problem found its true solution on the basis of Lenin's cooperative plan.

The building of socialism required a rise in the cultural level of the broadest masses of the people. This task, too, was successfully accomplished. A cultural revolution was carried out in the country. It brought the working masses out of spiritual enslavement and darkness and gave them access to the cultural riches accumulated by mankind. The country, the majority of whose population had been illiterate, took a huge stride to the heights of science and culture.

Socialism, the inevitability of which had been scientifically predicted by Marx and Engels—socialism, the plan for the construction of which was mapped out by Lenin, became a reality in the Soviet Union.

Socialism has done away forever with the domination of private ownership of the means of production, that source of the division of society into antagonistic classes. Socialist ownership of the means of production has become the solid economic foundation of society. Unlimited opportunities have opened up for the development of the productive forces.

Socialism has solved the great social problem of eliminating the exploiting classes and the causes of the exploitation of man by man. Two friendly classes remain in the U.S.S.R.—the working class and the peasantry. And furthermore, these classes themselves have changed. The common character of the two forms of socialist ownership has brought the working class and the collective farm peasantry close together; it has strengthened their alliance and made their friendship indestructible. A new intelligentsia, coming from the people and devoted to socialism, has arisen. The former antithesis between town and country-side, between mental and physical labor, has been eliminated. On the basis of the community of the fundamental interests of workers, peasants and intelligentsia, an indestructible socio-political and ideological unity of the Soviet people has arisen.

The socialist principle "From each according to his abilities, to each according to his labor" has been put into effect in the Soviet country. This principle ensures that the members of society have a material interest in the results of their labor; it makes it possible to harmonize personal and social interests in the best way and serves as a powerful stimulus for increasing the productivity of labor, advancing the economy and raising the people's standard of living. The working people's consciousness that they are working not for exploiters but for themselves, for their society, gives rise to labor enthusiasm, innovation, creative initiative and mass socialist competition. Socialism is living creativity by the working masses. The growing activeness of the masses of the people in the building of a new life is a law of the socialist epoch.

The aim of socialism is to satisfy the growing material and cultural requirements of the people ever more fully by constantly developing and improving social production.

The entire life of socialist society is based on the principle of broad democracy. Working people take an active part, through the Soviets, trade unions and other mass public organizations, in managing the affairs of the state and in solving problems of economic and cultural construction. Socialist democracy includes both political freedoms—freedom of speech, of the press and of assembly, the right to elect and be elected—and also social rights—the right to work, to leisure, to *free* education *and medical care,* to material security in old age and in case of illness or disability; equality of citizens of all races and nationalities; equal rights for women and men in all spheres of state, economic and cultural life. Socialist democracy, unlike bourgeois democracy, does not merely proclaim the rights of the people but makes it really possible for the people to exercise them. Soviet society ensures true freedom of the individual. The highest manifestation of this freedom is man's emancipation from exploitation. Genuine social justice lies in this above all.

Socialism has created *the most favorable* conditions for the flourishing of science. The successes of Soviet science are a vivid manifestation of the superiority of the socialist system and testify to the unlimited possibilities of scientific progress and to the growing role of science under socialism. It is only logical that the country of victorious socialism should have been the first to open the era of the utilization of atomic energy for peaceful purposes and that it should have been the first to blaze the trail into outer space. The artificial satellites of the earth and the sun, powerful space rockets and interplanetary spaceships, atomic power stations and the world's first triumphal *orbitings* [orbiting] of the globe, accomplished by Soviet man in a spaceship, have become symbols of the creative powers of ascendant communism and a source of pride for all mankind.

The solution of the national question is one of the greatest achievements of socialism. This question is of particular importance to a country like the Soviet Union, which has more than a hundred nations and nationalities. Socialist society has not only ensured the political equality of nations but has also abolished the economic and cultural backwardness inherited from the old system. Relying on mutual fraternal aid, and above all aid from the great Russian people, all the Soviet national republics have created their own modern industry, trained their own national cadres of the working class and intelligentsia, and developed cultures that are national in form and socialist in content. Many formerly backward *peoples* [nations] have attained socialism, bypassing the capitalist stage of development. The union and solidarity of equal peoples on a voluntary basis in a single multi-national state—the Union of Soviet Socialist Republics; their close cooperation in state, economic and cultural construction; fraternal friendship; and the flourishing of their economy and culture constitute a most important result of the Leninist national policy.

To the Soviet people fell the historic role of originator, pioneer and blazer of the new path of social development. This demanded of them special efforts, an untiring quest for forms and methods of building the new society and the testing of them in the crucible of practice. For almost two decades, out of slightly more than 40 years, the Soviet people were obliged to devote their energies to repelling invasions by the imperialist powers and to restoring the war-ravaged economy. The Soviet system underwent a particularly severe test during the years of the Great Patriotic War, the most grievous war in history. The victory of the Soviet people in that war proved that there are no forces in the world capable of halting the progress of socialist society.

What are the basic lessons to be learned from the path traversed by the Soviet people?

The experience of the U.S.S.R. has shown that peoples can achieve socialism only as a result of socialist revolution and the dictatorship of the proletariat. Despite certain specific features resulting from concrete historical conditions of socialist construction in the Soviet Union in the circumstances of a hostile capitalist encirclement, this experience has fully confirmed the fundamental principles of socialist revolution and socialist construction, principles that are of universal significance.

The experience of the U.S.S.R. has shown that socialism alone can put an end to the exploitation of man by man, to production anarchy, economic crises, unemployment and poverty of the masses, and can ensure planned, continuous and rapid development of the economy and steady improvement in the people's standard of living.

The experience of the U.S.S.R. has shown that the working class can fulfill its historic mission as the builder of a new society only in firm alliance with the nonproletarian working masses, above all with the peasantry.

The experience of the U.S.S.R. has shown that the victory of the socialist revolution alone provides all the possibilities and conditions for wiping out all national oppression, for the voluntary union of free and equal nations and nationalities in a single state.

The experience of the U.S.S.R. has shown that the socialist state serves as the basic instrument for the socialist transformation of society. It organizes and rallies the masses, carries out planned guidance of economic and cultural construction and safeguards the revolutionary gains of the people.

The experience of the U.S.S.R. has shown that socialism and peace are indivisible. The might of socialism serves the cause of peace. The Soviet Union saved mankind from fascist enslavement. The Soviet state, standing guard over peace and implementing the Leninist principle of peaceful coexistence *of states with different social systems,* is a mighty barrier in the way of imperialist aggression.

The experience of the U.S.S.R. has fully confirmed the Marxist-Leninist teaching on the decisive role of the Communist Party in the formation and development of socialist society. Only a party that unswervingly pursues a class, proletarian policy and that is armed with advanced revolutionary theory, only a party solidly united and closely linked with the masses, can organize the whole people and lead them to the victory of socialism.

The experience of the U.S.S.R. has shown that fidelity to and firm and unswerving application of the principles of Marxism-Leninism, the principles of proletarian internationalism and defense of these principles against any and all enemies and opportunists are necessary conditions for the victory of socialism.

The practical experience of the world's greatest revolution and of the socialist transformation of a society that has attained unprecedented heights in its development and flowering has confirmed the historical correctness of Leninism, has dealt a crushing blow to the ideology of social reformism.

As a result of the self-sacrificing labor of the Soviet people and the theoretical and practical activity of the Communist Party of the Soviet Union, mankind has received an actually existing socialist society and a science of socialist construction that has been tested in practice. The highroad to socialism has been built. Many peoples are already traveling along it. Sooner or later it will be taken by all peoples.

III. THE WORLD SYSTEM OF SOCIALISM.—The Soviet Union is not pursuing the tasks of communist construction alone but in the fraternal family of socialist countries.

The rout of German fascism and Japanese militarism in World War II, in which the Soviet Union played the decisive part, created favorable conditions for the overthrow of capitalist and landlord rule by the peoples in a number of countries of Europe and Asia. The peoples of Albania, Bulgaria, Hungary, the German Democratic Republic, the Democratic Republic of Vietnam, China, the Korean People's Democratic Republic, Poland, Rumania and Czechoslovakia [in Russian alphabetical order.—Trans.], and, earlier, the Mongolian People's Republic—forming together with the Soviet Union the socialist camp—took the path of building socialism. Yugoslavia also took the socialist path. But the Yugoslav leaders by their revisionist policy counterposed Yugoslavia to the socialist camp and the international Communist movement, creating a threat of the loss of the Yugoslav people's revolutionary gains.

The socialist revolutions in countries of Europe and Asia dealt a further powerful blow to the positions of imperialism. The victory of the revolution in China was of particular importance. The revolutions in countries of Europe and Asia constitute the biggest event in world history since October, 1917.

There arose a new form of the political organization of society—people's democracy, one of the forms of the dictatorship of the proletariat. It reflected the distinctive development of the socialist revolution in the circumstances of the weakening of imperialism and the change in the balance of forces in favor of socialism. It also reflected the distinctive historical and national features of the countries.

There emerged a world socialist system —a social, economic and political commonwealth of free sovereign peoples pursuing the path of socialism and communism, joined by common interests and goals and by the close ties of international socialist solidarity.

In the people's democracies socialist production relations prevail and the socio-economic possibility of the restoration of capitalism has been eliminated. The successes of these states have completely confirmed that in all countries, regardless of the level of their economic development, their area and population, true progress can be ensured only on socialist paths.

The united forces of the socialist camp reliably safeguard each socialist country against the encroachments of imperialist reaction. The consolidation of the socialist states in a single camp and its increasing unity and steadily growing might assure the complete victory of socialism within the framework of the system as a whole.

The countries of the socialist system have accumulated rich collective experience in changing the lives of hundreds of millions of people and have contributed much that is new and specific to the forms of political and economic organization of society. This experience is a most valuable asset of the international revolutionary movement.

It has been confirmed by practice and recognized by all the Marxist-Leninist parties that the processes of the socialist revolution and of socialist construction are founded on a number of major objective laws applicable to all countries that enter on the path of socialism.

The world socialist system is a new type of economic and political relationship among countries. The socialist countries have a uniform economic basis—public ownership of the means of production; a uniform type of state system—rule of the people headed by the working class; a single ideology—Marxism-Leninism; common interests in the defense of their revolutionary gains and national independence from encroachments by the imperialist camp; and a single great goal—communism. This common socio-economic and political nature creates an objective foundation for firm and friendly interstate relations within the socialist camp. Complete equality, respect for independence and sovereignty, and fraternal mutual assistance *and cooperation* are distinctive features of the relations among the countries of the socialist commonwealth. In the socialist camp or—which is the same thing—in the world commonwealth of socialist countries, no one has or can have any special rights or privileges.

The experience of the world socialist system has confirmed the need for the closest alliance of countries that have left capitalism, for uniting their efforts in the building of socialism and communism. The policy of building socialism in isolation, detached from the world commonwealth of socialist countries, is theoretically untenable because it conflicts with the objective laws governing the development of socialist society. It is harmful economically because it causes waste of social labor, retards the rates of growth of production and leads to dependence of the country upon the capitalist world. It is politically reactionary and dangerous because it does not unite but divides the peoples before the combined front of imperialist forces, because it nourishes bourgeois-nationalist tendencies and may ultimately lead to the loss of socialist gains.

Joining their efforts in the building of a new society, the socialist states are actively supporting and expanding political, economic and cultural cooperation with countries that have cast off the colonial yoke. They maintain—and are prepared to maintain—broad, mutually advantageous trade relations and cultural ties with capitalist countries.

The development of the world socialist system and the development of the world capitalist system are governed by diametrically opposed laws. Whereas the world capitalist system emerged and developed in fierce struggle among the states composing it, through the subjection and exploitation of weak countries by the strong, through the enslavement of hundreds of millions of people and the reduction of whole continents to the status of colonial appendages of the imperialist metropolitan countries, the process of the formation and development of the world socialist system proceeds on the basis of sovereignty, is completely voluntary, and accords with the fundamental interests of the working people of all the states of this system.

Whereas the world capitalist system is governed by the law of uneven economic and political development, leading to conflicts among states, the world socialist system is governed by opposite laws, ensuring the steady, planned growth of the economies of all the countries belonging to it. In the world of capitalism growth of production in one country or another deepens the contradictions among states and intensifies the mutual competitive struggle. But the development of each socialist country promotes the general progress and strengthening of the world socialist system as a whole. Whereas the economy of world capitalism develops slowly and experiences crises and upheavals, the economy of world socialism is marked by high and stable rates of growth and by the common uninterrupted economic advance of all the socialist countries.

All the socialist states make their contribution to the construction and development of the world socialist system and to strengthening its might. The existence of the Soviet Union greatly facilitates and accelerates the building of socialism in the people's democracies. The Marxist-Leninist parties and the peoples of the socialist states proceed from the fact that the successes of the world socialist system as a whole depend on the contribution and efforts of each country, and therefore they consider the greatest possible development of the productive forces of their country an internationalist duty. The cooperation of the socialist states enables each of them to use its resources and develop its productive forces most rationally and fully. A new type of international division of labor is taking shape in the process of the economic, scientific and technical cooperation of the socialist countries, the coordination of their economic plans and the specialization and cooperation of production.

The establishment of the Union of Soviet Socialist Republics and later of the world socialist system is the beginning of the historical process of developing the closest community of peoples. With the disappearance of class antagonisms in the fraternal family of socialist states, national antagonisms also disappear. The flowering of the cultures of the peoples of the socialist commonwealth is attended by a constantly increasing mutual enrichment of the national cultures and the active forming of the internationalist traits characteristic of the man of socialist society.

The experience of the peoples of the world socialist commonwealth has confirmed that their fraternal unity and cooperation conform to the supreme national interests of each country. The strengthening of the unity of the world socialist system on the basis of proletarian internationalism is an absolute requirement for the further successes of all the states belonging to it.

The socialist system must overcome certain difficulties stemming chiefly from the fact that in the past most of the countries in this system had a medium or even a low level of economic development, and also from the fact that world reaction is doing its utmost to impede the building of socialism.

The experience of the Soviet Union and the people's democracies has confirmed the correctness of Lenin's thesis that the class struggle does not disappear in the period of the building of socialism. The common trend of development of the class struggle within the socialist countries in the conditions of successful socialist construction leads to a strengthening of the position of the socialist forces and a weakening of the resistance of the remnants of the hostile classes. However, this development does not follow a straight line. Changes in the domestic or foreign situation may cause intensification of the class struggle in certain periods. This calls for constant vigilance in order to frustrate promptly the intrigues of hostile forces within and without which persist in their attempts to undermine the people's system and to sow strife in the fraternal family of socialist countries.

Nationalism is the basic political and ideological weapon used by international reaction and the remnants of the domestic reactionary forces against the unity of the socialist countries. Manifestations of nationalism and national narrow-mindedness do not disappear automatically with the establishment of a socialist system. Nationalist prejudices and survivals of former national friction are the sphere in which resistance to social progress may be most prolonged, stubborn, fierce and insidious.

The Communists consider it their prime duty to educate the

working people in a spirit of internationalism, socialist patriotism and intolerance of any manifestations of nationalism and chauvinism. Nationalism damages the common interests of the socialist commonwealth, and above all it harms the people of the country in which it appears, since estrangement from the socialist camp retards the country's development, deprives it of the possibility of making use of the advantages of the world socialist system and encourages attempts by imperialist powers to utilize the nationalist tendencies for their own purposes. Nationalism can gain the upper hand only where a consistent struggle is not waged against it. A Marxist-Leninist internationalist policy and a determined struggle to overcome survivals of bourgeois nationalism and chauvinism are an important condition for the further strengthening of the socialist commonwealth. Yet while Communists oppose nationalism and national egoism, they always show the utmost consideration for the national feelings of the masses.

The world socialist system is confidently advancing to decisive victory in the economic competition with capitalism. In the near future it will surpass the world capitalist system in total volume of industrial and agricultural output. The influence of the world socialist system on the course of social development in the interests of peace, democracy and socialism is growing more and more.

The majestic edifice of the new world being built by the heroic labors of the free peoples of vast areas of Europe and Asia is the prototype of the new society, of the future of all mankind.

IV. THE CRISIS OF WORLD CAPITALISM.—Imperialism has entered the period of decline and fall. The inexorable process of disintegration has seized capitalism from top to bottom —its economic and state system, its politics and ideology. Imperialism has irretrievably lost its power over the majority of mankind. The chief content, the chief direction and the chief features of the historical development of mankind are being determined by the world socialist system, by the forces fighting against imperialism and for the socialist reorganization of society.

World War I and the October Revolution ushered in the general crisis of capitalism. The second stage of the general crisis of capitalism developed at the time of World War II and the socialist revolutions in a number of countries of Europe and Asia. World capitalism has now entered a new, third stage of this crisis. A most important feature of this new stage is that its development was not linked with a world war.

The breaking away of more and more countries from capitalism; the weakening of the positions of imperialism in the economic competition with socialism; the disintegration of the colonial system of imperialism; the sharpening of the contradictions of imperialism with the development of state-monopoly capitalism and the growth of militarism; the intensified internal instability and decay of the capitalist economy, evidenced in the increasing inability of capitalism to make full use of productive forces (low rates of growth of production, periodic crises, constant underemployment of production capacity and chronic unemployment); the mounting struggle between labor and capital; an acute intensification of the contradictions within the world capitalist economy; an unprecedented growth of political reaction in all spheres, repudiation of bourgeois freedoms and the establishment of fascist and despotic regimes in a number of countries; and the profound crisis in the policy and ideology of the bourgeoisie—all these are manifestations of the general crisis of capitalism.

In the stage of imperialism state-monopoly capitalism receives extensive development. The emergence and growth of monopolies leads to the direct intervention of the state in the process of capitalist reproduction in the interests of the financial oligarchy. In its interests, the bourgeois state institutes various regulatory measures and resorts to the nationalization of some branches of the economy. World wars and economic crises, militarism and political upheavals have accelerated the evolution of monopoly capitalism into state-monopoly capitalism.

Oppression by finance capital keeps growing. Giant monopolies that have taken control of the bulk of social production dominate the life of the nation. A small handful of billionaires and millionaires wields untrammeled power over the entire wealth of the capitalist world and turns the life of entire nations into small change for the sake of their selfish deals. The financial oligarchy is becoming fabulously rich. The state is becoming a committee for the management of the affairs of the monopoly bourgeoisie. The bureaucratization of all economic life is increasing sharply. State-monopoly capitalism unites the power of the monopolies and the power of the state in a single mechanism for the purposes of enriching the monopolies, suppressing the working class movement and the national-liberation struggle, saving the capitalist system and unleashing aggressive wars.

The Right socialists and revisionists are trying to picture state-monopoly capitalism almost as socialism. Life is exposing this falsehood. State-monopoly capitalism does not change the nature of imperialism. Not only does it not alter the position of the principal classes in the system of social production; it widens the gap between labor and capital, between the majority of the nation and the monopolies. Attempts at state regulation of the capitalist economy cannot eliminate competition and anarchy of production, cannot ensure the planned development of the economy on the scale of the society, because capitalist ownership and the exploitation of wage labor remain the basis of production. The bourgeois theories of a "crisis-free" and "planned" capitalism have been laid in the dust by the entire course of development of the contemporary capitalist economy. The dialectic of state-monopoly capitalism is such that instead of strengthening the capitalist system, as the bourgeoisie expects, it further sharpens the contradictions of capitalism and shakes it to its foundations. State-monopoly capitalism is the fullest material preparation for socialism.

The new phenomena in the development of imperialism confirm the correctness of Lenin's conclusions about the fundamental objective laws of capitalism in its final stage and about its increasing decay. At the same time this decay does not signify complete stagnation, a paralysis of its productive forces, and does not exclude growth of the capitalist economy at particular times and in particular countries.

All in all, capitalism is increasingly fettering the development of contemporary productive forces. Mankind is entering a period of the greatest scientific and technical revolution bound up with the mastery of nuclear energy, the conquest of outer space, the development of chemistry, the automation of production and other major achievements of science and technology. But the production relations of capitalism are too narrow for the scientific and technical revolution. Socialism alone is capable of carrying out this revolution and of applying its fruits in the interests of society.

Technical progress under the rule of monopoly capital is being turned against the working class. Employing new forms, the monopolies are intensifying the exploitation of the working class. Capitalist automation is robbing the worker of his daily bread: Unemployment is rising and the standard of living is falling. Technical progress is throwing overboard more and more strata of small producers. Imperialism is using technical progress chiefly for military purposes. It is turning the achievements of the human mind against humanity itself. As long as imperialism continues to exist, mankind cannot feel secure about its future.

Modern capitalism has made the market problem extremely acute. Imperialism is incapable of solving this problem, for the lag of the purchasing power of the working people behind growth of production is one of its objective laws. Moreover, it retards the industrial development of the underdeveloped countries. The world capitalist market is shrinking relative to the more rapidly expanding production capacity. It is partitioned by countless customs barriers and restrictive fences and split into exclusive currency and finance zones. A sharp competitive struggle for markets, spheres of capital investment and sources of raw materials is under way in the imperialist camp. This struggle is acquiring an even sharper character since the territorial sphere of capitalist domination has been greatly narrowed.

Monopoly capital in the final analysis has doomed bourgeois society to low rates of production growth, which in some countries barely keep ahead of the growth of population. A considerable part of the production capacity lies idle, while millions of unemployed stand at the factory gates. Agricultural output is being artificially restricted, although millions in the world are hungry. People suffer a shortage of material goods, but imperialism is squandering *material resources and social labor* [them] on war preparations.

The liquidation of the capitalist system in a large group of countries, the development and strengthening of the world so-cialist system, the disintegration of the colonial system and the collapse of old empires, the breaking up of the colonial econom-ic structure that is beginning in the newly free countries and the expanding economic links between these countries and the world of socialism—all this is deepening the crisis of the world capitalist economy.

State-monopoly capitalism is intensifying militarism to an unprecedented degree. The imperialist states maintain im-mense armed forces even in peacetime. Military expenditures devour an ever-growing portion of the state budgets. The im-perialist states are turning into militarist, military-police states; militarization pervades the life of bourgeois society.

Militarism, while enriching some groups of the monopoly bourgeoisie, leads to the exhaustion of nations, to the ruin of peoples languishing under the burden of taxes, growing infla-tion and a high cost of living. Within the lifetime of one gener-ation imperialism plunged mankind into the abyss of two de-structive world wars. In World War I the imperialists anni-hilated ten million people and maimed twenty million. World War II claimed almost fifty million lives. In the course of these wars entire countries were ravaged, thousands of cities and villages were destroyed and the fruits of the labor of many generations were wiped out. The new war being hatched by the imperialists threatens mankind with unprecedented human losses and destruction. Even the preparations for it bring suffering and privation to millions of people.

The progress achieved in the development of productive forces and the socialization of labor is being usurped by the contempo-rary capitalist state in the interests of the monopolies.

The monopoly bourgeoisie has become a useless growth on the social organism, superfluous to the process of production. Plants and factories are run by hired managers, engineers and technicians. The monopolists lead a parasitic life, and together with their entourages swallow up a substantial portion of the na-tional income created by the labor of the proletarians and peas-ants.

Fear of revolution, the successes of the socialist countries and the pressure of the workers' movement oblige the bourgeoi-sie to make partial concessions with respect to wages, working conditions and social security. But right and left, rising prices and inflation reduce these concessions to nil. Wages lag behind the material and cultural requirements of the worker and his family, which are growing as society develops. Even the rela-tively high standard of living in the small group of capitalisti-cally developed countries rests on the poverty of peoples of Asia, Africa and Latin America, on unequal exchange, on dis-crimination against female labor and on brutal oppression of Negroes and immigrant workers, as well as on the intensified exploitation of the working people of these countries themselves. The bourgeois myth of "full employment" has proved to be a cruel mockery: The working class constantly suffers from mass unemployment and insecurity. In spite of individual successes in the economic struggle of the working class, on the whole its position in the capitalist world is deteriorating.

The development of capitalism finally dispelled the legend of the stability of small peasant farming. The monopolies have seized dominant positions in agriculture as well. Millions of farmers and peasants are being driven off the land and their farms sold under the hammer. Small farms survive only at the price of appalling hardships, underconsumption and excessive labor by the peasants. The peasantry is groaning under the burden of mounting taxes and debts. Agrarian crises are bring-ing ever greater ruin to the countryside. Incredible depriva-tions and poverty fall to the lot of the peasants in the colonial and dependent countries; they suffer under a double yoke—that of the landlords and that of the monopoly bourgeoisie.

The monopolies are also ruining small urban proprietors. Craft production is being driven out. Small-scale industrial and trade enterprises are fully dependent upon the monopolies.

Life has fully confirmed the Marxist thesis about the intensi-fication of proletarization in capitalist society. The expropriated masses have no other prospect of acquiring property than the establishment by revolutionary means of public ownership of the means of production, that is, making them the property of the whole people.

The uneven development of capitalism is changing the balance of forces among states and sharpening the contradictions be-tween them. The economic, and following that the political and military, center of imperialism has shifted from Europe to the U.S.A. American monopoly capital, bloated with war profits and the arms race, has seized the basic sources of raw materials, the markets and the spheres of capital investment, has created a *kind of* [covert] colonial empire and become the biggest world exploiter. Wrapping itself in the spurious flag of freedom and democracy, American imperialism is in effect performing the role of world gendarme, supporting reactionary dictatorial regimes and decayed monarchies, opposing democratic, revolu-tionary changes and unleashing aggressions against peoples who are fighting for independence.

The U.S. monopoly bourgeoisie is the chief bulwark of inter-national reaction. It has assumed the role of "savior" of capital-ism. The U.S. financial magnates are knocking together a "holy alliance" of imperialists and setting up aggressive military blocs. American troops and military bases are stationed at the most important points of the capitalist world.

But life is showing the utter futility of U.S. imperialism's claims to world domination. Imperialism has proved incapable of stemming the socialist and national-liberation revolutions. American imperialism's calculations that it would have a monop-oly of atomic weapons fell through. The U.S. monopolies have been unable to retain their share of the economy of the capital-ist world, although they remain its chief economic, financial and military force. The U.S.A., the strongest capitalist power, has passed its zenith and entered the stage of decline. Such impe-rialist states as Great Britain, France, Germany and Japan have also lost their former might.

The basic contradiction of the contemporary world—the con-tradiction between socialism and imperialism—does not elimi-nate the deep contradictions rending the capitalist world. The aggressive military blocs set up under the aegis of the U.S.A. repeatedly prove to be in a state of crisis. The international state-monopoly organizations springing up under the slogan of "unification" and the mitigation of the market problem are in reality new forms of the redivision of the world capitalist mar-ket and are becoming focal points of sharp friction and conflicts.

The contradictions between the principal imperialist powers are growing deeper. The economic reconstruction of the im-perialist states defeated in World War II is leading to the revi-val of old key points of imperialist rivalry and conflict and the emergence of new ones. The Anglo-American, American-French, Franco-*West* German, American-*West* German, Anglo-*West* German, [and] Japanese-American *and other* contradic-tions are becoming especially acute [while other contradictions are also becoming sharper]. Fresh contradictions will inevi-tably arise and deepen in the imperialist camp.

The American monopolies and their British and French allies are openly assisting the resurgence of West German imperial-ism, which is cynically advocating revanchist, aggressive aims and preparing a war against the socialist states and other Euro-pean countries. A dangerous focal point of aggression, menac-ing the peace and security of all peoples, is being revived in the center of Europe. In the Far East the American monopolies are reviving Japanese militarism *which is to a definite extent de-pendent on them;* this is another dangerous hotbed of war threat-ening the peoples of Asia, and above all, the socialist states.

The interests of the small group of imperialist powers are in-compatible with the interests of the other countries, the inter-ests of all peoples. Profound antagonism divides the imperial-ist states from the countries that have won national independence and countries that are fighting for liberation.

Contemporary capitalism is hostile to the vital interests and progressive aspirations of all mankind. Capitalism, with its exploitation of man by man, with its chauvinist and racist ide-ology, with its inherent moral decay, its rampant profiteering, corruption and crime, is debasing society, the family and man.

The bourgeois system was born with the alluring slogans of liberty, equality, fraternity. But the bourgeoisie used these slogans only to displace the feudal gentry and assume power. Instead of equality, a new gaping abyss of social and economic inequality has appeared. Not fraternity but ferocious class struggle reigns in bourgeois society.

Monopoly capital is baring its reactionary, antidemocratic essence more and more clearly. It does not tolerate even the former bourgeois-democratic freedoms, although it *hypocritically* [demagogically] proclaims them. At this stage of historical development the bourgeoisie finds it harder and harder to propagandize the slogans of equality and liberty as it used to. The advance of the international workers' movement restricts finance capital's freedom of maneuver, and it cannot quench the revolutionary sentiments *of the masses* and cope with the inexorably growing *revolutionary*, anti-imperialist movement by using the old slogans and by bribing the workers' bureaucracy.

Monopoly capital, having seized all the basic material means, refuses to share political power with anyone. It has established its own dictatorship, the dictatorship of the minority over the majority, the dictatorship of the capitalist monopolies over society. The ideologists of imperialism are disguising the dictatorship of monopoly capital under false slogans of freedom and democracy and, proclaiming the imperialist states to be countries of the "free world," they represent the ruling bourgeois circles as opponents of all dictatorship. In reality, however, freedom in the imperialist world means only freedom to exploit the working class and the working people not only in one's own country but in all the other countries that fall under the iron heel of the monopolies.

The bourgeoisie widely advertises the allegedly democratic nature of its election system, particularly glorifying the existence of many parties and the possibility of nominating many candidates. In reality, however, the monopolists deprive the masses of the people of the possibility of expressing their will and of electing true champions of their interests. Possessing such powerful resources as capital, the press, radio, the cinema and television and *utilizing* their henchmen in the trade unions and other mass organizations, the monopolists mislead the masses and impose their own candidates upon the electorate. The various bourgeois parties usually represent only various segments of the ruling bourgeoisie.

The dictatorship of the bourgeoisie also manifests itself in gross violation of the will of the electorate. Whenever the bourgeoisie sees that the working people, taking advantage of their constitutional rights, might elect a considerable number of champions of their interests to the legislative bodies, it brazenly discards the election system and arbitrarily limits the number of representatives of the working people in the parliament.

The financial oligarchy resorts to the establishment of fascist regimes, relying on the army, police and gendarmerie as a last refuge from the people's wrath, particularly when the masses of working people try to use even the curtailed democratic rights left to them, try to defend their interests and to end the omnipotent power of the monopolies. Although the naked German and Italian fascism smashed up, a fascist regime still survives in some countries and is being revived in new forms in others.

Thus the world imperialist system is rent by deep and acute contradictions. The antagonism of labor and capital, the contradictions between the people and the monopolies, growing militarism, the disintegration of the colonial system, the contradictions among the imperialist countries, conflicts and contradictions between the young national states and the old colonialist powers and—most important of all—the precipitous growth of world socialism are undermining and destroying imperialism and leading to its weakening and collapse.

The monopoly bourgeoisie cannot shoot its way out of the unalterable course of historical development even with nuclear weapons. Mankind has discerned the true face of capitalism. Hundreds of millions of people see that capitalism is a system of economic chaos and periodic crises, of chronic unemployment and mass poverty, of predatory waste of productive forces, a system constantly fraught with the danger of war. Mankind does not want to and will not tolerate the historically obsolete system of capitalism.

V. THE INTERNATIONAL REVOLUTIONARY MOVEMENT OF THE WORKING CLASS.

—The international revolutionary movement of the working class has won world-historic successes. Its greatest victory has been the world socialist system. The example of victorious socialism is exerting a revolutionizing influence on the minds of the working people of the capitalist world, inspiring them to struggle against imperialism and greatly easing the conditions of this struggle.

Within the womb of capitalist society the social forces called upon to bring about the victory of socialism are taking shape, multiplying and becoming steeled. A new detachment of the international proletariat—the young workers' movement of the newly liberated, dependent and colonial countries of Asia, Africa and Latin America—has entered the world arena. Marxist-Leninist parties have been established and have grown. They are becoming a more and more authoritative and generally recognized national force heading broad strata of the working people.

The international revolutionary movement has accumulated vast experience in the struggle against imperialism and its accomplices in the ranks of the working class. It has become ideologically more mature and possesses great organized might and a militant fighting spirit. The role of the trade union movement, which unites vast masses of working people, is increasing.

The countries of capitalism are constantly shaken by class battles. The working class is conducting militant actions in defense of its economic and political interests. The working class and the working people have more than once threatened the class rule of the bourgeoisie. In an effort to maintain its power, the finance oligarchy, in addition to methods of suppression, uses various means of deceiving and corrupting the working class and its organizations and of splitting the trade union movement on a national and international scale. It resorts to bribing the top stratum of trade union, cooperative and other organizations and enlarges the workers' bureaucracy, to which it allots lucrative positions in industry, the municipal bodies and the state apparatus. Anti-Communist and antilabor legislation, the banning of Communist Parties, mass dismissal of Communists and other progressive workers, blacklisting in industry, loyalty checks of office employees, police repression of the democratic press, and the suppression of strikes with the help of armed forces have all become routine methods of action for the governments of the imperialist bourgeoisie to preserve its dictatorship.

The reactionary forces in individual capitalist countries can no longer cope with the growing forces of democracy and socialism. The struggle and rivalry of the capitalist states does not preclude, however, a certain unity among them in the face of the mounting forces of socialism and the workers' movement. The imperialists form reactionary alliances; they enter into mutual agreements and set up military blocs and bases aimed not only against the socialist countries but also against the revolutionary workers' and national-liberation movement. The reactionary bourgeoisies of a number of European states have in peacetime opened the doors of their countries to foreign troops.

The bourgeoisie seeks to draw definite lessons from the October Revolution and the victories of socialism. It is using new methods to conceal the ulcers and evils of the capitalist system. Although all these methods complicate the activity of the revolutionary forces in the capitalist countries, they cannot weaken the contradictions between labor and capital.

The world situation today is more favorable to the workers' movement. The successes of the U.S.S.R. and the world socialist system as a whole, the deepening of the crisis of world capitalism, the growth of the influence of the Communist Parties among the masses and the ideological failure of reformism have brought about a substantial change in the conditions of class struggle in favor of the working people. Even in those countries where reformism still holds strong positions, considerable leftward shifts are taking place in the workers' movement.

In the new historical situation, the working class of many countries can compel the bourgeoisie, even before capitalism is overthrown, to carry out measures that transcend ordinary reforms and that are of vital importance both for the working class and the development of its *further* struggle *for the victory of the revolution,* for socialism, and also for the majority of the nation. By uniting *democratic and peace-loving forces* [large sections of the working people], the working class can force the ruling circles to cease preparations for a new world war, to renounce the idea of starting local wars and to utilize the economy for peaceful purposes. *By uniting the working people and the broad masses of the people, the working class* [It] can beat back the offensive of fascist reaction and achieve the accomplishment of a national program for peace, national independence, democratic rights and a definite improvement in the living standard of the people.

The capitalist monopolies are the chief enemy of the working class. They are also the chief enemy of the peasants, artisans and other small urban proprietors, of the majority of office employees and the intelligentsia [and of small capitalists] and even a section of the middle capitalists.

The working class directs its main blow against the capitalist monopolies. All the basic strata of a nation have a vital interest in eliminating the omnipotence of the monopolies. This makes it possible to unite all the democratic movements opposing the oppression of the finance oligarchy into one mighty antimonopoly stream.

The proletariat advances a program of struggle against the omnipotence of the monopolies with regard not only for the immediate but also for the future interests of its allies. It advocates broad nationalization on terms most advantageous to the people [and control by parliament and by trade union and other democratic and representative bodies over the nationalized branches of the economy and over the entire economic activity of the state]. It supports the peasants' demands for radical agrarian reforms and works for the realization of the slogan "The land to those who till it!"

The proletariat, together with other strata of the people, is waging a resolute struggle for broad democracy. It is mobilizing the masses for active opposition to the policy of the finance oligarchy, which strives to abolish democratic freedoms, to restrict the power of parliament, to revise the constitution with the aim of establishing the personal power of henchmen of the monopolies, and to change from the parliamentary system to one or another variety of fascism.

In this struggle is being forged the alliance of the working class and all working people. The working class rallies the peasantry, its basic ally, to combat feudal survivals and domination of the monopolies. Broad strata of the office employees and a considerable section of the intelligentsia, reduced by capitalism to the status of proletarians and recognizing the need for changes in public life, become allies of the working class.

The general democratic struggle against the monopolies does not delay the socialist revolution but brings it nearer. The struggle for democracy is an integral part of the struggle for socialism. The broader the democratic movement, the higher becomes the level of the political consciousness of the masses and the more clearly they see that only socialism opens up to them the path to genuine freedom and well-being. In the course of this struggle, Right-socialist, reformist illusions are dispelled and a political army of the socialist revolution is brought into being.

Socialist revolutions, anti-imperialist national-liberation revolutions, people's democratic revolutions, broad peasant movements, popular struggles to overthrow fascist and other despotic regimes, and general democratic movements against national oppression—all these merge into a single world revolutionary process undermining and destroying capitalism.

The proletarian revolution in each country, being part of the world socialist revolution, is accomplished by the working class and the masses of the people of the given country. The revolution is not carried out by order. It cannot be imposed on the people from without. It results from the profound internal and international contradictions of capitalism. A proletariat that has triumphed cannot impose happiness on *the people of another country* [another people] without thereby undermining its own victory.

Together with the other Marxist-Leninist parties, the Communist Party of the Soviet Union regards it as its internationalist duty to call on the peoples of all countries to rally, mobilize all their internal forces, take vigorous action and, relying on the might of the world socialist system, forestall or firmly repel the interference of the imperialists in the affairs of the people of any country that has risen in revolution, and thereby prevent the imperialist export of counterrevolution. It will be easier to prevent the export of counterrevolution if the working

people, defending the national sovereignty of their country, strive for the elimination of foreign military bases on their territory and for withdrawal from aggressive military blocs.

Communists have never held and do not hold that the road to revolution inevitably lies through wars between states. Socialist revolution is not necessarily linked with war. Although both world wars, which were started by the imperialists, culminated in socialist revolutions, revolutions are quite possible without wars. The great objectives of the working class can be realized without world war. Today the conditions for this are more favorable than ever.

The working class and its vanguard—the Marxist-Leninist parties—*seek to bring about the socialist revolution* [prefer to achieve the transfer of power from the bourgeoisie to the proletariat] by peaceful means [without civil war]. *This* [Realization of this possibility] would meet the interests of the working class and the people as a whole and would accord with the general national interests of the country.

In present-day conditions in a number of capitalist countries the working class headed by its vanguard has the possibility, on the basis of the workers' and popular front and other possible forms of agreement and political cooperation among various parties and public organizations, of uniting the majority of the people, winning state power without civil war and ensuring the transfer of the basic means of production to the hands of the people. The working class, relying on the majority of the people and firmly rebuffing opportunist elements that are incapable of renouncing the policy of compromise with the capitalists and landlords, has the possibility of defeating the reactionary, antipopular forces, winning a solid majority in parliament, transforming it from a tool serving the class interests of the bourgeoisie into a tool serving the working people, launching a broad mass struggle outside parliament, smashing the resistance of the reactionary forces and providing the necessary conditions for peaceful achievement of the socialist revolution. All this will be possible only through broad, constant development of the class struggle of the workers, the peasant masses and the middle urban strata against big monopoly capital, against reaction, for far-reaching social reforms, for peace and socialism.

Where the exploiting classes resort to violence against the people, the possibility of a nonpeaceful transition to socialism should be borne in mind. Leninism teaches, and historical experience confirms, that the ruling classes do not yield power of their own free will. The degree of bitterness of the class struggle and the forms it takes in these conditions depend not so much on the proletariat as on the strength of the reactionary circles' resistance to the will of the overwhelming majority of the people, and on the use of force by these circles at a particular stage of the struggle for socialism. In each country the real possibility of this or that means of transition to socialism depends on concrete historical conditions.

It is not excluded that in conditions of the ever-greater growth of the forces of socialism, of the strengthening of the workers' movement and the weakening of the positions of capitalism, a situation may arise in some countries in which it will be advantageous for the bourgeoisie, as Marx and Lenin foresaw, to agree to sell its basic means of production and for the proletariat to "buy it out."

The success of the struggle of the working class for the victory of the revolution will depend on how well it and its party master all forms of struggle—peaceful and nonpeaceful, parliamentary and extraparliamentary—and how well they are prepared to switch from one form of struggle to another as quickly and unexpectedly as possible. While the principal objective laws of the socialist revolution are common to all countries, the diversity of the national peculiarities and traditions that have arisen in the course of history gives rise to specific conditions of the revolutionary process and a diversity of the forms and tempos of the proletariat's advent to power. This determines the possibility and necessity, in a number of countries, of transitional stages in the development of the struggle for the dictatorship of the proletariat and of a diversity of forms of political organization of the society that is building socialism. But whatever the form in which the transition from capitalism to socialism is effected, it can come about only through revolution. However varied the forms of the new, people's state rule in the period of socialist construction, their essence is one—dictatorship of the proletariat, representing genuine democracy, democracy for the working people.

A bourgeois republic, however democratic, however sanctified by slogans about the will of the people or nation as a whole or a nonclass will, inevitably remains in practice—by virtue of the existence of private capitalist ownership of the means of production—a dictatorship of the bourgeoisie, a machine for the exploitation and suppression of the overwhelming majority of the working people by a handful of capitalists. In contrast to the bourgeoisie, which conceals the class character of its state, the working class does not conceal the class character of the state.

The dictatorship of the proletariat is a dictatorship of the overwhelming majority over the minority; it is directed against the exploiters, against the oppression of peoples and nations, and is aimed at wiping out any exploitation of man by man. The dictatorship of the proletariat expresses not only the interests of the working class but also those of all working people; its chief content is not force but creation, the building of a new, *socialist* [classless] society, and the defense of its gains against the enemies of socialism.

Overcoming schism in its ranks is an important condition for the fulfillment by the working class of its world-historic mission. Not a single bastion of imperialism can hold out against a closely knit working class that exercises unity of action. The Communist Parties stand for cooperation with the Social-Democratic Parties not only in the struggle for peace, for better living conditions for the working people and for the preservation and extension of their democratic rights and freedoms but also in the struggle to win power and build a socialist society.

At the same time the Communists criticize the ideological positions and Right-opportunist practice of Social Democracy; they expose the Right leaders of Social Democracy, who have openly sided with the bourgeoisie and renounced the traditional socialist demands of the working class.

The Communist Parties are the vanguard of the world revolutionary movement. They have demonstrated the vitality of Marxism-Leninism and their ability not only to propagandize the great ideals of scientific communism but also to put them into practice. The international Communist movement has now become so powerful that the combined forces of reaction cannot crush it.

The Communist movement is growing and being steeled in struggle against various opportunist trends. Revisionism, Right opportunism, as a reflection of bourgeois influence, is the chief danger within the Communist movement in present-day conditions. The revisionists, who mask their renunciation of Marxism with arguments about the necessity of taking account of the latest conditions of development of society and the class struggle, actually play the role of peddlers of bourgeois-reformist ideology within the Communist movement. They seek to deprive Marxism-Leninism of its revolutionary spirit, to undermine the faith of the working class and the working people in [the cause of] socialism, to disarm and demobilize the workers and the working people in their struggle against imperialism. The revisionists deny the historical necessity of the socialist revolution and of the dictatorship of the proletariat, deny the leading role of the Marxist-Leninist party, undermine the foundations of proletarian internationalism, and drift to nationalism. The ideology of revisionism is most fully embodied in the program of the League of Communists of Yugoslavia.

Another danger is dogmatism and sectarianism, which are in irreconcilable contradiction to the creative development of revolutionary theory; lead to the dissociation and isolation of Communists from the broad masses, doom them to passive waiting or incite them to Leftist adventurist actions in the revolutionary struggle; and hinder a correct appraisal of the changing situation and the use of new opportunities for the benefit of the working class and all democratic forces. Dogmatism and sectarianism, unless a consistent struggle is waged against them, can also become the chief danger at a particular stage of the development of individual parties.

The Communist Party of the Soviet Union proceeds from the fact that an uncompromising struggle against revisionism, dogmatism and sectarianism, against all departures from Leninism, is a necessary condition for the further strengthening of the unity of the international Communist movement and for the consolidation of the socialist camp.

The Communist Parties are independent and they work out their policies on the basis of the specific conditions prevailing in their own countries. They build relations between themselves on the basis of equality and the principles of proletarian internationalism. They voluntarily and consciously coordinate their actions as integral parts of a single international army of labor. The Communist Party of the Soviet Union, like all Communist Parties, regards it as its internationalist duty to abide strictly by the appraisals and conclusions jointly reached by the fraternal parties concerning their common tasks in the struggle against imperialism, for peace, democracy and socialism, and by the declarations and statements adopted by the Communist Parties at their international meetings.

Vigorous defense of the unity of the international Communist movement on the basis of the principles of Marxism-Leninism, of proletarian internationalism, and the refusal to permit any actions likely to disrupt that unity are an essential condition for victory in the struggle for national independence, democracy and peace, for the successful accomplishment of the tasks of the socialist revolution, for the construction of socialism and communism.

The C.P.S.U. will continue to *direct its efforts toward strengthening* [strengthen] the unity and solidarity of the ranks of the great army of Communists of all countries.

VI. THE NATIONAL-LIBERATION MOVEMENT.—The world is going through an era of tempestuous national-liberation revolutions. Whereas imperialism suppressed the national independence and freedom of the majority of peoples and fettered them with the chains of harsh colonial enslavement, the rise of socialism marks the advent of the era of liberation of oppressed peoples. A mighty wave of national-liberation revolutions is sweeping away the colonial system and undermining the foundations of imperialism. Young sovereign states have arisen or are arising in the place of the former colonies and semicolonies. Their peoples have entered a new period of development. They have emerged as makers of a new life and active participants in international politics and as a revolutionary force for the destruction of imperialism.

But the struggle is not yet over. The peoples who are throwing off the chains of colonialism have reached various levels of freedom. Many of them, having established national states, are striving for economic independence and stronger political sovereignty. The peoples of countries that are formally independent but actually depend politically and economically on foreign monopolies are rising in the struggle against imperialism and reactionary, pro-imperialist regimes. Peoples who have not yet cast off the chains of colonial enslavement are conducting a heroic struggle against their foreign enslavers.

The young sovereign states do not belong to either the system of imperialist states or the system of socialist states. But the overwhelming majority of them have not yet broken out of the world capitalist economy, even though they occupy a special place in it. They constitute a part of the world still being exploited by the capitalist monopolies. Until these countries put an end to their economic dependence on imperialism, they will have the role of a "world countryside," they will remain objects of semicolonial exploitation.

The existence of the world socialist system and the weakening of imperialism open up before the peoples of the liberated countries the prospect of a national renascence, of ending age-long backwardness and poverty and achieving economic independence.

A nation's interests call for elimination of the remnants of colonialism, the eradication of imperialist rule, the ousting of foreign monopolies, the establishment of a national industry, the abolition of feudal ways and survivals, the implementation of radical agrarian changes with the participation of the entire peasantry and in its interests, the pursuit of an independent peace-loving foreign policy, the democratization of public life and the strengthening of political independence. All the patriotic and progressive forces of the nation are interested in the accomplishment of the national tasks. This is the basis on which these forces can be unified.

Foreign capital will retreat only before a broad union of patriotic, democratic forces carrying out an anti-imperialist policy. The pillars of feudalism can crumble only under the pressure of a general democratic movement. Only profound agrarian reforms and a broad peasant movement can sweep away the remnants of medievalism that fetter the development of productive forces and can solve the food problem that so sharply confronts the peoples of Asia, Africa and Latin America. Political independence can be made secure only by a people that has won democratic rights and freedom and that participates actively in the governing of the state.

A consistent struggle against imperialism is a fundamental condition for solving national tasks. Imperialism seeks to keep former colonies and semicolonies in the system of capitalist economy and to perpetuate their unequal position within it. The imperialism of the United States of America is the chief bulwark of present-day colonialism.

The imperialists are trying by new methods and new forms to preserve the colonial exploitation of peoples. The imperialists are using every means (colonial wars, military blocs, conspiracies, terror, subversion, economic pressure, bribery) to keep the liberated countries in their power, to make a formality out of the independence they have won or to deprive them of independence. Under the guise of "aid," they are trying to retain their old positions in these countries and seize new ones, to enlarge their social base of support, to win the national bourgeoisie to their side, to implant despotic military regimes and to put obedient puppets in power. Using the poisoned weapon of national and tribal strife, the imperialists seek to split the ranks of the national-liberation movement. Reactionary circles of the local exploiting classes serve as allies of imperialism.

Imperialism thus remains the chief enemy and the chief obstacle to the accomplishment of the national tasks facing the young sovereign states and all dependent countries.

A national-liberation revolution does not end with the winning of political independence. This independence will be unstable and will turn into a fiction unless the revolution brings about radical changes in social and economic life and accomplishes the pressing tasks of national renascence.

The working class is the most consistent fighter for the consummation of this revolution, for national interests and social progress. As industry develops, its ranks will swell and its role in socio-political life will increase. The alliance of the working class and the peasantry is a fundamental condition of the successful struggle to carry out profound democratic changes and achieve economic and social progress. This alliance is called upon to form the nucleus of a broad national front. The extent to which the national bourgeoisie participates in the anti-imperialist and antifeudal struggle will depend in considerable measure on the firmness of the alliance of the working class and the peasantry. The national front [also] embraces *the working class, the peasantry,* the *national* [urban petty] bourgeoisie and the democratic intelligentsia.

In many countries, the liberation movement of the peoples that have awakened proceeds under the flag of nationalism. Marxists-Leninists draw a distinction between the nationalism of oppressed nations and the nationalism of oppressor nations. The nationalism of an oppressed nation has a general democratic content directed against oppression, and the Communists support it, considering it historically justified at a given stage. This element finds expression in the striving of the oppressed peoples to free themselves from imperialist oppression, to gain national independence and bring about a national renascence. At the same time, the nationalism of an oppressed nation has another aspect, one expressing the ideology and interests of the reactionary exploiter upper clique.

The national bourgeoisie is inherently dual in character. In modern conditions the national bourgeoisie in those colonial, formerly colonial and dependent countries where it is not connected with the imperialist circles is objectively interested in carrying out the basic tasks of an anti-imperialist and antifeudal revolution. Consequently, its progressive role and its ability to participate in the accomplishment of urgent national tasks are not yet exhausted.

But as the contradictions between the working people and the propertied classes grow and the class struggle inside the country sharpens, the national bourgeoisie shows an increasing inclination to compromise with imperialism and domestic reaction.

The development of the countries that have liberated themselves may be a complex process of several stages. By virtue of the diverse historical and socio-economic conditions in the newly liberated countries, the revolutionary initiative of the masses introduces much that is original in the forms and tempos of their development along the path of social progress.

One of the basic problems confronting the peoples of the countries that have freed themselves from the yoke of imperialism is which path to follow, the capitalist path or the noncapitalist path of development.

What does capitalism offer them?

Capitalism is the path of suffering for the people. It will not ensure rapid economic progress or eliminate poverty; social inequality will increase. The capitalist development of the countryside will still further ruin the peasantry. The lot of the workers will be either to engage in exhausting labor to enrich the capitalists, or to swell the ranks of the disinherited army of the unemployed. The petty bourgeoisie will be crushed in competition with big capital. The benefits of culture and education will remain inaccessible to the masses. The intelligentsia will be obliged to sell its talents.

What does socialism offer the peoples?

Socialism is the path to freedom and happiness for the peoples. It ensures rapid economic and cultural progress. It transforms a backward country into an industrial country within the lifetime of a single generation rather than in the course of centuries. By its very nature, a planned socialist economy is an economy of progress and prosperity. Abolition of the exploitation of man by man does away with social inequality. Unemployment disappears completely. Socialism provides all peasants with land, helps them to develop farming, combines their labor efforts in voluntary cooperatives and puts modern farm machinery and agronomy at their disposal. Peasant labor becomes more productive and the land can yield more. Socialism provides a high material and cultural standard of living for the working class and all working people. Socialism wrests the masses of the people from darkness and ignorance and gives them access to modern culture. Broad horizons for creative efforts for the benefit of the people open up to the intelligentsia.

It is for the peoples themselves to decide which path they are to choose. In view of the present balance of forces in the world arena and the real possibility of powerful support from the world socialist system, the peoples of the former colonies can decide this question in their own interests. Their choice will depend on the balance of class forces. The noncapitalist path of development is ensured by the struggle of the working class and the masses of the people, by the general democratic movement, and corresponds to the interests of the absolute majority of the nation. [This path will require concessions from the bourgeoisie, but these will be concessions on behalf of the nation. On the noncapitalist path of development, all strata of the population can find application for their energies.]

The path of the formation and development of national democracies opens broad prospects for the peoples of the economically underdeveloped countries. The political basis of a national democracy is a bloc of all the progressive, patriotic forces fighting for complete national independence and broad democracy and for carrying through to the end the anti-imperialist, antifeudal, democratic revolution.

A steady growth of the class and national consciousness of the masses is a characteristic of the present period of social development. The imperialists are stubbornly trying to distort the idea of national sovereignty, trying to emasculate it of its main content and to use it to inflame national egoism, to implant a spirit of national exclusiveness and to intensify national antagonisms. The democratic forces affirm the idea of national sovereignty in the name of equality of peoples, their mutual trust, friendship, mutual aid and closer contact, in the interests of social progress. The idea of national sovereignty in its democratic sense is becoming more and more firmly established; it is acquiring increasing significance and becoming an important factor in the progressive development of society.

The Communist Parties are actively fighting to press on consistently with the full anti-imperialist, antifeudal, democratic revolution, to establish national democracies and achieve social progress. The Communists' goals correspond to the supreme interests of the nation. The attempts of reactionary circles to disrupt the national front under the guise of anticommunism and their persecution of Communists lead to the weakening of the national-liberation movement, run counter to the national interests of the peoples, and threaten the loss of the gains that have been won.

The national states are becoming ever more active as an independent force on the world scene; objectively, this is in the main a progressive, revolutionary and anti-imperialist force. The countries and peoples that have freed themselves from colonial oppression are called upon to play an outstanding role in deciding the central question of our times—preventing another world war. The time is past when imperialism could use the manpower and material resources of these countries without hindrance in its predatory wars. The time has come when the peoples of these countries, overcoming the resistance of the reactionary circles associated with the colonialists as well as the vacillation of the national bourgeoisie, can put their resources at the service of world security and become a new bastion of peace. Their own fundamental interests and the interests of all peoples demand this.

Unification of the efforts of the peoples of newly liberated countries and the peoples of the socialist states in the struggle against the war danger is a major factor for universal peace. This mighty front, which expresses the will and strength of two-thirds of mankind, can force the imperialist aggressors into retreat.

The socialist countries are sincere and true friends of peoples fighting for their liberation and of those newly freed from the imperialist yoke, and render them all support. They stand for the wiping out of all forms of colonial oppression and promote in every way the strengthening of the sovereignty of the states rising on the ruins of colonial empires.

The C.P.S.U. considers fraternal alliance with the peoples who have thrown off the colonial or semicolonial yoke to be a cornerstone of its international policy. This alliance is based on the community of vital interests of world socialism and the world national-liberation movement. The C.P.S.U. regards it as its internationalist duty to assist the peoples who have set out to win and strengthen their national independence, all peoples who are fighting for the complete wiping out of the colonial system.

VII. THE STRUGGLE AGAINST BOURGEOIS AND REFORMIST IDEOLOGY.—A fierce struggle is going on between two ideologies—Communist and bourgeois—in the world today. This struggle is a reflection in the spiritual life of mankind of the historical process of transition from capitalism to socialism.

The new historical epoch has brought the revolutionary world outlook of the proletariat a genuine triumph. Marxism-Leninism has become the ruler of the minds of progressive mankind.

Bourgeois doctrines and schools have failed to withstand the test of history. They have been unable to furnish scientific answers to the questions posed by life and cannot furnish them. The bourgeoisie is no longer capable of putting forward ideas that can enlist the support of the masses. *More and more people in the capitalist countries are deserting the bourgeois outlook.* Bourgeois ideology is experiencing a profound crisis.

A revolutionary transformation in the minds of vast human masses is a complex and lengthy process. The more victories the world socialist system achieves, the deeper the crisis of world capitalism and the sharper the class struggle, the greater becomes the role of Marxist-Leninist ideas in unifying and mobilizing the masses in the struggle for communism. The ideological struggle is a most important element of the class struggle of the proletariat.

Imperialist reaction mobilizes every means of ideological influence on the masses in its attempts to blacken communism and its noble ideas and to defend capitalism. The chief ideological-political weapon of imperialism is anticommunism, the basic content of which consists in slander of the socialist system and falsification of the policy and objectives of the Communist Parties and the teaching of Marxism-Leninism. Under *the false slogans* [cover] of anticommunism, imperialist reaction persecutes and hounds all that is progressive and revolutionary and tries to split the ranks of the working people and to paralyze the proletarians' will to fight. United under this black banner today are all the enemies of social progress: the finance oligarchy and the military, fascists and reactionary clericals, colonialists

and landowners, all the ideological and political accomplices of imperialist reaction. Anticommunism is a reflection of the extreme decadence of bourgeois ideology.

The defenders of the bourgeois system, seeking to keep the masses in spiritual bondage, invent more and more new "theories" designed to mask the exploitative nature of the bourgeois system and to make capitalism look more attractive. They claim that modern capitalism has changed its nature and has become a "people's capitalism" in which there is taking place a "diffusion" of ownership and a "democratization" of capital, in which classes and class contradictions are disappearing, "incomes are being equalized" and economic crises are being eliminated. In reality the development of present-day capitalism is confirming the correctness of the Marxist-Leninist teaching on the mounting contradictions and antagonisms of capitalist society, on the sharpening of the class struggle within it.

The defenders of the bourgeois system call it a "welfare state." They propagate the illusion that the capitalist state is counterposed to the monopolies and can achieve social harmony and universal welfare. But the masses of the people are being convinced by their own experience that the bourgeois state is an obedient tool of the monopolies, while the vaunted "welfare" is welfare for the magnates of finance capital and torment and sufferings for the hundreds of millions of people of labor.

The "theoreticians" of anticommunism call present-day imperialism the "free world." In reality the "free world" is a world of exploitation and lack of rights, a world where human dignity and national honor are trampled underfoot, a world of obscurantism and political reaction, a world of rabid militarism and bloody treatment of the working people.

Monopoly capital gives birth to the ideology of fascism—an ideology of extreme chauvinism and racism. Fascism in power is open terrorist dictatorship by the most reactionary, most chauvinistic and most imperialistic elements of finance capital. Fascism begins always and everywhere with the frantic anticommunism that has as its purpose isolating and crushing the parties of the working class, splitting the forces of the proletariat and defeating them piecemeal, and then putting an end to other democratic parties and organizations and turning the people into the blind tool of the policy of the capitalist monopolies. Fascism strikes first of all at the Communist Parties, as the most consistent, stanch and incorruptible defenders of the interests of the working class and all working people.

Imperialist reaction makes wide use of chauvinism *and racism* to fan nationalist *and racial* conflicts, persecute entire nationalities and national groups (anti-Semitism, racial discrimination against Negroes and against the peoples of underdeveloped countries), becloud the class consiousness of the working people and divert the proletariat and its allies from the class struggle.

Clericalism is acquiring ever greater importance in the political and ideological arsenal of imperialism. It does not confine itself to using the Church and its ramified apparatus. It now has its own large political parties, which are in power in many capitalist countries. Setting up its own trade union, youth, women's and other organizations, it splits the ranks of the working class and of the working people. The monopolies generously subsidize clerical parties and organizations, which exploit the religious feelings of the working people, their superstitions and prejudices.

The shapes and forms of bourgeois ideology and the methods and means of deceiving the working people are diverse. But their essence is one—defense of the dying capitalist system. The ideological substantiation of rule by the monopolies, the justification of exploitation, the defamation of public ownership and collectivism, the glorification of militarism and war, the justification of colonialism and racism, the fanning of hostility and hatred among peoples—such are the ideas that imbue the political and economic theories, the philosophy and sociology, the ethics and esthetics of the present-day bourgeoisie.

Anticommunism is becoming the chief weapon of reaction in the struggle against the democratic forces of countries of Asia, Africa and Latin America. It is the meeting ground of imperialist ideology and the ideology of the feudal, pro-imperialist elements and reactionary groups of the bourgeoisie of the countries that have gained their freedom from the colonial yoke.

The antipopular circles of these countries seek to muffle the general democratic content of nationalism, to exaggerate its reactionary aspect, to push aside the democratic forces of the nation, to prevent social progress and to hinder the spread of scientific socialism. At the same time theories are advanced about a "national brand of socialism" and socio-philosophical doctrines are propagandized that represent as a rule variations of the petty-bourgeois illusions about socialism, which exclude class struggle. These theories mislead the masses of the people, retard the development of the national-liberation movement and imperil its gains.

National-democratic, anti-imperialist ideas are becoming widespread in the countries that have liberated themselves from colonial oppression. The Communists and other proponents of these ideas patiently explain to the masses the untenability of illusions about the possibility of [ensuring] national independence and social progress without an active struggle against imperialism and internal reaction; they actively oppose chauvinism and other manifestations of reactionary ideology justifying despotic regimes and the suppression of democracy. At the same time the Communists act as exponents of the socialist ideology, rallying the masses under the banner of scientific socialism.

The ideological struggle of the imperialist bourgeoisie is directed primarily against the working class and its Marxist-Leninist parties. Social Democracy in the workers' movement and revisionism in the Communist movement are a reflection of bourgeois influence on the working class.

Present-day Right Social Democracy remains a most important ideological and political support of the bourgeoisie within the workers' movement. It eclectically unites old opportunist ideas and the "latest" bourgeois theories. The right wing of Social Democracy has completely broken with Marxism and has set up so-called democratic socialism in opposition to scientific socialism. Its adherents deny the existence of antagonistic classes and the class struggle in bourgeois society; they have ranged themselves against the necessity of the proletarian revolution, against the abolition of private ownership of the means of production. They claim that a "transformation of capitalism" into socialism is going on.

The Right Socialists began by counterposing social reforms to the socialist revolution and ended up by defending state-monopoly capitalism. In the past they tried to convince the proletariat that their differences with revolutionary Marxism concerned not so much the ultimate goal of the workers' movement as the means of achieving it. Now they openly renounce socialism. The Right Socialists used to refuse to carry recognition of the class struggle to the point of accepting the dictatorship of the proletariat. Today they deny not only the class struggle but the very existence of antagonistic classes in bourgeois society.

Historical experience has shown the bankruptcy of both the ideology and the policy of Social Democracy. Even when reformist parties come to power they limit themselves to partial reforms that do not affect the rule of the monopoly bourgeoisie. Anticommunism has led social reformism into an ideological and political impasse. This is one of the chief causes of the crisis of Social Democracy.

Marxism-Leninism is winning more and more new victories. It is triumphing because it expresses the vital interests of the working class, of the vast majority of mankind, which seeks peace, freedom and progress, and because it expresses the ideology of the new society that is replacing capitalism.

VIII. PEACEFUL COEXISTENCE AND THE STRUGGLE FOR UNIVERSAL PEACE. — The C.P.S.U. considers that the chief aim of its foreign policy activity is to ensure peaceful conditions for the building of a communist society in the U.S.S.R. and for the development of the world socialist system and, together with all peace-loving peoples, to deliver mankind from a world war of extermination.

The C.P.S.U. proceeds from the fact that forces capable of preserving and consolidating world peace have arisen and are growing in the world. Possibilities are being created for establishing fundamentally new relations among states.

Imperialism knows no other relations among states than relations of domination and subordination, of oppression of the weak by the strong. It bases international relations on dictation and threats, on force and high-handedness. It regards wars of aggression as a natural means of settling international issues. For the imperialist states diplomacy has been and remains a tool for imposing their will upon other peoples, an instrument for preparing wars. In the period of the undivided rule of imperialism the question of war and peace was settled by the finance and industrial oligarchy in the utmost secrecy from the peoples.

Socialism counterposes to imperialism a new type of international relations. The foreign policy of the socialist states — based on the principles of peace, equality, self-determination of peoples and respect for the independence and sovereignty of all countries — and also the honest, humane methods of socialist diplomacy are exerting a growing influence on the world situation. At a time when imperialism has ceased to play a dominating role in international relations and the socialist system is playing a bigger and bigger role, and when the influence in world politics of the states that have won national independence and of the masses of the people in the capitalist countries has grown greatly, a real possibility is arising for the new principles advanced by socialism to win the victory over the principles of aggressive imperialist policy.

For the first time in history a situation has arisen in which not only big states but also small ones — countries that have taken the path of independent development, all states that seek peace — are in a position, irrespective of their strength, to pursue an independent foreign policy.

The question of war and peace is the basic question of our times. Imperialism is the only source of war danger. The imperialist camp is making preparations for the most terrible crime against mankind — a thermonuclear world war that can wreak unprecedented destruction upon entire countries and wipe out entire peoples. The question of war and peace has become a matter of life and death for hundreds of millions of people.

The peoples must concentrate their efforts on curbing the imperialists in time and depriving them of the possibility of loosing lethal weapons. The chief thing is to prevent a thermonuclear war, not to allow it to break out. The present generation is capable of doing this.

The strengthening of the Soviet state and the formation of the world socialist system were historic steps toward accomplishing mankind's age-old dream of banishing wars from the life of society. The socialist part of the world does not have classes or social groups interested in unleashing wars. Socialism, having outstripped capitalism in a number of important branches of science and technology, has placed in the hands of peace-loving peoples powerful material means for curbing imperialist aggression. Whereas capitalism established its rule with fire and sword, socialism does not require wars to spread its ideals.

Its weapon is its superiority over the old system in the organization of society, in state structure, in the economy, in raising the living standard and cultural level.

The socialist system is the natural center of attraction for all the peace-loving forces on earth. The principles of its foreign policy are gaining ever greater international recognition and support. A large peace zone has taken shape on the face of the globe. In addition to the socialist states, it includes a large group of nonsocialist states that for various reasons are not interested in unleashing war. The emergence of those states in the arena of world politics has substantially altered the balance of forces in favor of peace.

There is a growing number of countries that support a policy of neutrality and strive to safeguard themselves against the danger inherent in participation in *aggressive* military blocs.

In the new historical epoch the masses have an immeasurably greater opportunity of actively influencing the settlement of international issues. The peoples are more and more actively taking the settlement of the question of war and peace into their own hands. The antiwar movement of the masses, which takes the most diverse forms, is a major factor in the struggle for peace. The international working class, the most uncompromising and most consistent fighter against imperialist wars, serves as the great organizing force in this struggle of the entire people.

A world war can be prevented by the united forces of the mighty socialist camp, the peace-loving nonsocialist states, the international working class and all the forces championing the cause of peace. The growing superiority of the forces of socialism over the forces of imperialism, of the forces of peace over the forces of war, is leading to a real possibility of excluding world war from the life of society even before the complete victory of socialism on earth and while capitalism survives in part of the world. The victory of socialism throughout the world will completely remove the social and national causes of all wars. To abolish war and establish eternal peace on earth is a historical mission of communism.

General and complete disarmament under strict international control is a radical way of ensuring lasting peace. Imperialism has imposed an unprecedented burden of armaments on the people. Socialism sees its duty to humanity in delivering it from this senseless waste of national wealth. Accomplishment of this task would have historic significance for mankind. An active and determined struggle by the peoples can and must force the imperialists into disarmament.

Socialism has offered mankind the only reasonable principle of relations among states in the conditions of the division of the world into two systems—the principle of the peaceful coexistence of states with different social structures advanced by V. I. Lenin.

Peaceful coexistence of the socialist and capitalist states is an objective necessity for the development of human society. War cannot and must not serve as a means of settling international disputes. Peaceful coexistence or catastrophic war—such is the alternative offered by history. Should the imperialist aggressors nevertheless dare to unleash a new world war, the peoples will no longer tolerate a system that drags them into devastating wars. They will sweep imperialism away and bury it.

Peaceful coexistence implies renunciation of war as a means of settling disputes among states and their solution by negotiation; equality, mutual understanding and trust among states; consideration of one another's interests; noninterference in internal affairs and recognition of the right of each people to resolve all problems of its country independently; strict respect for the sovereignty and territorial integrity of all countries; the development of economic and cultural cooperation on the basis of complete equality and mutual benefit.

Peaceful coexistence serves as a basis for the peaceful competition between socialism and capitalism on an international scale and is a specific form of class struggle between them. The socialist countries, consistently pursuing a policy of peaceful coexistence, are steadily strengthening the positions of the world socialist system in its competition with capitalism. Peaceful coexistence affords more favorable opportunities for the struggle of the working class of the capitalist countries and facilitates the struggle of the peoples of the colonial and dependent countries for their liberation. Support for the principle of peaceful coexistence is also in accord with the interests of the part of the bourgeoisie that realizes that a thermonuclear war would not spare the ruling classes of capitalist society either. The policy of peaceful coexistence is in accord with the vital interests of all mankind except the big monopoly magnates and the militarists.

The Soviet Union has consistently championed and will continue to champion the policy of peaceful coexistence of states with different social systems.

The Communist Party of the Soviet Union sets the following tasks in the sphere of international relations:

—to use, together with the other socialist countries and peace-loving states and peoples, every means of preventing world war and creating the conditions for the complete elimination of war from the life of society;

—to pursue a policy of establishing healthy international relations and seek the disbanding of all military blocs opposing each other, the discontinuation of the "cold war" and the propaganda of hostility and hatred among peoples, and the abolition of all air, naval, rocket and other military bases on the territory of other countries;

—to seek general and complete disarmament under strict international control;

—to strengthen relations of fraternal friendship and close cooperation with states of Asia, Africa and Latin America that are fighting to attain or consolidate national independence, with all peoples and states that advocate the preservation of peace;

—to pursue an active, consistent policy of improving and developing relations with all capitalist countries, including the United States of America, Great Britain, France, the Federal German Republic, Japan and Italy [and others], in the interests of safeguarding peace;

—to contribute in every way to strengthening the militant solidarity of all the detachments and organizations of the international working class that oppose the imperialist policy of war

—consistently to pursue a policy of uniting all the forces fighting against war. All organizations and parties that strive to prevent war and the neutralist and pacifist movements and bourgeois circles that advocate peace and normalization of the relations among countries will meet with understanding and support on the part of the Soviet Union;

—to pursue a policy of developing international cooperation in the fields of trade, cultural relations, science and technology;

—to maintain high vigilance with regard to the aggressive circles that are seeking to violate the peace; to expose in good time the initiators of military adventures; to take all necessary measures to safeguard the security and inviolability of our socialist fatherland and the entire socialist camp.

The C.P.S.U. and the entire Soviet people will continue to oppose all and any predatory wars, including wars between capitalist states and local wars aimed at strangling people's liberation movements, and consider it their duty to support the sacred struggle of oppressed peoples and their just wars of liberation against imperialism.

The Communist Party of the Soviet Union will hold high the banner of peace and friendship among peoples.

PART II. THE TASKS OF THE COMMUNIST PARTY OF THE SOVIET UNION IN BUILDING A COMMUNIST SOCIETY

COMMUNISM—THE BRIGHT FUTURE OF ALL MANKIND.—The building of a communist society has become the immediate practical task of the Soviet people. The gradual evolution of socialism into communism is an objective law; it has been prepared by the whole preceding development of Soviet socialist society.

What is communism?

Communism is a classless social system with a single form of public ownership of the means of production and full social equality of all members of society; under it, the rounded development of people will be accompanied by growth of productive forces on the basis of constantly developing science and technology, all the springs of public wealth will yield abundantly, and the great principle "From each according to his abilities, to each according to his needs" will be applied. Communism is a highly organized society of free, socially conscious working people in which public self-government will be established, in which labor for the good of society will become a prime, vital need in everyone, a necessity recognized by all, and the abilities of each person will be employed to the greatest benefit of the people.

High communist consciousness, industry, discipline and devotion to the public interests are inalienable qualities of the man of communist society.

Communism ensures the constant development of social production and high labor productivity on the basis of rapid scientific and technological progress; it equips man with the best and most powerful machines, raises to tremendous heights his power over nature and enables him to control its elemental forces to an ever greater and fuller extent. The planned organization of the whole of the public economy reaches the highest stage, and the most effective and rational use of material wealth and manpower to meet the growing requirements of the members of society is ensured.

Under communism *there will be no classes* [classes will completely disappear, as will] *and* the socio-economic and cultural distinctions and differences in living conditions between town and countryside *will disappear;* the countryside rises to the level of the city in the development of productive forces, the nature of work, the forms of production relations, living conditions and the well-being of the population. With the victory of communism mental and manual labor in people's production activity will merge organically. The intelligentsia will cease to be a distinct social stratum, *and* [since] manual workers will have risen in cultural and technological level to the level of mental workers.

Thus communism *will end* [puts an end to] the division of society into classes and social strata, whereas the whole history of mankind, with the exception of its primitive period, has been a history of class society. Division into opposing classes led to the exploitation of man by man, class struggle and antagonisms among nations and states.

Under communism all people will have equal status in society, will stand in equal relation to the means of production, will enjoy equal conditions of work and distribution, and will participate actively in the management of public affairs. Harmonious relations will be established between the individual and society on the basis of unity of public and personal interests. For all their tremendous diversity, the requirements of people will express the healthy, reasonable requirements of persons of rounded development.

The goal of communist production is to ensure the constant progress of society and to provide each of its members with material and cultural benefits according to his or her growing needs, individual requirements and tastes. People's requirements will be met from public sources. Articles of personal use will come into the full ownership of each member of society and will be at his disposal.

Communist society, based on highly organized production and advanced technology, changes the character of work but does not release the members of society from work. By no means will it be a society of anarchy, idleness and inactivity. *Every able-bodied person* [Everyone] will participate in social labor and thereby ensure the steady growth of the material and spiritual wealth of society. Thanks to the change in the nature of labor, its greater mechanization and a high degree of consciousness, the inner need to work for the public benefit voluntarily and according to inclination will burgeon in all members of society.

Communist production demands high organization, precision and discipline, which are ensured not by compulsion but on the basis of understanding of public duty, and are determined by the whole way of life in communist society. Labor and discipline will not be a burden to man; labor will cease to be merely a source of livelihood—it will turn into a genuinely creative process and a source of happiness.

Communism represents the highest form of organization of the life of society. All production units, all self-governing associations will be harmoniously linked by a common planned economy and a single rhythm of social labor.

Under communism nations will draw closer and closer together in all spheres on the basis of a complete identity of economic, political and spiritual interests, of fraternal friendship and cooperation.

Communism is the system in which free men's abilities and talents and their best moral qualities blossom and fully show themselves. Family relations will be completely freed from material considerations and will be based entirely on mutual love and friendship.

Defining the basic tasks to be accomplished in building a communist society, the Party is guided by V. I. Lenin's inspired formula: "Communism is Soviet rule plus the electrification of the whole country."

As a party of scientific communism, the C.P.S.U. sets the tasks of communist construction and carries them out as the material and spiritual prerequisites are prepared and mature; in doing this, the C.P.S.U. is guided by the fact that one cannot leap over essential stages in development, any more than one can halt at an achieved level and check progress. The tasks of building communism are accomplished in successive stages.

In the current decade (1961-1970) the Soviet Union, creating the material and technical base of communism, will surpass the strongest and richest capitalist country, the U.S.A., in per capita production; the people's material well-being and cultural and technical level will rise substantially, everyone will be assured a material sufficiency; all collective and state farms will become highly productive and highly profitable enterprises; the demand of the Soviet people for well-appointed housing will in the main be satisfied; hard physical labor will disappear; the U.S.S.R. will become the country with the shortest working day.

By the end of [In] the second decade (1971-1980) the material and technical base of communism will be created *that will ensure* [and there will be ensured] an abundance of material and cultural benefits for the whole population; Soviet society will

come right up to the stage of application of the principle of distribution according to needs, and there will be a gradual transition to a single form of public ownership. Thus a communist society will be built in the main in the U.S.S.R. The construction of communist society will be completed in the subsequent period.

The majestic edifice of communism is being erected by the persevering labor of the Soviet people—the working class, the peasantry and the intelligentsia. The more successful their work, the closer the great goal—the building of communist society.

I. TASKS OF THE PARTY IN THE SPHERE OF ECONOMIC CONSTRUCTION, IN THE CREATION AND DEVELOPMENT OF THE MATERIAL AND TECHNICAL BASE OF COMMUNISM.—The chief economic task of the Party and the Soviet people is to create the material and technical base of communism in the course of two decades. This means the complete electrification of the country and the perfection on this basis of the equipment, technology and organization of social production in industry and agriculture; the integrated mechanization of production processes and their ever greater automation; extensive use of chemistry in the national economy; the comprehensive development of new, economically advantageous branches of production, new types of power and new materials; thorough and rational utilization of natural, *material and labor* resources; the organic fusion of science and production, and rapid scientific and technical progress; a high cultural and technical level for the working people; considerable superiority over the most highly developed capitalist countries in labor productivity, which constitutes a most important condition for the victory of the communist system.

As a result, the U.S.S.R. will possess productive forces of unprecedented might; it will surpass the technical level of the most highly developed countries and take first place in the world in per capita production. This will serve as a basis for the gradual transformation of socialist social relations into communist social relations and for such a development of *production* [industry and agriculture] as will make it possible to meet in abundance the requirements of society and all its citizens.

In contrast to capitalism, the planned socialist economic system combines accelerated technical progress with full employment of the entire able-bodied population. Automation and integrated mechanization serve as a material basis for the gradual development of socialist labor into communist labor. Technical progress will require of all working people considerably more efficiency and considerably higher specialized and general education. The development of new machinery will be used to improve radically the Soviet people's working conditions and make them easier, to reduce the length of the working day, to improve living conditions, and to eliminate arduous manual labor and later all unskilled labor.

The material and technical base will be steadily developed and improved as society develops along the road to the complete triumph of communism. The level of development of science and technology and the degree of mechanization and automation of production processes will constantly rise.

The creation of the material and technical base of communism will call for huge capital investments. The task is to utilize these investments most rationally and economically, with the maximum effect and gain of time.

1. The Development of Industry, *Construction and Transport; Their* [Its] Role in Creating the Productive Forces of Communism.—The creation of the material and technical base of communism and the task of making Soviet industry technologically the best and mightiest industry in the world require the further development of heavy industry. On this basis all the other branches of the national economy—agriculture, consumer goods industries, construction, transport, communications and the branches directly concerned with services for the population: trade, public catering, health services, housing and utilities—will be technically re-equipped.

A first-class heavy industry, the basis for the country's technical progress and economic might, has been built up in the Soviet Union. *The C.P.S.U. will continue to give unflagging attention to the growth of heavy industry and its technical progress. The chief task of heavy industry is to ensure fully the needs of the country's defense and the development of branches of the economy producing consumer goods in order to satisfy better and more fully the requirements of the people, the vital needs of Soviet man, and to ensure the development of the country's productive forces.* [The C.P.S.U. will continue to give unflagging attention to the growth of heavy industry, which ensures the development of the country's productive forces and defense capacity. In the new period of the Soviet Union's development, heavy industry must so grow that on the basis of technological progress it can ensure the expansion of branches of the economy producing consumer goods in order to meet ever more fully the requirements of the people.

[Thus the chief task of heavy industry is to ensure the needs of the country's defense in full and to satisfy the vital needs of man, of Soviet society, better and more fully.]

Proceeding from this, the C.P.S.U. plans to increase the volume of industrial output:

within the current ten years by approximately 150%, exceeding the [present] level of U.S. industrial output;

within 20 years by not less than 500%, leaving the present total volume of U.S. industrial output far behind.

For this it is necessary to raise labor productivity in industry by more than 100% within ten years and by 300% to 350% within 20 years. In 20 years' time labor productivity in Soviet industry will exceed the present level of labor productivity in the U.S.A. by approximately 100%, and, in view of the reduction of the working day in the U.S.S.R., by considerably more than this in terms of hourly output.

Such an intensive development of industry will call for major progressive changes in its structure. The role of new branches ensuring the greatest technical progress will particularly grow. The less efficient types of fuel and power and of raw and other materials will be increasingly superseded by highly efficient ones, and their integrated use will increase greatly. The proportion of synthetics, metals and alloys with new properties will increase considerably. New types of automatic and electronic machinery, instruments and apparatus will be rapidly and widely introduced.

Electrification, which is the backbone of the economy of communist society, plays a leading role in the development of all branches of the economy and in ensuring all modern technological progress. It is therefore important to ensure preponderant rates of production of electric power. The plan for the electrification of the country calls for almost tripling the per-worker supply of electricity to industry within the present decade; a considerable expansion of industries with a high rate of power consumption through the supply of cheap power; and extensive electrification of transport, agriculture and the household in town and countryside. The electrification of the whole country will be completed in the main in the second decade.

The annual production of electricity must be brought up to between 900,000,000,000 and 1,000,000,000,000 kwh. by the end of the first decade and to between 2,700,000,000,000 and 3,000,-000,000,000 kwh. by the end of the second decade. For this it will be necessary to increase the capacity of power plants accordingly in the 20 years and to build hundreds of thousands of kilometers of high-tension transmission and distribution lines in all regions of the country. A single power grid for the U.S.S.R. will be built, with sufficient reserves of capacity to transmit electric power from the eastern regions to the European part of the country. It will be linked with the power grids of other socialist countries.

As atomic energy becomes cheaper the construction of atomic power plants will be expanded, especially in areas that are poor in other power sources, and the use of atomic energy for peaceful purposes in the national economy, medicine and science will increase.

The further rapid expansion of the output of metals and fuels, constituting the foundation of modern industry, remains one of the major economic tasks. Within the 20 years ferrous metallurgy will attain a level making it possible to produce approximately 250,000,000 tons of steel a year. Steel output must fully meet the growing requirements of the national economy corresponding to the technological progress achieved in this period. The output of light, nonferrous and rare metals will be particularly speeded; the output of aluminum and its use in electrification, machine building and construction and for every-

day purposes will greatly increase. A consistent policy will be applied of priority *development of* extraction of oil and gas with their increasing use as raw material for the chemical industry. *Coal, gas and* oil output must fully meet all the requirements of the national economy. *The most progressive and economical methods of extracting mineral fuel will be widely applied.*

One of the major tasks is comprehensive development of the chemical industry and the full use in all economic fields of the discoveries of modern chemistry, which greatly expand opportunities to increase the national wealth and the output of new, better and cheaper means of production and consumer goods. Metal, wood and other building materials will be increasingly replaced by economical, practical and light synthetic materials. The production of mineral fertilizers and chemical weed and pest killers will rise sharply.

Of primary importance for the technical re-equipping of the entire national economy is the development of machine building, the all-round acceleration of the production of automated production lines and machines, automatic, remote-control and electronic devices, and precision instruments. The designing of machines with high technical properties, consuming smaller amounts of raw materials and power and leading to higher *labor* productivity, will develop rapidly. The requirements of the national economy for all types of modern machinery, machine tools and instruments *will* [must] be fully met.

On the basis of the development of machine building in the first decade integrated mechanization will be carried out in industry, agriculture, construction, transport [and loading and unloading operations] and in the communal economy. *Integrated mechanization will lead to the elimination of manual loading and unloading operations and will rule out heavy labor in the performance of basic and auxiliary production operations.* [Integrated mechanization will lead to the elimination of manual labor in both basic and auxiliary operations.]

In the 20-year period integrated automation of production will be carried out on a large scale, with an ever-growing shift to fully automated shops and enterprises *ensuring high technical and economic efficiency.* The introduction of highly perfected automatic control systems will be accelerated. *Cybernetics and electronic computers and control systems will be widely applied in production processes in manufacturing, the construction industry and transport, in scientific research, in planning and designing, and in accounting and management.* [It is necessary to organize the wide use of cybernetics and electronic computers and control systems in production, scientific work, designing and planning, and in accounting, statistics and management.]

The tremendous scale of capital construction calls for the rapid development and technological improvement of the construction industry and the building materials industry to a level meeting the requirements of the national economy and ensuring maximum reduction of construction periods, lowering of construction costs and improvement of quality through steady industrialization of construction and the most rapid completion of the change-over to the erection of completely fabricated buildings and installations from large factory-made structurals and elements on the basis of standard designs. [The tremendous scale of capital construction calls for the rapid development and technological improvement of the construction industry, a substantial increase in the volume and quality of building materials and reduction of their cost, a maximum acceleration of the tempos of construction and reduction in its cost through steady industrialization and the introduction of prefabricated structurals.]

The C.P.S.U. will direct its efforts toward ensuring a rapid rise in the output of consumer goods. The growing resources of industry must be applied more and more to meeting fully all the requirements of the Soviet people and to building and equipping enterprises and institutions serving the everyday and cultural needs of the public. Along with the accelerated development of all branches of light industry and the food industry, the share of consumer goods in the output of heavy industry will also increase. Electricity and gas will be employed on a larger scale for household use.

The growth of the national economy will require accelerated development of all types of transport. The most important tasks in the sphere of transport are: expansion of transport and road construction and meeting in full the requirements of the national economy and the public for all types of transportation; further technical re-equipment of the railroads and other transport systems; a considerable increase in speeds in rail, sea and river traffic; the coordinated development of all types of transport as integral parts of a single transport network. The share of shipments by pipeline will increase.

A single deep-water system will link the main inland waterways of the European part of the U.S.S.R.

A ramified network of improved roads will be built throughout the country. The country's motor vehicle fleet will increase sufficiently to meet fully all freight and passenger needs; car rental centers will be organized on a large scale. Air transport will become a means of mass passenger transportation and will extend to all parts of the country.

The latest jet technology will continue to develop rapidly, above all in air transport, and also for space exploration.

All means of communication (post office, radio, television, telephone and telegraph) will be further developed. All districts of the country will get good and reliable [telephone and radio] communications and will be linked in a network of television stations.

Full-scale communist construction demands a more and more rational geographical distribution of industries, which will save social labor and ensure the integrated development of districts and specialization of their industries, do away with overpopulation of big cities, facilitate elimination of the essential distinctions between town and countryside, and further equalize the level of economic development of different parts of the country.

To gain time, priority will be given to utilizing easily exploited natural resources that provide the greatest economic effect.

Industry in areas east of the Urals, where there are incalculable natural riches, raw material and power resources, will expand greatly.

The following must be ensured within the next 20 years: In Siberia and Kazakhstan—the creation of new power bases by using deposits of cheap coal and developing the water-power resources of the Angara and Yenisei Rivers, the organization of big centers of power-consuming industries and [the completion in Siberia of the country's third metallurgical base,] the development of rich new ore, *oil* and coal deposits, and the construction of a number of new machine-building centers; in areas along the Volga, in the Urals, the Northern Caucasus and Central Asia—rapid development of the power, oil, gas and chemical industries and the development of ore deposits. *Along with the development of the existing, old metallurgical bases in the Urals and the Ukraine, completion of the country's third metallurgical base in Siberia and the establishment of two new bases—in the center of the European part of the U.S.S.R. by exploiting the iron ore of the Kursk Magnetic Anomaly, and in Kazakhstan.* Soviet man will be able to carry out daring plans to change the courses of some northern rivers and regulate their waters for the purpose of utilizing the powerful water resources for the irrigation and watering of arid areas.

There will be further considerable development of the economy in the European part of the U.S.S.R., where the bulk of the country's population is concentrated and where there are great opportunities for expanding industrial production.

The maximum acceleration of scientific and technical progress is a major national task requiring constant effort to reduce the length of time spent on designing new technical means and introducing them in production. It is necessary to develop in every way the initiative of economic councils, enterprises, public organizations, scientists, engineers, designers, workers and collective farmers in creating and applying new technical improvements. Of prime importance is material and moral encouragement to mass invention and the rationalization movement, to enterprises, shops, *state and collective farms,* brigades and innovators mastering the production of new machinery and using it skillfully.

The Party will do everything to further increase the role of science in the building of communist society, to encourage research to discover new possibilities for the development of productive forces, the extensive and rapid application of the latest scientific and technical discoveries, a decisive advance in experimental work, including research directly at enterprises, and the exemplary organization of scientific and technical information and of the whole system of studying and disseminating advanced Soviet and foreign experience. Science will take its full place directly as a productive force.

Constant improvement in the technology of all branches and types of production is an absolute requisite for *their* [industrial] development. *Technical progress will make it possible to lighten the labor of man, substantially to intensify and accelerate production processes* [Technical progress will make it possible substantially to intensify and accelerate production processes without putting undue strain on the worker] and to achieve the highest precision in these processes, standardization of mass-produced items and maximum introduction of production lines. Machining will be supplemented and, when necessary, replaced by chemical methods, the technological use of electricity, electrochemistry, [electric heat treatment] etc.; radioelectronics, semiconductors and ultrasonics will occupy a more and more important place in production technology. The construction of new, technically improved enterprises should be combined with the reconstruction of those now in existence and the replacement and modernization of their equipment.

Development of specialization and cooperation *and also the expedient combining of allied enterprises* is one of the most important conditions for technical progress and the rational organization of social labor. The manufacture of articles of similar type should be concentrated primarily at large specialized enterprises, *with the most rational geographical distribution.*

New technology and the reduction of the working day call for shifting to a higher stage of labor organization. Technical progress and better organization of production must be fully utilized at every enterprise to increase labor productivity and reduce production costs. This presumes that labor productivity must grow faster than the payment of labor, that norm-setting be improved, loss of working time be prevented and cost accounting be introduced in all stages of production.

Most important will be the task of systematically raising the qualifications of those working in industry and other branches of the economy, in accordance with technical progress. Planned training, instruction and rational employment of those released from various jobs and transferred to other jobs as a result of mechanization and automation are essential.

Existing enterprises will be improved and developed into enterprises of communist society. Typical features of this process will be: new machinery, high standards of production organization and efficiency through increased automation of production processes and the introduction of automatic controls and automatic inspection; improvement of the efficiency and technical knowledge of the workers, the ever-increasing fusion of physical and mental labor and an increase in the proportion of engineers and technicians in industry; the expansion of experimental-research work, and closer links between enterprises and research institutes; development of the competition movement, application of scientific discoveries and introduction of the best forms of labor organization and models of labor productivity; the extensive participation of workers' collectives in the management of enterprises and the spreading of communist forms of labor.

2. The Development of Agriculture and Social Relations in the Countryside.—Along with a powerful industry, a flourishing, comprehensively developed and highly productive agriculture is an absolute requirement for the building of communism. The Party is organizing a mighty advance of productive forces in agriculture which will enable it to accomplish two basic, closely related tasks: (a) to achieve an abundance of high-quality food products for the public and of raw materials for industry; (b) to ensure a gradual transition to communist social relations in the Soviet countryside and to eliminate in the main the distinctions between town and countryside.

The chief means to an advance in agriculture and to satisfying the country's growing need for farm products are comprehensive mechanization and steady intensification: achieving high standards of crop farming and animal husbandry, based on science and advanced experience, on all collective and state farms, sharply raising the yields of all crops and increasing the output per hectare with the utmost economy of labor and resources. On this basis, it is necessary to secure an uninterrupted rise in farm output in accordance with the needs of society. Agriculture will approach the level of industry in technical equipment and the organization of production; farm labor will turn into a variety of industrial labor; and the dependence of agriculture upon the elements will decrease considerably and then will drop to a minimum.

The development of virgin and idle lands and the establishment of large new state farms, the reorganization of the Machine and Tractor Stations and the sale of implements of production to the collective farms, and the increasing of material incentives for the toilers of the countryside all constituted an important stage in the development of agriculture. *The Party will continue to devote considerable attention to developing agriculture in the areas where virgin and idle lands are being cultivated.*

The further advance of the countryside to communism will proceed through the development and improvement of the two forms of socialist farming—the collective farms and the state farms.

The collective farm system is an inseparable part of Soviet socialist society. This is the road charted by V. I. Lenin for the gradual transition of the peasantry to communism; it has stood the test of history and conforms to the distinctive features of the peasantry.

The collective farm form fully accords with the level and needs of development of modern productive forces in the countryside and makes possible the effective use of new machinery and scientific discoveries and the rational use of manpower. The collective farm blends the personal interests of the peasants with social, countrywide interests, blends individual with collective interest in the results of production, and affords extensive opportunities for raising the incomes and living standards of the peasants on the basis of growing labor productivity. It is essential to make the most of the possibilities and advantages of the collective farm system. By virtue of its organizational structure and democratic foundations, which will develop more and more, the collective farm is a social form that ensures the management of production by the collective farm masses themselves, the unfolding of their creative initiative and the education of the collective farmers in the spirit of communism. The collective farm is a school of communism for the peasantry.

The economic flowering of the collective farm system creates the conditions for gradually bringing closer together collective farm ownership and public ownership and in the long run for their merging in a single communist ownership.

The state farms, the leading socialist agricultural enterprises in the countryside, play an ever-increasing role in the development of agriculture. The state farms have the function of providing the collective farms with models of progressive, scientific, economically profitable methods of social production, efficiency and high labor productivity.

The C.P.S.U. proceeds from the fact that the further consolidation of the indestructible alliance of the working class and collective farm peasantry is of decisive political and socio-economic importance for the building of communism in the U.S.S.R.

A. Creating an Abundance of Farm Products. In order to satisfy fully the requirements of the entire population and of the national economy for farm products, the task is set of increasing the total volume of agricultural production by approximately 150% in ten years and by 250% in 20 years. The growth in the output of agricultural products must keep ahead of the growing demand for them. In the first decade the Soviet Union will overtake the United States of America in per capita output of basic agricultural products.

Accelerated growth of grain production is the basic link in the further development of all agriculture and the basis for rapid growth in animal husbandry. Gross grain output will more than double in 20 years, and yields will double. The output of wheat, corn, and cereal and leguminous crops will increase substantially.

Animal husbandry will develop at a rapid rate. Output of live-

stock products will increase: meat production will approximately triple in the first decade and almost quadruple in 20 years, and milk production will more than double in ten years and almost triple in 20 years. The planned increase in the output of livestock products will be achieved by increasing the numbers of livestock and poultry, improving breeds and raising productivity, and building up a stable fodder base, chiefly corn, sugar beets, fodder beans and other crops.

Labor productivity in agriculture will rise at least 150% in ten years and between 400% and 500% in 20 years. A rapid rise in the productivity of farm labor—at a higher rate than in industry—will make it possible to eliminate the lag of agriculture behind industry and will turn it into a highly developed branch of the economy of communist society.

The basis for the growth in productivity of farm labor will be further mechanization of agriculture, the use of integrated mechanization and of automation devices, and the introduction of highly efficient machinery adapted to the conditions of each zone.

The Party considers rapid electrification of agriculture to be one of the most important tasks. All state and collective farms will be supplied with electricity for production and domestic purposes from the state power grids and also by building rural power plants.

The technological re-equipping of agriculture must be combined with the most progressive forms and methods of organization of labor and production and the utmost improvement of the level of technical knowledge of the toilers in agricultural production. Skilled workers proficient in the use of new machinery and possessing special agricultural training will increasingly predominate on the collective and state farms. *Careful treatment of farm machines and their efficient use are of great importance.*

To ensure high, stable, steadily increasing harvests, to deliver agriculture from the harmful influence of the elements and especially drought, to raise the fertility of the soil sharply and to advance animal husbandry rapidly, it is necessary:

—to carry out a scientific distribution of agriculture by natural-economic zones and regions and a deeper and more stable specialization of agriculture, giving priority to increasing the output of the type of farm product for which the best conditions exist and which yields the greatest saving in expenditures;

—to introduce *on all collective and state farms* [in all parts of the country], in conformity with local conditions and the specialization of each farm, scientific systems of land cultivation and animal husbandry ensuring the most effective use of the land and the most economically advantageous combination of branches of agriculture, the best structure of sown areas with the substitution of high-yield and valuable crops for low-yield and less valuable ones; to see to it that every collective and state farm masters advanced methods of crop farming with the application of rational crop rotations and the sowing of only select seeds; to build up a stable fodder base in all districts and to spread advanced zootechnological achievements among collective and state farms;

—to carry out *rational* [consistent] and comprehensive introduction of chemicals in agriculture—to meet all its needs for chemical fertilizers and chemical means of killing weeds and plant and animal diseases and pests; and to ensure the best use of local fertilizers on all collective farms;

—to apply the discoveries of biological science widely, *especially of microbiology* [and make constantly increasing use of microbiology], which is assuming ever greater importance for improving soil fertility;

—to carry out an extensive program of irrigation construction, to irrigate and water millions of hectares of new lands in the arid areas and improve existing irrigation farming; to expand field-protective afforestation, the building of water reservoirs, irrigation of pastures and amelioration of overmoist land; and to combat water and wind erosion systematically. *Considerable attention will be given to the protection and rational use of forest, water and other natural riches and to restoring and increasing them.*

The Party will promote the development of agricultural science, direct the creative efforts of scientists toward working out key problems of agricultural advance, and work for the practical application and extensive introduction of scientific discoveries and advanced production experience in crop cultivation and animal husbandry. Research institutions and experimental stations must become important links in agricultural management, and scientists and specialists must become direct organizers of agricultural production. Each province or group of provinces of the same zonal type should have its agricultural research center, with its own large-scale farm and up-to-date material and technical base, to work out recommendations for state and collective farms applicable to the special features of the area. Agricultural research and training institutions should be located chiefly in rural areas and be directly associated with the process of farm production, so that students may learn while working and work while learning.

B. The Collective and State Farms on the Road to Communism; Remolding Social Relations in the Countryside. The economic basis for the development of the collective and state farms lies in the continuous growth and best use of their productive forces, improvement of the organization of production and methods of management, a steady rise in labor productivity and strict observance of the principle "The better the work and its results, the higher the payment." On this basis the collective and state farms will become to an increasing degree enterprises of the communist type in their production relations, the character of the work, and the living and cultural standard of their working people.

The policy of the *Party* [socialist state] toward the collective farms is based on blending countrywide interests with the material interest of the collective farms and their members in the results of their labor. The state will promote the growth of the productive forces of the collective farm system and the economic advance of all collective farms; at the same time, the contribution of the collective farm peasantry to the building of a communist society must also grow.

The state will ensure the full satisfaction of the needs of the collective farms for modern machinery, *spare parts*, chemicals and other means of production, will train new hundreds of thousands of skilled workers and will considerably increase capital investments in the countryside, in addition to greater investments by the collective farms themselves. There will be a great increase in the quantity of manufactured goods made available to the collective farm villages.

Strict observance by the collective farms and their members of their contract obligations to the state is an absolute principle of their participation in the development of the whole national economy.

The system of state purchases must be directed toward increasing the amount and improving the quality of the farm products procured, on the basis of an all-round advance of the collective farm economy. It is essential to coordinate the planning of state procurements with the production and economic plans of the collective farms, paying strict heed to the interests of agricultural production, its correct distribution and specialization.

The policy in the sphere of state purchase prices for agricultural products and selling prices of means of production for the countryside must take into account the interests of expanded reproduction in both industry and agriculture and the formation of the necessary accumulations on the collective farms. It is essential that the level of state purchase prices encourage the collective farms to raise labor productivity and reduce production costs, since greater farm output and lower production costs are the basis for higher incomes for the collective farms.

The proper ratio of accumulation and consumption in the distribution of income is a condition for successful collective farm development. The collective farms cannot develop without constantly enlarging their communal funds for production, insurance, cultural and community needs. At the same time, it must be an obligatory rule for every collective farm to increase its members' incomes from the communal economy and to raise their living standard in accordance with the growth in labor productivity.

Great importance attaches to improvement in the methods of norm setting and payment of labor on collective farms, the use of supplementary forms of labor payment and other material incentives to better economic results. Increasingly equal economic conditions must be provided that will improve the in-

comes of collective farms existing under unequal natural-economic conditions in different zones and also within the same zones, in order to apply more consistently the principle of equal pay for equal work on a scale embracing the whole collective farm system. Production on all collective farms must be conducted strictly on the basis of cost accounting.

By its organizational work and through economic policy measures, the Party will strive to overcome completely the lag of the economically weak collective farms and to turn all collective farms into economically strong, high-income farms in the course of the next few years. The Party sets the task of continuously reinforcing and educating collective farm cadres, of ensuring the further extension of collective farm democracy and developing the principle of collective leadership in the management of collective farm affairs.

As the collective farms develop, their basic production assets will increase and modern technical means will become dominant.

The economic advance of the collective farms will make it possible to perfect collective farm internal relations: to raise the degree of socialization of production, to bring norm setting and the organization and payment of labor closer to the level and forms employed at state enterprises, and to carry out the transition to a guaranteed monthly payment; and to develop community services (public catering, kindergartens and nurseries, everyday services, etc.) more widely.

At a certain stage the communal production of the collective farms will achieve a level at which it will be possible to satisfy the collective farmers' requirements fully out of its resources. On this basis, supplementary individual farming will gradually become economically obsolete. When collective farm communal production is able to replace in full the collective farmers' supplementary individual farming and when the collective farmers see for themselves that it is unprofitable for them to have personal plots, they will give them up of their own accord.

As productive forces increase, intercollective-farm production ties will expand and the process of the socialization of production will transcend the limits of individual collective farms. The practice of the joint building of intercollective-farm enterprises and cultural and service institutions, state-collective farm power plants and enterprises for the primary processing, storage and transportation of farm products, for various types of construction, for the manufacture of building materials, etc., should be encouraged. As their communal wealth increases, the collective farms will participate more and more in establishing enterprises and cultural and everyday-service institutions for general public use, boarding schools, clubs, hospitals and rest homes. All these developments, which must proceed on a voluntary basis and when the necessary economic conditions exist, will gradually impart to collective farm-cooperative property the nature of public property.

The state farms have a long way to travel in their development: *to steadily increase production and improve quality of output*, to *strive for* [attain] high rates of growth of labor productivity, to steadily reduce production costs and increase *profitability of production* [farm productivity]. This calls for the economically expedient specialization of state farms. Their role in supplying food to the urban population will grow. They must become mechanized and well-organized first-class factories of grain, cotton, meat, milk, wool, vegetables, fruit and other products and must develop seed farming and pedigreed animal husbandry to the utmost.

The material and technical base of the state farms will be enlarged and improved, and the living and cultural conditions on the state farms will approach those in cities. State farm management should follow a more and more democratic pattern, which will allot a greater role to the collectives of workers and employees, to general meetings and production conferences, in deciding production, cultural and community questions.

As the collective farms and state farms develop, their production ties with one another and with local industrial enterprises will grow stronger and the practice of joint organization of various types of output will expand. This will ensure a more even and fuller use of manpower and production resources throughout the year, raise the productivity of social labor and facilitate an advance in the living and cultural standards of the population. Agrarian-industrial associations will gradually emerge in proportion to their economic expediency; in these, with the rational specialization and cooperation of agricultural and industrial enterprises, agriculture will combine organically with the industrial processing of its products.

As the production of collective and state farms develops and social relations within them become perfected, agriculture *will rise* [rises] to a higher level, opening up the possibility of transition to communist forms of production and distribution. The collective farms will draw level in economic conditions with the publicly owned agricultural enterprises. They will turn into highly developed, mechanized farms. By virtue of high labor productivity, all collective farms will become economically strong, and the collective farmers will be well off and their needs fully met out of the collective farms' communal economy. They will have the services of dining rooms, bakeries, laundries, kindergartens and nurseries, clubs, libraries and stadiums. The payment of labor of the collective farmers will be the same as at publicly owned enterprises, and they will be provided with all forms of social security (pensions, vacations, etc.) out of collective farm and state funds.

The collective farm villages will gradually grow into amalgamated urban-type communities with modern housing, communal utilities, services and cultural and medical institutions. The rural population will ultimately draw level with the urban population in cultural and living conditions.

Elimination of the socio-economic and cultural-everyday distinctions between town and countryside will be one of the greatest results of communist construction.

3. Management of the National Economy and Planning.—The building of the material and technical base of communism calls for continuous improvement in economic management *and planning.* Chief attention in all links of planning and economic management must be focused on the most rational and effective use of material, labor, financial and natural resources and on the elimination of excessive expenditures *and losses.* It is an immutable law of economic construction to achieve, in the interests of society, the greatest results at the lowest cost. *The improvement of economic management must be accompanied by all-round simplification and reduction of the cost of the administrative apparatus.*

Planning at all levels must aim at the rapid development and introduction of new technology. It is essential that scientific, progressive norms for the use of means of production be *improved and* strictly observed in all sectors of the national economy.

The Party attaches prime importance to increasing the effectiveness of capital investments, the selection of the most advantageous and economical capital construction projects, the achievement [everywhere] of a maximum increase in output per ruble of capital invested, and quicker return on investments. It is necessary constantly to improve the structure of capital investments and to enlarge the proportion of them that is spent on equipment, machinery and machine tools.

Concentrating capital investments on decisive sectors, eliminating the scattering of capital expenditures and speeding the opening of enterprises under construction must become indispensable conditions of economic planning and organization.

Systematic improvement of the quality of output is an imperative requirement for economic development. The quality of goods produced by Soviet enterprises should be considerably higher than that of the output of the best capitalist enterprises. For this purpose it is necessary to employ a broad set of measures, including public control, and to heighten the role of quality indices in planning, in assessing the work of enterprises and in socialist competition.

Communist construction presupposes the maximum development of democratic principles of management coupled with a strengthening and improvement of centralized state management of the national economy. The economic independence and rights of local agencies and enterprises will continue to grow within the framework of the single national economic plan; plans and recommendations made at lower levels, beginning with enterprises, must play an ever-increasing role in planning.

Centralized planning should concentrate chiefly on working out and ensuring fulfillment of the major indices of the economic plans with utmost regard for proposals from below; on coordinating and dovetailing plans drawn up locally; on spreading scientific and technical discoveries and advanced experience; on carrying out a single state policy in the spheres of technical progress, capital investment, geographical distribution of production, payment of labor, prices and finance; and on introducing a unified system of accounting and statistics.

In the development of the national economy it is necessary strictly to observe balance, to avert in good time the rise of economic disproportions, to ensure sufficient economic reserves as a requirement for stable and high economic growth rates, uninterrupted operation of enterprises and continuous improvement in the people's well-being.

The growing scale of the national economy and the rapid development of science and technology call for an improvement in the scientific level of planning, *designing,* accounting and statistics [and industrial designing]. A better scientific, technical and economic grounding of the plans will ensure their greater stability, which also presupposes timely correction and amendment of plans in the course of their fulfillment. Planning must be continuous, and the annual and long-term plans must be organically integrated *and ensured financial, material and technical resources.*

Firm and consistent observance of discipline, day-to-day supervision and determined elimination of the elements of localism and of a narrow departmental approach in economic affairs are necessary requirements for successful communist construction.

There must be continued heightening of the role and responsibility of local agencies in economic management. The transfer of a number of functions of economic management from all-Union agencies to republic agencies, from republic to province agencies and from province to district agencies should be continued. It is necessary to improve the work of the economic councils, the most viable form of management in industry and construction, a form appropriate to the present level of productive forces. Improvement of the work of the economic councils within the economic administrative regions will be accompanied by greater coordination of the work of economic agencies in order to organize better the planned, integrated economic development of such major economic regions as the Urals, the Volga area, *Western* Siberia, *Eastern Siberia, the Far East,* Transcaucasia, the Baltic area, Central Asia, etc.

Operative independence and the initiative of enterprises on the basis of the state plan assignments must be increased in order to mobilize internal reserves and make more effective the use of capital investments, production facilities and funds. It is necessary greatly to raise the role *and interest* of enterprises in the introduction of the latest machinery *and the fullest possible use of production capacity.*

The selection, training and promotion of cadres that directly head enterprises and collective farms and engage in organizing and managing production are of decisive importance in economic management. The sphere of the creation of material values is the main sphere of the life of society. The best cadres must therefore be given leading posts in production enterprises.

The direct and most active participation of the trade unions in drafting and carrying out economic plans, in deciding matters concerning the labor of workers and employees and in setting up the agencies of economic administration and of management of enterprises must be extended more and more at the center and locally. The role of the collectives of workers and employees in deciding matters concerning the work of enterprises must be enhanced.

In the process of building communism, economic management will rely on material and moral incentives for high production indices. The proper combination of material and moral incentives for work is a great creative force in the struggle for communism. In the course of the advance to communism the importance of moral incentives for work, public recognition of results and the sense of responsibility of each for the common cause will become constantly greater.

The entire system of planning and assessing the work of central and local organizations, enterprises and collective farms must stimulate their interest in higher plan assignments and the maximum dissemination of advanced production experience.

Initiative and successes in finding and using new possibilities for improving the quantitative and qualitative indices of production should be especially encouraged.

There must be a continuous improvement in technical norm setting, in the system of labor payments and bonuses, in control by the ruble over the quantity and quality of work, in eliminating leveling and in intensifying collective forms of material incentives that raise the interest of each employee in a high level of operation of the enterprise as a whole.

In communist construction it is necessary to make full use of commodity-money relations in conformity with their new content in the socialist period. In doing so, the use of such instruments of economic development as cost accounting, money, price, cost, profit, trade, credit and finance play a big part. When the transition is made to a single communist form of public ownership and the communist system of distribution, commodity-money relations will become economically obsolete and will wither away.

The important role of the *state* budget in distributing the social product and national income will be retained throughout the period of full-scale communist construction. There will be a further strengthening of the monetary and credit system, a strengthening of Soviet currency, a greater and greater rise in the *purchasing power of the ruble* [rate of exchange of the ruble on the basis of its growing purchasing power] and a strengthening of the role of the ruble in the international arena.

It is necessary to intensify cost accounting in every way, to work for *the strictest economy and thrift, fewer losses*, lower production costs and higher profitability. The price system should be continuously improved and brought into conformity with the tasks of communist construction, technical progress, growth of production and consumption and reduction of production expenditures. Prices must to an ever-increasing extent reflect the socially necessary expenditures of labor, ensure return of costs of production and circulation and a certain profit for each normally operating enterprise. Systematic, economically justified price reductions based on growth of labor productivity and reduction of production costs are the main trend of the price policy in the period of communist construction.

Soviet society possesses tremendous national assets. For this reason the role of accounting and control over the maintenance and proper use of the national wealth increases. Thrift, rational use of every ruble belonging to the people, skillful use of funds, steady improvement of planning and methods of management, better organization and conscious discipline, and development of the initiative of the people are powerful means of accelerating the advance of Soviet society to communism.

II. THE TASKS OF THE PARTY IN IMPROVING THE MATERIAL WELL-BEING OF THE PEOPLE.—The heroic labor of the Soviet people has created a powerful and comprehensively developed economy. There is now every possibility of rapidly improving the well-being of the whole population— workers, peasants and intelligentsia. The C.P.S.U. sets a task of world-historic importance—to ensure a living standard in the Soviet Union higher than that of any capitalist country.

This task will be accomplished by: (a) raising individual payment [of working people] according to the quantity and quality of work, coupled with reduction of retail prices and the abolition of taxes paid by the public; (b) increasing the public funds *of consumption earmarked for satisfying the requirements of* [distributed among] members of society irrespective of the quantity and quality of their labor—that is, free of charge (education, medical treatment, pensions, maintenance of children at children's institutions, transition to cost-free use of public utilities, etc.).

The rise in the real earnings of the population will be more than covered by a rapid increase in the amount of commodities and services and by extensive development of housing, cultural and service construction.

The Soviet people will be more prosperous than *the working people* [the people] in the developed capitalist countries even if average incomes are equal, since in the Soviet Union the national income is distributed *in the interests of all* [fairly among] the members of society and there are no parasitic classes, as in the bourgeois countries, that appropriate and squander immense wealth plundered from millions of working people.

The Party proceeds from Lenin's thesis that communist construction should rest on the principle of material incentive. In the coming 20 years payment according to one's work will remain the principal source for satisfying the material and cultural needs of the working people.

At the same time the disparity between high and comparatively low incomes must gradually shrink. Greater and greater masses of unskilled workers and employees will become skilled, and the diminishing difference in labor skills and productivity will be accompanied by a steady reduction of disparities in the level of pay. As the living standard of the entire population rises, low income levels will approach the higher and the disparity between the incomes of peasants and workers, of low-paid and high-paid working people, and of the populations of different parts of the country will gradually decline.

Meantime, as the country advances toward communism, personal needs will be increasingly met out of public consumption funds, whose rate of growth will exceed the rate of growth of individual payment for labor. The transition to communist distribution will be completed after the principle of distribution according to work entirely exhausts itself—that is, when there is an abundance of material and cultural benefits and labor becomes a prime necessity of life for all members of society.

A. Provision of a High Level of Income and Consumption for the Whole Population; *Development of Trade*. The national income of the U.S.S.R. will increase almost 150% in the next ten years and about 400% in 20 years. Per capita real income will increase by more than 250% in 20 years. *In the first ten years the real incomes of all workers and employees (including public funds) per employed person will on the average almost double, while the incomes of workers and employees in low-paid categories will approximately triple. Thus by the end of the first decade there will no longer be low-paid groups of workers and employees in the country.* [In the course of the next ten years the real incomes of workers and employees (including public funds) per employed person will on the average almost double, and in 20 years they will increase by approximately 200% to 250%. The real incomes of workers and employees who receive relatively lower wages will be raised to a level that will bring about the elimination of low-paid brackets throughout the country within ten years. The real incomes of workers and employees receiving the minimum wages will be approximately tripled (including their benefits from public funds) in this period.]

On the basis of higher rates of growth of the labor productivity of collective farmers, their real incomes will rise more rapidly on the average than the incomes of workers and will, on an average per working person, more than double in the next ten years and increase more than fourfold in 20 years.

The pay of such numerically large strata of the Soviet intelligentsia as engineers and technicians, agronomists and zootechnicians, teachers and medical and cultural workers will rise considerably.

As the incomes of the population grow, the general level of public consumption will rise rapidly. The entire population will be able to satisfy amply its demand for high-quality and varied food products. The share of livestock products (meat, fats, dairy products) and of fruit and high-grade vegetables in the public diet will rise substantially in the near future. The demand of all sections of the population for high-quality consumer goods—well-made and attractive clothing, footwear and goods for improving and adorning the daily life of Soviet people, such as comfortable modern furniture, improved household articles, a wide range of goods for cultural purposes, etc.—will be amply satisfied. Production of automobiles for the public will be considerably expanded.

The output of consumer goods must fully meet the growing consumer demand and must conform to its changes. The timely output of goods in accordance with the varied demand of the public, taking into account local, national and climatic conditions, is an imperative requirement for *all* the consumer industries. [Good trade facilities will be arranged in all sections of the country and in all populated points; this is a necessary and important condition for satisfying the growing requirements of the public.]

Soviet trade will be further developed as a necessary condition for satisfying the growing requirements of the public. Good trade facilities will be arranged in all sections and populated points of the country, and progressive forms of service for the public will be widely applied. The material and technical base of trade—the network of stores, warehouses, refrigeration plants and vegetable storage facilities—will be expanded.

The consumer's cooperatives, which are called upon to improve trade in the countryside and to organize the marketing of farm surpluses, will be developed. Collective farm trade will also retain its importance.

The second decade will see an abundance of material and cultural benefits for the whole population, and the material prerequisites will be created for [completing] the transition in the subsequent period to the communist principle of distribution according to need.

B. Solution of the Housing Problem and Improvement of Living Conditions. The C.P.S.U. sets the task of solving the most acute problem in the improvement of the well-being of the Soviet people—the housing problem. *The housing shortage will be ended in the course of the first decade. Those families that still live in overcrowded and poor housing will receive new apartments.* By the conclusion of the second decade every family, including newlyweds, will have a well-appointed apartment meeting the requirements of health and cultured living. Peasant houses of the old type will in the main be replaced by new, modern dwellings, or where possible they will be rebuilt with necessary conveniences. In the course of the second decade housing will gradually be made rent-free for all citizens.

Urban development, architecture and planning are assuming great importance in creating modern, convenient cities and other populated points, as well as production, residential and public buildings, that are economical to build and maintain. Cities and settlements should represent rational, integrated organization of production zones, residential areas, a network of public and cultural institutions, service enterprises, transport, engineering installations and a power system ensuring the best conditions for the work, life and relaxation of people.

An extensive program of communal construction and of improvements in all cities and workers' settlements will be carried out in the coming period; this will require completion of their electrification, the necessary provision of gas, *telephone service,* public transport facilities, water supply *and sewer systems,* and measures for the further improvement of living conditions in cities and other populated points—including tree planting, pond building and a determined struggle against air, soil and water pollution. Well-appointed small and medium-sized cities will be increasingly developed, making for better and healthier living conditions.

Public transport facilities (streetcars, buses, trolleybuses and subways) will become free in the course of the second decade, and at the end of it such public utilities as water, gas and heating will also be free.

C. Reduction of Working Hours and the Further Improvement of Working Conditions. In the coming ten years the country will change to a six-hour working day with one day off a week or a *35-hour* [34- to 36-hour] working week with two days off, and in underground work and hazardous jobs to a five-hour working day or a 30-hour, five-day working week.

On the basis of a corresponding rise in labor productivity, transition to a still shorter working week will be begun in the second decade.

The Soviet Union will thus have the world's shortest and at the same time most productive and highest-paid working day. Working people will have much more leisure time, and this will create additional conditions for improving their cultural and technical level.

The length of the annual paid vacations of working people will be increased in addition to the reduction in the working day. The minimum vacation for all workers and employees will gradually increase to three weeks and then to one

month. Paid vacations will gradually be extended to collective farmers *also.*

Comprehensive improvement of working conditions to make work healthier and easier constitutes an important task in improving the well-being of the people. Modern labor safety and hygienic measures to prevent occupational injuries and diseases will be introduced at all enterprises. Night shifts will gradually be abolished at enterprises, except for those where around-the-clock operation is required by the technological process or the need to serve the population.

D. Health Care and Increasing Longevity. The socialist state is the only state that undertakes to protect and constantly improve the health of the whole population. This is provided for by a system of socio-economic and medical measures. An extensive program of measures will be carried out to prevent and decisively reduce illness, wipe out mass contagious diseases and further increase longevity.

The needs of the urban and rural population for all forms of highly qualified medical care will be met in full. Accomplishment of this task calls for the extensive construction of medical institutions, including hospitals and sanatoriums, the equipment of all medical institutions with modern apparatus, and regular medical checkups for the entire population. Special emphasis must be given to extending the urban and rural network of mother-and-child health institutions (maternity homes, medical consultation centers, children's sanatoriums and hospitals, forest schools, etc.).

In addition to the existing free medical services, sanatorium accommodations and medicines will be provided for the sick free of charge.

In order to afford the people an opportunity for recreation in an out-of-town environment, rest homes, boarding houses, country hotels and tourist camps will be built where working people will be accommodated at a reasonable charge or—by way of a bonus—at a discount or free.

The Party considers one of the most important tasks to be ensuring the upbringing from earliest childhood of a physically strong young generation, harmoniously developed physically and spiritually. This requires the utmost encouragement of all forms of mass sport and physical culture, including at schools, and the drawing of broader and broader strata of the population, particularly the youth, into the physical culture movement.

E. Improvement of Everyday Conditions and of the Position of Women; Maintenance of Children and Disabled Persons at Public Expense. The vestiges of the unequal position of women in domestic life must be completely eliminated; all social and living conditions must be provided to enable women to combine happy motherhood with increasingly active and creative participation in social labor and public activities and in scientific and artistic pursuits. Women must be given relatively lighter and at the same time sufficiently well-paid jobs. Maternity leave will be of longer duration.

It is essential to provide conditions to reduce and lighten woman's work in the home and later to make possible the replacement of this work by public forms of satisfying the everyday material needs of the family. Toward this end, improved, inexpensive domestic machines, appliances and electrical devices will be widely introduced in households, and the public's needs for service enterprises will be fully met in the next few years.

The extension of public catering—including dining rooms at enterprises and institutions and in big apartment houses—until it meets the demands of the population requires special attention. The service in dining rooms and the quality of food must be radically improved, so that dinners in the dining rooms will be tasty and nourishing and will cost the family less than meals cooked at home. Price reductions in public catering will keep ahead of price reductions for food products in the stores. Thanks to all of this, public catering will be able to take a preponderant place over home cooking within ten to 15 years.

The transition to free public catering (midday meals) at enterprises and institutions and for collective farmers at work will begin in the second decade.

To provide a happy childhood for every child is one of the most important and noble tasks of building a communist society. The further extensive development of the network of children's institutions will make it possible for more and more families, and in the second decade for every family, to keep children and adolescents free of charge at children's institutions if they so desire. *The Party considers it necessary to do everything possible to satisfy fully the need for preschool institutions within the next few years.* [State and public children's institutions will be able to accept the majority of preschool children within the next few years.]

In town and countryside the need for nurseries, kindergartens, playgrounds, *extended-day schools* and Young Pioneer camps will be satisfied fully and without charge; there will be mass extension of boarding schools with free maintenance; free hot lunches will be served at all schools, and extended school hours with free dinners for school children will be introduced; and school uniforms and textbooks will be issued without charge.

As the national income grows *state agencies* [the state], the trade unions and the collective farms will in the course of the 20 years gradually undertake the maintenance of all citizens incapacitated through old age or disability. Sickness and temporary disability grants and old-age pensions will be extended to collective farmers; old-age and disability pensions will be raised. In town and countryside the network of well-appointed homes for the aged and invalids will be greatly extended to provide free accommodations for all applicants.

By fulfilling the tasks set by the Party for the improvement of the well-being of the people, the Soviet Union will make considerable headway toward the practical realization of the communist principle of distribution according to needs.

At the end of the 20 years public consumption funds will account for approximately half of the total real income of the population. This will make it possible to provide at public expense:
—free maintenance of children at children's institutions and boarding schools (if parents wish);
—material security for nonable-bodied persons;
—free education at all educational institutions;
—free medical care for all citizens, including the supply of medicines and treatment of the sick at sanatoriums;
—rent-free housing and, later, free public utilities;
—free public transport;
—free provision of some types of everyday services;
—steady reduction of charges for, and partially free, use of rest homes, boarding houses, tourist camps *and sports installations;*
—increasingly broad provision of the population with benefits, privileges and stipends (grants to unmarried mothers, stipends for students);
—gradual change-over to free public catering (midday meals) at enterprises and institutions and for collective farmers at work.

The Soviet state will thus present to the world a model of truly full and all-embracing satisfaction of the growing material and cultural requirements of man. The faster the productive forces of the country and labor productivity grow and the more broadly the creative energy of the Soviet people comes into play, the faster will the living standard of Soviet people improve.

The planned program can be successfully fulfilled under conditions of peace. Complications in the international situation and the resultant necessity of increasing defense expenditures may retard fulfillment of the plans for improving the people's well-being. A lasting normalization of international relations, reduction of military expenditures, and in particular the realization of general and complete disarmament under an appropriate agreement among states would make it possible considerably to surpass the plans for raising the working people's living standard.

The fulfillment of the vast program for improving the well-being of the Soviet people will have world-historic significance. The Party calls on the Soviet people to work perseveringly, with inspiration. Every working person must do his duty in the building of a communist society, in the struggle to fulfill the program for improving the people's well-being.

III. TASKS OF THE PARTY IN THE SPHERES OF STATE CONSTRUCTION AND THE FURTHER DEVELOPMENT OF SOCIALIST DEMOCRACY.—The dictatorship of the proletariat, born of the socialist revolution, has played a world-historic role by ensuring the victory of socialism in the U.S.S.R. At the same time, in the process of the building of socialism it has undergone changes itself. In connection with the liquidation of the exploiting classes, the function of suppressing their resistance withered away. The chief functions of the socialist state—economic-organizational and cultural-educational—have developed comprehensively. The socialist state has entered a new *period of its development* [phase]. The process of the state's evolution into an organization of all the working people of socialist society has begun. Proletarian democracy is becoming more and more a socialist democracy of the people as a whole.

The working class is the only class in history that does not aim to perpetuate its power.

Having brought about the complete and final victory of socialism—the first phase of communism—and the transition of society to the full-scale construction of communism, the dictatorship of the proletariat has accomplished its historical mission and has ceased to be essential in the U.S.S.R. from the point of view of the tasks of internal development. The state that arose as a state of the dictatorship of the proletariat has *in the new, present stage* turned into a state of the entire people, an agency expressing the interests and will of the people as a whole. Since the working class is the most advanced and the best organized force of Soviet society, it performs its leading role in the period of full-scale construction of communism as well. The working class will have completed its function of leader of society when communism is built and classes disappear.

The Party proceeds from the principle that the dictatorship of the working class will cease to be necessary before the state withers away. The state as an organization embracing the entire people will survive until the total victory of communism. Expressing the will of the people, it is called upon to organize the creation of the material and technical base of communism and the transformation of socialist relations into communist relations, to exercise control over the measure of work and *the measure of* consumption, to ensure a rise in the well-being of the people, to safeguard the rights and freedoms of Soviet citizens, socialist law and order and socialist property, to instill in the masses of the people conscious discipline and a communist attitude to labor, reliably to ensure the defense and security of the country, to develop fraternal cooperation with the socialist countries, to champion the cause of universal peace and to maintain normal relations with all countries.

Comprehensive extension and perfection of socialist democracy, active participation by all citizens in the administration of the state and in the management of economic and cultural construction, improvement of the work of the state apparatus and intensification of control over its activity by the people—such is the main direction of the development of the socialist state system in the period of the building of communism. As socialist democracy develops further, the agencies of state power will gradually be transformed into agencies of public self-government. The Leninist principle of democratic centralism—which ensures the proper combination of centralized leadership with maximum development of the initiative of local agencies, the extension of the rights of the Union republics and greater creative activity of the masses—will be still further developed. It is necessary to strengthen discipline, to exercise day-to-day control over the activities of all links in the administrative apparatus, to check up on the execution of decisions and laws of the Soviet state and to heighten the responsibility of every official for their strict and prompt implementation.

1. The Soviets and the Development of Democratic Principles of State Administration.—The role of the Soviets, which have become all-inclusive organizations of the people embodying their unity, will grow in the course of communist construction. The Soviets, which combine the features of state and public organizations, operate more and more like public organizations, with the masses participating extensively and directly in their work.

The Party considers it necessary to perfect the forms of popular representation and to develop the democratic principles of the Soviet electoral system.

In nominating candidates for Deputies to Soviets, it is necessary to guarantee the widest and fullest discussion of the personal qualities and qualifications of the candidates at meetings and in the press in order to elect those who are most worthy and who enjoy the highest authority.

To improve the work of the Soviets and bring fresh forces

into them, it is desirable that at least one-third of the members of a Soviet be replaced by new Deputies at each election so that more [hundreds of thousands and] millions of working people may go through the school of administering the state.

The Party considers systematic renewal of the executive agencies necessary to bring a wider range of able persons into them and to rule out the possibility of abuses of authority by individual state officials. It is advisable to establish the principle that the leading officials of Union, republic and local agencies may as a rule be elected to their offices for not more than three consecutive terms. In cases where it is the general opinion that the personal talents of an official make his further activity in an executive agency useful and necessary, his re-election may be permitted; the election in such cases shall be considered valid only if at least three-fourths of the votes, and not a simple majority of them, are cast in his favor.

The Party regards the improvement of the principles of socialist democracy and their rigid observance as a most important task. It is necessary to employ to the full: regular accounting by the Soviets and Deputies to their constituents; the right of the electorate to recall Deputies who have not justified the confidence placed in them; publicity about all important questions of state administration and of economic and cultural construction, and free and full discussion of these questions at sessions of the Soviets; regular accounting by executive agencies of authority at all levels to sessions of the Soviets; checkup on the work of these agencies and control over their activity; regular discussion by the Soviets of interpellations by Deputies; criticism of shortcomings in the work of Soviet, economic and other organizations.

Every Deputy to a Soviet must take an active part in state affairs and carry on definite work. The role of the standing committees of the Soviets is increasing. The standing committees of the Supreme Soviets must systematically supervise the activities of ministries, agencies and economic councils and contribute actively to the implementation of decisions adopted by the respective Supreme Soviets. In order to improve the work of the legislative bodies and to increase control over the executive agencies, the practice shall be introduced of periodically releasing Deputies from the responsibilities of their regular jobs for full-time committee work.

A gradually increasing number of questions that now fall under the jurisdiction of the administrations and departments of executive agencies must be referred to the standing committees of the local Soviets for decision.

The rights of the local Soviets of Working People's Deputies (local self-government) will be enlarged. Local Soviets will make final decisions on all questions of local significance.

Strengthening of the district agencies deserves special attention. As collective farm-cooperative ownership and public ownership draw closer together, a single democratic agency administering all enterprises, organizations and institutions at the district level will gradually take shape.

The participation of public organizations and associations of the working people in the legislative activity of the representative agencies of the Soviet state will be increased. The trade unions, the Young Communist League and other mass public organizations as represented by their all-Union and republic agencies must be granted the right of legislative initiative, that is, the right to introduce draft laws.

Discussion by the working people of draft laws and other decisions of both statewide and local significance must become the rule. The most important draft laws should be put to nationwide vote (referendum).

The C.P.S.U. attaches great importance to improving the work of the state apparatus, which is largely responsible for the proper utilization of all the resources of the country and the timely decision of questions relating to cultural and everyday services for the working people. The Soviet apparatus must be simple, competent, inexpensive, efficient and free of any manifestations of bureaucracy, formalism and red tape.

Constant state and public control is an important means of accomplishing this task. In keeping with Lenin's instructions, control agencies combining state control with public inspection must function constantly at the center and locally. The Party regards inspection by people's control agencies as an effective means of drawing broad masses of the people into the manage-ment of state affairs and into control over the strict observance of legality, as a means of perfecting the government apparatus, eradicating bureaucracy, and promptly putting into effect proposals made by the people.

The socialist state apparatus serves the people and is accountable to them. Negligence by an official, abuse of power and bureaucracy must be resolutely cut short and the official must be severely punished regardless of who he may be. It is the duty of Soviet people to stand guard over legality and law and order, not to tolerate any abuses but to fight them.

The Party holds that democratic principles in administration must be developed still further. The principle of electivity and accountability to representative bodies and to the voters should be gradually extended to all the leading officials of state agencies.

Efforts must be directed toward ensuring that the salaried state apparatus is reduced, that ever broader masses learn the skills of administration and that work in the state apparatus eventually ceases to constitute a special vocation.

While every executive must be held strictly and personally responsible for the job entrusted to him, it is necessary consistently to apply the principle of collective leadership at all levels of the state and economic apparatus.

The broadest democratism must be combined with unwavering observance of comradely discipline by the working people and must promote the strengthening of this discipline and [through] checkup from above and below. The chief thing in the activity of all state agencies is organizational work among the masses; proper selection of officials and testing and evaluating them by their practical work; and control over the actual fulfillment of the assignments and decisions of executive agencies.

The further strengthening of socialist law and order and the improvement of legal norms governing economic-organizational and cultural-educational work and contributing to the accomplishment of the tasks of communist construction and to the all-round flowering of the individual assume great importance.

The transition to communism means the fullest development of personal freedom and the rights of Soviet citizens. Socialism has granted and guaranteed the working people the broadest rights and freedoms. Communism will bring the working people further great rights and opportunities.

The Party sets the task of ensuring the strict observance of socialist legality, the eradication of all violations of law and order, the abolition of crime and the removal of all the causes of crime.

Justice in the U.S.S.R. is exercised in full conformity with the law. It is based on truly democratic principles: electivity and accountability of the judges and people's assessors, the right to recall them, open hearing of court cases, and the participation of public accusers and defenders in court with strictest observance of legality and all the norms of trial procedure by the courts and by investigation and inquiry agencies. The democratic principles of justice will be developed and improved.

There should be no room for lawbreakers and crime in a society that is building communism. But as long as there are criminal offenses, it is necessary severely to punish those who commit crimes dangerous to society, violate the rules of the socialist community and do not wish to live by honest labor. Chief attention should be focused on preventing crime.

Higher standards of living and culture and greater social consciousness of the working people will create all the conditions for eradicating crime and for the ultimate replacement of measures of criminal punishment by measures of public influence and education. Under socialism anyone who has strayed from the path of a working man can return to useful activity.

The whole system of state and public organizations educates the working people in a spirit of voluntary and conscientious performance of their duties and leads to the organic fusion of rights and duties to form single norms of communist community life.

2. The Further Heightening of the Role of Public Organizations. The State and Communism.—The role of public organizations increases in the period of the full-scale building of communism. The trade unions acquire particular importance as

schools of administration and economic management, as schools of communism. The Party will help the trade unions to intensify their activity in economic management and to make the permanent production conferences increasingly effective agencies in improving the work of enterprises and exercising control over production. The trade unions are called upon:

—to concern themselves constantly with raising the communist consciousness of the masses, to organize competition for communist labor, to help the working people develop the skills for managing state and public affairs, and to take an active part in controlling the measure of labor and *the measure* of consumption;

—to develop the activeness of workers and employees, enlisting them in the struggle for constant technical progress, for further increasing labor productivity, for the fulfillment and overfulfillment of state plans and assignments;

—to show constant concern for improving the skills of workers and employees, for bettering their working and living conditions and for guarding the material interests and rights of the working people;

—to work for the fulfillment of plans for the construction of housing and of cultural and service facilities and for the improvement of public catering, trade, social insurance and sanatorium and health resort facilities;

—to ensure control over the use of public consumption funds and over the work of all enterprises and institutions serving the working people;

—to improve cultural services and recreation facilities for the working people and to develop physical culture and sports.

The Young Communist League, as a voluntary public organization of young people that is helping the Party to raise youth in a communist spirit, enlist them in the practical tasks of building the new society and train a generation of well-rounded people who will live, work and manage public affairs under communism, will play a greater role. The Party regards the youth as a constructive, creative force in the Soviet people's struggle for communism.

The Y.C.L. is called upon to display even greater initiative and enterprise in all fields of life and to develop the activeness and labor heroism of young people. A central place in the work of Y.C.L. organizations must be accorded to inculcating in youth a spirit of boundless devotion to the motherland, the people, the Communist Party and the cause of communism and a constant preparedness for labor for the good of society and for overcoming all difficulties, and to raising the general educational level and technical knowledge of young men and women. It is the sacred duty of the Y.C.L. to prepare young people for the defense of the socialist motherland, to rear them as self-sacrificing patriots capable of firmly repelling the attack of any enemy. The Y.C.L. educates the youth in a spirit of strict observance of communist moral principles and norms. By its *work* [influence] in the schools and Young Pioneer organizations, the Y.C.L. is called upon to take active part in molding a buoyant, industrious and physically and morally sound generation.

The importance of the cooperatives—collective farms, consumers', housing-construction and other cooperative organizations—will rise as one of the forms of drawing the masses into communist construction, as means of communist education and schools of public self-government.

Other public associations of the working people—scientific, scientific-technical *and scientific-educational* societies, rationalizers' and inventors' organizations, associations of writers, artists and journalists, cultural-enlightenment organizations, and sports societies—will likewise be developed.

The Party regards it as a major task of the public organizations to promote labor competition and encourage communist forms of labor in every possible way, to heighten the activeness of the working people in building communism, and to work for the improvement of the living conditions of the masses *and for satisfaction of their growing spiritual requirements*. Public organizations should take a greater part in managing cultural, health *and social security* institutions; within the next few years they should be entrusted with the management of theaters and concert halls, clubs, libraries and other cultural-enlightenment institutions now under state jurisdiction; they should extend their activity in strengthening public

order, particularly through the people's volunteer detachments and comrades' courts.

In order to develop membership participation, the Party considers it necessary further to reduce the salaried staffs of public organizations from top to bottom, to replace approximately half the membership of the governing bodies of the public organizations at each election, and to consider it advisable for the executives of public organizations to be elected, as a general rule, for not more than two consecutive terms.

As the socialist state system develops, it will gradually become public communist self-government, in which will be united the Soviets, trade unions, cooperatives and other mass organizations of the working people. This process will signify a further development of democracy, ensuring the active participation of all members of society in the management of public affairs. Public functions similar to the present state functions of economic and cultural management will be preserved under communism, changing and being perfected in accordance with the development of society. But the character of the functions and the ways in which they are carried out will be different than under socialism. The agencies for planning, accounting, economic management and cultural development, now state bodies, will lose their political character and will become agencies of public self-government. Communist society will be a highly organized community of men of labor. A single body of universally recognized rules of communist community life will be established, and the observance of these rules will become an inner need and habit of all people.

Historical development inevitably leads to the withering away of the state. For the state to wither away completely, it is necessary to create both domestic conditions—the building of a developed communist society—and external conditions—*the victory and consolidation of socialism in the international arena* [the final settlement of the contradictions between capitalism and communism in the world arena in favor of communism].

3. Strengthening of the Armed Forces and Defense Capacity of the Soviet Union.—Relying on the unanimous support of all the Soviet people, the Communist Party of the Soviet Union is steadfastly upholding and defending the gains of socialism and the cause of world peace and fighting tirelessly to deliver mankind for all time from wars of aggression. The Leninist principle of peaceful coexistence *of states with different social systems* has been and remains the general principle of the foreign policy of the Soviet state.

The Soviet Union is perseveringly seeking to bring about realization of the proposals it has made for general and complete disarmament under strict international control. But the imperialist states stubbornly refuse to accept these proposals and are intensively building up their armed forces. They do not want to reconcile themselves to the existence of the world socialist system and openly proclaim their insane plans for the liquidation of the Soviet Union and the other socialist states through war. This obliges the Communist Party, the armed forces, the state security agencies and all the peoples of the U.S.S.R. to show untiring vigilance toward the aggressive intrigues of the enemies of peace, to be always on guard over peaceful labor and to be constantly prepared for armed defense of their motherland.

The Party proceeds from the fact that as long as imperialism survives, the danger of aggressive wars will remain. The C.P.S.U. regards the defense of the socialist fatherland and the strengthening of the defense capacity of the U.S.S.R. and of the might of the Soviet Armed Forces as a sacred duty of the Party and the Soviet people as a whole and as a most important function of the socialist state. The Soviet Union sees it as its internationalist duty to ensure, together with the other socialist countries, the reliable defense and security of the entire socialist camp.

In terms of internal conditions, the Soviet Union does not need an army. But since the danger of war coming from the imperialist camp persists and since complete and general disarmament has not been achieved, the C.P.S.U. considers it necessary to maintain the defensive might of the Soviet state and the combat preparedness of its armed forces at a level ensuring the decisive and complete rout of any enemy who dares to encroach upon the Soviet homeland. The Soviet state will see to it that its armed forces are powerful, that they have the most up-to-date means of defending the homeland—atomic and thermonuclear weapons and rockets of every range—and that they keep all types of military equipment and all weapons up to standard.

The Party educates Communists and all Soviet people in the spirit of constant preparedness for the defense of their social-ist fatherland and of love of their army. *It will help in every way to develop further the activity of public defense organizations.* Defense of the fatherland and service in the Soviet Armed Forces is a lofty and honorable duty of Soviet citizens.

The C.P.S.U. is doing everything to see to it that the Soviet Armed Forces are an efficient and smoothly operating organ-ism, that they have a high standard of organization and disci-pline, carry out in exemplary fashion the tasks assigned them by the Party, the government and the people, and are prepared at any moment to administer a crushing rebuff to imperialist aggressors. Single command is a major principle of the organization of the Soviet Armed Forces.

The Party will work indefatigably to train army and navy of-ficers and political *and technical* personnel utterly devoted to the communist cause and recruited from among the finest rep-resentatives of the Soviet people. It considers it necessary for the officer corps persistently to master Marxist-Leninist theory, to possess high military-technical training, to meet all the requirements of modern military theory and practice and to strengthen military discipline. All Soviet soldiers must be trained in the spirit of boundless loyalty to their people and to the cause of communism and be prepared to give every effort and, if necessary, their lives in the defense of the socialist motherland.

Communist Party leadership of the armed forces and height-ening of the role and influence of the Party organizations in the army and navy are the keystone of military development. The Party devotes unremitting attention to increasing its organizing and guiding influence on the entire life and activity of the army, air force and navy, to unite the men of the armed forces around the Communist Party and the Soviet government, to strengthen the unity of the army and people, and to train the soldiers in the spirit of courage, bravery, heroism *and military cooperation with the armies of the socialist countries,* of readiness at any moment to defend the Land of Soviets, which is building commu-nism.

IV. TASKS OF THE PARTY IN THE SPHERE OF NATIONAL RELATIONS.—Under socialism nations flourish and their sov-ereignty is strengthened. The development of nations proceeds not along lines of strengthening national *discord* [barriers], national narrow-mindedness and egoism, as it does under capitalism, but along lines of their association, fraternal mutual assistance and friendship. The appearance of new industrial centers, the discovery and exploitation of natural resources, the plowing up of virgin lands and the development of all types of transport increase the mobility of the population and promote greater contact among the peoples of the Soviet Union. People of many nationalities live together and work in harmony in the Soviet republics. The boundaries between the Union republics within the U.S.S.R. are increasingly losing their former signifi-cance, since all the nations are equal, their life is organized on a single socialist foundation, the material and spiritual needs of each people are satisfied to the same extent, and they are all united into one family by common vital interests and are ad-vancing together to a single goal—communism. Common spiri-tual features deriving from the new type of social relations and embodying the finest traditions of the peoples of the U.S.S.R. have taken shape in Soviet people of different nationalities.

Full-scale communist construction signifies a new stage in the development of national relations in the U.S.S.R. in which the nations will draw still closer together and their complete unity will be achieved. The building of the material and technical base of communism is leading to still closer associa-tion of the Soviet peoples. The exchange of material and cultural wealth among nations is becoming more and more in-tensive, and the contribution of each republic to the common cause of communist construction is increasing. Obliteration of distinctions between classes and the development of communist social relations is intensifying the social homogeneity of nations and contributing to the development of common commu-nist traits in their culture, ethics and way of living, to a further strengthening of mutual trust and friendship among them.

With the victory of communism in the U.S.S.R., the nations will draw still closer together, their economic and ideological unity will increase and the communist traits common to their spiritual make-up will develop. However, the effacement of na-tional distinctions, especially of language distinctions, is a con-siderably longer process than the effacement of class distinc-tions.

The Party approaches all questions of national relationships arising in the course of communist construction from the posi-tions of proletarian internationalism and on the basis of un-swerving application of the Leninist national policy. The Party permits neither the ignoring nor the overemphasis of national characteristics.

The Party sets the following tasks in the sphere of national relations:

(a) to continue the all-round economic and cultural develop-ment of all the Soviet nations *and nationalities,* ensuring their increasingly close fraternal cooperation, mutual aid, solidarity and closeness in all spheres of life and achieving the utmost strengthening of the Union of Soviet Socialist Republics; to make full use of and improve the forms of the national state system of the peoples of the U.S.S.R.

(b) in the economic sphere, to continue to pursue the line of comprehensive development of the economy of the Soviet repub-lics; to ensure a rational geographical distribution of production and planned development of natural resources and to perfect the socialist division of labor among the republics, unifying and coordinating their labor efforts and properly combining the interests of the state as a whole and those of each Soviet repub-lic. Since the expansion of the rights of the Union republics in economic management has yielded substantial favorable results, such measures may also be carried out in the future, with due regard to the fact that the creation of the material and technical base of communism will call for still greater interrelationship and mutual assistance among the Soviet republics. The closer the contact between nations and the greater the understanding of the countrywide tasks, the more successfully can manifestations of localism and national egoism be overcome.

For the successful accomplishment of the tasks of communist construction and the coordination of economic activities, inter-republic economic agencies (especially for such matters as ir-rigation, power grids, transport, etc.) may be set up in particular zones.

The Party will continue to follow a policy of ensuring the ac-tual equality of all nations and nationalities with full considera-tion for their interests, devoting special attention to those areas of the country that are in need of more rapid development. Bene-fits growing in the process of communist construction must be fairly distributed among all nations and nationalities.

(c) to work for the further all-round flowering of the socialist culture of the peoples of the U.S.S.R. The vast scope of commu-nist construction and the new victories of communist ideology are enriching the cultures of all the peoples of the U.S.S.R., cultures socialist in content and national in form. The ideologi-cal unity of the nations and nationalities is growing, and there is a rapprochement of their cultures. The historical experience of the development of socialist nations shows that national forms do not harden; they change, improve and draw closer together, shedding all obsolete features that conflict with the new living conditions. An international culture common to all the Soviet nations is developing. The cultural treasures of each nation are increasingly augmented by works of an international character.

Attaching decisive importance to the development of the so-cialist content of the cultures of the peoples of the U.S.S.R., the Party will promote their further mutual enrichment and rap-prochement, the strengthening of their internationalist basis and thereby the formation of a future single worldwide culture of communist society. While supporting the progressive traditions of each people and making them the possession of all Soviet people, the Party will in all ways develop new revolutionary traditions of the builders of communism, traditions common to all nations.

(d) to continue ensuring the free development of the languages of the people of the U.S.S.R. and the complete freedom of each citizen of the U.S.S.R. to speak and to rear and educate his children in any language, ruling out all privileges, restrictions or compulsion in the use of this or that language. In the condi-tions of the fraternal friendship and mutual trust of peoples, national languages are developing on a basis of equality and mutual enrichment.

The existing process of voluntary study of Russian in addition to the indigenous language has favorable significance, since it facilitates mutual exchange of experience and the access of each nation and nationality to the cultural achievements of the other peoples of the U.S.S.R. and to world culture. The Russian language has, in effect, become the common medium of intercourse and cooperation among all the peoples of the U.S.S.R.

(e) to continue consistently applying the principles of internationalism in the field of national relations; to strengthen the friendship of peoples as one of the most important gains of socialism; to conduct an uncompromising struggle against manifestations and survivals of any kinds of nationalism and chauvinism, against trends of national narrow-mindedness and exclusiveness, idealization of the past and the veiling of social contradictions in the history of peoples, and against [obsolete] customs and ways *that impede communist construction*. The growing scale of communist construction calls for the continuous exchange of cadres among the nations. Any manifestations of national insularity in the rearing and employment of workers of different nationalities in the Soviet republics are impermissible. The elimination of manifestations of nationalism is in the interests of all nations and nationalities of the U.S.S.R. Each Soviet republic can continue to flourish and grow stronger only in the great family of fraternal socialist nations of the U.S.S.R.

V. TASKS OF THE PARTY IN THE SPHERES OF IDEOLOGY, UPBRINGING, EDUCATION, SCIENCE AND CULTURE.—Soviet society has achieved great successes in the socialist upbringing of the masses, in the molding of active builders of socialism. But even after the victory of the socialist system, survivals of capitalism persist in the minds and behavior of people and hamper the progress of society.

In the struggle for the victory of communism, ideological work becomes an increasingly powerful factor. The higher the social consciousness of the members of society, the more fully and broadly do they become creatively active in the building of the material and technical base of communism, in the development of communist forms of labor and new relations among people, and consequently the more rapidly and successfully are the tasks of building communism accomplished.

The Party considers that the paramount task in ideological work at the present stage is to rear all working people in a spirit of ideological integrity and devotion to communism and a communist attitude to labor and the public economy; to eliminate completely the survivals of bourgeois views and mores, to ensure the all-round, harmonious development of the individual, to create a truly rich spiritual culture. The Party attaches special importance to the rearing of the rising generation.

The molding of the new man is effected through his own active participation in communist construction and the development of communist principles in economic and public life, under the influence of the whole system of educational work carried on by the Party, the state and public organizations, work in which the press, radio, cinema and television play an important part. As communist forms of social organization are created, devotion to communist ideas will become stronger and firmer in life and work and in human relations and people will develop the ability to enjoy the benefits of communism in a rational way. Joint planned labor by the members of society, their daily participation in the management of state and public affairs, and the development of communist relations of comradely cooperation and mutual support lead to transforming the minds of people in a spirit of collectivism, diligence and humanism.

Increased communist consciousness of the working people furthers the ideological and political unity of the workers, collective farmers and intelligentsia and their gradual fusion into a single collective of the toilers of communist society.

The Party sets the following tasks:

1. In the Sphere of Inculcating a Communist Consciousness.—
(a) The Molding of a Scientific World Outlook. In conditions of socialism and of the construction of a communist society, when spontaneous economic development has given way to the conscious organization of production and of all public life and when theory is daily translated into practice, the molding of a scien-

tific world outlook in all the toilers of society *on the basis of Marxism-Leninism, an integral and harmonious system of philosophical, economic and socio-political views,* is of prime importance. [The ideological basis of this world outlook is Marxism-Leninism, an integral and harmonious system of philosophical, economic and socio-political views.] The Party sets the task of training the whole population in the spirit of scientific communism, striving to ensure that all working people [master the ideas of the Marxist-Leninist teaching, that they] acquire a deep understanding of the course and perspectives of world development, correctly interpret events within the country and in the international arena, and consciously build their life on communist lines. Communist ideas and communist deeds should blend organically in the behavior of every person and in the activities of every collective and every organization.

The theoretical elaboration and the timely practical solution of new problems raised by life are necessary to the successful advance of society to communism. Theory must continue to illumine the road for practice and help detect and overcome *obstacles and* difficulties [and contradictions] hindering successful communist construction. The Party regards one of its most important duties to be the further development of Marxist-Leninist theory through the study and generalization of new phenomena in the life of Soviet society and the experience of the world revolutionary workers' and liberation movement, and the creative combination of the theory and the practice of communist construction.

(b) Labor Upbringing. The Party places the development of a communist attitude toward labor in all members of society at the center of its upbringing work. Labor for the good of society is the sacred duty of every person. Any labor for the good of society, whether physical or mental, is honorable and commands respect. It is necessary to rear all working people after the best examples of labor and the best examples of managing the public economy.

Everything required for life and for the development of people is created by labor. Hence each *able-bodied* person must take part in creating the means that are necessary for his life and work and for the welfare of society. A person who received any benefits from society without participating in the work would be a parasite living at the expense of others.

It is impossible for a man in communist society not to work. Neither his own social consciousness nor public opinion will permit it. Work according to one's ability will become a habit, a prime necessity of life for every member of society.

(c) The Establishment of Communist Morality. In the process of the transition to communism, moral principles become increasingly important in the life of society; the sphere of operation of the moral factor grows and the importance of the administrative regulation of human relationships diminishes accordingly. The Party will encourage all forms of conscious self-discipline of citizens leading to the establishment and development of the basic rules of the communist community.

In contrast to the distorted, egoistic views and mores of the old world, the Communists, rejecting the class morality of the exploiters, present communist morality, the most just and noble morality, expressing the interests and ideals of all working mankind. Communism makes the simple standards of morality and justice, which were distorted or shamelessly flouted under the rule of the exploiters, into inviolable rules for relations both between individuals and between peoples. Communist morality includes the basic universal moral norms evolved by the masses of the people in the course of millenniums in the struggle against social oppression and vices. The revolutionary morality of the working class is of particular importance to the moral development of society. In the course of building socialism and communism, communist morality becomes enriched with new principles and new content.

The Party holds that the moral code of the builder of communism includes such principles as:

—devotion to the cause of communism, love of the socialist homeland, of the socialist countries;
—conscientious labor for the good of society: He who does not work, neither shall he eat;
—concern on the part of each for the preservation and growth of public wealth;

—a high sense of public duty, intolerance of violations of the public interest;

—collectivism and comradely mutual assistance: One for all and all for one;

—humane relations and mutual respect among people: Man is to man a friend, comrade and brother;

—honesty and truthfulness, moral purity, guilelessness and modesty in public and private life;

—mutual respect in the family and concern for the upbringing of children;

—an uncompromising attitude to injustice, parasitism, dishonesty, careerism *and money-grubbing;*

—friendship and brotherhood of all peoples of the U.S.S.R., intolerance of national and racial animosity;

—an uncompromising attitude toward the enemies of communism, peace and the freedom of peoples;

—fraternal solidarity with the working people of all countries and with all peoples.

(d) The Development of Proletarian Internationalism and Socialist Patriotism. The Party will untiringly rear Soviet people in the spirit of proletarian internationalism and will promote in every way the strengthening of the international solidarity of the working people. In developing the Soviet people's love of their fatherland, the Party proceeds from the fact that with the formation of the world socialist system, the patriotism of the citizens of socialist society is expressed in devotion and loyalty to their own homeland and to the entire commonwealth of socialist countries. Socialist patriotism and socialist internationalism organically embody proletarian solidarity with the working class and the working people of all countries. The Party will continue perseveringly to combat the reactionary ideology of bourgeois nationalism, racism and cosmopolitanism.

(e) All-Round and Harmonious Development of the Individual. In the period of transition to communism the opportunities increase for rearing a new man, in whom are harmoniously combined spiritual wealth, moral purity and physical perfection.

The conditions for all-round development of the individual have been created by historic social gains—freedom from exploitation, unemployment and poverty, from discrimination on account of sex, origin, nationality or race. Every member of society is provided equal opportunities for creative work and education. Relations of dependence and inequality between people in public and family life disappear. The personal dignity of each citizen is protected by society. Each is guaranteed an equal and free choice of field of endeavor and specialty, with due regard to the interests of society. As the time spent on material production is reduced, ever greater opportunities are afforded to develop abilities, gifts and talents in the fields of production, science, technology, literature and the arts. People's leisure will be increasingly devoted to public activities, cultural intercourse, mental and physical development and artistic endeavor. Physical culture and sports will become a firm part of the everyday life of people.

(f) Overcoming the Survivals of Capitalism in the Minds and Behavior of People. The Party regards the combating of manifestations of bourgeois ideology and morality and the remnants of private-property psychology, superstitions and prejudices to be an integral part of the work of communist upbringing.

The general public, public opinion and the development of criticism and self-criticism have a big role to play in the struggle against survivals of the past and instances of individualism and egoism. Comradely censure of antisocial acts will gradually become the principal means of eradicating manifestations of bourgeois views, customs and habits. The power of example in public affairs and in private life, in the performance of one's public duty, acquires tremendous educational significance.

The Party employs means of ideological influence to rear people in the spirit of the scientific-materialist world view, to overcome religious prejudices without permitting the sentiments of believers to be insulted. It is necessary *systematically to conduct broad scientific-atheist propaganda,* to explain patiently the untenability of religious beliefs, which arose in the past when people were ground down by the elemental forces of nature and by social oppression and were ignorant of the true causes of natural and social phenomena. Here it is necessary to rely on the discoveries of modern science, which is disclosing a

fuller and fuller picture of the world, extending man's power over nature and leaving no room for religion's fantastic fabrications about supernatural forces.

(g) The Exposure of Bourgeois Ideology. The peaceful coexistence of states with different social systems does not signify *weakening* [discontinuance] of the ideological struggle. The Communist Party will go on exposing the antipopular, reactionary nature of capitalism and all attempts to prettify the picture of the capitalist system.

The Party will systematically propagandize the great advantages of socialism and communism over the declining capitalist system.

To reactionary bourgeois ideology the Party opposes the scientific ideology of communism. This ideology, expressing the fundamental interests of the working class and all working people, teaches them to struggle, work and live for the sake of universal happiness. The communist ideology is the most humane ideology. Its ideals are to establish truly human relations among individuals and peoples, to deliver mankind from the threat of wars of extermination and to establish on earth universal peace and a free, happy life for all people.

2. In the Sphere of Public Education.—The transition to communism presumes the training and preparation of communist-minded and highly educated people, fitted for both physical and mental labor, for taking active part in various public, state, scientific and cultural fields.

The system of public education is so organized that the instruction and upbringing of the rising generation are bound up closely with life and productive labor and that members of the adult population may combine work in the production sphere with further education and training in accordance with their personal callings and the needs of society. [The organization of] Public education *based* on these principles will make for the molding of harmoniously developed members of communist society and for the solution of one of the major social problems—the elimination of substantial distinctions between mental and physical labor.

The basic tasks in the field of instruction and upbringing are:

(a) The Achievement of Universal Compulsory Secondary Education.

In the next decade compulsory secondary general and polytechnical 11-year education is to be introduced for all children of school age, and eight-year education for young people engaged in the national economy who have not had eight grades of schooling; in the subsequent decade everyone is to be provided an opportunity to get a full secondary education. Universal secondary education is guaranteed by the development of general and polytechnical education in combination with the participation of school children in socially useful labor within their physical capacity, as well as by a considerable expansion of the network of *all types of general-education schools, including* evening schools providing a secondary education in off-work hours.

Secondary education must furnish a solid knowledge of the fundamentals of the sciences, an understanding of the principles of the communist world view, and a labor and polytechnical training in accordance with the rising level of development of science and technology, with regard to the needs of society and the abilities and inclinations of the students, as well as to the moral, esthetic and physical education of a healthy rising generation.

In view of the swift development of science and technology, the system of technical vocational *education* and production training should undergo constant improvement, so that the work skills of those engaged in production may match the higher level of their general education in the social and natural sciences and their acquisition of specialized knowledge of engineering and technology, agronomy, medicine or other special fields.

(b) The Public Upbringing of Children of Preschool and School Age. The communist system of public education is based on the public upbringing of children. The influence that the family exerts on children's upbringing must be ever more organically combined with their public upbringing.

The development of the network of preschool institutions and boarding schools of various types will fully meet the requirements of all working people who wish to give their children of preschool and school age a public upbringing. The importance of the school, which is called upon to cultivate love of labor and of knowledge in children and to mold the young generation in the spirit of communist consciousness and morality, will increase in the public rearing of the rising generation. A lofty, honorable and responsible role in all this falls to the public teacher and the Young Communist League and Young Pioneer organizations.

(c) The Creation of Conditions Ensuring a High Level of Instruction and Upbringing of the Rising Generation. The Party plans to carry out a broad program of building schools and cultural-enlightenment institutions to meet fully the needs of upbringing and instruction. All schools will receive good buildings and will change to single-shift schedules. They will all have study workshops and chemistry, physics and other shops and laboratories; rural schools will also have their own farming plots; large factories will have production training shops for school children. The latest technical aids—cinema, radio and television—will be widely used in schools.

For physical and esthetic training, all schools and extra-scholastic institutions will have gymnasiums, sports grounds and facilities for the creative endeavors of children, for studies in music, painting and sculpture. The network of urban and rural children's stadiums, sports schools, tourist camps, skiing centers, water-sports facilities, swimming pools and other sports facilities will be enlarged.

(d) Higher and Specialized Secondary Education. In step with scientific and technical progress, higher and specialized secondary education, which must prepare highly qualified specialists with a broad theoretical and political background, will be further developed.

The reduction of the working day and a considerable improvement in the standard of living of the entire population will provide everyone with an opportunity to receive a higher or specialized secondary education if he so desires. The network of higher and specialized secondary schools, evening and correspondence schools in particular, as well as factory higher technical schools, agricultural institutes (on large state farms), [people's universities,] studios, conservatories, etc., must be increased in all areas of the country, with support from the factories, trade unions and other public organizations. The number of students at higher and specialized secondary schools is to be considerably increased each year. Tens of millions of people will obtain specialized education.

3. In the Sphere of Science.—Under the socialist economic system scientific and technical progress makes it possible to employ the riches and forces of nature most effectively in the interests of the people, to discover new types of energy and to create new materials, to develop means of influencing climatic conditions and to master outer space. The application of science becomes a decisive factor in the mighty growth of the productive forces of society. Scientific progress and the economic application of scientific discoveries will remain an object of special concern to the Party.

Most important are the following tasks:

(a) Development of Theoretical Research. The further perspectives of scientific and technical progress in the present period are determined primarily by the achievements of the leading branches of natural science. A high level of development in mathematics, physics, chemistry and biology is a necessary condition for the advance and for the effectiveness of the technical, medical, agricultural and other sciences.

Theoretical research will be developed most extensively, above all in such decisive fields of technical progress as electrification of the whole country, integrated mechanization and automation of production, transport and communications, the application of chemistry in the major branches of the national economy and the industrial uses of atomic energy [and transport and communications]. This applies to:

—studying the power and fuel balance of the country, seeking the best ways of utilizing natural sources of power, working out the scientific foundations for a single power grid, discovering new sources of power and methods for the direct conversion of thermal, nuclear, solar and chemical energy into electric power, and solving the problems of control of thermonuclear reactions;

—working out the theory and principles of designing new machines and automatic and telemechanical systems, intensively developing radioelectronics, working out the theoretical princi-

ples of computing, control and information machines and improving them technically;

—investigating chemical processes, working out new and more efficient technologies and creating inexpensive, high-quality artificial and synthetic materials for all branches of the economy: machine building, construction, the manufacture of household goods and mineral fertilizers; and also creating new preparations for use in medicine and agriculture;

—improving existing methods and devising new and more effective methods of mineral prospecting and of making integrated use of natural resources.

Big advances lie ahead in the development of the whole complex of biological sciences in order to solve medical problems and achieve further progress in agriculture. The main tasks to be solved by these sciences in the interests of mankind are the ascertainment of the nature of the phenomenon of life, *the discovery of the biological laws of development of the organic world, the study of the physics and chemistry of life, and the elaboration of various methods of controlling life processes, in particular metabolism, heredity and directed changes in organisms* [and the study and control of life processes, in particular metabolism and heredity]. *There must be broader and deeper development of the Michurinist school in biological science, which proceeds from the premise that conditions of life are fundamental in the development of the organic world.* Medicine must concentrate on discovering means of preventing and conquering such illnesses as cancer, virus diseases and cardiovascular and other dangerous ailments. It is important to study microorganisms and to make extensive use of them in the economy and public health work for, among other things, the production of foods and fodder, vitamins, antibiotics and enzymes, and for the development of new farming methods.

By enabling man to penetrate into outer space, artificial earth satellites and spaceships have provided great opportunities for discovering new phenomena and laws of nature and studying the planets and the sun.

In the age of tempestuous scientific progress, the working out of the philosophical problems of modern natural science on the basis of dialectical materialism, the only scientific [world outlook and] method of cognition, becomes still more urgent.

There must be intensive development of research in the social sciences, which constitute the scientific basis for the guidance of the development of society. In this sphere the chief thing is study and theoretical generalization of the practice of communist construction, investigation of the basic objective laws governing the economic, political and cultural development of socialism and its evolution into communism and the working out of the problems of communist upbringing.

The task of economics is to generalize new phenomena in the economic life of society and to work out problems of the national economy whose solution facilitates the successful building of communism. Economists must direct their attention to finding the most effective ways of utilizing resources and manpower in the economy and the best methods of planning and organizing industrial and agricultural production, and to working out the principles of rational geographical distribution of productive forces and the technical-economic problems of communist construction.

Study of the problems of world history and contemporary world development must disclose the law-governed process of mankind's advance toward communism, the change in the balance of forces in favor of socialism, the sharpening of the general crisis of capitalism, the downfall of the colonial system of imperialism and its consequences, and the upsurge of the national-liberation movement of the peoples.

It is important to study the triumphant, life-tested historical experience of the Communist Party and the Soviet people, the objective laws of development of the world socialist system and the world Communist and workers' movement.

It is necessary to continue stanchly championing and elaborating dialectical and historical materialism as the science of the most general laws of development of nature, society and human thought.

The social sciences must continue resolutely to oppose bourgeois ideology, Right-socialist theory and practice and revisionism and dogmatism, maintaining the purity of the principles of Marxism-Leninism.

(b) Linking of Science and Production. Indivisible ties with the creative labor of the people and the practice of communist construction are a guarantee of the fruitful development of science.

In conformity with the demands of economic and cultural development, it is necessary to extend and improve the network of scientific institutions, including those under the central agencies directing economic development and under the economic councils, and also the network of scientific laboratories and institutes at large industrial plants and in agricultural districts; to develop research at higher educational institutions; to improve the geographical distribution of research and higher educational institutions; and to ensure the further development of science in all the Union republics and major economic areas.

The scientific institutions must organize and coordinate their work along the most important lines of research in accordance with the plans of economic and cultural development. The role of the scientific community in directing scientific work will increase. Free comradely discussions promoting the creative solution of timely problems are an essential condition for scientific development.

The Party will take measures to strengthen and further improve the material base of scientific work and to enlist the most capable creative forces in scientific pursuits.

It is a matter of honor for Soviet scientists to consolidate the advanced positions that Soviet science has won in major branches of knowledge and to take a leading place in world science in all its basic lines.

4. In the Sphere of Cultural Development, Literature and Art.—Cultural development in the period of the full-scale building of communist society will constitute the crowning stage of a great cultural revolution. At this stage all the necessary ideological and cultural conditions will be created for the victory of communism.

The growth of productive forces, progress in technology and in the organization of production, increased public activeness of the working people, development of the democratic foundations of self-government, and the communist reorganization of everyday life depend in very large measure on the cultural advance of the population.

Communist culture, which *is absorbing and developing* [has absorbed and is developing] all the best that has been created by world culture, will be a new, higher stage in the cultural development of mankind. It will embody all the diversity and richness of the spiritual life of society and the lofty ideas and humanism of the new world. It will be the culture of a classless society, a culture of the entire people, a universal culture.

(a) All-Round Development of the Cultural Life of Society.
In the conditions of the transition to communism, creative work in all fields of culture becomes particularly fruitful and accessible to all members of society. Soviet literature, music, painting, cinema, theater, *television* and all the other arts will reach new heights in developing ideological content and artistry. Amateur theaters, mass amateur art, technical invention and other forms of creative endeavor by the people will become widespread. *The growth of the artistic and creative activity of the masses will contribute to the emergence of* [From the midst of the participants in amateur arts will come] gifted new writers, artists, musicians and actors. The development and the enrichment of the artistic wealth of society are achieved on the basis of a combination of mass amateur endeavor and professional art.

The Party will concern itself untiringly with the flourishing of literature, art and culture and the establishment of all the requirements for the fullest manifestation of the personal abilities of each individual, for the esthetic training of all the working people and for the molding of fine artistic tastes and cultural habits in the people. *Art will even more inspire labor, adorn life and ennoble man.*

For the further mighty advance of the material base for culture there will be assured:
—the utmost development of book publishing and the press, with corresponding expansion of the printing industry and paper production;
—an increase in the network of libraries, lecture halls, reading rooms, theaters, houses of culture, clubs and motion picture theaters;

—completion of countrywide radio receiving and broadcasting facilities and construction of television stations for all industrial and agricultural areas;
—wide development of people's universities, people's theater companies and other amateur cultural organizations;
—the organization of a large network of scientific and technical laboratories and of art and film studios for the use of all who have the inclination and ability.

The Party considers it necessary to distribute cultural institutions evenly throughout the country in order gradually to raise the cultural level of the countryside to that of the cities and to achieve rapid cultural progress in all newly developed areas.
[Great importance attaches to high standards in urban development and in the architecture and planning of cities, rural communities, industrial, cultural and service premises and housing. Art will even more inspire labor, adorn life and ennoble man.]

(b) Enhancement of the Educational Role of Literature and Art.
Soviet literature and art, imbued with optimism and life-affirming communist ideas, play a great part in ideological education and cultivate in Soviet people the qualities of builders of a new world. They are called upon to serve as a source of happiness and inspiration for millions of people, to express their will, sentiments and ideas, and to be means of their ideological enrichment and moral upbringing.

The chief line in developing literature and art lies in strengthening ties with the life of the people, in the truthful and highly artistic depiction of the richness and diversity of socialist reality, in inspired and vivid portrayal of all that is new and genuinely communist and exposure of all that hinders the progress of society.

In the art of socialist realism, based on the principles of Party spirit and popular quality,* bold originality in the artistic depiction of life goes hand in hand with the utilization and development of all the progressive traditions of world culture. Before writers, artists, musicians and stage and screen workers there open up broad horizons for individual creative initiative and skill, for a diversity of creative forms, styles and genres.

The Communist Party looks after the proper direction in the development of literature and art and their ideological and artistic standards; it helps public organizations and professional literary and art associations in their activities.

(c) The Development of International Cultural Ties. The Party considers it necessary to expand the cultural relations of the U.S.S.R. with the countries of the socialist system and also with other countries in the interests of exchange of scientific discoveries and cultural achievements and of mutual understanding and friendship among peoples.

VI. THE BUILDING OF COMMUNISM IN THE U.S.S.R. AND COOPERATION OF THE SOCIALIST COUNTRIES.—The C.P.S.U. regards the building of communism in the Soviet Union as a component part of the creation of a communist society by the peoples of the entire world socialist system.

The fact that socialist revolutions took place at different times and that the economic and cultural levels of the countries concerned are dissimilar predetermines the nonsimultaneous completion of socialist construction in those countries and their nonsimultaneous entry into the period of the full-scale construction of communism. Nevertheless, the fact that the socialist countries are developing as members of a single world socialist system and utilizing the objective laws and advantages of this system enables them to reduce the time necessary for the construction of socialism and affords them the prospect of effecting the transition to communism more or less simultaneously, within one and the same historical epoch.

The first country to advance to communism eases and speeds the advance of the whole world socialist system to communism. In building communism, the peoples of the Soviet Union are laying new roads for all mankind, testing their correctness by their own experience, discovering the difficulties, finding means of overcoming them, and selecting the best forms and methods of communist construction.

Since the social forces—the working class, the cooperative

*[The Russian words here are "partiinost" and "narodnost."—Trans.]

peasantry and the people's intelligentsia—and the social forms of economy (enterprises based on the two forms of socialist property) in the Soviet Union and in the other socialist countries are of a single type, there will be common basic objective laws for communist construction in the U.S.S.R. and in those countries, with due allowance made for the historical and national features of each country.

The building of communism in the U.S.S.R. corresponds to the interests of every country of the socialist commonwealth, for it increases the economic might and defense capacity of the world socialist camp and provides ever more favorable opportunities for the U.S.S.R. to deepen its economic and cultural cooperation with the other socialist countries and render them assistance and support.

The C.P.S.U. proceeds from the fact that the existing forms of economic relations among the socialist countries—foreign trade, coordination of national economic plans, and specialization and cooperation of production—will be developed and perfected more and more.

The socialist system creates the conditions for eliminating *the gap between countries in the level of economic and cultural development* [the economic and cultural gap]—a legacy of capitalism; for faster development of the states that lagged behind economically under capitalism; for the steady advance of their economy and culture; and for evening up the general level of development of the socialist commonwealth. This is ensured by the advantages of the socialist economic system and by equality in economic relations; by mutual assistance and the sharing of experience, in particular by mutual exchange of scientific and technological achievements and by coordinated research; and by the joint construction of industrial projects and cooperation in the development of natural resources. Comprehensive fraternal cooperation benefits each socialist country and the world socialist system as a whole.

The interests of socialist and communist construction demand that each socialist country combine efforts to strengthen and develop its national economy with efforts to strengthen and expand economic cooperation within the framework of the entire socialist commonwealth. The advance and the evening up of the general economic level of the socialist countries must be achieved primarily by each country's making full use of its internal resources and improving the forms and methods of economic guidance, consistently applying the Leninist principles and methods of socialist economic management, and making effective use of the advantages of the world socialist system.

The material prerequisites for the construction of communism are created by the constructive labor of the people of each country and by the country's constantly growing contribution to the common cause of strengthening the socialist system. This purpose is served by the application of the law of planned, proportionate development in socialist construction; the unfolding of the creative initiative and labor activity of the masses; constant improvement of the system of the international division of labor through the coordination of national economic plans; specialization and cooperation of production within the framework of the world socialist system on the basis of voluntary participation, mutual benefit and raising the level of science and technology in every way; the study of collective experience; the strengthening of cooperation and fraternal mutual assistance; undeviating observance of the principles of material incentive and the comprehensive development of moral incentives to work for the good of society, with control over the measure of labor and of consumption.

Socialism brings peoples and countries together. The [common] economic basis of world socialism will be strengthened in the process of extensive cooperation in all economic, sociopolitical and cultural fields.

The objective laws of the world socialist system, the development of the productive forces of socialist society and the vital interests of the peoples of the socialist countries predetermine an ever-increasing rapprochement of the various national economies. As V. I. Lenin foresaw, tendencies toward the future establishment of a world communist economy, regulated by the victorious working people according to a single plan, are developing.

The C.P.S.U. considers its tasks in cooperation with the Communist Parties of the other socialist countries to be:

in the political field—the utmost strengthening of the world socialist system, the development of fraternal relations with all the socialist countries on the basis of complete equality and voluntary cooperation, political consolidation of the states of the socialist commonwealth in a joint struggle *against the imperialist aggressors,* for universal peace and for the complete triumph of communism;

in the economic field—expansion of trade among the socialist countries, development of the international socialist division of labor, ever deeper coordination of long-range economic plans among the socialist states envisaging a maximum saving of social labor and accelerated development of the world socialist economy, the strengthening of scientific and technical cooperation;

in the cultural field—constant development of all forms of cultural cooperation and contact among the peoples of the socialist countries, reciprocal exchanges of cultural achievements, encouragement of joint creative effort by scientists, writers and artists; active encouragement of the mutual enrichment of national cultures, and bringing the mode of life and the spiritual cast of the socialist nations closer together.

The C.P.S.U. and the Soviet people will do everything possible to extend support to all the peoples of the socialist commonwealth in the building of socialism and communism.

VII. THE PARTY IN THE PERIOD OF THE FULL-SCALE BUILDING OF COMMUNISM.—As a result of the victory of socialism in the U.S.S.R. and the consolidation of the unity of Soviet society, the Communist party of the working class has become the vanguard of the Soviet people, a party of the whole people, and has extended its guiding influence to all aspects of the life of society. The Party is the wisdom, the honor and the conscience of our epoch, of the Soviet people, who are carrying out great revolutionary transformations. It looks keenly into the future and shows the people scientifically determined roads along which to advance, arouses titanic energy in the masses and leads them to the accomplishment of imposing tasks.

The period of the full-scale building of communism is characterized by a further rise in the role and importance of the Communist Party as the leading and guiding force of Soviet society.

Communist society, unlike all previous socio-economic formations, does not develop spontaneously but as a result of conscious and purposeful activity of the masses, led by the Marxist-Leninist party. The Communist Party—which unites in its ranks the most advanced representatives of *the working class and all* the working people, is closely linked with the masses, enjoys unbounded authority among the people and possesses knowledge of the laws of social development—ensures correct leadership in all the work of communist construction, giving it an organized, planned and scientific character.

The heightening of the role of the Party in the life of Soviet society in the new stage of its development is determined by:

—the growing scope and complexity of the tasks of communist construction, calling for a higher level of political and organizational leadership;

—the growth of the creative activity of the masses and the enlistment of new millions of working people in the administration of state affairs and of production;

—the further development of socialist democracy, the heightened role of public organizations, the expansion of the rights of the Union republics and of local organizations;

—the growing importance of the theory of scientific communism, of its creative development and propaganda; the necessity for intensifying the communist upbringing of the working people and for fighting to overcome survivals of the past in the minds of people.

There must be a new, higher stage in the development of the Party itself and of its political, ideological and organizational work that conforms with the full-scale building of communism. The Party will constantly improve the forms and methods of its work, so that the level of its leadership of the masses, through the building of the material and technical base of communism and the development of society's spiritual life, will keep pace with the growing requirements of the epoch of communist construction.

As the vanguard of the people building a communist society, the Party must also march forward in the organization of its inner-Party life, serving as an example and model in developing the most advanced forms of communist public self-government.

Undeviating observance of the Leninist norms of Party life and of the principle of collective leadership, heightening of the responsibility of Party agencies and their officials to the Party *masses* [mass], the ensuring of a growth in the activeness and initiative of all Communists and of their participation in working out and carrying into effect the policy of the Party, and the development of criticism and self-criticism are laws of Party life. This is an imperative condition of the ideological and organizational strength of the Party itself, of [a strengthening of] the unity and solidarity of the Party ranks, of comprehensive development of inner-Party democracy and of activization on this basis of all Party forces, and of the strengthening of ties with the masses.

The cult of the individual and related violations of collective leadership, inner-Party democracy and socialist legality are incompatible with the Leninist principles of Party life. The cult of the individual leads to a belittling of the role of the Party and of the masses of the people and hampers the development of the ideological life of the Party and the creative activity of the working people.

In order to apply the Leninist principle of collective leadership consistently, to ensure a wider influx of fresh new Party forces into the executive Party bodies and to combine old and young cadres properly, and also to rule out the possibility of an excessive concentration of power in the hands of individual officials and to prevent instances of loss of control over them by the collective, the Party considers it necessary to carry out the following measures:

(a) To introduce in practice a systematic turnover of a certain proportion of the membership of all elected Party bodies, from the primary organizations to the Central Committee, at the same time ensuring continuity of leadership.

At all regular elections of the Central Committee of the C.P.S.U. and its Presidium, not less than one-quarter of the membership shall be newly elected. Presidium members *may* [shall] as a rule be elected for not more than three successive terms. Certain Party workers may, by virtue of their recognized authority and high political, organizational or other abilities, be successively elected to executive bodies for a longer period. In such cases, election requires a majority of at least three-quarters of the votes cast by secret ballot.

At least one-third of the members of the Central Committees of the Union-republic Communist Parties and of territory and province Party committees chosen at each regular election, and one-half of the members of region [okrug], city and district (borough) Party committees and the committees or bureaus of primary Party organizations shall be new members. Furthermore, members of these executive Party bodies may be elected for not more than three terms, and secretaries of the primary Party organizations for not more than two consecutive terms.

A Party organization may, in consideration of the political and work qualities of an individual, elect him to an executive body for a longer period. In such cases election requires that not less than three-quarters of the Communists participating in the voting cast their ballots for him.

Party members who are not re-elected to an executive Party body on the expiration of their terms may be re-elected at subsequent elections.

It is established that a decision to remove a member from the Party Central Committee or other executive body shall be adopted solely by secret ballot and is valid when not less than two-thirds of the members of the body in question vote in favor of the decision.

(b) To extend the application of the elective principle and that of accountability in Party organizations from top to bottom, including Party organizations working in special conditions (army, navy).

(c) To heighten the role of Party meetings, conferences, Congresses and plenary sessions of Party committees and other collective bodies. To ensure favorable conditions for free and businesslike discussion within the Party of questions of its policy and practical activities and for comradely discussions of controversial or insufficiently clear matters.

(d) To reduce steadily the paid Party apparatus, enlisting Communists more extensively to do nonsalaried volunteer work.

(e) To develop criticism and self-criticism in every way, as a tested method of work and a means of disclosing and rectifying errors and shortcomings and of rearing cadres correctly.

In the period of full-scale communist construction the role and responsibility of the Party member will steadily increase. It is the duty of a Communist by his entire behavior in production, in public and in private life to be a model in the struggle for the development and strengthening of communist relations and to observe the principles and norms of communist morality. The C.P.S.U. will augment its ranks with the most politically conscious and active toilers and will keep pure and hold high the title of Communist.

The development of inner-Party democracy must ensure greater activity among Communists and heighten their responsibility for realization of the noble communist ideals, must promote the cultivation in them of an inner, organic need *always* to behave and act in all matters in full accordance with the principles of the Party and its lofty aims.

The Party will continue to strengthen the unity and monolithic character of its ranks and to keep pure the banner of Marxism-Leninism. The Party retains in the arsenal of its methods the organizational guarantees, provided by the Statutes of the C.P.S.U., against any manifestations of factionalism and clique activity incompatible with Marxist-Leninist Party principle. The indestructible ideological and organizational unity of the Party is a most important source of its invincibility, a guarantee of the successful accomplishment of the great tasks of communist construction.

The people are the decisive force in the building of communism. The Party exists for the people, and it is in serving the people that it sees the purpose of its activity. A further extension and deepening of the ties between the Party and the people is a necessary condition for success in the struggle for communism. The Party considers it its duty always to consult the working people on major questions of domestic and foreign policy, to bring these questions before all the people for discussion, and to attract nonmembers more widely into participation in all its work. The further socialist democracy develops, the deeper and more comprehensive must be the work of the Party among the working people and the stronger will be its influence among the masses.

The Party will promote in every way the expansion and improvement of the work of the Soviets, the trade unions, the Y.C.L. and other mass organizations of the working people and the development of the creative energy and initiative of the masses, and will strengthen the unity and friendship of all the peoples of the U.S.S.R.

The C.P.S.U. is an inseparable part of the international Communist and workers' movement. The tried and tested Marxist-Leninist principles of proletarian internationalism will continue to be inviolable principles that the Party will follow undeviatingly.

The Communist Party of the Soviet Union will continue to strengthen the unity of the international Communist movement, to develop fraternal ties with all the Communist and Workers' Parties, and to coordinate its actions with the efforts of all the detachments of the world Communist movement for joint struggle against the danger of a new world war, for the interests of the working people, for peace, democracy and socialism.

***

Such is the program of work for the construction of communism that the Communist Party of the Soviet Union sets forth.

The construction of communism in the U.S.S.R. will be the greatest victory mankind has won throughout its age-long history. Each new step made toward the shining peaks of communism inspires the working masses in all countries, renders tremendous moral support in the struggle for the liberation of all peoples from social and national oppression, and speeds the triumph of the ideas of Marxism-Leninism on a worldwide scale.

When the Soviet people enjoy the blessings of communism, new hundreds of millions of people on earth will say: "We are for communism!" It is not through war with other countries but by the example of a more perfect organization of society, by the flowering of productive forces, the creation of all the conditions for the happiness and well-being of man, that the ideas of communism are winning the minds and hearts of the masses.

The forces of social progress will inevitably grow in all countries, and this will give support to the builders of communism in the Soviet Union.

The Party proceeds from the Marxist-Leninist thesis that the people make history and that the establishment of communism is the work of the hands of the people, of their energy and intelligence. The victory of communism depends on people and communism is being built for people. Each Soviet man brings the triumph of communism nearer by his labor. The successes of communist construction spell abundance and a happy life for all and enhance the might, prestige and glory of the Soviet Union.

The Party is confident that Soviet people will accept the new Program of the C.P.S.U. as their own vital cause, as the greatest purpose of their life and as a banner of nationwide struggle for the building of communism. The Party calls on all Communists, on the entire Soviet people—men and women workers and collective farmers and workers of mental labor—to apply their energies to the successful fulfillment of the historic tasks set forth in the Program.

UNDER THE TESTED LEADERSHIP OF THE COMMUNIST PARTY, UNDER THE BANNER OF MARXISM-LENINISM, THE SOVIET PEOPLE HAVE BUILT SOCIALISM.

UNDER THE LEADERSHIP OF THE PARTY, UNDER THE BANNER OF MARXISM-LENINISM, THE SOVIET PEOPLE WILL BUILD COMMUNIST SOCIETY.

THE PARTY SOLEMNLY PROCLAIMS: THE PRESENT GENERATION OF SOVIET PEOPLE WILL LIVE UNDER COMMUNISM!

II. THE PARTY STATUTES

The Statutes of the Communist Party of the Soviet Union (below) are identical with the draft of the Statutes published Aug. 5—Current Digest of the Soviet Press, Vol. XIII, No. 31—except for the changes indicated: additions and substitutions by italics and deletions by square brackets.

THE STATUTES OF THE COMMUNIST PARTY OF THE SOVIET UNION.* (Pravda, Nov. 3, pp. 1-3. Complete text:)
The Communist Party of the Soviet Union is the militant, tested vanguard of the Soviet people, uniting on a voluntary basis the advanced, most socially conscious part of the working class, collective farm peasantry and intelligentsia of the U.S.S.R.

Founded by V. I. Lenin, the Communist Party, the vanguard of the working class, has traversed a glorious path of struggle and has led the working class and working peasants to the victory of the Great October Socialist Revolution, to the establishment of the dictatorship of the proletariat in the U.S.S.R. Under Communist Party leadership the exploiting classes were eliminated in the Soviet Union and the moral and political unity of Soviet society has taken shape and grown in strength. Socialism has triumphed completely and finally. The Communist Party, the party of the working class, has now become the party of the entire Soviet people.

The Party exists for the people and serves the people. It is the highest form of socio-political organization, the leading and guiding force of Soviet society. The Party directs the great creative activity of the Soviet people and imparts an organized, planned and scientific character to their struggle to achieve the ultimate goal, the victory of communism.

The C.P.S.U. organizes its work on the basis of unswerving observance of the Leninist norms of Party life—the principle of collectivity of leadership, the comprehensive development of inner-Party democracy, the activeness and initiative of Communists, and criticism and self-criticism.

Ideological and organizational unity, monolithic solidarity of its ranks and conscious discipline on the part of all Communists are the inviolable law of the life of the C.P.S.U. Any manifestation of factionalism or clique activity is incompatible with Marxist-Leninist Party principles and with Party membership.

In all its activity the C.P.S.U. is guided by the Marxist-Leninist teaching and the Program based on it, which defines the Party's fundamental tasks for the period of the construction of communist society.

The C.P.S.U., creatively developing Marxism-Leninism, resolutely combats any manifestations of revisionism and dogmatism, which are profoundly alien to revolutionary theory.

The Communist Party of the Soviet Union is an inseparable part of the international Communist and workers' movement. It firmly adheres to the tested Marxist-Leninist principles of proletarian internationalism, actively promotes strengthening of the unity of the entire international Communist *and workers'* movement and fraternal ties with the great army of Communists of all countries.

*[For the Statutes adopted at the 19th Party Congress in 1952, see "Current Soviet Policies—I," Frederick A. Praeger, Inc., New York, 1953.]

I. PARTY MEMBERS, THEIR DUTIES AND RIGHTS.—1. Any citizen of the Soviet Union who accepts the Party Program and Statutes, takes an active part in communist construction, works in one of the Party organizations, carries out Party decisions and pays membership dues may be a member of the C.P.S.U.

2. It is the duty of a Party member:

(a) to fight for the creation of the material and technical base of communism, to set an example of the communist attitude toward labor, to raise labor productivity, to take the initiative in all that is new and progressive, to support and propagate advanced experience, to master technology, to improve his qualifications, to safeguard and increase public, socialist property—the foundation of the might and prosperity of the Soviet homeland;

(b) to carry out Party decisions firmly and undeviatingly, to explain the policy of the Party to the masses, to help strengthen and broaden the Party's ties with the people, to be considerate and attentive toward people, to respond promptly to the wants and needs of the working people;

(c) to take an active part in the political life of the country, in the management of state affairs and in economic and cultural construction, to set an example in the fulfillment of public duty, to help develop and strengthen communist social relations;

(d) to master Marxist-Leninist theory, to raise his ideological level and to contribute to the molding and rearing of the man of communist society. To combat *resolutely* any manifestations of bourgeois ideology, remnants of a private-property psychology, *religious prejudices* and other survivals of the past, to observe the *principles* [rules] of communist morality and to place public interests above personal ones;

(e) to be an active proponent of the ideas of socialist internationalism and Soviet patriotism among the masses of the working people, to combat survivals of nationalism and chauvinism, to contribute by word and deed to strengthening the friendship of peoples of the U.S.S.R. and the fraternal ties of the Soviet people with the peoples of the socialist countries and the proletarians and working people of all countries;

(f) to *strengthen* [guard] the ideological and organizational unity of the Party in every way, to safeguard the Party against the infiltration of persons unworthy of the lofty title of Communist, to be truthful and honest with the Party *and people,* to display vigilance, to preserve Party and state secrets;

(g) to develop criticism and self-criticism, to boldly disclose shortcomings and strive for their removal, to combat ostentation, conceit, complacency and localism, to rebuff firmly any attempts to suppress criticism, to resist any actions detrimental to the Party and the state and to report them to Party bodies, up to and including the Central Committee of the C.P.S.U.;

(h) to carry out unswervingly the Party line in the selection of cadres according to their political and work qualifications. To be uncompromising in all cases of violation of the Leninist principles of the selection and training of cadres;

(i) to observe Party and state discipline, which is equally binding on all Party members. The Party has a single discipline, one law for all Communists, regardless of their services or the positions they hold;

(j) to help in every way to strengthen the defense might of the U.S.S.R., to wage a tireless struggle for peace and friendship among peoples.

3. A Party member has the right:

(a) to elect and be elected to Party bodies;

(b) to discuss freely questions of the Party's policies and practical activities at Party meetings, conferences and Congresses, at the meetings of Party committees and in the Party press; to introduce motions; openly to express and uphold his opinion until the organization has adopted a decision;

(c) to criticize any Communist, regardless of the position he holds, at Party meetings, conferences and Congresses and at plenary meetings of Party committees. Persons guilty of suppressing criticism or persecuting anyone for criticism must be held to strict Party responsibility, up to and including expulsion from the ranks of the C.P.S.U.;

(d) to participate in person at Party meetings and bureau and committee meetings at which his activity or conduct is discussed;

(e) to address questions, statements or proposals to Party bodies at any level up to and including the Central Committee of the C.P.S.U. and to demand an answer on the substance of his address.

4. Admission to membership in the Party is exclusively on an individual basis. Membership in the Party is open to socially conscious and active *workers, peasants and representatives of the intelligentsia, devoted to the cause of communism* [working people, devoted to the cause of communism, from among the workers, peasants and intelligentsia]. New members are admitted from among the candidate members who have completed their period as candidates.

Persons may join the Party on attaining the age of 18. Young persons up to 20 years of age inclusive may join the Party only via the Young Communist League.

The procedure for the admission of candidate members to full Party membership is as follows:

(a) Applicants for Party membership shall submit recommendations from three Party members who have a Party standing of not less than three years and who know the applicant from having worked with him on the job and in volunteer work for not less than one year;

Note 1. In admitting members of the Y.C.L. to membership in the Party, the recommendation of the Y.C.L. district* *or city* committee is equal to the recommendation of one Party member.

Note 2. Members and candidate members of the Central Committee of the C.P.S.U. shall refrain from giving recommendations.

(b) The question of admission to the Party is discussed and decided by a general meeting of the primary Party organization; the decision comes into force upon ratification by the district Party committee or, in cities where there is no district subdivision, upon ratification by the city Party committee.

The presence of the persons recommending admission is not essential at the discussion of the application;

(c) Citizens of the U.S.S.R. who formerly belonged to the Communist or Workers' Party of another country are admitted to membership in the Communist Party of the Soviet Union on the basis of rules established by the Central Committee of the C.P.S.U.

Persons who had formerly belonged to other parties are admitted to membership in the C.P.S.U. in conformity with the regular procedure, but only if their admission is approved by a province or territory Party committee or the Central Committee of a Union-republic Communist Party.

5. Those who recommend applicants are responsible to the Party organizations for the objectivity of their description of the applicant's *political, work and moral* [work and political] qualifications.

6. Tenure of membership dates from the adoption, by a general meeting of the primary Party organization, of a resolution to admit the candidate to Party membership.

---

*[The Russian "raion" is either an administrative division of a province or republic or an administrative division of a large city. The practice of the Current Digest is to translate the word "district" in the former sense and "borough" in the latter sense. Throughout the Statutes the word is translated "district," but applies in both senses.—Trans.]

7. The procedure for registering members and candidate members in the Party organization and for transferring them to another Party organization is determined in accordance with instructions of the Central Committee of the C.P.S.U.

8. If a Party member or candidate member has without valid reason failed to pay membership dues for three months, the matter shall be discussed in the primary Party organization. Should it turn out that the Party member or candidate member has in effect lost contact with the Party organization, he shall be considered to have dropped out of the Party; the primary Party organization shall adopt a decision to this effect and shall submit it to the district or city Party committee for ratification.

9. A Party member *or candidate member* who fails to perform the duties set forth in the Statutes or commits other offenses shall be called to responsibility and may be punished by admonition, by reprimand (or severe reprimand), or by reprimand (or severe reprimand) with entry in his registration card. The highest Party penalty is expulsion from the Party.

When it is necessary as a Party penalty, a Party organization may transfer a member of the Party to the status of candidate member for a period of up to one year. The decision of a primary Party organization to return a Party member to candidate status is *ratified* [subject to ratification] by the district or city Party committee. On expiration of the established period the person who has been returned to candidate status is admitted to Party membership on the regular basis and retains his former tenure of Party membership.

For minor offenses measures of Party education and influence, in the form of comradely criticism, Party censure, warnings or reproof, should be taken.

When deciding the question of expulsion from the Party, the maximum [prudence and] thoughtfulness must be exercised and a thorough examination must be made of whether the accusation against the Party member is justified.

10. The question of expelling a Communist from the Party is decided by a general meeting of the primary Party organization. The decision of the primary Party organization on expulsion from the Party is considered adopted if no less than two-thirds of the Party members present at the meeting vote for it, and it *is ratified by the district or city Party committee. The decision of a district or city Party committee on expulsion from the Party* comes into force after it is ratified by a province or territory Party committee or the Central Committee of a Union-republic Communist Party.

Until the province or territory Party committee or Union-republic Communist Party Central Committee ratifies the resolution expelling the Communist from the Party, his Party card *or candidate's card* remains in his hands and he has the right to attend closed Party meetings.

A person expelled from the Party retains the right to submit an appeal within two months to superior Party bodies, up to and including the Central Committee of the C.P.S.U.

11. Questions of Party penalty for a member or candidate member of the Central Committee of a Union-republic Communist Party or of a territory, province, region, city or district Party committee, and also of a member of an inspection commission, shall be discussed in the primary Party organizations.

Decisions of Party organizations on penalties for members and candidate members of these Party committees and members of inspection commissions shall be adopted by the regular procedure.

The proposals of the Party organizations regarding expulsion from the Party shall be reported to the Party committee of which the given Communist is a member. A decision to expel a member or candidate member of the Central Committee of a Union-republic Communist Party or of a territory, province, region, city or district Party committee or a member of an inspection commission shall be adopted at a plenary session of the respective committee by a two-thirds majority vote of its members.

The question of expelling from the Party a member or candidate member of the Central Committee of the C.P.S.U. or a member of the Central Inspection Commission shall be decided by a Party Congress or, in the interval between Party Congresses, at a plenary session of the Central Committee members.

12. If a Party member has committed an offense punishable under criminal procedure, he is expelled from the Party and held liable under the law.

13. Appeals by those expelled from the Party or subjected to

penalties, as well as decisions of Party organizations to expel members from the Party, shall be reviewed by the Party bodies concerned within a period of not more than one month from the day of their receipt.

II. CANDIDATES FOR PARTY MEMBERSHIP.—14. [All persons] *Those* entering the Party pass through a candidate stage, which is essential in order that the candidate may acquaint himself with the Party Program and Statutes and prepare for admission to the Party. The Party organization must help the candidate to prepare for admission to the Party and must verify his personal qualifications.

The period of candidacy is set at one year.

15. The procedure for admitting candidates (individual admission, presentation of recommendations, the resolution of the primary Party organization on admission and its ratification) is identical with that for admission to Party membership.

16. Upon expiration of the candidature, the primary Party organization takes up and decides the question of admitting the candidate to membership in the Party. If during his candidature the candidate has not proved himself and because of his personal qualifications *cannot be admitted* [has turned out to be unworthy of admission] to Party membership, the Party organization adopts a resolution to refuse him admission to Party membership, and after ratification of this resolution by the district or city Party committee, he is considered dropped from candidature for Party membership.

17. Candidates for Party membership take part in the entire activity of the Party organization and enjoy the right to a consultative vote at Party meetings. Candidates for Party membership may not be elected to executive Party bodies or as delegates to Party conferences and Congresses.

18. Candidates for Party membership pay the same Party dues as Party members.

III. ORGANIZATIONAL STRUCTURE OF THE PARTY. INNER-PARTY DEMOCRACY.—19. The guiding principle of the organizational structure of the Party is democratic centralism, meaning:

(a) election of all Party executive bodies from bottom to top;

(b) periodic accountability of Party bodies to their Party organizations and to higher bodies;

(c) strict Party discipline and subordination of the minority to the majority;

(d) the unconditionally binding nature of the decisions of higher bodies upon lower ones.

20. The Party rests on a territorial-production* basis: The primary organizations are created at the Communists' places of work and are territorially united in district organizations, city organizations, etc. The organization serving a given area is superior to all Party organizations serving parts of this area.

21. All Party organizations are autonomous in deciding local questions, provided that the decisions are not contrary to the Party's policy.

22. The highest executive body of a Party organization is the general meeting (for primary organizations), the conference (for district, city, region, province and territory organizations) and the Congress (for the Communist Parties of Union republics and the Communist Party of the Soviet Union).

23. The general meeting, conference or Congress elects a bureau or committee, which is the executive body and directs the entire current work of the Party organization.

24. Elections of Party bodies are held by closed (secret) ballot. In elections all Party members have the unrestricted right to challenge candidates and to criticize them. Voting must be on individual candidates. Candidates who receive more than one-half of the votes of the participants in the meeting, conference or Congress are considered elected.

25. The principle of systematic turnover of the membership of Party bodies and of continuity of leadership is observed in elections of Party bodies.

At all regular elections of the Central Committee of the C.P.S.U. and its Presidium, not less than one-fourth of the membership shall be newly elected. Presidium members shall as a rule be elected for not more than three successive terms. Particular Party workers may, by virtue of their recognized

*[Production is used to refer to industry, agriculture, transport, trade, etc.—Trans.]

authority and high political, organizational or other abilities, be successively elected to executive bodies for a longer period. In such cases, election requires a majority of at least three-fourths of the votes cast by closed (secret) ballot.

At least one-third of the members of the Central Committees of the Union-republic Communist Parties and of territory and province committees chosen at each regular election, and one-half of the members of region, city and district Party committees and the committees and bureaus of primary Party organizations, shall be new members. Furthermore, members of these executive Party bodies may be elected for not more than three successive terms. The secretaries of primary Party organizations may be elected for not more than two successive terms.

A *meeting, conference or Congress* [Party organization] may, in consideration of the political and work qualities of an individual, elect him to an executive body for a longer period. In such cases election requires that not less than three-fourths of the Communists participating in the voting cast their ballots for him.

Party members who are not re-elected to an executive Party body on the expiration of their terms may be re-elected in subsequent elections.

26. A member or candidate member of the Central Committee of the C.P.S.U. must by his entire activity justify the high trust placed in him by the Party. If a member or candidate member of the Central Committee of the C.P.S.U. has sullied his honor and dignity, he cannot remain a member of the Central Committee. The question of removing a member or a candidate member of the Central Committee of the C.P.S.U. from membership in the Central Committee is decided at a plenary session of the Central Committee by closed (secret) ballot. The decision is regarded as adopted if at least two-thirds of all the members of the Central Committee of the C.P.S.U. vote for it.

The question of removing a member or candidate member of the Central Committee of a Union-republic Communist Party committee from the given Party body is decided at a plenary session of the given committee. A decision is considered adopted if at least two-thirds of all the members of the committee vote for it by closed (secret) ballot.

If a member of the Central Inspection Commission does not justify the high trust placed in him by the Party, he must be removed from the Commission. This question is decided at a meeting of the Central Inspection Commission. A decision is considered adopted if at least two-thirds of all the members of the Central Inspection Commission vote for removal of a given member of the Central Inspection Commission from that body by closed (secret) ballot.

The question of removing members of inspection commissions of republic, territory, province, region, city and district Party organizations from these commissions is decided at meetings of the given commissions under the procedure established for members and candidate members of the Party committees.

27. The free and businesslike discussion of questions of Party policy in individual Party organizations or in the Party as a whole is an inalienable right of the Party member and an important principle of inner-Party democracy. Only on the basis of inner-Party democracy can criticism and self-criticism be developed and Party discipline, which must be conscious and not mechanical, be strengthened.

Discussions on disputed or insufficiently clear questions are possible within the framework of individual organizations or of the Party as a whole.

General Party discussion is necessary if:

(a) this need is recognized by several Party organizations at the province or republic level;

(b) if within the Central Committee there does not exist a sufficiently firm majority on major questions of Party policy;

(c) if the Central Committee of the C.P.S.U. considers it essential to consult with the entire Party on given questions of policy.

Broad discussion, especially discussion on an all-Union scale, of questions of Party policy must be carried out in such a way as to ensure the free expression of the views of Party members and to prevent the possibility of attempts to form factional groupings destructive to Party unity or of attempts to split the Party.

28. The highest principle of Party leadership is collectivity *of leadership*—the indispensable condition of the normal functioning of Party organizations, the correct rearing of cadres and the development of the activeness and initiative of Communists. The cult of the individual and the violations of inner-Party democracy connected with it cannot be tolerated in the Party; they are incompatible with the Leninist principles of Party life.

Collective leadership does not absolve officials of individual responsibility for matters entrusted to them.

29. *In the period between Congresses and conferences the* [The] Central Committees of the Union-republic Communist Parties and the territory, province, region, city and district Party committees shall keep Party organizations periodically informed about their work.

30. Meetings of the aktiv of district, city, region, province and territory Party organizations and of the Union-republic Communist Parties are called to discuss major Party decisions and to work out [practical] measures for implementing them, and also to consider questions of local life.

IV. THE SUPREME BODIES OF THE PARTY.—31. The highest body of the Communist Party of the Soviet Union is the Party Congress. Regular Congresses are convened *by the Central Committee* not less often than once every four years. Convocation of a Party Congress and the agenda are announced at least one and one-half months before the Congress. Extraordinary Congresses are convened by the Party Central Committee on its own initiative or on the demand of not less than one-third of the total Party membership represented at the preceding Party Congress. Extraordinary Congresses are convened on two months' notice. A Congress is considered valid if no less than one-half of the total Party membership is represented at it.

The norms of representation at the Party Congress are fixed by the Central Committee.

32. If no extraordinary Congress is convened by the Party Central Committee within the term indicated in Art. 31, the organizations demanding the convocation of an extraordinary Congress have the right to form an organizational committee possessing the rights of the Party Central Committee to convene an extraordinary Congress.

33. The Congress:

(a) hears and approves reports of the Central Committee, the Central Inspection Commission and other central organizations;

(b) reviews, amends and approves the Program and Statutes of the Party;

(c) determines the line of the Party on questions of domestic and foreign policy and considers and decides major questions of communist construction;

(d) elects the Central Committee and the Central Inspection Commission.

34. The number of members of the Central Committee and the Central Inspection Commission is determined and their members are elected by the Congress. In the event of vacancies in the membership of the Central Committee, they are filled from among the candidate members of the Central Committee of the C.P.S.U. elected by the Congress.

35. In the intervals between Congresses the Central Committee of the Communist Party of the Soviet Union directs the entire work of the Party and local Party bodies; selects and places executive cadres; directs the work of central state organizations and public organizations of the working people through the Party groups within them; creates various agencies, institutions and enterprises of the Party and directs their work; appoints the editorial boards of central newspapers and magazines that function under its control; and distributes the funds of the Party budget and supervises its implementation.

The Central Committee represents the C.P.S.U. in its relations with other parties.

36. The Central Committee of the C.P.S.U. keeps Party organizations regularly informed about its work.

37. The Central Inspection Commission checks on the promptness of the conduct of affairs in central bodies of the Party and audits the treasury and undertakings of the Central Committee of the C.P.S.U.

38. The Central Committee of the C.P.S.U. holds not less than one plenary session every six months. Candidate members of the Central Committee attend plenary sessions of the Central Committee with the right to a consultative vote.

39. The Central Committee of the Communist Party of the Soviet Union elects a Presidium to direct the work of the Central Committee between plenary sessions and a Secretariat to direct current work, chiefly in the selection of cadres and organization of checkup on fulfillment; it creates a Bureau of the C.P.S.U. Central Committee for the Russian Republic.

40. The Central Committee of the Communist Party of the Soviet Union organizes a Party Control Committee under the Central Committee.

The Party Control Committee under the Party Central Committee:

(a) verifies the observance of Party discipline by members and candidate members of the C.P.S.U.; calls to account Communists guilty of violating the Party Program and Statutes or Party and state discipline, as well as violators of Party ethics;

(b) examines appeals against decisions of the Central Committees of the Union-republic Communist Parties and of territory and province Party committees concerning expulsion from the Party and Party penalties.

V. THE REPUBLIC, TERRITORY, PROVINCE, REGION, CITY AND DISTRICT ORGANIZATIONS OF THE PARTY.—41. The republic, territory, province, region, city and district Party organizations and their committees are guided in their work by the Program and Statutes of the C.P.S.U.; carry out within the limits of the republic, territory, province, region, city or district the entire work of implementing Party policy; and organize execution of the directives of the Central Committee of the C.P.S.U.

42. The chief duties of republic, territory, province, region, city and district Party organizations and their executive bodies are:

(a) political and organizational work among the masses and their mobilization for accomplishment of the tasks of communist construction, for all-round development of industrial and agricultural production and for the fulfillment and overfulfillment of state plans; concern for a steady rise in the living standard and cultural level of the working people;

(b) organization of ideological work; propaganda of Marxism-Leninism; increasing the communist awareness of the working people; guidance of the local press, radio and television; supervision of the work of cultural-enlightenment institutions;

(c) guidance of the Soviets, trade unions, the Young Communist League, cooperative enterprises and other public organizations through the Party groups within them; the ever broader enlistment of the working people in the work of these organizations; development of the initiative and activeness of the masses as a necessary condition for the gradual transition from a socialist state system to communist public self-government.

Party organizations do not supplant Soviet, trade union, cooperative and other public organizations of the working people and must not permit a merging of the functions of Party and other agencies or unnecessary parallelism in work;

(d) selection and placement of executive cadres and the rearing of them in a spirit of communist ideology, honesty and truthfulness and a high sense of responsibility to the Party and the people for the work entrusted to them;

(e) broad enlistment of Communists in the conduct of Party work as unsalaried workers, as a form of public activity;

(f) organization of various institutions and enterprises of the Party within the bounds of their republic, territory, province, region, city or district and guidance of their work; distribution of Party funds within their organizations; systematic reporting to the higher Party body and accountability to it for their work.

The Executive Bodies of Republic, Territory and Province Party Organizations.—43. The highest body of the province, territory or republic Party organization is the province or territory Party conference or the Congress of the Union-republic Communist Party, and in the intervals between them the province committee, the territory committee or the Central Committee of the Union-republic Communist Party.

44. A regular province or territory conference or regular Congress of a Union-republic Communist Party is convened by the province or territory committee or the Central Committee

of the Union-republic Communist Party once every two years, and extraordinary sessions by decision of the province or territory committee or the Central Committee of the Union-republic Communist Party or upon the demand of one-third of the total number of members of the organizations belonging to the province, territory or republic Party organization. Congresses of the Communist Parties of the Union republics having province divisions (the Ukraine, Belorussia, Kazakhstan and Uzbekistan) may be held once in four years.

The norms of representation at the province or territory conference or Congress of a Union-republic Communist Party are fixed by the given Party committee.

The province or territory conference or Congress of a Union-republic Communist Party hears the reports of the province or territory committee or the Central Committee of the Union-republic Communist Party and of the inspection commission; discusses at its own discretion other questions of Party, economic and cultural work; and elects the province or territory committee or Central Committee of the Union-republic Communist Party, the inspection commission and delegates to the Congress of the C.P.S.U.

45. Each province and territory committee and Central Committee of a Union-republic Communist Party elects a bureau, which includes the secretaries of the committee. Party membership of not less than five years is compulsory for secretaries. The plenary sessions of the committees also approve the chairmen of Party commissions, the heads of the departments of these committees and the editors of Party newspapers and magazines.

Secretariats may be set up in the province and territory committees and Central Committees of the Union-republic Communist Parties to handle current questions and check on fulfillment.

46. The plenary session of the province committee, territory committee or Central Committee of the Union-republic Communist Party is convened not less than once in four months.

47. The province committees, territory committees and Central Committees of the Union-republic Communist Parties direct the region, city and district Party organizations, check on their work and periodically hear the reports of the region, city and district Party committees.

The Party organizations of the autonomous republics as well as of autonomous and other provinces within territories and Union republics work under the direction of the territory committees or the Central Committees of the Union-republic Communist Parties.

The Executive Bodies of the Region, City and District (Rural and Urban) Party Organizations.—48. The highest body of the region, city or district Party organization is the region, city or district Party conference or the general meeting of Communists convened by the region, city or district committee not less than once in two years, and the extraordinary conference convened by decision of the committee or on demand of one-third of the total number of members of the Party in the given Party organization.

The region, city or district conference (meeting) hears the reports of the committee and the inspection commission; discusses at its own discretion other questions of Party, economic and cultural work; and elects the region, city or district committee, the inspection commission and the delegates to the province or territory conference or Congress of the Union-republic Communist Party.

The norms of representation at the region, city or district conference are fixed by the given Party committee.

49. Each region, city or district committee elects a bureau, which includes the secretaries of the committee, and also approves the heads of the departments of the committee and the editors of newspapers. Party membership of at least three years is compulsory for secretaries of a region, city or district committee. The secretaries of the committees are approved by the province committee, territory committee or Central Committee of the Union-republic Communist Party.

50. The region, city and district committees organize and approve the primary Party organizations, direct their work, periodically hear reports on the work of the Party organizations and keep the records of the Communists.

51. The plenary session of the region, city or district committee is convened not less than once in three months.

52. The region, city or district committee has unsalaried instructors, sets up permanent or temporary commissions for various questions of Party work and employs other forms of enlisting Communists in the work of the Party committee as a public duty.

VI. PRIMARY ORGANIZATIONS OF THE PARTY.—53. The primary organizations are the foundations of the Party.

The primary Party organizations are set up at the places of work of Party members—at plants, factories, state farms and other enterprises, collective farms, units of the Soviet Army, offices, educational institutions, etc., wherever there are no fewer than three Party members. Primary Party organizations may also be set up on a territorial basis at the places of residence of Communists in villages or in apartment house administrations.

54. At enterprises, collective farms and offices where there are more than 50 Party members and candidate members, Party organizations may be set up within the over-all primary Party organization in shops, sectors, livestock sections, brigades, departments, etc., with the authorization of the district, city or region Party committee.

Party groups by brigades and other production units may be set up within shop organizations, sector organizations, etc., and also within primary Party organizations with fewer than 50 members and candidate members.

55. The highest body of the primary Party organization is the Party meeting, which is held not less than once a month.

In large Party organizations with more than 300 Communists, the general Party meeting is convened when necessary at times fixed by the Party committee or on the demand of several shop Party organizations.

56. The primary or shop Party organization elects a bureau for a term of one year to conduct current work; the number of its members is fixed by the Party meeting. Primary and shop Party organizations with fewer than 15 Party members elect a secretary and an assistant secretary of the Party organization instead of a bureau.

At least one year's membership in the Party is compulsory for secretaries of primary and shop Party organizations.

Full-time paid Party posts are as a rule not set up in primary Party organizations embracing fewer than 150 Party members.

57. In large enterprises and institutions with more than 300 Party members and candidate members, and also in organizations with more than 100 Communists in cases where special production conditions or geographical dispersion make it necessary, Party committees may be set up, with the authorization of the province or territory Party committee or the Central Committee of the Union-republic Communist Party; the shop Party organizations of these enterprises and institutions are granted the rights of primary Party organizations.

The Party organizations of collective farms that have 50 Communists may set up Party committees.

The Party committee is elected for a term of one year, and the number of its members is fixed by the general Party meeting or conference.

58. The primary Party organization is guided in its work by the Program and Statutes of the C.P.S.U. It conducts work directly among the working people, rallies them around the Communist Party of the Soviet Union and organizes the masses for carrying out the Party's policy and for the struggle to build communism.

The primary Party organization:

(a) admits new members to the C.P.S.U.;

(b) rears Communists in a spirit of devotion to the cause of the Party, ideological conviction and communist ethics;

(c) organizes the study by Communists of Marxist-Leninist theory in close connection with the practice of communist construction and opposes any attempts at revisionist distortions of Marxism-Leninism and at its dogmatic interpretation;

(d) concerns itself with enhancing the vanguard role of Communists in labor and in the socio-political and economic life of the enterprise, collective farm, office, educational institution, etc.;

(e) acts as the organizer of the working people in carrying out routine tasks of communist construction; heads socialist competition for the fulfillment of state plans and pledges *of the working people;* mobilizes the masses for disclosing and making better use of the internal reserves of enterprises and collective farms and for widely introducing in production the achievements of science, technology and the experience of leading workers; works for the strengthening of labor discipline and for a steady rise in labor productivity and an improvement of quality of output; shows concern for protecting and increasing public wealth at enterprises and state and collective farms;

(f) conducts mass agitation and propaganda work; rears the masses in the spirit of communism; helps the working people to develop skills in administering state and public affairs;

(g) on the basis of broad development of criticism and self-criticism, combats manifestations of bureaucracy, localism and violations of state discipline; thwarts attempts to deceive the state; takes measures against laxity, mismanagement and waste at enterprises, collective farms and institutions;

(h) assists the region, city and district Party committees in all their activity and accounts to them for its work.

The Party organization must see to it that every Communist observes in his own life and inculcates in the working people the moral principles set forth in the Program of the C.P.S.U., *in the moral code of the builder of communism:*

devotion to the cause of communism, love of the socialist homeland, of the socialist countries;

conscientious labor for the good of society: He who does not work, neither shall he eat;

concern on the part of everyone for the preservation and growth of public wealth;

a high sense of public duty, intolerance of violations of the public interest;

collectivism and comradely mutual assistance: One for all and all for one;

humane relations and mutual respect among people: Man is to man a friend, comrade and brother;

honesty and truthfulness, moral purity, guilelessness and modesty in public and private life;

mutual respect in the family and concern for the upbringing of children;

an uncompromising attitude to injustice, parasitism, dishonesty, careerism *and money-grubbing;*

friendship and brotherhood of all peoples of the U.S.S.R., intolerance of national and racial animosity;

an uncompromising attitude to the enemies of communism, peace and the freedom of peoples;

fraternal solidarity with the working people of all countries and with all peoples.

59. Primary Party organizations of production and trade enterprises, state and collective farms, and planning organizations, design bureaus and research institutes directly connected with production have the right to supervise the work of the administration.

The Party organizations of ministries, state committees, economic councils and other central and local Soviet and economic institutions and agencies, which do not have the function of supervising the work of the administration, must actively promote improvement of the work of the apparatus, foster among the personnel a high sense of responsibility for the work entrusted to them, take measures to strengthen state discipline and improve services to the public, vigorously combat bureaucracy and red tape, and inform the proper Party bodies in good time about shortcomings in the work of the institutions as well as of individuals, regardless of the posts they occupy.

VII. THE PARTY AND THE YOUNG COMMUNIST LEAGUE. —60. The All-Union Leninist Young Communist League is an independent public organization of young people, an active assistant and reserve of the Party. The Young Communist League helps the Party to rear young people in the spirit of communism, to enlist them in the practical work of building a new society and to train a generation of harmoniously developed people who will live, work and direct public affairs under communism.

61. Young Communist League organizations enjoy the right of broad initiative in discussing and submitting to the appropriate Party organizations questions of the work of an enterprise, collective farm or institution. They must be really active champions of Party directives in all spheres of communist construction, especially where there are no primary Party organizations.

62. The Y.C.L. *works* [conducts its work] under the guidance of the Communist Party of the Soviet Union. The work of local

Y.C.L. organizations is directed and supervised by the appropriate republic, territory, province, region, city and district Party organizations.

In their work in the communist education of young people, local Party bodies and primary Party organizations rely on Young Communist League organizations and support and disseminate their useful undertakings.

63. Y.C.L. members who *are admitted to* [become members or candidate members of] the Party leave the Young Communist League from the moment they join the Party, unless they occupy executive posts in Young Communist League organizations.

VIII. PARTY ORGANIZATIONS IN THE SOVIET ARMY. — 64. Party organizations in the Soviet Army are guided in their activity by the Program and Statutes of the C.P.S.U. and function on the basis of instructions approved by the Central Committee.

The Party organizations of the Soviet Army ensure the implementation of Party policy in the armed forces; rally their personnel around the Communist Party; educate servicemen in the spirit of the ideas of Marxism-Leninism and selfless devotion to the socialist homeland; actively help to strengthen the unity of the army and the people; show concern for strengthening military discipline; and mobilize personnel for fulfilling the tasks of combat and political training, mastering new equipment and weapons and irreproachably carrying out their military duty and the orders and instructions of the command.

65. The guidance of Party work in the armed forces is exercised by the Central Committee of the C.P.S.U. through the Chief Political Administration of the Soviet Army and Navy, which functions with the powers of a department of the Central Committee of the C.P.S.U.

Party membership of five years is compulsory for the heads of the political administrations of military districts and fleets and the heads of the political departments of armies, and Party membership of three years for the heads of the political departments of military units.

66. The Party organizations and political bodies of the Soviet Army support close contact with local Party committees and keep them periodically informed about political work in the military units. The secretaries of military Party organizations and the heads of political bodies participate in the work of the local Party committees.

IX. PARTY GROUPS IN NON-PARTY ORGANIZATIONS. — 67. Party groups are organized at congresses, conferences and meetings convened by Soviet, trade union, cooperative and other mass organizations of the working people as well as in the elective bodies of these organizations where there are at least three Party members. The task of these groups is to strengthen the influence of the Party in every way and to carry out its policy among non-Party people, to strengthen Party and state discipline, to combat bureaucracy and to check on the fulfillment of Party and Soviet directives.

68. Party groups are subordinate to the appropriate Party bodies: the Central Committee of the Communist Party of the Soviet Union, the Central Committee of the Union-republic Communist Party or the territory, province, region, city or district Party committee.

In all matters the Party groups must be guided strictly and undeviatingly by the decisions of the executive Party bodies.

X. PARTY FUNDS. —69. The financial resources of the Party and its organizations consist of membership dues, revenue from Party undertakings and other revenue.

70. The monthly membership dues for Party members and candidate members are established as follows:

Monthly earnings:	Dues	
up to 50 rubles	10 kopeks	
from 51 to 100 rubles	0.5% of monthly earnings	
from 101 to 150 rubles	1.0%	"
from 151 to 200 rubles	1.5%	"
from 201 to 250 rubles	*2.0%*	"
from 251 to 300 rubles	*2.5%*	"
[from 201 to 300 rubles	2.0%	"]
over 300 rubles	3.0%	"

71. An initiation fee in the amount of 2% of monthly earnings is assessed upon admission as a candidate member of the Party.

III. OPENING OF THE CONGRESS

22nd CONGRESS OF THE COMMUNIST PARTY OF THE SOVIET UNION.—Yesterday in the Kremlin Palace of Congresses. (Pravda, Oct. 18, p. 1. 2000 words. Condensed text:) The Kremlin Palace of Congresses, Moscow—here, in this majestic new building, the 22nd Congress of the Communist Party of the Soviet Union began its work yesterday, Oct. 17. Our whole country and all progressive mankind have awaited this historic day. The people have given the 22nd Congress the name of "congress of builders of communism." The Congress will adopt one of the greatest documents of our era, the new Party Program, the first program in history for building a communist society.

The solemn moment of the opening of the Congress approached. Those present in the hall warmly welcomed the appearance in the presidium of heads of the delegations of fraternal Communist and Workers' Parties who had arrived for the 22nd Congress.

At 10 o'clock the delegates and guests welcomed the appearance of the members of the Presidium of the Party Central Committee with stormy, prolonged applause. All rose.

The delegates and guests listened with tremendous attention to the introductory remarks of Comrade Nikita Sergeyevich Khrushchev, First Secretary of the Party Central Committee.

"The 20th regular Congress of our party was held in February, 1956. More than five and a half years have passed since then. In the life and work of the Party, of all the peoples of the Soviet Union, as well as in the whole world's development, this important period has been filled with events of historic significance," said N. S. Khrushchev.

"The extraordinary 21st Congress adopted a decision to convene a regular Congress in 1961.* The 22nd Party Congress begins its work today in accordance with this decision.

"Elected to the 22nd Party Congress were 4408 voting delegates and 405 with consultative votes; 4394 of the former and the 405 with consultative votes have arrived at the Congress. Fourteen delegates are absent for valid reason."

On behalf of the Party Central Committee, Comrade N. S. Khrushchev proposed that the Congress begin its work and declared the 22nd Congress of the Communist Party of the Soviet Union open.

Comrade N. S. Khrushchev said that since the 21st Congress the international Communist workers' movement had lost a number of outstanding leaders, including our unforgettable Comrades Wilhelm Pieck, William Foster, Harry Pollitt, Eugene Dennis, Waclaw Kopecky, Elias Laferte, Farajallah Helw and Gaston Monmousseau.

Patrice Lumumba, an outstanding leader of the national-liberation movement of Africa, fell in the struggle against colonialism.

Comrade Inejiro Asanuma, Chairman of the Socialist Party of Japan, prominent public figure and fighter for peace and democracy, died at the hands of a foul fascist assassin.

Comrade N. S. Khrushchev proposed that their memory be honored by a moment of silence. All rose.

* [For the documentary record of the 20th and 21st Congresses, see "Current Soviet Policies—II" (Praeger, New York, 1957) and "Current Soviet Policies—III" (Columbia University Press, New York, 1960).]

Comrade N. S. Khrushchev reported that delegations from 80 foreign Marxist-Leninist parties had arrived at the 22nd Party Congress.

"Allow me," he said, "to welcome warmly the delegations here from friendly fraternal parties." (Stormy applause.) [There follows a list of parties and delegation heads, punctuated by applause: Communist Party of China, Chou En-lai; Polish United Workers' Party, Wladyslaw Gomulka; Communist Party of Czechoslovakia, Antonin Novotny; Socialist Unity Party of Germany, Walter Ulbricht; Rumanian Workers' Party, Gheorghe Gheorghiu-Dej; Bulgarian Communist Party, Todor Zhivkov; Hungarian Socialist Workers' Party, Janos Kadar; Workers' Party of Vietnam, Ho Chi Minh; Korean Party of Labor, Kim Il Sung; Mongolian People's Revolutionary Party, Yumzhagiin Tsedenbal; French Communist Party, Maurice Thorez; Italian Communist Party, Palmiro Togliatti: Integrated Revolutionary Organizations of Cuba, Blas Roca; Communist Party of Indonesia, Dipa Aidit; Communist Party of India, Ajoy Ghosh; Communist Party of Japan, Sanzo Nosaka; Communist Party of Finland, Ville Pessi; Communist Party of Great Britain, John Gollan; Communist Party of Germany, Max Reimann; Communist Party of Spain, Dolores Ibarruri; Communist Party of Portugal, Alvaro Cunhal; Communist Party of the United States, Elizabeth Gurley Flynn, Henry Winston and James Jackson; Communist Party of Greece, Kostas Koliyannis; Communist Party of Belgium, Ernest Burnelle; Progressive Party of Working People of Cyprus, Ezekias Papaioannu; Communist Party of Austria, Johann Koplenig; Communist Party of Argentina, Victorio Codovilla; Communist Party of Brazil, Luis Carlos Prestes; Communist Party of Venezuela, Jesus Faria; Communist Party of Uruguay, Rodney Arismendi; Communist Party of Chile, Luis Corvalan; Communist Party of Colombia, Giberto Vieira; Communist Party of Canada, Tim Buck; Communist Party of Ecuador, Pedro Saad; Communist Party of Bolivia, Ruiz Gonzales; Communist Party of Mexico, A. Martinez Verdugo; Communist Party of Peru, Jorge del Prado; Communist Party of Australia, Lawrence Sharkey; Communist Party of New Zealand, George Jackson; Communist Party of Algeria, Larbi Bouhali; Communist Party of Iraq, Salam Adil; Communist Party of Syria, Khalid Bakdash; Communist Party of Lebanon, Nicholas Shawi; Communist Party of Jordan, Fuad Nassar; Communist Party of Morocco, Ali Yata; Communist Party of Tunisia, Mohammed Kharmel; People's Party of Iran, Reza Radmanesh; Communist Party of Sweden, Hilding Hagberg; Communist Party of Norway, Emil Lovlien; Communist Party of Denmark, Knud Jespersen; Communist Party of the Netherlands, Paul de Groot; Swiss Party of Labor, Edgar Woog; Communist Party of Luxembourg, Dominique Urbany; Communist Party of Israel, Samuel Mikunis; Communist Party of Ceylon, Pieter Keuneman; also "delegations from the fraternal parties of Burma, Haiti, Guadeloupe, Guatemala, Honduras, the Dominican Republic, Iceland, Costa Rica, Malaya, Martinique, Nicaragua, Panama, Paraguay, Reunion, El Salvador, San Marino, Northern Ireland, Sudan, Thailand, Turkey, the Republic of Ireland, the South African Republic, and parties of other countries."]

"Allow me also to extend friendly, sincere greetings to the dear guests present at our congress, the representatives of democratic national parties of the independent states of

Africa: the delegation of the Democratic Party of Guinea, headed by the Political Secretary of the party, President of the Guinean Republic National Assembly Saifoulaye Diallo (applause); the delegation of the Convention People's Party of the Republic of Ghana, headed by Chairman of the Accra Municipal Council Ebenezer Cethas Quaye (applause); and the delegation of the Sudan Union Party of the Republic of Mali, headed by Tidiani Traore, member of the Politburo of the party and Deputy to the National Assembly (applause)."

The Congress delegates warmly applauded the foreign guests who had arrived for the Congress.

The Congress proceeded to elect its executive bodies: presidium, secretariat, editorial commission and credentials commission.

The floor was given to I. P. Kazanets, a representative of the Ukraine Communist Party organization, on the question of the composition of the Presidium of the Congress. On behalf of the council [caucus] of representatives of delegations, he nominated a 41-man Congress Presidium. The Presidium was elected unanimously.

Presidium of the Congress

G. G. Abramov	L. N. Yefremov	N. A. Mukhitdinov
A. B. Aristov	M. T. Yefremov	A. J. Pelse
V. Yu. Akhundov	N. G. Ignatov	N. V. Podgorny
L. I. Brezhnev	M. V. Keldysh	D. S. Polyansky
G. I. Vorobyev	A. P. Kirilenko	Sh. R. Rashidov
G. I. Voronov	F. R. Kozlov	A. J. Snieckus
K. Ye. Voroshilov	A. N. Kosygin	I. V. Spiridonov
V. I. Gaganova	D. A. Kunayev	M. A. Suslov
A. V. Georgiyev	O. V. Kuusinen	Ye. A. Furtseva
V. V. Grishin	K. T. Mazurov	N. S. Khrushchev
A. A. Gromyko	F. P. Maximov	N. M. Shvernik
P. N. Demichev	R. Ya. Malinovsky	A. M. Shkolnikov
Ye. A. Dolinyuk	V. P. Mzhavanadze	V. V. Shcherbitsky
V. V. Yermilov	A. I. Mikoyan	

The floor was given to P. N. Demichev, a representative of the Moscow Communist Party organization. On behalf of the council of representatives of delegations he nominated a 19-man Congress Secretariat. The Secretariat was elected unanimously.

Secretariat of the Congress

Yu. V. Andropov	I. P. Kazanets	F. A. Surganov
A. F. Gorkin	I. G. Kabin	F. A. Tabeyev
A. A. Grechko	V. N. Malin	V. Ye. Chernyshev
G. D. Dzhavakhishvili	N. V. Popova	V. V. Shevchenko
Ya. N. Zarobyan	Z. T. Serdyuk	A. N. Shelepin
L. I. Lubennikov	N. A. Sobol	G. T. Shuisky
	T. I. Sokolov	

The floor was given to I. V. Spiridonov, a representative of the Leningrad Communist Party organization. On behalf of the council of representatives of delegations he nominated a 15-man Editorial Commission of the Congress. The Editorial Commission was elected unanimously.

Editorial Commission of the Congress

A. I. Adzhubei	T. Ya. Kiselev	P. N. Pospelov
A. V. Basov	V. N. Novikov	N. N. Rodionov
I. S. Grushetsky	N. N. Organov	P. A. Satyukov
O. I. Ivashchenko	S. P. Pavlov	V. V. Skryabin
L. F. Ilyichev	B. N. Ponomarev	F. Ye. Titov

Sh. R. Rashidov, representative of the Party organization of Uzbekistan, on behalf of the council of representatives of delegations, nominated a 35-man Credentials Commission of the Congress. The motion was adopted, and the commission was elected unanimously.

Credentials Commission

I. I. Bodyul	F. D. Kulakov	D. Rasulov
K. I. Galanshin	F. I. Loshchenkov	M. S. Sinitsa
F. I. Golikov	A. P. Lyashko	M. S. Solomentsev
F. S. Goryachev	T. K. Malbakhov	V. N. Titov
K. N. Grishin	S. I. Manyakin	N. P. Tolubeyev
A. D. Danialov	A. S. Mursyev	T. Usubaliyev
N. G. Yegorychev	Ya. S. Nasriddinova	P. Ye. Shelest
J. E. Kalnberzins	Z. N. Nuriyev	A. I. Shibayev
I. V. Kapitonov	B. Ovezov	A. P. Shitikov
A. A. Kokarev	G. I. Popov	V. A. Shurygin
N. S. Konovalov	S. O. Pritytsky	S. N. Shchetinin
D. S. Korotchenko		I. Kh. Yunak

The agenda of the Congress was then approved.

Comrade F. R. Kozlov, presiding at the session, gave the floor to Comrade N. S. Khrushchev, First Secretary of the Party Central Committee, for the Report of the Party Central Committee. The delegates and guests greeted Nikita Sergeyevich Khrushchev with warm applause. All rose.

Comrade N. S. Khrushchev's report, which continued through the morning and afternoon sessions, was heard with tremendous attention and was repeatedly interrupted by stormy, prolonged applause, [expressing] the approval of the entire hall.

The afternoon session heard a report by the Central Inspection Commission of the C.P.S.U., delivered by Comrade A. F. Gorkin.

The Congress continues its work today.

COMMUNIQUE ON 22ND PARTY CONGRESS. (Pravda, Oct. 18, p. 1. 200 words. Condensed text:) ... The following agenda was approved:

1. Report of the Party Central Committee—Comrade N. S. Khrushchev, First Secretary of the Central Committee, rapporteur.

2. Report of the Central Inspection Commission—Comrade A. F. Gorkin, Chairman of the Central Inspection Commission, rapporteur.

3. Draft Program of the Communist Party of the Soviet Union—Comrade N. S. Khrushchev, rapporteur.

4. On Changes in the Party Statutes—Comrade F. R. Kozlov, Secretary of the Party Central Committee, rapporteur.

5. Elections of central Party bodies. ...

IV. KHRUSHCHEV: CENTRAL COMMITTEE REPORT

22nd Congress of the Communist Party of the Soviet Union: REPORT OF THE CENTRAL COMMITTEE OF THE COMMUNIST PARTY OF THE SOVIET UNION TO THE 22ND PARTY CONGRESS.—Report by Comrade N. S. Khrushchev, First Secretary of the Central Committee, Oct. 17, 1961. (Pravda and Izvestia, Oct. 18, pp. 2-11. Complete text:) Comrades! Some six years have passed since the 20th Congress of the Communist Party of the Soviet Union. For our party, for the Soviet people, for all mankind these years have been of extraordinary, one might say world-historic, significance.

The Soviet motherland has entered the period of full-scale construction of communism along a wide front of great projects. The economy and culture of the Soviet Union are advancing sharply. The seven-year plan, a plan of mighty development of the productive forces of our motherland, is being successfully fulfilled. The creative forces of the masses of people are pouring forth as from thousands of springs throughout the whole country. The triumphant flights of Soviet men into outer space, the first in human history, are like a crown of splendid victories, a banner of communist construction raised high.

Socialism has been established within the framework of the whole world socialist commonwealth. The major events of recent years have been an expression of the chief law of our times: The process of growth and consolidation of the vital forces of the world socialist system has proceeded at a tempestuous pace.

The activity of our party and state has been conducted in a complex international situation. More than once the imperialists have tried to bring the world to the brink of war, to test the strength of the Soviet Union and the courage of its peoples. Many bourgeois politicians have comforted themselves with illusions that our plans would fail and that the socialist camp would disintegrate. They undertook many provocations and acts of subversion against us. The Party, the entire Soviet people, exposed the intrigues of enemies and emerged with honor from all trials. Today the Soviet Union is stronger and more powerful than ever! (Prolonged applause.)

Now, when the Land of Soviets is in the flower of its creative powers and we survey the triumphant path we have traversed, this path may seem to some an easy and simple one. No, the period since the 20th Congress was not easy or simple, it required great effort and sacrifice by our party and all the peoples of the Soviet Union. The great mission of being the pioneers of communist construction, of advancing to the victory of communism by uncharted paths, has fallen to the lot of the Soviet people, of the party of Communists of the Soviet Union.

History does not develop in a straight line, it takes tremendous bends, zigzags and sharp curves. What high qualities must a party possess not to lose the general perspective, to see clearly the road to communism, in the circumstances of tempestuous movement and sharp turns in the development of society! The party of Communists of the Soviet Union, founded by the great Lenin, possesses in full measure these qualities of a political leader. To find the correct solutions of the chief problems, to work out the general line in the sphere of domestic and foreign policy and to carry it out firmly, the Party, its Central Committee, had to have a deep understanding of events and revolutionary boldness and determination.

Life has fully confirmed the correctness of the theoretical conclusions and political course of the Party, its general line. The ten-million-strong party of Communists of the Soviet Union has come to its 22nd Congress united and closely rallied, indivisibly linked with the Soviet people. (Stormy applause.) The unity of Party and people is personified in the five thousand delegates to our Congress, the best sons and daughters of the great Leninist party. (Applause.)

The course taken by our party has had tremendous significance for strengthening the unity of the socialist countries, the unity of the international Communist and workers' movement, the preservation of peace and the prevention of a new world war. The prestige and authority of the Soviet state in the international arena have increased further. The conferences of representatives of Communist and Workers' Parties have given a high assessment to the role of the C.P.S.U. in the international Communist and workers' movement.

Allow me, on behalf of our Congress, on behalf of all the Communists of the Soviet Union, to express warm gratitude to the fraternal parties for their confidence in our party. (Prolonged applause.) Let me assure the delegates of fraternal parties present here as dear guests that the Communist Party of the Soviet Union will continue to fulfill its internationalist duty to the working people of all countries, to all progressive mankind. (Stormy applause.)

I. THE PRESENT WORLD SITUATION AND THE INTERNATIONAL POSITION OF THE SOVIET UNION.—Comrades! The competition of the two world social systems, the socialist and the capitalist, has been the chief content of the period since the 20th Party Congress. It has become the pivot, the foundation of world development at the present historical stage. Two lines, two historical trends, have manifested themselves more and more clearly in social development. One is the line of social progress, peace and constructive activity. The other is the line of reaction, oppression and war.

If we visualize the whole globe as the tremendous arena of this competition, we see that socialism has, step by step, won one position after another from the old world. Above all, socialism has pressed capitalism hard in the decisive sphere of activity, the sphere of material production. The share of the socialist system in world production has risen and its rates of development have considerably exceeded the rates of the most highly developed countries of capitalism. Everybody sees that the countries of socialism are capable of developing colossal productive forces and creating a genuine abundance of material and spiritual benefits on earth.

While unswervingly pursuing a policy of peace, we have not forgotten about the threat of war on the part of the imperialists. Everything has been done to assure our country's superiority in defense. The achievements of socialist production, Soviet science and technology have enabled us to carry out a real revolution in the military sphere. Our country and the whole socialist camp now possess such mighty power that it is quite sufficient for reliable defense of the great gains of socialism against attempts by the imperialist aggressors. (Applause.) The increased defense might of the Soviet Union and the other socialist countries and the peace-loving forces throughout the world have not allowed the imperialists to divert the competition of the two systems from peaceful rails to the path of armed conflict, the path of war. The Soviet Union, firmly pursuing a Leninist policy of peaceful coexistence, has exposed and resolutely checked the imperialists' provocations.

The fact that it has been possible to prevent war and that Soviet people and the peoples of other countries have been able to enjoy the benefits of peaceful life must be regarded as the chief result of the work of the Party, of its Central Committee, in increasing the might of the Soviet state and in carrying out a Leninist foreign policy; a result of the activity of the fraternal parties of the lands of socialism and the activizing of the peace-loving forces of all countries. (Prolonged applause.)

As we know, the imperialists have more than once in recent years tried to ignite the fire of a new war, to test the stability of the socialist system. In the past five years the U.S.A. and its closest allies have repeatedly resorted to gross force, have taken to arms. But each time the Soviet Union, all the socialist countries have stopped the aggressor in time. The actions of the socialist countries in defense of peoples fighting for freedom and independence have been of particular, fundamental importance. The realization that the Soviet Union and all the socialist countries are a reliable bulwark in the peoples' struggle for freedom and independence, for progress and peace, has sunk still deeper into the minds of the masses. (Applause.)

In the course of the peaceful competition of the two systems capitalism has suffered a profound moral defeat in the eyes of all peoples. The common people are daily convinced that capitalism is incapable of solving a single one of the urgent problems confronting mankind. It becomes more and more obvious that only on the paths to socialism can a solution to these problems be found. Faith in the capitalist system and the capitalist path of development is dwindling. Monopoly capital, losing its influence, resorts more and more to intimidating and suppressing the masses of the people, to methods of open dictatorship in carrying out its domestic policy and to aggressive acts against other countries. But the masses of the people offer increasing resistance to reaction's acts.

It is no secret to anyone that the methods of intimidation and threat are not a sign of strength but evidence of the weakening of capitalism, the deepening of its general crisis. As the saying goes, if you can't hang on by the mane, you won't hang on by the tail! (Laughter in the hall.) Reaction is still capable of dissolving parliaments in some countries in violation of their constitutions, of casting the best representatives of the people into prison, of sending cruisers and marines to subdue the "unruly." All this can put off for a time the approach of the fatal hour for the rule of capitalism. But such repressive measures still further expose the brigand nature of imperialism. The imperialists are sawing away at the branch on which they sit. There is no force in the world capable of stopping man's advance along the road of progress. (Stormy applause.)

Events have shown that our party's course worked out at the 20th Congress was correct and true: The Congress noted that the chief feature of our epoch is the emergence of socialism beyond the framework of a single country and its conversion into a world system. A new and important advance has occurred since the Congress: The world socialist system is becoming the decisive factor in the development of society.

The Party drew the conclusion that the collapse of colonialism is inevitable. Under the powerful blows of the national-liberation movement the colonial system has in effect caved in.

The Party propounded the important thesis that wars among states are not inevitable in the present epoch, that they can be prevented. The events of the past years have confirmed this conclusion also. They have shown that the mighty forces standing guard over peace possess great means in our times for preventing the imperialists from unleashing a world war. The superiority of the forces of peace and socialism over the forces of imperialism and war has become even more sharply delineated.

To put it briefly, comrades, for us these have been a fine six years on the global scale! (Stormy applause.)

1. Further Growth of the Might of the Socialist System. Its Conversion Into the Decisive Factor of World Development; Strengthening of the International Brotherhood of Socialist Countries.—In the period under review an important stage of the historical development of the world socialist system has been completed. Its characteristic features were these:

The Soviet Union set about the full-scale construction of communism; the majority of the people's democracies eliminated the mixed nature of their economies and are completing the building of socialism; fraternal cooperation and mutual aid have been thoroughly developed among the socialist countries. The social-economic possibilities for the restoration of capitalism have now been removed not only in the Soviet Union but in all the socialist countries. The increasing might of the new world system guarantees to the socialist countries permanence of their political and social-economic gains. The complete victory of socialism has been assured within the framework of the commonwealth of genuinely free peoples.

The economy of the world socialist system continues to develop at incomparably higher rates than the economy of capitalism. I shall cite data showing the growth of industrial output in the countries of socialism and in capitalist states (for a comparable area, in per cent of 1937):

Year	Socialist countries	Capitalist countries
1937	100	100
1955	362	199
1956	404	208
1957	445	215
1958	521	210
1959	610	231
1960	681	244

As you see, by 1960 the socialist countries had increased the volume of industrial production to 6.8 times that of 1937, while the capitalist countries had increased it to less than 2.5 times the 1937 figure. The socialist countries' share in world industrial output, 27% in 1955, rose by 1960 to approximately 36%.

In all the socialist countries the ratio of industrial to agricultural production has changed. The share of industrial production is growing rapidly. The average for the socialist camp is now approximately 75%. The development of the economy of the world socialist system has an industrial direction.

A great revolutionary event of these years was the completion in most of the people's democracies of the change to producer cooperatives in agriculture. The socialist sector's share of the total farmland area is now 90% for the system as a whole. As a result, the class structure of society changed, the alliance of the working class with the peasantry was strengthened, and economic bases for the exploitation of man by man were eliminated. The moral and political unity of the people, first established in our country, is growing stronger in all the socialist countries. Our people regard with deep sympathy the successes of the Chinese people and the other fraternal peoples in socialist countries and wish them further glorious victories. (Prolonged applause.)

On the basis of the successes in developing the economy in socialist countries, the living standard of the working people has risen. This is all the more gratifying because the revolutionary reorganization of society that went on in the early years in the fraternal countries was inevitably linked with serious losses and difficulties and required great expenditures for ending the economic backwardness inherited from capitalism. Now, with the completion of the important stage of social reorganization, more favorable conditions have been created for the further growth of the economy and culture, for improving the well-being of the working people.

With the appearance of a large group of sovereign socialist states in the world arena, life presented the problem of organizing mutual relations and cooperation among them on fundamentally new principles. By the joint efforts of the fraternal parties, new forms of interstate relations were found and are being perfected—relations of economic, political and cultural cooperation on the principles of equality, mutual benefit and comradely mutual aid. The process of undeviating fraternal rapprochement among the socialist countries and of their political and economic consolidation is one of the decisive factors in the firmness and indestructibility of the entire world system of socialism. We joined ranks voluntarily to advance together toward a common goal. No one imposed this union upon us. It is as necessary to us all as air.

In the first stage of development of the world system of socialism, ties between countries were effected chiefly through bilateral trade and scientific and technical exchange. The forms of aid and credits that generally predominated were aid and credits granted by one country to another.

In recent years the experience of the fraternal parties has brought into being a new form—direct production cooperation. Take, for example, the indices of development, correlated by the countries participating in the Council on Mutual Economic Aid, for individual branches of the economy in the years 1956-1960. This was an important step forward. Since 1959 the state plans of economic development have been coordinated. It has become the practice to hold periodic consultations and exchanges of views among the heads of parties and governments on major economic and political problems. The collective agencies of the socialist states—the Warsaw Treaty Organization and the Council on Mutual Economic Aid—have grown stronger.

There is every justification for speaking of the existence in the world arena of a durable socialist commonwealth of free peoples.

The profound qualitative changes that have taken place in the socialist countries and in the relations among them are vivid evidence of the increased maturity of the world system of socialism. It has now entered a new stage of its development. The chief thing now is, by steadily developing the economy of each and all of the socialist countries, to achieve a preponderance of the world socialist system over the capitalist in absolute volume of production. This will be a great historical victory of socialism. The achievements of our country, the first to enter on the path of full-scale construction of communism, facilitate and accelerate the advance of the other countries of the world socialist system toward communism.

Constant improvement of the forms and methods of economic management, the utmost rational employment of unutilized resources and potentialities, and observance of scientific proportions in the development of branches of the economy of each individual country—these now assume particular importance. There is likewise greater need than ever for making the wisest and most effective use of the advantages arising from the development of socialism as a world system—international socialist division of labor, specialization and cooperation in production, coordination of national economic plans, and the possibilities of the world socialist market.

Trade among the countries of socialism has grown at an exceptionally rapid tempo in the period under review, overtaking the tempo of growth of the capitalist countries' foreign trade. In the period 1950-1960 trade among countries of the socialist commonwealth more than tripled. During the same period trade among the capitalist countries only doubled. In the new stage of development of the world socialist system, mutually beneficial trade among the fraternal countries has a big role. In the long run it will evidently be conducted more and more on the same basis as trade within each socialist country, that is, with compensation for the socially necessary expenditures of labor. The more fully this principle is applied, the more effective will be the economic incentives within the economy of each country and the more rapid will be the development of interstate cooperation and international socialist division of labor on the basis of sovereignty and regard for national interests.

<u>A combination of efforts to develop the national economy of each socialist country with common efforts to strengthen and expand economic cooperation and mutual aid—such is the high road to a further upswing in the world socialist economy.</u>

Comrades! V. I. Lenin's declaration that socialism exerts its chief influence on world development by its economic achievements is more valid today than ever. The increasing influence exerted in every way upon the peoples of the nonsocialist countries by the construction of socialism and communism is a revolutionizing factor that accelerates the development of all mankind along the path of progress.

Socialism firmly holds first place in rates of economic development and is ahead of the capitalist countries in the development of major fields of world scientific and technical progress. The countries of imperialism have lost their former monopoly in supplying the world nonsocialist market with means of production, and also in granting credits and loans and providing technical services. The peoples of Asia and Africa who have freed themselves from foreign colonial oppression turn their gaze more and more often toward the socialist countries and borrow their experience in organizing individual spheres of economic and public life. They seek backing and support from the world socialist system in the struggle against the colonialists' encroachments on freedom and independence.

The growth of the might of the socialist states signifies an intensification of the material and moral factors of peace. The cardinal problems of our times, such as the problems of war and peace, can no longer be approached only from the standpoint of the operation of the laws of capitalism. Today it is not imperialism, with its wolfish customs, but socialism, with its ideals of peace and progress, that is becoming the decisive factor of world development.

The socialist countries have blazed the way for new norms of international life by showing the whole world a model of genuinely equal, fraternal relations among peoples. Under the influence of the ideas of socialism, the working people's liberation struggle and the general democratic movement of peoples are merging into a common worldwide flood that is washing away the underpinnings of imperialism.

As socialism wins new victories, the unity of peoples, both within each socialist country and on the scale of the world socialist system as a whole, is growing stronger and stronger.

Like a mighty tree that has put down deep roots and does not fear any storms, so no vicissitudes or upheavals frighten the new socialist world. The counterrevolutionary insurrection in Hungary, organized by domestic reaction with the support of imperialist forces, and the intrigues of enemies in Poland and the German Democratic Republic showed that class struggle may at times grow more intense and take sharp forms in the period of construction of socialism. The remnants of domestic reaction, with the support of imperialism, may continue to try to sever one country or another from the socialist system and seek to restore the old bourgeois ways. The reactionary forces speculate on the difficulties that are inevitable in such a new undertaking as the revolutionary transformation of society and send their agents into the socialist countries.

The ruling circles of some imperialist powers have elevated subversive activities against the socialist countries to the level of state policy. With cynical frankness, the United States of America is spending hundreds of millions of dollars on espionage and subversion against the socialist countries and organizing so-called "guerrilla units," assembling in them criminal elements and cutthroats prepared to undertake the vilest crimes for money. For several successive years the United States has been holding provocational "captive nations weeks." The hired agents of the monopolies call "captive" all those peoples who have liberated themselves from imperialist bondage and taken the path of free development. Truly, imperialist demagogy and hypocrisy know no bounds! The monopolists' howl about "captive peoples" is like the cry of the pickpocket who shouts "Stop, thief!" (Stir in the hall. Applause.)

The imperialists' intrigues must never be forgotten. Our tremendous successes in building a new life should not lead to complacency, to relaxation of vigilance. Of course, the greater the successes of socialism and the higher the living standard in each socialist country, the more the people rally around the Communist and Workers' Parties. This is one aspect of the matter, and a very gratifying aspect. But one must bear in mind another aspect also. As the solidarity of the peoples in all the socialist countries grows, the imperialists' hopes for the restoration of capitalist ways and for the degeneration of the socialist countries fade. World reaction therefore becomes more and more oriented toward striking a blow at the socialist states from outside in order through war to achieve the rule of capitalism throughout the world, or at least to check the development of the countries of socialism.

The most rabid imperialists, acting on the principle of "after us the deluge," openly voice their desire to undertake a new war venture. The ideologists of imperialism, intimidating the peoples, try to instill a kind of philosophy of hopelessness and desperation. Hysterically they cry: "Better death under capitalism than life under communism." They do not like free peoples to flourish, you see. They fear that the peoples in their countries too will take the path of socialism. Blinded by class hatred, our enemies are ready to doom all mankind to the catastrophe of war. The imperialists' opportunities to carry out their aggressive designs, however, are becoming smaller and smaller. They behave like a feeble and greedy old man whose powers have been exhausted, whose physical capacity has weakened, but whose avid desires remain.

The imperialists could, of course, set out on dangerous adventures, but they have no chance of success. They are prepared to try other ways. To weaken the socialist camp, the imperialists seek to set the peoples of the fraternal countries to quarreling or try to introduce discord into the relations among them, to stir up the remnants of national friction and artificially inflame nationalist sentiments.

A great historical responsibility rests upon the Marxist-Leninist parties, upon the peoples of the socialist countries—to strengthen tirelessly the international brotherhood among the socialist countries, friendship among peoples.

As long as the imperialist aggressors exist, we must be on guard, keep our powder dry, improve the defense of the socialist countries, their armed forces and the state security agencies. If, in the face of common sense, the imperialists dare attack the socialist countries and plunge mankind into the abyss of a world war of annihilation, this mad act of theirs would be their last, it would be the end of the whole system of capitalism. (Applause.)

Our party clearly understands its tasks, its responsibility, and will do everything in its power to see to it that the world socialist system continues to grow stronger, gathers fresh strength and develops. We believe that in the competition with capitalism socialism will win. (Prolonged applause.) We believe that this victory will be won in peaceful competition and not by way of unleashing a war. We have stood, we stand and we will stand by the positions of peaceful competition of states with different social systems; we will do everything to strengthen world peace. (Prolonged applause.)

2. Sharpening of Contradictions in the Countries of Capitalism. Growth of Revolutionary Struggle and Upsurge of the National Liberation Movement.—Comrades! The 20th Party Congress, analyzing the situation in the countries of capitalism, came to the conclusion that they were moving steadily toward new economic and social upheavals. Has this conclusion been borne out? Yes, it has. In the years that have elapsed there has occurred a further sharpening of contradictions, both within the capitalist countries and among them; colonial empires have collapsed, and the struggle of the working class and the peoples' national liberation movement have assumed tremendous proportions.

The general tendency of further decay of capitalism continued to operate with inexorable force. Although there has been some growth in production, the economy of the capitalist countries has become still more unstable and suggests a patient with a fever, so often do its short-lived upswings alternate with depressions and crises. The U.S.A., the chief country of capitalism, has experienced two critical drops in production in five years, and four such recessions have been recorded there in the postwar period as a whole. In 1957-1958 countries that account for almost two-thirds of the industrial output of the capitalist world were seized by crisis. While the incomes of the monopolies rose fabulously, the real wages of the working people grew extremely little, far more slowly than labor productivity. The social gains achieved by the working class in the past are gradually being reduced to nil. In general the situation of the working people, particularly in the economically underdeveloped countries, is growing worse.

In the past five or six years mankind has won substantial victories in the development of science and technology, particularly in the sphere of atomic energy, electronics and jet and rocket technology. But the evils of capitalist production that V. I. Lenin pointed out are hindering the rational utilization of these achievements. Back in 1913 he wrote: "Whichever way you turn, at every step you come up against problems that mankind is fully capable of solving immediately. Capitalism is in the way. It has amassed enormous wealth and has made people the slaves of that wealth. It has solved the most complex problems of technology—but has blocked the application of the technical improvements because of the poverty and ignorance of

millions of the population, because of the stupid miserliness of a handful of millionaires.

"The words civilization, freedom and wealth call to mind a rich glutton who is rotting alive but will not let what is young live." ("Works" [in Russian], Vol. XIX, p. 349.) How timely these words of Lenin's sound today!

The introduction of new scientific discoveries and technical progress not only do not eliminate but deepen the insoluble contradictions of capitalism. Capitalist automation has only begun, but millions of workers have already been thrown out of the production process. The imperialists counted on finding a way out of the difficulties by militarizing the economy. Their expectations failed.

Militarization has, of course, brought prosperity to branches of industry connected with arms production. Direct war expenditures of the U.S.A. alone for the past five years have exceeded $220,000,000,000, and all the NATO countries together have spent more than $500,000,000,000 on the arms race during the past ten years. But militarization gave rise to new disproportions, struck a serious blow at other branches of the economy and deprived more millions of working people of their employment. During the past five years the number of totally unemployed in the U.S.A. has rarely dropped below 3,000,000. In Italy, Japan and many other countries mass unemployment has acquired a chronic character. The more money spent on war production, the more unstable becomes the economy of capitalism and the more acute its contradictions. One of the most important of the contradictions of present-day capitalism shows in the fact that human labor is being used more and more to create means of destruction. The social system that creates such contradictions is discrediting and outliving itself.

No wonder the American millionaire Harriman proposed abolishing the word "capitalism." "To borrow Khrushchev's terminology, we should 'bury' the word 'capitalism,'" he said. He had to admit that to people outside America the concept of "capitalism" is synonymous with imperialism, exploitation of the poor by the rich, and colonialism; it is a sullied word, one that arouses horror. (Stir in the hall.) What is true is true! Not even the most thorough dry-cleaning could remove the blood and filth from that black word. There is an apt folk saying that "you can't wash a black dog white." (Laughter in the hall. Applause.) One can welcome the efforts of Mr. Harriman, who has taken up the spade to dig a grave for the word "capitalism." But the peoples of the capitalist countries will draw their own more correct conclusion and will bury not the word, but the thoroughly rotten capitalist system itself, with all its evils.

In recent years serious changes have taken place in the alignment of forces in the capitalist world.

First, the United States of America has lost its absolute supremacy in world capitalist production and commerce. The U.S. share of the capitalist world's industrial output dropped from 56.6% in 1948 to 47% in 1960, its exports from 23.4% to 18.1%, and its gold reserves from 74.5% to 43.9%. The result is that the United States of America today occupies approximately the same position among the capitalist countries as it did before the war.

Secondly, there has been a noticeable weakening of the position of Britain and France; these states, like Belgium and Holland, are losing their colonies forever. They have been unable to recover their prewar positions in world industrial production.

Thirdly, the defeated countries, especially West Germany and Japan, have taken a big leap forward. West Germany, Japan and Italy together account for approximately 17% of the industrial production of the capitalist world—that is, more than in 1937, on the eve of the second world war.

West Germany has caught up with Britain in industrial output, and in exports takes second place, after the U.S.A. In the postwar years U.S. monopolies have invested huge sums in the economy of West Germany and Japan. For a number of years these two countries were in effect relieved of the burden of their own war expenditure because the U.S.A. provided them with armaments at the expense of the American taxpayers. West Germany and Japan have made huge investments in key branches of the economy to modernize their fixed capital and reorganize production along modern lines. As a result, they are already serious rivals of Britain, France and even the United States in the world market.

The contradictions that existed among the imperialist powers before the war have reappeared and new ones have emerged. The struggle between the British and West German imperialists for supremacy in Western Europe is growing fiercer. French imperialism, in its struggle against British imperialism, is trying to find support in yesterday's enemy, the West German monopolies. This unnatural alliance—it is like a marriage of convenience—is more and more frequently operating against France herself. Major contradictions divide the U.S.A. and Britain and other imperialist states; they are manifested in NATO and other aggressive blocs.

It is becoming more and more obvious that the imperialist powers and their leaders fear a slackening of international tension, since in a tense situation it is easier for them to form military blocs and keep the peoples in fear of an alleged threat from the socialist countries. The imperialists are seeking to involve all countries in the arms race, to tie the economies of other countries to their own and direct them toward militarization. This line is particularly sharply expressed in U.S. policy toward West Germany and Japan. The U.S. imperialists are deliberately drawing West Germany into the arms race. In the event of the outbreak of war, it is to their advantage to pay for the new adventure mainly in the blood of the German people. At the same time they hope that this policy will exhaust the economy of West Germany and weaken her as a rival in world markets. Approximately the same policy is being pursued in respect to Japan.

In their statements the leaders of the Western powers do not conceal that their policy is one of arming West Germany. Their argument is something like this: If West Germany does not rearm and does not spend on armaments, she may become a still more powerful and dangerous rival. In short, acute contradictions are evident in the camp of imperialism.

In fear for the future, the imperialists are trying to unite their forces and strengthen their military-political, trade-tariff and other alliances. Reaction counts on finding a way out through aggression against the countries of socialism. In the period before the war it placed special hopes on Hitlerite Germany. Today the United States of America, which has become the center of world reaction, takes the role of the chief aggressive nucleus. The U.S. imperialists are acting in alliance with the West German militarists and revanchists and threatening the peace and security of peoples. In our times, however, it has become dangerous for imperialism to seek a way out of contradictions by using war as a pressure valve.

The positions of imperialism in Asia, Africa and Latin America, where the colonialists only quite recently oppressed hundreds of millions of people, are becoming more and more shaky. The revolutionary struggle of the peoples of those continents is rising stormily. In the past six years 28 states have won political independence. The 1960s will go down in history as years of the complete disintegration of the colonial system of imperialism. (Applause.)

It must not be forgotten, however, that although the colonial system has collapsed, its remnants have not been liquidated. Many millions of people in Asia and Africa are still suffering colonial slavery and waging a struggle for their liberation. For seven years the blood of Algerian patriots has been flowing in the fight for freedom. The French monopolies do not want an end to the war in Algeria, although this "dirty war" against a peaceful people is costing thousands of lives and lays a heavy burden on the shoulders of the French and Algerian peoples. Portugal, a small state with an area no more than two-thirds of our Vologda Province, holds in bondage colonies with an area nearly 25 times its own size. The Dutch colonialists stubbornly refuse to return to the Indonesian people their age-old land of West Irian. The U.S.A. is retaining its hold on the Chinese island of Taiwan which it has seized and the Japanese island of Okinawa. Against the will of the Cuban people it is making free with the Guantanamo military base on Cuban soil.

The forces of imperialism oppose any strivings by the peoples toward freedom and independence, democracy and progress. Under pretense of various commitments, the imperialists seek to smother the national-liberation movement and intervene brazenly in the internal affairs of young states by entering into deals with their reactionary forces. This was how they acted in Iran, Pakistan and the Congo, this is how they are acting now in Laos and Kuwait.

Throughout all these years the Soviet Union, unswervingly fulfilling its internationalist duty, has been helping peoples who are fighting against imperialism and colonialism. Some people do not like this stand. Too bad. Such are our convictions. Our people won freedom in a stubborn and long struggle against oppression by the landlords and the capitalists and against the intervention of international imperialism. We well remember what that struggle cost us, we remember the sacrifices that had to be made for the sake of victory. And from the bottom of our heart we wish success to all who are now fighting for their freedom and happiness against imperialism. We believe that it is the inalienable right of peoples to put an end to foreign oppression, and we shall support their just fight. Colonialism is doomed and a stake will be driven into its grave. Such is the will of the peoples, such is the course of history! (Stormy applause.)

The countries that have liberated themselves from the colonial yoke have achieved definite successes in national and cultural regeneration. But the economic development of the majority of the liberated countries of Asia and Africa is still proceeding slowly. The material position of the masses of the people remains difficult, while the wealth of their countries flows in streams of gold into the coffers of foreign banks and corporations. The U.S. monopolies are making two or three dollars' profit on every dollar they spend in the underdeveloped countries. Not long ago the U.S. monopolists announced that they wish to "allocate" $500,000,000 for aid to Latin American countries. What is $500,000,000 among 20 countries over a period of five years? These are miserly alms that the rich man throws to those whom he has been robbing to tatters for many years and whom he continues to rob. The peoples who have been plundered have the right to demand from the colonialists not aid but the return of what was stolen.

Now the colonialists, sensing that their rule is coming to an end, are putting on a good face in a losing game. They assert that they are leaving the colonies of their own accord. Who will believe them? Anyone can see that they are taking this step, knowing that all the same they will be driven out in disgrace. The more prudent of the colonialists succeed in leaving, so to say, five minutes before they are given "a kick in the pants," to put it in plain speech. (Stir in the hall. Applause.)

The colonial powers are imposing unequal treaties on the liberated countries, are locating military bases on their territories and are trying to involve them in military blocs, which is one of the new forms of enslavement. Almost half of the states that have arisen as a result of the disintegration of the colonial system are shackled by burdensome, unequal treaties. In the center of the system of refurbished but no less disgraceful colonialism stands the United States of America. In the role of its closest allies, and at the same time its rivals, are British colonialism and West German imperialism, the latter unceremoniously squeezing the British and French monopolies out of Africa and the Middle East.

The countries that have freed themselves from colonial oppression have entered a new period of their development. The struggle for political independence united all the national forces that suffered under the colonialists and were moved by common interests. But now that there appear on the agenda of the day the tasks of ripping out the roots of imperialism and carrying out agrarian and other urgent social reforms, the differences in class interests are beginning to show more and more distinctly. Broad strata of the working people, and also that considerable part of the national bourgeoisie interested in the accomplishment of the basic tasks of the anti-imperialist, antifeudal revolution, want to move farther along the path of strengthening independence and social and economic transformations. Within the ruling circles of these countries, however, there are also forces that are afraid of further collaboration with the democratic, progressive strata of the nation. They would like to appropriate the fruits of the people's struggle and retard the further development of the national revolution. Such forces follow a line of compromise with imperialism outside the country and feudalism within, and resort to dictatorial methods.

The example of Pakistan shows what this policy leads to. This country spends two-thirds of its budget for military purposes; the national industry is not developing, and foreign capital rules as if it were in its own bailiwick. The sad fate of Pakistan, whose people we wish nothing but good, should set the public thinking in some other countries where influential forces are destroying national unity and persecuting progressive leaders, especially the Communists, who have shown themselves to be the stoutest defenders of national independence.

To take the path of anti-Communism means to split the forces of the nation and weaken them in the face of the imperialists, the colonialists.

And, on the contrary, the firmer the unity of the democratic national forces, the more thoroughly will urgent social and economic transformations be effected and the stronger the young state. Why did the Cuban people, for instance, rally so solidly around their government? Because the Cuban peasants obtained land and extensive material support from the government. Because, now that industry has been nationalized, the Cuban workers are working for themselves and not for the American monopolies. Because the small and medium producers in Cuba have been given protection against the arbitrariness of the monopolies. The entire Cuban people have acquired broad democratic rights and freedoms, the road has been opened for them to better living conditions, happiness and prosperity! In the hour of danger, when the American imperialists organized the invasion of Cuba, the whole people stood like a solid wall in defense of the gains of their revolution. Under the leadership of the courageous patriot and revolutionary Fidel Castro, the Cubans quickly routed the American mercenaries and hurled them into the Bahia de Cochinos, which means "Bay of Pigs." The proper place for them! (Laughter in the hall. Stormy applause.)

The imperialists' agents more and more frequently advise the peoples of the liberated countries not to be in a hurry with reforms. They try to persuade the peoples of the same lengthy path that the capitalist countries of Europe and America traversed before they reached the present level of economic development. But they conceal how bloody and arduous this path was for the peoples. They prefer to say nothing about the fact that the roads and prisons in England, France and Germany from the 17th to the 19th centuries were filled with vagabonds and homeless people, that the workers in those countries were forced to work 14 to 18 hours a day even in the middle of the 19th century, and that the last plots of land were taken away from the peasants in England to make way for sheep pastures, so that, as was said at the time, "the sheep ate people."

The capitalist path of development would be still longer and more arduous for the peoples of the colonies at whose expense the Western powers built their own affluence. Why should this long and arduous road be imposed on peoples today, in the middle of the 20th century? The Communists believe that the age-old backwardness of peoples can be overcome through socialism.

We do not, however, impose our ideas on anybody, and we are firmly convinced that sooner or later all peoples will realize that there is no other road for them to happiness and well-being. (Applause.)

Comrades! The sharpening of the contradictions of imperialism confronts the working class of the capitalist countries with serious tests: Either throw yourselves upon the mercy of the monopolies and remain in your miserable plight or fight for your rights, for your future. The workers are choosing to fight, and are fighting stubbornly and persistently.

Bourgeois prophets have announced the advent of an era of "class peace." They have claimed that the time of class struggles is a thing of the past and that Marxist theory in general is, if you please, obsolete today. Life has made a mockery of such prophecies. The strike struggle of the working people is growing steadily. In 1960 alone more than 53,000,000 persons took part in it. The mass actions of the French and Italian working people, the Belgian workers' strike, the prolonged strike of American steelworkers, in which more than 500,000 took part, and the strike of British engineering workers will forever go down in the history of the working class movement.

The Japanese proletariat has demonstrated its militant strength on more than one occasion.

New detachments of the working class have stepped into the world arena in recent years. There are more than 100,000,000 workers and office employees in Asia, Latin America and Africa, about 40% of the total army of wage labor in the non-socialist world. The young working class is asserting itself more and more as a revolutionary force.

The struggle of the working people of the capitalist countries for their economic and social rights is becoming more and more acute. For today they are opposed, as a rule, not by individual employers but by powerful monopolies, which, moreover, have the entire power of the state on their side. More and more often the working people's actions assume a political character. In 1960 more than 40,000,000 persons, or about 73% of the total number of strikers, took part in political strikes. Powerful actions by the working class and the masses of the people in 1960 led to the fall of the governments in Japan, Italy and Belgium. The working people of France, united around the working class, foiled an attempt by the militarists, the ultra-reactionaries, to impose a fascist regime on that country.

Growth of a peasant movement has also been characteristic of the social situation that has taken shape in the large capitalist countries during the past five years. In France, Italy, West Germany and other countries monopoly domination is leading to the ruin of the peasantry, and it is participating ever more actively in the struggle against the monopolies.

The experience of recent years has again confirmed that all the gains of the working people have been the result of joint action. Nevertheless, the ranks of the working class remain split, and the subversive activity of the right-wing leaders of Social Democracy, who are making frantic efforts to divert their parties and the working class from the struggle against capitalism, is felt. The leaders of the Right Socialists and many trade union bosses have long betrayed the interests of the working class and faithfully serve monopoly capital. But among the rank-and-file Social Democrats, among the functionaries and even within part of the leadership there are many honest people who sincerely want to take part in the common struggle for working class interests. Of late they have put up increasingly active resistance to the policy of the leaders of the Right.

Therefore the Communists, while continuing to expose the ideological bankruptcy and disruptive actions of the Right Social-Democratic officials, want to cooperate with all the sound elements among the Socialists and act together with them in the struggle for peace, democracy and socialism. This is not a temporary tactical slogan, it is the general policy of the Communist movement, dictated by the vital interests of the working class.

Successes in the development of the workers' movement are inseparably bound up with the work of the Communist Parties. The Communist movement has emerged on the highroad of creative activity. In our day there is no longer a country with a more or less developed workers' movement where the political influence of the Communists is not felt. In recent years the close-knit Communist family has increased by 12 parties and the total number of Communists by 7,000,000 persons. (Applause.)

The Communist Parties are growing throughout the world despite the fact that reaction is fanning bitter anti-Communism with increasing ferocity. Communists are blacklisted, deprived of work, declared "foreign agents," imprisoned. In 36 capitalist countries the Communist Parties are obliged to operate deep underground. But the peoples are learning by experience that the Communists are the most loyal and dependable defenders of their interests. The ideas of Communism know no barriers; they cannot be shot or put behind stout prison bars. They are conquering the minds and hearts of people and are becoming an invincible force.

Of course in some major capitalist countries the Communist Parties are still small. But can this detract from their historical role? Strong in the conviction of the rightness of their cause, the Communists stand in the van of the working class under all conditions. For example, it is well known that the number of Communists in the U.S.A. is small. But that big capitalist power, for all its enormous military and police machinery, is afraid of the party of Communists and erects all kinds of obstacles to its work. It follows that the small contingent of U.S. Communists is working as befits Marxist-Leninists! Here one can say, in the words of the folk saying: "The nugget is small, but its value is great." (Applause.)

The Communists of the socialist countries never forget the difficulties and hardships borne by our brothers in the capitalist countries who are fighting for the victory of the working class, for the cause of all working people. Today, on behalf of the delegates to the 22nd Congress, on behalf of all Soviet Communists, we send the most heartfelt fraternal greetings to our comrades, the Communists in the capitalist countries, who bear aloft the victorious banner of Marxism-Leninism, to all those in the dungeons of reaction who have not bowed the head before the enemy, who are fighting courageously for the interests of their peoples! (Stormy, prolonged applause.)

The decisions of the 20th Congress, backed by the fraternal parties, multiplied the great creative forces of the Communist movement and helped restore the Leninist spirit and style in the life of the fraternal parties and the mutual relations among them. The conferences of representatives of Communist and Workers' Parties held in recent years were important milestones in the development of the world Communist movement. International conferences of Communists are one of the forms evolved by the fraternal parties that ensure their militant cooperation.

To Marxist-Leninists it is indisputable that the vital interests of the international Communist movement demand consistent and undeviating unity of action, and the Communist and Workers' Parties observe it faithfully. Only the leaders of the League of Communists of Yugoslavia, who plainly suffer from national narrow-mindedness, have turned from the straight Marxist-Leninist road on to a winding path that has landed them in the bog of revisionism. The Yugoslav leaders responded to the 1957 Declaration of the fraternal parties, which resounded throughout the world as a charter of Communist unity and solidarity, with a revisionist, anti-Leninist program that all the Marxist-Leninist parties criticized decisively and justly.

Revisionist ideas pervade not only the theory but also the practice of the leadership of the Yugoslav League of Communists. The line they have adopted—that of development in isolation, apart from the world socialist community—is harmful and dangerous. It plays into the hands of imperialist reaction, foments nationalist tendencies and may in the long run lead to the loss of socialist gains in the country, which has broken away from the friendly and united family of builders of a new world.

Our party has criticized and will continue to criticize the Yugoslav leaders' revisionist conceptions. As internationalists, we cannot but feel concern for the destiny of the fraternal peoples of Yugoslavia, who fought selflessly against fascism and after victory chose the path of socialist construction.

The historic conference of November, 1960, once again convincingly confirmed the will and resolve of the Communist Parties to uphold the purity of Marxism-Leninism, strengthen the unity of their ranks and continue the determined struggle on two fronts—against revisionism, as the main danger, and against dogmatism and sectarianism. The important propositions on the necessity for each party to observe joint decisions adopted collectively and likewise not to permit any actions that could undermine the unity of the Communist ranks are of tremendous importance for further strengthening the solidity of the working class parties.

The successes of socialist construction in the Soviet Union and in the people's democracies testify to the great power and vitality of Marxism-Leninism. They show the whole world what results can be achieved by workers and peasants who have taken their destiny into their own hands and are armed with the most progressive revolutionary theory.

Socialism is the result of the creative activity of the broadest masses marching under the banner of Marxism-Leninism. Communists are opposed to the forcible, artificial implanting of this or that socio-political system in other countries. We are convinced that in the end the socialist system will triumph everywhere, but this in no way means that we shall

seek to achieve this victory by interfering in the internal affairs of other countries.

Attempts are made to blame us Communists for any action by the masses against their oppressors. When the working people of any capitalist or colonial country rise in struggle, the imperialists begin to cry: "This is the handiwork of the Communists" or "the hand of Moscow." Of course we are glad to have the imperialists ascribe to Communists all the good actions of the peoples. By so doing, the imperialists are involuntarily helping the masses to gain a better understanding of Communist ideas. These ideas are spreading widely throughout the world. But of course this is not happening because the Soviet Union and the other socialist countries are imposing them on the peoples. Ideas cannot be carried on bayonets, as people used to say, or on rockets, as it would now be more accurate to say.

Of course, warring classes have always sought to rely on the support of kindred forces from outside. For a long time the bourgeois class had an advantage in this respect. The world bourgeoisie, acting in concert, stamped out centers of revolution everywhere and by every means, including armed intervention. Obviously, even at that time the international proletariat was not indifferent to the struggle of its class brothers, but more often than not it could express its solidarity with them only in the form of moral support. Now the situation has changed. The people of this or that country who rise in struggle will not find themselves engaged in single combat with world imperialism. On their side are powerful international forces, possessing everything necessary to give effective moral and material support. (Applause.)

The imperialists, alarmed by the scale of the revolutionary struggle, are not ceasing their attempts to interfere in the internal affairs of peoples and states. This is why they have reserved, in military pacts and agreements, the "right" to armed intervention in the event of so-called internal unrest, that is, to suppress revolutions, to put down actions by the masses of the people against reactionary regimes. The imperialists charge at every crossroads that the Communists export revolution. The imperialist gentlemen need this slander to camouflage in at least some way their claim to the right to export counterrevolution.

It is a strange logic these gentlemen have. Apparently they are still under the spell of the times when they were able to strangle the liberation movement of peoples. But those times have gone forever. The Communists are against the export of revolution, and this is well known in the West. But we do not recognize anybody's right to export counterrevolution, to perform the functions of an international gendarme. This too should be well known.

The attempts of the imperialists to interfere in the affairs of peoples rising in revolution would constitute nothing less than acts of aggression—a threat to world peace. We must state outright that in the event of imperialist export of counterrevolution the Communists will call on the peoples of all countries to rally, to mobilize their forces and, relying on the might of the world socialist system, firmly repel the enemies of freedom, the enemies of peace. In short, as ye sow, so shall ye reap! (Prolonged applause.)

3. Peaceful Coexistence Is the General Course of Soviet Foreign Policy. The Peoples Are the Decisive Force in the Struggle for Peace.—Comrades! In the period under review important changes have occurred in the alignment of forces in the world arena. The world socialist system has become a reliable shield protecting not only the peoples of countries friendly to us but all mankind against the military adventures of imperialism. And the fact that the preponderance of strength is on the side of the socialist commonwealth of peoples is extremely fortunate for all mankind. At the same time the forces of peace have continued to grow all over the world.

A few years ago only two opposing camps, the socialist and the imperialist, were active in international relations. Today the countries of Asia, Africa and Latin America that have freed or are freeing themselves from foreign oppression have also begun to play an active role in international affairs. These countries are often called neutralist, though they can be considered neutral only in the sense that they do not belong to any of the existing military-political alliances. But the majority of these countries are by no means neutral when it comes to the fundamental question of the day—the question of war and peace. As a rule they take their stand for peace and against war. The countries that have won their freedom from colonialism are becoming a serious factor in the world, a factor in the struggle against colonialism and imperialism; the basic issues of world politics can no longer be settled without regard for their interests.

In the capitalist countries themselves the masses are taking a more and more vigorous stand against war. The working class and all the working people are waging a struggle against the arms race and against the disastrous policy of the warmongers.

Thus the aggressive policy of the imperialist powers is today being countered by augmented forces. The struggle of the countries of socialism and all peace-loving forces against the preparations for new aggression and war constitutes the main substance of world politics today.

In the past few years the forces of war and aggression have time and again placed world peace in jeopardy. In 1956, simultaneously with the counterrevolutionary rising in Hungary, the imperialists staged an attack on Egypt. In the latter half of 1957 the imperialists prepared to invade Syria; this held the threat of a military conflagration. In the summer of 1958, in connection with the revolution in Iraq, they launched an intervention in Lebanon and Jordan and at the same time created tension in the region of Taiwan, an island that belongs to the Chinese People's Republic. In April and May of 1960 the American imperialists sent their military aircraft into the air space of the U.S.S.R. and wrecked the Paris summit conference. In the spring of 1961 they mounted an armed incursion into Cuba by gangs of hirelings and sought to bring Laos under their sway, to involve it in the aggressive SEATO military bloc. But these sallies of the imperialists all foundered.

It would be the greatest of mistakes, however, to imagine that the failures of their aggressive plans have brought the imperialists to their senses. The facts argue the reverse. They have not ceased their efforts to aggravate the international situation still further and bring the world to the brink of war. In recent months the imperialists have deliberately undertaken to create a dangerous situation in Central Europe by threatening to take up arms in response to our proposal to do away with the vestiges of the second world war, to conclude a German peace treaty and normalize the situation in West Berlin.

In circumstances of an exacerbated international situation, we were forced to take steps necessary to render our country secure against encroachments by aggressors and to save mankind from the danger of a new world war. The Soviet government was forced to suspend the reduction of its armed forces planned for 1961, to increase its defense expenditures, to postpone the transfer of servicemen into the reserves and to resume tests of more powerful new weapons. These are measures that we were forced to take; they were unanimously backed by our people and were correctly understood by the peoples of other countries, who know that the Soviet Union will never be the first to take the road of war. The Soviet people are well acquainted with the ways of aggressors. We have not forgotten the years of the Great Patriotic War, of the treacherous, villainous attack on the Soviet Union by Hitlerite Germany. In the face of the war threat created by the imperialists, there is no room and can be no room for complacency and unconcern. (Applause.)

Some people in the West are now claiming that the measures taken by the Soviet government to strengthen our homeland's defenses represent a renunciation of the policy of peaceful coexistence. This, of course, is plain nonsense. The policy of peaceful coexistence derives from the very nature of our system.

I should like to call to mind the following fact. In the days when our country was fighting off the fierce assaults of the White Guards and foreign interventionists, the Soviet government was discussing the question of a national emblem. The first design for the emblem showed a sword. Vladimir Ilyich was sharply opposed to it. "What is the sword for?" he asked. "We have no need of conquests. A policy of conquest is totally alien to us; we are not attacking our internal and external

enemies but defending ourselves against them; ours is a defensive war, and the sword is no emblem for us." As everyone knows, it was the hammer and sickle—the symbol of peaceful constructive labor—that became our country's emblem. (Stormy applause.)

The principles of peaceful coexistence worked out by V. I. Lenin and developed in our party's documents remain unalterably the general course of Soviet foreign policy. The entire foreign policy of the Soviet government attests convincingly to the fidelity of the Party and of all the Soviet people to this peaceful Leninist course. (Applause.)

But the threat of war is hard to avert unilaterally, just as a campfire is hard to put out if one person is pouring water on the fire and another kerosene. The Western powers, which should be no less interested than we are in avoiding a thermonuclear catastrophe, are obliged in their turn to show a readiness to seek ways of settling outstanding issues on a mutually acceptable basis.

Some pacifist-minded people in the West think in their naivete that if the Soviet Union were to make more concessions to the Western powers, there would be no aggravation of international tension. These people fail to consider that the policy of the imperialist powers, including their foreign policy, is determined by the class interests of monopoly capital, in which aggression and war are organically inherent. When under the pressure of the masses the advocates of a more or less moderate policy win the upper hand, a relaxation of international tension occurs, the war clouds are somewhat dissipated. But when the pressure of the masses relaxes and the day is carried by those groupings of the bourgeoisie that grow rich on the arms race and see in war a chance for more profit, the international atmosphere becomes aggravated.

Thus the peaceful coexistence of states with different social systems can be maintained and ensured only through the selfless struggle of all peoples against the aggressive aspirations of the imperialists. The greater the might of the socialist camp and the more vigorously the fight for peace is pressed in the capitalist countries themselves, the harder it is for the imperialists to carry out their aggressive plans.

Peace and peaceful coexistence are not quite the same thing. Peaceful coexistence is not simply the absence of war, not an unstable truce between wars. It is the coexistence of two opposing social systems, founded on mutual renunciation of war as a means of settling disputes between states.

The experience of history teaches that you are not going to appease an aggressor with concessions. Concessions to the imperialists on vitally important matters represent not a policy of peaceful coexistence but capitulation to the forces of aggression. That we will never accede to. (Applause.) The imperialists must at long last realize that they are no longer arbiters of mankind's fate, and that whether they like it or not socialism will continue to exist, develop and grow stronger. (Stormy applause.) But for the moment it does not look as though the imperialist gentry have assimilated this truth. One may expect from them adventurous actions that would spell disaster for hundreds of millions of human beings. Aggressors must not be humored, therefore, but bridled! (Prolonged applause.)

A big contribution to the struggle against the forces of aggression and war has been made by the partisans of peace organized in various associations and movements in many countries. Everyone remembers how at the beginning of the 1950s hundreds of millions of people called for outlawing the atom bomb, how angrily the peoples of Europe protested the establishment of the notorious European Defense Community and West Germany's membership in it. The pressure of the masses on parliaments and governments had a powerful effect.

The activities of the partisans of peace take on especially great importance today, when the danger of war has grown. Under the present circumstances men of good will can no longer confine themselves to merely voicing their hopes for peace. It is plain to see that despite the many actions of the public on behalf of peace, the forces of aggression and war are growing more and more brazen. Indeed, just a few years ago no Western politician would have dared, except at the risk of his career, to so much as mention arming the German Bundeswehr. But today the militarization of West Germany is proceeding full blast, and the Bundeswehr has now become the greatest military force in Western Europe. West Germany's War Minister Strauss cynically brags that the Federal Republic is not only a member of NATO but is in command there. More than that, something unheard-of has happened: The governments of Britain and France—that is, of countries that have in the past suffered from German militarism—have made training grounds and barracks available to the Bundeswehr on their own territories and have placed their armed forces under the command of former Hitlerite generals. Thus the soldiers of the Bundeswehr trample that British soil which they were unable to get to by force of arms in two world wars.

We share the feelings of bitterness and indignation of the French and British patriots who observe West German revanchists marching about their native lands.

Wind from words won't turn windmills, the saying has it. Still less can the war machine of the aggressors be held in check with talk of peace. Decisive and vigorous action is needed to stay the criminal hands of the warmongers in time, before it is too late. Needless to say, the struggle for peace, like any struggle, calls for exertion and perseverance. When you are fighting you not only strike blows but receive them too. But is that to be feared when the fate of all mankind is at stake? It must be realized that whether there is to be peace on earth or whether mankind is to be plunged into the catastrophe of a new world war depends above all on the peoples themselves, on their determination and vigorous action. The peoples' vigilance against the intrigues of the imperialist warmongers must be heightened. Their vigorous action against war cannot be delayed until war breaks out. They must launch the struggle full scale at once, without waiting for the nuclear and thermonuclear bombs to start falling.

The strength of the peace movement lies in its mass character, its organization and resolute actions. All peoples and all sections of society except for a narrow circle of monopolists have an interest in peace. And the peoples must insist that a policy of peace be pursued, must employ all forms of struggle to achieve that end. The peoples can and must pull the teeth of those who are obsessed with insane ideas of militarism and war. In the struggle for peace the peoples are the decisive force. (Stormy applause.)

4. Seek the Solution of International Problems by Peaceful Means. Expose the Intrigues and Maneuvers of the Warmongers. Improve Relations Between States.—Comrades! The situation that has developed demands that fundamental international problems be resolved without delay on the basis of the principles of peaceful coexistence. After the 20th Congress the Soviet Union put forward a broad and realistic program of action to ensure the preservation and consolidation of world peace. The essentials of this program, briefly stated, are: to rid mankind of the dangerous and burdensome arms race, to put an end to the vestiges of the second world war, and to remove the obstacles to normalization of the international situation.

The most important component of our party's foreign policy activities is the struggle for general and complete disarmament. The Soviet Union has been waging this struggle for many years now, and doing so firmly and perseveringly. We have always been resolutely opposed to the arms race, since rivalry in this sphere in the past not only saddled the peoples with a terrible burden but inevitably led to world wars. We are even more resolutely opposed to the arms race now that there has been a colossal technical revolution in the art of war and the use of today's weapons would inevitably entail the deaths of hundreds of millions of people.

The stockpiling of these weapons, proceeding as it is in a setting of cold war and war hysteria, is fraught with disastrous consequences. All that has to happen is for the nerves of some fellow in uniform to crack while he is on duty at a "push-button" somewhere in the West, and things may happen that will bring more than a little misfortune upon the peoples of the whole world.

Naturally, when we put forward a program of general and complete disarmament, we are talking not about the unilateral disarmament of socialism in the face of imperialism or vice versa, but about universal renunciation of arms as a means of solving problems at issue among states. Not daring to declare themselves opposed to disarmament, the ruling circles of the

capitalist countries—in the first place the United States, Britain and France—made up a story to the effect that the Soviet Union is opposed to control over disarmament. We exposed this maneuver and openly declared our willingness to agree in advance to any of their proposals on the most rigorous international control if they would accept our proposals on general and complete disarmament.

As a blind, the imperialists are now hypocritically making a great to-do over the fact that we have been forced to conduct experimental explosions of nuclear weapons. But this has not kept the peoples from realizing that we have done this only because the Western powers, having deadlocked solution of the disarmament problem and the nuclear-test talks, have pulled the throttle of their war machine all the way out in an effort to achieve a preponderance of strength over the socialist countries. We got the jump on them and thereby kept the advantage with the socialist camp, which is standing guard over the peace. (Stormy applause.)

Our measures were forced on us. It was known that the United States had been preparing for a long time to resume tests, while France had been conducting them repeatedly. Under the present circumstances it becomes even more obvious that a struggle by the peoples to get rid of the arms race is indispensable. The problem of disarmament affects the vital interests of every nation and of all mankind. And when it has been solved there will no longer be any need for atomic weapons or, consequently, for their manufacture and testing.

The problem of doing away with the vestiges of the second world war is of the greatest importance for the preservation and consolidation of peace. The fact that no peace settlement with Germany has been effected 16 years after the victory over the Hitlerite aggressors cannot be tolerated. The Western powers, headed by the United States, are wholly responsible for this inexcusable delay. Flouting the interests of the peoples, just as soon as the war was over they steered their course for the revival of German militarism.

The absence of a peace treaty has already played into the hands of the Bonn revanchists. With the aid of the American imperialists they have rebuilt their army for new aggression. The West German militarists dream in their sleep of how to take advantage of the unstable situation in Europe for bringing their former enemies—the powers in the anti-Hitler coalition—into conflict with one another. They dream of swallowing up the German Democratic Republic, enslaving other neighboring countries and taking revenge for their defeat in the second world war.

We have held all along that a peace treaty, having made permanent the German borders defined by the Potsdam Agreement, would tie the revanchists' hands and discourage them from adventures. The socialist countries have long held off on signing a treaty, hoping that common sense would prevail in Washington, London and Paris. We are still today prepared to join with the Western powers in seeking a mutually acceptable and agreed settlement through negotiations.

Recently, while attending the United Nations General Assembly, Comrade Gromyko, U.S.S.R. Minister of Foreign Affairs, had talks with the Foreign Secretary and Prime Minister of Great Britain. These talks left us with the impression that the Western powers were showing a certain understanding of the situation and that they were disposed to seek a settlement of the German problem and the question of West Berlin on a mutually acceptable basis.

However, a strange trait is to be discerned in the Western countries, and above all the United States. One thing is said there during talks between statesmen and another thing in the press, although there is every indication that the press has been informed of the character of the talks. The Western press has been presenting the question of a German peace treaty in unreasonable and unrealistic terms. The reproach is heard, for example, that someone is trying to give an apple in return for an orchard in settling the German question. This figure of speech may perhaps please its authors, but it fails to reflect the true picture in this case.

The Soviet government, as everyone knows, proposes that a German peace treaty be signed. The peace treaty is to be concluded for the purpose of clearing the way—as far as possible—

for the development of normal relations between states, and of not only heading off the threat of a new war but relaxing international tension.

We proceed from the actual situation that has taken shape since the crushing defeat of Hitlerite Germany, from the existence of two German states and of the borders that were fixed after the war. Any war, however grim and bloody, should end with the signing of a peace treaty. (Applause.) You must bear responsibility and must pay for aggression, for unleashing a war. That is the way things are. What has an orchard, what have apples, to do with it? (Stir in the hall. Applause.)

Certain Western politicians have been trying to give us some "good advice," so to speak, declaring that the signing of a peace treaty will be a dangerous thing for the Soviet Union and the other socialist countries. What should we take this to mean? Since when has war been considered dangerous for one side only? The days when the imperialist powers held sway are gone for good and all. The Soviet Union is today a mighty socialist power. Good progress is being made by the great socialist camp, which possesses well-developed industry and agriculture, advanced science and technology. (Stormy applause.)

I think the imperialist circles can surmise that if we have well-developed industry and agriculture, then the arms of our Soviet Army certainly measure up to the most up-to-date requirements. (Applause.)

We believe that the forces of socialism, all the forces that stand for peace, are today more powerful than the aggressive imperialist forces. But even if one agreed with the President of the United States that our forces are equal—he said this quite recently—it would plainly be unwise to threaten war. The fact that equality is conceded should lead to the drawing of appropriate conclusions. Nowadays it is dangerous to pursue a "position of strength" policy. (Applause.)

A German peace treaty must and will be signed, with or without the Western powers. (Applause.)

The status of West Berlin will also be normalized on the basis of this treaty: West Berlin will be a free, demilitarized city. The Western states and all other countries must enjoy the right of access to West Berlin in accordance with international law—that is, they must make appropriate arrangements with the government of the German Democratic Republic, inasmuch as all of West Berlin's communications with the outside world run through the territory of the G.D.R. (Applause.)

Some Western spokesmen say that our proposals that a German peace treaty be concluded this year are an ultimatum. But this is an erroneous contention. After all, the Soviet Union's proposals on concluding a peace treaty and on that basis settling the question of West Berlin, turning it into a free city, were put forward as early as 1958. A good deal of time has passed since then. We have not rushed settlement of the question, hoping for the achievement of mutual understanding with the Western countries. Where, may I ask, is the ultimatum? In proposing conclusion of a German peace treaty, the Soviet government has been presenting no ultimatum but has been moved by the necessity of finally settling this compelling question.

The Soviet government still insists that the German question be settled as promptly as possible and is against endlessly deferring its settlement. The question of a time limit for the signing of a German peace treaty will not be so important if the Western powers show a readiness to settle the German problem; we shall not in that case absolutely insist on signing the peace treaty before Dec. 31, 1961. The main thing is to settle the question, to do away with the vestiges of the second world war, to sign a German peace treaty. That is basic, that is the heart of the matter. (Applause.)

Solution of these problems will clear the way for further steps in the sphere of peaceful cooperation, both multilateral and bilateral, between states. But what else must be done to strengthen peace, besides concluding a German peace treaty?

The problem of basically improving the machinery of the United Nations is long overdue for solution. During the cold war years this machinery rusted and has begun jamming. The time has come to give it a cleaning, remove the incrustations from it and give it an infusion of fresh forces, with due regard for the changes that have occurred in the international situation in recent years. It is time to restore at long last the legitimate rights of the Chinese People's Republic in the United Nations. (Stormy, prolonged applause.) The time has come to settle the question of the German people's representation in the United Nations. (Prolonged applause.) Given the present situation, the most sensible thing would be to conclude a peace treaty with the two states that actually exist and admit them to membership in the U.N. The time has come to establish genuine equality in all U.N. agencies for the three groups of states that have formed in the world—the socialist, the neutralist and the imperialist. It is time to put a stop to the attempts to use this organization in the interests of the military alignment of the Western powers. (Applause.)

The problem of finally eliminating colonial oppression in all its forms and manifestations must be solved in accordance with the vital interests of the peoples. At the same time the peoples must be provided with effective aid, not in word but in deed; the consequences of colonialism must be overcome. They must be helped to rise as rapidly as possible to the economic and cultural level of the developed countries. As we see it, the way to accomplish this is first of all to get the colonial powers to give back to their victims at least part of what they looted from them. The Soviet Union and the other socialist countries are already giving the peoples friendly and disinterested support and assistance in the development of their economies and cultures. We shall go on rendering this assistance.

The solution of pressing regional political problems can play a role of considerable importance in the normalization of the international situation as a whole. We attach great importance to the problem of setting up atom-free zones, in Europe and the Far East first of all. A nonaggression pact between the countries in the Warsaw Treaty Organization and those in the North Atlantic military bloc could play an important part in strengthening security. An agreement might also be reached to set up a zone separating the armed forces of the military alignments, and a start might be made on reducing armed forces stationed on foreign territories. And the very best, the most radical, solution of the problem would be for the countries belonging to the military blocs to come to the wise conclusion that all military alliances should be dissolved and armed forces drawn back inside their own national boundaries.

In a word, given the mutual will, quite a few useful steps could be taken that would help the peoples to lessen the danger of war and then to remove it entirely.

As we see it, a way to improve the international situation is to be found in the further development of businesslike relations with all countries.

Our relations with the socialist countries have been, are and will continue to be relations of unbreakable fraternal friendship and cooperation. (Applause.) We shall continue developing and improving mutually advantageous economic and cultural ties with them on the basis of agreed long-range plans. This cooperation will enable us all to march ahead at an even faster pace on the road of socialism and communism. (Stormy applause.)

Soviet people derive deep satisfaction from the broadening of our cooperation with India and Indonesia, those great Asian powers. We are gladdened by their progress, we appreciate their difficulties and are willingly broadening the businesslike cooperation that is helping them to advance their economies and cultures. Our relations with other Asian and African countries that have won their freedom from an alien yoke—Burma, Cambodia, Ceylon, the United Arab Republic, Iraq, Guinea, Ghana, Mali, Morocco, Tunisia, Somalia and others—have been developing well on the same basis. We shall be expanding businesslike cooperation with the Arab Republic of Syria.

After a long and agonizing ordeal, a government that has declared itself to be the successor to the government of Patrice Lumumba has been set up in the Congo. The Soviet government stands ready to render the Congolese people assistance in accomplishing the difficult tasks that face them in the struggle to overcome the consequences of colonial oppression.

Our relations with the countries of Latin America have likewise expanded in the period under review, notwithstanding the artificial barriers erected by domestic reaction and by the American imperialists. The heroic people of Cuba have broken down these barriers and have been developing cooperation with other countries on a footing of equality. And although the U.S. imperialists have been stopping at nothing, up to and including the overthrow of legitimate governments, to prevent Latin American countries from pursuing an independent policy, life will take its own course just the same.

We intend to go on helping the peoples of the newly independent states to get on their feet, gain strength and play a worthy part in international affairs. The peoples of these countries are making a valuable contribution to the great cause of peace and progress. Traveling this road, they will always find reliable, loyal friends in the Soviet Union and in all the socialist countries. (Prolonged applause.)

We attach great importance to relations with the principal countries of the capitalist world, above all the United States of America. In recent years U.S. foreign policy has invariably been aimed at exacerbating the international situation. This occasions regret in all peace-loving peoples. As for the Soviet Union, it has always believed that the only way to prevent a global war of annihilation is to normalize relations among states regardless of their social systems. This being so, we must engage in a mutual search for ways of accomplishing this. No one asks the ruling circles of the U.S.A. to love socialism, just as they cannot ask us to love capitalism. The main thing is for them to renounce the settlement of disputed issues by war and to base international relations on the principles of peaceful economic competition. If realism wins out in U.S. policy, one of the serious obstacles to normalization of the entire international situation will have been removed. Not only the peoples of our countries but other peoples as well, and the cause of peace the world over, stand to gain from this kind of approach. (Applause.)

We also intend to broaden and reinforce normal businesslike economic and cultural ties with Britain, France, Italy, West Germany and other countries of Western Europe. Noticeable progress has been made in this matter in recent years, and now the matter rests entirely with our partners.

The Soviet Union is giving particular attention to the development of ties with its neighbors. The differences between our social and political systems have not been preventing the development of friendly, mutually beneficial relations between the U.S.S.R. and such countries as Afghanistan and Finland. Our relations with Austria and Sweden are coming along quite well. We have been making efforts to improve our relations with Norway and Denmark and shall continue doing so. Relations with neighboring Turkey have been improving of late. We want these relations to develop still further.

The Soviet Union would like to live in peace and friendship with such neighbors as Iran, Pakistan and Japan. Unfortunately, their ruling circles have thus far been unable or unwilling to disentangle themselves from the snares of the military blocs forced upon them by the Western powers and have failed to avail themselves of the opportunities for businesslike cooperation with our country. The present policy of the governments of these countries harbors a threat to their peoples. Especially conspicuous is the Shah of Iran, who has gone so far as to consent to having almost half his country turned into a zone of death to further the interests of the aggressive CENTO bloc.

The Soviet Union has been at considerable pains to improve its relations with Japan. But the government of that country, tied to the United States by an inequitable military treaty, still has no wish to do away with the vestiges of the second world war. The lack of a Soviet-Japanese peace treaty is materially hampering the development of cooperation between our countries. The Japanese people are becoming increasingly aware of how much Japan is losing by this. We trust that sooner or later common sense will prevail, and that our relations with Japan will be duly expanded to our mutual advantage.

Economic ties, as one of the important elements of peaceful coexistence, are coming to play an ever greater role in the development of international relations. The volume of Soviet foreign trade has almost doubled in the period under review. Stable trade relations have been established with more than 80 countries. Nevertheless, far more could be accomplished in this area if the Western powers stopped raising

obstacles and ceased their frequent highhanded behavior, which damages businesslike cooperation with the socialist countries. Incidentally, they do themselves more harm with these outmoded practices than they do us. Anyone who pursues a policy of discrimination, trade barriers and even blockade inevitably gives himself away as championing preparations for war and opposing peaceful coexistence.

Our country's cultural ties have been extensively developed in recent years. We now maintain such ties with more than 100 countries. More than 700,000 Soviet people have been going abroad each year, and an equal number of foreigners have been coming to visit us. We are prepared to continue the extensive development of these mutually profitable international contacts. They can and should play their part in improving cooperation and mutual understanding among people.

Contacts with the leaders of other countries have come to be one of the important elements of Soviet foreign policy. As we know, V. I. Lenin, who was directly engaged in guiding the foreign policy of the Soviet state, for all his busy schedule used to meet with figures from the United States, Britain, France, Finland, Afghanistan and other countries, conducted negotiations with them and was intending to participate in person in the Genoa Conference of 1922. The Central Committee has made a point of steadfastly observing this tradition established by Lenin. Carrying on active work in foreign policy, the members of the Party Central Committee's Presidium have often visited the countries in the socialist commonwealth and have made 65 trips to 27 nonsocialist states. I, too, have had occasion to do quite a bit of traveling the wide world over. It can't be helped—my position requires it, it is called for in the interest of our cause. (Prolonged applause.)

We have received many eminent foreign guests in our country, including the heads of state and government of European, Asian, African and Latin American countries. The leaders of the parties and governments of the socialist countries have been frequent and welcome guests of ours. We are prepared to continue both bilateral and multilateral meetings with heads of state and government.

Comrades! Events show our party's foreign policy line, framed at the 20th Congress, to have been correct. Keeping to this line, we have scored major victories. And although our strength has now grown substantially, we shall pursue the Leninist course just as unswervingly and consistently, seeking to make the idea of peaceful coexistence prevail. Present conditions have opened up the prospect of achieving peaceful coexistence over the entire period within which the social and political problems now dividing the world must be resolved. Matters are reaching a point where even before the total victory of socialism on earth, while capitalism holds on in part of the world, there will be a real chance of eliminating war from the life of society. (Applause.)

V. I. Lenin taught us to remain firm, unyielding and uncompromising where fundamental positions of principle are at stake. Under the most trying circumstances, when the only socialist state was withstanding the assaults of the whole capitalist world, when the enemy was attacking us at the front, in the rear and on the flanks, Vladimir Ilyich used firm and resolute language with the imperialists, at the same time pursuing a flexible line and constantly retaining the initiative.

What are the tasks for Soviet foreign policy that grow out of the present international situation? We must continue:

—unswervingly and consistently implementing the principle of the peaceful coexistence of states with different social systems, as the general course of the Soviet Union's foreign policy (applause);

—strengthening the unity of the socialist countries on the basis of fraternal cooperation and mutual assistance, and doing our part to reinforce the might of the world socialist system (applause);

—developing contacts and cooperating with all fighters for peace throughout the world; joining with all who want peace in a stand against those who want war (applause);

—strengthening proletarian solidarity with the working class and working people of the whole world, giving all possible moral and material support to peoples who are struggling for their liberation from imperialist and colonial oppression and for the consolidation of their independence (applause);

—developing international business ties, economic cooperation and trade on the broadest possible scale with all countries desirous of maintaining such relations with the Soviet Union (applause);

—carrying on a vigorous and flexible foreign policy, striving to secure settlement of urgent world problems through negotiations, exposing the intrigues and maneuvers of the warmongers and establishing businesslike cooperation with all states on the basis of reciprocity. (Applause.)

Experience has proved that the principle of the peaceful coexistence of states with different social systems, a principle put forward by the great Lenin, represents the way to preserve peace and prevent a global war of annihilation. We have been doing and we shall do everything in our power to achieve the triumph of peaceful coexistence and peaceful economic competition all over the world. (Stormy, prolonged applause.)

II. THE SOVIET UNION ENTERS THE PERIOD OF FULL-SCALE CONSTRUCTION OF COMMUNISM.—Comrades! The chief and determinant element in the Party's work since the 20th Congress has been the struggle to accomplish the basic tasks of the period of full-scale construction of communism: establishment of the material and technical base for communism; further strengthening of the economic might of the U.S.S.R.; the communist upbringing of the working people; and the ever fuller satisfaction of the growing material and spiritual requirements of the people.

The Central Committee reports to the Congress with satisfaction that all branches of the economy are developing at accelerated rates. The well-being of the people is rising steadily. Soviet science and culture have reached new heights. The seven-year plan is being carried out successfully. Our motherland has advanced far toward accomplishing the fundamental economic task of overtaking and surpassing the more highly developed capitalist countries in per capita output. And, it must be said, the population of the Soviet Union has increased considerably. At the time of the 20th Congress it was less than 200,000,000, whereas by the 22nd it had increased to almost 220,000,000. A fine increase, comrades! (Applause.)

We have adopted a rapid pace in developing the economy and are marching confidently along the Leninist path, taking one height after another. Our great goal is drawing nearer and nearer, and the bright peak on which the Soviet people in the near future will raise the banner of communism is already distinctly visible. (Stormy applause.)

1. The Struggle for an Upsurge in the Country's Economic Might. The Seven-Year Plan—an Important Stage in the Establishment of the Material and Technical Base for Communism.— Heavy industry, as the foundation of the entire economy, has a decisive role to play in the establishment of the material and technical base for communism. Permit me to cite data on the growth of industrial output since the 20th Congress. I shall quote figures that include preliminary estimates for 1961. Although 1961 has not yet come to an end, one can say that the plan goals will be exceeded for many important items of output.

The rise in industrial output over the past six years will come to almost 80%. Here are the indices for the major items:

		1955	1961 (est.)	% of 1955
Pig iron	(million tons)	33.3	51.1	153
Steel	(" ")	45.3	71.0	157
Rolled metal	(" ")	35.3	55.0	156
Coal	(" ")	391	513	131
Oil	(" ")	70.8	166	234
Gas	(billion cu.m.)	10.4	59.5	575
Electricity	(billion kwh.)	170	327	192
Chemical industry output	(billion rubles)	3.7	7.6	205
Output of machine-building and metalworking industries	(billion rubles)	17	38	224
Cement	(million tons)	22.5	51	226

Progress has been especially noteworthy in the key branches of heavy industry. In six years' time steel production has risen by 26,000,000 tons, an amount exceeding the total annual output of steel in Britain. Oil extraction has increased by 95,000,000 tons, or the equivalent of five new Bakus. Electric power production has increased by 157,000,000,000 kwh., which is to

say that our power installations grew, as it were, by the equivalent of 50 power plants the size of the V. I. Lenin Dnieper Hydroelectric Station. (Applause.)

Based on an up-to-date industry, all branches of the economy are making rapid progress; light industry and the food industry are developing well. The Party has been showing concern for raising the living standard of the people, for increasing the output of food products, clothing, footwear—everything that people need.

Here are some data on how the production of consumer goods has risen in our country:

	1955	1961 (est.)	% of 1955
Meat—slaughterhouse output (million tons)	2.5	4.5	178
Butter—dairy output (thousand tons)	463	794	171
Milk and whole milk products (million tons)	2.6	9.0	345
Vegetable fats (thousand tons)	1,168	1,730	148
Granulated beet sugar (million tons)	3.2	6.5	200
Fish catch (million tons)	2.7	3.7	136
Clothing and underwear (billion rubles)	6.0	9.2	152
Leather footwear (million pairs)	271	443	163
Textiles—total (million sq. m.)	5,543	6,661	120
incl. Woolen textiles	321	452	141
Radios and TV sets (thousands)	4,044	6,345	157
Household refrigerators (thousands)	151	731	380
Furniture (million rubles)	491	1,280	261

As you see, our output of consumer goods is growing more rapidly than in the recent past. We are now in a position to step up production of these commodities year by year. In the first three years of the seven-year plan alone, more than 1,000,000,000 meters of textiles and approximately 70,000,000 pairs of footwear have been turned out in excess of plan. But the needs of the Soviet population must be satisfied even more fully. For the remaining years of the seven-year plan the government is earmarking an additional sum of approximately 2,500,000,000 rubles for expanding the textile and footwear industries and their sources of raw materials. By the end of the seven-year plan our industry will be turning out more than 9,000,000,000 square meters of textiles a year and producing roughly three pairs of footwear per capita. The U.S.S.R.'s production of these articles will greatly exceed that of Britain, France and West Germany put together.

Naturally, cotton plantings will have to be expanded and the yield raised. This task is certain to be accomplished. When construction of the Nurek Hydroelectric Station has been completed, it will be possible to bring 1,200,000 hectares of irrigated land into use in Tadzhikistan and Uzbekistan and plant them to the most valuable, long-staple varieties of cotton. Development of the Golodnaya Steppe in Uzbekistan will bring with it a considerable increase in cotton production. But it is the program for building factories to produce artificial and synthetic fiber that, when completed, will result in providing the textile industry with its most dependable source of raw materials.

Our plans are plans for peaceful construction. The Party is concerned for increasing the country's economic power and is ever mindful of the need to strengthen its defensive capability. We have developed industries producing high-precision instruments and special-purpose metals; atomic, electronics and rocket industries; jet aircraft production, an up-to-date shipbuilding industry and the production of means of automation. These branches have already given a good account of themselves, not only on earth but in outer space. They are dependably serving the cause of peace, the cause of defense. We have at our disposal today intercontinental ballistic missiles, antiaircraft rockets and rockets for the land, air and naval forces.

The press has carried reports on the testing of our new rockets, which have a range of more than 12,000 km. Our vessels are standing by in the target area to determine when and with how much precision the rockets land in the prescribed area. We have been receiving communications to the effect that our rockets are performing with exceptional accuracy.

It should be pointed out that there are also American ships in this area, and they too are tracing the Soviet rockets in flight. The Americans have been publishing their respective data on these flights, and we have been comparing their figures with our own. Naturally, we have confidence in the comrades aboard our ships. But what we're getting in this case is something of a double check—ours and our adversary's. (Applause.)

Our adversaries—true, we wish we did not have to call them our adversaries, but the nature of imperialism must be reckoned with—confirm the fact that the Soviet rockets have been hitting the mark accurately. That's fine! We never doubted they would. (Applause.)

Since I have already wandered from my written text, I want to say that our tests of new nuclear weapons are also coming along very well. We shall shortly complete these tests—presumably at the end of October. We shall probably wind them up by detonating a hydrogen bomb with a yield of 50,000,000 tons of TNT. (Applause.) We have said that we have a 100-megaton bomb. This is true. But we are not going to explode it, because even if we did so at the most remote site, we might knock out all our windows. (Stormy applause.) We are therefore going to hold off for the time being and not set the bomb off. However, in exploding the 50-megaton bomb we are testing the device for triggering a 100-megaton bomb.

But may God grant, as they used to say, that we are never called upon to explode these bombs over anybody's territory. This is the greatest wish of our lives! (Stormy applause.)

I see in the audience some of the comrades who were involved in building our wonderful rockets, the engines for them, the precision instrumentation. I also see some of those who are working to improve our nuclear weapons. We take pride in these comrades, pay tribute to them, rejoice in their creative strides, which are helping to strengthen our homeland's defensive might, to reinforce peace throughout the world. (Stormy applause.)

The development of the Soviet submarine fleet is moving along well. Our adversaries are building a submarine fleet armed with ballistic missiles. We are arming our fleet with both ballistic and homing missiles. The situation makes this incumbent on us. Our adversaries in the military blocs are making preparations for firing upon the territories of both our country and the socialist countries from submarines. We are prepared to retaliate with strikes at targets on both land and water. The Soviet Union is a continental power. Those who choose to start a war against us will be forced to cross expanses of water. For this reason we are developing a powerful fleet of submarines armed with homing missiles, among other weapons, so that vessels approaching the boundaries of our country can be blown to pieces in the ocean hundreds of kilometers offshore.

The Soviet fleet of atomic submarines armed with ballistic and homing missiles is on the alert, guarding our socialist achievements. It will strike a crushing retaliatory blow at aggressors, and this includes their aircraft carriers, which in case of war will make a nice target for our submarine-launched missiles. (Stormy applause.)

I should like to inform the Congress that the rearming of the Soviet Army with nuclear and rocket weapons has been fully completed. Our armed forces are now in possession of weapons powerful enough to enable us to crush any aggressor. While providing the armed forces with rockets and a fleet of atomic submarines, we have not neglected the air force but are continuing to develop and improve it.

On behalf of the Congress, let me tender hearty thanks to the scientists, engineers and workers who have developed the most up-to-date weaponry for the Soviet Army. (Stormy applause.) They have done a great service to all mankind! The imperialists will now no longer be able to get away with military blackmail of peace-loving countries: In the hands of the Soviet people, the builders of communism, atomic and hydrogen weapons are reliable servants of the cause of peace. (Prolonged applause.)

The Soviet people have no need of war. Their thinking is directed toward the development of an economy of peace, the accomplishment of the great plans for communist construction, the creation of an abundance of material and spiritual benefits for all working people.

Substantial qualitative changes have occurred in industry, construction and transport since the 20th Congress, and a tremendous job has been done in the technical modernization of all fields of material production. Thousands of the latest types of machines, machine tools, apparatus, instruments and means of automation have been developed. The structure of the fuel balance has improved radically. In 1955 oil and gas accounted for 23.5% of total fuel production, while today they account for 42%. Savings from the use of cheaper fuels have been in excess of 3,000,000,000 rubles over these six years.

Electric power engineering has been shifted onto a new technical base. We are producing 200,000-kw. to 250,000-kw. steam and water turbines, while turbines of up to 500,000-kw. capacity are on the drawing boards. The largest power grids in the world have been set up and 500,000-volt transmission lines have been built. The supply of power available per worker has risen approximately 40%.

The chemical industry is using natural and casing-head gas as raw material on an ever greater scale. As a result we have been able to bring down output costs considerably and to save a large quantity of foodstuffs that would otherwise have been processed. A saving of 130,000,000 poods of grain is being effected in the current year simply from the use of other than food raw materials in the manufacture of alcohol. The production of plastics and chemical fibers has more than doubled in six years.

The big job of technically renovating all types of transport is in full swing: Freight capacity has grown 72%. More than 10,000 km. of railroad have been electrified. Half of all rail freightage is now being handled by electric and diesel locomotives, which has made possible a saving of some 2,500,000,000 rubles in the period under review. Ships under the Soviet flag call at the ports of more than 60 countries on all continents. Merchant-marine tonnage has increased almost 50%. The civil air lines, equipped with large, speedy airliners, daily carry up to 100,000 passengers. Centralized freight hauls by common-carrier truck transport have increased sixfold.

The industry producing precast reinforced-concrete items has to all intents and purposes been rebuilt from the bottom up; production has been raised to nearly 40,000,000 cubic meters, as against 5,300,000 in 1955. Basic changes have occurred in construction techniques in recent years. Large-panel construction is expanding rapidly. In the not very distant future construction will be shifted entirely to industrial methods and re-equipped with modern machinery. These are the most important features that have distinguished the development of industry, transport and construction in the period under examination.

Between 1956 and 1961 state capital investments in the national economy came to 156,000,000,000 rubles. This is more than was invested in all the years of the Soviet regime's existence prior to the 20th Party Congress. Some 6000 large state enterprises have been brought into operation. They include such giants as the V. I. Lenin and 22nd Party Congress Hydroelectric Stations on the Volga, the Karaganda and Kuibyshev Metallurgical Plants, huge ore-dressing combines in the Ukraine and Kazakhstan and at the deposits of the Kursk Magnetic Anomaly, and a large number of machine-building and chemical plants, sugar refineries and textile factories. More than 30,000 km. of oil and gas pipeline have been laid. A great victory has been scored by the builders of the Bratsk Hydroelectric Station, the world's largest: They have installed the first 225,000-kw. generating unit ahead of schedule.

The Congress has been presented with a fine gift by the builders of the Kremenchug Hydroelectric Station. They were well ahead of schedule in completing the third in the chain of Dnieper hydroelectric stations. The commissioning of this station will increase the stable, guaranteed capacity of the Dnieper Hydroelectric Station by 20%, and in addition conditions for the use of the Dnieper as a transport artery will be greatly improved. New cities have sprung up in recent years—Stavropol on the Volga,

Volzhsky, Temir-Tau, Rudny, Bratsk and many others.

These past years have been marked by a rapid rise in labor productivity. In 1961 it will exceed the 1955 level by 43% in industry, 60% in construction and 56% in rail transport. It has accounted for 70% of the total increase in industrial output. Production costs have been reduced by about 11% and rail freight costs by 22%. Last year industry and transport yielded twice the profits they did in 1955.

All the Union republics have made big strides in developing their economies and cultures. As compared with 1955, industrial output and capital investments have increased 50% to 100% and more in all the republics.

The productive forces of the country's eastern regions are being steadily developed in keeping with the policy adopted by the Party. Large power plants are being built to operate on the rich power resources of Siberia's rivers and on cheap coal. In Kazakhstan and Siberia large new iron ore deposits have been placed in the service of the people. Production of metal and coal is rising rapidly. With the exploitation of the huge deposits of natural gas in Uzbekistan, the Central Asian republics are being provided with a reliable source of fuel, and large quantities of cheap gas will be piped to Kazakhstan and the Urals. The chemical industry is developing at a rapid pace.

Reorganization of the management of industry and construction has been of vast importance for accelerating the movement forward. It has affected all sides of the country's economic life, heightened the role of the Union republics in economic development and given scope to the initiative of local Party, Soviet and economic agencies and the masses of working people at large, and has brought major reserves of the economy into play.

Comrades! The seven-year plan for development of the national economy of the U.S.S.R., adopted by the 21st Congress, is an important stage in the creation of the material and technical base for communism.

As you know, the control figures for the seven-year plan called for a rise of approximately 80% in gross industrial output. We planned to obtain as great an absolute increase over the seven years as had been achieved over the two previous decades. The seven-year plan was greeted with enthusiasm by all the peoples of the U.S.S.R. and by millions of working people abroad. As for bourgeois politicians, they saw it as a new challenge by the Soviet Union to the capitalist world. And it was in truth a challenge—to peaceful economic competition.

There were some bourgeois figures who repeated old fabrications from the days of the first five-year plans. They proclaimed in advance that this was more of the usual propaganda, that the Communists were framing economic plans without squaring them with their capabilities, that the seven-year plan would be revised. The seven-year plan has now been in effect for almost three years.

And what has happened? It must be conceded that we have indeed had to revise some of the seven-year-plan goals. Seven years, after all, is a long time, and it is impossible to anticipate everything. On a number of important points we have made adjustments in the plan, "heeded the criticism," so to say, of communism's adversaries. To be more precise, it was life itself that made the adjustments, it was the dedicated labor of the Soviet people. The seven-year plan envisaged an average annual increase of 8.3% in industrial output for the first three years. Actually it will be 10% for these three years. The industry of the Soviet Union will have produced approximately 19,000,000,000 rubles' worth of goods more than was contemplated for the first three years by the seven-year plan. (Applause.) In this period the country will have received above plan about 2,000,000 tons of pig iron, more than 9,000,000 tons of steel, approximately 8,000,000 tons of rolled metal, 10,000,000 tons of oil and much other output.

The adjusted targets for the last year of the seven-year plan look as follows:

—we had planned to smelt 65,000,000 to 70,000,000 tons of pig iron, and now expect to smelt 72,000,000 to 73,000,000 tons;

—indications are that we shall obtain not 86,000,000 to 91,000,000 tons of steel, but 95,000,000 to 97,000,000 tons or more.

There were some who suggested that steel output be boosted to 100,000,000 tons a year. But we restrained them. We said that all branches of the economy had to be developed proportionately, that along with metal output we had to remember

housing construction, children's institutions, the manufacture of footwear and clothing, etc. In this matter we must rigorously abide by the directives that were adopted by the 21st Party Congress (applause);

—production of rolled metal will amount to between 73,000,000 and 74,000,000 tons, rather than 65,000,000 to 70,000,000 tons;

—we will extract not 230,000,000 to 240,000,000 tons of oil but more than 240,000,000 tons;

—electric power output will amount not to between 500,000,000,000 and 520,000,000,000 kwh. but to more than 520,000,000,000 kwh.;

—the output of the machine-building and metalworking industries will reach 56,000,000,000 to 57,000,000,000 rubles in value, instead of the planned 49,000,000,000 rubles.

Of course the figures cited may change as plan fulfillment progresses; the need may arise to increase the appropriations for the development of a particular branch of industry or for cultural and everyday needs out of accumulations resulting from plan overfulfillment. It is evident that we will be obtaining substantial accumulations above plan. The Party Central Committee and the government will channel them into appropriate branches of the national economy on the basis of necessity and expediency.

The following items will be produced in greater quantities than envisaged by the control figures: cement, tractors and farm machinery, paper, footwear, butter, sugar, furniture, radios, television sets, refrigerators, washing machines and many other products for our country's economy and for its populace.

There's how we "miscalculated" in drawing up the seven-year plan! We are glad to own up to "miscalculations" of this kind! (Applause.) I do not think the Soviet people will be disappointed with these corrections. And as for those who prophesied that our plans would come to grief, let them figure out for themselves how to get out of the pickle they've landed in. That's not our worry. (Laughter in the hall. Applause.)

You recall, comrades, that even during the first five-year plans we outdid the United States in the rate of growth of industrial output, but we were considerably overshadowed with respect to its absolute increase, to say nothing of the substantial disparity in levels of production. In recent years our country, while continuing to outstrip the United States substantially in rate of growth, has also begun to leave it behind in absolute increase in the output of many major products. The question is now one of rapidly narrowing the gap between levels of production, of the Soviet Union's achieving first place in the world in the output of a number of food products and manufactured goods.

Let me cite some data. In the Soviet Union the average annual rate of increase of industrial output between 1956 and 1961 has been 10.2% and in the U.S.A. 2.3%; the average annual industrial output per capita has increased 8.2% in our country and 0.6% in the U.S.A.; the average annual increase in capital investments has been 12% in the U.S.S.R. over the past six years, while in the U.S.A. there has been no increase in investment, and it has even dropped somewhat.

And how do matters stand with respect to the absolute increase in output and the narrowing of the gap between levels of production? In the past six years the amount of steel smelted has increased by 26,000,000 tons in our country and declined by 15,000,000 tons in the U.S.A.; oil extraction has grown by 95,000,000 tons in the U.S.S.R. and by approximately 20,000,000 tons in the U.S.A.

The U.S.S.R.'s industrial production now stands at more than 60% of America's. Here are the comparative figures for major types of output in 1961 (according to preliminary estimates):

	U.S.S.R.	U.S.A.	U.S.S.R. in % of U.S.A.
Pig iron (million tons)	51.1	62.0	82
Steel (million tons)	71.0	91.0	78
Coal, oil, gas and other fuels, in terms of a single conventional fuel (million tons)	724	1,430	51
Electric power at the busbars (billion kwh.)	306	872	35

	U.S.S.R.	U.S.A.	U.S.S.R. in % of U.S.A.
Electric power used in industry (billion kwh.)	213	425	50
Cement (million tons)	51	54	94
Cotton textiles, un-bleached (billion sq.m.)	5.3	8.5	62
Woolen textiles (million linear meters)	353	270	131
Leather footwear (million pairs)	443	610	73
Granulated sugar (million tons)	6.5	3.7	175

It will be recalled that only ten or 11 years ago the Soviet Union was producing less than 30% of U.S. industrial output. At present the U.S.S.R. has already surpassed the United States in the extraction of iron and coal and in the production of coke, precast reinforced concrete, main-line diesel and electric loco-motives, lumber, woolen fabrics, sugar, butter, fish and several other foodstuffs and manufactured items. (Applause.)

Our country now accounts for almost one-fifth of total world industrial production, more than Britain, France, Italy, Canada, Japan, Belgium and The Netherlands combined. And these, after all, are highly developed countries with a total population of 280,000,000. The fact that our country, with a population of 220,-000,000, has surpassed them in total industrial output shows the confidence and speed with which the socialist economy is march-ing forward! (Applause.)

Completion of the seven-year plan will bring our nation to a stage where it will take little time to outdistance the United States economically. By accomplishing its basic economic task, the Soviet Union will win a world-historic victory in the peaceful competition with the United States of America. (Prolonged ap-plause.)

2. Make Fuller Use of Unutilized Reserves of the Socialist Economy. Eliminate Waste and Mismanagement. Achieve the Utmost Increase in Labor Productivity.—Comrades! As you see, things are going well with us. We have every possibility not only to fulfill but to overfulfill the seven-year plan and thereby lay a firm foundation for accomplishing the still greater tasks set forth in the draft Party Program. To realize these possi-bilities, however, we shall have to work a great deal, work better, make wiser use of unutilized reserves, and persistently improve the planning and management of the economy.

The chief thing on which attention must be concentrated is to achieve the utmost increase in labor productivity. Experience shows that the seven-year-plan goals for the growth of labor pro-ductivity can be exceeded. The task is a big and important one. Genuine heroism is needed to accomplish it. Heroism in our circumstances is not merely enthusiasm, persistence and effort. It is also skill, knowledge, high efficiency, advanced technology and innovation.

Our forefathers composed a familiar song about the dubinishka [the cudgel that drove men to work]. Although it is true that the words can't be taken out of a song, the people even before the revolution changed the word dubinishka in this song to mashi-nushka [the machine]—they realized the great power of the ma-chine even then. And today the Soviet Union is a technologically advanced country. In the struggle for high, genuinely communist labor productivity we must rely firmly on powerful machinery.

With due regard for the achievements in technical progress, one cannot fail to see that there are still many unsolved prob-lems. One still encounters instances in which new technology is applied in production slowly. Take Moscow's Likhachev Auto Plant, for example. It is turning out four-ton trucks that were first put into production 14 years ago and have been only in-significantly modernized in design. How do the executives of this plant and of the Moscow City Economic Council justify their de-votion to obsolete machines? Why has the designing of a new truck taken six years? After all, considerable help was given the plant to organize the production of an improved truck.

The introduction of the new sometimes involves certain pro-duction expenditures, extra worries and even disappointments. How much easier it is to go on calmly doing today what one did yesterday, and tomorrow what one is doing today! Unfortunate-ly, we still have executives who want to spend all their days in complete calm. But the Soviet executive cannot work that way. Routine and stagnation are alien to the very nature of socialist production—dynamic, revolutionary, always pressing forward. It is essential that we utilize more speedily and fully everything that science and technology discover in our country, that we take more boldly all the best that foreign experience offers, that we develop specialization and cooperation more extensively and accelerate the pace of complex mechanization and automation of production. In building a communist society we cannot tolerate technological conservatism. You can't clear high jumps on an old nag, as the saying goes!

At every plant, factory, mine and construction project we must thoroughly and painstakingly examine the machinery and replace whatever is obsolete; where there are no production lines, we must set them up. We must build new enterprises and technically re-equip existing ones, we must produce the most up-to-date machine tools, set up production lines, introduce automation and perfect technological processes.

Electrification plays a leading role in technical progress. It is the foundation for developing automation, radiotechnology, electronics, cybernetics and all the most highly developed means that determine the technical level of production. New power capacity must be put into operation more quickly and the electrification of all branches of the economy must proceed at a faster pace.

The thorough electrification of the country, the erection of powerful hydroelectric stations, will make it possible to begin simultaneously the solution of other, related economic problems. We must complete the chains of power stations on the Volga and the Dnieper, making it possible to provide deep waterways and irrigate millions of hectares of land.

On the Volga, the Kama and the Dnieper ten hydroelectric stations are in operation at full capacity and four are under construction. To complete the redevelopment of the Volga-Kama basin we have yet to build four hydrotechnical complexes and construct the installations for diverting part of the waters of the northern Pechora and Vychegda Rivers through the Kama and the Volga to the Caspian Sea. The sixth station of the Dnieper system—the Kanev Hydroelectric Station—is still to be built and the Pripet River redeveloped, and the Baltic Sea is to be linked with the Black Sea through the Neman River and a system of canals. (Applause.)

Such are the majestic plans being worked out by the Leninist party! We have the possibility of setting about them in the present seven-year period.

The question of questions, comrades, is capital construction. Under the seven-year plan we envisaged state investments in the amount of between 194,000,000,000 and 197,000,000,000 ru-bles. Some of our ill-wishers hissed at the time that we would not be able to make such huge capital investments. What has ac-tually happened? The average annual growth of investments was planned at 8.6%; the actual average has been 11% per annum for the three years. This overfulfillment of the capital investments plan means that in the course of the first three of the seven years we have invested more than 3,500,000,000 rubles addition-ally in the economy.

Unquestionably, we have begun to build better and faster. But there are still very many shortcomings in construction. At present there are more than 100,000 construction projects in the country, half of them industrial projects. With this huge number of projects under way simultaneously, materials and funds are scattered, and many enterprises are opened two or three years later than technical possibilities permit. Funds ex-pended are frozen over a long period, they lie idle, and the state does not get its money back.

Why does this happen? Here the desire for bigness operates as the enemy of the reasonable and realistic. Frequently a pre-tense of concern for the interests of the state as a whole conceals actual localism—to put it crudely, it conceals grabbing on a province, territory and at times even republic scale. Republic Councils of Ministers, the economic councils, ministries and local Party bodies try to get funds to start the greatest possible number of projects without regard for whether the necessary building materials, manpower and equipment can be provided, and the planning bodies do not prevent these antistate acts. This leads to stoppages, low labor productivity, the protraction of construction schedules, extra expense and higher building costs.

If we overcome this defect—and overcoming it depends entirely on the capacity to exercise leadership, on our will—we shall create conditions for a further rise in construction tempos. Evidently we should go so far as to stop undertaking new projects for a time, say for a year, and devote all the funds that accumulate in that period to the fastest completion of construction projects already begun. Exceptions can be allowed only for particularly important projects, and then only by decision of the Union government. The Central Committee and the Soviet government recently adopted a resolution setting up a schedule of priorities in capital construction.

Matters must be so arranged, the planning must be so organized, that proportions in the development of the economy are strictly observed and all unutilized reserves are employed to the full. An important role in this respect should be played by the recently organized major economic regions and their regional councils on coordination and planning of the work of economic councils.*

Of tremendous importance is the correct, economically justified choice of direction in the development of the individual branches of the economy. In planning the building of new enterprises and the reconstruction of existing ones, it is necessary to select the best technical variants and the best technological methods that can be used at lowest cost.

Considerable economic interest attaches, for example, to the question of how the steel industry is to develop. Experience has shown that the production of steel in converters with the use of oxygen is much more advantageous than in open-hearth furnaces; for each 1,000,000 tons of steel the saving amounts to approximately 6,000,000 rubles in initial investment alone and to more than 1,000,000 rubles in operating costs. Despite the clear advantages, far from sufficient attention is being paid to increasing the output of converter steel.

You remember that at the 20th Congress sharp criticism was leveled at conservatives who regarded themselves as specialists in rail transport. Their ideologist was Kaganovich, who called himself "the iron commissar." For a long time they clung to the steam locomotive and barred the way to electric and diesel traction. At that time we broke their resistance, and the technical re-equipping of the railroads went ahead at rapid speed. In some other branches of the economy too, conservatives cling to the old like the devil to a sinner's soul.

Socialist economic management demands an ability to analyze profoundly and knowledgeably the economic aspect of the work of enterprises, construction projects and industries. One cannot keep executives at the helm of economic construction who are either not used to counting state funds or unable to count them, who see their task as the fulfillment of plans at any cost. Take the leaders of the Perm Economic Council, for example. It would seem that all is going well with them, they punctually report fulfillment of the assignments for gross output. But look how they run their economy. Last year every third enterprise of the Perm Economic Region failed to fulfill its plan for profit, with the result that the accumulation funds were short 27,000,-000 rubles. The economic council paid more than 8,000,000 rubles in various fines, lost 7,000,000 rubles through spoilage and ended the year with a deficit of 26,000,000 rubles in working capital.

Do you think, comrades, that Comrade Soldatov, the chairman of the economic council, was seriously criticized? Nothing of the sort. He was promoted to a leading post in the All-Russian Economic Council. (Stir in the hall.)

Merciless war must be declared on the waste of raw materials, supplies and electric power. How many times has it been said, for instance, that a tremendous amount of metal is expended irrationally? Each year more than 4,000,000 tons of metal go into shavings, and furthermore, no little effort, working time, electric power and tools are expended on them.

And are we at all thrifty in the way we deal with natural and casing-head gas? During the past three years some 30,000,000,-000 cubic meters of gas have been released into the atmosphere or burned at the oil fields. To give you a clearer idea of what

*[See Current Digest of the Soviet Press, Vol. XIII, No. 41, pp. 16-17; Vol. XIV, No. 8, p. 23-24.]

such waste costs the state, it is enough to say that the natural gas lost would meet the annual needs of such big industrial centers as Moscow, Leningrad, Kiev, Minsk and Magnitogorsk combined, while the casing-head gas lost would be sufficient to produce approximately 1,000,000 tons of synthetic rubber.

Control through the ruble must be intensified in all spheres of production. Economy in big and little things, wise utilization of natural resources and material values, must be elevated to the level of state policy.

Planning practice must be radically improved. It must be stated that planning bodies often continue to make mistakes and miscalculations in determining the volume of production. Output plans do not always dovetail with plans for the supply of materials and machines and with integrated deliveries, and construction plans do not always dovetail with financial allocations, supplies of materials and deliveries of equipment. In any economy there must always be some reserves. The planning must not be from hand to mouth, so to say.

We now have all the conditions for creating the necessary material operating reserves at the enterprises themselves. It was difficult to do this in the past, when dozens of ministries operated in each economic region and each of them tried to isolate itself behind its own boundary posts. These boundary posts have been removed. The economic region is a single economic entity, its manager is the economic council, and this body must provide its enterprises and construction projects with materials for both production and repair needs.

It is necessary to heighten the responsibility of Party and economic agencies for the fulfillment of the decisions and directives of the Party and government, and Party and state discipline must be raised at all the levels of the apparatus. No arbitrariness or lack of discipline can be tolerated in a planned economy. A number of economic councils—the Dnepropetrovsk, Bryansk and Uzbek councils, for instance—expended more than their quotas of certain materials and equipment on the needs of "their own" economic regions, to the detriment of the plans for deliveries to other economic regions. This is the way of those who are guided by the principle, "How can you refuse a friend a favor?" Unprincipled executives who are prepared to "do a favor" for local leaders at state expense, who deliberately violate Party and state discipline, must be severely punished.

The task is to increase output substantially by improving the organization of production, by extensive application of the methods of advanced workers in all branches of industry and construction.

The best methods must be introduced more vigorously, and lagging and so-called average enterprises must be brought up to the level of leading ones.

The splendid successes of our industry, construction and transport have been achieved by the devoted labor of the Soviet working class, engineers, technicians, designers and scientists. By continuing to rely on their experience, knowledge and political and labor activeness, we shall accomplish those great tasks of communist construction that the 22nd Congress will define. (Prolonged applause.)

3. A Highly Developed Agriculture Is a Requirement for Building Communism. The Development of the Virgin Lands Is a Great Achievement of the Soviet People.—Comrades! Problems of the development of agriculture occupied the Party's particular attention in the period under review. This is understandable. Agriculture was in a difficult position as a result of the war's consequences and also of errors and shortcomings in the leadership of collective and state farms.

There arose before the Party an urgent and vital task—to eliminate the lag in agriculture quickly and to meet the people's food requirements and industry's needs for raw materials. The September (1953) and subsequent plenary sessions of the Central Committee disclosed the roots of the errors and shortcomings in the leadership of agriculture and devised a comprehensive program for its advance. The 20th Congress unanimously approved the measures taken and instructed the Central Committee to struggle with unflagging energy for a rapid increase in the output of grain, industrial crops, meat, milk and other products.

In these years very important measures have been carried out in agriculture, which have already had a deep effect on communist construction and will have an even deeper effect in the future. With the active participation of the whole people, the Party effectively solved many cardinal problems of the development of agriculture.

—The material and technical base of the collective and state farms has been strengthened. Total capital investments in agriculture in 1956-1960 amounted to 27,200,000,000 rubles as compared with 13,900,000,000 rubles in the preceding five years, or almost twice as much. Agriculture was supplied with 747,000 tractors (compared with 427,000 in the preceding five-year period) and large quantities of other machinery.

—The Machine and Tractor Stations have been reorganized, which has made it possible to concentrate the land and the machinery in the same hands and to create conditions for better utilization of the productive forces in agriculture.

—Immense tracts of virgin and idle land have been put to the plow. As a result, decisive successes have been achieved in increasing grain output and creating the prerequisites for faster development of animal husbandry.

—The role of the state farms in communist construction has been raised. In seven years more than 3000 new state farms have been set up, and there are now altogether about 8000 state farms. Many state farms are actually models of highly productive farming that set an example of socialist organization of agricultural production. The sown area of the state farms has increased from 15,000,000 to 80,000,000 hectares, and the state farms account for the following percentages of the total state procurements of farm products: grain, 43%; meat, 28%; milk, 32%; wool, 31%.

—A new system of planning has been introduced, based on the principle of combining state direction with the utmost development of the creative initiative of the people. This has increased the activeness of the toilers of the countryside and heightened the responsibility of the collective farms and local agencies for better use of the land and machinery.

—There has been a restoration of the Leninist principle of material incentives for collective farmers, state farm workers and specialists to increase agricultural output. The state has changed over from obligatory deliveries to the purchase of farm products, it has substantially raised purchase prices and it has reduced the prices charged for rural producer goods.

—The collective and state farms have been reinforced with management cadres and specialists. Hundreds of thousands of Communists and non-Party members have gone to work in the countryside at the call of the Party.

Such are the chief measures carried out by our party. They have had truly revolutionary significance for an upsurge in agriculture, for development of the whole socialist economy. The gross output of agriculture in the past five years has been 43% higher than in the preceding five years. The output of grain, meat, milk and other farm products has increased greatly. The monetary income of the collective farms and their indivisible funds have doubled because of the upsurge in communal production. The development of the communal economy has been the basis for an improvement in the collective farmers' well-being.

Let us look at the state of the major branches of agriculture.

The Central Committee has been directing the efforts of the toilers of the countryside toward increasing the output of grain as the basis of development of agriculture. The Party criticized the stereotyped use of the grass-crop rotation system, measures were taken for a considerable enlargement of the area under the higher-yield and more valuable crops—wheat and corn—and the seed situation was improved substantially.

The cultivation of virgin and idle lands occupies an outstanding place in the system of measures carried out by the Party. The Central Committee reports to the Congress with satisfaction that the task of developing the virgin lands has been successfully accomplished. In the boundless steppes of Kazakhstan, Siberia, the Volga region, the Urals and other eastern areas, 41,800,000 hectares of new land has been plowed and put in the service of the people. The new lands now yield more than 40% of all the country's grain procurements. The development of the virgin lands is a great feat that our heroic people have performed in building communism, an achievement that will live through the ages! (Prolonged applause.)

The virgin lands have radically changed the grain balance of many areas of the country. One cannot speak without pride and elation of such a historic fact as the increase achieved in the country's grain output through the development of the virgin lands. Before the new lands were developed, the regions concerned produced an annual average of 386,000,000 poods of grain, whereas between 1956 and 1960 the annual average was 3,363,000,000 poods! (Applause.)

Grain procurements, too, have increased sharply. Here are some data showing average annual state grain procurements (in millions of poods):

	1949-1953	1956-1960
Russian Republic including:	1,196	1,734
Altai Territory	49	245
Orenburg Province	43	115
Omsk Province	36	89
Novosibirsk Province	26	80
Krasnoyarsk Territory	44	73
Kazakh Republic including:	111	705
Virgin Land Territory	63	508
Tselinograd Province	13	152
Kustanai Province	17	138
Kokchetav Province	12	93
Pavlodar Province	5	74
North Kazakhstan Province	16	51

There it is, the power of virgin soil! Such are the fruits of our party's policy! It is gratifying to note that the peoples of all the fraternal republics of the Soviet Union, particularly our glorious young people, the Leninist Young Communist League, took part in the development of the new lands. At the call of the Party hundreds of thousands of patriots set off for the uninhabited steppes, showed labor heroism and brought glory upon their great motherland. (Prolonged applause.)

The significance of the virgin lands goes beyond the additional billions of poods of grain our country obtains. Thanks to the development of the virgin lands, tremendous areas in the East are being radically transformed. Large state farms, modern settlements and scientific and educational institutions have arisen in the steppes, and railroads, highways and power transmission lines have been built. The Party and the people created a very large industrial base in the East. Now, with the development of the virgin lands, we have created in the eastern regions a very large base for raising grain and livestock products. Thus the entire complex of riches of the Soviet East will serve the great cause of building communism. This is a truly communist renovation of the land. (Applause.)

While solving the task of an upsurge in grain farming, the Party has undertaken a struggle to increase the output of sugar beets, cotton, sunflower seed, flax, potatoes, vegetables, fruit (including citrus fruits) and melons, grapes and tea. Here, too, substantial progress has been attained. The growth of output of farm products is characterized by the following data showing average annual output:

	1951-1955	1956-1960	% of '51-'55
Grain (million poods)	5,442	7,742	142
Sugar beets for refining (million tons)	24	45.6	190
Cotton (thousand tons)	3,888	4,365	112
Sunflower seed (thous. tons)	2,456	3,672	150
Flax (thousand tons)	234	438	187
Potatoes (million tons)	69.5	88.3	127
Vegetables (million tons)	11.2	15.1	134
Melons and fruit (thous. tons)	2,100	2,905	138
Grapes (thousand tons)	1,021	1,592	156
Tea (thousand tons)	105.8	134	127

Agricultural output thus has increased considerably in the five years. As a consequence, purchases of grain and all other farm products have increased greatly. Whereas the state used to purchase approximately 2,000,000,000 poods of grain, it has been buying 3,000,000,000 and more in recent years.

Problems of an upsurge in animal husbandry occupy a special place among the most urgent problems of the development of agriculture. It is well known that this vitally important branch was only quite recently in an extremely neglected condition and that great difficulties occurred in supplying the public with food. Tremendous efforts were required to overcome the protracted lag. Above all, it was necessary to solve the problem of increasing fodder production. The introduction of corn planting was a most important requirement—along with the development of the virgin lands—for improving the fodder base. Growing corn for ensilage at the lactic-waxen stage extended the boundaries of cultivation and made it possible to extend this valuable crop into almost all regions of the country. Whereas in 1953 the area under corn was 3,485,000 hectares, today it is almost 26,000,000 hectares. The collective and state farms have begun to produce more fodder grain and have sharply increased the amount of silage. Much has been done in building livestock premises and mechanizing labor-consuming operations in animal husbandry.

We now have every justification for saying that radical changes have come about in developing communal animal husbandry. Let us look at the growth in the number of livestock. For a long time the figures remained at a standstill, and only in the past few years has the situation changed substantially. This is how the number of livestock has increased on farms of all categories (in millions):

	1955	1960	% of 1955
Cattle	58.8	75.8	129
incl. cows	27.7	34.8	126
Pigs	34	58.7	173
Sheep	103.3	133	129

It is important to note that the number of livestock is growing chiefly in the communal economy. In the past five years the number of cattle on the collective and state farms has increased 68% and of pigs 150%.

The growth in state purchases of meat, milk and other products vividly reflects the work carried out in animal husbandry. Here are annual averages:

	1951-1955	1956-1960	% of '51-'55
Meat, live weight (tons)	3,523,000	6,111,000	173
Milk (tons)	10,987,000	22,231,000	202
Eggs	2,582,000,000	4,841,000,000	187
Wool (tons)	190,600	310,600	163

As you see, state purchases of livestock products have greatly increased. It should be particularly stressed that the collective and state farms have now become the decisive force in supplying the country with livestock products. They accounted for 87% of the sales of meat to the state last year and 93% of the sales of milk to the state. This is a big victory for the policy of our party, a victory for the socialist economic system. (Applause.)

Comrades! The successes in agriculture are indisputable and substantial. But the question arises: Why do we still not have enough of some products, particularly meat? Why, despite the general substantial achievements, do we still encounter considerable difficulty in supplying the public with livestock products?

This is explained, above all, by the fact that the rate of growth of agricultural output still lags behind the rate of growth of industry and the increasing requirements of the public.

Let us look at the changes that have occurred in our country in recent years. Our population has risen considerably. As I have already said, it has increased by more than 20,000,000 since 1955. The earnings of the working people have been growing year by year. Thanks to higher wages, the abolition of taxes, discontinuing the floating of state loans, and increased pensions, the income of the public in 1960 was 24,000,000,000 rubles higher than in 1955. Obviously, the worker or office employee does not tuck this money away in a cookie jar but spends it on food and other items. It is natural, therefore, that meat, milk and butter consumption have increased sharply. State and cooperative sales of live-

stock products to the public have increased as follows (thousands of tons):

	1953	1960
Meat and meat products	1,757	4,158
Milk and whole milk products	1,980	8,214
Butter	330	613

We all rejoice in this rise in the consumption of the more valuable food products. The Party is seeking to see to it that the Soviet people eat better, that the well-being of the people improves. Consumption will continue to grow steadily. But it follows that we must always keep agricultural problems in the center of attention and ensure such a rate of agricultural growth that output of farm products is always ahead of demand. Yet many Party and Soviet organizations slackened attention to agriculture in 1959-1960, with the result that the rate of output, especially of meat and milk, lagged seriously behind seven-year-plan assignments.

This aroused the Party's justified alarm. The Central Committee plenary session held in January, 1961, sharply criticized shortcomings in the leadership of agriculture and condemned any manifestation of complacency and self-satisfaction. The tasks of further developing agriculture were deeply and thoroughly surveyed at the Central Committee plenary session and zonal conferences, and concrete measures were drawn up to increase the output of agricultural products.

Soviet people warmly supported the measures set forth by the Party, believed in their feasibility and by their heroic labor are successfully carrying out the decisions of the January plenary session of the Central Committee. Of course, little time has passed, and the measures adopted by the Party could not yet have had their full impact on the state of affairs in agriculture. But what has been accomplished thus far, the results achieved in this year, warrants confidence that output of farm products will increase sharply in a short time.

What has 1961 brought us? The gross grain harvest will be higher than last year's. State grain purchases have increased: 3,086,000,000 poods of grain had been purchased by Oct. 15, or 354,000,000 poods more than on the same date last year. This year the state will buy a total of approximately 3,300,000,000 poods of grain, 450,000,000 more than last year. This is a great victory of the Party and the people. It is all the more valuable because it has been won in a year that has not offered the best in weather conditions. (Applause.)

What, then, enabled us to reach a higher level of grain production and purchases? The decisive role was played by the fact that the collective and state farms, carrying out the decisions of the Central Committee plenary session, revised the structure of the sown area and replaced less productive crops with more productive ones, particularly corn and legumes—although it must be noted that not all the collective and state farms carried out these very important measures.

How favorably the measures taken by the Party influenced the state of agriculture is clearly evident from the case of the Ukraine. You remember that the leaders of the Ukraine Communist Party, Council of Ministers and province Party and executive committees were sharply criticized at the January plenary session for shortcomings in agricultural management, and particularly for the low level of grain production. In 1960 only 359,000,000 poods of grain were procured by the state in the Ukraine.

You Ukrainian comrades of course remember this, you have not forgotten it.

Voice from the hall: We have not forgotten, and it is not only the Ukrainians who remember.

N. S. Khrushchev: Good!

The Party organizations of the Ukraine accepted the criticism correctly. They rallied the masses of the toilers of the countryside and led them in solving great new tasks. The republic's collective and state farms made better use of the land, mobilized their potentialities more fully and launched a competition for fulfilling pledges and plans. Millions of persons were taught advanced methods of corn growing. The area under grain corn was greatly enlarged this year, and there was a considerable rise in the yield per hectare. Sowings of peas increased by 342,000 hectares, and the average yield was 17.4

centners per hectare. All this played a decisive role in increasing grain production and state purchases.

Look how the situation has changed in sales of grain to the state by individual provinces of the Ukraine (millions of poods):

Province	By Oct. 15, 1961	Annual av., 1956-1960
Poltava	73	22
Dnepropetrovsk	70	44
Kharkov	60	25
Kirovograd	60	31
Zaporozhye	54	41
Vinnitsa	41	27
Lugansk	40	10
Cherkassy	37	20

Altogether, the collective and state farms of the Ukraine will sell the state this year approximately 850,000,000 poods of grain (applause); by Oct. 15 they had already sold 774,000,000 poods. (Applause.) It is important to note that, although the collective and state farms have sold so much grain, they provided themselves with full seed stocks and laid in more fodder grain than they ever had in the past. The collective farms are issuing their members a sufficient amount of grain in workday payments and are paying high-yield bonuses in full.

Comrades, this is a pleasing phenomenon. I lived in the Ukraine for many years, I know the industrious Ukrainian people well, I worked with them both before the war and after the war, in the restoration of the economy. But I confess that we could not imagine then that the Ukraine would reach the level it has attained today in grain production. We often say that being determines thinking, and sometimes we remark in jest that a beating spurs thinking. (Applause.) The criticism levelled at the Ukrainian comrades was severe but justified. It was correctly received and correctly understood. The criticism roused people, and they showed what they could do. We praise the Ukrainian comrades and expect them to raise the level of agricultural output still higher. (Applause.)

The Communist Party of the Ukraine and the entire Ukrainian people have won an outstanding victory. Honor and glory to the working people of the Ukraine, who greeted the 22nd Congress with such splendid achievements! (Prolonged applause.)

The working people of many provinces of the Russian Federation achieved gratifying successes this year in the struggle for grain. By Oct. 15 the republic's collective and state farms had sold the state 1,828,000,000 poods of grain, or 91,000,000 poods more than by the same date last year. Evidently a total of 2,000,000,000 poods of grain will be purchased by the state throughout the republic. Here, as in the Ukraine, corn played an important part in enlarging food and fodder grain production.

A high harvest of this crop was raised on large areas. Take Krasnodar Territory, for example. Because of the spring drought, the yield of ear grain in the Kuban came to 19 centners per hectare in 1961, or four centners less than last year, when 23 centners was gathered per hectare. Yet considerably more grain was sold to the state this year. By Oct. 15, 1961, the collective and state farms of the territory had sold the state 116,000,000 poods of grain, or 35,000,000 more than by the same date last year. What happened? The territory's collective and state farms raised a good corn crop over an area of 400,000 hectares. As a result, the state bought 33,000,000 poods of corn by Oct. 15, 1961, whereas by that date last year it had bought 16,000,000 poods of grain corn.

The collective farmers and state farm workers of provinces of the Central Black-Earth Zone and many districts of the Volga region, the Urals and Siberia this year achieved substantial results in increasing grain production, showing that the Russian Federation possesses tremendous reserves for increasing the output of farm products. Here are comparative data on the growth in grain sales to the state for some provinces (in millions of poods):

	By Oct. 15, 1961	Annual av., 1956-1960
Stalingrad	125	75
Voronezh	66	38

This is the same Voronezh Province which, as you recall, demonstrated the "innovation" of harvesting corn by using a tractor-drawn rail.* The Voronezh comrades were criticized, and they changed their means of tilling the soil and, as you see, achieved good results! (Stir in the hall.)

	By Oct. 15, 1961	Annual av., 1956-1960
Tambov	42	28
Penza	42	27
Belgorod	37	19
Kursk	36	23
Lipetsk	28	17

The successes are the result of the devoted labor of the collective farmers, state farm workers and agricultural specialists and the great organizing and political work of the Party organizations, which launched a nationwide competition for the fulfillment of pledges.

If in 1961 the Ukrainians demonstrated what they could do, the comrades from the Russian Federation should take good note of their experience and draw appropriate conclusions. The Russian Federation has great opportunities and should realize its strength and tackle matters energetically. (Stir in the hall.)

Many Western politicians declare at times: "We believe in the achievements of your industry, but we cannot see how you will right matters in agriculture!"

In talking with them, I have said: "Just wait, we'll show you a thing or two† in output of farm products as well."

We have inexhaustible opportunities. But they must be fully appreciated and utilized. Evidently after the Party Congress it will be necessary to repeat the experience of holding conferences of agricultural personnel in the republics, territories and provinces. It will be necessary to give some people in some places a good shaking up, as we say, to cleanse the pores a bit, as is done by those who are fond of Russian steam baths, so that the organism receives a more normal supply of oxygen. (Stir in the hall.)

Allow me to express confidence that the working people of the Russian Federation will make still fuller use of their potentialities and achieve fresh successes in developing all branches of agriculture. (Applause.)

The January plenary session of the Central Committee noted an intolerable lag in the production of cereals and legumes in a number of areas. This year the situation noticeably improved in the production and sale of these crops to the state. Whereas 21,000,000 poods of legumes were purchased in 1960, this year the figure was 41,000,000 poods. More buckwheat and millet were procured.

The production of cotton, sugar beets, sunflower seeds and other crops also increased. In the face of the complex conditions this year, when there was a shortage of water for irrigation, the collective farmers and state farm workers of the spring Uzbek, Tadzhik, Turkmenian and Kirgiz Republics and of South Kazakhstan Province in the Kazakh Republic showed great perseverance and tenacity in their work. They raised a good cotton crop and are successfully meeting the pledges made. By Oct. 15 state cotton procurements for the country as a whole were 3,000,000 tons, or 663,000 tons more than by this date last year; procurements in Uzbekistan, the biggest cotton producer among the republics, are 1,982,000 tons, or 453,000 tons more than last year.

The collective and state farms of Georgia achieved considerable successes in tea growing, as they did last year. They have sold the state 154,000 tons of tea leaves, fulfilling the plan 107%.

---

*[See Current Digest of the Soviet Press, Vol. XIII, No. 7, p. 17. The officials of a state farm that Khrushchev was expected to pass on an inspection trip to an atomic power plant knocked down the unharvested corn on 300 hectares so that it would appear from the road to have been cut.—Trans.]

†[Literally, "We'll show you the beetle's mother" (kuzkina mat), which the "Dictionary of the Russian Language," edited by Prof. D. N. Ushakov, Moscow, 1935, defines as "a colloquial vulgar oath."—Trans.]

Such are the year's preliminary results in the development of agriculture. As for animal husbandry, some successes have been achieved in this sphere also. The number of cattle on the collective and state farms has increased by 4,000,000 during the year, including 1,700,000 cows; the number of pigs has increased by 5,000,000 and of sheep by 3,000,000. Output and state purchases of livestock products have increased.

However, the rate of growth in production of meat and milk is far from the level we need. Much hard work remains to be done, and in particular we must utilize more fully the possibilities for considerably increasing the output of these products as early as by 1962.

4. Consolidate and Multiply Successes in the Development of Agriculture. Satisfy the Population's Demands for Farm Products More Fully.—Comrades! We have vast unutilized reserves. They will permit us to bring procurements of grain up to 4,200,000,000 poods, of meat to 13,000,000 tons and of milk to 50,000,000 tons a year within the next few years, as envisaged in the decisions of the January plenary session of the Central Committee. What must be done to achieve a substantial increase in agricultural output and to bring procurements up to these levels?

The main thing in increasing grain production is a further improvement in the structure of sown areas and the raising of yields. Low-yield crops must be decisively eliminated and replaced by high-yield ones, and sound crop rotations must be introduced. This, comrades, is one of the most pressing and fundamental tasks in agriculture. Farming is still carried out irrationally in many of our areas. Kirov, Kostroma and Yaroslavl Provinces are especially representative in this respect.

Kirov Province, for instance, planted 477,000 hectares to oats and 515,000 hectares to annual and perennial grasses in 1960. A total of 1,000,000 hectares, or 44% of the planted area, was taken up with these crops. In addition, there were 514,000 hectares of so-called clean fallow. If you consider that the annual grasses yielded seven or eight centners of hay and the oats five to seven centners of grain per hectare, it is plain that to all intents and purposes more than half of all the arable area was nonproductive. At the same time there were 155,000 hectares of corn and peas in the province, or a mere 7% of the sown area. Where, one may ask, is the grain to come from, where is the fodder to come from, and how can animal husbandry be expanded with such a planting structure? A good many speeches were made in Kirov Province about efficient farming, but they forget about the main thing.

What do we mean when we speak of highly efficient farming? Above all we mean producing a maximum per hectare of land and per unit of expended labor. But this can be achieved only if the crops with the highest yield are introduced and crop rotations are properly organized, and if the collective and state farms draw extensively upon the achievements of science and the experience of production innovators. The system of farming should serve precisely this purpose: maximum output, better utilization of land and improvement of soil fertility.

Unfortunately, many of our scientists, experts and practical farmers are still prisoners of the grass-crop rotation system, the indiscriminate application of which has done great harm to agriculture. The sooner we rid ourselves of stereotype in farming, the more creatively we go about solving the urgent problems of agriculture and the more fully we take the experience of the best collective and state farms and scientific institutions into account, the faster will we accomplish the task of increasing the output of grain and other farm products.

In revising the structure of sown areas, special attention should be given to expanding the production of grain and corn, as well as legumes. In the areas most favorable for growing corn—the Ukraine, the southern part of the Russian Federation, Moldavia, Georgia, Azerbaidzhan, southern Kazakhstan and the republics of Central Asia—we can get 50 centners of dry grain per hectare on large areas. We must select suitable varieties and hybrids and grow corn for grain in the Central Black-Earth provinces, in the Volga area and in other regions, pushing the crop northwards.

It must be understood, comrades, that without corn the collective and state farms will not achieve the required level of grain production. Corn has shown its possibilities in all parts of the Soviet Union. If in certain areas of the country corn is introduced for form's sake only and the collective and state farms harvest small crops, it is not the climate that is to blame but the people in charge. Where corn does not thrive, there is an "ingredient" that is not conducive to its growth. This "ingredient" is to be sought in the leadership. On what level? First and foremost, on the collective and state farms, and also at the district, province, territory and even the republic level. Officials who have themselves withered and are letting a crop like corn wither, giving it no chance to develop for all it's worth, must be replaced. (Applause.)

The experience that many thousands of collective and state farms have had this year has shown convincingly that along with corn one of the main sources of increased grain output lies in sharply heightening the share of peas and beans in the spring crop area. From the foothills of the Carpathians to the virgin-land steppes of Siberia and Kazakhstan, peas yield a crop of 20 to 30 and more centners per hectare. The extensive introduction of corn, peas and fodder beans is not an incidental task but a major line of development for our agriculture.

There are great reserves for increased grain production in the further development of virgin lands and the improvement of their use. At least 8,000,000 additional hectares are to be brought under cultivation in the next few years, so that 50,000,000 hectares of new land will have been put into use. Proper utilization of these huge tracts of land is a matter of statewide importance. It should be said that there are at present major shortcomings in the way the virgin lands are being utilized. In Kazakhstan, for example, a single-crop system in effect prevails; the state and collective farms have for years been sowing nothing but spring wheat, that is, grain on grain. This has caused the fields to become weed-infested and has checked a rise in the yield. The Central Committee of the Kazakhstan Communist Party and the republic's Council of Ministers have given no thought to the virgin land's future and have taken an erroneous position in their decisions on the development of virgin-land farming.

The errors that have been committed must be set right and the virgin lands must be comprehensively utilized; the area of row crops must be extended, plantings of corn, peas, fodder beans and sugar beets must be introduced and, where necessary, there must be clean fallow. The fallow and row-crop system on the virgin lands must have its own corresponding system of machines. The introduction of row crops in the virgin-land districts can proceed only on a highly mechanized basis.

It is important to establish the strictest agronomical discipline, to see to it that the complex of agrotechnical measures is as mandatory as the technological production procedures at a factory and that the role of the agronomist on the collective and state farms is raised to as high a level as that of the engineer in industry.

The development of the virgin lands, comrades, is the accomplishment of our party, a source of pride for our people! We must work to make virgin-land farming a symbol of efficient socialist agriculture.

Increasing the production of grain will also make for the more rapid development of animal husbandry. We are purposely dealing with the problems of grain, meat and milk production as a single task. It would be wrong to consider solution of the grain and livestock problems separately. They must be dealt with in their indivisible oneness, must be solved as a complex. What does solving the grain problem mean? It means achieving the level of grain output required both for food purposes and for the needs of animal husbandry. What does solving the livestock problem mean? It means above all increasing the output of meat, milk and butter. As the saying goes, a dry spoon scratches the tongue. If a man is to find the bread he eats appetizing, he must be able to spread something on it, and that takes butter, lard, meat and other livestock products, which you will not get unless you have enough grain. Solution of the livestock problem will bring with it an increase in the production of organic fertilizers and thereby help to raise yields.

Drawing support from the progress that has been made and bringing accumulated experience to bear, the collective and state farms must fully provide for the people's meat and milk needs and must overtake and surpass the United States in per capita output of livestock products.

Present here are some American journalists, who like to make fun of this slogan of ours. But let me tell you, gentlemen, that if we say this, our people are sure to accomplish it. (Applause.) When our party advances a slogan, our people back it up and translate it into action. It will be done! (Applause.)

Our immediate task is to produce an average for the country of at least 75 centners of meat per 100 hectares of plowland and 16 centners per 100 hectares of other farmland. We now have all we need for every collective and state farm to achieve that level. Needless to say, these are average indices for the country. A far larger quantity of meat and milk, figured per 100 hectares of plowland and other farmland, can and should be produced by many districts in the Russian Federation and by the Ukraine, Belorussia, Lithuania, Latvia, Estonia and Moldavia.

Comrades! I have already spoken of the role that the virgin lands have played in increasing the production of grain. But this has served to accomplish only the first task; the first stage in the development of virgin-land agriculture has been passed. We must move on. Farming in the virgin-land areas cannot develop one-sidedly, in the form of grain production alone. The job today is to tackle the development of animal husbandry with the same persistence and drive, making use of the resources of grain farming. This will be the second stage in the development of the virgin lands.

Large-scale, well-organized livestock raising in the virgin-land areas will provide one of the important sources of increased meat, milk and butter supplies, enabling us to meet the public's needs more fully. The virgin lands have given our people billions of poods of grain; along with grain, they must now give our people millions of tons of meat, milk and other livestock products.

Corn, legumes and sugar beets are a dependable basis for the development of animal husbandry. If we learn how to get big harvests of these crops everywhere, we shall be able to produce any quantity of meat, milk and other products we decide on.

Before us is the important task of fully meeting the demand of the population in the cities and industrial centers for fresh milk and dairy products, high-quality potatoes and the broadest assortment of vegetables. As you know, a good deal was said not long ago about developing sources of vegetable and dairy supplies around cities, but in practical terms progress was slow.

The Party Central Committee and the government have now found the most rational way of quickly meeting the public's needs for these foods. The Party is engaged in a broad program of establishing specialized state farms around cities and industrial centers. We must pursue with still greater purpose and persistence the task of fully meeting the public's requirements for fresh milk, potatoes and vegetables through their production on specialized state and collective farms surrounding these cities and industrial centers.

It is in the interests of the state that the production of cotton be rapidly increased. The seven-year plan calls for a rise of almost 50% in the cotton crop in the remaining years of the plan.

It is important to expand cotton plantings and to speed up the extension of irrigated areas in Central Asia. At the same time, the paramount task is still to increase the yield through improved use of irrigated lands and the mechanization of cotton growing.

The cotton-growing regions of the Uzbek, Tadzhik, Turkmen, Kirgiz, Kazakh, Azerbaidzhan and Armenian Republics are today faced with two tasks: to obtain a high yield of cotton, the staple crop, and to build up a well-developed animal husbandry. While producing more cotton for industry, the cotton-growing regions must see to developing a fodder supply for livestock raising and must provide the public with meat, milk and other food products. To accomplish this, they must make a close study of their crop rotations, so that while increasing the output of cotton they also increase the output of feed. The task of building up the fodder supply can be accomplished in the first place by introducing corn on the irrigated lands and raising the yields of alfalfa and sugar beets.

Every collective and state farm should increase its cotton yield in the next few years to at least 25 centners per hectare. The country would then obtain more than 1,000,000 additional tons of cotton from the area now under this crop. Twenty-five centners is the yield on average collective farms; many of the advanced ones are getting 40 and more centners of cotton per hectare.

Attention must also be given to raising the yield and introducing mechanization on a broad scale in the production of sugar beets, sunflower seed, flax, hemp, potatoes, vegetables, fruit, grapes, tea and other crops. This is the way to reduce labor expenditures and produce cheaper products.

Comrades! Our tasks in the field of agriculture are dictated by the fundamental interests of communist construction. We all proceed from the premise that progress in agriculture is one of the chief requirements for the steady improvement of the people's well-being.

The Party is laying down a long-range plan for the development of agriculture over 20 years. It is setting the task of greatly increasing production of grain, meat, milk and other farm products. Accomplishment of this objective will call for raising the productivity of labor in all branches of agriculture, for labor heroism, for a high level of organization in production, for providing the collective and state farms with up-to-date machinery and for its improved utilization. It is important for workers and collective farmers, Communists and non-Party members and the Soviet people as a whole to understand that the foundations for successful accomplishment of the great plan are being laid today in the effort to bring the seven-year plan to fulfillment. By fulfilling the seven-year plan we shall have built a solid foundation, relying on which we can seize new heights in the development of agriculture.

A further advance in agricultural production is the concern of the whole Party, of all the people. It is a frontier of communism that we must cross by bringing the entire might of the Soviet system to bear. (Prolonged applause.)

5. Improvement of the People's Well-Being. The Flowering of Science, Education, Literature and the Arts.—Comrades! Our party conceives the whole point of its activity to lie in raising the people's well-being, in cultivating the material and spiritual demands of Soviet man and satisfying them more fully. The socialist system in our country has now entered a period of maturity where all its capabilities are being revealed to the fullest. The superiority of socialism in rates of economic development is having a more and more salutary effect not only in the sphere of material production but in the area of consumption as well.

Under socialism the higher the national income, the higher the people's standard of living. In the Soviet Union three-fourths of the national income goes to meet the personal needs of the working people. In 1960 the national income of the U.S.S.R. was more than 50% higher than in 1955, and in the last ten years the national income per capita has risen 120%. The per capita national income is increasing much more rapidly in the Soviet Union than in the most highly developed capitalist countries.

On the basis of the growth in the national income, the real incomes of workers and employees calculated per working person have risen over the past five years by 27% and the incomes of collective farmers by 33%. In the course of the seven-year plan the real incomes of workers, employees and collective farmers will increase as much as 40%.

We have undertaken the task of surpassing the most advanced capitalist countries in living standards. But in setting this task the spheres we have in mind are those in which our country really must overtake and outdistance the capitalist countries. In terms of many criteria the Soviet Union already possesses unarguable advantages over the most highly developed capitalist countries. Free education, free medical care, absence of unemployment, and many other benefits that socialism offers have long been commonplace for Soviet people; they are taken for granted, as it were. But all these, comrades, are very great achievements, of which our people have reason to be proud. In these respects we long ago left the capitalist countries behind. The working class in the capitalist countries will be called upon for great efforts, will have to wage a stubborn struggle, to achieve the same gains. (Applause.)

Public consumption has been rising steadily in the Soviet Union. In 1960 retail state and cooperative trade was more than 50% higher than in 1955; the rate of growth of goods turnover in the first three years of the seven-year plan has been higher than envisaged by the control figures. Soviet people are consuming more and more meat, milk and dairy products and sugar; sales of clothing, footwear, furniture and cultural and everyday goods are growing. Even so, the public demand for these goods is not yet being fully satisfied. Our performance is to be seriously criticized for the absence of certain commodities from store shelves. To meet the growing requirements of the population, the Party and government have taken a decision to step up production of consumer goods.

The time has come to emphasize more strongly the need for sharply improving the quality of all goods. Often the stores offer a narrow selection, and meanwhile the warehouses can be crammed with so-called "unsalable goods." What sort of goods are these? They are products of poor quality, which customers turn away from. The demand for footwear, for example, is not being fully met, yet more than 1,500,000,000 rubles' worth of footwear has collected in the trade network. Or take the quality of clothing. Everyone says that Soviet fabrics wear very well, but there has been unfavorable criticism of the styles and finish of suits and topcoats. Often we turn out poor articles made from good materials and then spend money eliminating the defects and imperfections, acting as in the old joke:

—Akulya, why are you sewing it crooked?

—Well, I'm going to rip it apart anyhow, Mother. (Laughter in the hall. Applause.)

How long are some of our management people going to continue using the method of this Akulya in their work?

The work of the enterprises of light industry must be improved. We must see to it that all consumer goods are not only well made but are attractive and outstanding.

In its effort to improve people's lives, the Party has been giving a great deal of attention to matters that determine the improvement of living standards. The adjustment of the wages of workers and employees is being completed and the minimum wage raised. In five years some 4,000,000,000 rubles have been expended for raising wages. At the same time the excessively high pay received by certain categories of personnel has been brought down.

The new pay scales have already gone into effect for about 40,000,000 workers and employees. In the next few years the new rates will be introduced throughout the national economy. It is planned to raise the salaries of large contingents of the intelligentsia, such as teachers and doctors. In the remaining years of the seven-year plan the minimum wage will be brought up to 50 to 60 rubles. The wage rates and salary scales of middle-income workers and employees will also rise.

The working people are receiving a new and very appreciable increase in their pay as a result of the measures being put through to abolish taxes. Since Oct. 1, 1960, when the abolition of taxes was initiated, this increase has already amounted to 360,000,000 rubles for the year. The second stage in the abolition of taxes began on Oct. 1, 1961; when it has been carried through the working people will have received an additional 400,000,000 rubles, calculated for the year. By the end of 1965 the public will be paying no taxes. The abolition of taxes represents a signal social gain for the Soviet people. (Prolonged applause.)

In 1960 all workers and employees went over to a seven- or six-hour working day. The work week has thus diminished by six and a half hours, with no reduction but even a rise in wages at the same time that the working day was being shortened. It is contemplated that in the next few years a 40-hour week will be introduced for workers and employees working a seven-hour day.

The raising of wages and shortening of the working day and week must be accompanied by a rise in labor productivity. The higher the productivity of labor, the more chance society has of improving the people's living standards. Each gives to society and society gives to each—this is our unshakable principle. (Applause.)

Important measures have been carried through of late to improve pension provisions. The average old-age pension has more than doubled, and pensions for disability and in cases of loss of support have been increased. The state's expenditure on pensions has grown from 3,000,000,000 rubles in 1955 to 7,600,000,000 rubles in 1961. In 1963 minimum pensions will again be raised. As the collective farm economy advances, pensions for collective farmers will be introduced on a broader scale.

Housing construction has acquired truly unprecedented scope in the Soviet Union. One is tempted to say that the construction crane has become our symbol. The program of state housing construction mapped for 1956-1960 has been successfully completed. More housing has been put up in the last five years than in the preceding 15 years. Think a minute, comrades! Some 50,000,000 persons—nearly one-fourth of the total population—have received new housing accommodations! (Prolonged applause.) The Soviet Union leads the world in the volume and rate of housing construction. In the past few years our country has been building twice as many apartments per 1000 people as the United States and France and more than twice as many as Britain and Italy. (Applause.)

And still we have a housing shortage, and the housing problem remains extremely acute. In the past few years the growth of the urban population in the U.S.S.R. has run substantially ahead of estimates. By the end of the seven-year plan the population of the cities will have risen by approximately 15,000,000 more than had been contemplated. Still more housing will therefore be needed. The Central Committee and the Soviet government are taking steps to speed up housing construction. About 400,000,000 square meters of housing, or 60% more than in the Fourth and Fifth Five-Year Plans combined, is scheduled to be built in the remaining four years of the seven-year plan. More than 4,000,000 houses will be built in rural localities.

The problems of rural housing construction merit special attention. Dwellings with greater conveniences and fine schools, clubhouses, hospitals and stores have been erected in the villages in the past few years. Yet rural construction is often carried out without regard for the anticipated development of the economy or for the betterment of living conditions. Villages being built are spread out and without the everyday conveniences they should have, even though large sums of money are being put into construction. The settlements being newly established in rural areas, especially on the virgin-land state farms, should be of the urban type.

We are building in quantity. But we must give some earnest thought to another aspect of the matter: Sometimes, in the rush, houses with major defects are turned over for occupancy, and this makes the working people indignant. And rightly so! The shoddy workers in housing construction must be taken to task; with the participation of the public, stricter order must be introduced in the distribution of housing, and people whose need is most acute must be given priority in receiving apartments.

In the Soviet Union the state has undertaken to provide health care for the working people. Eloquent evidence of the way it has been coping with this noble task is the fact that mortality in the U.S.S.R. is the lowest in the world, while life expectancy is increasing all the time. (Applause.) We must continue improving medical services for the population, promoting physical culture and sports, and building more hospitals, sanatoriums, polyclinics and other medical facilities, especially in the rural localities and the country's eastern regions.

Providing everyday services for the population is no small thing, no matter of secondary importance. The mood of people and the productivity of their labor depend in large measure on the extent of amenities in their daily lives, on the standard of services provided them. The way to improve their lives is to establish highly efficient, technologically up-to-date stores, dining rooms, everyday-service combines and meal-preparation factories.

Our party's policy is pervaded with the great communist idea: Everything in the name of man, for the benefit of man! (Prolonged applause.)

Ought we to pursue the task of further improving the material living standards of the working people solely through direct wage raises and price reductions? To be sure, the wage will for a long time continue to be the principal form of material incentive for workers, and will depend on their labor contribution to social production. But at the same time the Soviet people are deriving an ever greater portion of their material and cultural benefits from public sources.

A huge share of the working people's requirements is already being met out of public funds at the present time. In 1940 payments and benefits received by the population out of public funds came to 4,200,000,000 rubles, whereas in 1960 the figure was 24,500,000,000 rubles. Under the seven-year plan—allowing for adjustments in it—the public consumption funds will grow to as much as 40,000,000,000 rubles in 1965. More than 20,000,000 pensioners are now being maintained out of these funds; about 4,000,000 students in higher, secondary and technical vocational schools are being provided with state stipends and dormitory accommodations; more than 600,000 boarding school pupils are being maintained for the most part at state expense. More than 7,000,000 workers, collective farmers and office employees and their children take vacations and receive treatment in sanatoriums, rest homes, and Young Pioneer camps each year on funds that come out of social insurance and from the collective farms. Some 7,000,000 mothers receive allowances from the state. This is what public funds mean! (Applause.)

Comrades! We are rightly proud that Soviet society has become the most highly educated society in the world and that Soviet science has come to occupy a leading place in major fields of knowledge.

When the first Soviet artificial earth satellite orbited our planet, a special commission was set up in the United States to investigate the school situation. Comparing schooling in the U.S.A. and the U.S.S.R., the commission concluded that the Soviet system was superior. But it was just at that time that our party began reorganizing the schools so that they would provide pupils with an even more solid foundation of knowledge and would link the schools still closer to life.

The experience of reorganizing the schools has confirmed the timeliness and validity of the Party's measures. On the whole, the schools now have stronger ties with life and with production, and the labor training of the pupils has improved. Secondary school graduates are doing good work in the national economy. The number of schools for working and rural youth is growing year by year, and hundreds of thousands of young people are pursuing their studies without leaving their jobs.

A big job has been done. But there have been cases of bureaucratic attitudes toward the matter of school reorganization. Not all workers in education have as yet understood the tasks in the field of polytechnical education.

New types of educational institutions—boarding schools and extended-day schools and groups—have been established in our country and have met with popular approval. The boarding schools and extended-day schools and groups have about 1,500,000 pupils; 2,500,000 children will be attending the boarding schools alone by 1965.

Universal compulsory eight-year schooling has been introduced in the Soviet Union, and conditions have been created so that all who wish to receive a complete secondary education can do so. The next task in the field of public education is to move on to universal secondary education.

The rearing of the man of communist society places new and higher demands upon the schools. The schools must keep up with the rapid development of modern science and industry. The training of pedagogical cadres must be expanded so that there are enough to staff all schools, and the teacher must be the object of general consideration and respect. Enterprises and collective farms must help the schools to reorganize and the students to acquire a good background of knowledge and to learn needed vocations. We must build more schools and do away entirely with shifts. This is a big task, considering that in 1965 there will be about 43,000,000 children in school.

The development of higher and specialized secondary education and vocational training is proceeding in close interconnection with the school reorganization. Here too, as we know, the task has been set of bringing schooling closer to life and to production. More than half the students admitted this year to the day-time branches of the higher schools have had practical work experience. Approximately 500,000 specialists with higher education have been trained during the past five years through the system of evening and correspondence education.

The Soviet Union is training three times as many engineers as the United States, while the total number of persons engaged in mental work in our country is more than 20,000,000! When these figures were published they proved highly disquieting to the adversaries of socialism, who had often portrayed our society as backward and lacking in culture. They are now being forced to make an agonizing reappraisal of values and, not infrequently, to resort outright to stupid inventions. To bamboozle people they have given currency to the notion that the more educated people there are in the Soviet Union, the greater the chance that Soviet people will turn their backs on communism. (Stir in the hall.)

What answer can we make to the ideologists of capitalism? Let them demand of their governments larger appropriations for public education—for if you follow their logic, the more educated a society is, the more firmly it cleaves to capitalism. But not even those who make up these fables believe them any longer. (Applause.) Communism offers knowledge to all; from the masses' knowledge, from their high level of culture, it derives strength and confidence for its successful onward march! (Prolonged applause.)

The flourishing of Soviet science is striking evidence of this. We have more than 350,000 scientific workers. There are some 4000 scientific institutions in the country, and, what is especially noteworthy, in the past five or six years there has been a sharp increase in the number of scientific institutions in the Union republics. A big role in developing scientific research in the eastern part of the country is being played by the Academy of Sciences' Siberian Division.

Soviet scientists and scholars are creditably discharging their duty to their homeland. Our scientists are widely celebrated for their achievements in the development of physics, mathematics and cybernetics, in the creation of high-speed computers, in the working out of the chemical theory of chain reactions and of the chemistry of polymers, in biology, in the discovery and prospecting of major mineral deposits, in the development of automation and telemechanics, radio engineering and electronics, metallurgy, machine building and other fields of science. Soviet scholars in the field of the social sciences also have a number of achievements to their credit.

Soviet scientists are engaged on a broad front in an effort to solve one of the most important problems of the day—to accomplish a controlled thermonuclear reaction. The work done by Soviet scientists and their cooperation with the scientists of other nations have already won recognition all over the world. The further progress of thermonuclear research in our country will contribute to the achievement of the earliest peaceful use of thermonuclear energy for the benefit of all mankind. A brilliant new age in the evolution of mankind's scientific knowledge was ushered in by the successes of our science in exploring outer space. The Soviet Union launched the world's first artificial earth satellite. Soviet space rockets were the first to overcome the force of earth's gravity and set out on interplanetary pathways. We were the first to put our pennant on the moon and to photograph the moon's reverse side. The first men to dare forsake the cradle in which they were nurtured—earth—and to make triumphal space flights were citizens of the Soviet Union, Yury Alexeyevich Gagarin and German Stepanovich Titov, who are delegates to the 22nd Party Congress! (Stormy, prolonged applause.)

How can we help priding ourselves on the great accomplishments of Soviet science! From this lofty tribune allow me to tender heartfelt thanks, comrades, to all Soviet scientists and wish them big new creative victories for the glory of the Soviet fatherland and in the name of the triumph of communism! (Prolonged applause.)

The Soviet Union's successes in conquering space drove the capitalist world to revise its attitude toward the achievements of socialist society, toward the development of science and industry in the U.S.S.R. The American statesman Chester Bowles declared, for example, that "before the first Soviet sputnik hardly anyone questioned America's industrial, military and scientific superiority. Suddenly the sputnik appeared, circling the earth, and millions of people began to ask themselves:

Can it be that communism is after all destined to gain the victory?" (Stir in the hall. Applause.)

It is so destined, Mr. Bowles, it is! Even Wernher von Braun, the German rocket expert who is now working in the United States and who thinks as you do, gives the following answer to this question: "On the basis of their philosophy the Russians have developed the kind of system that assures them these successes. Unfortunately, our system does not permit us to match Russia's successes." Rather well stated, comrades! (Applause.)

Now that our country is carrying into effect the magnificent plans for building communism, Soviet science is faced with new and even grander tasks. Scientific research must be pursued more purposefully and science must open its doors wider to young people. Our task is to lead the world in all the major fields of science and technology. (Prolonged applause.)

Comrades! Soviet literature and art have won great and enduring prestige throughout the world for the richness of their ideological content. The artistic skill of Soviet writers, composers, painters and workers in the motion pictures and the theater has won high recognition. The past few years have seen the production of new works of literature and art that reflect socialist reality truthfully and vividly.

The achievements and traditions of our arts are of enormous significance; they mark an important stage in the artistic evolution of mankind. The experience of our country has proved that only under socialism are the most favorable opportunities created for the flowering of free artistic creativity and for active participation by the masses in the creation of cultural values. Soviet art is enriching the spiritual treasure house of all humanity and is paving the way for the triumph of communist culture.

V. I. Lenin pointed out that the road to a unified culture for communist society lay through the flowering of the national cultures of all peoples who had gained their freedom from capitalist oppression. In the process of artistic association within the community of socialist nations new features arise and develop and exert a mutually beneficial effect, features common to Soviet culture as a whole. Our task is to give solicitous support to the international unity of socialist cultures and to further its development. The people are confidently waiting for writers and people in the arts to produce new works in which our heroic epoch of the revolutionary transformation of society will find fitting embodiment. The Party's premise is that art is called upon to educate people first and foremost on the basis of positive models in life, to educate people in the spirit of communism. The strength of Soviet literature and art, of the method of socialist realism, lies in the truthful reflection of the most important and decisive elements of reality. Under present conditions serious attention must be given to the esthetic education of all Soviet people, to the molding of their artistic tastes, and a comprehensive struggle must be launched on bad taste however it may manifest itself—in formalist enthusiasms or in philistine notions of "the beautiful" in life and in everyday surroundings.

That which is most beautiful is man's labor, and there is no task nobler than to portray man the toiler, the new man—the richness of his spiritual interests, his struggle against the old, the moribund. We must give Soviet people absorbing works that reveal the romance of communist labor, that cultivate initiative and perseverance in the achievement of the goal.

Our party is confident that Soviet literature and art will continue to be the Soviet people's reliable weapon and their kindly and sensible counselor on all aspects of their lives! (Applause.)

6. The Evolution of Socialist Relations Into Communist Ones. The Development of Soviet Democracy. Socialism and the Freedom of the Individual. Comrades! In translating the decisions of the 20th Congress into action, the Party has given a great deal of attention to the development and improvement of socialist production relations and other social relations. Our party sees this as the main way of effecting the transition to communist social relations—the most perfect type of relations between free, comprehensively developed people with a high degree of political consciousness, relations based on friendship and comradeship. Recall that the first international workers' organization, formed under the leadership of K. Marx, was called the International Workingmen's Association. The word "associate" [the Russian word is tovarishch, which also means "comrade"—Trans.] connotes identity of views, equality, fraternity, respect and cooperation.

The principle that operates under socialism is "From each according to his ability, to each according to his work." In order to move on to the communist principle "From each according to his ability, to each according to his needs" time and certain specific conditions are necessary. The principles of communism are noble, beautiful and alluring! We would all like to see them come into our lives as soon as possible.

Why, then, do we not introduce them right away, why does the Party provide for two decades to build communist society in its basic outlines? Are we not dragging out the time needed to realize these communist principles? No, comrades, we are not! Of course we would like to introduce these principles sooner, but the subjective wish is not enough. We must proceed on the basis of objective conditions, must take the laws of social development into consideration.

The transition to communist principles is practicable, but not before the material and technical base has been created, not before the people have reached a high level of political consciousness and the principles of socialism have completely evolved and revealed their progressive potentialities to the fullest degree. There is no other path to communist social relations than through the development and perfection of socialist relations.

In recent years the Party has carried out important socioeconomic measures in all spheres of Soviet life. They are of revolutionary significance not only because they have helped strengthen our material and technical base but also because they have played an important role in the development of social relations and in bringing the two forms of socialist property still closer together.

The shoots of new features in the character of labor and in relations among industrial workers are more and more clearly visible. The most important thing is that ever wider sections of the working people are growing accustomed to working conscientiously, to the full extent of their powers and capabilities. For many Soviet people, work today is no longer simply a means of making a living but a public calling, a moral obligation. Recall the example of Valentina Gaganova, who is now here in the presidium of this Congress. It was not selfish aims that guided her when she voluntarily shifted from an advanced sector to a lagging one but a high degree of political awareness and her ideological dedication to our common cause. Gaganova's lead was followed by many other working people.

The Party has encouraged and will continue to encourage the desire of Soviet people to learn to work and live in a communist way. We attach great importance to the movement of Communist Labor Collectives and Shock Workers. There can be no doubt but that as time goes on life will prompt the appearance of even better forms of socialist competition.

Another sphere in which social relations have been developing vigorously is in the distribution of material and cultural benefits. In what has this manifested itself?

First of all, in the further development of the socialist principle of distribution according to work as the paramount precondition for transition to the communist principle of distribution according to needs. The Party has consistently implemented the principle of personal material incentive and has emphatically opposed wage leveling. We start from the position that until an abundance of material goods has been created and labor has become a prime necessity of life for every individual, there are no grounds for giving up the socialist principle of distribution, for relaxing control by society and the state over the measure of labor and the measure of consumption.

The entire experience of socialist construction in our country has served to confirm the soundness of Lenin's principle of material incentive. Lenin's genius lay in his ability to analyze social phenomena deeply and draw profound generalizations from them, and to reach sound decisions for each specific period of socialist construction.

Recall how V. I. Lenin, with his inherent insight and daring, called for a fundamental revision of policy just as soon as the Civil War had ended, and veered sharply from the policy of War Communism to the New Economic Policy.

The transition to the New Economic Policy was not easy and caused difficulty in the Party itself. There were even Communists who left the Party because of their inability to grasp the essence of the New Economic Policy. V. I. Lenin clearly perceived the complexity of the situation, but he firmly proceeded to inaugurate NEP, and the Party as a whole backed up Lenin's policy in the fight for the victory of socialism. Had not Lenin's line prevailed at that time, we would have been unable to accomplish the task of building socialism. It was a matter of strengthening the alliance between the working class and the peasantry, of providing all toilers of town and countryside with a material stake in the development of the economy, in socialist construction. Instead of the leveling principle, the principle was established that people should be paid according to the quantity and quality of their output.

V. I. Lenin teaches us to be realists in our policy. You can paint the rosiest prospects, schedule the highest rates of economic development, but unless the working people themselves appreciate the necessity of reconstructing society, unless they have a material incentive, the plans that have been projected will fail to materialize. To ignore the principle of material incentive is to be ruled by subjective considerations in managing affairs, to skip over a stage, which means to wreck the cause of socialist and communist construction.

We must constantly learn from V. I. Lenin how to work with people as they are. It does not do to be subjectivists in politics, to operate by the rule "I do as I please." We must look closely at the life of the people, must study it, must heed the voice of the people. In the combination of material and ideological incentives the Party sees the true road that is leading us and will necessarily bring us to the creation of abundance and to distribution according to need, to the victory of communist labor.

The concept of abundance as the limitless growth of personal property is not ours; it is a concept alien to communism. The worker's personal ownership of a number of objects, as a form of personal consumption, does not conflict with communist construction as long as it remains within sensible limits and does not become an end in itself. But under certain conditions exaggeration of the importance of personal property can, and often does, turn into a brake on social progress, into fertile soil for the growth of private-property mores; it can lead to petit-bourgeois degeneration. It happens that things gain the upper hand over a person and he becomes a slave to them.

Communists reject the morality of bourgeois society, where the concept of "mine" is the sovereign principle and the wealth of some is possible only at the cost of the ruin of others, where the corrupting psychology of egoism, money-grubbing, lust for wealth is fostered. Against the world of private ownership the Communists set the world of public ownership, and against bourgeois individualism they set the principle of comradeship and collectivism.

The progress of all aspects of socialist production relations is leading as a natural development to the gradual effacement of distinctions between town and countryside, between classes and social groups in Soviet society, and to the extension and consolidation of communist principles in relations between workers, peasants and the intelligentsia. The two friendly classes of our society, the working class and the collective farm peasantry, are drawing closer and closer together, their unbreakable alliance is growing stronger. The Soviet peasantry are approaching the working class in the level of their skills, in their working conditions and in their cultural and technical levels. The peasants and workers enjoy the same political rights, and they have common basic interests. The distinctions between the working class and the peasantry have been eliminated in their major, decisive aspects; the final eradication of class differences will now proceed at an ever-faster pace.

The essential differences between mental and physical labor are being eliminated on the basis of technological progress and the raising of the cultural and technical levels of the working people. The labor of worker and collective farmer, armed with up-to-date machinery and knowledge, incorporates elements of both physical and mental labor. Today 40% of the workers and more than 23% of the collective farmers have a secondary or higher education. In many cases it is already hard to tell a leading worker from an engineer, a leading collective farmer from an agronomist.

As matters stand today, therefore, class relationships in our country have entered a new stage in their evolution. Proletarian democracy is developing into a socialist democracy of all the people. It gives us great satisfaction to note that we are today close to realizing the goal set by V. I. Lenin, which was to draw all citizens without exception into the performance of government functions. Tens of millions of Soviet people are participating in the management of the country's affairs as members of Soviets and their committees and of the elective bodies of cooperatives and of trade union, Young Communist League and other public organizations and are carrying out public assignments.

Every Soviet person should take an active part in managing public affairs—this is our slogan, our task. (Applause.)

While regarding the development of state agencies and the transformation of the Soviets of Working People's Deputies into agencies of public self-government as the tasks of uppermost importance, our party will at the same time continue its course of handing over an ever greater number of government functions to public organizations. It is important, however, to take into account the level of development of the public organizations themselves, how much their independent activity has grown. It is not a formal change of signboards that we want but substantive transformations.

The transfer of many important government functions to public organizations and the gradual evolution of persuasion and education into the basic method of regulating the life of Soviet society do not and cannot imply a relaxation of control over strict observance of the norms of Soviet law, labor discipline and everyday living. We must instill a respect for Soviet laws. Both the power of the law and the power of public action, public influence, must be used to the full.

Our party has been working and will continue to work on the development of social relations in every province of life. Not only economics and politics but everyday life, culture, psychology and people's consciousness offer a field for the active shaping of new relations—relations of friendship, comradeship, mutual aid and collectivism. The true freedom and comprehensive flourishing of the individual, the harmonious coupling of personal interests with the interests of society as a whole are possible only in a socialist society, on the basis of new relations between people.

Our ideological adversaries incessantly repeat their allegation that communism inevitably creates conflict between the individual and society, leads to the repression of the individual. The enemies of socialism are even quite willing to concede our gains in the sphere of material production, but they are quick to contend that we scored these gains by infringing human freedom and rights. The imperialists gauge ideas by their own yardstick, and they see freedom of the individual as meaning the anarchic opposition of the personal to the public, of the private individual to the collective. They know only one ethic: "Either claw your way or sink into the mud."

The social system that represents the criterion of genuine freedom and happiness is one that frees man from the yoke of exploitation, accords him broad democratic rights, assures him a chance of proper living conditions, gives him confidence in the future, unlocks his individual aptitudes and talents and makes him keenly aware that his labor is of benefit to the whole of society. Socialism is just such a social system. Of all the values created by the socialist system, the greatest is the new man, the active builder of communism. The Soviet people are providing more and more proof of what the truly free man of the new world is capable of. (Applause.)

The ideologists of imperialism call the world of capitalism the "free world." But what has capitalism to set against the Soviet Union's genuine freedom, economic growth, rising living standard and cultural level, and flourishing of the individual? Freedom for the rich to exploit and rob the poor, "freedom" from work for millions of people, rising taxes, the runaway arms race, racial discrimination, the dictatorship of the moneybags, the banning of democratic organizations? What sort of free world is this? No, this is not a free world, it is a world of slavery and exploitation!

The ideologists of imperialism term the capitalist countries "open societies" and the Soviet Union a "closed society." We agree. Our socialist state is indeed closed to exploitation and plunder at the hands of monopoly capital, to unemployment, to banditry, to the corrupting ideology of decadence. The imperialist gentry would of course like to see socialist society open to espionage activity. But Soviet society is closed, shut tight, to subversive activity against socialism! (Applause.)

Our society is open to those people who come to us from abroad with open hearts. It is open to honest trade, to scientific, technical and cultural exchanges, to the exchange of truthful information. If it's an iron curtain we're talking about, where it really exists is in the world of capitalism, which, though dubbing itself the "free world," every now and then fearfully slams its gates shut to Soviet people, one moment to our cooks, the next to our chess players. There was a case where one state, which calls itself the "most open," was afraid to let in Soviet dancers. Can they really have feared that Russian folk dancing might shake the foundations of the capitalist world?! (Stir in the hall.)

We have long proposed to the capitalist world that we compete not in an arms race but in improving the working people's lives. We are confident that capitalism cannot stand up under that kind of competition! We are confident that in the end all peoples will make the correct choice, will give their preference to the truly free world of communism and turn their backs on the so-called "free world" of capitalism. (Applause.)

***

Comrades! When the Party mapped the major measures for expanding our country's economy, bourgeois politicians and economists had quite a good deal to say about how the Communists were sacrificing the people's vital interests to heavy industry, about how production in the Soviet Union exists only for production's sake. What a vicious libel on socialism! Production not for the sake of production but for the sake of man is the sacred principle governing the activities of the Party and the Soviet state. Now everyone, even the most incorrigible skeptic and doubter, can once more see for himself that our party always honors its pledges to the people. (Applause.)

In the area of domestic policy, our party is setting Communists and the Soviet people the following tasks for the next few years:

1. The entire effort of the people must be directed toward fulfillment and overfulfillment of the seven-year plan—an important stage in the creation of the material and technical base for communism. We must continue to raise the level of material production and to keep the country's defenses up to the mark. As we seize new heights in the economic development of the Soviet homeland, we should bear in mind that only steady progress will assure us complete superiority and bring closer the day of our victory in the peaceful economic competition with capitalism.

2. We must strive to accelerate technical progress in all branches of socialist industry without exception. We must move forward particularly in power engineering, chemistry, machine building, metallurgy and the fuel industry. We must specialize enterprises on a broader scale, see to the integrated mechanization and automation of production processes and apply the achievements of modern science and technology and the experience of innovators more rapidly in production. Steady growth of labor productivity and reduction of production costs and an improvement in the quality of output must become law for all Soviet enterprises.

3. We must strive for a level of industrial and agricultural development that will enable us to meet the public's demand for manufactured goods and foodstuffs ever more fully. Funds that accumulate as a result of overfulfillment of industrial output plans should be channeled primarily into agriculture, light industry, the food industry and other consumer goods industries.

4. The development of agriculture is a matter for the whole Party, for the people as a whole. Party and Soviet agencies are obliged to concern themselves with farm production on a day-to-day basis and make full use of the experience of advanced collective and state farms. We must make sure that the seven-year-plan assignments for the production and procurement of grain, cotton, sugar beets, oil-bearing crops, tea and other crops and of meat, milk, wool, eggs and other farm products are met and exceeded.

5. We must advance along the entire front of cultural and social development. There must be continuous progress in Soviet science, public education, literature and art. We must raise the working people's living standards, complete the adjustment of wages and the planned measures for shortening the working day and week, maintain a rapid pace in housing construction, and improve the pension system, trade, public catering, and medical and everyday services for the working people.

Our country is experiencing a great upsurge of creative effort. All the many nationalities of the Soviet Union look upon the building of communism as a cause near and dear to them and are working hand in hand and making invaluable contributions toward our common victory. Consciousness of the grandeur of the tasks we pursue is multiplying the efforts of Soviet people tenfold, causing them to be more exacting of themselves and more intolerant of shortcomings, stagnation and inertia. We must take maximum advantage of the enormous motive forces inherent in the socialist system. (Prolonged applause.)

III. THE LENINIST PARTY IS THE ORGANIZER OF THE STRUGGLE FOR THE VICTORY OF COMMUNISM.—Comrades! Our great successes in the fields of both foreign and domestic policy have been achieved through the steady and consistent implementation of the Party's Leninist general line, which was given profound expression in the historic decisions of the 20th Congress. The Central Committee considers it necessary to report that the political course of the 20th Congress has triumphed completely. Dictated by life itself and filled with Leninist revolutionary creativity, it has become the cause of all our Soviet people. The Party has strengthened its ties with the people still further and, relying on their mighty energy, has further exalted the Soviet Union. (Stormy applause.)

The extraordinary 21st Congress was a major milestone. Its historical significance is that it adopted the seven-year plan for the development of the national economy and announced the entry of the Soviet Union into the period of the full-scale building of communism.

The 22nd Party Congress is destined to play a world-historic role: It will consider and adopt the new Party Program, a program for building a communist society that will become the victory banner and ideological weapon of the Party and the people in the struggle for the triumph of communism. (Stormy applause.)

The Leninist party of Communists—flesh of the flesh of the working class and all working people, their brain, their heart, the voice of their vital interests and their revolutionary will—has traveled a long, difficult and glorious road. There is no other party in the world that in the years of its existence has achieved so many great victories in the transformation of society. (Prolonged applause.) You remember the prophetic words of Vladimir Ilyich Lenin: "Give us an organization of revolutionaries and we will turn Russia upside down!" Sixty years have passed since those times. The whole world now sees that the Bolsheviks really did turn the country upside down. Former tsarist Russia has been transformed from a backward capitalist country into a mighty and flourishing Soviet state. (Stormy applause.) And today we cordially greet the old guard of Bolsheviks who for decades waged a brave revolutionary struggle for the happiness of the peoples and for socialism. We warmly greet the glorious representatives of this old guard who have come as elected delegates to the 22nd Party Congress! (Prolonged applause.)

Our party is justly proud that it has successfully implemented its first and second Programs. Our Leninist party has achieved the complete and final victory of socialism in the Land of Soviets and has honorably performed both its national task and its international duty to the proletarians of all countries, to the international Communist movement! (Prolonged applause.)

In the new Party Program, the draft of which was warmly approved by the Party and the entire Soviet people during the days of preparation for the Congress, the building of a communist society is posed as the main and immediate practical task. Besides the new Program, the Congress will also consider the draft of the new Party Statutes, on which Comrade F. R. Kozlov will deliver a report. We have always adhered and now adhere to Lenin's teachings on the unbreakable unity of the Party Program and the Party Statutes. The organizational principles contained in the Statutes must assure successful fulfillment of the Program and strengthen the unity and solidarity of the Party, the militant vanguard of the Soviet people in the struggle for communism! (Applause.)

1. Overcoming the Consequences of the Cult of the Individual. Developing Leninist Norms of Party Life and Principles of Leadership. Increasing the Party's Combat Readiness.—Comrades! The restoration and further development of the Leninist norms of Party life and principles of leadership is a highly important aspect of the activities of our party during the period covered by the report. The 20th Congress, by condemning the cult of the individual, which is alien to the spirit of Marxism-Leninism, opened a broad vista for the creative forces of the Party and the people and furthered the expansion and strengthening of the Party's ties with the people and the increasing of its combat readiness.

On the eve of the 20th Congress the question was this: Either the Party would openly and in a Leninist manner condemn the errors and distortions committed during the period of the cult of J. V. Stalin and reject those methods of Party and state leadership that had become an impediment to progress, or the forces that had chained themselves to the old and were resisting everything new and creative would gain the upper hand in the Party. This is exactly how serious the problem was.

Was it necessary to make such sharp and frank criticism of the major errors and the serious consequences of the cult of the individual?

Yes, it was necessary. After the inveterate enemy and adventurer Beria had been unmasked, a careful analysis and profound study of a number of documents was made, as a result of which there were fully revealed to the Central Committee instances of the grossest violations of socialist legality, abuses of power, instances of arbitrary action and repression against many honest people, including outstanding figures in the Party and the Soviet state. The Central Committee, profoundly aware of its responsibility to the Party and the people, could not enter upon a course of concealing or glossing over the errors and distortions that had taken place in the past. Following Lenin's behests, the Central Committee decided to tell the truth about the abuses of power during the period of the cult of the individual. This was the inner moral requirement and obligation of the Party and its leadership. It was a correct decision. It was of enormous importance for the fate of the Party and for the building of communism. (Prolonged applause.)

Vladimir Ilyich Lenin called upon the Party not to conceal mistakes but to criticize and correct them openly. "The attitude of a political party toward its errors," he wrote, "is one of the most important and truest criteria of the seriousness of the party and of its actual performance of its duties to its class and to the masses of working people. To admit a mistake openly, to ascertain its causes, to analyze the situation that gave rise to it and to discuss attentively the means for correcting it—this is the sign of a serious party, this is the fulfillment of its obligations, this is the rearing and training of the class, and later of the masses." ("Works" [in Russian], Vol. XXXI, p. 39.) (Applause.)

What would have happened to the Party and the country had the cult of the individual not been condemned, had its harmful consequences not been overcome and had the Leninist principles of Party and state activity not been restored? This would have threatened to cut the Party off from the masses and the people, to cause serious violation of Soviet democracy and revolutionary legality, to slow down the country's economic development and to reduce the rate of communist construction and, consequently, to detract from the well-being of the working people. In the field of international relations it would have led to a weaker position for the Soviet Union in the world arena and to a worsening of relations with other countries, which would have been fraught with serious consequences. This is why the criticism of the cult of the individual and the overcoming of its consequences was of great political and practical importance. (Applause.)

Marxism-Leninism has always sternly condemned any evidence of the cult of the individual and has considered it alien to the spirit of the proletarian revolutionary movement, alien to the spirit of communism. Marx, Engels and Lenin saw the people as the true creator of history; they emphasized the leading and organizational role of the party of the working class. Marxism-Leninism does not deny the importance of leaders and chiefs of the working class, but it is decisively against the exaltation and certainly against the deification of any person. The exaltation of one individual inevitably pushes the Party and the people into the background and reduces their role and importance.

The Soviet people, through labors and heroic struggle under the leadership of the Party, have achieved great successes in socialist construction. They gained an outstanding victory in the Great Patriotic War against fascism. But, as you remember, all the successes and victories gained by the Party and the people were ascribed during the period of the cult of the individual to one man. Of course J. V. Stalin did make great contributions to the Party and the Communist movement, and we give him his due. However, it was incorrect to associate all the victories of the Party and the people with the name of one man. This was a gross distortion of the true state of affairs. (Applause.)

The 20th Congress restored justice, eliminated distortions and emphasized the great role of the people, and the role of the Party as the vanguard of the working class and all the people and as the leading and guiding force in the struggle for communism. The Congress instructed the Central Committee to consistently implement measures that would ensure that the cult of the individual was completely overcome, that would eliminate its consequences in all fields of Party, state and ideological work and that would bring about strict observance of the norms of Party life and the principle of collective leadership elaborated by Vladimir Ilyich Lenin. (Prolonged applause.)

In its principled and decisive criticism of the cult of the individual our party was guided by the teachings of Vladimir Ilyich Lenin and by his testament. It is known that while Lenin valued Stalin, he also perceived his shortcomings, even vices. In December, 1922—i.e., soon after Stalin's election as General Secretary of the Central Committee—Vladimir Ilyich, concerned for the fate of the Party and the Soviet state, wrote in a letter to the regular Party Congress:

"Having become General Secretary, Comrade Stalin has acquired immense power, and I am not sure he will always know how to use this power with sufficient caution.***Stalin is too rude, and this failing, which is quite tolerable in our midst and in relations among us Communists, becomes intolerable in the office of General Secretary. Therefore, I propose to the comrades that they think of a way of removing Stalin from this post and appointing to it another person who in all other respects differs from Comrade Stalin in one advantage alone, namely, that he be more tolerant, more loyal, more courteous and more considerate to comrades, less capricious, etc."

As you see, Vladimir Ilyich understood very well that Stalin's negative qualities could do great harm to the Party and the state. Unfortunately, Lenin's warning and advice were not heeded in time, and as a result the Party and the country had to live through a good many difficulties that were due to the cult of the individual. At the 20th Congress the Party severely criticized the cult of the individual. In carrying out the decisions of the Congress, it overcame the distortions and errors and drew up measures that would preclude the possibility of such phenomena in the future. This was a bold decision, and was new evidence of the political maturity of our party and its Central Committee. (Stormy, prolonged applause.)

Of course, the Party was aware that the disclosure of the errors, distortions and abuses of power might arouse a certain feeling of bitterness and even dissatisfaction in Party ranks and among the people, that it might entail certain costs and minuses and create temporary difficulties for the Communist Party of the Soviet Union and the fraternal Marxist-Leninist parties. But the Party boldly met the difficulties head on, and it honestly and frankly told the people the whole truth, with profound faith that the line it had taken would be correctly understood by the people. The Party was not mistaken. Our progress along the road to communism became faster. Now we can straighten our backs more freely, breathe easier and see more clearly. The whole internal life of the country is developing rapidly. Our industry, agriculture, science and culture have conquered great new frontiers. As we know, millions of Soviet people are taking a more and more active part in the management of state and public affairs.

Soviet Communists can say with pride: We have not sullied the honor and dignity of the Leninist Party; its authority has grown immeasurably and the international Communist movement has climbed to a new and higher stage. Our party is now united and monolithic as never before! (Stormy, prolonged applause.)

The Leninist course expressed by the 20th Congress was at first carried out against the fierce resistance of anti-Party elements, zealous partisans of the methods and practices prevailing under the cult of the individual, revisionists and dogmatists. The factionalist anti-Party group consisting of Molotov, Kaganovich, Malenkov, Voroshilov, Bulganin, Pervukhin and Saburov, and Shepilov, who joined them, came out against the Party's Leninist course.

At first the strong resistance to the Party's line on condemning the cult of the individual, fostering inner-Party democracy, condemning and rectifying all abuses of power, and exposing the individuals guilty of repression was rejected by Molotov, Kaganovich, Malenkov and Voroshilov. Their stand in this matter was no accident. They bear personal responsibility for many mass repressions against Party, Soviet, economic, military and Y.C.L. cadres and for other similar manifestations that took place during the period of the cult of the individual. At first this group was only an insignificant minority in the Presidium of the Central Committee.

But when the Party launched the struggle to restore Leninist norms of Party and state life, when it set about such urgent tasks as developing the virgin lands, reorganizing the management of industry and construction, enlarging the rights of the Union republics, improving the well-being of Soviet people, and restoring revolutionary legality, the factional group activized its anti-Party subversive work and began to recruit supporters in the Central Committee Presidium. It added Bulganin, Pervukhin and Saburov, and Shepilov joined them. Realizing that they had succeeded in throwing together an arithmetical majority in the Presidium, the participants in the anti-Party group went into open attack, seeking to change the policy in the Party and the country—the policy set forth by the 20th Party Congress.

Having reached agreement at their secret gatherings, the factionalists demanded an extraordinary meeting of the Presidium. They counted on carrying out their anti-Party designs, on seizing the leadership of the Party and country. The anti-Party group wanted to confront the members of the Central Committee and the whole Party with a fait accompli.

But the factionalists miscalculated. Members of the Central Committee who were then in Moscow, learning of the factional actions of the anti-Party group within the Presidium, demanded the immediate calling of a Central Committee plenary session.

The Central Committee plenary session, held in June, 1957, resolutely exposed the anti-Party group and routed it ideologically. The June plenary session demonstrated the political maturity, monolithic unity and close cohesion of the Central Committee on the basis of the Leninist line of the 20th Congress. (Stormy applause.) Ideologically routed in the course of the plenary session and faced with unanimous condemnation by the Central Committee session, the participants in the anti-Party group came forth with the confession that they had conspired and with an admission of the harmfulness of their anti-Party activity. Comrade Voroshilov came forth at the plenary session with an admission of his mistakes, saying that "the factionalists misled" him and that he fully recognized his errors and firmly condemned them, together with the whole subversive work of the anti-Party group.

As you know, the resolution of the Central Committee plenary session on the anti-Party group was adopted unanimously; the participants in the anti-Party group also voted for it, except Molotov, who abstained from voting. Later, at a primary Party organization's discussion of the results of the plenary session, Molotov too declared that he considered the plenary session's decision correct and accepted it.

The struggle against the anti-Party group was a struggle of principle, a sharp political struggle, a struggle between the new and the old. The issue was whether our party would continue to carry out the Leninist policy set forth by the 20th Congress or whether the methods of the period of the cult of the individual, methods condemned by the whole Party, would be revived.

This struggle was complicated by the fact that the Party line, the course set by the 20th Congress, was opposed by a group of political leaders including persons who had long held prominent positions in the Party and state. There have been many public figures in history who proved themselves at certain periods in their lives and played a notable role but then came to a standstill, as it were, and even began gradually to fade out.

Such phenomena happen for various reasons: One person's powers deteriorate; another loses touch with life, becomes conceited, does not work; a third proves an unprincipled, spineless turncoat without stanchness in the struggle for the cause of the Party. Meantime, in the course of the struggle new political figures arise who oppose everything that hampers the development of the new and who overcome the resistance of the old. What happens is something like the phenomenon that astronomers call light from extinct stars. Some very distant stars seem to continue to shine even though they have actually been extinct for a long time. The trouble with some people who have found themselves in the position of stars on the public horizon is that they think they are continuing to radiate light although they have long since turned into dying embers. This is what happened to some political figures who fell into the path of factional anti-Party struggle. (Stormy applause.)

The decisions of the June plenary session of the Central Committee were unanimously approved by our whole party, by the entire Soviet people. Somewhat later, in October, 1957, a plenary session of the Party Central Committee firmly rebuffed attempts by the former Minister of Defense, Zhukov, to take an adventurist path and to pursue a policy of separating the armed forces from the Party, of opposing the Soviet Army to the Party leadership. By casting aside the bankrupt factionalists and scheming careerists, the Party rallied its ranks closer, strengthened its ties with the people and mobilized all forces for the successful implementation of its general line. (Prolonged applause.)

The policy of the 20th Congress encountered ardent approval from the international Communist movement, from the fraternal Marxist-Leninist parties. This was reflected in the decisions of Congresses and other materials of the fraternal parties and in the documents of the conferences of representatives of Communist and Workers' Parties in 1957 and 1960.

Thus the statement of the Moscow conference of 1960 pointed out that "the historic decisions of the 20th Congress of the C.P.S.U.***initiated a new stage in the international Communist movement and contributed to its further development on the basis of Marxism-Leninism."*

At the same time it should be noted that, as it later turned out, our party's policy of overcoming the harmful effects of the cult of the individual did not meet with due understanding from the leaders of the Albanian Party of Labor; indeed, they began to conduct a struggle against this policy.

Everyone knows that until recently the relations between the Soviet Union and the People's Republic of Albania and between the Communist Party of the Soviet Union and the Albanian Party of Labor were friendly and good. The peoples of our country gave Albania comprehensive, disinterested help in developing its economy, in socialist construction. We sincerely wanted and want to see Albania a flourishing socialist republic and its people happy and enjoying all the benefits of the new life.

For many years the Albanian leaders signified their complete unity of views with the Central Committee of our party and the Soviet government on all questions of the international Communist movement. They repeatedly declared their support of the 20th Congress policy. Enver Hoxha, First Secretary of the Central Committee of the Albanian Party of Labor, stated this in his speeches at the 20th and 21st Congresses of our party. At the Third Congress of the Albanian Party of Labor, held soon after the 20th Congress, the criticism of the cult of the individual as well as measures to overcome its harmful con-

*Current Digest of the Soviet Press, Vol. XII, No. 49, p. 8.

sequences were fully and completely approved.

We Soviet people believed the Albanian leaders and considered that mutual understanding and unity of views existed between our party and the Albanian Party of Labor.

The facts show, however, that recently the Albanian leaders, despite their former declarations and the decisions of their own Party Congress, sharply changed political course without any excuse and took the path of acute deterioration of relations with our party, with the Soviet Union. They began to depart from the commonly agreed line of the whole world Communist movement on the major questions of our times, something which became particularly manifest from the middle of last year.

Now the Albanian leaders do not conceal the fact that they do not like the course, taken by our party, of firmly overcoming the harmful consequences of the Stalin cult, of sharply condemning the abuse of power, of restoring Leninist norms of Party and state life.

Evidently the Albanian leaders in their hearts disagreed with the conclusions of the 1957 and 1960 conferences of fraternal parties, which, as everyone knows, approved the decisions of the 20th Congress and our party's policy of overcoming the harmful consequences of the cult of the individual. This stand of the Albanian leaders is explained by the fact that they themselves, to our regret and distress, are repeating the methods that occurred in our country in the period of the cult of the individual.

We are following events in Albania with a feeling of anxiety for the destinies of the heroic Albanian people. We are pained to see that rank-and-file Albanian Communists and the whole Albanian people, who are vitally interested in friendship and cooperation with all the socialist countries, are obliged to pay for the mistaken line of the Albanian leaders. We are deeply troubled by this situation and have persistently sought and are seeking ways of overcoming the differences that have arisen.

The course drawn up by the 20th Congress of our party is a Leninist course, and we cannot concede on this fundamental question to either the Albanian leaders or anyone else. To depart from the 20th Congress line would mean not heeding the wise instructions of Lenin, who discerned the danger of the appearance of the Stalin cult even when it was in embryo. It would mean disregarding the costly lessons of history, forgetting the price that our party paid for not having heeded in time the instructions of its great leader.

Now the Albanian leaders, opposing the 20th Congress policy, are trying to pull our party back to ways that they like but that will never be repeated in our country. Our party will continue firmly and unswervingly to carry out the line of its 20th Congress, a line that has withstood the test of time. No one will succeed in diverting us from the Leninist path! (Stormy, prolonged applause.)

If the Albanian leaders hold dear the interests of their people and the cause of building socialism in Albania, if they really want friendship with the C.P.S.U., with all the fraternal parties, they should renounce their mistaken views and return to the path of unity and close cooperation in the fraternal family of the socialist commonwealth, the path of unity with the whole international Communist movement.

As for our party, it will continue, in keeping with its internationalist duty, to do everything it can so that Albania may march shoulder to shoulder with all the socialist countries.

From the rostrum of the 22nd Congress we declare that purity of the Marxist-Leninist teaching and irreconcilability with any kind of distortions of its great principles are law for our party. (Prolonged applause.) Communists hold the cause of the revolution, the cause of the people, above all else, and its leaders are worthy of the name only when they express the vital interests of the working people and follow the true path. Such leaders and chiefs are forged in the course of the struggle itself, they win authority by their service to the people, to the cause of communism, they serve the people and should be under the people's control. (Stormy applause.)

Comrades! There is not one major question of either domestic or foreign policy that is not discussed collectively in our party, and the decisions adopted are the expression of the Party's collective experience. This is true application of Leninist principles. It has become the practice to hold broad Party-wide and nationwide discussion of the questions that are introduced for consideration at Central Committee plenary sessions and U.S.S.R. Supreme Soviet sessions. The measures to restore revolutionary legality, to develop Party and Soviet democracy, to expand the rights and raise the role of local Party and Soviet bodies and unleash the working people's creative initiative have had fruitful effects.

The Central Committee has paid particular attention to the regular convening of elected bodies, beginning with Party Congresses and Central Committee plenary sessions. We know how regularly the Party Congresses were held during V. I. Lenin's lifetime: In the difficult first seven years of Soviet rule they were held each year, and they discussed the main tasks of the Party and of the young Soviet state. In the period of the cult of the individual this custom was grossly violated: A Congress was not held for almost 14 years after the 18th, despite the fact that the country had gone through the Great Patriotic War and a stage of great and difficult work on economic reconstruction. Plenary sessions of the Party Central Committee were convened extremely rarely. This provided a situation for abuse of power, for some leaders to put themselves beyond the control of the Party and the people.

Such things do not and cannot occur now in the Party. In the nine years since the 19th Congress, the 20th, the extraordinary 21st and the present 22nd Party Congresses have been convened. The major questions of the life of the Party and country are examined at regularly held plenary sessions of the Central Committee, and the work of a number of Party organizations and their leaders, including the work of individual members of the Central Committee and members of the Party Central Committee Presidium, has been sharply criticized. Officials who have not justified the Party's trust have been relieved of their posts.

In the past, in the period of the cult of the individual, such bad features of Party, state and economic leadership as highhanded rule by fiat, the hushing up of shortcomings, working with a cautious or fearful glance over the shoulder, and fear of anything new were widespread. In this situation many sycophants, hosanna-singers and falsifiers appeared. The Party is waging and will continue to wage a determined struggle against violators of Party and state discipline, against persons who take the path of deceiving the Party and state. It is boldly developing principled criticism and self-criticism, using them as the sharpest and most effective weapon.

The development of inner-Party democracy, expansion of the rights and heightening of the role of local Party bodies, and observance of the principle of collective leadership have made the Party still more effective, have strengthened its ties with the masses. The Party's indivisible ties with the people are vividly manifested in the growth of the Party ranks, in the continuous influx of fresh forces into the Party.

During the period under review the membership of our party has increased by almost 2,500,000. Whereas the Party had 7,215,505 Communists in its ranks at the time of the 20th Congress, their number had risen to 9,716,005 by the time of the 22nd Congress (by Oct. 1, 1961). Among those admitted to the Party, 40.7% are workers, 22.7% are collective farmers, 35.6% are office employees and professionals and 1% are students. What is represented in our times by the category of office employees and professionals admitted to the Party? Almost two-thirds of them are engineers and technical personnel, agronomists, zootechnicians and other specialists.

It must be said that the very concept of office employees and professionals has now changed. In the early years of Soviet rule the intelligentsia consisted chiefly of persons who until the revolution had been connected with the propertied classes. Therefore definite restrictive measures were applied toward the category of office employees and professionals. Now the situation is quite different: The overwhelming majority of the office workers and professionals nowadays are former workers and collective farmers or their children. This is why the attitude to office employees and professionals has changed. In the process of development of science and technology and the automation and mechanization of production, the category of those whom we call office employees and professionals will increase and will play an ever greater role in production. In time we shall have no need to divide Party members into workers, collective farmers and office employees-professionals, since class distinctions will completely disappear and all will be toilers of communist society. (Applause.)

It is gratifying to report, comrades, that the number of educated people in the ranks of our party is constantly increasing. Now every third Communist among us has a higher or secondary education. It is particularly important to note that more than 70% of all Party members and candidates for membership are working in the sphere of material production. The great majority of the Communists are working in the decisive sectors—industry and agricultural production.

The ranks of the C.P.S.U. contain representatives of more than 100 nationalities and peoples inhabiting the U.S.S.R. Our party arose and is developing as an internationalist organization of the working class, and it embodies the great unity and fraternal friendship of equal socialist nations making up the close-knit family of builders of communism. (Applause.)

In selfless service to communism lies the supreme calling of a member of the Leninist party. The communist must toil passionately, must give heart and soul to the people's cause. And if a Party member does not live up to his lofty obligations, he does not belong in the Party ranks. More than 200,000 persons have been expelled from the Party in the past six years for various reasons. The Party has become stronger and firmer by ridding itself of these people who entered it by chance. (Applause.)

It must be admitted that there are still people who regard their membership in the Party as an opportunity to advance their personal careers. How are we to safeguard the Party from such time-servers? In the early years of the revolution and in the period of the Patriotic War, the Communist's qualities were tested in the fire of struggle. When one of our military units entered a village liberated by the Red Army, a local teacher turned to me with the question: "What position will you give me if I enter the Bolshevik party?"

"The highest—we'll give you a rifle and send you to fight the bourgeoisie for Soviet rule," I told him.

"No, that job doesn't suit me," he said. (Stir in the hall.) It was all clear as the palm of your hand. You know that there were many intellectuals in our party, including teachers, who honorably defended the achievements of the Great October Revolution, who fought for the Party cause.

Now that we are fighting for communism, we must demand of each person who enters the Party that he be a leading fighter on any sector of communist construction. The Party Statutes require each Communist to set an example of a communist attitude to work, lofty devotion to our ideas, intolerance of shortcomings, money-grubbing and parasitism, considerateness and attentiveness to people, and dedication to the Party and the people. The Communist must set an example in the struggle for establishing the lofty principles of communist ethics. (Applause.)

This is why all the Party organizations must strictly observe the principle of individual selection and carry out a thorough check of the personal qualities of applicants for membership. It is necessary to continue to admit to the C.P.S.U. leading individuals of the working class, the collective farm peasantry and the Soviet intelligentsia, the best representatives of the Soviet people.

Our party, with almost 10,000,000 members in its ranks, will continue to hold sacred Lenin's behest to raise the title of Communist ever higher and higher! (Stormy applause.)

2. Organizational Work of the Party and the Rearing of Cadres. The Active Participation of the Masses in Public Activities Is the Key to New Successes.—Comrades! In recent years the Party has abruptly shifted toward questions of the concrete guidance of the national economy. The Central Committee has turned the attention of Party organizations and executive cadres to the careful study and extensive dissemination of progressive experience in industry and agriculture; it has taught through specific positive examples how to conduct our great communist construction correctly.

How are we to assess the work of a Party official? What must be our criterion for considering one person an able and energetic organizer while finding another wanting and criticizing him? As we know, the labor of the smelter, the labor of the sower or the builder lends itself readily enough to both qualitative and quantitative measurement. The performance of leaders of Party agencies should be judged by the concrete results of the work of the plant or construction project, the collective or state farm, the scientific institution, the district, province or republic.

Success in organizational work and the standard of leadership depend in large measure on the leaders' ties with the masses, on their skill in organizing human effort and directing it toward accomplishment of the cardinal tasks. But ties with the masses can differ in nature: They may be deep and vital, they may be shallow and perfunctory. To maintain close ties the Party leader needs many qualities: He must know the job and have a progressive approach to the various aspects of economic and cultural construction. The leader is obliged to enrich his knowledge unceasingly by strengthening his ties with life and studying the advanced experience of production innovators and the achievements of science and technology. Knowledge of this kind is accumulated when a Party worker holds firmly to the Marxist analysis of social phenomena, when he has an eye for the new, stands up for it and helps clear a path for it.

This certainly does not mean that the Party functionary must be a specialist in all fields of knowledge. He must, of course, know a great deal, must be a broadly educated and well-informed person, but he must have a particularly good grasp of the tasks assigned him, must have a profound understanding and love of personal work with people. The strength of Party leadership lies in its collective character, which is what helps to knit the talents, knowledge and experience of many people into a single talent, as it were, capable of doing great things.

The decisions of the 20th Congress stated the necessity of heightening the role of primary Party organizations and district Party committees in organizational and political work. It is in these primary organizations, in the districts, that the most diverse and compelling problems of economic and cultural development are dealt with. The primary organizations, which carry on day-to-day work in the thick of the masses, are the backbone of the Party. There are 41,830 primary organizations at industrial enterprises, 10,427 at construction projects, 18,938 in transport, 44,387 on the collective farms and 9,206 on the state farms. The success of our whole cause depends in large measure on the standard of organizational and political work on the lower Party levels.

With a view to raising the standards of the primary organizations in the performance of their work, the Central Committee has kept all Party members regularly informed on the most important measures in the field of domestic and foreign policy and on questions of the international Communist movement and ideological work. The Central Committee has time and again sent the primary Party organizations and district Party committees messages explaining urgent tasks in communist construction.

We can all agree that there is nothing more interesting or important for us as Communists than Party work, the heart of which is close association with the masses, with the people. To devote your life to this work, making no distinction between small and large concerns; to be tactful with people whatever the reason that has brought them to see you; to look at things broadmindedly and from the standpoint of Party principles, and not to lose touch with life—these constitute our duty and our obligation to the Party and to the people. Only inspiration and creative work of this kind can fire people's hearts, kindle enthusiasm in them for the accomplishment of great deeds in labor and in struggle. (Applause.)

We must always remember that the Party is strong by virtue of the activeness, political consciousness and militant solidarity of Communists. Party work is basically a sphere of public activity, and it is the duty of every Communist to take an active part in it. We are moving toward communism, under which the people themselves will manage the affairs of society without special apparatus.

In our country the socialist system of government is in process of evolving into public self-government. As the vanguard of a people engaged in building a communist society, the Party must also take the lead in organizing its own inner-Party life; it must set an example, be a model in developing the very best forms of communist public self-government. In practice this may mean, for instance, that the apparatus of the Party agencies will steadily shrink while the ranks of Party aktivists grow. The Party agencies should have more and more commissions, departments, instructors and district and city committee secretaries who work on a public [unpaid] basis. Stronger ties with the masses, Leninist affability, eagerness to be with the people, to live as one with them and share their concerns, an impassioned Party spirit in the fight for the new— these are the features that should identify the Party leader. (Applause.)

Comrades! The Party has trained large cadres of mature and ideologically seasoned leaders for all fields of endeavor. Dedicated service to the people is for them the supreme duty. It used to be that many local officials would in every situation wait for directives and instructions from above, and frequently they had no opportunity to show any initiative of their own, whereas today, in view of the expanded rights and heightened responsibilities of the local agencies, these officials are asked to be more independent in their activities and to show a more creative approach to matters. We do have cadres of this kind, and they are setting the tone in all our activities.

But are there really no leaders left whose work is spiritless and lacking in initiative, who have grown used to seeing their enterprise or their district, province or republic lagging behind? We still are not always as exacting of these cadres as we should be, and they hold on to their positions for a long time. If an enterprise fails to fulfill its monthly or quarterly plans, its director obviously is not going to be able to stay on very long. Nonfulfillment of the plan at an industrial enterprise is rightly considered intolerable and impermissible.

But why is the same principle not always applied to officials in agriculture? We have not only collective farms but whole districts and provinces that have "won" for themselves the "right" not to fulfill plans, if it can be put this way, the "right" to be listed in the consumer column, not the producer column. They come to be consumers because their farming standards are extremely poor and they settle for crops of five to seven centners of oats per hectare. I have already described how matters stood in Kirov Province, where for more than eight years the position of secretary of the province Party committee was held by Comrade Pchelyakov. When he was finally relieved of his position for making a bad job of things and for hoodwinking, he was surprised and demanded an explanation. On what grounds, he asked, for what reasons was he being dismissed? Can this sort of official possibly stand at the head of a Party organization?

Let us take another type of official, the type who likes to live off the state. There are some enterprise directors, collective farm chairmen and heads of state farms and various departments who make a specialty of requesting year after year that their production assignments be reduced and their payrolls and capital investments increased. Such officials cannot be called real leaders: They do not get people to give their best to the job, do not set them an inspiring example but implant a parasitical frame of mind in them. If such leaders, who consider themselves Communists, gave some serious thought to what would happen if all enterprises and collective and state farms sought to have their production assignments reduced and their state appropriations increased, they would realize that we would be unable to make any progress with that kind of approach. For it should be plain to all that we can create abundance and satisfy the people's requirements, which are growing year by year, only if each enterprise and each Soviet man and woman contributes to the common cause of communist construction. (Applause.)

A great deal of harm is done our cause by conceited leaders. More often than not they are people who are indifferent about raising their job qualifications and ideological and political level and therefore often slide into unprincipled attitudes, turning into shrewd operators and windbags.

In general, work with cadres, the ability to select and rear them properly, is a very delicate and complicated matter. It may happen that a man is promoted to a particular position and fails to cope with it. There may be various reasons for this, and they do not all necessarily reflect on the individual. But it becomes increasingly clear that the promotion was a mistake, and that the cause is beginning to suffer as a result. Obviously the mistake must be rectified. But just try to move a comrade back to his old job—a job that he had done well.

This proves next to impossible. Why? He has acquired the right, you see, to call himself a province or republic or even a Union official, and he considers it all but a mortal insult if he is offered a job within the scope of his talents. To show ambition, conceit and arrogance in a case like this is to display qualities unbefitting a Party member. (Voices in the hall: "Correct!" Applause.)

In working with cadres we must abide strictly by Lenin's principle that mature, experienced personnel tempered in the struggle for the Party line must be properly matched with vigorous young organizers who are highly competent at their jobs. It is extremely important to maintain continuity in our work; it fosters the preservation and development of the finest Party traditions and an influx of young people, who are imbued with a feeling for the new, full of initiative in their work, and efficient. It is altogether inadmissible for a hoodwinker or confirmed bureaucrat to function in the position of a Party leader. Persons guilty of hoodwinking and fraud will continue to be indicted by the Party with the full strictness of Party and Soviet laws. (Applause.)

Our party and the Soviet people are rich in talented individuals. The promotion and rearing of cadres for various fields of Party and government work and of economic and cultural construction are a primary obligation of Party organizations. The best school for the training and political tempering of cadres is the school of life, the school of practical experience. The traits that mark a Party or government leader of the Leninist type are evolved in the struggle to carry out the Party line and to accomplish the tasks of communist construction. We must take pains to nurture such cadres!

Comrades! The question of Party, state and public control from top to bottom and from bottom to top is taking on paramount importance at the present time. Control is an effective means of perfecting leadership in communist construction. The work of this or that organization, of any leading Party agency, should be gauged primarily by the way it actually implements the requirements of the Program and Statutes of the C.P.S.U. and the directives of the Party.

If in the earliest years of the Soviet regime V. I. Lenin attached such enormous importance to control in all its forms and to checking on the execution of Party decisions, how attentive must we be to this today, now that our national economy has experienced such prodigious growth! Like the good mechanic whose ear is attuned to the working of an enormous engine and who is able from a scarcely audible sound to tell where the trouble lies, who seems to see every little speck of dust that might cause the engine to stop running, we too are obliged to listen day by day and hour by hour to the heartbeat of the huge Soviet land, to eradicate evidence of bureaucracy and red tape and be prompt to notice and clear out of our way every obstacle to our successful progress.

The Party organizations should be the first to start intensifying control and checking on the execution of decisions. A strict procedure must be instituted for the rendering of accounts by local Party agencies to higher Party committees and to the Communist rank and file on the implementation of Party decisions. We must keep in mind and rigorously comply with Lenin's insistence that people be checked on, that actual performance be checked on.

There is much to be done in improving state control. Until very recently there were major shortcomings in the work of the Soviet Control Commissions. Most significant was their poor contact with life and the masses, for without the active participation of the broad masses, without their help, the state control agencies cannot function properly.

The system of Party, state and public control is a potent means of improving leadership in communist construction on the basis of genuinely democratic principles: it is a wonderful school of communist education for the broadest masses of people. This is why we must, with due attention to present circumstances, take fuller advantage of the advice offered by Vladimir Ilyich Lenin in his article "How We Should Reorganize the Workers' and Peasants' Inspection."

Public control involving strict verification of the execution of decisions is one of the methods for giving effect to the principle of criticism and self-criticism. We must pay careful attention to the new things that are coming into being, to the shoots of communism, must clear the weeds and wild growth from the field in which communist society is growing, must foster the creative activity of the great army of builders of the communist society.

The great strides our people have made under the Party's leadership are apparent to all. They gladden all Soviet people and instill confidence that in the future we shall surge forward even more successfully and rapidly.

Lenin taught the Party never to tolerate conceit and complacency, to see not only the achievements but also the shortcomings in our work and to focus efforts on the solution of unresolved problems. And we still have many such problems. There are quite a few shortcomings in the work of Party and Soviet agencies that must be eliminated.

We must direct our efforts to achieving more rapid economic growth and raising the people's standard of living. We must strive for further increases in agricultural production, for the fulfillment of housing plans, for higher labor productivity in all branches of the economy and for a considerable improvement in the quality of output, especially consumer goods.

The more vigorously we support and the more extensively we apply in production everything that is new and progressive, and the more sharply we expose shortcomings and the more uncompromising we are in eliminating them, the sooner will the tasks we face be accomplished. The cause of communist construction is the great cause of millions, the cause of the entire people.

Marching with the Party in all its undertakings are the mass organizations of the working people—the Soviets, the trade unions, the Young Communist League and the cooperatives.

Born in the fires of revolution as the people's agencies in their struggle for power, the Soviets have now become all-encompassing organizations of the people, the embodiment of their unity; they have developed into a school of public activity for millions, a school such as mankind has never before known in the history of its development.

The entire activity of the Soviets constitutes the best confirmation of the highly democratic nature of our society. After all, the mere fact that the total number of the Deputies to the Soviets comes to about 2,000,000 persons says a great deal. In addition, more than 2,000,000 aktivists participate in the work of the Soviets' standing committees. What other system can offer such confirmation of its truly democratic character, of being genuinely rooted in the people?! The Soviets must make their ties with the masses still stronger and must concern themselves more deeply and comprehensively with the problems of government and of economic and cultural development.

Over the past quarter of a century, since the present Constitution of the U.S.S.R. was adopted, there have been big changes in the life of our country. The Soviet Union has entered a new stage of its development, and socialist democracy has risen to a higher level. The new Constitution of the U.S.S.R. that we are beginning to draft must reflect the new features in the life of Soviet society in the period of the full-scale building of communism.

Under present conditions the role and the importance of the trade unions are growing all the time. After the 20th Congress the rights and functions of the trade unions in the handling of all matters affecting the vital interests of the working people were substantially broadened. The Soviet trade unions, with their membership of more than 60,000,000, are a school of upbringing, of administration, of economic management, a school of communism, for our country's working people. Most important in the activities of the trade unions at the present stage should be the effort to accomplish the program of communist construction. Concern for the working man is the noble duty and obligation of the trade unions. Our trade unions are called upon to make vigorous efforts, drawing upon traditional principles of trade union work and enriching them with new communist procedures and methods, to involve the masses of working people in the management of production and of all the affairs of society.

As Soviet society advances toward communism, the functions of the trade unions will broaden and the range of their

activities will come to include more and more problems that were previously handled by agencies of the state. Our party will promote the intensification of trade union activity in economic management, and will in particular promote the development of the permanent production conferences into ever more effective agencies for helping to improve the operations of enterprises.

Special stress must be laid on the tasks of the trade unions in raising the level of communist political consciousness among the working people, organizing Communist Labor competitions and cultivating in the masses the ability to manage state and public affairs.

The trade unions are faced with the need to improve their working procedures and methods. At this stage in our development it is imperative that the principle of public [unpaid] work be introduced ever more extensively in the activities of the trade unions and that the paid staffs of their organizations be reduced. The more widely the principle of public work is applied, the more actively will the working people be participating in the life of society.

We all set great store by the activities of the Party's militant helper—the wonderful Leninist Young Communist League. The lives of many of us are linked with it. Many of the Party's members have been through the school of the Y.C.L. The Y.C.L. is our future, our reserve. At all stages of socialist construction Soviet youth, members of the Y.C.L., have shown a clear understanding of the tasks set by the Party. With their labor they are proving themselves worthy to inherit the great revolutionary traditions, to carry on the glorious cause of their fathers and mothers.

It is hard to enumerate the splendid exploits of the Y.C.L., of Soviet youth. Our people are proud, and rightly proud, of their young people.

Youthful Leninists are growing up in the Young Pioneer organization, and the Party has charged the Y.C.L. with nurturing them carefully and solicitously and with leading them along the difficult and adventurous paths into life.

We must not forget that the old world is still trying to trip us up with old ideas and habits. It must be borne in mind that young people do exist who have the sticky mud of the past clinging to them, who are being sucked in by philistine ways, upon whom bourgeois ideology is exerting a pernicious influence.

The primary task of the Leninist Young Communist League is to bring up young men and women on the heroic traditions of revolutionary struggle, on the examples of the devoted labor of workers, collective farmers and the intelligentsia, on the great ideas of Marxism-Leninism.

Magnificent vistas, great and alluring goals, are unfolding before young people. The Program of the Communist Party of the Soviet Union throws open to them the door to the future. To build communism—how great and beautiful a goal! But building communism means first of all expanding the economy, increasing the production of material and cultural wealth, and cultivating in every individual the traits of the man of communist society. Young people will be called upon to exploit new mineral wealth, to build factories, state farms, plants and cities. But the mineral wealth lies not near Moscow or Leningrad but in the taiga, in the mountains, in the deserts. If these riches are to serve the people they must be taken out of the ground.

Muscovites and Leningraders, Kievans and Gorkyites, all the youth of the older settled localities must, fearless of hardships, set out on a great expedition to provide new wealth for our people. Where man is, where he is at work, there will be everything. Nekrasov said, back in his time: "The will and the labor of man work wonders!" Such was the case in Nekrasov's time, when man's work was done with pick and shovel, with ax and saw. Soviet youth today head for the construction sites armed with thorough knowledge and the most up-to-date equipment. How many fine things have they already accomplished in our land, and how many more will they accomplish armed with the great plans for communist construction!

The Party believes in the Y.C.L., in Soviet youth, and it summons our young generation forward to the attack, to the construction projects of communism! (Stormy applause.)

3. The Ideological Activity of the Party and the Strengthening of Ties With the Life of the People. The Building of Communism and the Development of Revolutionary Theory.— Comrades! The 20th Congress opened broad vistas for the creative development of Marxism-Leninism. We note with satisfaction that in the years since the Congress the Party has restored and developed Leninist principles in ideological work and has been fruitfully solving urgent theoretical problems of Communist construction. After overcoming the negative consequences of the cult of the individual, the Party has reoriented ideological work toward the requirements of life and has pursued a course of strengthening the unity of theory and practice. It has based its policy on a scientific, Marxist-Leninist foundation and has subordinated all its theoretical and ideological-educational activity to the solution of specific tasks of communist construction.

The publication of the second edition of the "Works" of K. Marx and F. Engels, of the fifth, complete "Collected Works" of V. I. Lenin, of collections of Party decisions, of a scholarly biography of V. I. Lenin and of textbooks and other books on questions of theory and Party history, on philosophy and political economy and on the history of the Civil War and the Great Patriotic War has had great importance for raising the level of ideological and theoretical work. By decision of the Central Committee, work has begun on the preparation of a multivolume history of the C.P.S.U. that will generalize the experience of the struggle of the Party and the Soviet people for the victory of communism.

The Party proceeds from the Leninist directive concerning the steady rise in the role of the conscious historical creativity of the masses. The Party consults with the people on all the most important, most burning questions of the day. The ideological work of the Party organizations enhances the communist consciousness and the work and political activeness of the masses and is a highly important and constantly operating factor in the building of communism.

An important role in deepening and broadening the Party's ideological influence on the masses is played by political education, lecture propaganda, mass-political and cultural-educational work, the press, radio, television, motion pictures, literature and art. It is very indicative that in the past five years the per-issue circulation of newspapers has increased in our country by 20,000,000 copies, while the annual circulation of magazines and other periodicals has increased by 417,000,000 copies. The Soviet Union now holds first place in the world in the number of books published. This, comrades, is a great achievement of the Party in the development of socialist culture and in the dissemination of communist ideology. (Applause.) The Party and the Soviet people highly value the activity of propagandists and agitators, of workers in science, education and culture, of the whole army of ideological workers, active fighters for the triumph of the ideas of Marxism-Leninism. (Applause.)

The task of thoroughly explaining to the working people the new Party Program, which arms the Party and the whole people with a great plan of struggle for the full triumph of communism, is today being put to the fore in ideological work. Our new Program is the foundation for educating the masses in the spirit of communism. Vladimir Ilyich Lenin pointed out that the Party program is the strongest material for propaganda and agitation. "In our program," he said, "every paragraph is something that each worker must know, learn and understand." ("Works" [in Russian], Vol. XXIX, p. 168.)

Ideological work is not an end in itself but a highly important means for solving the basic tasks of communist construction. Therefore, the essence of the demands on ideological-educational work in present-day conditions is that it be highly efficient and effective.

The building of communism requires great labor efforts on the part of the people, of literally every Soviet individual. Without labor there can be no prosperous society, no well-being and happiness for man. The good things of life are not going to fall upon us like manna from heaven. Every working person must understand this and contribute his share to the cause of all the people, the building of communism.

You know about the great industriousness of bees: Each bee carries its own drop of nectar into the common hive. Soviet society is, so to speak, a big communist hive. In our society everyone must multiply by his labor the public wealth, and then as time goes on we shall be able to satisfy all the requirements of people. But just as in the bee family there are drones whom the bees themselves and the beekeeper try to drive out, so in our Soviet collective there are still people who want to live at society's expense while giving nothing in return. There are still people among us who are inclined to view communism as a society of indolence and idleness. Unfortunately, oral and even printed propaganda not infrequently presents a one-sided and oversimplified picture of the future society; some might think that under communism man will neither sow nor reap but only eat pie. (Stir in the hall.) Such views of communism are characteristic of people who are lacking in spirit, of philistines and loafers.

Communism and labor are inseparable. The great principle "He who does not work, neither shall he eat" will be in force under communism as well; it will indeed become a sacred principle for all. Man is beautiful and glorious by his labor, by his deeds, by what he has created, what he has accomplished. The abilities and talents of people, the genius of man, are revealed in labor. In labor lies mankind's immortality. (Applause.)

The preparation of a man for labor activity, the labor tempering of people, the fostering of love and respect for labor as the prime vital necessity constitute the essence, the core of all work in communist education.

The rearing of the new man is a long and complex process. People cannot be mechanically resettled from the realm of capitalism to the realm of communism. A person overgrown with the moss of capitalist prejudices cannot be taken into communism. We must first see to it that he is freed from the burden of the past. The struggle against survivals of capitalism in people's minds, the changing of the customs and mores of millions of people evolved through the centuries that was begun by our revolution is a long task and not a simple one. Survivals of the past are a terrible force that weighs like a nightmare on the minds of the living. They remain rooted in the mores and the consciousness of millions of people long after the economic conditions that engendered them have disappeared.

At the present stage of communist construction it is necessary to wage an even more resolute struggle against such survivals of capitalism as idleness and parasitism, drunkenness and hooliganism, swindling and money-grubbing, against relapses into great-power chauvinism and local nationalism, bureaucratism, an incorrect attitude toward women and so forth. There must be no place for such weeds in our life. (Applause.)

Communist education presupposes the emancipation of the consciousness from religious prejudices and superstitions which still prevent some Soviet people from manifesting their creative forces to the full. We need a well-considered and orderly system of scientific-atheist education that will embrace all strata and groups of the population and will prevent the dissemination of religious concepts, especially among children and adolescents.

Also, it should not be forgotten that the overcoming of survivals of capitalism in the consciousness of people and the upbringing of the new man are proceeding in a situation of fierce struggle between the world of socialism and the world of capitalism. The ideologists of imperialism are doing all they can to bolster and invigorate bourgeois mores and prejudices in the minds of Soviet people and to halt our movement toward communism.

The upbringing of the new man requires great effort and a rational approach. After all, we are dealing with real human beings. Everything in a person is ingeniously interconnected. But this is not the kind of interconnection that exists between the parts of a machine; it is a far more complicated matter. Once, during the construction of the Dnieper Hydroelectric Station, M. Gorky was watching the blasting on the rapids. The workers placed a charge under the rocks, a silent impact was felt, the water began to seethe, the snags in the rapids settled to the river bottom and the Dnieper flowed on, smooth and broad. And Gorky mused: If one such explosion were possible in human society as well, to remove all the rapids, all that is outmoded, dark and barbaric, how wonderful that would be! But in rebuilding a society everything is more complex and more difficult. Human society cannot be rid of all that prevents a happy and joyful life without sweat and spiritual suffering.

The rearing of the new man, a man of lofty ideals and high principles, is one of the main achievements of the Party. Our adversaries are frightened by the political and cultural growth of Soviet people and by their devotion to the cause of communism. Needless to say, all this did not come about by itself but has been achieved through many years of educational work by the Party. Now we are in a position to set forth and to realize the noblest principles in relations among people, which have been the dream of many generations of working people. These principles are embodied in the specific points of the Code of Communist Morality.

The interests of communist construction demand that questions of communist education be at the center of attention and activity of each Party organization and of the public as a whole.

It is time to have done completely with undervaluation of ideological work and with its divorce from organizational activity. Any counterposition of ideological and organizational work is wrong and harmful. An ideological worker, if he really aspires to make his activity fruitful, must invariably be a political organizer of the masses. On the other hand, it must always be remembered that the basic methods of organizational work itself are persuasion and indoctrination of people. Raising the level of ideological work is a mandatory condition for the success of our practical activity.

Comrades! The strength of our Party lies in the fact that it has been able in its revolutionary and reforming activity to weld the theory and the practice of scientific communism into a single whole. The world-historic victories won by the Soviet people are the most convincing evidence of its proper application and creative development of Marxist-Leninist theory. In the past few years the scope and significance of the Party's theoretical activity have grown immensely.

The great teaching of Marx, Engels and Lenin has always been and remains our guide to action. The Party will continue in the future as well to carry high and keep spotless the all-conquering banner of Marxism-Leninism and to sweep resolutely from its path those revisionists and other renegades who try, under cover of "renovating" communist theory, to distort it by stripping it of its revolutionary principles.

The architects of scientific communism foresaw that life would pose more and more new questions and that Communists would be obliged to develop revolutionary theory constantly in unbreakable conjunction with the socialist transformation of society. This directive rings forth with special timeliness and force in our days, days of a rapid and revolutionary breakdown of social relations and of radical changes of direction in the history of mankind. Now that the founding geniuses of scientific communism are no longer with us and life is constantly raising new questions, the disciples and followers of Marx and Lenin must provide the answers.

The defining characteristic of the epoch of the full-scale building of a communist society is the fact that we are confronted by more and more theoretical questions of the kind whose answers must be sought not in books alone but in the life-giving practice of communist construction itself. We would be untrue to the spirit of our teaching if, in these new conditions, we were incapable of applying and developing Marxism-Leninism creatively, if we did not enrich it with new theoretical propositions and conclusions, if we lacked the boldness to adjust the formulas and propositions that no longer conform to new historical experience.

Life is immeasurably richer than any formulas. Theoretical propositions must be adjusted and modified in the light of changes in the life of society. Our party has furnished wonderful examples of this truly Marxist-Leninist approach to revolutionary theory.

The period of the Party's life under review has been marked by creative solutions to many large questions of communist construction and to urgent problems in the international liberation movement. These include highly important theoretical conclusions concerning the dictatorship of the proletariat in present-day conditions; the laws of the transition of socialism

into communism; the ways for creating the material and technical base of communism; the formation of communist social relations and the rearing of the new man; the variety of forms of transition from capitalism to socialism; the more or less simultaneous entry of the socialist countries into communism; the possibility of preventing a world war in our time; the nature of the modern epoch, etc.

The great theoretical work of the Party is most fully embodied in its new Program, which represents the philosophical, economic and political foundation for building communism in our country. The working out of the Program not only attests to historic victories in the fields of economic and cultural development but also indicates the great and many-sided theoretical work of the Party. The development of revolutionary theory has become the business of the entire Party. (Applause.)

Our practical successes in communist construction are at the same time successes in the development of theory. This is the standpoint from which the important social and economic measures carried out by our Party in the past few years must be considered. These include: the reorganization of the management of industry and construction, the reorganization of the Machine and Tractor Stations and the further strengthening of the collective farm system, the improvement of the planning of the national economy, the bringing of the schools closer to life, the development of the public education system and a number of others. The measures carried out by the Party constitute a great and truly revolutionary step in the development of Soviet society and at the same time a major contribution to Marxist-Leninist theory. These were highly important decisions dictated by the requirements of the objective laws of communist construction. The Party proceeded from a need for changes in certain methods of economic and cultural management, which, though they had played a positive role in the past, had ceased to correspond to the demands of life in the new conditions and might have become an obstacle to our development. When the Party introduces important measures, it does so with a view both to the need for solving current economic and political tasks and to the prospects for the movement of the Soviet Union toward communism.

Creative Marxism-Leninism is intransigent toward stagnation of thought and toward submission to formulas that no longer correspond to the actual state of affairs or to the objective situation. Nothing is so contrary to the essence and creative spirit of revolutionary theory as an attempt to cling to propositions that life has proved to be untenable. In our economic literature, for example, and not only economic literature, one thesis that persisted for a long time was that under socialism public demand backed by purchasing power supposedly must always keep ahead of production; it was even alleged that this represented some kind of special superiority of socialism over capitalism and was one of the moving forces of our society. This clearly erroneous assertion, which contradicts Marxist-Leninist teaching on the relation between production and consumption, arose on the basis of an uncritical, dogmatic acceptance of J. V. Stalin's mistaken thesis that in the U.S.S.R. "the growth of mass demand (purchasing power) exceeds the growth of production at all times."

Those who adhered to this view were not embarrassed by the circumstance that they were in fact justifying the shortage of articles of prime necessity and were perpetuating the procedures and psychology of the rationing system.

A socialist economy is a planned economy. In planning the volume and nature of output, we can and must take public demand into account at every step. V. I. Lenin pointed out that socialism means "the planned organization of the public production process to ensure the welfare and comprehensive development of all members of society." He repeatedly emphasized the need to ensure rates of development of production that would permit the creation of an abundance of goods for the people. We must be guided by this Leninist directive. Our party fights for the full satisfaction of the people's material and spiritual requirements. (Applause.)

The creative development of Marxism-Leninism is the cornerstone of the Party's activity and a decisive condition for our successes in building communism. Guided by the Leninist principle of the unity of theory and practice, our party will continue to regard the defense and creative development of the principles of Marxism-Leninism as its most important duty to the peoples of our country and to the working people of the entire world.

Comrades! Our Congress will discuss the great tasks of building a communist society and the attainment of this cherished goal, for which the great thinkers and revolutionaries Marx, Engels and Lenin supplied the scientific basis. The Party Program will determine all the political, organizational and ideological work of the Party.

What are the chief tasks in the field of Party construction?

1. The Party first of all will direct the efforts of the Soviet people toward creating the material and technical base of communism, toward perfecting the new social relations and toward the upbringing of all Soviet people in a spirit of communist consciousness. The Party, its organizations and all Communists must provide the proper guidance for communist construction, must set an example, must be in the vanguard, must bring organization and planning into all the work of communist construction and must develop the initiative and activeness of the masses.

2. The Party's attention must be focused on the fulfillment of the seven-year plan, the steady growth of labor productivity and a rise in the well-being of the working people. The Party organizations must head the struggle for technical progress in all branches of the national economy, for a broad dissemination of the experience of innovators and advanced workers in socialist competition and for the full-scale development of the Communist Labor movement.

3. In conformity with the demands of the new Program and Statutes, the Party will steadfastly observe the Leninist norms of Party life and the principles of collective leadership, will raise the responsibility of Party agencies and their officials to the Party and the people, will ensure a growth in the activeness and independent action of all Communists and their participation in formulating and implementing Party policy, and will develop criticism and self-criticism. The Party will cement the unity and monolithic solidarity of its ranks, will guard the purity of Marxism-Leninism and will wage a resolute struggle against any manifestations of factionalism and clique activity, which are incompatible with a Marxist-Leninist Party spirit.

4. The Party will assist in every possible way in expanding and improving the activity of Soviets, trade unions, the Young Communist League and other mass organizations, in raising their role in communist construction and in communist education, in developing the creative initiative of the masses and in strengthening friendship among all the peoples of the U.S.S.R. The increasing scope and complexity of the tasks of building communism insistently demand a strengthening of Party, state and public control and systematic checking on the fulfillment of decisions taken. Work on improving control must be based on public principles so that control will truly be a cause of the people.

5. In order to raise the level of ideological work as a mighty factor in the struggle for the victory of communism, the Party will continue to work out new theoretical questions posed by life and to rear all Soviet people in a spirit of loyalty to Marxism-Leninism and intransigence toward any and all manifestations of bourgeois ideology and in a spirit of increased political vigilance against the intrigues of communism's enemies.

6. The Party considers the building of communism in the U.S.S.R. to be the fulfillment of its international duty to the working people of all countries. It will continue to fight tirelessly for the strengthening of the world socialist system and for the unity of all the international Communist and Workers' Parties and, jointly with them, will wage a resolute struggle for the purity of Marxism-Leninism and against various manifestations of opportunism and present-day revisionism, the chief danger, and against dogmatism and sectarianism.

Loyalty to the great teaching of Marxism-Leninism and ties with the people constitute the basis of all our past, present and future victories and the guarantee of the triumph of communism! (Stormy applause.)

***

Comrades! Majestic plans for building a communist society will be considered and discussed at our Congress. These are plans for peaceful creative work, for the tempestuous growth of the economy and culture, for an upsurge in the people's well-being. All the countries of the powerful socialist commonwealth are in a mighty upsurge. Great and clear prospects have opened before us.

The peoples who are building socialism and communism do not need war. They are adhering firmly to and putting into effect the principle of peaceful coexistence that the great Lenin bequeathed to us.

In the name of the Communist Party and the Soviet people, we solemnly state from the platform of the 22nd Congress: The Soviet Union will continue unswervingly to implement the peace-loving Leninist foreign policy and to strive for the establishment of mutual trust and cooperation with all states regardless of their social system. The Soviet Union will continue to strive for a relaxation of international tension and for general and complete disarmament under strict international control. (Applause.)

We have appealed and we appeal anew to the governments and peoples of the countries that fought together with the Soviet Union against Hitlerite Germany to liquidate the vestiges of the second world war, to remove everything that prevents the strengthening of peace and friendship among peoples and that carries with it the threat of a new war. The proposals of the Soviet Union on concluding a peace treaty with Germany and deciding the West Berlin question on that basis cause no harm to other states. These proposals are filled with concern for strengthening peace among peoples. We would like to believe that in the end reason will triumph! (Applause.)

In present-day conditions, when the great powers have weapons of terrible destructive power in their hands, it is especially dangerous and criminal to play with the fire of war. We appeal to the governments of all countries for mutual understanding and cooperation and for the solution of pressing international problems by peaceful means. It is the sacred duty of peoples to use all the means available in waging a persistent and vigorous struggle for the preservation and strengthening of peace on earth. (Applause.)

***

Comrades! The 22nd Congress is being held on the eve of the anniversary of the Great October Socialist Revolution. The fact that our party is adopting a new Program at its Congress is an indication of the world-historic victories of socialism and communism, the success of the cause of the Great October, a new triumph for Marxism-Leninism. (Prolonged applause.)

Only 44 years ago, in the revolutionary days of 1917, our country faced the crucial question of choosing a path, a question of how to save Russia from an impending national catastrophe. In those days a leader of the Mensheviks declared that we had no party that could assume responsibility for the fate of the country. It was then, in the perilous days of 1917, that the inspired words of Lenin, the leader of the proletarian revolution, sounded boldly and proudly all over the world:

"Yes, there is such a party!" (Stormy, prolonged applause.)

Speaking at the First All-Russian Congress of Soviets, Vladimir Ilyich declared in the name of the Central Committee that the party of Bolsheviks was ready to take power and to assume responsibility for the fate of our homeland. He laid out a bold program of struggle for the victory of the revolution and for the transformation of Russia on the basis of socialism. Now everyone can see that the prophetic words of our beloved Ilyich have come true. Our party has assumed an enormous burden, has accepted a high responsibility for the fate of the country and for the future of the people. The hero party of Communists has been equal to this burden. Placing itself at the head of the working class and of all working people, the Party in a short historical period has fulfilled honorably its pledge to transform the homeland and to make it powerful and prosperous. (Stormy applause.)

Everyone sees and admits this now. But in those days, when Vladimir Ilyich declared that the party of Communists was ready to assume the leadership of the country, the bourgeois press of Russia embarked on a furious harassment campaign against the Communists, railed at us and derided us. Here is what the monarchist newspaper Nashe vremya [Our Times] wrote in those days:

"Let us assume for a minute that the Communists will win. Who will govern us then? Cooks, perhaps? Or firemen? Stable boys? Stokers? Or will nursemaids perhaps run to sessions of the State Council in between diaper-sessions? Who, then? Who are these statesmen? Stable boys, nursemaids and cooks—these are the people who the Communists apparently think are called upon to rule the country. Will this happen? No! Is it possible? History will provide the Communists with an authoritative answer to this insane question."

History has indeed answered this question authoritatively. The great victories of the Soviet people in the building of socialism and communism, in all spheres of economic activity and in the development of science and culture have dispelled like fog the legend that the working masses are incapable of creation or of governing the states. These victories have shown convincingly that the laboring people—workers, peasants, miners, stokers and cooks—after taking power in their hands, are able to govern the state better and more intelligently and to develop the economy, science and culture far more successfully than was done, for example, by the members of the Russian State Council, the princes, counts, capitalists and landholders whose paths ended ingloriously on the trash heap of emigration. (Applause.)

The example of the Soviet Union inspires all progressive mankind. Never has the great vital force of Marxist-Leninist teaching been so clearly evident as in our days, now that socialism has triumphed fully and finally in the Soviet Union, the cause of socialism is winning new victories in the countries of the world socialist commonwealth, and the international Communist and workers' movement and the national liberation struggle of peoples are growing and expanding tempestuously. The revolution awakened the great energy of peoples, which is transforming the world on the principles of socialism and communism. Colossal changes are taking place and will take place throughout the world under the influence of the successes of communism.

The victory of communism is inevitable! (Stormy applause.)

When Marx greeted the heroic exploit of the Paris Communards 90 years ago, he enthusiastically called them heroes who were storming the skies. This was high praise for the exploit of the Paris Commune fighters and a passionate call to revolutionary struggle. Now we can say with pride that the peoples of the Soviet Union, who have built socialism and are now successfully erecting the edifice of a communist society, are indeed storming the skies, in the figurative and in the literal sense of the word. (Prolonged applause.)

The great army of Communists and of Marxist-Leninists acts as the vanguard of the peoples in the struggle for peace, for social progress and for communism, the bright future of mankind. New and ever newer millions of people will assemble and rally under the great banner of communism. The cause of progress, the cause of communism will triumph! (Stormy applause.)

Long live the great and heroic Soviet people, the builders of communism! (Stormy applause.)

Long live the indestructible unity and fraternal friendship of the peoples of the world socialist camp! (Stormy applause.)

Long live the heroic party of the Communists of the Soviet Union, created and tempered in struggle by the great Lenin! (Stormy applause.)

Long live the indestructible unity of the international Communist and workers' movement and the fraternal solidarity of the proletarians of all countries! (Stormy applause.)

Long live peace the world over! (Stormy applause.)

Under the all-conquering banner of Marxism-Leninism, under the leadership of the Communist Party, forward to the victory of communism! (Stormy, prolonged applause, turning into an ovation. All rise.)

V. GORKIN: CENTRAL INSPECTION COMMISSION REPORT

REPORT OF PARTY CENTRAL INSPECTION COMMISSION TO 22ND CONGRESS OF THE COMMUNIST PARTY OF THE SOVIET UNION.—Report by Comrade A. F. Gorkin. (Pravda and Izvestia, Oct. 18, pp. 11-12. Complete text:) Comrades! We have listened to Comrade N. S. Khrushchev's report on the work of the Central Committee of the Communist Party of the Soviet Union in the period since the 20th Congress with close attention and a feeling of deep satisfaction.

The vivid, all-encompassing report elucidated the glorious path traversed by the Party and the people in these years, a path of struggle and of brilliant victories won by the Party, under the leadership of the Leninist Central Committee, in communist construction and in the struggle to strengthen the forces of peace, democracy and socialism.

Thanks to the wise policy of the Party Central Committee, our people have achieved unprecedented successes in developing industry and agriculture and in advancing their material and cultural well-being; they are living and creating in the conditions of peace. The achievements of Soviet science have forever glorified our great socialist homeland.

The theoretical and practical importance of the draft of the new Party Program prepared by the Central Committee and submitted for the approval of the 22nd Congress—a program for building a communist society in our country—is truly inestimable. The draft of the Program is a model of the creative application and development of Marxist-Leninist theory in the present historical epoch. It arms the Party with a clear understanding of the situation, of the unfolding perspectives and of the specific paths of communist construction.

The draft Party Program reflects the collective wisdom of our party and of its Central Committee headed by Comrade N. S. Khrushchev, First Secretary of the Central Committee. (Applause.)

Comrades! In accordance with the directives of the 20th Party Congress, the Party Central Committee has done substantial work to restore the Leninist norms of Party life violated in the period of the cult of J. V. Stalin. In the period under review plenary sessions of the Central Committee were convened regularly, aktiv meetings and broad all-Union and zonal conferences were held on questions of agriculture, industry, construction and culture, and the drafts of major legislative acts were submitted for nationwide discussion. The aktiv and Party members were extensively informed about the decisions of the Central Committee both on questions of the country's internal life and foreign policy and on inner-Party questions. This ensured collegiality of leadership and high activeness on the part of Communists in the Party.

In the period under review large-scale changes were made in the sphere of state administration and the management of industry and agriculture, the rights of the Union republics and local Soviets were extended, the role of the public in the work of the state apparatus was enhanced, and legality was strengthened in the country. Major measures were carried out in reorganizing the system of public education, in the pension system and in financial-tax policy.

Life has fully confirmed the correctness of the Party's policy, outlined in the decisions of the historic 20th Congress. And a great contribution of the Central Committee and of Comrade N. S. Khrushchev personally to the Party is that the Central Committee succeeded in overcoming the serious opposition that arose to implementation of this Leninist policy of the Party. The June, 1957, plenary session of the Party Central Committee exposed the subversive, schismatic activity of the anti-Party group of Molotov, Kaganovich, Malenkov, Voroshilov, Bulganin, Pervukhin, Saburov and Shepilov, who joined them, which tried to swerve the Party from the Leninist path, to disrupt fulfillment of the historic decisions of the 20th Congress and to return to the old, outdated methods of leadership.

The Central Inspection Commission unanimously condemned the anti-Party activity of the group of bankrupt people who divorced themselves from the Party and people, and it added its voice to the decision unanimously adopted by the Central Committee plenary session on this question.

A Party Central Committee plenary session removed Zhukov from membership in the Central Committee and its Presidium for having failed to justify the trust placed in him by the Party and for having taken the path of adventurism. While Minister of Defense, he grossly violated the Leninist principles of leadership of the armed forces, pursued a policy of curbing Party work in the army and of isolating the army from the Party, and lost his sense of modesty, considering himself the sole hero of all the victories won by the people and the armed forces under the leadership of the Communist Party in the Great Patriotic War.

In their decisions, the Party Central Committee and the Central Inspection Commission proceeded from the Leninist thesis that the struggle to strengthen the unity of the Party was and remains the prime duty of every member of the Party.

In presenting the report of the Party Central Committee's Central Inspection Commission for the approval of the Congress, it is necessary to report to the Congress that the members of the Central Inspection Commission took an active part in the work of the Party Central Committee plenary sessions and in carrying out the decisions of the Party Central Committee.

Comrades! In accordance with the Party Statutes, the Central Inspection Commission supervised the conduct of affairs in the apparatus of the Party Central Committee. It should be noted that the successful implementation of the Party's decisions in the guidance of socialist construction largely depended on the smooth organization of the work of the Secretariat of the Party Central Committee. In considering questions at its regular meetings, the Secretariat of the Central Committee focused the attention of the apparatus on verification of the execution of Party decisions and on strengthening ties with local Party organizations and assisting them in practical work. The Central Committee Secretariat gave serious attention to the question of the selection and placement of executive Party and Soviet cadres.

The formation of the Party Central Committee's Bureau for the Russian Republic and the establishment of corresponding departments in the Party Central Committee are of great importance for strengthening leadership of the province Party organizations in the Russian Republic.

In the view of the Central Inspection Commission, the Central Committee apparatus is doing a great deal of work in preparing the drafts of decisions of the Central Committee and in bringing up specific questions of economic and cultural construction arising from checkup on the execution of adopted decisions, is carefully heeding letters and petitions received by the Central Committee and is promptly carrying out the instructions of the Secretariat and the Presidium of the Party Central Committee.

***

The Central Inspection Commission has given considerable attention to questions of the Party's finances and fulfillment of the Party budget.

The income part of the Party budget is comprised of membership dues, revenue from publishing and other receipts, which include interest on current accounts and payments for blank Party document forms. Membership dues comprised 67.8% of the Party budget in 1961, income from publishing 31.7% and other revenue 0.5%.

In the period under review the income of the Party budget increased considerably as regards both membership dues and revenues from publishing.

Revenue from membership dues increased 25.9% from 1955 through 1960. This increase was primarily the result of the growth in the membership of the Party and the rise in the earnings of Communists, along with all workers and employees.

The province and territory Party Committees and the Central Committees of the Union-Republic Communist Parties noticeably improved management of the collection and accounting of Party membership dues. The city and district Party committees as well as inspection commissions have begun to check more regularly on the state of payment of membership dues in the primary Party organizations, giving these organizations the necessary assistance in this matter. Members and candidate members of the Party usually pay their membership dues punctually each month in the amounts stipulated in the Party Statutes.

However, by no means all primary Party organizations are as yet observing the established procedure and period for the payment of membership dues. As a checkup shows, individual Party members and candidates pay their dues late or not in the amounts specified in the Statutes. Some secretaries of primary Party organizations permit Communists to fall three months or more in arrears in their membership dues without discussing the matter in the bureau or at a general Party meeting. There are cases where primary Party organization secretaries accept membership dues from Communists without calculating their earnings from all sources.

In its report to the 20th Congress, the Party Central Inspection Commission called the attention of local Party agencies to the violation by primary Party organization secretaries of the established periods for depositing the membership dues received from Communists in savings banks.

In the majority of Party organizations this matter has been put into proper order. But some secretaries of primary Party organizations keep the membership dues received from Communists for a long time before depositing them in the bank. It should be noted that the fact that primary Party organization secretaries hold on to cash sums for a long time does not always ensure their safekeeping and sometimes leads to the spending of them.

By no means all primary Party organizations examine reports on the collection of Party membership dues at sessions of the Party committee or bureau or at Party meetings, and reports that are submitted do not always fully show the amount of arrears and the number of Communists who have not paid their membership dues on time.

In seeing to the prompt and correct payment of membership dues and regularly hearing reports on the collection of these dues, Party organizations should explain to Communists the importance of prompt payment of Party dues as one of the principal conditions of membership in the Party and as an index of the awareness and discipline of the Communist and of his bond with the Party organization.

Revenue from publishing is of great importance in the Party budget's income. In the period under review the volume of publishing by Party agencies increased considerably, printing facilities were expanded both by the construction of new printshops and the modernization of old ones, and equipment was replaced. The circulation of newspapers published by Party publishing houses was 85.2% higher and of magazines 109.4% higher in 1961 than in 1955.

In order to get Pravda, Sovetskaya Rossia and other news-

papers to the reader as quickly as possible, they are being printed from matrices in 21 cities; as a result the residents of cities and districts far from Moscow can receive the newspapers on the day of publication. In the future the number of these publishing centers will be increased.

As a result of the growth of circulation and the increased number of publications and of the decline in costs and the reduction of excessive administrative expenditures, revenue from publishing increased by 44.7% in the period 1955-1960.

In 1960 considerable work was done to shift printshops and publishing houses of central, republic, territory and province newspapers to a seven-hour working day and to new conditions of labor payment. This made it possible to adjust the wages of workers, to increase their material incentive, and to raise labor productivity and profits in publishing.

Construction and modernization of a number of printshops of publishing houses of the Central Committees of the Union-republic Communist Parties and of the territory and province Party committees and their provision with up-to-date equipment is continuing. With the completion of this construction the capacity of printing facilities will increase 100% for newspapers, 200% for magazines and more than 50% for books in the next two or three years.

The Central Committees of the Union-republic Communist Parties and the territory and province Party committees must undertake supervision of the construction and modernization of printshops and help the Party publishing houses to complete planned work promptly and to ensure high quality of work.

A checkup has shown that Party publishing houses are still making nonproductive expenditures for the payment of idle time and overtime work resulting from violations of the schedule for sending newspapers and magazines to press and from late delivery of matrices to the places where they are being printed. Some publishing houses are exceeding the budget for administrative expenditures. It is necessary that Party publishing houses observe strict economy, make no unproductive expenditures and work for a further reduction in unit costs and the cost of publications.

The successful fulfillment of the income part of the Party budget made it possible to ensure uninterrupted financing of all measures carried out by the Central Committee and local Party agencies.

After the 20th Party Congress the Party Central Committee carried out a number of measures for further improving the Party apparatus and reducing staffs and expenditures for its maintenance.

As a result of the amalgamation of provinces and districts, 12 province and 1,186 rural and urban district Party committees were abolished in the period from Jan. 1, 1956, to October 1, 1961. This made it possible to reduce the number of officials by 25.2% and staff personnel by 22.7%. This measure, along with the reduction in expenditures for maintenance of the Party apparatus, made it possible to eliminate unnecessary units and to send a large number of workers to bolster the cadres of collective and state farms. One hundred seventy-three buildings released by Party agencies were turned over for hospitals and polyclinics, 91 for general schools, 120 for boarding schools, 41 for children's institutions and 14 for higher educational institutions and technicums.

The Central Inspection Commission considers it necessary to note that some province and territory Party committees, contrary to the March 24, 1956, resolution of the Party Central Committee "On Reducing the Staffs of Province and Territory Party Committees and Central Committees of Union-republic Communist Parties" and without sufficient grounds, have begun to increase the number of personnel in the province and territory committees. Thus in the recent period the apparatus of the Kostroma Province Party Committee has increased by six officials and one staff worker, of the Maritime Territory Committee by five officials and one staff worker, of the Tambov Province Committee by seven officials and of the Kemerovo Province Committee by three officials and four staff workers. The apparatuses of province committees are frequently increased by reducing the apparatuses of lower Party bodies.

The Party Central Committee considers the tendency to expand the paid staffs of Party agencies to be incorrect and calls the attention of province and territory Party committees and the Central Committees of the Union-republic Communist Parties to the necessity of more broadly enlisting the Party <u>aktiv</u> in work as nonpaid instructors, lecturers and propagandists and in other Party work. This fully conforms to the draft Party Statutes, which provide for the broad enlistment of Communists as nonpaid workers in carrying out Party work by way of public activity and the establishment of permanent or temporary commissions for various questions of Party work.

The Central Committee has devoted considerable attention to questions of the propaganda of the ideas of Marxism-Leninism. Party education clubs and offices, the Institute of Marxism-Leninism and its branches, Party archives, the V. I. Lenin Central Museum and its branches, home-museums, and lectures and seminars by propaganda personnel are supported with funds from the Party budget.

The Party Central Committee has done a great deal to restore and ensure the maintenance of historic places associated with the life and work of the great leader and teacher of the working people Vladimir Ilyich Lenin.

In the period under review considerable work was done in the training and refresher training of Party and Soviet personnel. About 40,000 Party and Soviet workers completed a course of instruction in Party educational institutions in this period.

In order to improve the training and refresher training of personnel, republic and interprovince, higher Party schools with a four-year course of instruction have been set up on the basis of the three-year Party schools in accordance with the decisions of the Party Central Committee. These schools offer graduates a higher Party and political education. Soviet and Party schools with a three-year course of instruction have been set up to train cadres of district Party workers, Party organization secretaries and executive personnel for collective and state farms and rural Soviets. New curriculums have been introduced in the Academy of Social Sciences and the Higher Party School under the Party Central Committee.

These measures have also made it possible to reduce expenditures under the Party budget. Eleven vacated academic buildings and 16 dormitories have been turned over to higher educational institutions, technicums and other organizations.

Expenditures under the budgets of Party agencies have been reduced considerably in connection with the decision of the Party Central Committee and the U.S.S.R. Council of Ministers concerning improved use of passenger cars. The number of automobiles in Party agencies has been reduced by more than 30% and expenditures on transport maintenance by 22.5%.

In the period 1955-1960 the expenditure part of the Party budget was reduced 8% for local Party agencies and Party institutions and 18.9% for the apparatus of the Party Central Committee and central Party institutions.

In summing up the results of fulfillment of the expenditure part of the Party budget, the Central Inspection Commission deems it necessary to report to the Congress that the funds allocated under the Party budget are being spent both in the Party Central Committee and in the majority of local Party agencies in strict accordance with approved allocations.

At the same time it must be noted that in some Party organizations there were serious violations of budget discipline, manifested in overexpenditure of approved allocations, chiefly on such budget items as transport maintenance and postal, telegraph and other administrative expenditures. In the first six months of the current year 16 out of the 29 district and city Party committees in Kirov Province permitted overexpenditures for maintenance of transport. According to the reports of the inspection commissions of Ulyanovsk, Tula and other provinces, some city and district Party committees also permitted overexpenditures for transport maintenance and office, postal and telegraph expenses.

The Central Committee exercised systematic supervision over fulfillment of the Party budget by means of local checkups on the financial and economic activity of Party agencies and analysis of the financial reports received from province and territory Party committees and the Union-republic Communist Party Central Committees and of the audits of the province, territory and republic inspection commissions.

The results of the checkups were usually considered at meetings of the respective Party committees, which adopted the measures necessary to eliminate the disclosed shortcomings and violations of financial and budget discipline. The Party Central Committee adopted decisions on the materials of the checkups on the financial and budget work of the Kazakhstan Communist Party Central Committee and the Tatar Province Party Committee.

The inspection commissions of the Union-republic Communist Parties and of territory, province, region, city and district Party organizations are doing considerable work in supervising the financial and budget activity of local Party bodies. They are giving serious help to Party agencies in organizing their finances and in eliminating shortcomings disclosed in the course of audits.

But some city and district inspection commissions have a formal attitude toward audits, carry them out irregularly, confine themselves to copying down the balances from the ledgers and do not disclose existing violations in the financial activity of city and district Party committees or check on the payment of membership dues in primary Party organizations.

It should also be noted that the recommendations of inspection commissions on the elimination of violations of financial and budget discipline by individual city and district Party committees are not always carried out, and the same violations are again disclosed in subsequent audits.

The Central Committees of the Union-republic Communist Parties and the territory and province Party committees must make higher demands on accountable Party organizations in financial work, striving for strict observance of budget discipline and economy in the expenditure of Party funds, and must further improve and reduce the cost of the Party apparatus.

***

Comrades! The tasks of further strengthening and developing Soviet socialist democracy and overcoming bureaucracy and red tape in the work of the state apparatus demand a more attentive attitude toward the consideration of letters, complaints and petitions from the working people and toward organization of the reception of visitors.

In their letters the working people disclose shortcomings in the work of enterprises and state and collective farms, in construction and in cultural and everyday services for the population, warn of violations of legality and abuses by individual workers, and submit valuable proposals for improving the work of Party, Soviet, economic, trade union and other organizations. Since the January plenary session of the Party Central Committee and the zonal conferences of agriculture there has been an increased flow of letters reporting cases of hoodwinking and deception of the state, mismanagement, and pilfering of socialist property. Many of them cite cases of unsatisfactory quality of housing, cultural and service construction and repair work and serious shortcomings in the organization of trade and public catering and in the work of children's institutions; they also report a slackening of the struggle against law violators and antisocial parasitic elements on the part of the militia, the courts, prosecutors' offices and the public.

Letters from the working people are an expression of their initiative and their political consciousness; they reflect concern about further improving the work of the state apparatus and strengthening the might of the socialist homeland.

Among the letters and petitions received by the Party Central Committee from the working people that contain personal requests, a large number concern questions of improving housing conditions. Some letters contain requests for repairs and for the improvement of courtyards and playground equipment and cite cases of an incorrect distribution of apartments in newly built apartment houses. Complaints about violations of labor legislation, about incorrect dismissal or transfer to other, less skilled work, continue to come in. A large number of complaints concern pensions. Petitions dealing with other questions are also received.

The Central Committee and Comrade N. S. Khrushchev personally are devoting exceptional attention to letters and requests from the working people.

In a speech at the zonal conference of leading agricultural

workers in Voronezh on Feb. 11, 1961, Comrade N. S. Khrushchev stressed that "it is the duty of every leader to pay careful heed to critical warnings, to every letter received by the province Party committee and the province executive committee and by other Party and Soviet agencies, because behind each letter stands a living person who awaits an attentive, benevolent attitude toward his letter and toward his petition."

The letters received by the Party Central Committee, regardless of their nature, are considered in departments of the Central Committee or sent to the appropriate central and local organizations, which must resolve the questions touched upon in the letters. Many letters were the subject of consideration in the Secretariat and the Presidium of the Party Central Committee, and some of them were given attention at plenary sessions of the Party Central Committee.

The Aug. 2, 1958, resolution of the Party Central Committee "On Serious Shortcomings in the Consideration of Letters, Complaints and Petitions From the Working People" is of great importance in putting the settlement of complaints from the working people into proper order. In accordance with this resolution, most Party and Soviet organizations have noticeably improved work with letters and have brought order into the reception of visitors. Petitions and complaints from the working people are considered more carefully and the necessary decisions are adopted on them. Many questions touched upon in letters from working people are discussed at meetings of the bureaus and secretariats of province and territory committees and the Central Committees of the Union-republic Communist Parties, as well as at meetings of Soviet executive committees.

The Party Central Committee exercises systematic supervision over the work of local Party and Soviet agencies in the consideration of working people's petitions. In the recent period alone, Central Committee personnel checked on the state of work in the consideration of letters, complaints and petitions from the working people in Party and Soviet agencies of the Azerbaidzhan and Armenian Republics, the Karelian and Dagestan Autonomous Republics, Krasnoyarsk and Krasnodar Territories, and Kharkov, Pskov, Orel and other provinces. In order to verify individual warnings, personnel of the Party Central Committee visited Kiev, Lvov and Pavlodar Provinces, the Kara-Kalpak Autonomous Republic, a number of districts of the Lithuanian, Tadzhik and Georgian Republics, and Tyumen and other provinces of the Russian Republic.

The results of the checkups were discussed at meetings of the bureaus and in the secretariats of the above-mentioned province committees and Central Committees of the Union-republic Communist Parties. Thus the question of the consideration of working people's letters, petitions and complaints on the basis of the results of the checkup was discussed in April of this year in the bureau of the Azerbaidzhan Communist Party Central Committee with the participation of the heads of republic ministries and agencies, secretaries of the district Party committees and chairmen of the district executive committees, and later at a plenary session of the Central Committee, which outlined a number of measures to improve this important work.

The Central Committee devoted special attention to checking on the letters that reported serious shortcomings and distortions in the work of Party and Soviet agencies.

Last year, in 1960, the Party Central Committee received a letter from collective farmers of the Soviet Russia Collective Farm in Yaroslavl Province on the violation of collective farm democracy and socialist legality. A checkup established that the Yaroslavl District Party Committee, without taking economic feasibility into account and contrary to the wishes of the collective farmers, adopted a decision to merge the Soviet Russia, Ray and Red Cornfield Collective Farms into one collective farm. At a meeting of the collective farmers the district Party committee secretary displayed high-handedness, attempting to impose the district committee's decision on the collective farmers.

This conduct on the part of the district Party committee secretary evoked the just indignation of the collective farmers. They wrote a letter to the Party Central Committee in which they asked that the Soviet Russia Collective Farm not be merged with the other collective farms. Instead of drawing the correct conclusions and honestly admitting and rectifying the

mistake that had been made, the district Party committee officials undertook a search among the collective farmers for the authors of this letter.

The decision of the Party Central Committee recognized the collective farmers' demands to be well founded and the actions of the district committee leaders unlawful; those to blame were duly punished.

Upon receipt by the Party Central Committee of a letter from women miners in the Chechen-Ingush Autonomous Republic reporting cases of unequal treatment of women, Central Committee officials were sent to the republic; they established that work in the political education of women and in their enlistment in public activities was being conducted unsatisfactorily in the republic. The province, city and district Party committees were tolerating infringements of the principle of equality for women and were not waging an active struggle against those who harbored survivals of a feudal, tribal attitude toward women. The question of the unsatisfactory state of work among women in the Chechen-Ingush Autonomous Republic was discussed in the Party Central Committee.

An Aug. 2, 1958, resolution of the Party Central Committee advised the editorial boards of central and local newspapers to adopt specific measures to improve work with letters, to publicize cases of bureaucracy and red tape in the examination of petitions and complaints from the working people, and to publish readers' letters regularly, as well as reports on what action had been taken in response to them. It can be noted that newspapers have increased attention to working people's letters, are making wider use of them in the press, and are giving the Party considerable help in eliminating shortcomings in the work of Party and Soviet agencies.

The central newspapers have begun to publish working people's letters more often and to make fuller use of them in editorials, articles, surveys and feuilletons. In the first nine months of 1961 the editors of Pravda, the Party's central organ, used about 1500 letters in various forms. Pravda daily receives between 150 and 200 replies to letters sent to the proper organizations for verification and action. Pravda, Izvestia and other central newspapers regularly report on what has been done in response to working people's petitions and complaints. But institutions and agencies do not always react correctly to critical statements in the press and sometimes respond with stereotyped replies and unsubstantiated refutations.

It should also be noted that the press is not yet making adequate use of its possibilities in the struggle against bureaucracy and red tape and is not expanding its ties with readers toward this end. A checkup showed that the editors of the province newspaper Kurskaya pravda [Kursk Truth] maintain poor contact with the workers' and rural correspondents and do not heed the warnings contained in letters from the working people. For example, in the first five months of 1961 the editors received from Besedino District 70 letters, many of which spoke of the incorrect organization of labor on the collective farms and of violation of the principle of material incentive. But the editors did not respond to these serious warnings, did not check them on the spot and did not criticize the shortcomings noted in the letters.

The Party Central Committee called the attention of the Kursk Province Party Committee and the editors of Kurskaya pravda to the necessity of ensuring the broad participation of workers, collective farmers and the intelligentsia in the newspaper's work and of dealing with letters attentively, since only under these conditions will the newspaper enhance its organizational role and help to develop criticism and self-criticism, eliminate shortcomings and expose hoodwinking and abuses.

The Party Central Committee devoted considerable attention to a checkup on the examination of petitions and complaints from the working people and the organization of the reception of visitors in central Soviet institutions.

A checkup on the state of this work in the U.S.S.R. Ministry of Public Health showed that the leadership and public organizations of the ministry have begun to pay more attention to letters and complaints from the working people and to follow the practice of sending ministry officials to the localities to check on individual petitions. However, the complaints being received indicate serious shortcomings in the work of public health agencies. Many complaints point to the still unsatisfactory organization of matters in certain medical institutions and to instances of an inattentive attitude toward the sick on the part of doctors and service personnel. The ministry must increase its demands on republic and local public health agencies in examining petitions from the working people and ensure proper supervision of action on them.

Communications offices receive a large number of complaints about delays in the delivery of newspapers, magazines and mail. There are many complaints about garbling and late delivery of telegrams, the poor organization of long-distance telephone calls and delays in payment of money orders and late dispatch of tax payments. There are cases of loss of letters and even of pilfering of parcels and valuable shipments.

In view of the fact that the complaints represent just demands on the part of citizens, the U.S.S.R. Ministry of Communications must see to it that they are acted upon as quickly as possible. Yet the periods for consideration of letters are still being violated and the ministry has not yet organized proper supervision over the handling of complaints, the majority of which are sent to republic and local communications agencies. Proper order has not yet been established in the reception of visitors.

Serious shortcomings in the examination of working people's petitions exist in the Russian Republic Ministry of Trade, although a number of measures have been adopted recently to improve this work. The leadership of the ministry is not exacting enough on the directors of administrations, departments, chief administrations and republic offices and does not supervise the prompt consideration of working people's complaints and petitions and the adoption of effective measures with respect to them.

There is an unsatisfactory state of affairs in the examination of letters in the Russian Republic Central Statistical Administration. As a checkup showed, the administration does not keep proper track of the letters and petitions received, and in the case of many letters no indication is made as to who has been instructed to handle them. The staff is indifferent to losses of letters, telegrams and other documents. The consideration of some letters that contain critical comments is exceedingly prolonged, the letters are verified superficially and no specific measures are taken on petitions and warnings.

In order to implement the May 19, 1961, resolution of the Party Central Committee and the U.S.S.R. Council of Ministers "On Measures to Prevent Deception of the State and to Strengthen Supervision Over the Reliability of Reports on the Fulfillment of Plans and Pledges," state statistical agencies must pay the greatest heed to documents, letters and petitions and respond promptly and vigorously to the warnings contained in them.

The inspection commissions of the republic, territory and province Party organizations cite a number of violations of the established procedure for examining letters, petitions and complaints from the working people in local Party and Soviet organizations. This indicates that not all organizations are

meeting the necessary standards in the consideration of questions raised in the letters and do not always exercise the proper supervision over their disposition.

A thoughtful attitude toward the examination of letters, petitions and complaints from the working people and the proper reception of visitors should be regarded by all Party, Soviet, trade union and other public organizations as a requirement stemming from the essence of our state and social system that is truly of the people.

**

Approximately 5,500,000 Party cards and candidates' cards have been issued to persons admitted as candidate members and members of the Party in the period since the 20th Party Congress. The report materials for all these documents that were received from local Party organizations have been checked and recognized to be correct.

The Party Central Committee attaches great importance to the prompt issuance of Party documents to Communists. Those who have joined the Party but have not received their Party documents promptly do not feel that they are Communists with full rights and are not included in the active life of the Party organization. But some district and city Party committees violate the established period for issuing Party documents, a period of ten days from the time of approval of admission to the Party, and wait one or two months before issuing them.

Party organizations have been repeatedly reminded of the necessity of adopting proper measures to prevent the loss of Party cards and candidates' cards by Communists and to inculcate in Communists a sense of responsibility for the safekeeping of Party documents. But losses of Party documents continue to remain quite high.

Party organizations must pay more attention to questions of the registration of Communists and issue Party documents promptly, seeing to it that all Party members and candidates have an attitude of responsibility for the safekeeping of Party and candidates' cards and remembering that this is one of the statutory requirements of the Party.

**

Comrades! Our party has come to its 22nd Congress monolithic as never before, ideologically and organizationally rallied around the Leninist Central Committee.

Not one Congress represented the Party so broadly and comprehensively as does the present 22nd Congress, which embodies the strength and unconquerable will of our great Leninist Party.

The pre-Congress discussion of the drafts of the Party Program and Party Statutes showed that the magnificent plan for building a communist society in our country—the most just and the brightest society on earth—has found warm response in the hearts and minds of the Soviet people.

Under the leadership of the glorious Leninist Party, the people will achieve the great goals formulated in the draft of the new Program of the Communist Party of the Soviet Union—the program for building communism in our country. (Prolonged applause.)

VI. KHRUSHCHEV: REPORT ON THE PARTY PROGRAM

ON THE PROGRAM OF THE COMMUNIST PARTY OF THE SOVIET UNION.— Report by Comrade N. S. Khrushchev at the 22nd Congress of the Communist Party of the Soviet Union Oct. 18, 1961. (Pravda and Izvestia, Oct. 19, pp. 1-10. Complete text:) Comrades! The 20th Congress instructed the Central Committee to draft a new Program of the Communist Party of the Soviet Union. The Central Committee has carried out this instruction and is now submitting the draft Program to the Congress for consideration following its discussion by the Party and the people.

Our Congress will go down in history as the Congress of the builders of communism, as the Congress that considered and adopted the great program for creating the first communist society in the history of mankind.

From the rostrum of our Congress we would first address our words of love and devotion to those geniuses of mankind, the great leaders of the working class Marx, Engels and Lenin. (Prolonged applause.) Socialism, whose inevitability was scientifically predicted by Marx and Engels; socialism, the plan for whose construction was outlined by Lenin, has become a living reality in the Soviet Union. Now our country is moving on to new heights—the heights of communism. (Applause.)

The working class and its Communist Party pass in their struggle through three world-historic stages: the overthrow of the rule of the exploiters and the establishment of the dictatorship of the proletariat; the building of socialism; and the creation of a communist society.

Our party and people have traversed the first two stages. And if our party was invariably successful in both these stages, this is to an enormous extent attributable to its having had an unerring compass—its militant revolutionary programs, which were based on the granite foundation of Marxism-Leninism. The first two Programs were drawn up with the direct participation of Vladimir Ilyich Lenin and under his supervision. In preparing the third Program we constantly consulted with Lenin, were guided by his clear-sighted outlines, his inspired ideas on the building of socialism and communism. So we have every reason to call this program, too, a Leninist one. (Prolonged applause.)

The 20th century is the century of triumphal victories for communism. In the first half of the century socialism firmly established itself on our planet, and communism will establish itself in the latter half. The way to this is pointed by our party's new Program, which is justly called the Communist Manifesto of the modern era. (Applause.)

The draft Program embodies the collective thinking of the Party. All Soviet people say: This is our Program, it accords with our hopes and aspirations.

The ideas contained in the Program express the bright dreams of all humanity. The draft Program of the C.P.S.U. has been heartily endorsed by the fraternal parties. It has been received with great enthusiasm by the proletariat, by the working people, of the whole world. And this testifies to the strength of communism and the great significance of our Program for the destinies of mankind.

I. THE HISTORIC VICTORIES OF SOCIALISM. 1. Lenin's Program Has Been Translated Into Reality.—Comrades! In October, 1917, the Party achieved the first great victory on its historic road to communism: The rule of the exploiters was overthrown and the dictatorship of the proletariat was established. The Party Program adopted at the Second Congress had been carried out. The country had set foot on the glorious but untried path of socialist transformation.

On the bridge of the Soviet ship of state stood a dauntless helmsman—our beloved Ilyich. He outlined a brilliant plan for the building of socialism. Lenin's Party Program, adopted at the Eighth Congress, was at once a daring scientific forecast, a coherent plan for building a new society and a fervent revolutionary appeal to the masses. The Party's premise was that we had all we needed to build socialism. It had profound faith in the revolutionary potentialities of the new system and in the heroism of the working people.

The difficulties entailed in founding the new order were incalculable. The fires of war raged over the vast reaches of our country. The combined forces of international reaction and internal counterrevolution scourged the Republic of Soviets, seeking at the very outset to bar mankind's way to socialism.

The imperialist war and the intervention wrecked the national economy of Russia, which already lagged economically 50 to 100 years behind the principal capitalist countries. The country's industrial output in 1919 was one-fifth the 1913 figure. Agriculture, too, was at a low ebb.

The difficulties were compounded by the lack of experience in organizing life on socialist lines, by the necessity of blazing new historical trails. The Soviet people were unable to obtain any material or technical assistance from without. The country found itself in a hostile capitalist encirclement and was forced to live the life of a beleaguered fortress.

Truly titanic efforts were required of the Party and the people to surmount these incredible difficulties and help the country to its feet so that it might build a new life.

We Communists were portrayed by our enemies as good at tearing down but incapable of building and creating. We did indeed tear down the exploiters' system so hated by the people. But we did this so that on soil cleansed of the filth and abomination of capitalism we might build the new and most equitable of social systems—communism. In the history of mankind the Communists emerge as the greatest creative force, a force that is remaking and regenerating the world. (Prolonged applause.)

It has been borne out by historical experience that Communists are the most consistent patriots, the most loyal sons of their homeland, the most valiant defenders of its interests. We Bolsheviks saved the country from national disaster, from enslavement by foreign imperialists, and exalted it in the eyes of all mankind.

The bourgeois parties, politicians and ideologists greeted the plan for building socialism in Russia with fierce hatred and venomous derision. With one voice they cried that the "Bolshevik experiment" would inevitably founder. Churchill predicted the complete breakdown of all forms of life in Russia and the total failure of the socialist and communist theories. We might well ask Mr. Churchill today who it was that proved the failure. Our country, which economically had been at the bottom of the list of the world's principal countries, has now become the second-ranking industrial power and is in the van of historical progress. And Great Britain, which had

been the world's foremost power, has lost her place for good.
Here is graphic evidence for you of the enormous transforming power of the ideas of socialism and the utter failure of
the ideas of the imperialists. (Applause.)

Among those who sought to prove the impossibility of building socialism in Russia were the leaders of the Second International. "The radical destruction of capitalism is out of
the question.***Capitalism will, it must, rise again, and
probably very soon"—such was the fate foretold for our
country by Karl Kautsky. He stated outright that the Bolshevik
Party would be unable to carry out its program. The Mensheviks and Right Social Revolutionaries echoed this sentiment.
An official document of the Central Committee of the party of
Right Social Revolutionaries declared: "The attempts to turn
an economically backward country with a demolished industry
and a disrupted transport system into a basis for socialism
can only effect the utter ruination of the economy and plunge
the country into chaos and anarchy."

The bourgeois and Social-Democratic false prophets suffered ignominious failure. If the right-wing socialist leaders
had had an ounce of conscience they would have conceded that
the Bolsheviks were right. The Communist Party proved to
be the only party that knew in which direction to lead the people.
It overcame enormous difficulties, swept the Trotskyites, right-
wing opportunists, nationalist deviationists and other defeat-
ists out of its way and translated its plans into reality, thereby
demonstrating a unity of word and deed that was without parallel.
(Applause.)

The primary result of the activities of the Party and the
people has been the complete and final victory of socialism in
the U.S.S.R. A great feat has been accomplished, a feat of
world-historic importance. Mankind has now been armed with
a science, verified by experience, of the establishing and development of socialism. It is now easier for other peoples to
move on to socialism.

The basic achievement of the Party and the people in the
political sphere has been the creation and consolidation of a
new type of state, the socialist state, and of a higher type of
democracy, socialist democracy. The U.S.S.R. is a country of
genuinely popular sovereignty, freedom and equality.

Our most important historical accomplishment in the economic
sphere has been the affirmation of public ownership and the
liquidation of private ownership of the means of production,
which breeds the most violent collisions between classes and
nations. The bourgeoisie proclaimed private ownership, which
had existed for millenniums, to be eternal and immutable. We
Communists boldly assaulted that principle. Socialism has
ushered in the era of public ownership and has put an end to
production anarchy, economic crises and other social convul-
sions.

Within an astonishingly short time we built a powerful industry, which constitutes the material base of socialism, the foundation of our country's might and prosperity. Armed with
Lenin's plan for cooperatives, the Party accomplished the most
difficult task it had faced since the taking of power: It helped
the peasants switch to socialist rails. The voluntary organization of the peasantry into cooperatives was a signal event in the
social and economic history of mankind.

Take in our country at a glance with your mind's eye and compare it with what it was like in the past, and you will see how
startlingly the face of our homeland has changed, what a long
way we have come in these years.

Russia was considered a country of sledge hammers and wheel-
barrows, of wooden plows and spinning wheels. It was one-
tenth as well equipped with machinery as the United States and
one-fifth as well as Germany. Today the Soviet Union is a
country of advanced technology, high-powered machines and
high-precision instruments, automatic production lines, electronic computers and spaceships. In 1961 the output of our
machine-building and metalworking industries was 350 times
as great as in 1913 and nearly 1000 times as great as in 1919.

Russia was considered a country of wood, straw and bast
and was actually starving for metals. Now the Soviet Union
is a country of steel and aluminum, cement and plastics. We
smelt almost as much steel as Britain, the Federal German
Republic and France put together.

Russia was considered a country of oil lamps and wood
torches. When the delegates to the Eighth Congress of Soviets
discussed GOELRO [the State Plan for the Electrification of
Russia], there was barely enough electricity in Moscow to light
the building in which the Congress held its meetings. Today the
Soviet Union is a country of giant power stations, the largest in
the world. We are generating more than 300,000,000,000 kwh.
of electrical energy. In 1961 we shall produce roughly 160 times
as much power as in 1913 and 650 times as much as in 1919.

In the days when the country was getting started on socialist
construction, Lenin, speaking of the enormous tasks we would
have to accomplish, recalled Nekrasov's famous lines, permeated with the poet's anguish for his homeland and his passionate faith in its powers:

> Thou are at once
> Poor and abundant,
> Thou art at once
> Mighty and impotent,
> Mother Russia!

The unswerving resolve of the Bolsheviks, Lenin proclaimed,
was "to see to it at any cost that Russia ceased to be poor and
impotent and became mighty and abundant in the full sense of
the words" ("Works" [in Russian], Vol. XXVII, p. 134). And
we have seen to it! (Stormy applause.)

In the social sphere the Party has realized the age-old
hopes of the masses. Oppression of man by man has been
done away with in all its forms. The exploiting classes have
been eliminated. The working class has become the guiding
force in society. The peasantry has gone over to socialist
farming. A socialist unity of the whole Soviet people has
been established. Women have been given equal rights with
men and have received every opportunity for vigorous creative
activity for the good of society.

In the ideological sphere an upheaval has occurred, profound
in substance and great in its social significance and consequences. The Communists have raised aloft the torch of
learning and science. In the course of the cultural revolution
illiteracy has been wiped out and millions of people have
familiarized themselves with the achievements of culture and
science. A people's intelligentsia has been called into being.
We have long since attained world leadership in the training
of engineers. A socialist culture, the prototype of the future
universal culture of mankind, has been molded. Marxism-
Leninism has become the ideology of Soviet society. The
misanthropy born of private ownership has receded into the
past. Collective principles have triumphed in the life and activities of Soviet man.

The Party has solved one of the most complex of problems,
which has plagued mankind for ages and remains acute in the
world of capitalism to this day—the problem of relations between nations. Tsarist Russia was called the "prison of the
peoples." The Soviet Union is called the fraternal family of
peoples, the country of the friendship and flowering of nations. The Soviet system has roused to a new life and brought
to their flowering all the formerly oppressed and rightless
peoples who had been at various levels of historical development, from the patriarchal clan to capitalism. With the aid
of the more highly developed peoples, above all the great
Russian people, previously backward peoples by-passed the
capitalist stage and rose to the level of the advanced nations.
There has formed in the Soviet Union a new historical community of people who are of different nationalities but have
characteristic features in common—the Soviet people. They
have a common socialist homeland, the U.S.S.R.; a common
economic base, the socialist economy; a common social-
class structure; a common world view, that of Marxism-
Leninism; a common goal, the building of communism; and
many common traits in their spiritual makeup, in their
psychology. (Applause.)

The result of all these colossal transformations has been a
fundamental change in the people's living conditions. In
Tsarist Russia the workers' toil was arduous, and they often
worked a 12- to 14-hour day. They were paid starvation
wages. Many workers lived in slums. The peasants were
starved for land. Every third family was without a horse.
Taxes and other exactions claimed the greater part of the
crop. The diet of most peasants was very poor: They had
meat only on important holidays, and sugar was considered
a luxury beyond their reach. Every year thousands of peas-

ants were ruined and departed for the cities to swell the army of unemployed.

Socialism has brought the peoples a different kind of life. Unemployment, that dread scourge of working people, has long since been eliminated. The real earnings of the workers, taking into account the elimination of unemployment and the shortening of the working day, have increased 480% and the real incomes of the peasants more than sixfold under the Soviet regime. Gas, electricity, television, radios, refrigerators, books and newspapers have come into the homes of the working people. Apartment rents in the U.S.S.R. are the lowest in the world. A law abolishing taxes is being implemented. Striking evidence of our progress is the fact that average life expectancy has increased to 69 years, meaning that it has more than doubled under socialism. Communism will bring a further rise in life expectancy, and the poet's dream — "A hundred years' life for us, without old age" — will come to pass. (Applause.)

Socialism, for the first time in history, has really secured for man his basic social rights: the right to work, the right to leisure, the right to material security in old age and in the event of illness or disability, and the right to education. Socialism has given the Soviet people a great feeling of confidence in their own futures and in the futures of their children, a sense that the well-being they have attained is secure; it has instilled in people a spirit of historical optimism.

The heroic strength of socialism was demonstrated during the Great Patriotic War, which saw the utter defeat of German fascist hordes that had been considered invincible.

With the victory of socialism colossal changes have occured in the nature of social development. For thousands of years people had been the victims of the elemental workings of social laws, had been the pitiful playthings of these laws. Under socialism people not only come to know objective laws but gain mastery over them. The workers and peasants, whom the exploiters had dealt with contemptuously as a faceless, inert mass, under socialist conditions have shown truly limitless creative powers, have displayed wondrous heroism, legendary courage, the strength of giants. The example of the Soviet Union has bred in the hearts of the working people of all lands confidence in their own strength.

The fundamental advantages that have been demonstrated by the socialist system in our country have been the most telling reply to the question of which road mankind should take. We have seen that all the plans of the bourgeois and Social-Democratic parties have come to nothing; these parties have failed to redeem their promises and have not solved, and could not solve, a single basic social problem. It is a fact borne out by history that the Communists are the only socio-political force that is really solving the social problems that disturb mankind and that carries out its programmatic plans.

2. Principal Results of the World's Development. — Comrades! The Party Program adopted at the Eighth Congress stated that the development of imperialism and of its contradictions had "made inevitable the collapse of capitalism and the transition to a higher type of social economy." The program proclaimed that the era of world-wide proletarian, communist revolution had been launched. The whole subsequent course of historical events has been as the Marxist-Leninists predicted.

Let us compare the political map of the world as it was in 1919 and as it is today [see table below].

What does this comparison indicate? That the great revolutionary forces of our time have decisively altered the world's appearance. That imperialism has permanently lost its sway over the greater part of the world's peoples. It has become apparent that the main highway along which mankind is advancing is the highway of socialism.

The principal result of the forward movement of society in our time has been the formation of the world socialist system. The victories of the socialist revolutions in China and in a number of other European and Asian countries represent the most important development in the history of the world since October, 1917.

The world socialist system is a young system. But it has already amassed sufficient experience to permit conclusions that are of vast significance for the determination of the course of mankind's future development.

The inevitability of the replacement of capitalism by socialism has now been confirmed by the experience not of one country alone but of a large group of states, and socialism has proved its decisive advantages. The new system has ensured the rapid development of productive forces, a steady improvement of the working people's living standards, freedom from exploitation, and broad social and political rights for the individual.

The glorious Marxist-Leninist parties of the fraternal countries have made a vital contribution to the collective experience of socialist revolution and socialist construction. Along with the vast experience of the U.S.S.R., the international working-class movement can today draw upon the experience in developing a new form of dictatorship of the proletariat—people's democracy; upon the experience of peaceful transition from the democratic stage of the revolution to the socialist stage; the experience of making use of parliaments and multiparty systems in the furtherance of socialist construction; the experience of building a socialist society in industrially developed countries; the experience of the bypassing of the capitalist stage of development by economically underdeveloped countries in their transition to socialism; the experience of socialist transformation of the countryside without nationalization of the land, taking into account the lingering tradition of deep peasant attachment to private ownership of land.

Socialism has produced a new type of economic and political relationship between states and peoples. The principal features of the relations in the socialist commonwealth are socialist internationalism, all-round comradely cooperation, fraternal mutual aid and the complete equality of all sovereign countries. In the socialist commonwealth age-old antagonisms between nations have been done away with and the principles of brotherhood and friendship between peoples prevail. (Prolonged applause.)

The socialist system is turning into a factor that is increasingly shaping the course of world development in the interests

	1919				1961			
	Area		Population		Area		Population	
	million sq. km.	%	millions	%	million sq. km.	%	millions	%
I. Whole world	135.4	100	1,777	100	135.4	100	3,017	100
including: 1) Socialist world	21.7	16.0	138	7.8	35.1	25.9	1.072	35.5
2) Rest of the world	113.7	84.0	1,639	92.2	100.3	74.1	1,945	64.5
II. Major imperialist powers (U.S.A., Britain, Germany—F.G.R., France, Japan, Italy) and their colonies	60.3	44.5	855	48.1	18.6	13.7	541.5	17.9
III. All colonies, semicolonies and dominions	104.5	77.2	1,230	69.2	14.2	10.5	85.4	2.8
IV. Ex-colonies and semicolonies that have won independence since 1919 (excluding socialist states)	-	-	-	-	72.2	53.4	1,228	40.7

of peace and social progress. The socialist commonwealth, by force of example, is inspiring the working class and all the working people of other countries to step up the struggle against capitalist oppression and for their vital rights and interests, for social and national liberation and for lasting peace. The facts of life are bringing the masses to the realization that socialism is the world's true prime of youth, while capitalism is its yesterday. (Applause.)

The second most important result of world development, from the historical standpoint, is the collapse of the colonial system. The rise and consolidation of socialism marked the advent of the era of liberation for oppressed peoples. Such a historic development as the liberation of more than 1,500,000,000 people from colonial oppression could have occurred only under circumstances where socialism had become a mighty force. The national-liberation revolutions dealt the Bastille of colonialism a shattering blow. On the wreckage of the colonial empires 42 sovereign states have sprung into being.

Imperialism transformed whole continents into prisons of the peoples. It put the shackles of slavery upon hundreds of millions of people and for centuries kept them removed from civilization; it warped the economies of Asian, African and Latin American countries, giving them a one-sided, agrarian-raw materials character. Judge for yourselves, comrades. Countries that have more than two-thirds of the population of the nonsocialist world produce only about one-tenth of the output of the manufacturing industries, roughly 3% of the machinery and equipment and 5% of the metallurgical output of the capitalist economy. The average per capita income in the underdeveloped countries of Asia and Africa is between a twentieth and a twenty-fifth that of the United States.

After the many years in which the capitalist "civilizers" have been "looking after" the colonies, millions of people in Asia, Africa and Latin America are literally starving to death. Life expectancy in those regions is little more than half that of the former mother countries. In Africa infant mortality is exceptionally high. More than 80% of the adults in Africa and more than 40% in Latin America are unable to read or write. This is the terrible price that has been paid for the so-called civilization of the "free world." Not unnaturally, the peoples are engaged in demolishing the disgraceful system of relations that was built up by the colonialists.

The third result of world development has been an acute all-round weakening of capitalism and a fresh sharpening of its general crisis. The course of events has fully corroborated the analysis of capitalism and of its highest stage, imperialism, given by Lenin in our party's second Program. This is why we saw fit to reproduce the fundamental tenets on this question in the new Party Program.

Socialist and national-liberation revolutions, the growth of the world socialist system and the break-up of the colonial system are the decisive factors in the deepening of the general crisis of capitalism, which in recent years has arrived at a new, third stage in its development. But the play of these factors is not the only thing that has sharpened the general crisis of capitalism. The crisis of world capitalism is a far-reaching, all-embracing process that takes in all aspects of the life of bourgeois society: the economy, domestic and foreign policy, and the ideological superstructure.

First of all, it is essential to note that the economic instability of capitalism and the unevenness of the development of some countries in relation to others have become much more marked. The rates of economic development are falling off in the capitalist system, barely keeping ahead of population growth in a number of countries, and economic crises are becoming more frequent, especially in the U.S.A. War production has become a permanent feature of the economy. Militarism has run wild: 15% to 20% of the national income is being spent on armaments. A considerable part of the labor force is not being used to produce material wealth. The chronic underutilization of production facilities is assuming ever greater proportions. During crises the utilization of capacity drops to as low as 50% in a number of industries. In many countries mass unemployment, not to speak of agrarian overpopulation, has become a real national calamity. According to official statistics, in the developed capitalist countries of North America and Western Europe plus Japan and Australia, out of an industrial proletariat of 85,000,000 there are 8,000,000 to 10,000,000 totally unemployed. This means that on the average one person in nine is jobless.

The political instability of world capitalism has increased, especially as a result of sharpening class antagonisms. This is cogently attested by the deepening of the contradictions between the handful of monopolists and all sections of the people, by the vast scope of the struggle that the working class is waging, by the mounting struggle of the peasants, and by the mass action of the working people in defense of democracy and against fascism and tyrannical military regimes. The steady rise in the role and influence of the Communist Parties also furnishes eloquent evidence.

The edifice of imperialism, from its foundation to its pinnacle, is in the grip of a deep and acute crisis. This does not mean, of course, that imperialism is at a total standstill, that its productive forces are immobilized. In particular periods, under the influence of transitory factors, there may be a more rapid economic growth in certain capitalist countries than in others. But viewed as a whole, capitalist production relations are to an ever greater extent inhibiting the development of modern productive forces. Nowadays the criterion of their development is the rate at which production is growing in the socialist countries. Over the past decade the average annual rate of growth for the capitalist economy as a whole has been no more than 5%, while in the socialist world it has amounted to almost 14%.

The ideologists and politicians of imperialism are straining to prove that there are still big possibilities and "reserves" for development in capitalism. The right-wing socialists and other champions of imperialism, seizing upon new manifestations in the capitalist economy, have been representing things as though capitalism were changing its nature and all but evolving toward socialism. This, needless to say, is all nonsense. As a matter of fact, these new manifestations constitute the most striking possible substantiation of Lenin's analysis of imperialism. They show that what is under way is no "transformation" of capitalism but a process of its ever greater weakening, of the ever greater sharpening of its contradictions, of its ever-intensifying decay and parasitism.

On just what are the apologists of imperialism pinning their hopes? Above all, on state-monopoly capitalism. But state-monopoly capitalism, as we know, is not a new-born thing. And what have events shown? They have proved that state-monopoly capitalism by no means signifies the appearance of some new stage of capitalist development distinct from imperialism, or the transformation of the bourgeois state into an arbiter, into a kind of supra-class force that provides equal safeguards for private and public interests, for the interests of labor and those of capital. State-monopoly capitalism represents a fusion of the power of monopolies with the power of the state to form a single mechanism that subordinates all aspects of the nation's life to the interests of the financial oligarchy. The monopolies remain the backbone of the economy, and not merely within the confines of particular countries but on a scale encompassing the whole capitalist world. Suffice it to say that nearly one-third of world capitalist production is concentrated in the hands of just 200 great monopolies. Like giant octopuses, the monopolies have wrapped their tentacles around whole countries and continents, sucking the lifeblood out of the peoples.

The emergence of state monopolies and the state's ever-increasing intervention in the process of capitalist reproduction do, of course, offer an opportunity for exerting definite influence on the development of productive forces and facilitate the mobilization of resources in the interests of the financial oligarchy. The state's intervention in economic relations in the interests of the monopolies has had a definite effect in bringing about a certain increase in production and renewal of fixed capital in the postwar years. Aware of the dread social consequences that an economic crisis on the 1929-1933 scale might entail, the monopolistic bourgeoisie is seeking by the method of government regulation to blunt the destructive force of the economic upheavals inherent in capitalism. But state-monopoly capitalism does not nullify, nor can it nullify, the economic laws of capitalism; it does not eliminate the spontaneous, anarchic nature of production, or economic crises, or the other evils of the capitalist system.

In the U.S.A. state-monopoly capitalism has reached a high level of development. Well, what has it done for the country?

It is precisely there that underutilization of plant capacity is at its greatest. At a time when multitudes of people are going hungry in the world of capitalism, the American monopolists are financing contraction of the crop area and reduction of agricultural output. Instead of the vaunted "full employment" there is a standing army many millions strong of totally and partially unemployed.

It turns out that there are no substantial reasons for banking on state-monopoly capitalism as a means of saving imperialism.

American imperialism lays claim to the role of bulwark and savior of world capitalism. There is no denying that the United States is the richest and strongest power in the capitalist world. But more and more it is coming to be the epicenter of capitalism's economic troubles. And another fact deserves mention: For a whole decade now the U.S. share in world capitalist production and trade has been declining steadily. American capitalism has passed its zenith, and its sun is setting.

There is still another reason why the plans of the U.S.A. for "uniting" the whole capitalist world under its aegis have proved bankrupt. This is the ineradicable economic discord among the imperialist states. The international state-monopoly organizations that come into being under the slogan of the unity of the capitalist countries and the easing of the market problem are in actual fact a new means of redividing the world capitalist market, and they turn into hotbeds of acute friction and conflict. There are two trends objectively at work and intertwined in the camp of imperialism: One is toward the rallying of all its forces against socialism, and the other is toward mounting contradictions between the imperialist powers themselves and also between them and the other states in the capitalist world. The United States has been unable, and will be unable, to overcome this latter trend. The U.S. financial oligarchy lacks the power and means to make good its claim to the role of savior of capitalism, much less its claim to world domination.

Comrades! The more plainly capitalism shows its exploiting nature, shows that its ideology stands opposed to the people, shows its moral degradation, the louder do the advocates of the bourgeoisie extol it. But just what has capitalism given to humanity? It perverts the achievements of man's creative genius and directs them against him. It has made of the liberation of atomic energy a threat to mankind. Capitalism turns against man every new forward stride in technology. The wealth of certain countries is sustained by the poverty of the peoples of many other countries. Even the pure light of science, to quote Marx, is able to shine under capitalism only against the dark background of ignorance.

An insignificant handful of billionaires and millionaires not only exercise unchecked control over the entire wealth of the capitalist world but even use whole nations as small change. Within the span of one generation the imperialists have unleashed two world wars. Approximately 80,000,000 dead and crippled, to say nothing of property destruction beyond calculation—this is the price mankind has paid for the policies of imperialism. According to the estimates of some students of the subject, the sums spent on wars and on preparations for wars in the first half of the 20th century (1900-1953) add up to a truly astronomical figure for the world as a whole—more than $4,000,000,000,000.

Let us take a look at what could have been done for the benefit of man with these funds. The entire population of our planet could have been supplied with free bread for half a century. Comfortable housing for 500,000,000 families—i.e., two-thirds of the world's population—could have been built with this sum. At present imperialism is forcing mankind to spend at least $100,000,000,000 a year for military purposes. If even 20% of this sum were applied annually for 25 years toward helping the underdeveloped countries, it would be possible to build power plants with a total capacity of 230,000,000 kw. and metallurgical plants with a capacity of 185,000,000 tons of steel a year, to irrigate more than 100,000,000 hectares of land and to carry out many other great projects for improving the life of these people. This all goes to show once again the vital importance for the peoples of the struggle for disarmament.

To summarize the principal results of the world's development, it can be said: History is moving as Marx and Lenin predicted. The forces of socialism, all the forces of progress in the world, are growing; the peoples are breaking more and more decisively with imperialism. The doom of imperialism and the triumph of socialism on a world scale are inevitable. (Prolonged applause.)

II. COMMUNISM IS THE GREAT GOAL OF THE PARTY AND THE PEOPLE.—Comrades! The adoption of the new Program marks the beginning of a new era in the history of the development of our party and of all Soviet society. Each new Program of our party corresponds to a specific stage in the country's development. Yet all our Programs are interrelated. Taken as the component parts of a united whole, they provide a harmonious Marxist-Leninist theory, tested and confirmed by experience, of socialist revolution, of the building of socialism and communism. The Party Programs may be compared to a three-stage rocket. The first stage wrenched our country out of the capitalist world, the second stage lifted us to socialism and the third is to carry us into the orbit of communism. This is a remarkable rocket, comrades. (Stormy applause.) It is moving precisely along the course laid down by the brilliant Lenin and by our revolutionary theory, and it is fed by the greatest energy of all—the energy of the builders of communism. (Applause.)

What are the basic features of the draft Program?

The principal feature is that it is a concrete and scientifically grounded program for the building of communism. The draft indicates clear paths toward the erection of the bright edifice of communism. We see how it should be built, how it should look both inside and out, what kind of people will inhabit it and what they must do in order to make the edifice of communism still more comfortable and beautiful. To him who wishes to know what communism is, we can say with pride: "Read the Program of our party." (Prolonged applause.)

The draft Program marks a new stage in the development of the revolutionary theory of Marx, Engels and Lenin. The Program gives a clear answer to all basic questions of the theory and practice of the struggle for communism and to the major problems of contemporary world development. The 20th and 21st Party Congresses, which introduced a great deal that was new in principle into the solution of basic problems of the life of the Party and Soviet society and into the analysis of the processes of world development, were of enormous, truly historic importance in preparing the draft Program. If the 20th and 21st Party Congresses had not taken place, it would have been much more difficult for us to work out such a Program.

The whole spirit and the whole content of the draft reflect the unity and consistency of Marxist-Leninist theory and the practice of communist construction. The Program gives specific delineations of the tasks in the fields of industry, agriculture, the development of the state, science, culture and communist education. Just think, comrades, of the heights Soviet man has raised himself to if he can map the prospects for social development over such a considerable historical period!

The third Party Program is a program of all Soviet people. When the Party adopted its first Program it was followed by small groups of advanced workers. When the Party adopted the second Program it was followed by the working class and the major part of the toiling peasantry. The entire Soviet people now follows the Party. Our people have accepted the Party Program as a cause close to their hearts and as the great goal of their lives. (Prolonged applause.)

The new Program is the full embodiment in life of the Party slogan: "Everything in the name of man, for the benefit of man." Further improvements in the material well-being and culture of the people and the flowering of the human personality are given a leading place in the Program. This is very much as it should be. The Bolsheviks raised the banner of revolution in the name of making the life of the working people joyful and happy. The third Program marks the beginning of a period in which all the difficulties and deprivations the Soviet people have borne in the name of their great cause will be rewarded a hundred-fold.

The draft Program is based on new international conditions: The building of communism is no longer proceeding within a capitalist encirclement but in the conditions of the existence of a world socialist system, an increasing balance in favor of the forces of socialism over the forces of imperialism and of the forces of peace over the forces of war. Of course, the imperialist states are making every effort to impede the economic and social progress of the Soviet land by compelling it to make expenditures for defense. If this were not so, the rate of our development would be still higher. Nevertheless, as the forces of socialism grow stronger and the forces of world imperialism grow weaker, there will be more favorable conditions for our economic and cultural construction.

Our Program is imbued with the spirit of socialist internationalism. The Leninist Party has always honorably fulfilled its obligations to its foreign brothers. In October, 1917, it lighted the dawn of liberation over the world. It raised the beacon of socialism that is visible to all peoples and lights their way toward the new system. The Leninist Party will continue to bear the banner of internationalism on high. The Party sees as its chief international obligation the building of communism in a historically short period of time. (Applause.)

The draft Program is a document of true communist humanism; it is permeated with ideas of peace and the brotherhood of peoples. We place the constantly growing might of our state at the service of peace and the progress of mankind. When the Soviet Union becomes the first industrial power, when the socialist system has been transformed completely into the decisive factor in world development and when the forces of world peace have multiplied still further, the scales will be tipped permanently in favor of the forces of peace and the barometer of the international climate will point to "Clear. The danger of world war is gone forever." (Prolonged applause.)

Comrades! Communism is the age-old dream of mankind. The masses of working people believed that slavery and dependence, arbitrary rule and poverty, the fierce struggle for bread, and wars between peoples would be followed by a society ruled by Peace, Labor, Freedom, Equality and Brotherhood. (Applause.) The spontaneous movement of the masses gave rise to utopian theories of the golden age of the future.

The representatives of utopian socialism sharply criticized the system of exploitation and 'its vices. They painted a picture of the society of the future. But the utopians were closer to the truth when they talked about what would be absent from this society than when they talked about ways of bringing socialism into being. Nevertheless, we even now find the germs of brilliant ideas under the fantastic surface of these pictures of the ideal system. With gratitude we recall the names of the great utopian socialists Saint-Simon, Fourier, Owen, Campanella and More, and the names of our Russian revolutionary democrats Chernyshevsky, Herzen, Belinsky and Dobrolyubov, who came closer than the others to scientific socialism.

But only Marx, Engels and Lenin created the theory of scientific communism and pointed out the true paths toward the establishment of the new society and the revolutionary forces that were to destroy the old world and build the world of communism.

Marx and Engels defined the most characteristic features of communism. Now that we are actually building a communist society, we cannot but admire the brilliant foresight of our teachers. Their gaze truly penetrated an entire century.

Lenin, the great founder of our party, further developed the Marxist teaching on the communist society, gave a precise definition of the two stages of communism, worked out a plan for building socialism and revealed the laws of its development into a communist society.

Our concept of the communist system is based entirely on the scientific conclusions of the founders of Marxism-Leninism. Nonetheless, we have one important advantage over them: We live in the second half of the 20th century, and we have at our disposal enormous and invaluable practical experience in the building of socialism and communism. And we have been building not on a tiny Island of Utopia lost in oceanic wastes, as Thomas More imagined it, and not in some City of the Sun like the one Tommaso Campanella describes, and not on some patch of ground in distant America, as Robert Owen planned. No, the new life is being built on a great land mass.

Now not only can we picture the communist society more clearly but, most important, we can define practical ways for building it and give concrete meaning to the principles of scientific communism. We see more sharply and distinctly much that was concealed from our predecessors by the veil of time, for the tendencies in the development of socialist society that will lead to the victory of communism have already been fully discerned. Of course, even now we follow the example of our teachers in not attempting to define all the details of a fully developed communist society.

The draft Program gives the following definition of communism:

"Communism is a classless social system with a single form of public ownership of the means of production and full social equality of all members of society; under it, the rounded development of people will be accompanied by growth of productive forces on the basis of constantly developing science and technology, all the springs of public wealth will yield abundantly, and the great principle 'From each according to his abilities, to each according to his needs' will be applied. Communism is a highly organized society of free, socially conscious working people in which public self-government will be established, in which labor for the good of society will become a prime, vital need in everyone, a necessity recognized by all, and the abilities of each person will be employed to the greatest benefit of the people."

I shall dwell on several problems of the characteristics of communist society. Communism proposes highly organized and centralized production on the scale of society as a whole, the management of which is to be carried out on the basis of the broadest democratic principles. Communist society is not an alliance of closed, separate economic organisms. No, communist society, more than any other, needs a single system for planning the economy, organized distribution of labor and regulation of working time. The need for these follows from the requirements of the development of production forces, from the profound mutual ties between the various branches of the economy, from the need for steady technical progress and from the communist principles of distribution and consumption. The development of the communist economy is impossible without the most active participation of all the people in the management of production.

The draft Program is the first exposition of the problem of the specific forms and means for implementing the great slogan of Communists "From each according to his abilities, to each according to his needs." The way toward the implementation of the principles of communist equality is the correct combination of material incentives to labor with growing distribution through public funds.

There are some people who have an incorrect and philistine concept of living conditions under communism. They take only the second half of the formula—"according to needs"—and reason approximately thus: "Under communism you can work if you want to, or if you want to you can roam from the Far East to the West and from the West to the South and you will still receive according to your needs." The only way these people are preparing for communism is by equipping themselves with the biggest spoon. (Laughter in the hall. Applause.)

These people must be disillusioned right from the beginning. Their ideas have nothing in common with communism. Communist society will have the most highly developed technology, the most highly developed and organized production and the finest machines. But man will control the machines. Therefore accuracy, organization and discipline are sacred rules and obligatory norms of behavior for every worker. The working people will fulfill their obligations not under the scourge of hunger, as is the case under capitalism, but consciously and of their own will. Each will understand his duty and contribute his labor to the creation of both material and spiritual goods. All Soviet people must labor in such a way that they will be able to say when the bright edifice of communism is built: "Here is my contribution."

The classical writings of Marxism-Leninism emphasized that communism is not separated from socialism by a wall, but that they are rather two phases of the same socio-economic formation, different from each other in the level of economic development and in the maturity of social relations.

Socialism does not develop on its own foundation: For all its gigantic, world-historic achievements, socialism in many respects—economic, moral, legal and in the minds of people—still bears the stamp of the old order from whose depths it sprang. Communism is a higher and more perfect phase of social life, and it can be developed only after socialism has achieved its full strength. Under communism all consequences of the capitalist system will have disappeared.

The fact that communism develops on its own foundation predetermines the features of the process of its creation. The transition from capitalism to socialism occurs under conditions of class struggle and requires a complete break in social relations, a profound social revolution and a dictatorship of the proletariat. As distinct from this, the transition to communism takes place in the absence of exploiting classes and in a situation in which all members of society—workers, peasants and intelligentsia—have a vital stake in the victory of communism and deliberately set about achieving it. It is therefore natural that the building of communism should proceed by the most democratic methods, through the improvement and development of social relations, the atrophying of old forms of life, and the rise of new forms and their interweaving and interaction. Society will never again know the difficulties caused by the continuing class war within a country. All this will make it possible to increase the tempos of social development in the period of the transition to communism.

The draft Program covers a historical period of 20 years. Why did we decide on this particular span of time? During the discussion of the draft Program, some comrades asked if this was not too much time to allow for the accomplishment of this task. No, comrades. In order to prepare society for the principles of communism, we must achieve an enormous development of productive forces and provide an abundance of material and spiritual goods. A certain amount of time is needed to do this. The cup of communism is the cup of abundance, and it must always be filled to the brim. Everyone must make his contribution to it and everyone must drink from it. It would be an irremediable error to decree the introduction of communism before all the necessary conditions were ripe for it. If we stated that we were introducing communism at a time when the cup was not yet full, it would not be possible to drink from it according to need. We would only be compromising the ideas of communism, disrupting the initiative of the working people and retarding progress toward communism. We are guided by strictly scientific calculations. These calculations show that in 20 years we will have built in the main a communist society. (Prolonged applause.)

What will it mean to have built communism in the main? It will mean that:

in the economic field, the material and technical base of communism will have been created; the Soviet Union will surpass the economic level of the most highly developed capitalist countries and will take first place in per capita production; it will have the highest living standard in the world; and conditions will have been created for achieving an abundance of material and cultural goods;

in the field of social relations, the remaining distinctions between classes will be eliminated and they will be merged into a classless society of the working people of communism; the basic distinctions between city and country, and later the distinctions between physical and mental labor, will in the main be eliminated; the economic and ideological community of nations will increase; and the characteristics of the communist man will be developed, harmoniously combining lofty ideology, broad education, moral purity and physical perfection;

in the political field, it will mean that all citizens will take part in the management of public affairs and, as a result of the broad development of socialist democracy, society will prepare itself for the complete implementation of the principles of communist self-government.

III. FROM A SOCIALIST TO A COMMUNIST ECONOMY.
1. The Creation of the Material and Technical Base of Communism.—Comrades! The draft Program indicates magnificent prospects for the creation in our country of unprecedentedly powerful productive forces and for the transformation of the Soviet Union into the world's leading industrial power. V. I. Lenin said: "We value communism only when it is economically grounded." The draft Program provides this grounding.

In two decades the U.S.S.R. will create the material and technical base of communism. This is the main economic task, the foundation of the general line of our party.

The building of the material and technical base of communism is the decisive link in the chain of economic, social and cultural tasks and is dictated by both the internal and the external condi-

tions of the development of our motherland. It will make it possible for us to accomplish the following important tasks:

first, to create unprecedentedly powerful productive forces and to take first place in the world in per capita production;

second, to attain the highest labor productivity in the world, which is in the final analysis the most important, the principal factor in the victory of the new social system, and to arm Soviet people with the most modern equipment and to transform labor into a source of joy, inspiration and creativity (applause);

third, to develop the production of material goods to satisfy all the requirements of Soviet man, to achieve the highest standard of living for the entire population and to create all conditions for the ultimate transition to distribution according to need;

fourth, gradually to transform socialist production relations into communist ones, to create a classless society and to eliminate the basic distinctions between city and country and, later, the distinctions between mental and physical labor.

Finally, it is only by building the material and technical base of communism that we can win the economic competition with capitalism and maintain the country's defense at a level sufficient to destroy any aggressor who dares raise a hand against the U.S.S.R., against the socialist world as a whole. (Prolonged applause.)

Do we have all we need to create the material and technical base of communism in two decades? Yes, comrades, we have. We have a social system of gigantic creative power, enormous production capacities and inexhaustible natural resources. We have a first-class technology and the world's most advanced science. The Soviet Union has produced remarkable skilled cadres, capable of performing the tasks of communist construction. The Soviet people are guided by a wise Party that has been tempered in battle. (Applause.)

Of course, the creation of the material and technical base of communism will require enormous means. In the next 20 years it is planned to make capital investments in the national economy of the U.S.S.R. amounting to about 2,000,000,000,000 rubles. This, comrades, is now the scale of our capital construction; it has to be reckoned in trillions!

Will the mobilization of such enormous means bring with it difficulties and sacrifices such as attended the period of industrialization? We have every reason to answer that question in the negative. And the chief reason is that our country has created a mighty industry.

The role of heavy industry in the growth of the people's wellbeing, as well as in solving the problem of accumulations, now presents itself in a new way. It is known that heavy industry is made up of two types of enterprises: First, there are those that produce means of production for enterprises that in their turn also produce means of production, and second, there are the enterprises that produce means of production for the enterprises of light industry and the food industry, for agriculture, for housing construction and for cultural and everyday services for the population. When our heavy industry had just been created we were obliged to direct accumulations primarily toward the development of enterprises of the first type and to limit investments in those of the second type. We are now able to increase capital investments considerably in the second type of enterprise as well, and this will raise the growth rate of the consumer goods industry. By 1980 the output of enterprises of the first type will have increased approximately sixfold over the 1960 level, while the output of enterprises of the second type will have increased thirteenfold. In addition, heavy industry enterprises will produce more and more cultural-everyday and household goods to meet the growing demands of the population. In developing heavy industry, we proceed from the Leninist principle that "means of production are manufactured not for the sake of the means of production themselves but only because more and more means of production are required by those branches of industry making articles of consumption."

The plan for the development of the national economy over a period of 20 years (the general long-range plan) calls for bringing the rates of development of the production of the means of production and the production of articles of consumption much closer together. In the period 1929-1940 the average annual rates of growth of the production of the means of production were almost 70% higher than the rates of growth of the production of articles of consumption, whereas in the period 1961-1980 the differential will be about 20%.

Heavy industry has always played and will continue to play a leading role in expanded reproduction. The Party will continue to show concern for its growth, for it sees this growth as the decisive factor in the creation of the material and technical base and in rapid technical progress and as the basis for strengthening the defense capability of the socialist state. At the same time, the Party will see to it that heavy industry makes an ever greater contribution to increasing the production of consumer goods.

We are also capable of making capital investments on the planned scale because all social production and the national income will rise sharply. The further we move forward, the more "weight" each percent of the national income used for accumulation will have, and consequently the more funds will be available for capital investment. There is one other important factor. The further development of technology and rise in labor productivity will make it possible to increase the increment in production growth per ruble of capital investment.

On the basis of our experience and of realistic calculations for the future, we can draw up plans for approximate production scales and can speak in the concrete language of figures about the time required to create the material and technical base of communism. The table [see box] gives some estimates made by planning agencies for the development of the U.S.S.R.'s industry from 1960 through 1980 (in July 1, 1955, prices).

The most general index of all branches of social production is the gross social product. In the forthcoming 20 years it is planned to increase it approximately fivefold. Industrial output will rise at least sixfold and gross agricultural output will rise about 250%. This is equivalent to creating on our bountiful land five additional industrial countries and two agrarian countries with output equal to that of the·present-day Soviet Union. (Prolonged applause.) In 20 years the U.S.S.R. will have almost twice the present industrial output of the entire nonsocialist world.

In the next 20 years the production of means of production will increase almost sevenfold. Our country will have basic production facilities five times greater than those it has at present. This means that there will be a virtually complete renewal of production on the basis of the latest technology and that the production apparatus of the Soviet Union will be the most powerful, the newest and the most highly developed. The growth of new production facilities is a gradual process. Therefore it is necessary to make determined use of all existing means of production and all available machinery while constantly increasing its efficiency.

The Soviet economy will continue to develop rapidly. In the next 20 years the average annual rate of growth of industrial output will be at least 9% to 10%. This means that the rates of growth of our economy will continue to be substantially higher than the rates in capitalist countries.

The draft Party Program indicates the basic trends in the creation of the material and technical base of communism.

The creation of the material and technical base of communism involves transition to a new level of production technology, standards and organization and a steadily increasing development of the processes of concentration, specialization, cooperation and the formation of combines. Science will become more and more a direct productive force and production will become more and more a technological application of modern science. As V. I. Lenin emphasized many times, communism cannot be built without the latest technology and without new scientific discoveries.

What new implements of labor—to use Marx's words—will form the bone and muscle of the system of communist production? It will be a system of machines for integrated mechanization and automation. During the building of communism automation will open up a new era in the development of machine technology. In production, a greater and greater role will be played by the creation and use of chemical products, new and highly efficient substances and new materials and by the broad use of chemical methods. Great importance is now attached to a sharp increase in the strength and reliability of metals and other materials, especially those subject to extremely high pressures, temperatures and speeds. There are prospects for expanding raw material sources by penetrating into deeper layers of the earth and using the biological and mineral resources of giant bodies of water.

The draft Program discloses the high importance of the electrification of the entire country. "Electrification on the basis of the Soviet system will achieve final victory for the foundations of communism," said V. I. Lenin. Lenin's idea of complete electrification is the pivot of the entire program for building the economy of communism.

Vladimir Ilyich put forward the first plan for the integrated development of the country's economy—the GOELRO plan [State Plan for the Electrification of Russia]—describing it as the second program of the Party. It called for increasing electric power production to 8,800,000,000 kwh. a year. This plan was fulfilled ahead of schedule. By 1947 our country was first in Europe and second in the world in electric power production.

By 1960 the capacity of all our power plants was 66,700,000 kw.

We are progressing toward the mastery of new sources of energy and new means of generating it. The solution of the problem of the direct transformation of various types of energy into electrical energy, with a resultant sharp increase in the efficiency of power installations, will take on great importance.

	1960	1970	1980	1980 ÷ 1960
Gross industrial output in wholesale factory prices (billion rubles)	155	408	970-1,000	6.2-6.4
including:				
Production of means of production—group "A" (billion rubles)	105	287	720-740	6.8-7.0
Production of consumer goods—group "B" (billion rubles)	50	121	250-260	5-5.2
Electric power (billion kwh.)	292.3	900-1,000	2,700-3,000	9.2-10.3
Steel (million tons)	65	145	250	3.8
Oil (million tons)	148	390	690-710	4.7-4.8
Gas (billion cu. m.)	47	310-325	680-720	14.4-15.2
Coal (million tons)	513	686-700	1,180-1,200	2.3-2.34
Output of machine-building and metalworking industries (billion rubles)	34	115	334-375	9.8-11
Mineral fertilizers, in conventional units (million tons)	13.9	77	125-135	9-9.7
Synthetic resins and plastics (thousand tons)	332	5,300	19,000-21,000	57-63
Artificial and synthetic fiber (thousand tons)	211	1,350	3,100-3,300	14.7-15.6
Cement (million tons)	45.5	122	233-235	5.1-5.2
Textiles, all types (billion sq.m.)	6.6	13.6	20-22	3-3.3
Leather footwear (million pairs)	419	825	900-1,000	2.1-2.4
Cultural-everyday and household goods (billion rubles)	5.9	18	58-60	9.8-10.1

The general long-range plan calls for a preponderant rate of development of electric power output. It is planned to increase production to between 2,700,000,000,000 and 3,000,000,000,000 kwh. by 1980, or nine or ten times the level of 1960.

By 1980 our country will be producing about one and one-half times as much power as is now produced by all other countries of the world combined. This will mean an eight- or ninefold increase in the electrification of industrial labor. (Applause.)

By this time the U.S.S.R. will have overtaken the U.S.A. both in the amount of electric power produced and in kilowatt-hours per capita.

As a result of this increase in electric power output, transportation and agriculture and urban and rural homes will make extensive use of electricity.

Thus the electrification of the entire country will play a leading role in the development of all branches of the national economy and in the movement of the country along the path of technical progress.

What magnificent and truly thrilling plans, comrades! The sun of communism is indeed rising over our motherland! (Prolonged applause.)

The Party and the people are fully resolved to implement consistently the construction plans that will result in fulfillment of the Leninist program for the complete electrification of the country.

Planning agencies have worked out a tentative scheme for the construction of major thermal and hydroelectric power stations. Every station in the plan is to be given careful consideration. Substantial changes may result from further technical progress.

In 20 years we are to build 180 large hydroelectric stations, about 200 regional thermal power plants with capacities of up to 3,000,000 kw. each, and about 260 large thermal heat-and-power plants.

In addition to the completion of the Bratsk and Krasnoyarsk Hydroelectric Stations, the plans for Eastern Siberia call for the construction of several more large hydroelectric stations on the Angara and Yenisei Rivers, such as the Sayanskaya, Ust-Ilim, Boguchany, Yeniseisk and Osinovo Stations, as well as a station on the Lower Tunguska River, by 1980. The capacity of each is to exceed 4,000,000 kw. (Applause.)

In addition, two groups of highly economical thermal power plants will be built here to use coal from the Kansk-Achinsk Basin: the Itat-Bogotol complex in the Krasnoyarsk area and the Irsha-Borodinskaya complex in the Kansk-Taishet area. Each will have a capacity of 3,000,000 kw. or more.

Large hydroelectric stations are to be erected in Central Asia for both electrification and irrigation purposes. Among these are the Nurek and Rogunskaya Stations on the Vakhsh River and the Toktogul and Toguztorouskaya Stations on the Naryn River. A number of large power plants will be built in Kazakhstan, including an Irtysh group.

The Volga-Kama power chain will be completed with the construction of the Saratov, Lower Volga and Cheboksary Hydroelectric Stations and two hydroelectric stations on the Kama. The Lower Ob Hydroelectric Station with a capacity of up to 6,000,000 kw. will produce power for the unified power grid of the European part of the country. In addition, there are plans for building a number of large thermal power plants in the vicinity of Saratov, Stalingrad, and Gorky and in the Kuibyshev-Ufa-Orenburg area.

Large thermal power plants will rise in the Central and Central Black-Earth regions of the European part of the Union; to the south and northeast of Moscow; in the Ukraine near Kiev, Kirovograd and Nikolayev; and in the Donets Basin, Latvia and Belorussia. The development of power production in the Caucasus will be based on the use of water resources and other sources of energy.

The implementation of this plan will solve such important problems as the problems of the Greater Volga and the Greater Dnieper. This, of course, will require considerable capital investment, but it will pay for itself in a relatively short time. Calculations indicate that the production of cheap electric power at the Volga-Kama and Dnieper hydroelectric stations will be almost doubled. More than 20,000,000 hectares of arid land in the Volga area and the South will be insured against the caprices of the weather, and it will become possible to drain more than

4,000,000 hectares of swampy land in the Polesye and the Baltic region.

The great flow of freight from the northwestern and other parts of the country, and also freight coming from Baltic ports, could then move through Black Sea ports into the Mediterranean, bypassing the Gilbraltar route, and freight from the southern regions could travel along the Dnieper through the Pripet and Neman Rivers to the Baltic. The route to the eastern part of the Mediterranean would be cut almost in half.

The Party Program calls for enormous development in machine building. Only thus will it be possible to implement the plan for integrated mechanization and automation. We must arrange for the mass production of many types of highly productive and economical machines, instruments and apparatuses and various automatic and electronic devices and create an improved system of machines for industry, agriculture and construction. In the next 20 years 2,800 new machine-building and metalworking enterprises will be built, chiefly in the eastern part of the country, and 1,900 old enterprises will be rebuilt. This will make it possible to increase production in the machine-building and metalworking industries 10 to 11 times and to increase the output of automatic and semiautomatic lines more than 60 times.

The chemical industry is taking on exceptional importance. In the 20-year period there will be an intensive program to increase the number of chemical items produced, and output will be increased about 17 times. Polymer chemistry will become very widespread. The production of synthetic resins and plastics will increase about 60 times. The output of artificial and synthetic fibers, of great importance in consumer goods production, will increase about 15 times. The production of mineral fertilizers will rise nine- or tenfold.

The general long-range plan devotes a great deal of attention to those highly important branches of heavy industry, the fuel and metallurgical industries. The production of all types of fuel will approximately quadruple. It is planned to increase gas production 14 to 15 times in the 20-year period and to increase coal extraction from the 1960 figure of 513,000,000 tons to 1,200,000,000 tons in 1980. By 1980 oil extraction will have risen to between 690,000,000 and 710,000,000 tons. For comparison I will point out that in 1960 the U.S.S.R. extracted 148,000,000 tons and the U.S.A. 348,000,000 tons.

The ferrous metallurgy industry will be in a position to pour 250,000,000 tons of steel annually. In 1960 the U.S.S.R. produced 65,000,000 tons of steel and the U.S.A. 90,000,000 tons. In only nine years, the Soviet Union will be producing some 55,000,000 tons more steel than the present U.S. output. Economists' estimates show that we can raise steel production to a still higher level, but for the time being we have adopted the figure of about 250,000,000 tons. It is possible that rapid development of the production of substitutes for ferrous metals and successes in increasing the quality of metals, introducing metal-saving procedures and improving the design and manufacture of machines will enable us to do with a smaller quantity of steel. In that case the appropriate corrections will be made in the plans for the development of metallurgy.

In view of the requirements of such rapidly developing branches of industry as power engineering, chemistry, electronics, machine tool making, atomic and space technology and high-speed transport, the proportion of nonferrous metals in the total metals balance will rise. It is necessary to increase the output of nonferrous metals for alloys and of rare metals and materials for semiconductors. There will be a particularly great expansion of the applications of aluminum.

The production of building materials must be developed at a high rate. In 1980 cement output will reach 235,000,000 tons, a fivefold increase for the 20-year period.

In the next 20 years the output of all consumer goods industries must be increased about five times. For example, it is planned to more than triple textile production by 1980, bringing the annual output to between 20,000,000,000 and 22,000,000,000 square meters, while the output of leather footwear will rise to 1,000,000,000 pairs per year. The output of cultural and everyday goods, the demand for which will increase rapidly, will be increased tenfold. To do this it is necessary to accelerate and improve the utilization of capital investments in light industry

and the food industry and to build hundreds of plants and factories. The concern for consumer goods and household goods
and appliances, for anything that makes life easier and more
beautiful for Soviet people, must be no less than the concern
for, say, the metallurgical equipment industry.

Comrades, we must be fully aware of the decisive importance
of labor productivity in the attainment of a communist level of
production. The increase in the productivity of social labor is
the measure of our progress and an important source of improvements in the people's living standard. Any other approach
to the question is empty Manilovism.*

We face gigantic tasks in increasing production and creating
abundance. How is this to be achieved, considering that there
are limits to the increase in the number of workers—during the
20-year period the increase will be about 40%, and a considerable part of this will go into the nonproductive sphere, particularly into education and public health—and also considering the
shortened working day? There can be only one answer to this
question: We must bring about a corresponding rise in labor
productivity. According to estimates of the planning agencies,
more than nine-tenths of the rise in the national income in the
years 1961-1980 must be provided by increased labor productivity. In the next ten years labor productivity in the U.S.S.R.'s
industry will approximately double, and in 20 years it will increase four to 4.2 times. In view of the shortened working day,
the increase in output per working hour will be even higher.

In the next 20 years it is planned to make further improvements in the distribution of production forces. This will make it
possible to achieve the maximum economy of social labor,
achieve high rates of production development and put colossal
new sources of natural wealth at the service of society.

In the field of the distribution of productive forces it is
planned:

to create mighty fuel and power bases in areas of Siberia
where there are deposits of cheap coal that can be mined by the
opencast method and in areas where the hydroelectric resources
of the Angara and Yenisei can be put to use;

to transform Central Asia into a major power-producing region, using the enormous resources of gas and water power to
be found there;

to create mighty new metallurgical bases, so that by 1980
there will be five all-Union bases: in the Urals, the Ukraine,
Siberia and the Far East, Kazakhstan, and the central regions
of the European part of the U.S.S.R.;

to organize large chemical industry complexes where there
are concentrations of cheap natural and petroleum gases, and
also petroleum industry complexes, particularly in the Urals,
the Volga area, the Ukraine, the Northern Caucasus, Siberia and
Central Asia;

to create mighty machine-building bases in the regions east
of the Urals in order to satisfy the greater part of the demand of
these regions for machinery and equipment;

to carry out major projects for diverting large amounts of
water from the northern regions of the European part of the
U.S.S.R. into the Volga basin and into the water supply system
for Central Kazakhstan, the Virgin Land Territory, the Donets
Basin and the Urals; to build regulating reservoirs in Central
Asia and on the Volga, the Dnieper, the Bug and the Dniester;
and to develop farming on irrigated and reclaimed land on a
large scale.

These are the general prospects for the development of our
industry. They are truly magnificent prospects. But we are
positive that today's plan will be tomorrow's reality. The
guarantee of this is the determination of our party and our people, a hero people! (Stormy, prolonged applause.)

2. The Development of Agriculture and Social Relations in the
Countryside.—Comrades! The draft Program of our party gives
a thorough description of the social, economic and political
changes that have taken place in the countryside as a result of
the victory of the collective farm system and the adoption of a
socialist system of agriculture. The establishment of a socialist
system of agriculture in the U.S.S.R. is a historic victory of our
party and of all the Soviet people.

When the working class under the leadership of Lenin's party
carried out the revolution, our enemies comforted themselves

---

*[Idle daydreaming—from Manilov, a character in Gogol's
"Dead Souls."—Trans.]

with the hope that the Bolsheviks would not succeed in solving
the peasant question, that the peasant would never give up his
strip of land and that the peasant-proprietor could not be bred
into a peasant-collectivist.

But the enemies' hopes dispersed like smoke. Vladimir
Ilyich Lenin worked out his brilliant cooperative plan. Guided
by this plan, the Party lifted millions and millions of peasants
to a new life. The deep socialist furrow not only plowed across
the boundaries of individual holdings but also transformed the
private-property psychology of the peasant. We today are the
witnesses of the triumph of Lenin's ideas in the reorganization
of agriculture, in bringing millions of toilers of the land into
the building of communism. Our party can rightly be proud that
it has reared a new peasant who is marching in step with the
heroic working class and is an active builder of the new life.
(Prolonged applause.)

Along with industry and its striking force—heavy industry—
U.S.S.R. agriculture constitutes a powerful socialist economy
that does not know crises or upheavals.

We have carried out the first part of Lenin's cooperative
plan—we have swung the peasantry onto the path of collective
farms, established an extensive network of state farms and
consolidated the collective and state farms. Now we must take
a decisive new step forward—we must ensure the flourishing of
all collective and state farms and raise their production to a
level worthy of communism.

In the present stage of communist construction, the Party
considers the following to be the chief tasks in the sphere of
agriculture:

—to achieve an abundance of high-quality products for the
people and of raw materials for industry;

—on the basis of a mighty expansion of the productive forces
of agriculture, to ensure the gradual transition of the Soviet
countryside to communist social relations and to eliminate in
the main the distinctions between town and countryside.

Permit me to take up the basic problems of the development
of agriculture posed by life and the practice of communist construction and comprising major propositions in the draft Party
Program.

The Communist Party has proclaimed a great and noble goal
—the full satisfaction of man's growing material and cultural
needs. The achievement of this goal requires an unprecedentedly high level of material production. Therefore the draft of the
Party Program unfolds before the people an imposing plan for
the development of agriculture. In discussing the Program, we
speak specifically both about our stirring times and about the
future of the socialist economy. This is how V. I. Lenin taught
us to approach the solution of the tasks of communist construction. In the spring of 1920, in a letter to Party organizations on
preparations for the Ninth Party Congress, Vladimir Ilyich
stated: "We must go forward, we must look ahead, we must
bring to the Congress considered practical experience of economic construction, and carefully analyzed by the common labor,
the joint efforts of all Party members" ("Works" [in Russian],
Vol. XXX, p. 379).

Such practical experience of economic construction is embodied in our economic plans and in the assignments for the
development of agriculture. The draft Program provides for increasing total agricultural output approximately 250% in 20
years, the gross output of grain more than 100%, of meat almost
300% and of milk almost 200%.

How much and what kind of products must we produce in order to satisfy fully the people's needs, taking into account the
prospects of development of Soviet society? Upon the instructions of the Party Central Committee, the State Economic
Council has submitted estimates of the volume of production
that our country must achieve in the next 20 years. Let me
cite these estimates.

Agricultural Output in 1960-1980

	1960	1970	1980
Grain (billion poods)	8.2	14	18-19
Meat (million tons in slaughter weight)	8.7	25	30-32
Milk (million tons)	61.7	135	170-180
Eggs (billions)	27.4	68	110-116
Wool (thousand tons)	357.0	800	1,045-1,155
Raw cotton (million tons)	4.3	8	10-11

Agricultural Output in 1960-1980

	1960	1970	1980
Sugar beets (at refineries, million tons)	57.7	86	98-108
Oil-bearing seeds (million tons)	4.3	8	9-10
Potatoes (million tons)	84.4	140	156
Vegetables and melons (million tons)	19.2	47	55
Fruit, berries and grapes (million tons)	4.9	28	51

As you see, the Party is outlining big tasks. Such a large volume of agricultural output may seem too bold to some people. The figures are indeed staggering. As a matter of fact, for many decades, right up to 1954, the gross grain harvest in our country amounted to about 5,000,000,000 poods. It is only in the past few years, thanks to the development of the virgin lands and the introduction of corn, that we have begun to harvest 8,000,000,000 to 8,500,000,000 poods. For a long time the state procured about 2,000,000,000 poods of grain, and only in recent years have procurements reached 3,000,000,000 to 3,500,000,000 poods. By 1980 grain production is to be increased to between 18,000,000,-000 and 19,000,000,000 poods and purchases to 7,000,000,000 poods!

In outlining these great plans, we firmly believe that they will be successfully carried out. This confidence is based on realistic calculations, on the rich reserves of the socialist system of economy, and on the selfless and well-organized labor of the Soviet people.

Let us examine the prospects for a rise in grain production in the major republics—the Russian, Ukraine and Kazakh Republics. We shall speak with the Belorussians in Belorussia. We shall whisper into each other's ears—there is something to whisper about. (Laughter in the hall. Applause.)

What contribution are the working people of the Russian Federation to make in accomplishing the tasks outlined by the draft Party Program? In 1960 the collective and state farms of the Russian Republic produced 4,800,000,000 poods of grain and sold the state 1,800,000,000 poods. By 1980 they are to increase production to 12,000,000,000 poods and the sale of grain to 4,000,000,000 to 5,000,000,000 poods.

Perhaps the bourgeois press will write about this: You see what an imagination Khrushchev has about the plans for agricultural production! Let these gentlemen write, but let them not forget that this is being said at the Party Congress on the instructions of the Central Committee. The Congress will call on the Party and the people, and the people will move mountains! (Stormy, prolonged applause.)

Thus the Russian Federation is to increase grain production and procurements 150%. Of course with the present structure of sown areas, with millions of hectares planted to oats and other low-yield crops and with vast areas in the humid zone idle under so-called clean fallow, this task is insoluble.

I might say in jest: If certain workers continue to be stubborn and to plant the land to oats, we will feed them oatmeal. (Laughter in the hall, applause.) And not the kind of oatmeal that is fed to children, but coarse oatmeal, the kind about which the Red Army said during the Civil War: Damn it all, you don't know whether you're on rations of food or fodder! (Laughter in the hall. Prolonged applause.)

But if we rely on the experience of the leading farms and scientific institutions, revise the structure of sown areas, replace low-yield crops more boldly and resolutely, and make wide use of possibilities for increasing yields, the planned level of grain production will be achieved, and before 1980.

What reserves do we plan to use in order to accomplish this task? A certain amount of grain will be obtained by cultivating lands that are now idle. But the chief source for increasing grain output lies in replacing low-yield crops with higher-yield ones and increasing the yields of all crops.

The Party Central Committee's Bureau for the Russian Republic and the Russian Republic Council of Ministers, together with scientists and specialists, have worked out a new structure of sown areas that opens up big possibilities for increasing the output of grain. What is new about this structure? The areas under unprofitable and low-yield crops are being sharply reduced: the area under oats by 6,000,000 hectares and the area under grasses by 9,000,000 hectares. Clean fallow in the humid zone is being eliminated on an area of 9,000,000 hectares.

A total of 24,000,000 hectares is being freed for more valuable crops. Sowings of corn for dry grain, peas, fodder beans and other valuable crops are being increased by using these lands.

The collective and state farms are planning to increase the area under corn for dry grain from 2,400,000 hectares to 7,000,000 hectares. Given a yield of 40 centners of corn per hectare, this will provide 1,700,000,000 poods of grain.

The area under leguminous crops in the republic will be increased from 2,600,000 to 19,000,000 hectares, including up to 16,500,000 hectares under peas and fodder beans. Given a yield of approximately 20 centners per hectare, this will provide 2,300,000,000 poods of grain.

The area under wheat and other cereals, as well as groat crops, will amount to 68,000,000 hectares. Given a yield of 20 centners per hectare, the gross harvest of these crops will exceed 8,000,000,000 poods.

Thus the introduction of grain corn, peas and legumes and a rise in the yields of all crops will enable the collective and state farms of the Russian Republic to produce more than 12,000,000,000 poods of grain a year and to sell the state 4,000,000,000 to 5,000,000,000 poods. In order to give you a more graphic idea of the feasibility of obtaining such a quantity of marketable grain, I would like to call attention to the following figures. In 1961 the Russian Federation, according to the plan, is to sell the state 2,100,000,000 to 2,200,000,000 poods of grain. If legumes are planted instead of the 9,000,000 hectares of low-yield grasses and the 9,000,000 hectares of clean fallow mentioned above, and a yield of 20 centners per hectare is obtained, this alone will provide 2,200,000,000 poods of grain. This will in effect be marketable grain, since at present the collective and state farms to all intents and purposes obtain nothing from these areas. Consequently another 2,200,000,000 poods of grain will be added to the present level of grain sales envisaged by the plan, and purchases will then total more than 4,000,000,000 poods of grain. So the sale of 4,000,000,000 to 5,000,000,000 poods of grain to the state is not too high a hurdle for the collective and state farms of the Russian Federation. Let us all applaud, comrades. (Applause.)

We are confident that when the decision is adopted, the workers of the Russian Federation will mobilize their forces and the task will be accomplished! (Stormy applause.)

In the calculations for the Russian Federation, the yield of wheat and other cereals, as well as of leguminous crops, has been set at 20 centners per hectare. Comrades, an average yield of 20 centners per hectare has been achieved for a whole 20 years. Does such a figure represent our power, are these our potentialities? No, we have far greater potentialities.

In the near future the Soviet Union will occupy a position in the international grain market that will make the Messrs. Imperialists feel how our agriculture is growing! (Stormy applause.)

Such an estimated yield for a period of 20 years is even understated. In our country many collective and state farms are already obtaining 25 to 30 and even 40 centners of wheat and other grain crops per hectare. They are obtaining these yields with the present level of production organization and of agricultural science and technology. But with every year science will move forward and furnish practice with new possibilities. Better strains and hybrids of agricultural plants will appear, and the production of organic and mineral fertilizers, herbicides and other chemicals will increase sharply. The collective and state farms will be equipped with more up-to-date farm machinery. All this will make it possible not only to achieve but to surpass the planned level of grain production and purchases.

Take the estimates submitted by the Central Committee of the Ukraine Communist Party and the republic Council of Ministers. Prior to the extensive introduction of corn, the potentialities of the Ukraine in grain production amounted to approximately 1,300,000,000 to 1,500,000,000 poods and in grain procurements to 400,000,000 to 500,000,000 poods.

Now that they are armed with such strong crops as corn, peas and fodder beans, the working people of the Ukraine, firmly confident of success, are planning to increase grain output to 3,800,000,000 poods and grain purchases to 1,500,000,000 poods.

What changes in the structure of sown areas will take place on the collective and state farms of the Ukraine? Winter wheat will be planted on 6,500,000 hectares; corn on more than 5,-000,000 hectares, or 28% of the area under grains; and legumes on about 4,000,000 hectares, or 21% of the area under grains. Corn and legumes, as the most productive crops, will account for almost half the area under grains in the republic, and the share of these crops in gross grain production will reach 60%.

It is planned to obtain the following yields per hectares:

All grain crops	35 centners
incl:	
Winter wheat	30 centners
Corn	50 centners
Peas	30 centners
Fodder beans	32 centners

The experience of this year, when many collective and state farms obtained 70 to 80 centners of grain corn and 30 to 40 centners of wheat and peas per hectare, confirms that these figures are realistic.

The Party assigns Kazakhstan a big role in increasing grain production. This republic has its distinctive features. Corn is grown there, with the exception of the southern regions, mainly for silage. Therefore grain output will be increased by raising yields, widely introducing leguminous crops and further developing new land. In the future, when scientists provide agriculture with corn varieties having a shorter vegetation period, corn will presumably be grown for grain on the virgin lands as well.

I must tell you that while I was preparing for this report I received a letter from a selection expert in Azerbaidzhan. He announced that he had succeeded in creating a variety of corn with a vegetation period of approximately 60 days. If this is really the case, then simply colossal opportunities open up for expanding and extending corn sowings for grain to the North.

Mr. Rusk told me in Vienna that in America there is supposedly a similar variety of corn. But his statement has not been confirmed, although Mr. Rusk promised to prove that this was so. Americans who know corn—Mr. Garst, for example—say that there is no such corn variety in America. But if there is none in America, it would be good to create such a variety of corn in the Soviet Union. (Prolonged applause.)

But it must be realistically understood that this is a very difficult task. And we are not making the development of agriculture dependent on the solution of this problem. If such a variety of corn is not developed, then even with the varieties that do exist we will not only fulfill but overfulfill our plans. (Applause.)

How is the structure of sown areas taking shape in the virgin-land areas of Kazakhstan? Taking into account the development of new lands, a total of approximately 32,000,000 hectares will be planted to wheat and other cereal crops and to leguminous crops and corn for silage. Wheat and other cereal crops will account for 50% to 55% of this area, peas and fodder beans for 30% to 35% and corn and sugar beets for livestock fodder for 10%. I am citing tentative estimates for the principal crops alone. Naturally, the economy will require a wider range of crops; potatoes, vegetables and oil-bearing crops are also needed. Nevertheless, wheat, peas, fodder beans, corn for grain and silage, and sugar beets for livestock fodder will occupy the chief place in the virgin land regions.

With this structure the grain balance will be made up as follows:

Wheat and other cereal crops will be planted on 17,600,000 hectares. Given a yield of 20 centners, this will provide 2,150,-000,000 poods of cereals. Of this quantity the state and collective farms will be able to sell about 1,500,000,000 poods to the state.

Peas and fodder beans will be planted on 11,000,000 hectares, and a yield of 20 centners per hectare is contemplated. The gross harvest will be 1,350,000,000 poods. Approximately 600,000,000 poods of this can be sold to the state.

Thus it is possible to increase Kazakhstan's gross grain harvest to 3,500,000,000 poods and to sell the state more than 2,000,000,000 poods of grain.

Like the other republics, Kazakhstan has enormous possibilities for increasing yields. When the Party set the task of developing the virgin lands, the yield was estimated at eight centners per hectare. As experience was amassed and the system of

agrotechnology was improved, the yield indices of many farms rose considerably. Today there are state and collective farms in the virgin-land areas that obtain 20 and more centners of grain, chiefly wheat, per hectare over large areas.

The Mamlyutka State Grain Farm in North Kazakhstan Province annually obtains a yield of 20 to 22 centners of grain per hectare. High yields are obtained by the Kustanai, Petropavlovsk, Kiyalinsky, Chandaksky and other state farms.

Especially good results are being achieved by those farms that are widely introducing row and leguminous crops which are good predecessors to spring wheat. The Fedorovsky State Farm in Kustanai Province this year obtained the following yield of spring wheat sown after corn: 26 centners per hectare from field No. 3 and 22 centners per hectare from field No. 7.

Such examples exist not only in Kazakhstan. Many of you know of the Altai Agricultural Research Institute. For a number of years it has been obtaining high stable grain yields on the basis of the extensive introduction of corn, legumes and other row crops. In 1961 the institute's collective obtained 20 centners of grain from an area of 6,359 hectares, including 20.4 centners of wheat per hectare from 5,140 hectares. The new wheat variety Barnaulka-32 yielded 44 centners per hectare. The Land of Soviets Collective Farm in the Altai Territory has obtained an average grain yield of 20.5 centners per hectare over the past five years. The brigade of Alexander Bekker, a delegate to our Congress, obtained an average grain yield of 23 centners per hectare.

The experience amassed by collective and state farms makes it possible to draw a conclusion on ways of developing virgin-land farming. We can no longer run agriculture on the basis of a single crop—spring wheat. Along with wheat, it is necessary to introduce corn, peas, fodder beans and sugar beets for livestock fodder on a wider scale; this is a major factor in raising farming standards, increasing the grain harvest, rapidly developing animal husbandry and making the virgin-land state farms highly productive farms.

Why does the Party attach so much importance to corn and leguminous crops in solving the grain and livestock problem? Many years' experience has shown that in terms of yield and other qualitites these crops have no equal. The Central Committee report has already noted the role corn has played in increasing grain output in the Ukraine, Krasnodar Territory and other regions of the country.

Evidently we will be correct in putting leguminous crops on a par with corn in importance. Peas and beans are old crops, known to the peasants for centuries. There is scarcely a peasant in the Russian Federation, the Ukraine, Belorussia or the Baltic republics who could not grow good pea harvests. Unfortunately, the leaders who for a long time headed the U.S.S.R. Ministry of Agriculture ruined leguminous crops.

But there have been leading agricultural workers who have cultivated leguminous crops with loving care and have showed all the collective and state farms the path that must be taken to increase grain output.

Vasily Mikhailovich Kavun, Chairman of the Stalin Collective Farm in Vinnitsa Province, is a delegate to the 22nd Congress. He has opened the eyes of many to leguminous crops. Year after year the collective farm grows big pea harvests. He obtained 27 centners per hectare from an area of 520 hectares in 1960 and 31 centners from an area of 708 hectares in 1961. On this collective farm considerable attention is given to corn. Sixty centners of corn grain per hectare has been obtained from an area of 900 hectares. Peas account for 21% and corn for 30% —or together for more than half—of the area under grain crops. Thanks to this, the average yield of grain crops on the collective farm came to 38 centners per hectare. (Applause.)

This year Vinnitsa Province as a whole harvested 20.7 centners of peas per hectare from an area of 180,000 hectares and Cherkassy Province harvested 21.5 centners from 89,000 hectares. (Applause.)

Not only in the Ukraine are good pea harvests gathered. The Petrovsky State Farm in Lipetsk Province, which is headed by Comrade Volovchenko, a delegate to the 22nd Party Congress, obtained 36 centners of peas per hectare on an area of 110 hectares. Depending on the sowing methods and the seeding norms, the yields were as follows (in centners per hectare):

wide-row method, with rows 45 cm. apart and a seeding norm of 110 kg. per hectare	22
ordinary-row method, with rows 15 cm. apart and a seeding norm of 270 kg.	33
narrow-row method, with rows 7.5 cm. apart and a seeding norm of 270 kg.	42.2

This experience warrants serious attention. (Applause.)
Even before the war, the late Academician Pyotr Ivanovich
Lisitsyn told me that Shatilov Station, where he worked, used
the narrow-row method of sowing and obtained the highest
yields. It is important that we widely verify the leading methods
and assess them on their merits in order to open before them a
wide road into production.

Many examples can be cited of collective and state farms in
the central regions of the Russian Federation, in Belorussia,
Latvia, Lithuania and Estonia and in provinces of Siberia and
Kazakhstan that obtain high pea yields over large areas.

For the next year or two we will probably not have the necessary amount of bean seeds, whereas there are more peas.
Fodder beans could be replaced by peas, which are an equally
valuable grain crop.

The extensive introduction of leguminous crops offers agriculture big new possibilities. Leguminous crops simultaneously solve three tasks:

First, they yield good harvests and are an important source
of increasing grain output both for food purposes and for the
needs of animal husbandry. They have a comparatively short
vegetation period and are resistant to spring frosts; this is
especially valuable for regions of Siberia and Kazakhstan. The
early ripening of leguminous crops makes it possible to take the
strain off the harvesting there, to free the fields more quickly
and prepare them for the next crop.

Peas can be planted early; this is very important in southern
Ukraine, the Volga area and certain other regions that are subject to hot winds. Peas will ripen earlier there and escape the
hot winds. In Krasnodar and Stavropol Territories and the
Kabardino-Balkar, North Ossetian and Chechen-Ingush Republics the early sowing of peas and the short vegetation period
make it possible to use them as the first crop in growing two
harvests. As is known, corn is sown at a soil temperature of
ten to 12 degrees centigrade. Peas can be sown considerably
earlier—approximately two or three weeks earlier. They have a
vegetation period of 70 to 80 days. If peas are sown at the end
of March or early in April, they ripen in the second ten days of
June. After harvesting of the peas, which are a good predecessor, corn can be planted on this area in the last ten days of
June. Four months are left to grow the latter crop. That is ample time for the corn to ripen for grain. Thus peas afford big
possibilities for obtaining two crops a year in the southern
regions of the country.

Second, leguminous crops contain a large percentage of protein and make possible a fundamental solution of the problem of
providing animal husbandry with protein fodders.

Third, leguminous crops are a means for increasing the fertility of fields, a kind of factory for obtaining nitrogen from the
air, while other agricultural crops do not take nitrogen from the
air but use up only soil nitrogen for their growth. Let me cite
figures supplied by specialists.

—Given a yield of 20 centners per hectare, peas take 105 kg.
of nitrogen from the air, leaving 47 kg. of nitrogen per hectare
in the soil after harvesting. With a yield of 30 centners, they
take 160 kg. of nitrogen from the air and leave 70 kg. in the
soil.

—Given a yield of 20 centners per hectare, fodder beans take
142 kg. of nitrogen from the air and leave 63 kg. per hectare in
the soil. With a yield of 30 centners, they take 213 kg. from the
air and leave 95 kg. in the soil.

In the future leguminous crops will be planted on approximately 30,000,000 hectares, and perhaps more. Consequently enormous quantitites of nitrogen, a highly valuable and essentially
free fertilizer, will accumulate in the soil. In order to produce
this fertilizer in the chemical industry, it would be necessary to
build many large plants and spend hundreds of millions of rubles.

Some officials of planning agencies will probably think:
"Fine! The plants will procure their own fertilizer from the
air, and we can build fewer chemical factories."

No, comrades, one of today's most urgent tasks is to develop
the chemical industry and to increase the output of mineral fertilizers, including nitrogen fertilizers, as well as herbicides and
other chemicals for combating weeds and crop pests. It is no
exaggeration to say that we must put the production of fertilizers
on a par with the mechanization of agriculture, for both are decisive conditions for increasing the output of agricultural products. (Applause.)

The Party plans to increase the output of mineral fertilizers
to between 125,000,000 and 135,000,000 tons, as against 14,000,-
000 tons in 1960. It is important that we do everything necessary
to obtain the greatest possible increase in the supply of fertilizers to agriculture in the current seven-year period.

Implementation of an extensive program for the production of
mineral fertilizers, a sharp increase in the area under leguminous crops, an increase in the density of livestock and the
accumulation of organic fertilizers—all this will make it possible to raise yields sharply.

In every zone there are collective and state farms that have
shown in specific conditions what methods should be used for
rapidly increasing yields. It is not possible to name these
farms for every zone. I will cite only one example.

Many of you know the collective farm at Kalinovka Village in
Kursk Province, about which I have spoken many times. V. V.
Grachev, chairman of the collective farm, is a delegate to the
22nd Party Congress. This collective farm has 6,000 hectares
of land. In 1961 it obtained the following yields (in centners per
hectare):

Winter wheat	32.6
Rye	24.3
Barley	21.6
Millet	20
Peas, with a seeding norm of 320 kg.	28
Fodder beans, with wide-row sowing	25.6
Sugar beets	350
Corn with ears for silage	700
Clover (hay in one mowing)	39

How was it possible to obtain such yields on heavy loamy
soil? The answer lies in the large number of livestock and the
resultant fertilizer. Only a few years ago Kalinovka (together
with the collective farms that merged with it) had 91 cows; today it has 1,050. The grain yield then was eight to ten centners
per hectare; today it is 25 to 30 centners.

Why are there now so many livestock? Because the collective
farmers began growing corn and eliminated the clean fallow,
sowing it to valuable crops. This meant more fodder, more
livestock, more fertilizer, higher yields.

There are such farms in other regions of the country also.
They have paved the way to high yields, and now the task is to
pull all the collective and state farms up to their level. But to
"pull up" is not to make speeches but really to raise the lagging farms to the level of the leading ones or to "pull down"
from the leadership of collective and state farms those who do
not understand matters and stifle production. (Prolonged applause.)

The growth of grain production opens up big possibilities for
a rapid advance of animal husbandry. Given an ample supply of
grain, silage and other fodder, we can increase the number of
livestock in a short period and ensure the level of output of
meat, milk and other products necessary for fully satisfying
the people's needs.

In outlining the plan for the development of agriculture, our
party attaches special importance to the irrigation and watering
of fields. Irrigation is an integral part of Lenin's plan of
electrification. Vladimir Ilyich Lenin regarded the problem of
power plant construction and the development of irrigation as
an indivisible whole. Even in the first years of Soviet rule Lenin
dreamed of irrigating the fields of Transcaucasia and Central
Asia and of bringing water to the arid Volga steppes.

Now that we have a powerful industry, the time has come to
outline and implement a broad plan for irrigation in order to
create a stable base guaranteeing agricultural production under
any conditions.

Upon the instructions of the Party Central Committee, the
State Economic Council is drafting a long-range plan for irrigation construction. There are today 9,000,000 hectares of irrigated land in the country. The task is being set of increasing

this area to approximately 28,000,000 hectares.

It is planned:

—to create a large new cotton-growing region in the basin of the Syr-Darya River, where, according to preliminary estimates, it is possible to irrigate 800,000 to 850,000 hectares of the Golodnaya Steppe in the Uzbek, Kazakh and Tadzhik Republics;

—to build the Nurek Hydroelectric Station to irrigate up to 1,200,000 hectares of land for cotton, rice and other crops in the Uzbek and Tadzhik Republics;

—to irrigate and develop 600,000 hectares of land in Turkmenia on the basis of the Kara-Kum Canal in order to develop cotton farming;

—to establish new rice-growing regions in the lower reaches of the Amu-Darya and Syr-Darya Rivers, with irrigated land amounting to about 900,000 hectares;

—to make integrated use of the lands and water resources of the Volga-Akhtuba floodlands and the Volga River deltas to develop irrigation farming and the production of vegetables, rice and corn and to create the best conditions for fish and waterfowl breeding;

—to develop irrigation of land in the Volga area by using the power of the V. I. Lenin and 22nd Party Congress Hydroelectric Stations on the Volga;

—to use the water resources of the Don, Kuban and other rivers in the south of the European part of the Russian Federation to irrigate more than 1,000,000 hectares of land and increase the production of rice, grapes, vegetables and industrial crops;

—to develop irrigation of 4,500,000 hectares of land in the Crimea and other southern regions of the Ukraine Republic and in Moldavia on the basis of the water resources of the Dnieper, Bug, Dniester and Danube Rivers in order to increase the production of rice, corn, sugar beets, grapes, fruits and vegetables and to develop animal husbandry;

—to carry out large-scale irrigation projects in the Transcaucasus.

Once the program for irrigation construction is completed, our country will be able to produce millions of tons more cotton, corn, rice and sugar beets and a great deal of additional livestock products.

Our party will achieve the deliverance of man from the domination of the elements and make him master over nature. (Prolonged applause.)

Comrades! In analyzing the paths of development of our industry, I spoke about increasing labor productivity as a major problem of communist construction. It is no less pressing a problem for agriculture.

In the draft of its Program the Communist Party envisages an increase of at least 150% in labor productivity in agriculture in the first ten years and a five- to sixfold increase in 20 years. This is a difficult task. But the paths to its solution have been paved. In all branches of agriculture we already have models of labor worthy of a communist society.

Take a look at the level of labor productivity achieved by leading people of the countryside in major branches of agricultural production.

Grain farming. The average expenditure on the production of a centner of grain on the country's state farms is 2.1 hours, at a cost of four rubles ten kopeks per centner.

On the Gigant State Farm in Rostov Province, meanwhile, the expenditure on a centner of grain is 38 minutes, less than one-third as much, and the cost is one ruble 53 kopeks.

Sugar beet production. For the country as a whole, the expenditure on the production of a centner of sugar beets on the state farms is 3.2 hours and the cost one ruble 80 kopeks, while the brigade of V. A. Svetlichny in Krasnodar Territory, which has mechanized the cultivation of sugar beets, expends 17 minutes per centner of sugar beets, or one-eleventh as much, at a cost of 30 kopeks, or one-sixth the average for the country as a whole.

Cotton production. On the state farms of the Uzbek Republic the average expenditure per centner of cotton is 52 hours and the cost 25 rubles 30 kopeks. At the same time Comrade Kuchiyev's comprehensively mechanized brigade on the Malek State Farm in Tashkent Province expends ten hours per centner of cotton, at a cost of seven rubles 30 kopeks.

Output of livestock products. For all the state farms using manual labor one milkmaid tends ten to 12 cows and milks 30 to 40 tons of milk a year. Zinaida Ivanovna Zabotina, a milkmaid on the Shuisky State Farm in Ivanovo Province, gets different results. She works on a mechanized livestock section equipped with herringbone-type installations. In 1960 Comrade Zabotina tended 150 cows and milked 307 tons of milk. In 1961 she began working at the section with her husband Dmitry Ilyich Zabotin, a mechanic. Together they tended 300 cows, pledged to milk 650 tons of milk and have already milked 510 tons. They have expended 4.8 man-hours per centner of milk, while the average for the country's state farms is 14 hours.

What conclusions can be drawn from these examples? The leading state and collective farms are already exceeding by five to six times and more the level of labor productivity achieved by the majority of state and collective farms. Here it is important to stress that it did not take them decades to make this advance in labor productivity but only the last few years. We are faced with the task of organizing production in such a way that the entire mass of collective and state farms attains this level of labor productivity in the near future.

This is a difficult task. Its accomplishment will require intensive efforts on the part of the Party and the people and the material resources of the state. But this is not the whole story. We must stop letting things drift, a situation that still impedes the development of agriculture in many ways. There is still no active intervention and competent influence on agricultural production on the part of some Party organizations. The old still prevails here, when the number of people engaged in agriculture was dictated not by the interests of production but by their availability on the collective farm.

The situation is different now. Agriculture is becoming more and more mechanized and the demands made on it are increasing. It is necessary to discard the old approach, to abandon outdated concepts about agriculture. The main thing is to ensure maximum output with minimum expenditure of labor.

Therefore one of the most important tasks is the struggle for further mechanization and electrification of agriculture in literally all units and for better use of equipment. This depends to a decisive extent upon the experience and organizational capabilities of our personnel, on the people to whom the equipment has been entrusted. Labor productivity on the collective and state farms should be increased not by overexerting muscular power but by further equipping agriculture with more up-to-date machinery. It is necessary in as short a time as possible to provide all collective and state farms with a complex of machines conforming with the advanced technology of agricultural production and to show special concern about developing machines for introducing more progressive methods of grain harvesting, for fully mechanizing the cultivation of corn, cotton, flax, sugar beets and potatoes and for mechanizing work in animal husbandry.

It is necessary to introduce more productive machinery, especially tractors, combines and transport vehicles. We can and must, for example, organize the production of powerful new high-speed tractors of 200 to 220 h.p., and the appropriate implements for them, for the steppe regions of the country. A decision on this has been adopted by the Party Central Committee and the U.S.S.R. Council of Ministers. Such tractors will be three to four times more productive than the DT-54 tractors now in use, and their introduction in production will yield enormous economic advantages. Let me cite the estimates of specialists on the effectiveness of using powerful tractors in working 1,000,000 hectares of plowland.

	DT-54 tractor	200-220 hp. tractor
Average area plowed per day	7.6 hectares	21.2 hectares
Tractors needed for autumn plowing (20 days, two shifts a day)	6,600	2,400
Number of tractors needed	13,200	4,800

These are estimates for 1,000,000 hectares. But there are approximately 80,000,000 hectares of plowland in the country on which powerful tractors could be used. Consequently the economic advantages resulting from the introduction of such tractors will be many times greater.

We must take serious measures for further developing the manufacture of tractors and farm machines. It is necessary to expand production capacity at tractor plants and other enterprises producing equipment for agriculture, to provide them with more modern equipment and to reinforce the design bureaus with experienced personnel capable of successfully solving the problems of developing new equipment.

Comrades! The draft Party Program regards the development of productive forces in the countryside and the formation of communist social relations as an indivisible whole. This is quite logical, since communist social relations are born in the process of labor, in the process of the development of production, in the nationwide struggle to build communism.

What will typify our countryside in its advance along the road to communism? In terms of technical equipment and production organization, socialist agriculture will approach the level of industry. This means that large qualitative changes will take place in the nature of labor. As the cultural and technical level of collective farmers and state farm workers rises and all branches of agriculture are equipped with up-to-date machinery, agricultural labor will develop into a variety of industrial labor.

In solving the tasks of communist construction in the countryside, we must rely on the wealth of experience amassed by our country in developing socialist agriculture. What does this experience show? Two forms of socialist enterprise have developed in Soviet agriculture—state farms and collective farms.

The state farms were established on the initiative of V. I. Lenin as state socialist agricultural enterprises. They were called upon to show the advantages of large-scale socialist farming over small-scale individual peasant farming and to serve as models for the peasants around them.

Our party has successfully carried out Lenin's plan for the development of state farms. The state farms have grown into a big force and have become highly productive enterprises; making wide use of modern machinery and the achievements of science, they attain higher labor productivity and consequently produce cheaper agricultural products. Labor expenditures per centner of output in 1960 were as follows: for grain (excluding corn)— 2.1 hours on the state farms and 7.2 hours on the collective farms; for milk—14.2 hours and 20.8 hours, respectively. The expenditure per centner of added weight of cattle was 66 man-hours on the state farms and 118 man-hours on the collective farms. Labor expenditure per centner of added weight of pigs was 57 man-hours on the state farms and 133 man-hours on the collective farms.

As was already noted in the Central Committee report, the growth of the role of the state farms in agricultural production has been especially marked in recent years. The advantages of state farms made themselves felt with new force in the development of the virgin lands and in solving the problem of supplying large cities and industrial centers with milk, potatoes and vegetables.

Of course, not all state farms today are models of organization of agricultural production; much must still be done so that every state farm makes fuller and better use of the reserves and possibilities of large-scale mechanized farming.

The other form of large-scale socialist agriculture is the collective farm. This is the path charted by V. I. Lenin to effect the transition of millions of individual small-scale peasant farms to socialism. The collective farms were a school of communism for the Soviet peasantry. They did much to overcome centuries-old private-property habits and to accustom the peasants to collective labor and to large-scale communal farming. The collective farms have come a long way in their development. The present-day collective farms are no longer the original agricultural artels, with their primitive equipment, low level of labor organization and distribution according to the mouths-to-feed principle. Today the collective farm is a large-scale mechanized enterprise. As a result of the measures adopted by the Party, the collective farms have become considerably stronger in the past few years; their communal economy has grown, the output of farm products has increased and the living standard of the collective farmers has risen.

Some comrades ask: What path will the further development of agriculture take—the collective farm or the state farm path? The Party bases itself on the premise that the building of communism in the countryside will proceed through the devel-

opment and improvement of both forms of socialist production. One socialist form of farming must not be counterposed to the other. Both the collective farms and the state farms are large-scale socialist enterprises that make possible the effective use of the achievements of technology and science and a rapid expansion of social production. Given equal material possibilities, good organization of production and competent management, both forms can produce good results.

If at present labor productivity on many collective farms is lower and unit production costs are higher than on the state farms, this is not because the collective farm form has exhausted itself and ceased to correspond to the level of development of present-day production forces. The reason must be sought elsewhere—above all in the organization of production, in management and in the level of technical equipment. Wherever there are experienced personnel, good organizers and specialists, where concern is shown for the mechanization of production, where the principle of material incentive of workers is applied, both the state farms and the collective farms flourish. It is important to stress here that objective conditions for the rapid development of the collective farm economy exist literally everywhere.

The main thing is to help the collective farms to improve production organization, to make skillful use of modern machinery and scientific achievements and thereby to achieve higher labor productivity. It is important to reinforce the weak collective farms with cadres—collective farm chairmen, brigade leaders and agricultural specialists. The task is to raise all the collective farms to the level of the leading state farms.

The state shows enormous concern for strengthening and developing the collective farms. In turn, each collective farm must make it a sacred rule to fulfill state plans strictly, to increase production and other communal resources and to ensure that the collective farmers' incomes rise as their labor productivity increases.

The role of the state farms as the leading socialist enterprises in the countryside will grow even more as agriculture continues to develop and as the task of creating an abundance of farm products is carried out. We must make the state farms first-class factories for the production of grain, cotton, meat, milk, wool, vegetables, fruit and tea. It is also important that the state farms become models not only in better production organization but also in the organization of everyday life, culture and the communist education of man.

In the course of the development of production on the collective and state farms and improvement of social relations on them, agriculture will advance to a higher level that will make it possible to change over to communist forms of production and distribution. The principle of material incentive will play an important role in achieving this goal. We must continue to combine moral and material incentives, to encourage those who produce more for society and to inculcate, by means of the best labor models, high discipline and communist awareness.

Comrades! Our party is outlining a great plan for the development of agriculture. We all remember the difficult conditions in which socialist agriculture was built up. The Communist Party, guided by V. I. Lenin's behests, skillfully overcame the difficulties and led the peasantry along the path of socialism. Now we have emerged onto the broad road of communist construction. Wonderful prospects have opened up before us. This does not mean, of course, that our advance will be smooth and easy, without strain and without difficulties.

In the struggle to create an abundance of agricultural products, we must climb many steep slopes and solve many complex problems. Enriched by its great historical experience, the Party will boldly and confidently lead the peasantry forward, to the building of communism. (Prolonged applause.)

3. Improving the People's Well-Being and Achieving the Highest Standard of Living.—Comrades! The C.P.S.U. is setting a great task—to achieve in the next 20 years a standard of living higher than that of any capitalist country and to create the conditions necessary for achieving an abundance of material and cultural benefits.

Within the first ten years all sections of the Soviet population will enjoy sufficiency, will be materially provided for. Communism will thereby have demonstrated its decisive advantages over capitalism in an area of immediate concern to literally every individual. For the first time in history insufficiency will have been fully and finally eliminated. This will be a wonderful accomplishment for the new society. No capitalist country can undertake a task of this kind.

Two basic circumstances ensure the achievement of the highest standard of living by the Soviet people. First is the growth of labor productivity and of total social production and national income, a growth that is beyond capitalism's capabilities. Second is the utilization of the growing productive forces and social wealth in the interests of the whole people. The communist program for abundance rests, therefore, on a firm foundation, while the many well-advertised bourgeois projects for bringing about "public prosperity" are nothing but the usual attempts to deceive the masses.

The Party's position is that in the period directly ahead, while further developing heavy industry and other branches of the national economy, we can and must step up the rate of improvement of the people's living standard. Real income per capita will double in the next ten years, and in 20 years it will increase more than 250%. This increase in the real income of the population will have its source in the growth of the national income of the U.S.S.R. By 1980 the national income will amount to between 720,000,000,000 and 750,000,000,000 rubles, or five times the 1960 figure.

What are the basic lines along which the improvement of the people's well-being will proceed?

In the years immediately ahead we shall see to it that all sections of the population enjoy a good diet of high quality. In the next ten years the per capita consumption of food is to rise as follows: meat and meat products, 150%; milk and milk products, 100%; butter, 50%; vegetable fats, 100%; eggs, 120%; fish and fish products, 50%; sugar, 50%; vegetables and melons, 130%; and fruit and berries, almost 400%, while the consumption of bread and potatoes will fall off somewhat. This means that the most nutritious foods and foods of higher quality will account for a larger share of the diet. Everything possible will be done to develop public catering. It will expand more than threefold in the next ten years and approximately thirteenfold in 20 years and will gradually take precedence over the home preparation of meals. Prices in public dining rooms will decline steadily.

Within the next decade all Soviet people will be able to acquire a sufficiency of consumer goods, and in the following decade the demand for them will be met in full. According to plan estimates, per capita consumption will increase over the 20 years as follows: clothing and footwear, approximately 250%; articles of cultural and everyday use, 450%. The output of furniture is to rise six- to eightfold. The electrification of daily life will be carried out on the basis of improved household electrical equipment and appliances.

Retail state and cooperative trade in town and countryside will increase 150% (in comparable prices) in ten years and 400% in 20 years. The demand for public laundries and shops for the repair of clothing, footwear and articles of cultural use will be satisfied. We must expand all types of public services, so that all who wish can rely on them instead of doing household work themselves.

The Communist Party and the Soviet government attach particular importance to the final solution of the housing problem. Not one social system has been able to solve this problem. Housing construction has now assumed unprecedented dimensions in our country. In the past five years alone some 50,000,-000 people have received new housing accommodations. We must put an end to the housing shortage within this decade. By the end of the following decade every family will have been provided with a separate comfortable apartment. This means that the country's housing must be approximately tripled in 20 years' time. The average annual volume of housing construction will rise from approximately 135,000,000 square meters in 1961-1965 to 400,000,000 square meters in 1976-1980. A truly colossal program!

While preserving large cities as industrial and cultural centers but at the same time preventing their excessive growth, we must develop and build small and medium-sized towns having all facilities. Our communities should increasingly conform to the concept of "green cities," "garden cities." They will combine all that is best in the modern city—up-to-date dwellings,

transport thoroughfares, communal services, children's and cultural institutions and sports facilities—with all the best that rural localities have to offer—abundant greenery, lakes and ponds, and clean air.

The draft Program provides for further reduction of the working day, thus giving the people scope for the rapid advancement of their cultural and technical level, for the useful employment of their leisure time. We have already carried out the changeover to a seven-hour, and in a number of branches a six-hour, working day. In the first decade a six-hour day or 35-hour week will be instituted for the majority of the working people and a shorter work period (30 hours a week) for the rest. The country of communist construction will have the shortest working day in the world. The growth of labor productivity will make possible further reductions in working hours.

At the same time paid vacations for workers and employees will be lengthened to three weeks and later to a month. The system of paid vacations will gradually be extended to collective farmers.

Comrades! We shall move on from the socialist principle of distribution according to work to the communist principle of distribution according to need. In addition to an abundance of material and cultural benefits, this will call for another, no less important precondition—the transformation of labor into a prime necessity of life for everyone. Until this precondition has been realized, attempts to "introduce" communist distribution irrespective of the worker's labor contribution would mean the spread of leveling, which undermines production. The Party is resolutely opposed to a "line" of this sort.

The Party's premise is that for the next 20 years payment according to work will remain the chief means for the satisfaction of material and cultural needs. Payment according to work is a potent method of increasing output; it stimulates working people to raise their cultural and technical level, thereby furthering the gradual elimination of the essential distinctions between mental and physical labor; it is an important means of augmenting the real incomes of the population; and it makes possible a gradual reduction of the disparity between higher and lower wage levels as social wealth increases. While doing our utmost to promote and reinforce moral incentives to labor, we must employ the principle of distribution according to work consistently and to the fullest degree, as a key factor in the building of a communist society.

The U.S.S.R. will accomplish a task of historic importance within this decade: The category of low-paid workers and employees will disappear. The process of reducing the disparity in wage rates has nothing to do with leveling, since it goes hand in hand with the supplanting of unskilled labor by skilled labor. The wages of skilled workers must rise as the productivity of labor rises. On the collective farms, where the productivity of labor will be rising more rapidly, the average pay will increase over the next 20 years at a faster rate than will the pay of industrial workers. Plans call for raising the wages of such categories of the Soviet intelligentsia as engineers, technicians, agronomists, medical personnel, teachers and people in the cultural field.

The enlargement of public consumption funds will also assume ever greater importance as a way of improving the public well-being. Distribution among the members of society through these funds is not contingent upon the quantity and quality of their labor—that is to say, it is free of charge. The draft Program calls for public consumption funds to grow more rapidly than individual wages, since they lead directly to communist distribution. Over the 20-year period an increase of more than tenfold is contemplated in the annual volume of public consumption funds—from 24,500,000,000 rubles in 1960 to between 255,000,000,000 and 265,000,000,000 rubles in 1980. At the end of the 20 years these funds will account for about half the total incomes of the people.

It is important that the growth of public funds be properly coupled with the principles of material incentives and distribution according to work. The draft Program envisages the following as the chief trends in the development of the public consumption funds over the 20 years ahead: a gradual shift to the maintenance of children and all incapacitated individuals at society's expense; free education and medical services for the population; free housing, public utilities and transport. The maintenance of children and the incapacitated at society's expense is a noble and humane undertaking, which accords with the lofty ideals of the new system. And we are proud, comrades, that the time is at hand when we shall be equal to tasks like these. (Prolonged applause.)

The day is not far off when we shall be able to introduce free lunches in all schools and to furnish school children with textbooks and school uniforms free of charge. This will be followed by the total abolition of charges for the maintenance of children in nursery schools, kindergartens and extended-day schools. At present the workers themselves bear most of the cost of the children's maintenance, but by the end of the next 20 years approximately 75% to 80% of the cost of maintaining and rearing the children will be borne by the state. The state's expenditures on the maintenance of children and adolescents will increase more than ten-fold between 1961 and 1980.

The fact that society is to an ever-increasing extent undertaking the maintenance and rearing of children and the provision of everyday services is of enormous social significance, for it ensures the total elimination of the vestiges of woman's inequality in daily life. These measures are also doing away with the inequality entailed in having a large family.

Provision will be made at the same time for the full maintenance at public expense of all who are unable to work. Pensions will gradually increase. The network of homes for the aged and disabled will be expanded sufficiently to meet the need. In the second decade it will be possible to shift gradually to a single system of pensions for all who are unable to work.

As a result of all these measures, conditions will be created for a further improvement in the health of Soviet people and for an extension of their life expectancy. Expansion of the network of public health institutions will play a big part in this. The needs of the urban and rural population for competent medical care of all types will be fully satisfied. Special stress will be laid on developing preventive medicine. A substantial increase is planned in the number of hospitals, sanatoriums, rest homes and boarding houses. To the free medical treatment that our country has long had we are going to add free sanatorium care for the sick and free medicines.

The provision of free modern living quarters and free basic utilities for every family will be one of the wonderful accomplishments of communist construction. The second decade will see a start made on the implementation of another important social measure—free public catering (meals) at enterprises and institutions—and for collective farmers while they are at work.

The Soviet people already enjoy social benefits that are out of reach of the working people in capitalist countries. They are strangers to exploitation, unemployment, depressions, and racial or other discrimination in pay, and they are confident of the future. (Applause.) At present, however, the Soviet Union still lags behind the United States in average per capita consumption standards and in the general level of real income per person. But there are two circumstances that must not be lost sight of: the level from which we started, and the cost of the war to us as compared with its cost to the United States. In 1980 real income per capita in the U.S.S.R. will exceed the present income level of U.S. working people by approximately 75%. But when average per capita consumption standards are discussed, it should be borne in mind that the U.S. figures conceal millions of fully and partially unemployed and of low-paid semiskilled and unskilled workers, who live in slums and lack the most basic necessities. In our country every family will be assured a sufficiency, and later on an abundance, of material and cultural benefits. (Applause.)

The draft Program points out that the projected plans for improving the people's well-being can be successfully fulfilled only if there is peace. Furthermore, a relaxation of international tension and the accompanying reduction in military expenditures would enable us to raise the people's standard of living even higher. Our struggle for peace is an integral part of the struggle for communism, for the prosperity of the Soviet country and the improvement of the people's well-being.

Comrades! The magnificent program for raising the living standard of the Soviet people is imbued with tremendous social meaning. It vividly reveals the noble features of our people's regime and has evoked the admiration of the broadest

sections of the world's population. Western bourgeois propaganda recognizes that the goals set by the draft Program are practicable, and it finds in this the "principal challenge" to the Western powers.

Well, we consider it a noble thing to issue a challenge to a competition in providing the best living conditions for the people. Why shouldn't the capitalist gentry, who have made fortunes from plundering the peoples, take up a challenge of this kind? Why should they not shift their war industries to the production of civilian goods, and raise the workers' wages? We believe the working people in the capitalist countries, too, would welcome the abolition of rent for housing, which in a number of countries eats up almost one-third of their pay. Surely the American people, who in 1960 alone spent some $20,000,000,000 for medical attention, would applaud the introduction of free medical care?

But, as we know, capitalism's motto is "Squeeze a man dry." And when a man can no longer work, capitalist society leaves him to the mercy of his fate: If he has no money, let him starve to death; if he has no place to live, let him spend the night under a bridge. That is what the "free world" means, what bourgeois "freedom" means. Socialism has put an end to such misanthropic ways. The motto of communism is "Everything in the name of man, for the benefit of man." And under communism, which is being built by the people and for the people's happiness, the word Man will have a prouder ring than ever! (Prolonged applause.)

4. Planning and Economic Management Must Measure Up to the Demands of Communist Construction.—Comrades! If the tremendous tasks set by the draft Program are to be carried out successfully, we must see to it that planning and economic management are adequate to the demands of the full-scale building of communism. The factors dictating this are: first, the vastly growing scale of production and construction and the development and extension of economic interdependence; second, the rapid progress of science and technology; third, the huge social, cultural and technical changes in the sphere of labor; fourth, the extension of democratic principles in economic management and the increasing activeness of the masses.

The building of communism requires sound and efficient utilization of all productive resources and the intelligent economizing of labor. Lenin's wise words "Socialism means accounting" take on even greater significance in the period of the construction of communism.

Here is what the figures tell. In the period of the general long-range plan, savings from the reduction of industrial production costs alone are to amount to between 1,400,000,000,000 and 1,500,000,000,000 rubles, or nearly three-fourths of the total investments in the national economy. Today every saving of one percent in production and construction costs develops into an enormous source of additional increases in production and improvements in living standards. And at the same time even seemingly insignificant planning error or irrationality in the use of funds means losses of many millions of rubles.

The amount to be invested over the 20 years—2,000,000,000,000 rubles—is six times the total investment in all the years of the Soviet regime. With magnitudes of this kind, we literally cannot take a single step without observing the popular injunction to "measure seven times, and cut only once." This is a case where we absolutely must have the most precise calculations as to what, where and how to build in order to derive the greatest advantage with the least expenditure. The slightest slow-down in schedules for bringing such a multitude of new projects into operation would mean freezing enormous funds. And at the same time, what great resources would be freed by speeding up these schedules, how many dwellings, children's institutions, schools, hospitals and rest homes over and above plan could be opened for use!

Life itself requires of planning and economic management a new and far higher order of scientific substantiation and economic calculation. The drafting of plans and approval of economic measures should be preceded by a thorough scientific analysis of the problems of economic and technical development. The correct solution of economic problems must be facilitated by economic and technical studies. It is a matter of determining the most advantageous proportions in the national economy, of making the most effective use of natural resources, productive capacity and new equipment, of apportioning national income and capital investments soundly, of marshaling additional resources for accelerating the rate of economic development, etc.

What demands are made of planning in our times? First, it is essential that we have progressive planning standards for the utilization of all kinds of implements of labor and of raw and other materials and for technological methods and project timetables; the introduction and the strictest observance of these standards should become law for every economic manager. Second, it is essential that every plan be precisely balanced in all its component elements and that it be backed with the necessary resources.

The work of planning and economic organization must be oriented even more strongly toward modern technology, which must be given the "green light," as they say. After all, the material and technical base of communism is being laid right now in technological designing, in the plants that are being commissioned today but that will also be operating 15 to 20 years from now. The task is to see to it that the latest scientific and technical discoveries and advances are promptly and fully reflected in the new blueprints produced by design organizations. It is important that the centralized system for the introduction of new equipment from above be made more efficient and that a mass nationwide movement for technical progress be launched from below.

Material and moral encouragement must be extended to enterprises that have been successful in mastering the operation of new equipment and the output of new types of products, and they must be given preferential treatment as compared with those that show conservatism and cling to the past. We must see to it that all over the country specialized enterprises turning out the various parts of each type of new equipment are smoothly organized on cooperative lines, with coordinated schedules. A matter that is assuming particular importance is the organization of close, businesslike cooperation among scientists, designers, technologists and workers at every stage, starting with designing and surveying, moving through the making of test models and ending with mass production. Finally, it is essential that any technical project in the production field be considered and approved only after thorough substantiation of its economic effectiveness.

It is no exaggeration to say that the success of our whole movement toward communism and our success in raising the living standards of the Soviet people depend to a very great degree on how much we are able to speed up construction, lower its cost and improve its quality, how efficiently and wisely we are able to use capital investments and production resources and how successful we are in achieving maximum output per unit of productive capacity with minimum expenditure. This will call for the reorganization of planning and accounting, state and public control, competition, and the whole system for assessing and encouraging the work of every worker, brigade, shop, enterprise, and economic council, in order to get the most efficient performance from every machine tool and all other machinery and equipment and in order that our investments pay for themselves as soon as possible. We must thoroughly eradicate the deplorable practice of scattering or "spreading" resources over a great number of construction projects. I have already spoken of this in the Central Committee report.

In accelerating the construction, commissioning and full-scale operation of enterprises, it would be no sin for us to learn from the best capitalist examples. In his day Lenin said that we had to learn how to trade. Much water has flowed under the bridge since then. We have amassed vast experience in construction and economic management, and have an incomparable advantage over capitalism. But even today we should not disregard useful foreign experience but should critically adopt anything the West has that is of value from the technical and organizational standpoints, including ways of accelerating the turnover of funds and securing greater results from investments.

In the course of communist construction the steady improvement of the quality of output becomes a paramount economic and political task. The slogan advanced in the period immediately preceding the Congress—"Soviet Means the Best"—should be the guiding principle in the work of every enterprise.

Running through the entire draft Program is the thought that the bedrock of communism is highly productive, scientifically organized labor equipped with up-to-date machinery. Rational use of labor resources is therefore a most important aspect of planning and management.

The introduction of new technology will release millions of people, including those employed in auxiliary, subsidiary jobs. Many people will be released from jobs in agriculture. Administrative and management personnel and office staffs will be sharply reduced. Millions of women will be relieved of household duties. They will swell the ranks of working people engaged in the national economy. As a result of the vast expansion of public health services, education and cultural activities, the number of persons engaged in these and other nonproduction spheres will experience the greatest increase—almost threefold in the 20 years.

All this will require a whole complex of carefully worked out measures, covering the entire country, for the mass training of workers and improvement of their skills and for the planned redistribution of manpower on a purely voluntary basis and with strict observance of the principle of material incentive. Suitable living conditions and cultural facilities must be provided to encourage people to move to jobs in other regions.

The growing scale of construction and the accelerated pace of technical progress necessitate continuity in planning. It is by now quite impossible to set an annual plan for production, machinery, capital investment or labor without full consideration of all aspects of long-range development. Every annual plan must become an organic part of the long-range plan covering a number of years. And at the same time the long-range plans must be "down-to-earth," so to speak, and corrected through the agency of the annual plans, taking into account their actual fulfillment.

Unified planning, coordinating all spheres and branches of our economy, plays a role of growing importance in the period of communist construction. To see to it that the interests of the entire state come first, to keep an effective check on the strict observance of state discipline in economic activities everywhere and by everyone without exception, and to be resolute in eliminating any manifestations of localism or of a narrowly departmental approach—these are essential prerequisites for progress toward communism.

The draft Program contains a clear-cut formulation of the Leninist line that democratic principles of economic management must be promoted to the utmost in combination with centralized state direction. Centralized direction should draw upon the creative initiative of the masses and give it ever broader scope. This assumes the further gradual extension of the economic rights and responsibility of local agencies as well as of enterprises. Everything possible must be done to enhance the role and rights of trade union and other public organizations, especially on the lower levels, and to see to it that participation by workers' collectives in the management of enterprises becomes broader and more active all the time.

The sound coupling of material and moral incentives—this is our policy, our line for the entire period of communist construction. While society is at the socialist stage, we cannot dispense with distribution according to work, with commodity-money relations and with such categories as price, profit, finance and credit. With us these economic instruments are socialist in substance and serve the building of communism. When communism has been established they will have become obsolete and will be replaced with the superior economic categories of the direct calculation and distribution of social labor.

Our task in the course of building communism is to make ever greater use of and to improve the finance-and-credit levers, ruble control, prices and profits. We must enhance the importance of profits, of profitability. It is in the interest of better plan fulfillment that enterprises be given greater opportunity to determine the use of their profits, to make broader use of them for encouraging their collectives to do good work and for expanding production. (Applause.) It is very important to devise and introduce forms of collective inducement, so as to provide every worker with a material stake in the results not only of his own work but of the labor of the collective as a whole.

Comrades! The plan for developing our country's productive forces over the next 20 years is truly magnificent. It does not merely present exciting figures for increases in the output of coal, steel, oil, grain, meat and milk. It is a majestic plan for building a society in which man will be the true master of nature and of social relations and in which a high standard of living will be attained by all the people. (Prolonged applause.)

Such great goals are worth living, working and fighting for. Party, trade union and Young Communist League organizations have no task loftier, more meaningful or interesting than the task of organizing the struggle to carry out the general long-range plan, the struggle to build communism. (Prolonged applause.)

IV. THE DEVELOPMENT OF COMMUNIST SOCIAL RELATIONS AND THE MOLDING OF THE NEW MAN.—Comrades! In the transition to communism, the mighty expansion of productive forces is attended by the gradual evolution of socialist social relations into communist ones. The formation of a communist economy, the development of social relations and the molding of the new man are interconnected processes. Whereas economics constitutes the basis for changes in social relations and the consciousness of people, the development of social relations and the growth of man's communist convictions, cultural level and activeness constitute a necessary condition for economic progress.

1. The Building of a Classless Society in the U.S.S.R.—The U.S.S.R. has now arrived at the historical period in its development in which it is directly pursuing the task of building a classless communist society of free and politically conscious working people.

The extremely rich experience of Soviet society bears out the conclusions of Marxism-Leninism that in order to abolish classes and class distinctions it is necessary:

First, to overthrow the rule of the exploiter classes—landlords and capitalists—and to abolish their private ownership of the means of production, which is the economic basis of the exploitation of man by man. This task was accomplished in our country as a result of the October Revolution, the nationalization of land and capitalist property, and the restriction and forcing out of capitalist elements.

Second, to transform individual small-scale commodity production into large-scale collective commodity production, to complete the establishment of a single socialist economic system and to eliminate the last exploiter class, the class of kulaks. This task was accomplished by the collectivization of the countryside and the organization of handicraft production on cooperative lines, and by the elimination of the kulaks as a class.

Third, to remove class distinctions between workers and peasants and the essential distinctions between town and countryside and to create conditions for the organic fusion of physical and mental labor. How is this third task being pursued? Our continued advance toward a classless society unquestionably depends above all on the rapid expansion of our productive forces. The effacement of distinctions between the classes of working people proceeds on the basis of a high level of development of productive forces and socialist production relations.

And it is not only from theory that we know this, comrades. We are witnessing it in practice. The extensive use of machinery and electric power has been changing the character of the peasant's labor and his mentality. He is steadily approaching the factory worker in the level of his technical knowledge.

Public property is the basis of the life of the entire population, including the collective farm peasantry. At the same time, features distinctive to the system of public property are emerging and becoming rooted in the system of cooperative-collective farm property. Life itself has been steadily bringing public and cooperative forms of ownership closer together and will ultimately lead to the establishment of a single, communist form of ownership and a single, communist principle of distribution.

As the building of communism proceeds, the major changes in production technology and in the character of labor will result in the accomplishment of another social task of the utmost importance—the elimination of essential distinctions between physical and mental labor. We are observing these processes in our everyday lives at this very moment. Millions of people with a secondary education have gone to work in industrial enterprises and on the fields of collective and state farms.

Among workers and collective farmers there are tens of thousands who are getting a higher education without dropping their jobs. The labor of the workers is gradually beginning to resemble the work of engineers. Take the foreman, for instance. Unquestionably, he is in the category of engineers and technicians, in the intelligentsia, yet he is also a worker. Or take the army of production innovators, of worker-rationalizers. After all, they too often make the kind of creative contributions to technological development that are the responsibility of major specialists. The same can be said with good reason of the leading workers in agriculture, who are veritable professors in their field.

The obliteration of distinctions between classes, a process that is fully under way, is leading to the ever greater social homogeneity of society. It goes without saying that this is a long and gradual process. The final elimination of all class distinctions will occur only when a full communist society has been built.

Simultaneous with this process and inseparably bound up with it will be the establishment of complete social equality among human beings—communist equality, signifying an identical relationship to the means of production, complete equality in distribution, and harmony between the individual and society based on the organic combination of personal and public interests. The classless communist society will thus be the highest form of organization of the human community.

2. From a State of the Dictatorship of the Proletariat to a State of the Entire People.—The draft Party Program poses and resolves a most important new question of communist theory and practice—the evolution of the state of the dictatorship of the working class into a state of the entire people, the character and tasks of this state, and its destinies under communism. A state of the entire people represents a new stage in the development of the socialist state, a most important milestone in the evolution of socialist statehood into communist public self-government.

Half a century ago our party was the only party to have incorporated into its program the Marxist-Leninist idea of the dictatorship of the proletariat. If we were able to hold out in a desperate struggle against internal and world reaction, if we have been able to make a reality of socialism, the age-old dream of man, we owe all this very largely to the fact that we had in our hands a powerful instrument for the transformation of society—the state of the dictatorship of the working class. The experience of the Soviet Union and the people's democracies has fully confirmed the Marxist-Leninist teaching that it is possible to achieve the victory of socialism only if the dictatorship of the proletariat has been established.

The dictatorship of the proletariat is born of conditions of class struggle between the proletariat and the bourgeoisie. On the way to its establishment, socialism is forced to overcome resistance, often of the most savage kind, from the reactionary forces of the old world. Think back, comrades, to the fierce resistance we encountered from the landlords and capitalists, who had the most active support from the forces of world reaction. One might also cite an event of the comparatively recent past—the counterrevolutionary insurrection in Hungary in 1956. This example served to re-emphasize that for the transition to socialism the working class needs a regime capable of suppressing the resistance of the exploiters, consolidating the victory of the revolution, promptly heading off attempts to restore the rule of the bourgeoisie and ensuring defense against the aggressive acts of international reaction.

It must be emphasized that the proletariat resorts to coercion only against the capitalists and landlords and their confederates, and not against the laboring classes. This gives the proletarian regime its profoundly democratic nature. The bourgeois state signifies the dictatorship of the exploiting minority over the overwhelming majority of society, whereas the proletarian state represents the interests of the enormous majority of the people. The working class guides the peasantry and the other sections of society's laboring people, its allies and brothers-in-arms, helps them voluntarily shift to the path of socialism. This guidance, as a characteristic feature of the proletarian regime, differentiates it fundamentally from the bourgeois state, which knows no other relationship than that of dominance and subservience.

V. I. Lenin taught us that the working class needed a dictatorship to establish a socialist society and abolish all exploitation of man by man. "This goal," V. I. Lenin explained, "cannot be realized at once; it requires quite a lengthy period of transition from capitalism to socialism—because the reorganization of production is a difficult thing, because it takes time to effect radical changes in all spheres of life, and because the enormously powerful effect of habituation to management by the petty bourgeoisie and the bourgeoisie can be overcome only by a long, hard struggle. That is precisely why Marx speaks of an entire period of dictatorship by the proletariat, as a period of transition from capitalism to socialism" (Works" [in Russian], Vol. XXIX, p. 358). According to Marx and Lenin, therefore, a state of the dictatorship of the proletariat is a state of the period of transition from capitalism to socialism.

Naturally, when socialism had triumphed fully and finally in our country and we entered the period of the full-scale building of communism, the circumstances necessitating the dictatorship of the proletariat disappeared; its internal tasks had been accomplished.

The working class is the only class in history that does not set the goal of perpetuating its rule. When the conditions that gave rise to its dictatorship disappear and when society has exhausted the tasks that could not be accomplished without its aid, the state proceeds to evolve under working-class leadership into an all-inclusive organization of the working people of socialist society. With the victory of socialism and the entry of our country into the period of the full-scale building of communism, the working class of the Soviet Union, on its own initiative and proceeding from the tasks of communist construction, transformed the state of its dictatorship into a state of the entire people. Comrades, this is a fact without a parallel in history! Until now the state has always been the instrument of dictatorship by one class or another. For the first time there has arisen in our country a state that is not a dictatorship of any one class but the instrument of society as a whole, of all the people. (Stormy applause.)

The dictatorship of the proletariat is not needed for building communism. All the working people in our society enjoy equal rights. Naturally, during the transition to communism the working class continues to play the leading role in society. The working class retains this role by virtue of the fact that it is the most advanced and most highly organized class, the class that is associated with machine industry, and the most consistent bearer of communist ideals.

It would be wrong to think that the state of the dictatorship of the proletariat, which represents the interests of the overwhelming majority of society, is separated by a wall of some kind from the state of the entire people. From its very inception the dictatorship of the proletariat incorporates features of universal socialist democracy. As socialism develops these features are reinforced, and when socialism has fully triumphed they become determinative. From an instrument of class rule the state becomes an agency representing the will of the entire people.

With the evolution of the dictatorship of the proletariat into a state of the entire people the might of our society and state, far from being impaired, increases many times over, for to the earlier sources of our strength new ones are now added. Coupled with the steady growth of our state's economic potential has been the strengthening and broadening of its social base; society has grown more unified and monolithic than ever before. And this is the state's chief source of strength. Every worker, every peasant, every member of the intelligentsia can say: We are the state, its policy is our policy, and the task of developing and strengthening it and of defending it against any and all encroachments is our common task. (Prolonged applause.)

But just why is the state itself being retained, when the main thing that produced it—class antagonism—has disappeared? The explanation for this is that society has not yet exhausted the tasks that it can solve only with the help of the state. These tasks and functions of the socialist state are clearly defined in our party's draft Program.

The state will endure long after the first phase of communism has triumphed. The withering away of the state will be a most protracted process, which will embrace an entire historical epoch and will be completed only when society has fully matured for self-government. Features of state guidance and public self-government will be interwoven for a definite period. In the course of this process the domestic functions of the state will develop to the full, be transformed and gradually lose their political character. Only when a developed communist society exists in the U.S.S.R., and provided socialism has triumphed and been consolidated internationally, will there be no further need for the state; it will then wither away completely.

The fact that the dictatorship of the proletariat has ceased to be a necessity does not in the least signify any slackening in the maintenance of public order or of legality. The Party attaches great importance to the further strengthening of legality and order, to the protection of citizens' rights. The rights, freedom, honor and dignity of Soviet people will be strictly protected by society and by the state. People who expect that public order will be maintained less firmly in our state are in for a cruel disappointment. Side by side with the state agencies, the mass organizations of the working people will be playing an increasing role in combating antisocial and criminal elements. The struggle against embezzlers of public property and against parasites and hooligans will be even more effective, since it will become the concern of working people and their organizations.

Comrades! You know that in the past few years, particularly since the 20th Party Congress, an enormous job has been done of re-establishing Leninist norms of Party and state life and further broadening Soviet democracy. Needless to say, we do not consider that the task of perfecting our political system has already been completed. Everything necessary must be done to improve and develop the state of the entire people, to draw the masses ever increasingly into the administration and control of state agencies.

I want to say something first about the role of the representative agencies of authority. The powers of the Soviets will be broadening, and the Soviets will be to an even greater extent what Marx and Lenin had in mind when they analyzed the nature of a genuine people's regime—"working corporations," engaged in the practical work of directing economic and social processes. Many of the questions that today fall within the competence of executive agencies of authority and administration will be handled directly by the Soviets and their committees.

The transition to communism calls for a constant improvement in the work of the state and economic apparatus, and for promoting democratic principles and voluntary participation in that apparatus. The apparatus of the Soviet, economic and other agencies must become even simpler, less costly and more efficient, and must respond promptly and sensitively to the citizens' needs. Such survivals of the past as bureaucracy, callousness, formalism and red tape must be thoroughly eradicated, and officials guilty of a bureaucratic attitude to the needs and requirements of the working people should not only be arraigned before the bar of public opinion but called to strict account by administrative action and through the courts.

The unfolding of socialist democracy entails heightening the role of the public organizations—the trade unions, the Young Communist League, the cooperatives, and cultural and educational groups.

Lenin termed the trade unions a school of administration, a school of management, a school of communism. This fundamental assessment by Lenin of the trade unions' role takes on special significance in the transition to communism. Through the trade unions the workers and employees are exerting an ever greater influence on economic activity, are helping to improve the operations of enterprises and control over production. The growing importance of the trade unions' role is due also to the fact that they are being granted the right of legislative initiative and that a number of functions formerly exercised by state agencies are being turned over to them.

Of great importance in the life of our society is the work of the Young Communist League, the militant organization of Soviet youth. The young are our successors, comrades, our country's future. They are a vigorous creative force capable of moving mountains in the struggle for our ideals. We must show day-to-day and truly fatherly concern for the rearing of the Young Communists.

Our state is run for the working people and by the working people themselves. We are setting ourselves the task of drawing every citizen without exception into the management of public affairs.

How do we expect to accomplish this task?

First, by constantly improving the material and cultural living conditions of all working people.

Second, by constantly perfecting the forms of popular representation and the democratic principles of the Soviet electoral system.

Third, by extending the practice of nationwide discussion of the most important problems of communist construction and of drafts of Soviet state legislation.

Fourth, by doing everything possible to expand the forms and heighten the effectiveness of popular control over the activities of agencies of authority and administration.

Fifth, by regularly renewing the composition of administrative agencies, more and more consistently implementing the elective principle and the principle of accountability with respect to leading officials of the state apparatus and public organizations, and gradually extending these principles to all leading officials of state and public organizations, and also of cultural institutions.

Our ideological adversaries never stop yelling that capitalism is the world of freedom and seeking in every way to vilify our Soviet democracy. But the truth about socialist democracy —the brightest democracy on earth—cannot be suppressed. For it is a fact beyond dispute that the world of socialism is steadily and consistently following a course of developing and broadening democracy and the world of capitalism a course of more and more constricting and curtailing bourgeois democracy, limited as it already is.

Never before has real power in the leading imperialist states been concentrated in the hands of so narrow a group of monopolists as it is today. The Americans themselves called the Eisenhower administration an administration of big business, and the fact is that more than a score of that administration's members were either millionaires themselves or held positions in the biggest corporations. In the British government, 12 out of 19 cabinet Ministers are directly linked with monopolies, while 12 out of 18 members of the Adenauer government are direct representatives of concerns and corporations. The only thing that changes in the governments of the imperialist states is the personalities; some millionaires or their proteges take the place of others, but all of them work for the interests of the monopolists.

The ideologists of the bourgeoisie talk about equality in capitalist society. But what sort of equality do they refer to? Let us take a look at the social structure in the capitalist countries. Confronting us is a monstrous pyramid of social inequality. At its apex are a handful of industrial and financial oligarchs. Like the corrupt nobility in the decline of the Roman Empire, they are wallowing in luxury and utterly sated. At the same time the hundreds of millions of people who comprise the base of that pyramid are condemned to privation and lack of rights. In the United States a narrow circle of rich men—one percent of the population—controls about 60% of the nation's wealth. In Britain more than 50% of the wealth is concentrated in the hands of a group that does not exceed one percent of the country's population.

And let us take the electoral system in the capitalist countries. It is perpetually being revised and readjusted so as to safeguard the interests of the monopolies to the maximum degree and to pervert the true will of the electorate. The present electoral system of France can serve as an illustration. At the last elections, 3,882,204 voters cast their ballots for the Communist Party, yet it obtained a mere ten seats in the National Assembly. Yet the Union for the New Republic, a reactionary party that polled 3,603,958 votes—fewer, that is, than the Communists—obtained 188 seats. Is this not the naked dictatorship of monopoly capital? Is this not making a mockery of the people's will? Working people make up the vast majority of the voters. But are they represented in the parliaments? Is it not a fact that in the United States, where there are more than 50,000,000 workers, employees and working farmers, there is not one worker or small farmer in Congress?

The monopolistic bourgeoisie uses all levers—the press,

the radio, television and other means of ideological influence— to deceive the masses, to stupefy them, to paralyze their will. Whose will, for example, can be reflected by the press that is in the hands of millionaire Hearst? Only one will—the will of the monopoly bosses.

The bourgeoisie has been making steadily greater use of the police and army in the struggle against the people. How much of the people's blood has been spilled in the capitalist countries in the past decade! The policeman's club and bullet occupy a place of ever-increasing importance in bourgeois democracy's arsenal of "arguments."

This is their "free world"—a society in which there is no real freedom and democracy, a society based on social and national oppression and inequality, on the exploitation of man by man, on contemptuous disregard for human dignity and honor.

The flowering of democracy in the socialist countries and the ever greater abridgment of an already circumscribed democracy in the capitalist countries—these are the two contrasting lines in the political development of the contemporary world. We are doing and shall continue to do all we can to improve our socialist system and our democracy still further as a model of the socialist way of life for all peoples. (Prolonged applause.)

3. The Drawing Together of Nations and the Consolidation of Friendship Among the Peoples.—The draft Program charts a course toward the further economic and cultural flowering of Soviet republics and a drawing together of nations still more closely and comprehensively during the full-scale building of communism.

Under socialism two interconnected, progressive tendencies operate in the national question. In the first place, each nation is undergoing a tempestuous all-round development and the rights of the Union and autonomous republics are expanding. In the second place, under the banner of proletarian internationalism the socialist nations are drawing ever closer together and their influence on one another and mutual enrichment are intensifying.

The full-scale building of communism represents a new stage in the development of national relations in the U.S.S.R. The key to intensified cooperation among the nations is above all sound economic policy. The draft Program calls for integrated development and specialization of the Union-republic economies. The economy of each of them will continue to develop as an integral part of the single economy of the Soviet Union as a whole. The greater the contribution made by each republic to the common task of building communism, the broader and more diversified the relations among the Soviet nations.

The economic development of each Soviet republic is the result of fraternal cooperation and mutual assistance among all the Soviet peoples. Take, for example, the plowing up of Kazakhstan's virgin lands. By itself the republic could not have coped with this gigantic task. Russians, Ukrainians, Belorussians and representatives of many other nationalities came to its aid. Or take our enterprises and construction projects. They are harmonious multinational collectives in which workers are judged not by the color of their skin or the language they speak, but by their attitude to their work, by their effort in the cause of communism. The republic populations are becoming more and more heterogeneous in their national composition. The Soviet republics have been exchanging skilled cadres among themselves. This all helps to reinforce the internationalist bonds between the peoples of the U.S.S.R.

The development of the socialist nations also finds expression in the improvement of the national state system of the peoples of the U.S.S.R. The Party will continue to respond to the needs that arise in this sphere. Full advantage must be taken of all the potentialities inherent in the Soviet principles of federation and autonomy. Life already indicates the need for setting up several interrepublic zonal agencies to improve the coordination of the republics' efforts in carrying out the plans for communist construction.

Cultural development and ideological work have also been helping to draw our country's nations and nationalities closer together. The exchange of spiritual riches among them is quickening. The cultural achievements of the various nations are becoming the property of others also. This leads to mutual enrichment of the cultures of U.S.S.R. peoples, to strengthening their internationalist basis, and this is helping to mold the future single universal culture of communist society.

National cultural forms are not ossifying but are evolving progressively; outdated forms that are inconsistent with the tasks of communist construction are fading away while new ones are emerging. It is quite natural that literature and the arts should make use of local national color. But we often run into instances of archaism in this field. In architecture, for instance, obviously outmoded forms are occasionally derived from remote antiquity, forms that are wholly unsuitable to the living conditions and requirements of people of our day. Only forms appropriate to our age have a future.

The Party will continue to make sure that the languages of the peoples of the U.S.S.R. develop freely and will prevent any restriction, privilege or compulsion in the use of a particular language. Every citizen of the U.S.S.R. enjoys and will continue to enjoy full freedom to choose the language of instruction for his children. Nothing impedes the development of national languages in our country. But their development must tend not to reinforce barriers between peoples but to draw nations closer together.

One cannot help noticing the growing eagerness of non-Russian peoples to master the Russian language, which has become virtually a second native tongue for the peoples of the U.S.S.R., a means of intercourse among them, a vehicle for bringing each nation and nationality into contact with the cultural achievements of all the peoples of the U.S.S.R. and with world culture. (Applause.) This voluntary study of Russian is a process of positive significance for the development of cooperation among the nations. (Applause.)

The nations are drawing closer together in our country and their social homogeneity is growing. In the course of the full-scale building of communism the nations will achieve complete unity. But even after communism has in the main been built, it will be premature to pronounce the fusion of nations. Lenin, as we know, said that state and national distinctions would exist long after the triumph of socialism in all countries.

People are to be encountered, of course, who complain about the effacement of national distinctions. Our answer to them is that Communists are not going to freeze and perpetuate national distinctions. With the building of communism under way, the nations and nationalities are drawing closer and closer together on a voluntary and democratic basis, and we shall support this objective process. We must intensify the education of the masses in a spirit of proletarian internationalism and Soviet patriotism. With uncompromising Bolshevist implacability we must eradicate even the slightest manifestation of nationalist survivals.

The friendship of the peoples of the U.S.S.R. is one of our greatest achievements. We must cherish it as the apple of our eye! (Stormy applause.)

4. The Communist Education and All-Round Development of the Individual.—Comrades! The education of people in the spirit of communism is a most important element of communist construction.

The raising of labor productivity to the highest possible level, the development of communist social relations and the establishment of rules of communist community life are inconceivable without a rise in the political consciousness and cultural level of all members of society. The greater the political consciousness of the members of society and the more fully and broadly they display creative activeness, the sooner and the more successfully shall be accomplish the program for building communism.

What tasks do we have in mind when we speak of the molding of the new man? They include:

—consolidation of the communist world outlook: deep belief in the ideals of communism, a conscientious attitude to one's duty to society, socialist internationalism and patriotism, devotion to the homeland and readiness to defend it with one's life;

—labor upbringing, the cultivation of a communist attitude to work, to social production;

—reinforcement of the principles of communist morality, voluntary observance of the rules of communist community life;

—cultural development, mastery of the fundamentals of science, general and polytechnical education, esthetic and physical education.

Communism ennobles man. Communism is the highest flowering of mankind and the human personality.

While inculcating the new communist traits of character in all members of our society, the Party attaches particular importance to the communist upbringing and education of youth. The Party and the people have reared a wonderful generation of dedicated builders of socialism and heroic defenders of the homeland, who have earned undying fame. Now we are preparing people for life in communist society. The generation of communism must be molded from childhood, must be cared for and tempered in youth. We must make sure that it has no moral cripples—victims of improper upbringing and bad example. If young fruit trees have been damaged to any extent, how much trouble must be taken to nurse them back to health, and even then this cannot always be accomplished. It is the same with the people of the new generation.

The molding of the new man is influenced not only by the educational work of the Party, the Soviet state, the trade unions and the Young Communist League but by the entire pattern of society's life: the mode of production, forms of distribution, everyday services, social and political activities, legal regulations and judicial practice. All economic, social, political and legal levers must be used to develop people's communist consciousness and to eradicate the survivals of bourgeois psychology and morality.

The bourgeoisie associates the freedom of the individual with private property. But millions of people in the capitalist countries are without property, and for them bourgeois property is not a guarantee of freedom but a grievous yoke. For the petty proprietors property is not the condition for their development as individuals but a chain that keeps them in a state of total dependence upon monopoly capital. It is only the capitalists to whom private property means complete freedom to exploit the workers and make fabulous profits. The wealth of experience amassed by our country and by the world socialist system as a whole indicates that it is not private but public ownership that releases man from all forms of social dependence and provides broad opportunities for the free development of the individual. The noble feelings of collectivism, comradeship, and dedication to one's duty as a member of society have become the flesh and blood of our people.

The draft Program attaches great importance to the further molding of the progressive scientific world outlook of Soviet people. This is quite natural. For man cannot progress in his spiritual development if his head is stuffed with mysticism, superstitions and false notions.

For the first time in history the world view of millions of people rests on the scientific foundation of Marxism-Leninism, which has become the ideological weapon of the masses in their struggle for a better life and for the victory of communism. Marxism-Leninism has launched mankind into the correct, accurately calculated orbit leading to the bright communist future! (Applause.)

We are revolutionaries and internationalists, and therefore we cannot remain indifferent to the propagation of reactionary views; we cannot be reconciled to the befuddling and corrupting of people's minds, the stirring up of chauvinistic passions, by the bourgeoisie. The Party will continue to expose imperialist ideology.

Communist consciousness develops and is reinforced in the active struggle for communism, in work for the common good. Communist ideas must be organically coupled with communist deeds in the behavior of every individual and in the work of every collective, organization and institution.

The basis of communist education, of the all-round development of the individual, is creative labor. Labor always has been and always will be the means of people's subsistence and development. In their various languages, and in various forms, all peoples have the precept "He who does not work, neither shall he eat."

The Communists have set the goal of freeing people not from labor but from the exploitation of their labor. Man's work and the provision of all benefits are in full accord in the communist principle "From each according to his abilities, to each according to his needs."

One of the most important tasks of communist education is to instill in everyone the firm realization that man cannot live without working, without creating the means of life. All the good that Soviet man does he does for himself and for society as a whole. To be conscientious in your work, to do everything on time and do it well actually means to show regard for your fellows, who are also working for everyone, including you. Comradely cooperation and mutual assistance among the people of the new society manifest themselves in this way.

The bourgeoisie oppresses and demeans laboring people. The Communists glorify and exalt free labor as the source of life and well-being for all people and as the assurance of progress and prosperity for society! (Applause.)

The draft Program contains the moral code of the builder of communism, the ethical standards of the new society, its moral precepts.

For more than a hundred years now bourgeois ideologists have accused Communists of denying morality, of undermining the moral bases of society. The bourgeoisie needs these fabrications to cover up its own immorality. What underlies the moral precepts of the exploiting classes? The clearest possible answer to this is provided by sayings such as: "Anything goes for the strong and the rich"; "Rob or be robbed"; "Money has no smell"; "Man is a wolf to man."

We do indeed repudiate these cruel and cynical maxims. Against them we range the moral principles of collectivism and humanism beautifully expressed as: "One for all and all for one," "Man is to man a friend, comrade and brother." (Prolonged applause.)

Our task is to see to it that the new moral requirements become an inner need for all Soviet people. We still have a great deal of work to do in eradicating survivals of the past. In the life of society the progressive is not fenced off from the old and backward. In the end the progressive prevails, but survivals of the old impede forward movement. The force of good example has an increasing effect, and our educational effort is founded on this fact. But as everyone knows, weeds spread rapidly if their growth is not checked in time.

The public must be asked to pay more attention to people's conduct and be more exacting with regard to it. After all, the persons who commit misdeeds are generally members of some collective, some organization—members of trade unions, the Y.C.L., collective farms, cultural-enlightenment associations and societies, and sometimes even members of our party. The moral weight and authority of public opinion must be brought to bear more vigorously in dealing with those who trespass against the norms and rules of socialist community life.

We want to make well-rounded individuals of all the people. What class other than the working class, what ruling party other than the Communist Party has set its sights on developing the capacities and endowments of all working people?

The Party sees the rapid cultural advance of the people as the guarantee of victory in the building of communism. Our country's cultural revolution has reached its crowning stage, at which its principal purpose is to establish all the necessary ideological and cultural preconditions for communism. The paramount task at this stage is to raise the cultural and technical level of all the workers and peasants to that of the intelligentsia so as to eliminate in the main the essential distinctions between mental and physical labor.

In the next 20 years the greater part of the members of society will through one channel or another receive a complete secondary, specialized secondary or higher education. This is a big but entirely practicable task.

Within the present ten-year period general and polytechnical secondary (11-year) education is to be introduced for all school children. Under the school law, upon completing the eight-year school they must work at enterprises or collective farms and at the same time continue their schooling until they obtain a complete secondary education. This paves the way both to the obtaining of a higher education and to the performance of more highly skilled work in production.

We must also make sure that in the coming ten years young

people employed in the national economy who do not have a secondary education receive an education equivalent to at least eight years of schooling. This is an important and urgent task. It must not be forgotten that during the war many boys and girls were unable to obtain a secondary education. Proper concern must be shown for these young citizens of our country.

The Soviet school plays an especially important part in the all-round and harmonious development of our people. The schools must rear their pupils in the spirit of communism, implanting the finest qualities and habits in them and preparing them to work conscientiously according to their abilities, make sensible use of public wealth, and steadfastly observe the standards of communist morality and the rules of community life. The public schoolteachers, who may rightly be considered the spiritual mentors of youth, play a great role in bringing up the rising generation. Everything possible should be done to elevate this role and to surround the teacher with consideration and regard! (Applause.)

The Party attaches great importance to further developing the institutions of public upbringing: the boarding schools, extended-day schools and preschool institutions. Public and family upbringing do not conflict; the influence of the family in the children's upbringing must be coupled with their public upbringing.

People who take the position that the family is of dwindling importance in the transition to communism and that it will in time disappear altogether are quite mistaken. As a matter of fact, the family will grow stronger under communism; family relations will finally be cleansed of material considerations and attain a high level of honesty and stability.

While the Party is directing its efforts toward making universal secondary education a reality, its Program at the same time sets the goal of making all forms of higher education still more widely accessible. There are now 2,600,000 people enrolled in our higher schools. It is contemplated that by 1980 the number of students in higher educational institutions will have been brought up to 8,000,000—that is, increased by more than 200%. The program of evening and correspondence education will be expanded in particular.

The still considerable lag in the cultural and technical level of the rural population behind that of the urban population must be overcome in order that the essential distinctions between town and countryside can be eliminated in this sphere as well. All organizations dealing with cultural matters must heighten their attention to raising the cultural level in the countryside.

Extensive measures are to be taken in the next few years to achieve a great expansion of the material base of culture—paper mills and printshops, radio and television stations, theaters, film studios and motion picture theaters, clubs and libraries. This will naturally necessitate large financial expenditures. But our society, engaged in building communism, will not begrudge funds for the fullest satisfaction of Soviet people's cultural requirements.

In our age of tempestuous scientific and technical progress, the development of society and of the individual is inconceivable without planned and comprehensive utilization of scientific achievements. V. I. Lenin once said: "No force of darkness will be able to withstand the alliance of science, the proletariat and technology" ("Works"[in Russian], Vol. XXX, p. 376). These prophetic words have become living reality. We have smashed and destroyed the dark forces of the exploiters and have put an end for good to all forms of economic and spiritual oppression. And today we are steadily intensifying our efforts to overcome man's dependence on the elemental forces of nature, to make him their master. This will mean for mankind clearing the last hurdle on the road to the true realm of freedom.

Science is called upon to respond to the needs of the day, to serve as a militant and effective weapon in the solution of pressing problems of the national economy and in the development of society's productive forces. In the long run science must discover ways of controlling thermonuclear reactions so that the limitless sources of nuclear energy can be harnessed for peaceful purposes; it must find ways of modifying climate and weather conditions, conquering disease and lengthening the span of human life, controlling the vital processes of organisms, developing a countless multitude of artificial materials with desired properties, mastering outer space and laying down dependable routes of communication in the universe. This will comprise a whole epoch in the history of world science and technology, will provide man with inexhaustible energy resources and make him truly the lord of nature.

The social sciences are playing a role of ever-growing importance in the study of the historic path of mankind's movement to communism, in the investigation of the processes of capitalism's collapse, in the working out of scientific principles for the planned guidance of the development of social, economic and cultural construction, the molding of a materialist world outlook in people, in the rearing of the man of communist society and in the struggle against bourgeois ideology. The Party will concern itself with the flourishing of all fields of human knowledge.

It is a matter of honor and a patriotic duty for Soviet scientist to consolidate the forward positions that Soviet science has already won in major fields of knowledge and to ensure for it the leading role in all the main areas of development in world science. (Applause.)

Literature and the arts play a big part in the molding of the new man. By upholding communist ideas and true humanism, literature and the arts cultivate in Soviet man the qualities needed by the builders of the new world and further the artistic and moral development of people. The Party summons all writers and workers in the arts to bold, inventive treatment of contemporary themes.

The amateur arts, which are continually gaining in scope, offer a broad arena for the display and development of the people's talents and gifts. This does not, however, obviate the necessity of developing the professional arts. The amateur arts will continue to find models for emulation in the creative artistic work of professional groups and outstanding artists. In its turn, the art of the people will serve as an inexhaustible source of enrichment for professional literature and art and will foster their rich growth.

The culture of socialism and communism is a new and higher stage in the cultural development of mankind. We have all that is required for successfully traveling the path to the heights of communist culture. (Prolonged applause.)

V. COMMUNISM AND THE PROGRESS OF MANKIND.—Comrades! Carrying out our Party Program will have the most profound effect on the course of world history.

By the power of example, communism in the making will attract to the banner of Marxism-Leninism additional hundreds of millions of people of labor throughout the world. The example is above all an example of rapid development of productive forces, of a great rise in the people's living standard and cultural level, of the creation of the conditions for a peaceful and happy life for people. The whole course of social development confirms Lenin's prediction that the countries where socialism triumphs would exert their chief influence on the development of world revolution through economic construction. Peaceful economic competition is the chief arena of the contest between the socialist and capitalist systems.

The outcome of this competition will be decided in tremendous measure by the competition between the Soviet Union and the United States of America.

The Party sets the task of making our country the world's leading industrial power within the next decade and within that time achieving preponderance over the U.S.A. both in absolute and in per capita volume of industrial output. Within approximately the same period the U.S.S.R. will surpass by 50% the present U.S. level of per capita output of farm products and will exceed the U.S. level of national income.

This is but the first objective. We shall not stop there. In the course of the second decade—by 1980—our country will leave the United States of America far behind in per capita output of industrial and agricultural goods.

The economy not only of the Soviet Union but of all the countries of the world socialist system is developing far faster than the economy of capitalism. The countries of the socialist commonwealth as a whole have increased the volume of industrial production to sevenfold the prewar level, whereas the countries of capitalism have increased their industrial output less than two and a half times over the prewar figure.

Preliminary estimates by economists show that the world socialist system will account for approximately two-thirds of world industrial production by 1980.

Some say figures are dull. But it is pleasant to recite the figures showing the growth of our system, and I think it is pleasant to listen to them. I recall that in our youth we used to sing, "Fly forward, our locomotive! Stop at the commune!" Now we and the whole socialist system are being drawn forward not by an ordinary steam locomotive but by a powerful electric one. There is no doubt that the socialist express will overtake and pass capitalism. Capitalism does not have the power, the traction! (Prolonged applause.)

The building of communism in our country is an integral part of the building of communist society in the whole socialist commonwealth. The successful development of the world system of socialism opens up a prospect of a more or less simultaneous transition of the socialist countries to communism within a single historical epoch. The law of uneven economic and political development, leading to the deepening of contradictions and the intensification of the competitive struggle among states, is characteristic of the world system of capitalism. The world system of socialism develops by diametrically opposite laws. It is characterized by the steady and planned economic growth of each country, faster development of those states that lagged economically under capitalism, and the evening up of the general level of development of all the countries.

Within the framework of the world system of socialism, countries that once lagged behind because of specific features of their historical development have already come far toward the level of the advanced socialist countries in a brief period, with the comprehensive assistance and support of the latter. However, the productive forces in these countries are not yet developed to the same degree. It is these objective factors that account for the circumstance that there cannot be any one definite "hour" for all the socialist countries to enter the higher phase of the new society. It is natural that the full-scale building of communist society will begin in those countries as the necessary conditions for it arise. This is in accordance with the interests of the entire socialist system, since it will accelerate the process of the common advance of the peoples toward communism and will create more favorable conditions for increasing aid and support by the countries of victorious communism to other socialist states.

To Marxist-Leninists it is indisputable that the fundamental interests of the socialist states imperatively require the utmost strengthening of their commonwealth. Any policy of building socialism in isolation, separately from the world socialist commonwealth, runs counter to the objective laws of development of a socialist society. Such a policy is harmful, since it could weaken the forces of socialism in the face of the united front of imperialist reaction; it nourishes nationalist tendencies and in the long run it could lead to the loss of socialist gains.

Nationalism, in whatever guise it wraps itself, represents the most dangerous political and ideological weapon employed by international reaction against the unity of the socialist countries. "The Communists consider it their prime duty to educate the working people in a spirit of internationalism, socialist patriotism and intolerance of any manifestations of nationalism and chauvinism," our draft Party Program emphasizes. "Nationalism damages the common interests of the socialist commonwealth, and above all it harms the people of the country in which it appears, since estrangement from the socialist camp retards the country's development, deprives it of the possibility of making use of the advantages of the world socialist system and encourages attempts by imperialist powers to utilize the nationalist tendencies for their own purposes."

Soviet people have the most friendly feelings for their brothers in the socialist countries of Europe and Asia. They rejoice at their successes and take pride in their victories. They have helped and will help them to build the new life. In fair weather and foul, the people of the socialist countries act according to the principle "All for one and one for all." Whoever raises a hand against the socialist gains of the people of our commonwealth will receive a crushing rebuff from the billion builders of socialism and communism. (Prolonged applause.)

As for Yugoslavia, as already stated in the Central Committee report, we have fought and will fight against the revisionist positions of the leadership of the League of Communists of Yugoslavia; at the same time, we have stood and we stand for the utmost development and strengthening of relations with Yugoslavia along state lines. On questions of the struggle for peace, our position and that of Yugoslavia coincide in many ways. The Soviet Union stands for the rapprochement and consolidation of all forces fighting against the imperialist warmongers, for peace and friendship among peoples.

Comrades! The draft of the new Party Program reflects the indisputable fact that communism has become the greatest force of our age. Communist Parties are now operating in 87 countries of the world and unite in their ranks approximately 40,000,-000 persons. And what tremendous masses of people follow the Communists, sharing their views and convictions, approving and supporting their policy! Communism has struck deep roots in the soil and is developing mightily; more than a third of mankind is building a new life under its banner. And in many nonsocialist countries the working class is dealing thousand-ton sledgehammer blows at the foundations of capitalism.

The world is going through an epoch of revolutions. Socialist revolutions, anti-imperialist national-liberation revolutions, people's democratic revolutions, broad peasant movements, the struggle of the masses to overthrow fascist and other tyrannical regimes, the general democratic movements against national oppression—all these merge into a single world revolutionary process undermining and destroying capitalism.

The draft Program illumines the paths of the peaceful and the nonpeaceful development of revolution. In this question, as in all others, our party stands fully on the principles collectively formulated by the international Communist movement in the 1957 declaration and the 1960 statement.

In the present epoch more favorable international conditions have arisen for the development of the world revolutionary movement. This is due above all to the strengthening of the forces and the growth of the influence of the socialist system. The example of socialism is exerting a powerful influence on the minds of people, making them active fighters for the establishment of the new system. Peoples rising in revolution have the opportunity to rely on the support of the socialist countries in the struggle against the attempts of world reaction to export counterrevolution. They can obtain comprehensive help from the socialist countries in building a new society.

In the present epoch internal conditions for the transition of new countries to socialism have also become more favorable. Among these conditions are: the general weakening of capitalism and the deepening of its contradictions; the growth in the size, organization and unification of the working class and the intensification of its influence in society; the growth in the numbers of the allies of the working class objectively interested in the struggle against imperialism, in liquidating the monopolies' omnipotence; the rise and strengthening of Communist Parties in almost all countries of the world.

But one should not forget about the difficulties in the way of the revolutionary forces. In the postwar period the monopoly bourgeoisie has created a new reactionary "holy alliance"—military blocs aimed not only against the socialist countries but against the revolutionary workers' and national-liberation movement. It has monstrously inflated the apparatus of violence and suppression. At the same time it is resorting to new and subtle methods of splitting the working class and corrupting the trade union movement, making active use for this purpose of the reactionary leaders of Social Democracy and reactionary trade union officials. It has launched a rabid campaign of anticommunism, uniting all the enemies of the working people under this black flag. By no means should the possibility be excluded that the monopoly bourgeoisie would resort to the most extreme, the bloodiest means of preserving its domination. In these circumstances Lenin's words sound more pertinent than ever: the working class must "master all—without the slightest exception—forms or aspects of public activity***," must be prepared "for the swiftest and most unexpected replacement of one form by another" ("Works" [in Russian], Vol. XXXI, p. 76).

The tasks of people's democratic, national-liberation and socialist revolutions are drawing closer together and becoming more intertwined in the present epoch. The logic of social development has caused all these revolutions to be directed primarily against one chief enemy—imperialism, the monopoly bourgeoisie.

The question is often asked: How will the world liberation movement proceed?

Obviously, the prerequisites for a transition to socialism have fully matured in the highly developed capitalist countries. The seething, underdeveloped states of Asia, Africa and Latin America, upon carrying the anti-imperialist national-liberation revolution to the end, will be able to make the transition to socialism. In the present epoch almost any country, regardless of the level of its development, can embark on the path that leads to socialism.

The world revolutionary process is developing more and more widely, embracing all the continents. At one time imperialism, unable to destroy the world's first socialist state by military means, tried to fence it off from the rest of the world by a "cordon sanitaire." But the revolutionary energy of peoples of Europe and Asia extended the borders of socialism from the Elbe to the South China Sea. The imperialists did everything to confine the ideas of the revolution within these bounds. But neither mountains nor oceans serve as barriers to the ideas of freedom. Vivid evidence of this is the triumphant revolution in Cuba. (Stormy applause.)

The freedom-loving Cuban people, having raised the banner of the people's anti-imperialist revolution, have cleansed their land of the foreign plunderers and their henchmen. The workers, peasants, intelligentsia and middle strata of the urban population have closed ranks under the banner of the revolution. Here is one of the chief sources of the strength of the Cuban revolution and a guarantee of its further development along the path of social progress. The small island, lost in the seas, has now become an undying beacon lighting the way to progress for all the peoples of Latin America. (Stormy, prolonged applause.)

Cuba lies far from the Soviet Union. But our peoples are close. Our hearts are with you, heroes of Cuba, who are defending your independence and freedom from American imperialism and who have inscribed socialist goals on your battle standards! (Stormy applause.) Our people have extended and will extend help to the fraternal Cuban people in their sacred struggle for their just cause. (Prolonged applause.)

As the socialist system grows stronger and as its advantages over capitalism are more and more fully revealed and the socialist and democratic forces throughout the world increase, more and more countries at various levels of development will embark on the path of revolution and will join the system of socialism as streams add their waters to a huge and mighty river.

The working class, in its revolutionary struggle, will continue to come up against various opportunist trends hindering the rallying of its forces and attainment of its goals. As long as capitalism exists, these trends will appear over and over under various guises. This is why the draft Program emphasizes the need to fight the ideology of Social Democracy and revisionism as well as dogmatism and sectarianism.

The Communist Party of the Soviet Union will continue to do everything to fulfill with honor its internationalist duty to the international working class and the working people of the whole world; will continue to direct its efforts toward strengthening the unity and solidarity of the ranks of the great army of Communists of all lands. (Prolonged applause.)

Comrades! Our successes in communist construction will be of extraordinary significance to the destinies of the peoples of Asia, Africa and Latin America, those huge and long-suffering continents, who are now rising to their full stature to become makers of their own history and are seeking ways for rapid development of their economy and culture.

The national-liberation movement has entered the final stage of liquidation of colonial regimes. The peoples who have freed themselves are setting themselves the task of consolidating their political independence, launching an offensive against economic backwardness and eliminating it, and wiping out all forms of dependence on imperialism.

But this path is not easy. Imperialism, losing against the national-liberation movement in open battle, is not laying down

its arms. Its methods are becoming more subtle. The monopolists are seeking to carry out a far-reaching plan for preserving
and consolidating their positions in the world of underdeveloped
countries, and are concealing the true essence of this plan with
pious talk of aid. In this, too, the palm goes to the American
imperialists.

Of course there can be no question of the imperialist powers
giving disinterested aid to underdeveloped countries. The
monopolies cannot give up their superprofits.

The monopolies' aims were—and they remain the same—to
keep the underdeveloped countries in the position of agrarian-
raw materials appendages, to exploit their peoples. If the
imperialists nevertheless proclaim a policy of "aid," it is an
insincere and forced step. The finance oligarchy did not dream
of extending any aid to underdeveloped countries as long as
imperialism ruled the world undividedly. The situation changed
when the Soviet Union and the world socialist system broke the
imperialist powers' monopoly of supply of equipment, granting
of loans and credits, technical experience and knowledge. The
imperialists were obliged to adjust, if one may put it this way,
and had to begin to talk of economic "aid" to underdeveloped
countries.

They expected that prayers would be sent up and gratitude
expressed to those who threw them a few dollars. Instead, the
American imperialists heard themselves cursed. Why? Because the U.S.A. is giving an essentially insignificant handout
from the tremendous sums that it extracts from the underdeveloped countries. Indeed, from 1946 to 1959 for each dollar
invested in all the underdeveloped countries the U.S.A. took
$2.50 profit from these countries. Soviet economists calculate
that the monopolies of the U.S.A. and other Western countries
squeeze $20,000,000,000 a year from the underdeveloped
countries. If this is called help, what is robbery called? Rob-
bers are not thanked, they are cursed. (Applause.)

The monopolists try to keep the underdeveloped countries in
imperialism's harbor, to anchor them in an unequal position in
the system of the capitalist world economy. But this is a vain
effort. The peoples of the underdeveloped countries do not want
to remain tied to imperialism. They see the example of socialism. It is not from books alone that people judge socialism now,
but most of all by its actual achievements. The peoples see that
Soviet rule has put an end to the country's age-old backwardness, the Soviet Union has become a mighty world power not in
centuries but within the lifetime of a single generation.

The achievement of political independence by the former
colonies has had a favorable influence on their economic development. The rates of growth of production have increased.
Whereas the average annual rate of growth of production in
these countries was 1% before the second world war, it has
risen to 4% in recent years. A state sector has been established
in many countries and national industry has begun to develop.

But these are only the first steps. The heritage of colonialism is still quite strong. The major economic tasks still await
resolution. Meantime, the upper crust of the bourgeoisie and the
feudal landlords, who have linked their destinies with foreign
capital, are seeking to fasten the underdeveloped countries in
the system of world capitalism. The path onto which the imperialists and their henchmen are pushing these countries cannot in the least ensure solution of the problems because of which
the peoples rose in struggle against the colonialists.

What is the way out? History provides a clear answer to the
question: The way out must be sought in a noncapitalist path of
development. Let whoever wants to know what fruits it yields
look at the flourishing republics of Soviet Central Asia and other
parts of our country that since the October Revolution have
bypassed the agonizing path of capitalist development. (Applause.)

Entering on the noncapitalist path of development cannot be
achieved by drifting into it. Only active struggle by the working
class, by the masses of working people, and the unification
of all democratic and patriotic forces in a broad national front
can lead the peoples onto this path.

By deep study of the objective course of development,
Marxist theoretical thought has discovered the form in which
all the sound forces of a nation can be most successfully unified. This form is the national-democratic state. Such a state,
reflecting the interests not of any one class but of broad strata

of the people, is called upon to carry through the tasks of the
anti-imperialist, national-liberation revolution.

It is the good fortune of peoples who have won national independence that they are emerging on the road of independent
development in a situation in which the forces of imperialism
and its ability to influence the course of developments are
steadily declining, while the forces and influence of socialism
are growing more and more. In these circumstances it will be
immeasurably easier for them to solve the tasks of economic
and social development.

The Soviet Union, like the other socialist countries, has no
intention of interfering in the internal affairs of the young, free
states, of imposing socialism upon anyone. Socialism has not
been, is not being and will not be exported. But there must also
not be any imposition of colonialism, there must not be export
of counterrevolution.

The Communist Party of the Soviet Union regards alliance
with peoples who have thrown off the colonial yoke as one of the
cornerstones of its international policy. Our party considers it
our internationalist duty to help peoples who are taking the path
of winning and consolidating national independence, all peoples
fighting for the complete destruction of the colonial system.
(Applause.)

Comrades! Fulfillment of our vast plans will be of decisive
help in accomplishing communism's historic mission of
abolishing war and establishing everlasting peace on earth.

Historical experience has confirmed that war is as indivisible from imperialism as the struggle against imperialist
wars, the policy of strengthening peace, is inherent in socialism. Events inscribed in history's annals not in ink but in the
blood of millions cannot be eradicated from human memory.
Beginning in 1898, when the United States of America unleashed
the first war of the imperialist epoch, imperialism has loosed
upon the peoples one "local war" after another, and twice it
has plunged mankind into world holocausts of unparalleled
bloodshed; moreover, the ruins of cities and villages were still
smoldering and the wounds in the hearts of millions of people
who lost relatives in the flames of the second world war had
not yet healed when the U.S. imperialists were already "asking"
for a third world war.

In the imperialist camp, and above all in the United States of
America, groups are operating that behave like gamblers. They
give no thought to the calamity that the new war they are preparing would cause to mankind. The use of thermonuclear and
rocket weapons would turn all the continents of the globe into a
zone of mass annihilation of people and destruction of material
values. In the conditions of a thermonuclear world war the
factor of distance would lose its former significance. And the
Western Hemisphere would become an area in which a holo-
caust of destruction would rage. In our times war cannot and
must not serve as the means of settling international disputes.

It may be asked: Is there not a contradiction between the
recognition on the one hand of the existence of a danger of war,
and on the other hand our striving to eliminate war from the
life of society? No, comrades, there is no contradiction here.

The Party's confidence that the present generation already
has every possibility of preventing a world war is based on
comprehensive and profound analysis of the forces operating
in the international arena. This analysis leads to the indisputable conclusion that the balance of world political, economic
and military forces has already changed in favor of the peace-
loving camp.

What gives this camp its superiority? Above all, the following basic factors:

First—The mightiest power of our times, the Soviet Union,
is directing all its efforts toward the preservation and strengthening of universal peace. Whereas the rise of the might of any
large imperialist power has inevitably been accompanied by
intensification of its aggressive aspirations and consequently
has led to sharpening the menace of war, the growth of the
forces of the world's first socialist state has created and is
creating effective guarantees against the danger of war and is
increasing the chances of preventing it. Since the time when the
Soviet Union won first place in the world in the decisive branches of science and technology and placed this superiority in the
scales in the struggle for peace, the possibility of assuring universal security has increased manyfold.

Second—In the way of the imperialist aggressors there now stands, together with the Soviet Union, a new and mighty force, all the countries of the world socialist camp. Whereas under the conditions of imperialism the appearance of any grouping of states is aimed at preparing new wars, the countries of the socialist commonwealth unite their efforts exclusively for the sake of the triumph of the cause of peace and social progress.

Third—Another new force, a large group of young national states of Asia, Africa and Latin America interested in the preservation of peace in order to accomplish the tasks of national regeneration, has entered the world arena. Most of these states champion a policy of peace. Coincidence between the vital interests of the peoples of these countries and the interests of the peoples of the socialist states is the objective basis for combining their efforts in the cause of defending peace. This mighty front, expressing the will and power of two-thirds of mankind, can force the imperialist aggressors to fall back.

Fourth—The role of the masses of people of the capitalist countries in international politics has increased unprecedentedly. In the face of the menace of thermonuclear war there is taking place a process of formation of a coalition, such as history has never seen, of the most diverse mass movements, united in the desire to rid mankind forever of the catastrophe of war. The international working class, which is becoming more and more aware of its historical responsibility for the destiny of mankind, has become the great organizing force of this coalition. The banner of peace is in the dependable hands of the many-millions-strong army of the Communists of all countries.

Such are the principal forces of our times blocking the way to war. These forces are truly countless already. Tomorrow they will be more powerful still. The accomplishment of our plans proclaimed in the Program will make even more powerful the material base on which the defenders of peace rely.

Mankind can and must prevent war. But this task can be accomplished only given the most active and decisive actions by all the peace-loving forces. To curb the imperialists in good time, to deprive them of the possibility of loosing lethal weapons, to prevent war, to keep it from breaking out—this is now the chief thing. (Applause.)

It was a great service on the part of V. I. Lenin and our party that they worked out the only correct foreign policy principle for the period of existence of two social systems, a principle now being applied: peaceful coexistence of states with different social systems. The principle of peaceful coexistence is winning the minds of hundreds of millions of people. Even representatives of bourgeois circles who are capable of sober thinking recognize the telling force and role of this principle.

Genuine stability in the relations among states with different social systems can be achieved only when the Damocles' sword of the arms race ceases to hang over the peoples, that is, in conditions of general and complete disarmament. A truly reliable system of international security can be established not on the basis of military power but on the basis of general disarmament. This is why our party, the Soviet government and our entire people are filled with determination to fight for disarmament, to seek ways to it, until this historic task is finally accomplished.

Imperialism wants to turn the policy of balancing on "the brink of war" into a permanent norm of international relations. We want to turn lasting peace and the universal security of nations into a permanent norm of international relations. The selfish interests of a handful of monopolists are expressed in the policy of imperialism. The interests of all mankind are embodied in the policy of socialism. This is why we are convinced that the general principle of socialism's foreign policy—the principle of peaceful coexistence—will become the banner under which all peoples, all who want true peace and prosperity for mankind, will rally. (Applause.)

In adopting our new Program, our great party solemnly proclaims before all mankind that it sees as the principal goal of its foreign policy not only the prevention of world war but its exclusion, within the lifetime of our generation, from the life of society for all time. (Prolonged applause.)

The policy of peace is our principled, honest, socialist policy. We are championing the cause of peace not because we are weak. We were able to rout our enemies and ensure ourselves peace-

ful conditions even when the young socialist republic was hemmed in on all sides by the imperialist wolves, when it was incomparably weaker than the imperialists militarily and economically. In the years of the second world war the Soviet Union made the decisive contribution to the rout of the Hitler military machine and saved mankind from fascist enslavement. Can there be any doubt of the fate that awaits the imperialist maniacs if they dare make an attempt against the socialist gains of the peoples in the new situation, when the U.S.S.R. possesses great might, when the mighty socialist commonwealth marches with it in solid ranks, when hundreds of millions of people throughout the world support us? In these conditions the starting of a war will be the end of the antipopular imperialist system. (Stormy applause.)

Our unshakable confidence in this does not by any means signify even the slightest underestimation of the forces of imperialism. We know that imperialism is still strong. The possibility that the imperialists may unleash a new war cannot be excluded. The imperialist maniacs may throw themselves into adventures to stay the course of history. In this situation we have only one path: to strengthen our might, to create the most powerful weapons, to be prepared every minute to hurl back an attack by aggressors. (Applause.) We have declared more than once and we declare again that we are prepared fully to disband the army, to sink atomic bombs and rockets in the sea, but of course only on the condition of general and complete disarmament under strict international control. Until the imperialist powers accept that, we shall see to it that our armed forces possess the most modern means of defending the motherland—atomic and thermonuclear weapons and rockets of all ranges, so that all types of war materiel are maintained at the necessary level. Strengthening the defense of the U.S.S.R., the might of the Soviet Armed Forces, is the task of tasks of the Soviet people. (Stormy applause.)

Communists must look history boldly in the eye. As long as the war danger exists, as long as the imperialist jungles and the predatory tigers inhabiting them exist, we must educate our whole people, our youth, in boundless love of their homeland, in preparedness to defend it without sparing strength or life itself. Our cause is great, and the Soviet people will give all their efforts to defend it. If the imperialists cast a military challenge at us, we will not only take it up without hesitation but will loose a blow of devastating force upon the enemy, with all the wholehearted courage and bravery inherent in Communists. (Stormy, prolonged applause.)

Comrades! By its entire content our new Program confirms that communism serves the cause of peace, the creation of conditions for excluding war from the life of society. It is clear to everybody that he who sets himself such unprecedented tasks in the economy, culture and improvement of the people's well-being cannot be seeking war. The Program of the building of communism is at the same time a world-historic program for strengthening peace and international security. (Prolonged applause.)

VI. RESULTS OF THE DISCUSSION OF THE DRAFT PROGRAM.—Comrades! The draft Program has been at the center of the Soviet Union's political life since the day of its publication. What is more, its ideas have spread far beyond the borders of our country and have evoked a broad response in the hearts of millions of people in all countries and on all continents.

The discussion of the draft Program has demonstrated with special force the vital, indissoluble bond between the Party and the people and the democratic nature of Soviet society, in which the people are masters of their own fate.

Allow me to tell at some length about the results of the discussion of the draft Program in the Party and in the country and then to speak briefly about the responses it has evoked throughout the whole world.

1. Unanimous Approval of the Draft Program by the Party and the People. Additions and Amendments to the Draft.—The discussion of the draft Program acquired a scope unprecedented even in the history of our party and of the Soviet state. And this is natural, since the goals of the Program and the tasks set forth in it touch and stir one and all.

The draft Program was thoroughly and comprehensively discussed at meetings of all primary Party organizations, at district, city, province and territory Party conferences and at Congresses of the Communist Parties of the Union republics. More than 9,000,000 Communists, or the entire Party, took part in these. More than 500,000 meetings of working people were held at enterprises, collective farms and institutes and in military units and trade union and Y.C.L. organizations to discuss the draft Program. About 73,000,000 people participated in these meetings. More than 4,600,000 individuals delivered speeches about the draft Program at Party meetings and conferences, Congresses of the Union-republic Communist Parties and meetings of the working people.

Besides this, the C.P.S.U. Central Committee and local Party agencies and the editorial offices of newspapers, magazines, radio and television received more than 300,000 letters and articles.

But no statistics are able to give the exact number of participants in the discussion. After all, the discussion constituted the very content of the country's ideological life and was carried on in the most diverse forms: at meetings of the collectives of plants, factories, state and collective farms, offices, institutes and schools, and in earnest conversations at work and in the home. It is possible to say without exaggeration: The draft Program was discussed by the whole people and was taken up by the people as their own program, their life's cause. (Stormy applause.)

The Congress has every ground for declaring that the draft Program has been unanimously approved by all Communists and by the whole Soviet people. (Stormy, prolonged applause.) The ideas of the Program and the plans set forth in it have been welcomed into the mind and heart of each Soviet individual. The speeches and letters of Party members and non-Party people have been filled with inspired thoughts and emotions. In their letters—and some of them might more properly be called poems, so inspired and impassioned are they—people welcome the new Party Program with all their heart and express their unbending will and aspiration to incorporate its designs in life. The thoughts and sentiments of the people are reflected in these letters as the sun is reflected in a drop of water. (Applause.)

The discussion of the draft Program was principled and businesslike and proceeded on a high ideological and political level. This attests once more to the political maturity of the millions-strong army of Communists and of Soviet people. It is impossible not to be delighted at the deep knowledge of theory and life with which Soviet people approached the consideration of large and complicated new questions connected with the building of a communist society. The draft Program has widened the ideological horizons of Soviet man; now he can see more clearly his great purpose and the tasks that must be solved. The Program spurred vast creative forces in the all-Union pre-Congress competitions. And this is convincing proof that the Party and the people have already taken the Program into their arsenal and are unfurling a practical struggle for its incorporation in life. (Stormy applause.)

Comrades! The countless proposals made in connection with the draft Program are marked with the imprint of creative quests for the best solutions to the tasks posed and are permeated with the profound interest of all Soviet people in the most successful unfolding of the construction of a communist society.

Permit me to report to the Congress that all proposals have been studied carefully by the Central Committee. I shall deal first with the proposals that, in the Central Committee's opinion, can be accepted. I shall point out only the most substantial of these.

1. The Central Committee supports the proposal that the Program lay stronger emphasis on the significance of the acceleration of technical progress and the fuller and more rational use of production capacity.

2. The Party Central Committee considers proper the proposal to refer specifically in the Program to the necessity for raising the effectiveness of capital investments and the inadmissability of scattering them and to stress the importance of concentrating capital investments in the decisive sectors.

During the discussion, attention was properly called to instances of a lack of coordination between the construction of new industrial projects and the supplying of them with equipment. Indeed, we are suffering large losses because of this lack of coordination. For example, as of Jan. 1, 1961, there were millions of square meters of ready production space that had not been completely equipped, while at the same time there were hundreds of millions of rubles' worth of ready equipment for which there was no production space. The Central Committee and the government have already drawn up measures for the further improvement of capital construction in the country. Our urgent task is to impose firm order on this highly important matter.

3. At some Party meetings and conferences proposals were made that the Program provide for the creation of a metallurgical base in the Central European part of the U.S.S.R. to make use of the world's largest ore deposit, the Kursk Magnetic Anomaly. This proposal coincides with projected plans. As I have already said, it is intended by the end of the 20-year period to complete the construction of the country's third metallurgical base, in Siberia, and to create two more mighty metallurgical bases. We consider it advisable to indicate in the Program the areas where they will be created. This will raise the responsibility of Party organizations, planning agencies and all officials of the metallurgical industry for the implementation of the projected plans.

4. In connection with innumerable proposals received, the Party Central Committee considers it necessary to add to the appropriate section of the Program a special clause on the conservation of nature and the proper use of natural riches. Our forest, fish, water and other natural resources are a great national asset. As we move toward communism we must guard nature carefully, must use its resources sensibly and economically and must restore and multiply the natural riches of our forests, rivers and seas.

5. Comrade Nektov, Hero of Socialist Labor, and many other toilers of agriculture have rightly proposed that the Program indicate the necessity for a scrupulous attitude toward farm machines. The fact that on many state and collective farms tractors and machines are used inefficiently and, most important, go out of commission prematurely because of poor maintenance and care cannot be tolerated. A wasteful and sometimes barbaric attitude toward machinery slows the growth of agricultural production and in effect amounts to embezzlement of the people's property.

The Central Committees of the Union-republic Communist Parties and the Union-republic Councils of Ministers should without delay work out a system of economic, organizational and technical measures to ensure good storage and careful maintenance of tractors, combines and other machines.

6. There have been many proposals from working people, especially women, on shortening the schedules for the solution of such an important task as the further expansion of the network of preschool institutions. The draft Program provides for the creation of a wide network of children's institutions so that in the second decade each family will have an opportunity to maintain its children in these institutions. In consideration of the desires expressed during the discussion of the draft Program, the Central Committee deems it necessary to respond to these desires and to do everything possible to satisfy the demand for children's institutions in the next few years. (Applause.)

There have also been proposals to establish a shorter working day for women with large families at their request and to remunerate their labor accordingly. The Central Committee deems it necessary to instruct our government and trade union agencies to consider this question and to prepare recommendations.

Many people expressed at Party gatherings and working people's meetings and in letters to the Central Committee a desire to accelerate the solution of the housing problem. Taking into account the innumerable proposals on this question, the Central Committee has recognized the necessity of indicating in the Program that by the end of the first decade the families that are still living in poor and overcrowded apartments will receive new apartments. (Applause.)

During the discussion proposals were received touching on literally every aspect of life of our society and permeated with a profound concern for the all-round improvement of our economic and cultural construction. There have been many proposals on specific questions of the development of industry and agriculture, on planning and administration and on improving the work and lowering the cost of the state and economic apparatus. A large group of proposals has to do with questions of strengthening scientific research on various problems, the chief one being the application of the achievements of science in industry, agriculture, transportation, construction and communications. The proposals give an important place to ideological work, communist morality, education, culture, and intensification of the struggle against parasitism, money-grubbing and other manifestations of a private-property psychology. Valuable proposals have been submitted on questions of urban development, particularly housing construction and public improvements in cities and villages. There has been a substantial number of proposals on other problems as well. The basic lines to be taken in solving all the tasks to which these proposals are addressed are expressed in the draft Program. But many of these proposals touch upon important questions of state, economic and cultural construction and of political and ideological educational work. They deserve serious attention. As the final revision of the text of the draft Program proceeds, these proposals are being taken into consideration. The Central Committee will give attentive consideration to all proposals received and will instruct the appropriate Party, state and other agencies to take the necessary practical measures.

Party members and non-Party people made a large number of critical remarks and proposals concerning the work of local Party, Soviet, economic and trade union organizations and institutions. Shortcomings in production, trade, public catering, the distribution of housing space, the maintenance of housing, etc., were pointed out. Manifestations of bureaucratism and red tape and instances of abuse of office on the part of individual officials were exposed. Our Congress should charge the province and territory Party committees and the Central Committees of the Union-republic Communist Parties with considering the specific criticisms and proposals, with taking measures to eliminate the exposed shortcomings, and with reporting on the action taken to their respective plenary sessions and then to the regular Party conferences and Congresses.

It is true that a very few proposals were submitted whose authors showed an unrealistic approach to the solution of certain tasks of communist construction. For example, certain comrades recommend writing into the Program that the full electrification of the country, including agriculture, must be completed within the next ten, or even five, years. It is proposed that the Program provide also for a number of other measures, equally "decisive" in form but economically unrealistic. It is possible to understand such comrades, but not to agree with them. It would be incorrect to include in the Program that which we are as yet unable to accomplish. Such pledges and promises would only serve to discredit the Program. (Applause.)

There are proposals of another sort, which I would say are presented from the standpoint of a scholarly but uncreative approach to the processes going on in life. For example, in the opinion of certain comrades, the dictatorship of the proletariat must be preserved right up to the complete victory of communism. Such comrades take absolutely no account of the objective conditions that have developed in our country but base themselves solely on arbitrarily excerpted quotations, while losing sight of the essence of the teachings of Marx, Engels and Lenin concerning the state of the dictatorship of the proletariat as the state form in the transitional period from capitalism to socialism, the first phase of communism. They do not consider that in our socialist society there are now only laboring classes, which are engaged in socialist production and are unified in their socio-political and ideological attitude. After the full and final victory of socialism in our country, there is no soil for the dictatorship of one class. Indeed, over what class can we have a dictatorship? We have no such class.

Further, these comrades believe that, inasmuch as the alliance of the working class and the peasantry has remained, the dictatorship of the proletariat must remain as well. But these comrades do not realize that the workers' and peasants' alliance needed the dictatorship of the proletariat for the fight against the exploiter classes, for the socialist transformation of the peasant economy and the re-education of the peasants, and for the building of socialism. With the accomplishment of these tasks, the alliance of the working class and the peasantry

is successfully developing and growing stronger without the dictatorship of the proletariat, in the conditions of a socialist state of the entire people. (Applause.)

These comrades also use the argument that the organizational-economic and cultural-educational functions inherent in the dictatorship of the proletariat are retained in the period of the transition to communism. But these functions will remain under communism as well. If one is to be consistent, the dictatorship of the working class too must be preserved, in the logic of these comrades, under communism. The fallacy of this reasoning is obvious to everyone.

The propositions formulated in the Program on the evolution of the state of the dictatorship of the proletariat into a state of the entire people fully correspond to what occurs in life. The state of the entire people has been generated by life, and it expresses our policy in the political organization of society—the all-round development of democracy. (Applause.)

Some comrades propose that collective farm trade be prohibited, and the most zealous among them even demand that trade be done away with altogether and replaced with direct distribution. Must it be demonstrated that these comrades' proposals are considerably premature? The question of whether there should or should not be trade cannot be decided according to someone's desire or by decree. The transition to direct distribution requires the necessary material and technical base and an abundance of material goods. Until these exist we must not curtail but on the contrary must develop and improve Soviet trade. (Applause.) Nor is it possible to prohibit collective farm trade, which still plays a conspicuous role in supplying the population with food products. Collective farmers have to sell part of their produce, and the administrative establishment of fixed collective farm market prices suggested by some comrades is impossible. It is necessary to work for the reduction of collective farm market prices primarily by increasing the output of farm products and not by administrative measures, which should be resolutely applied only against speculative elements. At the same time the work of the cooperatives, which should help the collective farmers sell their surplus products, must be improved.

In view of the great importance of the further expansion of Soviet trade, the Central Committee deems it necessary to include in the Program a point on trade and on its improvement in the period of communist construction.

Our party, being a party of scientific communism, advances and carries out the tasks of communist construction only as the necessary conditions develop and mature. I have already spoken at length about the Party's plans in the field of production and the people's well-being. But some comrades propose going beyond the planned goals and in the very near future extending the principle of free satisfaction of the requirements of society's members to a wider range of material and cultural goods, thus virtually establishing equal pay for all, regardless of the skill and complexity of their work. Such proposals are profoundly erroneous. To embark on this path would mean to undermine the material incentive for raising labor productivity and to slow down the building of communism. (Applause.)

As is known, upon the initiative of the Party Central Committee a great deal of work has been done in the past few years in adjusting wage scales. As a result of the measures that have been taken, the high incomes and official salaries of certain categories of personnel have been considerably reduced. At the same time the minimum wage scale has increased. The system for eliminating the income tax that has been introduced also contributes to narrowing the gap between the earnings of the different categories of working people. In short, much has been done toward reducing the differences in the earnings of various population groups. The draft Program clearly indicates that the Party will continue to pursue this line consistently and unwaveringly and will see to it that the very category of low-paid workers ceases to exist in the U.S.S.R. by the end of the first ten-year period and that the well-being of the entire people rises. (Applause.) Along with wages, there will be an accelerated growth of public funds, designed to bring about the elimination of differences in earnings and a speedier rise in the well-being of the working people with low and medium wages. Any leveling tendencies are contrary to the interests of advancing production and the people's well-being and to the cause of educating the working people in the spirit of a communist attitude toward labor.

We must strictly enforce the principle "He who does not work, neither shall he eat," the principle of payment according to work. At the same time, any and all loopholes through which antisocial elements can rob society, acquire nonlabor incomes and lead a parasitic way of life must be tightly closed. Speculation and other machinations must be resolutely done away with, using to this end the full force of Soviet law and the force of public opinion.

We are for a steady growth in the well-being of the entire people, but at the same time we are against the overacquisition of goods by people, which nurtures a private-property psychology.

Many amendments and corrections of an editorial nature were suggested in the course of the discussion. The Central Committee has considered these corrections also. Some of them will improve the text and have been incorporated in the draft of the Program that has been handed to you.

These have been the basic questions advanced in the course of the discussion of the draft Program.

2. International Response to the Draft Program.—Comrades! The draft Program of the C.P.S.U. has acquired the character of a document of truly world significance and has already exerted an enormous influence on the political climate of the world. It has attracted the closest attention of the broadest popular masses in the countries of the socialist camp, of public circles in the imperialist states and of the peoples who have already won independence or are still groaning under the boot of the colonialists. It has penetrated to the remotest corners of the globe and has found its way to the pages of even the most reactionary bourgeois publications.

We Soviet Communists naturally feel a deep satisfaction in the fact that the fraternal Marxist-Leninist parties and the many-millions-strong army of ·Communists of all countries have given a high appraisal to the draft Program. As internationalists we are happy when Communists of other lands declare that they draw from the Program of the C.P.S.U. inspiration for their practical activity and struggle and that our party's successes multiply their forces, the forces of freedom, peace and socialism throughout the world. Permit me, on behalf of the delegates to the 22nd Congress, on behalf of the members of our party and of the entire Soviet people, to express heartfelt gratitude to all the fraternal parties and to all the Communists of the world for their support of our plans and our goals. (Prolonged applause.) We assure you, our brothers in other lands, that our Leninist party, bearing high the banner of proletarian internationalism, will do everything in its power to bring mankind closer to a society of peace, happiness and prosperity—a communist society. (Stormy applause.)

All the people of advanced and democratic views note that the Program provides answers to the most acute problems and that it will play an outstanding role in the social movements and progressive transformations of our time. As for the bourgeoisie and its press, even they cannot help but admit that the Program and its fulfillment will exert an exceptional impact on the state of affairs throughout the world.

An analysis of the statements about the draft Program of the C.P.S.U. by bourgeois and right-wing socialist figures enables us to draw a number of conclusions that are important in principle.

First of all, it must be noted that a real battle between the two ideologies, the communist and the bourgeois, has arisen around the ideas of the Program. We can boldly say that the communist ideas that are embodied in the imposing plans for construction have demonstrated with the utmost clarity their immeasurable superiority to bourgeois ideology, an ideology of violence and destruction, and are winning new victories over it. (Applause.)

The first victory consists in the fact that the bourgeois ideologists now admit that communism, as a new socio-economic organization of society, is becoming an ever more powerful force in our times. In the 19th century the bourgeoisie declared the communist ideals utopian and harassed and persecuted their adherents. In the first third of the 20th century it carried out several "anticommunist" crusades on an international scale and declared communism buried forever in a number of our

countries. In the 1950s it shouted about the "incurable crisis" of communism. Only a few years have passed, and imperialist reaction has been forced to note the colossal growth of communism, its life-asserting force and its constantly growing significance in world history. (Applause.)

The statements of such a solid bourgeois magazine as Britain's Economist are characteristic of the evolution of the views of the bourgeoisie. The same Economist that after our party's adoption of its second Program announced that Bolshevism had one foot in the grave is now forced to admit that the new Program contains "a plan for the development of already existing tendencies" and that "the promises of this manifesto do not appear fantastic." (Applause.)

The Communists have proved that they do not merely cast their words to the wind, that they fulfill all their promises. They have compelled even their opponents to respect their plans. (Applause.) Communism has entered contemporary social life "palpably" and "visibly," has occupied leading positions in it, and there is no force that can stop its triumphant march. (Stormy applause.)

An analysis of the international response makes it possible to draw another important conclusion: The great idea of the Program that communism and peace are inseparable is becoming ever more widespread among the populations of the capitalist countries. Even many representatives of the bourgeoisie cannot help recognizing that a country that proclaims such great creative plans cannot but be interested in peace. Even in the citadel of imperialism, the U.S.A., the democratic public contrasts the Program of the C.P.S.U., this great charter of peace and humanism, with the military mobilization plans of the American imperialists, fraught with grief, sweat and blood. Australia's Sydney Morning Herald, an old hand at anti-Soviet slander, has been forced to admit that the Soviet Union is calling for peace, since it is confronted with such a tremendous plan. And here is what a bourgeois newspaper in another part of the world, Lebanon's An Nahar, writes: "The proponents of war have been dealt a crushing blow. Once everyone understands the essence of this Program, the flags of peace will be raised everywhere."

What do such admissions indicate? That the Program has dealt a great new defeat to the aggressive forces and to the idolaters of the hydrogen bomb.

The anticommunist myths and fabrications of the bourgeoisie and its lackeys are disintegrating under the blows of the great ideas of the Program. The attractive power of the ideas of communism is growing and winning more and more new supporters. The new Program will help ever broader masses to understand that communism is superior to capitalism economically and politically and morally, and that the future belongs to it. It is not difficult to see the causes of the anxiety that has seized the bourgeoisie and its defenders: After all, they clearly have nothing to counterpose to the Program of the C.P.S.U. They can say nothing about the future; they cannot plan for a single year, let alone 20 years. This was well expressed by the Burmese writer Dau A Ma: "The United States is the monarch of capitalist society, the 'commander-in-chief' in the struggle against communism," she wrote. "This country, even if it wanted to do so out of pique, could not draw up any plan to compete with the Soviet one. The same is true of Britain. It is in no position to offer even a single plan resembling the Soviet one."

The imperialist bourgeoisie is especially alarmed by the influence of the ideas of the Program on the peoples of Asia, Africa and Latin America. Albert Gore, a member of the U.S. Senate's Foreign Relations Committee, anxiously warns: "We must not underestimate the appeal of the draft Party Program for the deprived nations."

The appeal of the Program's ideas is indeed great for all the people exploited by capitalism. The newspaper Times of India writes: "Since the time of the Communist Manifesto there has not been a more inspiring communist document. Nor can the feasibility of the Program be doubted. The Afro-Asian nations, at least, are impressed by the Soviet achievements, which have convinced them that Russia fulfills all its promises." An excellent testimonial for our Program and for our activities! (Applause.)

Imperialist propaganda constantly invents new means of extolling the capitalist system and frightening the peoples of the newly liberated countries with the difficulties of the noncapitalist path. But the more the imperialist bourgeoisie does this, the more obvious does it become that it fears the advanced ideas that inspire the peoples to the final liquidation of colonialism and the struggle for social progress. As far as we are concerned, we do not impose our ideas on anyone. But if the peoples of the liberated countries arm themselves with the ideas of socialism, the ideas of progress, we can say from our own experience that they are doing the right thing. (Applause.)

Imperialism's ideological servants try to comfort their masters with the timeworn allegation that the ideas of communism have no appeal for the populations of the Western countries. Enough of that, gentlemen! The ideas of communism live and gain strength wherever there are toiling people humiliated by capitalism. Do you want to know what millions of people in the countries of your vaunted "civilization" think? Ask the workers who live in fear of what the next day may bring, the ruined farmers, the unemployed who stand in soup lines; ask all those who want peace and happiness for their children. And you will learn that millions of people in your own countries long for communism. I would like to read a letter sent to Pravda by Arthur Stone, an unemployed American: "The draft Program," he writes, "is the answer to the daily murder of workers in all capitalist countries, to all the crimes committed by the monopolists against the peoples of the entire world.***The people of the Soviet Union cannot imagine what a great source of strength this Program is for us, who are living under the domination of the capitalists." Arthur Stone appeals to the Soviet people: "Hurry to fulfill this task. The entire world is looking to you in the Soviet Union with the hope that you will carry out this Program as quickly as possible; thereby you will save millions of people who otherwise would die from exploitation, would be crushed and ruined." This document was written with the heart's blood; it contains the genuine thoughts and feelings of our brothers in the countries of capital.

The ideas of the Program, the ideas of communism are marching triumphantly across the earth because hundreds of millions of the downtrodden and disinherited see in them the embodiment of their best sentiments and aspirations. The capitalist quacks cannot fence off the peoples from the idea of progress with police cordons or "iron curtains." Communism is the hope of the peoples, the guarantee of their radiant future! (Stormy applause.)

Naturally, the imperialist bourgeoisie still does not want to admit its ideological defeat. This is understandable: After all, this would be tantamount to political suicide. It is making feverish attempts and using every means to minimize the significance of the draft Party Program, to weaken its influence on the popular masses.

The ruling elite of capitalist society is making vain attempts to counterpose to our Program its own platform, a plan of sorts for saving capitalism. How many times already have we read and heard about plans for rejuvenating capitalism? But decrepitude is inexorably overtaking capitalism. And this stands to reason. There are no means for saving a system that is doomed. Such a system has not and cannot have any ideas that would inspire peoples. A devastating testimonial to the poverty of bourgeois ideology was provided by none other than the American newspaper the New York Post. "For several years," it wrote on the occasion of the publication of the draft Program, "a number of American leaders have been working intensively on the concept of 'national purpose,' and they have come up with only empty, abstract conclusions."

And so capitalism has no positive program. Nor has it any arguments for criticizing our Program. Finding themselves in such an unenviable situation, the army of defenders of the bourgeoisie searched in an arid desert for anticommunist arrows. But they found only the poisoned arrows of slander, insinuation and distortion. Hence the utter confusion and impotent rage in the camp of the enemies of communism.

The bourgeois critics began shouting in chorus, as if upon command: "The Program cannot be fulfilled." Incantations familiar from the first Soviet five-year plans reappeared on the pages of the reactionary newspapers: "utopia," "mirage," "illusion." Do the opponents of our Program have figures, calculations, facts? Nothing of the sort. We offer substantiation for every proposition in our Program. They offer only shrill pronouncements. We have calculated and proved every figure. They fear figures as the devil fears incense. We have given a precise and scientific analysis of the trends of historical development. They offer nothing but sorceresses' spells and tea-leaf prophesies. They are so zealous in this that they do not even notice when they fall into obvious contradictions and are unable to tie loose ends together. More than that, they contradict one another. Whereas one group of critics shouts "The Program is unfeasible!," another proclaims "This is a challenge! On guard, save yourselves!" The French newspaper Figaro asserts that the new Soviet plans are "castles in air." But the Austrian newspaper Das Kleine Volksblatt appeals to the West "not to regard the gigantic goals set by the Kremlin as mere castles in air, because these goals are a challenge to the West in the truest sense of the word." Indeed, comprehend that if you can! As can be seen, these critics have lost their way not in a forest and not even among three pine trees, but among two.

A second card the critics of our Program try to play consists of wearisome assertions about the absence of individual freedom under communism. The Austrian Social-Democratic newspaper Die Arbeiter Zeitung has tried to build some kind of "foundation" under this stupid assertion. Listen to what it writes: "We believe that the Soviet citizen actually will have free train rides the day after tomorrow, but we consider it quite unlikely that he will have the right to travel where he wants." (Laughter in the hall.) If someone were to ask a Soviet person whether he can go wherever he wants, he would look at his questioner as he would at a mentally deranged person who has escaped from an asylum. (Laughter in the hall. Applause.) Soviet people travel wherever they wish. And how would the hundreds of Americans who went on "freedom rides" through the southern states and found themselves in jail answer this question?

No less laughable is the following trick of bourgeois propaganda. It asserts without the slightest blush that the living standards the Soviet people want to attain under communism allegedly already exist in the U.S.A. and in some other capitalist countries. It would be difficult to imagine a greater mockery of the facts and of the living conditions of people of labor in the countries of capital. Just think: The American press admits that the "level of unemployment remains a national scandal" and that millions of people are simply starving. And an attempt is made to convince these people, who have experienced all the marvels of the American way of life, that they are provided for according to their needs! American newspapers have reported year after year that medical services are ruinously expensive in the U.S.A. But now, it turns out, medical care is allegedly free. Only yesterday the American press declared for all to hear that apartment rents spell actual ruin for millions of families; but today, if we listen to the hired word merchants, housing in the U.S.A. is all but free. How hopelessly have our wretched critics entangled themselves in lies!

The Party Program consistently develops the idea of coexistence and peaceful competition. But as we see, peaceful coexistence frightens those who do not want peace. Some bourgeois newspapers go so far as to label peaceful coexistence "an instrument of world revolution." The New York Times, the leading newspaper of the capitalist world, in commenting on the Program shouts: "This is a new declaration of war on the free world—a military, political, economic and propaganda war."

This, gentlemen, is hysteria. Your nerves have given way. Where in the Program did you find any hint whatever of a declaration of military action against the capitalist world? What clause, what proposition in the Program gives any grounds for assertions of this sort? There are no such grounds, nor can there be. And if the hacks of The New York Times still insist on droning their monotonous song, this merely confirms once more that they fear peace and are afraid of coexistence, because they know that capitalism cannot withstand peaceful competition with socialism. The imperialist circles rest their hopes on war, thus proving again and again how hostile their intentions are to the vital interests of peoples.

We are not the least bit pained by the fact that our Program is viciously attacked by obscurantists and reactionaries. We would be pained if they had praised us. If the obscurantists howl against our Program, this means it is hitting the mark. We are marching confidently along our path, the path of communism, firmly convinced that sooner or later all mankind will follow this path. (Stormy, prolonged applause.)

VII. THE PARTY IN THE PERIOD OF THE FULL-SCALE BUILDING OF COMMUNISM.—Comrades! The grandeur of the new Program testifies to the grandeur of our Leninist party. Expressing the lofty ideals of communism, it is fulfilling with honor the mission of leader of the revolutionary transformation of society. Our Marxist-Leninist party, which arose as a party of the working class, has become the party of the whole people. This is a manifestation of the monolithic unity and might of the Soviet state, welded together by common interests and a common world view. Always—when the sun shines brightly or when the sky is overcast, in days of victory or in days of grave trial—the Party is with the people, the people are with the Party. (Stormy applause.) The Communist Party is the force that concentrates the will, the efforts and the energy of our people on the solution of the tasks that have arisen in the new stage of historical development.

Now, when the country possesses enormous material possibilities and a highly developed science and technology and when the initiative of the masses flows like a mighty flood, the speed of our advance depends chiefly on correct local as well as state-wide pursuit of the political line set forth, on the correct and effective functioning of the entire system of our state and public organizations and on their ability to make good use of the advantages of the socialist system. From this there ensues the need to heighten the directing and organizing role of the Party in the period of the full-scale building of communism. (Applause.)

What major lines will the development of the Communist Party follow in this period? We believe that the directions will be:

—a further heightening of the role of the Party as the highest form of socio-political organization and a strengthening of its directing influence on all sectors of communist construction;

—a strengthening of the unity of Party and people, enrichment of the forms of the Party's ties with the non-Party masses and the rise of ever broader strata of the working people to the level of the Party members' consciousness and activeness;

—a further development of inner-Party democracy, a heightening of the significance of the title of Party member, a still greater growth of the activeness and initiative of all Communists, and strengthening of the unity and solidarity of the Party ranks. (Applause.)

It is necessary to emphasize that a new and higher level of Party political work and of Party organizational leadership should correspond to the period of full-scale communist construction. The adoption of the new Program is a great historic act. But this is nevertheless only the beginning. The main thing is to carry out the Program. The vast tasks posed in the Program make unprecedentedly high demands on the Party as a whole and on each Party organization.

The draft of the Party Statutes that our Congress will adopt on the basis of the new Program develops organizational principles for the Party corresponding to the conditions and tasks of the period of full-scale communist construction.

The question of the formation of elective Party bodies is of great fundamental importance. The draft Program proposes a new system that ensures systematic renewal of the membership of leading Party bodies. It would be advisable, in our opinion, to extend the principle of renewal to the formation of the elective bodies of state administration and public organizations.

The change to this system will be a big step in the development of our democracy. It corresponds to the nature of the new period in the political organization of Soviet society, when the state has become the state of all the people and the Party the exponent of the will and interests of the whole people. This period is characterized by an enormous growth of the ranks and ideological might of the Party and of its cadres and an unprecedented advance in the political and cultural level of the people. (Applause.)

When the Party was in its infancy it was made up of small groups of advanced workers and intellectuals who took to

Marxism because they strove to comprehend the laws of history and looked for a revolutionary way out of the contradictions that existed in society. These professional revolutionaries, selflessly devoted to the cause of communism, formed the leading core of the Leninist party that organized and enlightened the working class and the working masses, led them in storming the old exploiting system and ensured the victory of socialism. From the very beginning the strength of our party lay in the high devotion to ideas, the solidarity and the discipline of its ranks, in its ties with the masses and in the support of the working class and the toiling peasantry.

The strength of our party multiplied, its ranks grew and its cadres became tempered in the battles for the victory of the October Revolution, in the fire of the Civil War, at the fronts of the building of socialism, in the severe tests of the Great Patriotic War and in the conditions of the postwar period. In our times non-Party people too are actively building communism arm in arm with the Communists, and the overwhelming majority of them reason like Communists.

Whereas in the first years of the revolution the circle of Communist executive cadres was narrow, now the possibilities for promoting new people to executive posts are inexhaustible. A system must be established whereby comrades elected to executive posts do not bar the way to new forces but, on the contrary, open the path to others for the application of their knowledge and intelligence in executive work in Party, Soviet, trade union and other public organizations, in the leadership of the Party and the country. We have many able and well-educated people. They lack only experience. It is here that the role of executive personnel as educators of new cadres must manifest itself.

Each organism consists of individual cells and constantly renews itself through the death of some and the formation of other cells. The Party and society as a whole are subject to the same process and follow this same law of life. One cannot halt or disturb this natural process without damaging the development of the Party organism and of society as a whole.

It is no secret that we have comrades who were deemed meritorious and elected to executive posts long ago and have been occupying those posts for decades. In that time some of them have lost the capacity to work creatively and lost the sense of the new; they have become an obstacle. To go on keeping these people in their posts merely because they were once elected would be wrong. Should we of all people confine ourselves in a circle of one and the same persons who were elected to executive bodies? This is not our course. (Applause.) Naturally, the failure to re-elect a Party member to a Party body because he has completed the established period in office should not serve as a basis for discrimination against the Party member. If a Communist has worked well for the established tenure in a post entrusted to him, honor and glory to him. (Applause.)

The task is to enlist in executive Party and state work younger comrades who have matured in work. The fresh forces, relying on the theory of Marxism-Leninism and the experience of generations of revolutionaries and builders of socialism, will, in cooperation with tested cadres, successfully strengthen the might of our homeland and advance the economy, science, technology and culture. If one bears in mind that there are hundreds of thousands of elective bodies in our whole ramified system of primary and higher Party, Soviet and public organizations, it becomes clear that each new round of elections can draw millions of new persons into executive work.

The constant renewal of cadres, the promotion of new comrades who have matured in work, the combination in our Party and state orchestra of young personnel with those wise in experience--this is a law of development of the Marxist-Leninist party. This conclusion of our party is based, in particular, on the lessons ensuing from the consequences of the J. V. Stalin cult. I have spoken about this on more than one occasion, including the Central Committee report at the present Congress. The drafts of the Program and Statutes, those principal Party documents, formulate propositions that should establish guarantees against relapses into a cult of the individual and erect reliable barriers against it. We declare from the rostrum of the

Congress: The Party must take all necessary measures to close the way forever to a cult of the individual. (Prolonged applause.)

The systematic renewal of elective Party bodies must henceforth become an inviolable norm of Party life, a norm of state and public life. On this basis there will arise new opportunities for still more consistent realization of the principle of collectivity of leadership.

The Party relies on the collective experience and collective thought of the Communists and of all the people and develops in every possible way the initiative of public organizations and of all Soviet people. Each good undertaking, each good idea and each valuable proposal must be most attentively considered, actively supported, and carried out. But there are officials among us who are deaf to the manifold manifestations of initiative on the part of the broad masses. For them only what they themselves think or say is important. This is not a communist but a bureaucratic point of view. To utilize the talents and abilities of each person for the sake of building communism—this is the calling of leaders and of all Party organizations. (Applause.)

The proposed system of forming elective Party bodies offers new opportunities for the development of criticism and self-criticism and for resolute eradication of instances of personal dependence of officials on their superiors, of elements of nepotism and of mutual concealment of shortcomings and mistakes in work. The principle of renewal of cadres makes it possible to rid elective bodies of persons who are inclined to disregard the opinion and will of the executive collective and the broad masses and who lose the sense of responsibility to the Party and the people. Elective bodies must henceforth be renewed regularly and take in the most gifted persons who have matured and are devoted to the cause of communism.

The interests of the cause demand a combination of old and young cadres and a continuity of leadership, especially in the higher bodies. Without continuity it would be difficult to carry out a correct foreign and domestic policy and successfully guide economic and cultural development. Continuity of leadership is one of the fundamental Leninist principles. V. I. Lenin taught: "The importance of the Party organization and of Party leaders worthy of the name lies precisely, among other things, in evolving, through the prolonged, persistent, diversified and comprehensive efforts of all the thinking representatives of the given class, the necessary knowledge, the necessary experience, and—over and above knowledge and experience—the necessary political intuition for speedy and correct solution of complicated political questions" ("Works" [in Russian], Vol. XXXI, p. 50).

The authority of the Party's officials and of its leading figures is a great asset of the Party. In rejecting the cult of the individual we do not in the least eliminate the question of developing leading Party figures and strengthening their authority. What is necessary is that the leading Party figures be promoted from the Party masses by virtue of their talent, their political qualities and their qualifications and that they be closely tied with the Communists and the people. That was the process of formation of Party figures in Lenin's lifetime. That is how it should be now. (Stormy applause.)

We must unswervingly observe and develop the Leninist norms of Party life and the principle of collectivity of leadership and ensure the strict control of the Party masses over the work of executive bodies and their officials, growth of the activeness and initiative of all Communists and their truly creative participation in the working out and application of Party policy, and the development of criticism and self-criticism.

If the Party constantly looks forward, if it constantly turns to the people and their wisdom, supplementing and expanding its experience—then it need fear no tests. Our party, created and reared by Lenin, is indeed that kind of a party. (Stormy applause.) Let us then, comrades, always hold sacred and ever more consistently carry out the behests of our immortal leader and teacher! Then we shall have still more majestic successes. (Prolonged applause.)

At the new stage of our development the improvement of the Party's guidance of Soviet, economic, trade union, Y.C.L., cooperative and other mass organizations acquires particular importance. This is a prime condition for heightening the degree of organization of the people and mobilizing their creative forces. While bearing responsibility for the state of work on all sectors of communist construction, the Party organizations must at the same time not supplant the state and public agencies. The main thing in the Party's guidance of the mass organizations is mobilization of their efforts for the building of communism, a systematic improvement of the membership of their executive bodies and a concern for the promotion, correct placement and rearing of cadres.

At the present stage the role and the responsibility of the Party members are especially heightened. The title of Communist is a lofty one. Today more than ever the Communist is called upon to be in the front line of the struggle for carrying out the Party policy. Through honest service to the people and through his whole behavior in public and personal life, a Communist must be a model in the development and strengthening of communist relationships and in observance of the norms of communist morality. (Applause.)

A most important source of the Party's strength and invincibility lies in its indestructible ideological and organizational solidarity. The Party keeps in the arsenal of its methods organizational guarantees against any manifestations of factionalism and clique activity, which are incompatible with a Leninist Party spirit.

The measures proposed in the draft Program for the renewal of cadres, for preventing a cult of the individual and for the thorough development of inner-Party democracy are truly revolutionary measures. They bear a close, organic relationship with the general plan worked out by the Party, with its tactics and strategy in the struggle for communism. The application of the proposed measures will make it possible to carry out on a still wider scale the rearing of gifted cadres loyal to communism and to develop the activeness of the Party, of all public organizations and of the entire people. This means that the whole cause of economic and cultural construction, of communist construction, will proceed even more successfully.

Comrades! The working out of the program for the full-scale building of communism is evidence of the enormous theoretical power of our party and of its Central Committee. Armed with the new Program, we Soviet Communists are rising, as it were, to a new height, from which we see our communist future still more clearly. (Applause.) What gives us this strength? Above all, Marxism-Leninism—our all-conquering and eternally developing teaching. The process of building socialism and communism is at the same time a process of enrichment of Marxist-Leninist theory on the basis of the practical experience of the millions-strong masses. The new Program is an outstanding theoretical and political document in which are concentrated the major propositions of Marxist-Leninist theory on communism and new conclusions flowing from the experience of applying these propositions in the practice of socialist and communist construction.

We are advancing on an untrod path. We must work out all kinds of problems that arise in the course of building communism and must develop theoretical propositions and learn how to apply them. Just as a living organism cannot grow normally without sunlight, so the building of communism cannot be successfully realized if its path is not illumined by Marxist-Leninist science. The Party's task is to show unflagging concern for the development of our Marxist-Leninist theory, this most reliable compass pointing the way to new victories of communism. (Prolonged applause.)

***

Comrades! To us delegates to the 22nd Congress has fallen the great honor of considering and adopting the new Party Program, the program of building communism. The implantation of this Program will mark the onset of the happiest era in the history of mankind.

For centuries mankind has lived with the dream of a society in which there would be no exploitation, no social or national oppression, in which there would be no exploitation, no social or national oppression, in which the bloody scourge of wars would not hang over people. Many heroes died the death of the brave in the struggle for the people's cause. But happiness remained a dream and grief and tears the fate of peoples. The greatness of the Marxist-Leninist teaching lies in the fact that it pointed a real way to achieve the aspirations of people of labor. To our party has fallen the happiness of establishing socialism, the first phase of communism, and leading the Soviet people now to the higher phase, communism. (Stormy applause.)

Our party, having raised the torch of freedom and the banner of socialism and communism over the world, shed glory on the 20th century as a century of radical changes in the destinies of mankind. The heroic struggle of the great army of Communists of all countries who led the masses has accelerated the course of history and brought the brightest ideals of mankind closer to realization. But how much faster will history gallop when a communist society has been built in the Soviet Union!

The cause of communism is advancing with giant steps. The standard-bearers of communism—the Marxist-Leninist parties—have proved that they are parties of revolutionary innovators, forging the people's happiness. Progressive people of all countries now associate the best and the brightest things with the Communists. The forces of communism are incalculable. The truth of life and the truth of history are on the side of communism. (Prolonged applause.)

The triumph of communism has always been the cherished ultimate goal of the Leninist party. Now this dream—communism—is becoming reality. Not only our descendants but you and I, comrades, our generation of Soviet people, will live under communism! The awareness of this gives wings to every Soviet person and generates in him the desire to live and work with an unprecedented enthusiasm. (Prolonged applause.)

The Program points out to everyone his place in the ranks of the builders of communism. It shows how one must work and study in the name of communism and how to prepare oneself for life in communist society. Let us then, comrades, give all our efforts and all our energy to bringing closer as quickly as possible the day when the sun of communism will shine over our earth. (Stormy applause.)

The banner of Lenin inspired us in the struggle for the triumph of socialism. And we were victorious! (Stormy applause.)

The banner of Lenin inspires us at the new historical stage of development of our homeland, the stage of building communism. (Stormy applause.)

Under the banner of Marxism-Leninism, under the leadership of the Communist Party—forward to the victory of communism! (Stormy, prolonged applause, turning into an ovation. All rise. Shouts: "Hurrah!" "Hail to the Communist Party!" "Hail to Leninism!" "Hail to the Leninist Central Committee!" "Hail to communism!")

VII. TITOV: CREDENTIALS COMMISSION REPORT

REPORT OF THE CREDENTIALS COMMISSION OF THE 22ND PARTY CONGRESS.—Report by Comrade V. N. Titov. (Pravda, Oct. 22, pp. 5-6; Izvestia, pp. 4-5. 4,000 words. Condensed text:) ... In the period that has elapsed since the 20th Congress the Party has been enlarged by 2,500,000 members, or more than one-third. (Applause.) The largest Party organizations, such as those of Moscow, Leningrad, Sverdlovsk, Gorky, Chelyabinsk and others, have grown considerably. The Communist Parties of the Ukraine, Belorussia, Uzbekistan, Latvia, Estonia, Moldavia and Tadzhikistan have increased their membership by more than 50%.

At present the Communist Party of the Soviet Union numbers 8,872,516 Party members and 843,489 candidates for membership in the Party—9,716,000 Communists in all. (Stormy applause.) The Communist Party of the Soviet Union has thus arrived at the 22nd Congress a mighty army nearly 10,000,000 strong, the tested and steeled vanguard of the whole Soviet people. (Stormy applause.)

An exceptionally important role in strengthening the monolithic unity of the Party's ranks was played by the 20th Party Congress. The severe criticism of the cult of the individual—criticism based on Leninist principles—contained in the report made by Comrade N. S. Khrushchev at the 20th Congress and the report's resolute condemnation of the harmful consequences of that cult were fully and unanimously approved by our whole party and by the entire Soviet people. Only a wretched little group of dogmatists who had lost touch with life, the Party and the people tried to turn our party from its general line, from the Leninist path.

Having smashed the anti-Party group and thrown it into the discard, the Party rallied even more closely around its Leninist Central Committee and accelerated its advance to new victories in the building of communism.

And for the fact that our party can now live and create in a Leninist way, can set and pursue the most daring tasks and realize mankind's brightest ideals, it is indebted to the Leninist Central Committee and to Comrade Nikita Sergeyevich Khrushchev personally—that stalwart revolutionary-Leninist and outstanding personality of our party and of the entire international Communist and workers' movement. (Prolonged applause.) His unflagging energy, courage and tireless work for the happiness of the Soviet people should serve as an example for every Communist in the discharge of his duty as a Party member.

Carrying out the decisions of the 20th and 21st Party Congresses, the Party organizations have done a large amount of work in restoring Leninist standards of Party life and the principle of collective leadership and in comprehensively developing inner-Party democracy, independent initiative on the part of Communists, and criticism and self-criticism. The primary Party organizations have been further strengthened organizationally and politically, and their role and responsibility for the performance of tasks set by the Party and government have been further heightened.

The Party has a total of 296,440 Party organizations, including 75,681 at enterprises in industry, transport, communications and construction; 41,387 on collective farms and 9,206 on state farms. The ratio of large primary Party organizations has been constantly increasing, and the number of shop Party organiza-

tions and Party groups has been growing rapidly. The number of primary Party organizations that have Party committees has increased tenfold over this period, while the number of shop Party organizations has grown by nearly 150%.

The Credentials Commission's report at the 20th Party Congress noted that as of that time there were 7,356 collective farms without Party organizations. At present almost all collective farms have Party organizations. Before the 20th Party Congress collective farm Party organizations with memberships of 26 to 100 Communists accounted for only 7.5% of the total number of collective farm Party organizations; they now account for 53%. The primary Party organizations of the state farms have also grown considerably larger; 2,604 of them, or 28%, have more than 100 Communists.

Comrade delegates! Consistently implementing the line calling for the development of inner-Party democracy, the Party Central Committee has considerably broadened the norms of representation at the 22nd Congress. At the 19th and 20th Party Congresses each voting delegate who had been elected represented 5,000 Party members. At this Congress one voting delegate represents 2,000 Party members and one delegate with a consultative vote represents 2,000 candidates for Party membership.

In conformity with the established representation norm, 4,408 voting delegates and 405 delegates with consultative votes were elected to the 22nd Congress, a total of 4,813 delegates, or three and a half times as many as there were at each of the three preceding Congresses. There are 4,394 voting delegates and 405 delegates with consultative votes present at the Congress; 14 delegates are absent for valid reasons.

The delegates to the 22nd Party Congress were elected by secret ballot at province and territory Party conferences and Union-republic Communist Party Congresses. By decision of the Party Central Committee, the elections of delegates to the 22nd Congress from the Moscow City and Leningrad Province Party organizations were held at borough and district Party conferences.

The Communists who are members of Party organizations in the Soviet Army and Navy, the internal and convoy guards and border units elected delegates to the Congress together with the other Party organizations at province and territory Party conferences or Union-republic Communist Party Congresses. Communists in Party organizations of units of the U.S.S.R. Armed Forces that are stationed abroad elected delegates to the Party Congress at Party conferences of their respective units. ...

The largest delegations at the 22nd Party Congress are the delegation from the Party organization of the capital of our nation, the city of Moscow, comprising 345 persons (applause); the Leningrad delegation of 199 (applause); Moscow Province, 124; Gorky, 87; and Sverdlovsk, 86. The Party organizations of the Communist Party of the Ukraine elected 783 delegates to the 22nd Party Congress, including 77 from the Kiev Province Party organization, 75 from the Stalino organization, 66 from the Kharkov organization and 65 from the Dnepropetrovsk organization. (Applause.) The Communist Parties of the other Union republics have at the 22nd Congress delegations of the following strength: Kazakhstan, 187 delegates; Belorussia, 141; Uzbekistan, 122; Georgia, 118; Azerbaidzhan, 89; Armenia, 47;

Latvia, 45; Lithuania, 36; Kirgizia, 35; Moldavia, 34; Turkmenistan, 30; Tadzhikistan, 28; and Estonia, 25. (Applause.) Participating in the proceedings of the Congress as part of the delegation from the Communist Party of Kazakhstan are 51 delegates from the Party organizations of the newly formed Virgin Land Territory. (Applause.)

The Party report-and-election meetings and the district, region, city, province and territory Party conferences and Union-republic Communist Party Congresses held before the 22nd Party Congress proceeded in an atmosphere of unprecedented political enthusiasm and monolithic solidarity of all the Party's organizations in support of its Leninist Central Committee. (Applause.) ...

Every one of the Soviet republics has reared and educated wonderful cadres for all branches of the national economy, science and culture and for the manifold spheres of state and public activity. Represented at the Congress are the delegates of 65 nationalities and peoples, among them Russians, Ukrainians, Belorussians, Uzbeks, Kazakhs, Georgians, Azerbaidzhanians, Lithuanians, Moldavians, Latvians, Kirgiz, Tadzhiks, Armenians, Turkmenians and Estonians and Communists of the indigenous nationalities and peoples of the autonomous republics, autonomous provinces and national regions.

The nationality breakdown of the delegates elected from the Communist Parties of the Union republics indicates that a steady exchange of skilled cadres between nations is under way in the country. And as Comrade Nikita Sergeyevich Khrushchev has said, the broader the scale of communist construction, the greater will this exchange be. It is a teaching of the Party that without mutual fraternal assistance in the way of cadres it is impossible to ensure rational development of productive forces and properly combine state interests with the interests of the separate republics. The draft Party Program points out the inadmissibility of any manifestations of national exclusiveness in the Soviet republics in the training and employment of workers of various nationalities.

The inviolable friendship of the peoples of the U.S.S.R. has stood every test in the course of peaceful socialist construction and in the grim years of the war. There is no force capable of disrupting this sacred friendship. (Applause.)

The occupational composition of the delegates to the Congress fully reflects the thesis inscribed in the drafts of the Party's Program and Statutes that the Communist Party is a party of the whole people. Attending this Congress are workers of Party, Soviet, trade union and Young Communist League agencies, people from industry, transport and communications, construction, agriculture, science, education, public health, literature and the arts, and members of the Soviet Army and Navy.

The number of Party workers with voting rights elected to the Congress is 1,158, of workers in the Soviets 465 and of trade union and Y.C.L. workers 104. Of the Party and Soviet workers, 50.2% are workers on the district level, 37.2% work in province, territory and republic Party and Soviet agencies and 6.3% of the delegates are personnel of the central Party and state agencies and of ministries and departments of the U.S.S.R. These data testify to the heightened role and responsibility of local Party and Soviet bodies in accomplishing the tasks of communist construction. (Applause.)

There are 1,391 people from industry, transport, communications and construction among the voting delegates to the Congress, including 984 workers, brigade leaders and foremen, who comprise 22.3% of the total number of voting delegates. (Applause.) This figure was 12.2% at the 20th Congress. Participating in the proceedings of the Congress are many innovators, brigade leaders and Communist Labor Shock Workers known to the whole country, true revolutionaries in the production sphere, whose great deeds constitute bright pages in the story of the countrywide competition for completion of the seven-year plan for development of the U.S.S.R. national economy ahead of schedule. ...

The voting delegates elected to the Congress include 748 agricultural workers, of whom 469, or 10.6% of the voting delegates to the Congress, are collective farmers, state farm workers, brigade leaders and heads of collective and state farm sections. At the 20th Party Congress the figure for collective farmers, state farm workers and brigade leaders was 4.9%. Among the delegates to the Congress there are many outstanding masters and organizers of collective farm production, people who are carrying high the banner of the struggle to create an abundance of farm products in our country, who are bringing to light more and more unutilized reserves in agriculture and inspiring millions of working people in the countryside by their example.

As everyone knows, the Soviet Union leads the world in the preparation of highly skilled specialists. As compared with 1941, the number of specialists with a higher education who are employed in the national economy has increased 290% and of specialists with a secondary education 250%. ...

The steady rise in the cultural level of the U.S.S.R.'s working people is also shown by the data on the educational backgrounds of the Party's membership. As of July 1, 1961, there were 3,076,237 specialists with a higher, incomplete higher or specialized secondary education in the Party, which is over 1,000,-000 more than there were at the time of the 20th Party Congress. Out of 4,408 voting delegates, 2,312 have a higher education, 230 an incomplete higher education and 665 a secondary education. Thus 72.8% of the voting delegates to the Congress have a higher, incomplete higher or secondary education. (Applause.) The delegates elected to the Congress include 975 engineers and economists, 260 agronomists, veterinarians, zootechnicians and other farm specialists, and 379 teachers, doctors, lawyers and journalists. Among the voting delegates to the Congress, 17.1% have received a Party-political education.

Taking part in the proceedings of the Congress are 226 scientists and scholars, among them 38 Academicians and corresponding members of the U.S.S.R. Academy of Sciences, 24 members and corresponding members of the branch Academies and the Union-republic Academies of Sciences and 139 doctors and candidates of science. ...

The world had not yet had time to fully appreciate the greatness of Yury Gagarin's unexampled voyage in space before it was followed by the even more daring flight of German Titov. (Stormy applause.) Hero Cosmonauts Yury Alexeyevich Gagarin and German Stepanovich Titov, valiant sons of the great Soviet people, sons of the Leninist party, have been elected delegates to the 22nd Party Congress. (Stormy applause.)

Among the delegates elected to the Congress are 45 writers, painters, composers and performing artists. Our party is carefully and sensitively orienting literature and art toward stronger links with the people, profound portrayal of their many-sided spiritual life, and the inculcation of high principles and communist ethics in Soviet man. Literature and art are asked to make an important contribution to the cultural development of our society and to the common effort to achieve communism.

In our country the people and the Communist Party have always devoted a great deal of attention to the armed forces. The voting delegates elected to the 22nd Party Congress include 305 members of the Soviet Army and Navy. Renowned commanding officers—marshals, generals and admirals—are delegates to the Congress.

The building of communism in the U.S.S.R. is proceeding in a complicated international setting where the bosses of the imperialist states' military-political blocs are making feverish preparations for war. The Party at every turn admonishes Communists, the Soviet people as a whole, the armed forces and the state security agencies against any manifestations of smugness and complacency, and educates Soviet people in a spirit of day-to-day readiness to defend the socialist homeland. (Applause.) Every Soviet individual understands the necessity of the measures recently taken by the Party Central Committee and the government to strengthen our state's defenses. These measures have met with approval and support from the whole people.

At the 21st Party Congress there was criticism of shortcomings in the promotion of young cadres to positions of leadership. Party organizations drew definite conclusions from this and have shown greater concern for the proper combination of experienced, tested cadres with young people. And this is reflected in the composition of the delegates to the 22nd Party Congress. The age breakdown of the voting delegates is as follows: under 35, 22%; between 36 and 40, 16.6%; between 41 and 50, 37.9%; and over 50, 23.5%.

With respect to length of Party membership the delegates to the Congress are distributed as follows: 42 delegates joined the Party before the Great October Socialist Revolution. (Stormy, prolonged applause.) Those who joined the Party in the period 1917-1920 total 1.3%; in 1921-1930, 7.7%; in 1931-1940, 22%; in 1941-1945, 26.6%; and in 1946-1955, 23.1%; while those who joined in 1956 and the subsequent years total 18.4%. Present at our Congress side by side with those who have been in the Party's ranks since it set out on its glorious path more than half a century ago are the people who have joined its ranks in our heroic times, who hand in hand with the older generation are to carry the great Leninist banner forward to communism. (Applause.)

The Party organizations have sent to the Congress as delegates such Party elders as Fyodor Nikolayevich Petrov, a Party member since 1896; Nikolai Alexandrovich Alexeyev, since 1897; Yelena Dmitriyevna Stasova and Vyacheslav Alexeyevich Karpinsky, since 1898, and many others. (Applause.) The election to the 22nd Party Congress of representatives of the old Bolshevik guard who, under Lenin's leadership, went through the heroic school of class struggle for the victory of the dictatorship of the proletariat and the establishment of the Soviet regime is an expression of the deep respect that Communists have for the revolutionary traditions of our great party. (Applause.) ...

There are at present 1,898,759 women in the ranks of the Communist Party of the Soviet Union, almost 500,000 more than at the time of the 20th Party Congress. (Applause.) Of the total number of delegates elected to the 22nd Party Congress 1,073, or 22.3%, are women. (Applause.) At the 20th Congress the figure for women delegates was 15.3%.

Among the women delegates to the 22nd Congress are workers, collective farmers, engineers, teachers, doctors, scientists and scholars, Party and Soviet workers and prominent public figures. Women are represented in the greatest numbers in the following delegations: the Ivanovo Province Party organization, 36.8% (applause); Kostroma, 32% (applause); Novgorod, 30% (applause); Smolensk, 29.2% (applause); the Krasnodar Territory organization, 28.2% (applause); and in the delegations from the Communist Parties of Moldavia, 26.5% (applause); Kirgizia, 25.7% (applause); and Uzbekistan, 25.4% (applause). The delegates to the Congress include 110 women Deputies to the U.S.S.R. Supreme Soviet and the Supreme Soviets of the Union and autonomous republics. (Applause.)

Comrades! The composition of the delegates with consultative votes is shown by the following data: The total number of delegates with consultative votes is 405, of whom 116 work in industry, construction and transport, 105 in agriculture, 55 in Party and 30 in Soviet agencies and 24 in trade union and Y.C.L. organizations, while 45 are serving in the Soviet Army and Navy and in the border troops. The delegates with a higher or incomplete higher education number 186, or 46%, and those with a secondary education 85, or 21%. In length of Party membership the delegates with consultative votes are distributed as follows: those who joined the Party in 1921-1930, 2.2%; in 1931-1940, 9.4%; in 1941-1945, 24.2%; in 1946-1955, 32.3%; and since 1956, 31.9%.

The Party organizations have sent the best of the best to the 22nd Congress—the Congress of the builders of communism. Of the total number of delegates with voting rights and with consultative votes, 84.1% have been decorated with orders and medals of the Soviet Union. (Applause.) Among the Congress delegates there are 99 Heroes of the Soviet Union, 478 Heroes of Socialist Labor and 203 holders of Lenin and Stalin Prizes. (Applause.) ...

VIII. DISCUSSION OF KHRUSHCHEV-GORKIN REPORTS

Podgorny

SPEECH BY COMRADE N. V. PODGORNY, FIRST SECRE-
TARY OF THE UKRAINE COMMUNIST PARTY CENTRAL
COMMITTEE. (Pravda, Oct. 20, pp. 2-4; Izvestia, Oct. 21,
pp. 2-3. 7500 words. Condensed text:) Comrades! ... The
Party Central Committee has done a great deal of important and necessary work in eliminating the cult of the individual and its harmful consequences and in restoring the
Leninist norms of Party life; this has enhanced the role and
developed the creative initiative of the masses. Today we are
being convinced once again of how very important it was to expose and rout the anti-Party group, which isolated itself from
the people and, taking the road of factionalism, tried to swerve
the Party from the Leninist course worked out by the 20th
Party Congress. ...

The entire activity of Comrade N. S. Khrushchev, his inexhaustible, ebullient energy and truly revolutionary, Leninist
approach to the solution of complex problems of theory and
practice, his inseparable bond with the people, humanity and
simplicity, his ability constantly to learn from the masses and
to teach the masses are an inspiring example for the entire
Party and for every Communist. (Stormy, prolonged applause.) ...

We are happy to report to the Congress that the Ukrainian
people are firmly keeping their word to the Party: The assignments of the seven-year plan are being fulfilled throughout the
republic a year ahead of time, and in some branches of the
economy two years ahead of time. (Applause.)

The sharpness with which Comrade N. S. Khrushchev
criticized the leaders of a number of economic councils, including the Dnepropetrovsk council, for arbitrariness and
lack of discipline is quite understandable and justified. The
Ukraine Communist Party Central Committee and the republic's
Party organizations are doing everything to prevent a repetition
of such faulty phenomena in the future and will persistently
raise the responsibility of every official for the work entrusted
to him and for strict observance of Party and state discipline.

The task advanced in the Party Central Committee report of
radically improving the practice of planning is dictated by life
itself. The mistakes and miscalculations that are made by local
planning agencies, and also by the U.S.S.R. State Planning Committee, create considerable difficulties in the work of enterprises, construction projects and even whole branches of
industry.

Despite the fact that the republic's coal industry has been
operating at a high level in recent years, the growth of its
capacity is behind the seven-year-plan control figures. At the
same time metallurgy and the power industry are developing
considerably faster than called for by the assignments. This
could lead to a gap between the needs of metallurgical enterprises for coking coal and the amount that can be extracted.
Therefore the U.S.S.R. State Planning Committee and the
U.S.S.R. State Scientific-Economic Council, jointly with the
Ukraine Republic Council of Ministers, should take this circumstance into account in considering questions of the further development of the coal industry in the Ukraine, above all in the
Donets Basin. ...

Time has fully confirmed the correctness of the Party's

course, adopted on Comrade N. S. Khrushchev's initiative, of
strengthening and comprehensively developing grain farming.

In the period 1956-1960 the average annual gross harvest of
grain increased by 211,000,000 poods in comparison with the
preceding five-year period. ...

The number of cattle increased by 5,200,000, including cows
by 1,700,000, and of pigs by 6,500,000. Communal animal husbandry developed at an even faster rate. The number of cattle
on the collective and state farms increased almost 100% and
the number of pigs 130%. ...

This year, according to preliminary figures, the gross grain
harvest will exceed 2,100,000,000 poods. The Ukraine has never
yet had such a harvest! This will enable the collective and
state farms to sell the state more than 800,000,000 poods of
grain, i.e., more than the republic has ever sold, at the same
time creating the necessary seed stocks, increasing the amount
of grain issued to the collective farmers and providing more
fodder for animal husbandry. (Applause.)

The improvement of the structure of sown areas, above all
the expansion of sowings of corn, peas and winter wheat and
increased yields of other crops, has been of decisive importance in the achievement of these successes.

The Party organizations of the Ukraine consider the year
1961 a turning point in corn production. Although on an area of
3,000,000 hectares we failed to obtain 50 centners of grain per
hectare, the results already achieved instill confidence that
such a yield is not the limit. ...

Communists and all workers in the socialist fields are deeply
convinced that in a very short period of time the Ukraine will
harvest the highest corn yields in the world! (Applause.) ...

The Communist Party of the Ukraine has set itself the task
of expanding the area under grain corn and of raising 40 to 50
centners of grain per hectare from the entire area under corn
in 1962. ...

Increasing importance attaches to irrigation of lands in the
republic. After thoroughly studying this question, we worked
out long-range measures for increasing irrigated areas to
7,200,000 hectares, and it is planned to irrigate 450,000 hectares in the most arid regions by the end of the seven-year
period. This will completely transform the face of the southern
part of the Ukraine.

More funds should be allocated for land irrigation in order to
carry out the plans outlined more rapidly, since the country will
obtain considerably more farm products and the expenditures
will be quickly recouped.

As is known, only one enterprise in the country—the Kherson
Plant—produces corn-harvesting combines, and in the next two or
three years it will not be able to satisfy the needs of collective and
state farms for these machines. Therefore, relying on the experience accumulated in the republic, we shall take the course of converting silage-harvesting combines for this purpose. At the
same time, we feel that it is necessary to speed implementation
of the Party Central Committee's decision on organizing the
industrial production of universal combines for the harvesting
of corn for both grain and silage.

As is known, every year the collective and state farms are
provided with more and more equipment. Nevertheless, agriculture is still experiencing a shortage. We all realize that it
is not easy to satisfy the growing requirements all at once.

But it seems to us that, taking into account the prospects for the further development of agricultural production, the U.S.S.R. State Planning Committee, jointly with the Union-republic Councils of Ministers, should once again carefully calculate the possibilities of increasing the output of tractors, trucks and machines in the next few years and also of producing fertilizers, chemical poisons and materials for agricultural needs, and submit the recommendations prepared on this question for consideration by the Party Central Committee and the U.S.S.R. Council of Ministers. (Applause.) ...

The Communist Party of the Ukraine numbers 1,500,000 members and candidate members of the C.P.S.U. (Applause.) In the period under review it grew even stronger organizationally and became hardened ideologically, and its mobilizing and organizational role in the struggle to accomplish economic and political tasks increased.

A major place in the work of the republic's Party organizations is occupied by cadres, and the success of any undertaking decisively depends on their correct selection, placement and training. Today every third person among the secretaries of city and district Party committees and chairmen of city and district Soviet executive committees is an industrial or agricultural specialist.

Much has been done to strengthen the administrative cadres of state and collective farms. In the period since the January plenary session of the Party Central Committee alone, almost 20,000 Communists have been sent to leading sectors of agricultural production, about 1,500 of them as collective farm chairmen. ...

In order to picture the grandeur of our successes, let us recall that before the October Revolution the Ukrainian people were under a double yoke--social and national--and were deprived of statehood. Hunger, poverty and lack of rights drove them to foreign lands. Hundred of thousands of Ukrainians emigrated in search of a crust of bread. ...

Today you can't recognize the Ukraine! In the fraternal Union of Soviet Socialist Republics it has burgeoned luxuriantly. Every honest, unprejudiced person sees this.

Thousands of foreign tourists annually visit the Soviet Ukraine. Hundreds of Ukrainian emigrants have also come. Returning from our country, many of them truthfully relate how rich and happy are the Ukrainian people they saw. They indignantly refute the ravings of imperialist and nationalist propaganda, which claims that the Ukrainian people continue to "live in poverty."

The Soviet Ukraine has outdistanced many capitalist countries in its development and occupies a prominent place in the Union economy and in the world economy. Our republic's products are exported to 61 countries.

The culture of the Ukrainian people is developing tempestuously. About 13,000,000 people in the republic now have a seven-year, secondary or higher education. The ten-day festival of Ukrainian literature and art held in Moscow in 1960 vividly demonstrated the flowering of the spiritual life of the working people. The organic ties of Ukrainian Soviet culture with the culture of the great Russian people and all peoples of our homeland are growing stronger and stronger. (Applause.) A mutual enrichment of the fraternal socialist cultures takes place in the process of their uniting and drawing together. ...

The Central Committee report states with absolute correctness that Molotov, Kaganovich, Malenkov and Voroshilov opposed the Party line of condemning the cult of the individual and developing inner-Party democracy, of condemning and rectifying all the abuses of power and exposing those specifically guilty of repressions, since they bear personal responsibility for many mass repressions against Party, Soviet, economic, military and Young Communist League cadres.

In this connection one cannot but tell of Kaganovich's provocational activities in the Ukraine. After becoming Secretary of the Ukraine Communist Party Central Committee in 1947, he surrounded himself with a pack of unprincipled people and toadies, betrayed cadres devoted to the Party, and trampled upon and terrorized leading officials of the republic. Like a true sadist, Kaganovich found satisfaction in mocking activists and the intelligentsia, belittled their human dignity and threatened them with arrests and imprisonment. It is no accident that many Party, Soviet and professional workers still call the period of Kaganovich's tenure the "black days" of the Soviet Ukraine.

Kaganovich inflated the cult of Stalin, pandered to him, exploited his weak sides for his own careerist purposes and at the same time created his own cult of the individual, representing himself as the "leader" of the Ukrainian people. To this end the press carried articles extolling his activities in the Ukraine in the 1930s, although it is known that even at that time he was recalled from the Ukraine for serious mistakes. Matters reached a point where he demanded, for example, that artists add his portrait to already completed paintings representing the liberation of the Ukraine from the German occupiers, although he had nothing to do with these events. (Laughter, stir in the hall.)

Considering himself infallible, Kaganovich personally, bypassing the Central Committee, decided major questions of the life of the republic, and very frequently decided them incorrectly. Being a master of intrigues and provocations, he accused leading writers of the republic, as well as a number of executive Party officials, of nationalism, literally without any grounds. Upon Kaganovich's instructions, abusive articles against a number of writers devoted to the Party and the people appeared in the press.

However, this did not satisfy Kaganovich. He began working to convene a plenary session of the Central Committee with the agenda: "The struggle against nationalism as the chief danger in the Ukraine Communist Party (Bolsheviks)," although in reality there was not even a trace of such a danger. There couldn't be, since, to our good fortune, the Central Committee of the Ukraine Communist Party was for many years headed by the stanch Leninist Nikita Sergeyevich Khrushchev, who instilled in Communists and the Ukrainian people a spirit of internationalism (stormy applause), friendship of peoples and selfless devotion to the great ideas of Leninism. (Stormy, prolonged applause.)

Comrade N. S. Khrushchev enjoyed enormous prestige among the Communists and all the working people of the Ukraine and, relying on them, disrupted by every means the provocations of Kaganovich. And if today the remarkable poet-Communist and Lenin Prize Winner Maxim Faddeyevich Rylsky is among us delegates to the 22nd Congress, and if many other figures in Ukrainian literature continue to fight actively for the cause of the Party, they owe this above all to the courage and inflexible will of our Nikita Sergeyevich Khrushchev. (Stormy applause.)

In the conditions of the prevalence of the Stalin cult, this was truly a heroic struggle, particularly since in the end Kaganovich pursued the aim of compromising and making short work of executive cadres of the Ukraine Communist Party, and above all he set out to compromise Comrade N. S. Khrushchev. This is now totally clear to us.

When in June, 1957, the Party Central Committee routed the anti-Party factional group, it was clear to many that Kaganovich's participation in it was not a chance "fall" but the culmination of his many anti-Party crimes. But at that time not everything had yet been fully disclosed, and punishment was confined solely to his removal from membership in the Party Central Committee.

After the June plenary session of the Central Committee new facts became known that proved Kaganovich guilty of the grossest violations of revolutionary legality, of abuses of power, of arbitrary action and unfounded repressions against honest officials devoted to the Party and the Soviet regime. As was stated at the Central Committee plenary session, while Kaganovich was Minister of Transportation he mocked his subordinates, arrested them without grounds, tortured them, etc.

I believe, comrades, that Kaganovich did the Party and the people a great deal of harm. He is a degenerate, in whom there has been nothing communist for a long time. We think his actions are incompatible with the title of member of the great party of Communists. (Stormy applause.) ...

The bosses of the imperialist camp are resorting to all sorts of tricks to defame our national policy, to discredit it in the eyes of the working people of the capitalist and colonial countries. In the U.S.A., for example, so-called "Captive Nations Weeks," "Ukraine Days," etc., are held with the government's blessing. But all these provocational measures are suffering disgraceful failure.

No one will ever succeed in splitting the unity and solidarity of the Soviet peoples or in undermining the fraternal solidarity of the working people of the whole world. (Applause.)

As for the organizers of these silly undertakings, we can advise them: "Direct your zeal, gentlemen, first of all toward eliminating racial discrimination against 17,000,000 Negroes and the remnants of the indigenous Indian population in the U.S.A. itself, and at stopping the black deeds of the colonialists in Africa, Asia and Latin America." But they are scarcely even trying to do this. Such is the wolfish nature of the imperialists. ...

Spiridonov

SPEECH BY COMRADE I. V. SPIRIDONOV, FIRST SECRETARY OF THE LENINGRAD PROVINCE PARTY COMMITTEE. (Pravda, Oct. 20, p. 4. 2,800 words. Condensed text:) Comrades! ... The Central Committee acted wisely and in a Leninist way when, upon the initiative of Nikita Sergeyevich Khrushchev, it submitted the question of the cult of the individual for discussion by the 20th Party Congress and then by the entire Party. The criticism of the cult of the individual, the elimination of the distortions in Party and state work, and the restoration of Leninist norms of Party life and the principles of collective leadership have brought a new revivifying spirit into the life of our party and the entire people and into the international Communist movement and have helped to raise the level of political and organizational work of the Party and all its organizations. It is as if every member of the Party began to see clearly, saw the chains of the cult of the individual that bound him, shook them off and felt a new surge of strength for the struggle for the cause of the Leninist party. The scales seemed to fall from people's eyes and they began to orient themselves more freely in the surrounding environment.

Only the participants in the anti-Party group did not see this, or, more accurately, did not want to see it. The Party Central Committee report correctly notes that this was not happenstance, since Malenkov, Molotov, Kaganovich and Voroshilov bear personal responsibility for many mass repressions against the best cadres of our party and state. Along with the adventurist Beria, Malenkov took a hand in the so-called "Leningrad case," which was fabricated and slanderous from beginning to end. On Malenkov's conscience lie the deaths of totally innocent people and numerous repressions. On his conscience lie the belittling of the dignity and the compromising of the Leningrad Party organization. Could such a man as Malenkov accept the denunciation of the cult of the individual with an open heart? Of course not. He himself was not only a participant in but an organizer of the distortions and lawlessness of that period.

A similar burden also weighed on Molotov, Kaganovich and Voroshilov and united their efforts to seize leadership of the Party and the country for a struggle to retain the ways that existed in the period of the cult of the individual. Winning Bulganin, Pervukhin, Saburov and later Shepilov over to their side, the anti-Party group openly opposed the Party's Leninist course. ...

The Leningrad Party organization suffered especially great losses from the distortions in the period of the cult of the individual, from arbitrariness and lawlessness. Thousands of honest people devoted to the Party were subjected to severe repressions in the period 1935-1937. And four years after the end of the war, during which many leading officials were killed and when new cadres of Party, Soviet and economic leaders had just begun to be formed, numerous repressions were again visited upon innocent people.

For the complete rehabilitation of the Leningrad Party organization, for the restoration of its honor and dignity and for the greatest insight into the conduct of the Leninist general line in the building of communism, the Leningrad Communists from the bottom of their hearts thank the Party Central Committee and especially Nikita Sergeyevich Khrushchev, who did so much for the struggle against the consequences of the cult of the individual, for the exposure and routing of the anti-Party group and for the disclosure of the provocational "Leningrad case." (Stormy applause.)

Invested with the high trust of the Central Committee, the Leningrad Party organization strengthened and rallied its ranks, unanimously approved the decisions of the 20th Party Congress and welcomed with profound satisfaction the resolution of the June, 1957, plenary session of the Party Central Committee on the anti-Party group. Several days after this historic plenary session, members of the Presidium of the Central Committee visited Leningrad and witnessed the 500,000-strong demonstration of the working people, who unanimously condemned the schismatic activities of the anti-Party group and expressed their ardent feelings of love for and devotion to the

Foreign Speakers

With the exception of the speeches by Chou En-lai and Wladyslaw Gomulka, the greetings delivered by foreign guests at the Congress have been omitted in the interests of space. A list of the foreign speakers, as well as of the Communist Parties and other parties on whose behalf messages were read, follows. An asterisk denotes those who mentioned Albania and supported the Soviet position in the Soviet-Albanian dispute.

October 19.--Chou En-lai, Vice-Chairman and member of the Politburo, Central Committee of the Communist Party of China; Wladyslaw Gomulka,* First Secretary, Central Committee of the Polish United Workers' Party; Maurice Thorez,* General Secretary, French Communist Party.

October 20.--Antonin Novotny,* First Secretary, Central Committee of the Communist Party of Czechoslovakia; Walter Ulbricht,* First Secretary, Central Committee of the Socialist Unity Party of Germany; Palmiro Togliatti,* General Secretary, Italian Communist Party; Gheorghe Gheorghiu-Dej,* First Secretary, Central Committee of the Rumanian Workers' Party; Janos Kadar,* First Secretary, Central Committee of the Hungarian Socialist Workers' Party.

October 21.--Todor Zhivkov,* First Secretary, Central Committee of the Bulgarian Communist Party; Kim Il Sung, Chairman, Central Committee of the Korean Labor Party; Ho Chi Minh, Chairman, Central Committee of the Workers' Party of Vietnam; Yumzhagiin Tsedenbal,* First Secretary, Central Committee of the Mongolian People's Revolutionary Party; Blas Roca,* member of the directorate, Integrated Revolutionary Organizations of Cuba; Dipa Nusantara Aidit, Chairman, Central Committee of the Communist Party of Indonesia; Ajoy Kumar Ghosh, General Secretary, National Council of the Communist Party of India.

October 23.--Sanzo Nosaka, Chairman, Central Committee of the Communist Party of Japan; Elizabeth Gurley Flynn,* Chairman, National Committee of the Communist Party of the U.S.A.; Max Reimann,* First Secretary, Central Committee of the Communist Party of Germany; Dolores Ibarruri,* Chairman, Communist Party of Spain; Ville Pessi,* General Secretary, Communist Party of Finland; Larbi Bouhali, First Secretary, Central Committee of the Algerian Communist Party; Luis Corvalan,* General Secretary, Central Committee of the Communist Party of Chile; John Gollan, General Secretary, Executive Committee of the Communist Party of Great Britain; Salam Adil,* First Secretary, Central Committee of the Iraqi Communist Party; Alvaro Cunhal,* General Secretary, Portuguese Communist Party; Johann Koplenig,* Chairman, Communist Party of Austria

October 24.--Victorio Codovilla,* Secretary, Central Committee of the Communist Party of Argentina; Kostas Koliyannis,* First Secretary, Central Committee of the Communist Party of Greece; Tim Buck, General Secretary, Communist Party of Canada; Khalid Bakdash,* General Secretary, Central Committee of the Syrian Communist Party; Saifoulaye Diallo, Political Secretary of the Democratic Party of Guinea and Chairman of the Guinean Republic National Assembly; Ebenezer Cethas Quaye, head of the delegation of the Convention People's Party, Republic of Ghana; Tidiani Traore, member of the Politburo of the Sudan Union Party of the Republic of Mali and Deputy to the National Assembly; Emil Lovlien, Chairman, Communist Party of Norway; Ernest

Party and its Leninist Central Committee. (Applause.) ...

Carrying out the historic decisions of the 21st Party Congress, the working people of Leningrad and the province are successfully fulfilling the assignments of the seven-year plan and their socialist pledges for preschedule achievement, in five years, of the level of production and labor productivity called for in the seven-year plan. ...

It is more than four years since the reorganization of the management of industry and construction. But the experience of management in the new conditions is still being studied poorly and the necessary measures are not being taken to improve the structure of the economic councils and the state planning agencies. Certainly no one will assert that once a good system has been established, it does not require improvement. A new central organization has arisen in this period—the All-Russian Economic Council. Apparently it is this agency that, with the help of scientists, was to have undertaken an analysis of the work of industry and an improvement of its management and to have submitted its views on these questions to the Central Committee.

The practice of the planning of industry and construction still lags very far behind the requirements in economic management set forth in Nikita Sergeyevich Khrushchev's report on the Party Program.

One of the principles of planning is the material and moral incentive to introduce new technology. Unfortunately, this principle is violated in many cases. Frequently labor expenditures for new products per 1000 rubles of gross output are higher than for old products, especially in cases where the expenditure of costly materials is greatly reduced. Under the present method of calculating economic indices, enterprises are not interested materially—or morally—in increasing the share of new products in the over-all plan.

Personnel in industry and we local Party officials have gained the impression that the Union State Planning Committee and the Russian Republic State Planning Commission are merely a conglomeration of various agencies, called branch administrations and departments, in which the right hand often does not know what the left is doing, while the heads of these agencies spend their time plugging up countless gaps and rectifying the no less countless mistakes of their own apparatus. (Applause.)

Let me cite a specific example. For the third year in a row

the Russian Republic State Planning Commission's plans for the Izhora Plant have called for the supply of castings for the production of excavators from the Building Materials Machinery Plant in Bryansk. In 1959 only 18 tons were received out of the 3,000 tons that should have been delivered. When the Izhora Plant appealed for a fine against the supplier, Comrade Balandin, Vice-Chairman of the State Planning Commission, submitted a report to the arbitration board in which he stated that the Building Materials Machinery Plant in Bryansk had been unable to supply the Izhora Plant with 3,000 tons of shaped castings in 1959.

In 1960 it was again planned to supply the Izhora Plant with 4,200 tons of castings from the Bryansk plant, of which it received only 1,600 tons. Comrade Siry, then Vice-Chairman of the Russian Republic State Planning Commission, vetoed an assessed fine for nondelivery. He wrote: "The Bryansk plant has not yet completed construction of the heat-cutting shop and it does not have a pattern shop or a scrap-reduction shop; because of this, the plant could not supply the steel castings."

This, however, did not stop either the Russian Republic State Planning Commission or Comrade Siry, who is now Vice-Chairman of the All-Russian Economic Council, from again this year allocating stocks from the Bryansk plant and again confronting the Izhora plant with a disruption of the excavator production plan because of a breakdown in the supply of castings. Is this state planning? This is chaos, deception of the Party and state, for which, unfortunately, no state official bears responsibility. (Applause.)

As a result of this same departmentalization in the administrative structure the state planning agencies are displaying helplessness in applying the principle of specialization and rational cooperation. Instead, there now exists the principle of so-called cooperation "as it has developed"; this in effect has legalized the cooperation that existed previously under the ministries, which in many instances was clearly irrational and attributable only to departmental interests.

Here are concrete facts. Many Leningrad enterprises continue senselessly to use a great deal of metal making items for which they are not specifically adapted. The heads of the Union State Planning Committee and the Federation's State Planning Commission agree on this, but beyond that they do nothing. Back in 1959 the U.S.S.R. State Planning Committee approved

---

Burnelle, Chairman, Communist Party of Belgium; Rodney Arismendi,* First Secretary, Central Committee of the Communist Party of Uruguay.

October 25.--Jesus Faria,* General Secretary, Central Committee of the Communist Party of Venezuela; Knud Jespersen, Chairman, Communist Party of Denmark; Paul de Groot,* General Secretary, Central Committee of the Communist Party of the Netherlands; Gilberto Vieira,* Political Secretary, Central Committee of the Communist Party of Colombia; Lawrence Sharkey, General Secretary, Communist Party of Australia; Nicholas Shawi,* Secretary, Central Committee of the Lebanese Communist Party; Pieter Keuneman,* General Secretary, Central Committee of the Communist Party of Ceylon; Ali Yata,* First Secretary, Central Committee of the Moroccan Communist Party; Martinez Verdugo,* Secretary, Central Committee of the Mexican Communist Party; Ezekias Papaioannu,* General Secretary, Progressive Party of Working People of Cyprus; Pedro Saad,* General Secretary, Central Committee of the Communist Party of Ecuador; Reza Radmanesh,* First Secretary, Central Committee of the People's Party of Iran.

October 26.--Camille Silvestre, General Secretary, Martinique Communist Party; Samuel Mikunis,* General Secretary, Central Committee of the Communist Party of Israel; Fuad Nassar,* General Secretary, Central Committee of the Jordanian Communist Party; George Jackson, Chairman, National Committee of the Communist Party of New Zealand; Edgar Woog, General Secretary, Swiss Labor Party; S. Pierre-Justen, member of the Politburo, Central Committee of the Communist Party of Guadeloupe; Communist Party of San Marino;* Communist Party of Luxembourg;

Guatemalan Party of Labor; Paraguayan Communist Party; Mohammed Kharmel,* Secretary, Central Committee of the Tunisian Communist Party; Yakup Demir,* member of the Politburo, Central Committee of the Communist Party of Turkey; South African Communist Party; head of the delegation of the Communist Party of Burma; head of the delegation of the Communist Party of Malaya; Ruiz Gonzales,* Secretary, Central Committee of the Communist Party of Bolivia; Communist Party of North Ireland; Nicaraguan Socialist Party;* Irish Workers' League.

October 27.--Communist Party of Honduras; Communist Party of Pakistan; Communist Party of Thailand; African Party of Independence, Senegal; Party of People's Comrades, Burma, and Burman Workers' Party.

October 28.--Hilding Hagberg, Chairman, Communist Party of Sweden; Geraldo Rodriquez dos Santos,* member of the national directorate, Brazilian Communist Party; Ibrahim Mustafa,* member of the Politburo, Central Committee of the Sudanese Communist Party; Oscar Vargas,* Secretary, National Committee of the People's Vanguard Party of Costa Rica; Jorge del Prado,* Secretary, Central Committee of the Peruvian Communist Party; Paul Verges,* First Secretary, Reunion Communist Party; Gudmundur Vigfusson, member of the Executive Committee, Central Committee of the United Socialist Party of Iceland; Jose Sanchez Verde,* Secretary, Central Committee of the Communist Party of El Salvador; Juan Docoudray, Secretary, Central Committee of the Dominican Popular Socialist Party; Ruben Castellanos,* Secretary, Central Committee of the People's Party of Panama.

October 30.--People's Unity Party of Haiti.*

plans for measures to improve the specialization of enterprises under the Leningrad Economic Council. But the State Planning Committee itself is not fulfilling them. The Leningrad Metals Plant, for example, was to have specialized in the production of powerful steam, hydraulic and gas turbines and to be released as of 1961 from the production of jaw crushers, charging machines and other items requiring a great deal of metal and not suited to the plant's specialization. But the decision remained on paper, and even the draft of the 1962 plan for the plant again includes these items. ...

When we carried out a mass inspection of the quality of output at the beginning of 1961, we found that various shortcomings in the quality of machinery, instruments and apparatus were due in large measure to last-minute-rush work in assembly operations. Rush work, in turn, is the result of unsatisfactory use of equipment. In Leningrad's metalworking industry the coefficient of use of equipment is not much more than 50%. The share of machine operators in the total number of workers does not exceed 18% to 20%, and as a result the machine shops do not provide the assembly shops promptly with the parts they need. This gives rise to last-minute-rush work, and quality of output drops.

We submitted recommendations on improving the use of equipment which the Russian Republic State Planning Commission was instructed to consider. Various committees and departments of the commission have long been studying these recommendations, but no results are evident. The impression one gets is that they are solidly buried there.

It is known, too, that at a great number of enterprises, including ones in Leningrad, there are cases of high turnover of machine operators. The reason for this is that machine operators are frequently paid less than workers in many other occupations. As a result, skilled machine operators transfer to work that pays more. ...

It is necessary in general to outline measures for combating high turnover of workers. (Applause.) ...

Mazurov

SPEECH BY COMRADE K. T. MAZUROV, FIRST SECRETARY OF THE BELORUSSIAN COMMUNIST PARTY CENTRAL COMMITTEE. (Pravda, Oct. 20, pp. 4-5; Izvestia, Oct. 21, pp. 3-4. 7,000 words. Condensed text:) Comrades! ...
At the June, 1957, plenary session of the Central Committee materials were cited testifying to the fact that Molotov, Kaganovich and Malenkov were personally guilty of mass slaughter of Party cadres and the grossest violations of Soviet legality. They confessed at the plenary session and hypocritically admitted their direct guilt in the crimes committed by Yezhov, Beria and their assistants. At that time not everything was yet known to members of the Central Committee. After the rout of the anti-Party group, Communists helped the Central Committee completely expose the organizers of the anti-Party group, Malenkov in particular.

The results of this man's activity were particularly serious and tragic in the Belorussian Party organization. As is known, in 1935-1936 there took place a verification and exchange of Party cards in the Party. Malenkov, who worked in the Central Committee apparatus at that time, used this operation to slaughter honest Communists and, together with Yezhov, concocted a story about the existence in Belorussia of an extensive anti-Soviet underground, which was supposedly headed by Party and Soviet leaders of the republic. On the basis of this story more than half of the entire membership of the Belorussian Communist Party was expelled from the Party at the time of the exchange of Party cards.

When, at a plenary session of the Belorussian Communist Party Central Committee, Goloded, Chairman of the Council of People's Commissars of the republic, cast doubt upon the results of the verification and exchange of Party cards, Malenkov went to Belorussia and routed the leading cadres of the republic. As a result of his activity at the time of his stay in Belorussia, almost the entire leadership of the republic, including Central Committee secretaries, the chairman of the Council of People's Commissars, people's commissars, and many leaders of local Party and Soviet bodies and representatives of the creative intelligentsia were expelled from the Party and many of them were arrested.

All of these totally innocent people have now been rehabilitated, many of them posthumously.

Now the conduct of Malenkov and the other factionalists, who tried in every way to cover up the traces of their crimes before the people, is even more understandable. The Communists of Belorussia consider it impossible that Malenkov continue to remain in the Party. (Applause.) ...

The measures directed at specialization and cooperation in machine building that we have carried out have made it possible to free a large amount of production space, which has been used, with small capital expenditures, for the organization of new specialized enterprises for the production of machines, machine tools and sets of parts.

All this has made it possible to increase the volume of industrial output in the republic almost 100% in six years, and in the first three years of the seven-year period to increase output in machine building 85%, in the machine tool, tool and radioelectronic industries 100%, and in the electrical equipment and instrument industries 200%. (Applause.)

The chemical industry is developing successfully in the republic. Construction of the first section of the Soligorsk Potassium Combine, the largest in Europe, is nearing completion and construction of a second enterprise of this kind has begun. Construction is under way on an oil refinery in Polotsk, the Grodno Nitrogen Fertilizer Combine, the Svetlogorsk Artificial Fiber Plant and a number of other chemical enterprises. In the near future Belorussia, which has large reserves of chemical raw material, will become a region of large-scale chemistry. ...

The volume of industrial production in 1961 will exceed the 1958 level by more than 40%, as against the 27% increase envisaged in these years by the seven-year-plan control figures. Labor productivity increased more than 23%, as against the 18.7% called for in the seven-year plan. ...

There is no way to explain why in our country even machines in the same class differ sharply from one another in terms of design. Is it not possible, let us say, to build motors of various capacities that differ from each other only in number of cylinders, and to standardize widely used, frequently replaced parts, such as pistons, piston rings and connecting rods, for all motors in a given class? It is even easier to organize the production of tractors, trucks and metal-cutting machine tools on the basis of standardized units.

Extensive standardization of widely used units and parts would make it possible to set up centralized production of them at specialized automatic plants, to reduce production costs sharply throughout the entire U.S.S.R. economy and to raise labor productivity. The U.S.S.R. Council of Ministers' State Automation and Machine-Building Committee should seriously tackle this matter. ...

There are still major shortcomings in planning. Nikita Sergeyevich Khrushchev correctly stated in the report that planning agencies do not always coordinate volume of production and construction with material and technical supply; this often disrupts fulfillment of production plans and prolongs construction periods. For example, the plan for 1961 called for the Belorussian Economic Council to manufacture 145 units of crane equipment, but special electrical apparatus has not been allocated to complete it and the national economy will fail to receive a large number of cranes.

Upon the instructions of the Party Central Committee and the government, measures are now being worked out, with the participation of the republics, to improve planning. It is necessary to expand the list of products whose output is planned by the State Planning Committee, with a detailed itemization of them by dimensions, assortment and group characteristics. Along with the production plans, it is necessary to approve plans at the center for interrepublic deliveries not provided for in the plans for the development of the U.S.S.R. national economy, so that every economic region will know at the beginning of the year what it must produce and when and to whom it is to make deliveries, with the directors of the economic councils bearing personal responsibility for this.

Belorussia's construction workers carried out twice as much work in 1961 as in 1955. After the example of Moscow and Leningrad, housing construction combines have been set up in the republic for erecting large-panel housing by industrial methods. ...

But we still have many shortcomings in capital construction also. N. S. Khrushchev correctly criticized the practice of scattering capital investments. In Belorussia, too, there are managerial personnel who frequently display a localist approach to capital construction and seek allocations only to "latch on to" a construction site, as they say. Our builders often disrupt periods for putting installations into operation, turn out poor-quality work and do not use up all the funds allocated. The plan for construction and installation work in the first nine months of 1961 was only 95% fulfilled.

The Belorussian Communist Party Central Committee and Party organizations are taking the necessary measures, and the plan for capital work in 1961, as in 1960, will be fulfilled, and installations nearing completion will be put into operation.

The successful accomplishment of capital construction tasks is also being impeded by defects in planning. In recent years the Party Central Committee and the U.S.S.R. government have adopted a number of resolutions calling for a sharp increase in capacity for the production of precast reinforced concrete and nonmetallic minerals and the organization of the production in the republic of new types of building materials, such as foam plastic, polyvinyl chloride linoleum, wall linoleum, asbestos-cement and reinforced-concrete conduit pipes, rock wool, etc. But the annual plans for capital work are drawn up without taking proper account of the adopted decisions, and therefore the construction industry not only fails to keep ahead of the growth in the volume of capital work but is even behind in its development. There is a particularly acute shortage of large-capacity hoisting and transport equipment for construction.

Housing construction plans are fulfilled and overfulfilled in the republic every year, but because of the tempestuous growth of cities the housing problem in our republic is being solved slowly. The allocations for housing construction in 1962 are smaller than the seven-year-plan control figures for this year. Even more acute for us is the problem of building children's preschool institutions, as well as schools and hospitals.

Officials of the U.S.S.R. State Planning Committee evidently underestimate the difficulties that exist in this matter locally, do not have a clear enough idea of the need for a rapid solution of this problem and lack a differentiated approach to the republic in allotting capital investments for cultural and everyday needs.

In the period under review definite successes have been achieved in the development of the republic's agriculture. Gross output of agriculture increased almost 50% in five years. ...

The output of milk for all categories of farming increased 50% in five years and of meat 22%. Output of milk on the collective and state farms increased 170% in five years and output of meat 100%; this year output of milk on the collective and state farms has risen 10%. Eleven percent less meat has been produced than in 1960.

Khrushchev.—Meat production has declined in your republic. Do the Belorussians want to become vegetarians?

Mazurov.—The Belorussians will increase the output of meat. By the end of the year we will rectify the mistake—the lag will be overcome.

Khrushchev.—Good, the Congress hears your statement.

Mazurov.—The plan for grain purchases has been fulfilled. Fifteen million poods of grain has been sold to the state, or 4,-800,000 poods more than in 1960. The plans for purchases of other products have also been met. ...

Despite the substantial growth in the output of livestock products, the assignments of the seven-year plan are still being fulfilled unsatisfactorily; the republic produces 380 kg. of milk and only 50 kg. of meat per capita. ...

Upon Nikita Sergeyevich Khrushchev's advice, the structure of sown areas is being revised in the republic. We in effect no longer have any clean fallow. Oats accounted for about 6% of the entire sown area in our republic in 1961, while 12% of the grains were grain legumes. In addition, leguminous crops were planted in the same amount for green fodder and grain. The collective and state farms assigned 10% of the sown areas to corn. This year many farms planted sugar beets for livestock fodder. ...

However, for the republic as a whole the average agricultural yields are still low. We realize that we have many internal unutilized reserves for further increasing the output of all farm products substantially. ...

But in Belorussia's agriculture there are problems that the collective farms cannot solve without the active help of the state. There are only 6,000,000 hectares of plowland in the republic, but there are 7,000,000 hectares of swamp and excessively moist land that brings scarcely any benefit. About 2,500,000 hectares of land is used as hayfields and pastures and yields only two to 2.5 fodder units per hectare a year. Reclamation of this land is still proceeding slowly, although its high quality is obvious, because on drained peat lands the collective and state farms are obtaining 45 to 50 fodder units per hectare.

The drainage and active agricultural use in the future of 4,-500,000 to 5,000,000 hectares of swampland in Belorussia will make it possible considerably to increase the area of plowland and to produce about 200,000,000 poods more grain, at least 600,000 tons more meat and 3,000,000 tons more milk.

In working out the general long-range control figures, we plan to improve the structure of sown areas radically, to increase the area under grain crops from 2,500,000 to 4,000,000 hectares and the area under grain legumes from 200,000 to 1,300,000 hectares, and, given an average grain yield of 22 centners per hectare, to increase the gross grain harvest to 500,000,000 poods; this will make it possible to satisfy fully all the requirements of the republic's population and animal husbandry. ...

Reclamation of a large part of the swampland in the republic is linked with the plan for creating an inland waterway from the Black Sea along the Dnieper, Pripet and Neman Rivers to the Baltic Sea, about which N. S. Khrushchev spoke in his report, and can be carried out as a subsidiary task.

The electrification of agriculture is quite an acute problem in Belorussia. A third of the republic's collective farms are not yet electrified, and the farms that are electrified make little use of electricity in production because of the inadequate capacity of the transformers and the shortage of electric motors and electrical equipment. The State Planning Committee continues to plan rural electrification on the basis of understated norms. The use of low-voltage networks belonging to the collective farms has not been organized and there has been no systematization of rates for electric power supplied to collective farms. Along with more vigorous expansion of power capacities serving agriculture and broad development of high-voltage transmission lines, the question has arisen of transferring the operation of all the collective farms' power facilities to state organizations. (Applause.) ...

The integrated mechanization of farming is being hampered above all by the shortage of tractors. Yet the supply of them in the republic not only has not increased but has even declined of late. The needs of the republic's state and collective farms for grain- and silage-harvesting combines, beet-harvesting machines, earth-moving equipment, tractor attachments and loaders are not being fully met.

Guided by the advice of Academician T. D. Lysenko, our state and collective farms are improving the production of organic fertilizers with every year. On the majority of collective farms genuine factories have been set up for the production of peat-manure, manure-earth and organic-mineral composts. But the norms of application of these fertilizers are still inadequate. In order to obtain high yields, our collective and state farms must annually apply at least ten tons of organic fertilizers per hectare of sown area. With the equipment they have at their disposal, labor expenditures simply to produce and apply this quantity of fertilizer come to three and four man-days per hectare. This largely explains the high cost of agricultural production on our collective and state farms.

Integrated mechanization in animal husbandry is proceeding slowly: There is a shortage of pipe and pumps, motors, electrical equipment, milking equipment, machines for distributing fodder and other equipment.

The January plenary session of the Party Central Committee recognized the need for a considerable increase in capital investments in agriculture from above-plan accumulations obtained in certain branches of heavy industry. This plenary session decision should be implemented more rapidly.

The draft of the Party Program calls for a fundamental reorganization of the collective farm village. ... Unfortunately, the republic Construction and Architecture Committee and also Union organizations are doing little in this direction. Intercollective-farm construction organizations have existed locally for several years now. They are doing considerable work, but they have not yet been legally recognized as contract organizations and therefore cannot even obtain bank credits. They are being poorly supplied with materials and receive hardly any equipment. These problems should be resolved in the U.S.S.R. government. ...

Rashidov

SPEECH BY COMRADE SH. R. RASHIDOV, FIRST SECRETARY OF THE UZBEKISTAN COMMUNIST PARTY CENTRAL COMMITTEE. (Pravda, Oct. 20, pp. 5-6. 3,100 words. Excerpts:) ... The economy and culture of Soviet Uzbekistan are developing at rapid, unprecedented rates. ... In the past five years the industry of the Uzbek Republic produced 50% more than in the preceding five-year period. ...

By the will of the Party and the people, incalculable resources of natural gas, which lay dormant for centuries in the region of Bukhara, have been placed at the service of man. According to estimates, reserves of "blue fuel" there exceed 2,000,000,000,000 cubic meters. The gas pipeline that extended to Tashkent has gone farther and entered fraternal Kazakhstan. Construction has begun on the large new Bukhara-Urals trunklines, which will be more than 2,000 km. long. (Applause.) ...

The average annual rates of industrial development in Uzbekistan in the first three years of the seven-year period are outstripping the control figures. The republic's industry fulfilled the nine-month plan ahead of schedule and is now completing the ten-month program. ...

With Comrade Khrushchev's name are linked radical changes in Soviet cotton farming, as in all branches of the national economy. We are indebted to the wisdom, boldness and devotion to principle of Nikita Sergeyevich and to his constant concern for easing the labor of cotton growers for the fact that cotton farming is now developing on a firm basis of technical progress. It is thanks precisely to this that our republic in the past five years gave the homeland 2,200,000 tons more cotton than in the preceding five-year period. The peoples of Uzbekistan with all their souls, from pure hearts, name Nikita Sergeyevich Khrushchev their closest friend, their dear and beloved teacher. (Applause.)

The cotton growers of our republic, selflessly overcoming the difficulties arising from the lack of water this year, have now grown a rich harvest. They have already sold the state more than 2,150,000 tons of cotton—almost 400,000 tons more than in 1960. (Applause.) ...

All basic processes in cotton cultivation are now mechanized. The problem of machine harvesting of the crop is being successfully solved. Tests are now going on in the republic of wonderful new models of cotton-harvesting machines, the best of which will be put into series production. ...

There has been large-scale modernization of existing irrigation systems and construction of new ones, and the supply of water to irrigated lands has been improved through the construction of large new reservoirs. This has made it possible to irrigate and put into cultivation more than 200,000 hectares of virgin land and to improve 400,000 hectares of land. ...

Utilizing the wealth of experience of the subjugators of the Golodnaya Steppe, we can in a short period establish a large new cotton region in the Karshinskaya Steppe. The construction in the republic of the Garvak, Tyuya-Muyun and Takhia-Tash hydroelectric systems will make possible the integrated solution of the task of irrigating and increasing power capacities, and the construction of the Kamnyr-Ravat reservoir will make it possible to increase the supply of water to the Fergana Valley and fraternal Kirgizia. We ask prompter consideration of questions pertaining to the development of these and other projects in the sphere of irrigation and reclamation. ...

In the years since the 20th Party Congress science and culture have undergone further tempestuous development. We now have 120 scientific institutions, among them a nuclear physics institute; there is a large computing center with modern electronic machines. The number of specialists graduated annually from higher or secondary specialized schools has reached almost 30,000. We joyously report to the Congress that approximately 96% of the republic's schools have changed over to single-shift instruction. (Applause.) ...

Kunayev

SPEECH BY COMRADE D. A. KUNAYEV, FIRST SECRETARY OF THE KAZAKHSTAN COMMUNIST PARTY CENTRAL COMMITEE. (Pravda, Oct. 20, pp. 6-7. 3,700 words. Condensed text:) In the year since the 20th Party Congress more than 9,000,000,000 rubles has been invested in the republic's economy, or 50% more than in the preceding 35 years. ...

The republic's working people, carrying out the decisions of the 20th and 21st Party Congresses, laid the firm foundation of a powerful new metallurgical base in the eastern part of the country. With the commissioning of two blast furnaces, three coking batteries and chemical shops at the Karaganda Metallurgical Plant and of the Sokolovka-Sarbai Ore-Enriching Combine and the Atasu mines, Kazakhstan has begun to produce pig iron and coke for the first time and has increased its extraction of iron ore thirtyfold. A reliable raw material base has thereby been created not only for Kazakhstan's Magnitka but for the entire metallurgical industry of the Southern Urals.

Nonferrous metallurgy, one of the leading branches of industry in our republic, has developed at a rapid pace. The opening of new capacity in Dzhezkazgan and in the Ore Altai and the modernization of such large enterprises as the Balkhash and Ust-Kamenogorsk Lead and Zinc Combines and the Chimkent Lead Plant have made it possible to increase the output of copper, lead and zinc. The foundations of an aluminum industry have been laid. The Karaganda and Ekibastuz coal basins, where 13 pits and a large opencast mine have been built since the 20th Party Congress, now yield approximately 35,000,000 tons of coal a year. The output of the machine-building and chemical industries, light industry and the food industry has grown considerably. With the preschedule opening of the Chimkent, Semipalatinsk and Karaganda Plants, a cement industry has been established with a capacity of about 3,000,000 tons a year. Construction of the Dzhetygara Asbestos Combine, one of the largest in the country, has begun on the basis of the rich deposits in the Turgai Steppe.

Great changes have taken place in the power industry. The opening of the Bukhtarma Hydroelectric Station on the Irtysh and of a number of large thermal power plants has increased the republic's power supply by almost 1,000,000 kw. ...

Kazakhstan's industry is successfully fulfilling the assignments of the seven-year plan and on the basis of technical progress is developing at faster rates than envisaged by the control figures. In the first two years of the seven-year period gross industrial production increased 28%, instead of the planned 22%. Labor productivity in 1960 was 20.7% higher than in 1958.

Far-reaching changes have taken place in agriculture. ... In the steppes of Kazakhstan 834 state farms have now been set up where the field tents of the first settlers once stood. (Applause.) ...

Life has cruelly mocked the would-be prophets of the anti-Party group that was exposed and routed by the Central Committee. The very virgin lands they considered barren have enabled Kazakhstan to increase grain output immeasurably. Whereas in the eight years prior to 1954 the republic produced only 799,000,000 poods of grain for the market, in the subsequent eight years, despite the unfavorable climatic conditions that marked several of them, 4,370,000,000 poods of grain were sold to the state. (Applause.) ...

Practical measures have now been worked out and are being implemented that will make it possible in the future to triple the gross grain harvest, increasing it to 3,500,000,000 poods or more, and to increase the output of marketable grain to at least 2,000,000,000 poods a year. (Applause.) ...

First and foremost we set ourselves the task of considerably improving the structure of sown areas, eliminating the dominance of a single crop and carrying out a complex of measures that will guarantee a sharp rise in yields. ...

In the near future Kazakhstan will become one of the chief rice regions of the country, and in 1962 it will considerably increase the output of grain corn. It must be said that corn has made a fine showing in all zones of the republic, including the virgin lands. ...

In order to increase the output of grain, we must also develop new tracts of virgin land and increase areas under grain crops from 22,000,000 to 28,000,000 hectares; spring wheat will account for 50% to 55% of the entire sown area, leguminous crops for 30% to 35% and corn for up to 10%. ...

Thanks to the construction of new enterprises and the expansion of existing ones, it is possible to organize the production of fertilizers in quantities that will fully meet the needs not only of our republic but of all the republics of Central Asia. ...

It is quite feasible to increase the number of sheep in Kazakhstan to 100,000,000 in the near future. In this connection it is necessary to develop millions of hectares of pasturelands, to carry out large-scale work on installations for supplying water to them and to set up 400 to 500 new state sheep-raising farms. Questions of developing sheep raising warrant special consideration. In our conditions sheep raising is an exceedingly advantageous branch of animal husbandry. Economists have estimated that every sheep that our state farms had at the beginning of the year will yield the state 21 rubles net profit. This confirms once again the enormous economic effectiveness of sheep raising and the possibility of producing a large quantity of cheap mutton and wool in the republic. ...

We wholly agree with Nikita Sergeyevich Khrushchev's opinion, stated in the report, that in order to achieve the greatest economic effectiveness of capital investments and to gain time, the organizations of new, large-scale metallurgical production in the eastern part of the country should proceed through the accelerated development of the rich resources of our republic. In the Greater Turgai region alone, where about 20% of all the country's iron ore reserves are concentrated, it is expedient to speed the construction of the Kachar and Lisakovo Ore-Enriching Combines and to increase the capacity of the Sokolovka-Sarbai Combine to 55,000,000 to 60,000,000, instead of 26,000,000 tons of ore a year. This will make it possible not only to supply plenty of ore to the entire metallurgical industry of the Southern Urals, but also to build next to the Karaganda Plant a second enterprise of equal capacity. The existence of an already operating production base and the proximity of deposits of coking coal and fluxes are convincing evidence that the establishment of a similar enterprise, and also of two large metallurgical plants in Kustanai Province, would be economically advantageous to the state. Kazakhstan geologists have discovered valuable oil-bearing deposits on the Mangyshlak Peninsula. In view of the fact that the construction of roads has begun on Mangyshlak, the question now arises of developing the oil-bearing deposits of this peninsula. Our republic can become a major new oil base of the country, which will eventually yield up to 100,000,000 tons of liquid fuel a year. ...

The extensive use of the rich resources of both industry and agriculture sharply demands a fundamental solution to the water problem. Even today the development of the republic's production forces is being hampered in a number of cases by a shortage of water. This is why, in addition to considerably improving the use of underground waters, it is necessary to take measures to build the Irtysh-Karaganda and Volga-Urals Canals in the next few years, as well as reservoirs on the Chu, Syr-Darya and Ili Rivers. ...

The population is growing at an unprecedented rate. It has increased by almost 3,000,000 since 1956. The gigantic construction projects and virgin-land expanses are attracting patriots from all parts of the country. Representatives of more than 100 peoples and nationalities of the Soviet Union today live and work in Kazakhstan in a single fraternal family. ...

Chou En-lai

SPEECH BY COMRADE CHOU EN-LAI, VICE-CHAIRMAN OF THE CENTRAL COMMITTEE OF THE COMMUNIST PARTY OF CHINA AND MEMBER OF THE POLITBURO OF THE CHINESE COMMUNIST PARTY CENTRAL COMMITTEE. (Pravda, Oct. 20, p. 7. 2,300 words. Condensed text:) Dear comrades! The delegation of the Communist Party of China considers it a great honor to be present, by invitation of the Central Committee of the Communist Party of the Soviet Union, at the 22nd Congress of the Communist Party of the Soviet Union. On behalf of the Central Committee of the Communist Party of China and in the name of all members of the Communist Party of

China and of the Chinese people as a whole, let me convey to this Congress, and through the Congress to the great Communist Party of the Soviet Union and the great Soviet people, the warmest fraternal congratulations and expressions of the highest respect. (Applause.)

We wholeheartedly wish the 22nd Congress of the Communist Party of the Soviet Union success in its work.

Since the 21st Congress of the Communist Party of the Soviet Union, the Soviet people, led by the Central Committee of the Communist Party of the Soviet Union with Comrade Khrushchev at its head, have scored brilliant victories in the full-scale building of communism. (Applause.)

We are delighted to see the national economy of the Soviet Union making steady advances. ...

Twice this year the Soviet Union has successfully launched into space manned spaceships, which triumphantly orbited the earth and returned to it. This new exploit in man's conquest of space is still more conclusive evidence that the Soviet Union is leaving the U.S.A. farther and farther behind in major fields of science and technology. It demonstrates strikingly that the socialist system is incomparably superior to the capitalist system. (Applause.)

This Congress of the Communist Party of the Soviet Union will adopt a new Party Program. ...

The Chinese Communists and the Chinese people are certain that under the leadership of the Communist Party of the Soviet Union, the Soviet people will score great new victories in their efforts to make a reality of this magnificent plan for the building of communism. (Applause.)

Together with the peoples of the other socialist countries, the Soviet people are exerting enormous efforts to uphold world peace, relax international tension, bring about general disarmament, maintain the peaceful coexistence of states with different social systems and extend support to the national-democratic movement in Asia, Africa and Latin America. A short while ago the Soviet Union advanced proposals that a German peace treaty be concluded and the situation in West Berlin normalized on that basis. In the face of the serious situation that had resulted from intensification of the arms race and military preparations, the breakdown of the conference on the cessation of nuclear testing and the rejection of disarmament by the U.S.A., the Soviet Union was forced to take very important steps such as the resumption of test explosions of nuclear weapons. These proposals and these steps represent important moves to uphold world peace and protect the security of the socialist camp, and to put a stop to imperialist military adventures; they are fully consistent with the interests of the peoples of the whole world. The Chinese people fully support all of these important moves by the Soviet Union aimed at defending world peace. (Applause.)

The way in which the present international situation is developing fully substantiates the scientific Marxist-Leninist analysis given in the Statement of the 1960 conference of representatives of Communist and Workers' Parties.

The forces of the socialist camp and its international influence are growing very rapidly. The strides in construction in all the countries of the socialist camp are reinforcing the positions of peace and socialism all over the world. The burgeoning national-democratic movement in Asia, Africa and Latin America, supported by the socialist camp, has already become a great force in the struggle against the new and the old colonialism and internal reaction. The class struggle in the capitalist world is becoming ever sharper, the capitalist system is continuing its decline and decay and the imperialist camp headed by the U.S.A. is day by day nearer the point of breaking up. This means that the preponderance of the forces of socialism over the forces of imperialism, of the forces of peace over the forces of war, is today becoming more and more apparent in the world arena. The correlation of forces in the world has created a situation that is extremely favorable for the peoples' struggle for universal peace, national liberation, democracy and socialism. (Applause.)

The struggle of the peoples of the socialist countries for the cause of revolution and construction, the revolutionary struggle of the peoples of the capitalist countries, the liberation movement of oppressed nations and the general democratic movement and struggle of the masses for peace all over the world are today flowing together into a common stream which is undermining and demolishing the imperialist system. The Cuban revolution is advancing with giant strides and successfully parrying the aggressive and interventionist intrigues of the U.S.A. The Laotian people, despite U.S. interference, have won tremendous victories in the struggle to uphold their independence and neutrality. The peoples of the southern part of Vietnam and the southern part of Korea are engaged in a selfless struggle for the peaceful unification of their countries. The Algerian people are steadily gaining strength in the struggle for their independence. The peoples of the Congo, Angola and Cameroon and other African peoples still being oppressed by the new and the old colonialism have engaged colonialism in fierce combat, seeking to smash its chains. In Japan and Brazil, everywhere the fiendish grip of American imperialism extends, the patriotic struggle of the peoples against that imperialism, their struggle to uphold national independence, is building up.

In the principal capitalist countries the masses of workers and peasants are waging a struggle against oppression, a struggle to win and defend democratic rights and to improve their living conditions. The struggle of the masses to defend world peace is spreading to every corner of the globe. No matter how savagely the imperialists and reactionaries of various countries may behave, and no matter how tortuous the path of struggle may be, the oppressed nations and peoples, encountering support from the socialist camp, are certain to win out over imperialism; the forces of peace, with the socialist camp and the international working class as their nucleus, are certain to win out over the forces of war. Inevitable doom awaits the imperialists and all reactionaries. (Applause.)

As the Statement of the Moscow conference points out, however, as long as imperialism lasts, the soil for aggressive wars will remain. The worst enemy of peace is American imperialism. It is the bulwark of present-day colonialism and international reaction, the prime force of aggression and war. The whole world sees today that the Kennedy administration is even more insidious and adventurous. Seeking to make itself more attractive with an "olive branch," it spouts "peace," "progress" and "the prosperity of mankind," while under the cloak of "peace" it is actually making even more frenzied efforts in the arms race and in preparing for war. This administration has been the direct organizer of an attack on Cuba and has provoked civil war in Laos, and it is preventing the reaching of an agreement at the Geneva conference. It is this administration which, making use of the so-called Berlin crisis, is raising a frantic war clamor and threatening war, incessantly engineering military provocations in Berlin, Cuba, Laos, South Vietnam and South Korea and on territory belonging to our country—Taiwan. It is this administration which is appropriating the largest sums the U.S.A. has ever spent for military purposes in time of peace, which is making intensive preparations for local wars and nuclear war against the peoples of the whole world. The face of American imperialism as the common enemy of the peoples of the whole world has been completely exposed.

All the actions of American imperialism indicate that we still face the danger of war and that the peoples of all lands must redouble their vigilance. The struggle against imperialist aggression and the defense of world peace remain, as they have been, a task of extreme urgency for the peoples of all countries. If the socialist camp, the international working class, the national-liberation movement and all peace-loving peoples and states make common cause, form a united front to combat the policy of aggression and war being pursued by the imperialist circles headed by the U.S.A. and wage an unflagging struggle, world peace is certain to be preserved. (Applause.)

Our country steadfastly upholds solidarity with the Soviet Union and the other socialist countries and, together with them, is carrying on an unflagging struggle for world peace and the progress of mankind. We are actively supporting the liberation struggle of oppressed nations and oppressed peoples and resolutely opposing the policy of aggression and war being pursued by the imperialist circles headed by the U.S.A. We stand at all times for the peaceful coexistence of countries with different social systems on the basis of the five principles and are exerting tremendous efforts to achieve it. In recent years China has concluded treaties of friendship or treaties of friendship and non-aggression with many countries of Asia and Africa, including Yemen, Burma, Nepal, Afghanistan, Guinea, Cambodia, Indonesia and Ghana. The conclusion of these treaties not only strengthens and develops the friendly relations between China and these

countries but also makes a useful contribution to the defense of world peace.

The Chinese people, under the leadership of the Central Committee of the Communist Party of China headed by Comrade Mao Tse-tung, and holding high three red banners—the banners of the general line, of the great leap and of the people's commune—are struggling to turn China into a socialist country with modern industry, modern agriculture and modern science and culture. We are aware that we are bound to encounter difficulties on the path of our advance. In the past three years our country's agriculture has suffered natural calamities. But no difficulties can daunt the solidly united and tempered Chinese people. We are positive that we shall be able with our own hands, by hard work, to surmount the difficulties and realize our great goal. (Applause.)

The Moscow conferences of representatives of Communist and Workers' Parties held in 1957 and 1960 were conferences of great historic importance for the international Communist movement. The Declaration of 1957 and the Statement of 1960 are the common program of action for the Communist and Workers' Parties. The Declaration and the Statement point out that the solidarity of the socialist camp and of the international Communist movement is the guarantee of victory in the struggle of the peoples of all countries for universal peace, national liberation, democracy and socialism. Upholding this great solidarity is an internationalist duty for us as Communists. (Applause.)

The Declaration and Statement point out that the solidarity of the socialist camp and of the international Communist movement is the nucleus for even broader cohesion on a world-wide scale. This solidarity of ours is cemented by common ideals and a common cause. It has been reinforced and developed in the joint struggle against common enemies. It rests on the foundation of Marxism-Leninism and proletarian internationalism. This solidarity of ours has stood up under testing, and there are no forces capable of undermining it. Our socialist camp of 12 fraternal countries, from the Korean People's Democratic Republic to the German Democratic Republic and from the Democratic Republic of Vietnam to the People's Republic of Albania, constitutes a single whole. Our socialist countries and our Communist Parties fraternally support and cooperate with one another on the basis of independence and complete equality. We must unite as closely as possible, must cherish our solidarity as the apple of our eye and on no account permit any statements or actions detrimental to that solidarity. (Applause.)

We hold that if, unfortunately, disputes and disagreements have arisen among the fraternal parties and fraternal countries, we should resolve them patiently, being guided by the spirit of proletarian internationalism and by the principles of equality and the achievement of identity of views through consultations. Open unilateral condemnation of a fraternal party does not make for solidarity, does not help settle issues. Openly exposing disputes between fraternal parties and fraternal countries for enemies to see cannot be regarded as a serious, Marxist-Leninist approach. Such an approach can only pain friends and gladden foes. The Communist Party of China sincerely hopes that the fraternal parties between which the disputes and disagreements exist will reunite on the basis of Marxism-Leninism and on the basis of mutual respect for independence and equality. I think that this is the position that we Communists should take on this question.

At present the imperialist circles headed by the U.S.A., using the struggle against communism as a facade, are engaged in aggressive and expansionist activities. American imperialism and the Yugoslav revisionist group are doing all they can to drive a wedge into the progressive forces of the world and to undermine their solidarity. Under the circumstances the solidarity and unity of the whole socialist camp and of the whole international Communist movement take on supreme importance. In solidarity there is strength. If there is solidarity any difficulty can be surmounted. In the face of the solidarity of the forces of world socialism, the solidarity of oppressed nations and peoples and of the peace-loving peoples and states of the whole world, the mad designs of the imperialists and their stooges are all sure to founder. (Applause.)

Between the peoples of China and the Soviet Union there is a deep friendship of long standing. Both in revolution and in construction our people have received and are continuing to receive support and assistance from the Soviet people and the Communist Party of the Soviet Union, for which we here once more tender sincere thanks. (Applause.) Both in the building of socialism and communism and in the struggle against imperialist aggression and for world peace, the peoples of our two countries and the peoples of the other socialist countries have always rendered each other assistance, cooperated with one another, waged a joint struggle and advanced shoulder to shoulder. This great solidarity and friendship between the peoples of our two countries will live forever, even as the Yangtse and the Volga will flow eternally. (Applause.)

Let me now read a message of greetings to the Congress from the Central Committee of the Communist Party of China, signed by Comrade Mao Tse-tung, Chairman of the Central Committee of the Communist Party of China. (Applause.)

"To the 22nd Congress of the Communist Party of the Soviet Union. Dear Comrades! ... Close solidarity and friendship have always existed between the C.P.C. and the C.P.S.U. and between the peoples of China and of the Soviet Union. This solidarity and friendship, which rest on the foundation of Marxism-Leninism and proletarian internationalism, are of exceptional importance for the triumph of the common cause of the peoples of the whole world—the struggle against imperialism, for world peace and for the progress of mankind. The solidarity and

Chou Leaves Moscow

COMRADE CHOU EN-LAI LEAVES MOSCOW. (Pravda, Oct. 24, p. 1. Complete text:) In connection with the forthcoming session of the All-China Assembly of People's Representatives, Comrade Chou En-lai, Vice-Chairman of the Chinese Communist Party Central Committee and Premier of the State Council of the Chinese People's Republic, and head of the C.P.R. delegation to the 22nd Congress of the C.P.S.U., left Moscow for home by plane Oct. 23, 1961.

Comrade Chou En-lai was seen off at Vnukovo Airport by Comrade N. S. Khrushchev, First Secretary of the C.P.S.U. Central Committee; Comrade F. R. Kozlov, member of the Presidium and Secretary of the C.P.S.U. Central Committee; Comrade N. V. Podgorny, member of the Presidium of the C.P.S.U. Central Committee and First Secretary of the Ukraine Communist Party Central Committee; Comrade A. A. Gromyko, member of the C.P.S.U. Central Committee and U.S.S.R. Minister of Foreign Affairs; Comrades Yu. V. Andropov and N. R. Mironov, department heads of the C.P.S.U. Central Committee; Comrade S. V. Chervonenko, U.S.S.R. Ambassador to the Chinese People's Republic; Comrade L. N. Tolkunov, assistant department head in the C.P.S.U. Central Committee; and high-ranking officials of the C.P.S.U. Central Committee apparatus.

Comrade Chou En-lai was also seen off by Comrade Peng Chen, acting head of the C.P.R. delegation to the 22nd C.P.S.U. Congress and member of the Secretariat of the Chinese Communist Party Central Committee; Comrades Kang Shen, Tao Chu and Liu Hsiao, members of the C.P.R. delegation; and staff members of the C.P.R. Embassy in the U.S.S.R.

TO COMRADE N. S. KHRUSHCHEV, FIRST SECRETARY OF THE C.P.S.U. CENTRAL COMMITTEE, THE KREMLIN, MOSCOW. (Pravda, Oct. 25, p. 1; Izvestia, Oct. 26. Complete text:) Dear Comrade N. S. Khrushchev:

In leaving the borders of our great ally, I express to you and to the Central Committee of the Communist Party of the Soviet Union sincere gratitude for the cordial welcome and warm concern shown us. May the great eternal and indestructible friendship between the peoples of China and the Soviet Union flourish forever. From aboard the plane.   CHOU EN-LAI

friendship between our two parties and our two peoples have stood up under testing and are eternal and inviolable. (Applause.)

"With all our hearts we wish the 22nd Congress of the Communist Party of the Soviet Union success in its work. We wish the Soviet people, led by the Communist Party of the Soviet Union, great new strides in the struggle to build communism, uphold world peace and further the progress of mankind. (Applause.)

"Hail to the great Soviet people! (Applause.)

"Hail to the great and glorious Communist Party of the Soviet Union! (Applause.)

"Hail to the eternal and inviolable solidarity and friendship of the peoples of China and the Soviet Union! (Applause.)

"Hail to the great solidarity of the socialist camp! (Applause.)

"Hail to the great solidarity of the peoples of the whole world! (Applause.)

"Hail to Marxism-Leninism! (Applause.)—MAO TSE-TUNG, Chairman of the Central Committee of the Communist Party of China. Oct. 14, 1961." (Stormy, prolonged applause. All rise.)

Gomulka

SPEECH BY COMRADE WLADYSLAW GOMULKA, FIRST SECRETARY OF THE CENTRAL COMMITTEE OF THE POLISH UNITED WORKERS' PARTY. (Pravda, Oct. 20, p. 8; Izvestia, Oct. 21, pp. 7-8. 2,300 words. Condensed text:) Dear comrades! ... The 22nd Congress of the Communist Party of the Soviet Union is an event worthy of our epoch, eloquently symbolic of our time. ...

In no corner of the globe is there a people that could be unconcerned about the question that was the keynote of both reports—the central question of the day, the question of war and peace. And although no one could have had any doubt about the stand the Soviet Union would take on this question, still, everything that Comrade Khrushchev has said on the subject from this rostrum is of tremendous significance for the whole world. (Applause.) The 22nd Congress of the Communist Party of the Soviet Union is attracting the eyes of all the world's peoples, who are following it with sympathy, confidence and hope, since on the question that is most important for them—the question of averting the threat of a new world war and ensuring the peaceful coexistence of states regardless of their social systems—Comrade Khrushchev's reports express their will, their innermost hopes, their vital interests. (Applause.) The world public, and especially the peoples of Europe, waited with great impatience to hear what position the 22nd Congress would take on the question that today heads the list in international affairs—the question of concluding a peace treaty with Germany and settling the West Berlin problem on that basis.

What Comrade Khrushchev has said on this subject—expressing the position of the Central Committee of the Communist Party of the Soviet Union and, it can confidently be said, the position of the entire Congress—will meet with full approval and gratitude from the peoples of Europe and of the whole world. (Applause.) Our party and the Polish people, deeply and vitally interested in seeing all the vestiges of the second world war done away with, fully identify ourselves with this position. (Applause.)

The 22nd Congress of the Communist Party of the Soviet Union is a tremendous new contribution to the cause of world peace. (Applause.)

It has become the historic mission of the international Communist movement to save mankind from the catastrophe of a nuclear war. Last year's Moscow conference of 81 Communist and Workers' Parties laid special emphasis on this. But the decisive force preventing a new world war and frustrating the war plans of imperialism is the Soviet Union. (Applause.)

On behalf of our party and all the Polish people, allow me to express to you, comrade delegates, our very greatest appreciation for the decisive contribution that the Communist Party of the Soviet Union—the great party of Lenin—and the Soviet people as a whole are making to the preservation and consolidation of world peace. (Applause.) For it is you who bear the main burden of the noble historic mission of saving mankind from a new world war, from a nuclear catastrophe. Your Party Congress is of vast importance for all the world's peoples in this respect. (Applause.) ...

The drafts of the basic documents of the 22nd Congress of the Communist Party of the Soviet Union—the Party Program and Statutes—aroused enormous interest among our party's activists and its membership as a whole from the moment of their publication. Polish Communists regard them as a great achievement of creative Marxism-Leninism. These documents, drawing sound generalizations from the experience both of the Communist Party of the Soviet Union and of the entire international Communist movement, contain an admirable analysis of the social and political situation in today's world and outline in masterly fashion ways of solving the principal problems of our time. (Applause.)

The Polish United Workers' Party also considers the creative elaboration of the Leninist principles of Party life and the theory of the socialist state in the drafts of the new Program and Statutes of the Communist Party of the Soviet Union to be of very great theoretical and political importance. We see this as the logical extension of the ideas and decisions of the 20th Congress, which, having been implemented in the political practice of the Communist Party of the Soviet Union and taken up by the other Communist Parties, have become the motive power for the mighty growth of socialism's forces and of its ideological and moral influence on the minds of the masses. (Applause.)

The development of socialist democracy and its future prospects as concretely outlined in the new Program of the Communist Party of the Soviet Union show the paltriness of bourgeois pseudodemocratic phrasemongering and are convincing evidence that only socialism can create genuine democracy and ensure all-round freedom for man and his full development. (Applause.)

The decisions of the 20th Congress, which were of vast importance for the Communist Party of the Soviet Union, for the peoples of the Soviet Union and for all our parties—a fact emphasized in the 1957 and 1960 Statements of the Communist and Workers' Parties—at the same time helped to strengthen substantially the unbreakable unity of the socialist states on the basis of Leninist principles. It is six years since the 20th Congress. The Soviet Union's tremendous strides in this period, which delight and gladden us, and the wonderful prospects for further triumphs that will predetermine the future of mankind, prospects which were opened up to us by the new Program of the Communist Party of the Soviet Union and which Comrade Khrushchev has treated so thoroughly in this report, the strengthening of the socialist camp and the new strides made by the socialist states—these are all evidence of how wonderfully the decisions of the 20th Congress have passed the test of actual practice. (Applause.)

Only the leadership of the Albanian Party of Labor failed, to the detriment of its party, its people and the international workers' movement, to profit from these decisions and draw the necessary conclusions from them; this is now finally pushing that leadership onto the fatal path of defection from the basic principles of proletarian internationalism, from Marxism-Leninism and from the unity of all the countries in the socialist camp. (Applause.)

Speaking of the decisions of the 20th Congress, I want to reemphasize here at the 22nd Congress of the Communist Party of the Soviet Union that thanks to those decisions and to the Leninist policy of the Central Committee of the Communist Party of the Soviet Union headed by Comrade Khrushchev, our party, too, has grown stronger, routing revisionism and dogmatism, and has mustered new creative energies, and that relations between the Communist Party of the Soviet Union and our party and between the Polish and Soviet peoples have grown warmer and more fraternal than ever before. (Prolonged applause.) ...

Comrades! ... Just as the October Revolution in Russia ushered in a new epoch in the history of mankind and exerted a decisive influence on the formation of the world socialist system and the liberation of hundreds of millions of people on all continents from the yoke of imperialism, so implementation of the program of communist construction in the Soviet Union will open a new stage in the history of mankind, raise the class consciousness of working people in the capitalist countries to a high level and create unprecedented conditions for the worldwide victory of socialism. (Applause.)

This is the substance of the vanguard role performed by the Communist Party of the Soviet Union in the international Communist movement. (Applause.)

Your sessions, comrades, your decisions, your proceedings are of enormous significance for all the Communist and Workers' Parties, for all the socialist countries, for all peoples and for all mankind. (Applause.)

The proceedings of your Congress are being followed with special attention by our party, the Polish working class and our people as a whole. Deep and wonderful traditions of fraternity and solidarity unite the revolutionary movements of our peoples. Our fraternity and solidarity were born of common struggle and sealed with blood jointly shed. Today we are united by a common goal, the common struggle to build socialism and communism. We are with you in your unflagging struggle for a relaxation of international tension, for general disarmament, for the peaceful coexistence of all states and the elimination of the threat of war from the life of mankind, and for enduring world peace. (Applause.)

We are with you in your unrelenting struggle against imperialism, against the West German militarists and revanchists, for a peace treaty with Germany, for the conversion of West Berlin into a free city, in the struggle to win full respect for the sovereign rights of the German Democratic Republic, the first workers' and peasants' state in the history of Germany, and in the struggle for the security of Europe and of the whole world. (Applause.)

The Polish people, who were menaced with annihilation by Hitlerism, well know what liberation from the Hitlerite occupation by the Soviet Army meant for them and what the fact that the Soviet Union with its strength and invincible power, the socialist camp with its strength and might stand guard over our Oder and Neisse borders means for Poland today. (Applause.) Poland is trying to make the greatest possible contribution to the over-all strength of the Warsaw Treaty states, the strength that guards security and peace in Europe. (Applause.) ...

Hail to the great, glory-crowned party of Lenin—the Communist Party of the Soviet Union! (Applause.)

Hail to its tried and tested Leninist leadership headed by Comrade Khrushchev! (Applause.)

Hail to the inviolable fraternal friendship between the Polish and Soviet peoples! (Applause.)

Hail to the unshakable unity of all the countries in the socialist camp! (Applause.)

Hail to the unity of the international Communist movement! (Applause.)

Hail to mankind's common cause of socialism and peace, and may it triumph! (Stormy, prolonged applause. All rise.)

Brezhnev

SPEECH BY COMRADE L. I. BREZHNEV, CHAIRMAN OF THE PRESIDIUM OF THE U.S.S.R. SUPREME SOVIET. (Pravda, Oct. 21, pp. 2-3; Izvestia, pp. 4-5. 6,500 words. Condensed text:) Comrades! ... The Central Committee of our party pursued a genuinely Leninist general line in carrying out truly magnificent tasks in the sphere of domestic and foreign policy in the period under review. The overcoming of the consequences of the Stalin cult, the restoration of Leninist norms of Party life, the further development of socialist democracy, the successful struggle for fulfillment of the seven-year plan, the consistent implementation of the Leninist policy of peaceful coexistence and the persistent struggle for peace—these above all characterize the activity of our party and its Central Committee. ...

These successes were assured thanks to the correct leadership of the Leninist Central Committee of our party. We owe these successes to the fact that the Central Committee is headed by an outstanding state and Party figure—Nikita Sergeyevich Khrushchev. (Stormy, prolonged applause.) His indefatigable energy and revolutionary ardor inspire all of us to militant deeds. Comrade Khrushchev is distinguished by great faith in the people and in the strength of our party, firmness and steadfastness in the conduct of its policy, implacability toward the enemies of communism, and boldness and determination in carrying out the domestic and foreign policies of the Party and the Soviet state. (Prolonged applause.) These qualities best characterize Comrade Khrushchev as a true Leninist who is consistently and creatively developing the great teaching of Marxism-Leninism. (Prolonged applause.) ...

As you know, comrades, at this sharp turn not everyone

proved capable of understanding the enormous importance that the restoration of Leninist norms of Party and state life and the all-round development of democracy had for our party. It was precisely on this abrupt frontier that the factionalists, dogmatists and skeptics who broke their ties with the people—Molotov, Kaganovich, Malenkov, Voroshilov, Bulganin, Pervukhin and Saburov, and Shepilov, who joined them—entered into an anti-Party collusion directed against the Leninist policy worked out by the 20th Party Congress. Burdened with the weight of the past and the mistakes and crimes that had been committed in this soil and for which they should bear responsibility to the Party and the people, they did not want to reconcile themselves to the restoration of Leninist principles and norms in the life and policy of our party. In both domestic and foreign policy they were and remained revisionists, sectarians and hopeless dogmatists, clinging to old, outdated forms and methods, refuting everything new that is born of life and stems from the interests and development of Soviet society. ...

The change and improvement in the style of all Party and state work are living evidence of the new element that we won in the struggle against the dogmatists and revisionists. This new element is now evident in everything—in the consistent implementation of the Leninist principle of collective leadership, in the regular conduct of Party Congresses and Central Committee plenary sessions, in the all-round development of criticism and the vitalization of the work of primary Party organizations and of every Communist. Today not one important state decision of the Party or government is adopted without consulting with the people, without their weighty word and direct participation. ...

Comrades! In noting the remarkable results of the implementation of the Leninist course restored by the 20th Party Congress, one cannot speak without a feeling of alarm and concern about the actions of the Albanian leaders, who of late have been undermining step by step the foundations of the friendship between our countries and between the C.P.S.U. and the Albanian Party of Labor.

As members of a Leninist party and as internationalists, we can state with complete confidence that everything necessary was done on the part of our party, its Central Committee and Comrade N. S. Khrushchev personally to ensure that Soviet-Albanian relations would develop and grow stronger. The leaders of the Albanian Party of Labor have themselves stated this many times. ...

The Albanian leaders, whipping up an atmosphere of the cult of the individual in their country, do not like the course of the 20th Congress of our party, the course of completely eliminating the consequences of the cult of the individual and ensuring inner-Party democracy and revolutionary legality. Today we speak with bitterness of this attempt of the leaders of the Albanian Party of Labor to sow dissension in the fraternal family of socialist countries. And we do so out of a deep conviction that there is only one way to prevent a fatal development of events, as Comrade N. S. Khrushchev pointed out in his report. This is the return of the Albanian leaders to the positions of internationalism, to the positions of friendship and cooperation with all the socialist countries in the interests of our great common cause. (Applause.)

Comrades! ... In our times, when the socialist system has become the decisive factor in world development, the Leninist peace-loving foreign policy of the Soviet Union and the other countries of the socialist camp assumes special importance, and in this sphere, too, new paths have been laid in recent years. Hardened methods and ossified dogmas have been discarded. The Party has restored in all its fullness and developed in accordance with the new conditions in the world the Leninist policy of peaceful coexistence, a policy that is deeply principled and at the same time flexible and closely linked with life. (Applause.) ...

Never has the prestige of our socialist homeland in the international arena been as great as today. Never has its peace-loving foreign policy been as active and at the same time as calm, confident and effective as in our times. ...

Our successes in the sphere of foreign policy in the period under review are indissolubly linked with the ebullient activity of Nikita Sergeyevich Khrushchev, indefatigably defending the cause of peace and the freedom of peoples. In his report Nikita Sergeyevich mentioned almost casually that he had to travel around the wide world to maintain direct contacts with

the leaders of other countries. He stated that there was nothing one could do, the situation demanded it. But we and you are well aware what a titanic task this was! Since the 20th Party Congress, Comrade N. S. Khrushchev has made more than 30 trips to 18 states of Europe, Asia and America. The routes of these trips extend on the map of the world from Sofia to New York, from Peking to London, from Helsinki to Jakarta, and each of them marked a new stage in strengthening the foreign policy positions of our country, developing fraternal friendship with the countries in the socialist camp or expanding cooperation with other states. And how many state and public figures, members of parliaments and representatives of business circles and the press has Comrade N. S. Khrushchev received in these years in the Soviet Union for extensive and frank talks on vital questions of international life! Sincerity and forthrightness, inflexible adherence to principle in upholding the interests of socialism and in defending universal peace and the rights of peoples to a free, independent life, fidelity to the principles of proletarian internationalism, invariable readiness for friendly cooperation with all countries on the basis of peaceful coexistence—all these are inalienable features of the Leninist foreign policy so successfully being carried out by our Soviet government and its head, Nikita Sergeyevich Khrushchev. (Prolonged applause.) ...

Direct contacts between the U.S.S.R. Supreme Soviet and the parliaments of other states and regular exchanges of delegations with different countries of the world have been developed extensively. In the past six years parliamentary figures from 57 countries, including delegations from a number of states of Asia, Africa and Latin America and many statesmen of the East and West representing the most diverse political parties and trends, have come to the Soviet Union. ...

Comrades! ... The Soviets have become truly all-embracing organizations of the people, an embodiment of their unity, and have turned into a school of public activity for millions of people. Suffice it to say that 1,822,000 Deputies, representing 138,000,000 voters, were elected to local Soviets alone in 1961. The Soviets, like a magnet, attract the broadest masses of the people. The Soviet aktiv now totals more than 20,000,000 people. All these people, by their sometimes unobtrusive but exceedingly important work, are making an invaluable contribution to our common cause.

Such new forms of enlistment of the working people in the work of the Soviets as the standing committees of Soviets, public departments of executive committees, people's public inspection services, groups of unsalaried instructors, and public councils in cultural, health and public education institutions have arisen in our country and have already become widespread. Millions of people from all segments of the population of our country—workers, collective farmers, the urban and rural intelligentsia, students and pensioners—are voluntarily participating in state administration, finding true moral satisfaction in this and not demanding any remuneration. This, comrades, is a living manifestation of the truly popular foundation of our state. It is one of the forms of implementation of the Party's line of gradual transformation of the agencies of state authority into communist public self-government.

Our party is responding to this new element in the work of the Soviets and creating all the conditions for the Soviets' development in this direction. In order that more and more hundreds of thousands and millions of people may pass through the school of state administration by way of the Soviets, the Party has set the task of renewing at least one-third of the membership of the agencies of state authority at each election. ...

Our party and government are not sparing funds to advance the public well-being. The state budget for 1961 calls for allocations of more than 27,000,000,000 rubles, or 35% of all budget expenditures, for social and cultural measures alone. ...

Not all our local organizations, including the Soviets, have had the proper sense of responsibility in the use of funds allocated by the state for these purposes. Is this not indicated, for example, by the fact that in Azerbaidzhan the plan for the first nine months of this year for opening general-education schools was only 66% fulfilled and for hospitals only 14%? Many new schools in Tambov and Kamchatka Provinces also were not ready to open at the beginning of the school year.

Matters fare no better with the use of funds allocated for the construction of preschool institutions. In the Belorussian and Armenian Republics, for example, in the first nine months of

1961 the plans for opening children's preschool institutions were met only 26% to 30%. In this same period the plans for putting children's preschool institutions into operation were not fulfilled in Belgorod and Magadan Provinces and in the Kabardino-Balkar Autonomous Republic. This situation is all the more intolerable in view of the fact that we have a shortage of children's institutions, and, as stated in Comrade N. S. Khrushchev's report, the Party deems it necessary to accelerate the construction of children's institutions. ...

The Leninist style of work that the Party and the Central Committee teach us presupposes leadership not by orders and instructions but above all by persuading people and organizing them, by thorough explanation and by giving practical consideration to the opinions and proposals of the masses themselves. ...

Great importance in this connection attaches to work with letters and complaints from the working people and the reception of voters by Deputies and Soviet officials. What official has not learned from the voters during a public reception true, if sometimes bitter, instances of shortcomings and defects in his work? ...

In receiving the working people and looking into their requests and petitions, every Soviet official must constantly remember that it is by his attitude toward visitors and the investigation of complaints, by his sincerity and adherence to principle, that the Soviet man judges our state apparatus. For all of us the day-by-day activity of Nikita Sergeyevich Khrushchev serves as an excellent example of a profoundly Party-like and sensitive attitude toward the working people's proposals, an ability to heed the voice of the common people. We all know well his ability to explain to the people in understandable and clear form the most complex questions, his constant vital bond with the people, the ability to draw inspiration and popular wisdom from this pure and bright source, his enormous organizational talent. These qualities have rightly won Nikita Sergeyevich the love and deep respect of our party and of all the Soviet people. (Prolonged applause.) ...

Mzhavanadze

SPEECH BY COMRADE V. P. MZHAVANADZE, FIRST SECRETARY OF THE GEORGIAN COMMUNIST PARTY CENTRAL COMMITTEE. (Pravda, Oct. 21, p. 3; Izvestia, pp. 5-6. 3,300 words. Excerpts:) ... Our entire party unanimously approved the Central Committee decision concerning the anti-Party group and rallied its ranks even more closely around the Leninist Central Committee. We must display constant vigilance and wage a struggle against those who distort the vital creative essence of Marxism-Leninism, against dogmatists and revisionists, against all those who try to shake the unity and solidity of the ranks of our party. The Party has always unwaveringly cast, and it will continue to cast, from its path factionalists of all shades and colors. (Applause.) ...

Comrades! ... In the past five or six years industry has further developed in Georgia. ...

It is necessary to note in particular that in this period new branches of industry have been established in the republic. We are proud that our industry is turning out both precise complex electronic devices and powerful up-to-date main-line electric locomotives. ...

In the first two years of the seven-year period alone, gross industrial output rose 15%, as against the 12% envisaged in the control figures. ...

The tea industry is developing successfully. Beginning in 1960, Georgia's tea growers have been giving the country more than 150,000 tons of tea leaf a year, whereas prior to 1960 the annual harvest of tea leaf was no more than 100,000 tons. This year, too, our tea growers have overfulfilled the plans and ensured the country the needed quantity of tea.

In his report Nikita Sergeyevich Khrushchev stressed the importance of carrying out irrigation and drainage work in the Transcaucasus; in particular, the further development of the subtropical economy of Georgia is directly linked with the draining of the Colchis swampland, only 60,000 hectares of whose 220,000 hectares have been drained. On the other hand, in order to increase farm output considerably in Eastern

Georgia and obtain stable harvests, it is necessary to carry out large-scale irrigation work in Kakhetia. It must be noted that the funds invested for these purposes will be recovered with interest in a very brief period. ...

Permit us delegates to the Congress from the Georgian Party organization, on behalf of the 220,000-strong detachment of Communists of Georgia and all the working people of the republic, to assure the Congress, the Party Central Committee and you, dear Nikita Sergeyevich, that the Communists and all the working people of Georgia, under the leadership of the Leninist Party Central Committee, will not spare efforts to carry out the decisions of the Congress and to fulfill the great program for the construction of communism in our country. (Prolonged applause.)

Voronov

SPEECH BY COMRADE G. I. VORONOV, VICE-CHAIRMAN OF THE PARTY CENTRAL COMMITTEE'S BUREAU FOR THE RUSSIAN REPUBLIC. (Pravda, Oct. 21, pp. 4-5; Izvestia, pp. 6-7. 7,000 words. Condensed text:) Comrades! ...

Comrades! ... Our Congress will serve as a new, grave warning to all sorts of apostates from Marxism, revisionists and dogmatists, who are trying to impede the socialist development of the peoples and to push the Communist and Workers' Parties from the correct, Leninist path.

Expressing the will of the almost 6,000,000-strong army of Communists of the Russian Federation and the aspirations and hopes of the entire population of the republic, we wholly and fully approve the political line and practical activity of the Leninist Party Central Committee headed by Nikita Sergeyevich Khrushchev. (Applause.) ...

Comrades! The Russian Federation has an enormous role to play in the establishment of the material and technical base of communism. ...

Our industry is successfully coping with the assignments of the seven-year plan. In 1959-1960 the Federation's gross industrial output increased 21%, as against the 16% stipulated in the control figures. ...

The growth of the technical equipment of our industry and the high creative activeness of the working people have made it possible, with a reduced working day, to increase labor productivity 14%. (Applause.)

All these, comrades, are good prerequisites for storming the new heights outlined in the draft Party Program. The present level of industrial output in the republic will be exceeded by 160% in the next ten-year period and by 480% in 20 years. (Applause.) In order to achieve this growth, it is necessary to make fuller use of our inexhaustible reserves and possibilities, to introduce automation and mechanization of production processes on a broader scale and to eliminate the substantial shortcomings in the work of industry and construction.

And we still have many shortcomings. Who does not know that the national economy is experiencing considerable difficulties with metal, that there is a shortage of tubing, that little new equipment and mineral fertilizer is being produced for the countryside, that hundreds of thousands of vehicles are without tires and that paper production is lagging? These difficulties could be overcome more quickly if the work of enterprises and construction projects were properly managed. Would it not be possible to move up the schedule for the opening of new capacity at the Cherepovets, Novo-Tulsky, Novolipetsk, Novosibirsk and Chelyabinsk Metallurgical Plants, at Magnitogorsk and at the Pervouralsk New Pipe Plant? If we were to speed up construction at the Yaroslavl, Moscow, Krasnoyarsk and Omsk Tire Plants, there would be no "famine" of automobile tires either. And is everything being done to obtain greater output at existing enterprises? If the modernized machines at the Solikamsk and Balakhna Pulp and Paper Combines were mastered more rapidly, for example, there would be no need to speak of the lag of these enterprises.

Thus, comrades, these shortcomings depend on us, on the level of management of industry and construction. Planning agencies are making many mistakes. Comrade Spiridonov correctly stated here today that they often do a poor job of coordinating production assignments with material and technical supply. The recently established All-Russian Economic Council is still directing industry and construction weakly and is giving little assistance to economic councils in practical questions of production development. ...

In recent years the Party Central Committee has done truly titanic work in advancing all branches of agriculture. It is now especially clear how dangerous and shameful were the attempts of the participants in the anti-Party group to swerve the Party and people from the true Leninist course. Our successes confirm again and again the utter bankruptcy of the skeptics and whiners, whom life has cast on the dump heap of history. These remarkable successes are clearly evident from the example of the Russian Federation also.

A total of 16,300,000 hectares of virgin and idle land has been developed and brought under cultivation in six years; this has already enabled the state to obtain an additional 3,200,000,000 poods of cheap grain. (Applause.) Last year 1,800,000,000 poods of grain was sold to the state, or 425,000,000 poods more than in 1955, prior to development of the virgin lands. By Oct. 15, 1961, the Federation's collective and state farms had gathered 1,828,000,000 poods of grain into the homeland's granaries. (Applause.)

Our animal husbandry has also moved ahead. Output of meat in 1960 was 31% higher, of milk 40% higher, of wool 27% higher and of eggs 46% higher than in 1955.

It should be admitted, however, that these achievements are more than modest. The republic's collective and state farms are not yet fully meeting the public demand for certain products, especially meat. Many provinces and territories of Siberia and the Urals have today not given what they promised and are still in debt to the country in the sale of grain, meat and milk. Thus little has yet been done. ...

In his report to the Congress, Nikita Sergeyevich Khrushchev quite rightly stated that by the end of the 20-year period the Russian Federation should produce up to 12,000,000,000 poods of grain a year. This is more than twice what was harvested in 1960. The Federation's collective and state farms will annually sell the state 4,000,000,000 to 5,000,000,000 poods of grain.

What must be done to achieve this? The main thing is to increase yields. ...

At the same time, we must do a great deal to raise farming standards sharply. In many territories, provinces and autonomous republics the fields are full of weeds, spring crops are planted on spring plowland and with poor seeds and low sowing norms, and very little local fertilizer is applied. Can there be a good harvest in, say, Omsk Province when the sowings there are sparse and choked with weeds? Or in Vladimir Province, where year after year they sow on spring plowland and essentially without fertilizers? ...

In animal husbandry as in no other branch of agriculture, backward methods of labor and production organization still prevail in our republic. It is no secret that there are large losses of livestock in a number of provinces, territories and autonomous republics because of lack of fodder and poor maintenance. Many lightweight and thin livestock, including young stock, are delivered.

It must be admitted that the blame for all this rests with the Party Central Committee's Bureau for the Russian Republic and the republic Council of Ministers, which have not always made the proper demands on local Party and Soviet agencies and have sometimes ignored glaring cases of mismanagement. ...

The main trend in the development of animal husbandry is the change-over to year-round stall maintenance of livestock. We have many farms that have become convinced from experience that livestock must be fed rather than pastured. ...

The new method, combined with untethered maintenance of livestock, the use of the "herring-bone" type of milking unit and large-group feeding of pigs and poultry, will make communal animal husbandry a highly mechanized branch in which expenditures of manual labor will drop to a minimum. Then it will be possible for one person to tend at least 100 cows, or 1,500 to 2,000 pigs. or 10,000 to 12,000 hens. These figures are not fantasy; they reflect the achievements of our best livestock farmers.

Unfortunately, we still have managers who avoid the new,

do not understand the economic advantage of progressive methods and assess the labor of livestock raisers from old positions. ...

In the Russian Federation it is planned to have 40 head of cattle, including 17 cows, per 100 hectares of land by 1980. This is more than a twofold increase.

This is why the question of livestock premises arises especially acutely at present. It is necessary to build more facilities and to build from standard designs with maximum use of local materials. ...

In 1955-1960 labor productivity on the republic's collective farms increased 44% and on the state farms 28%. But these rates of growth cannot be considered satisfactory. In order to carry out the instructions of the 21st Party Congress on raising labor productivity, the annual increase in the time remaining to the end of the seven-year period must be 13% to 15% on the collective farms and 9% to 10% on the state farms. The path to this is clear: the integrated mechanization of all processes and the use of means of automation and systems of machinery with high technical-economic indices. ...

We have not yet completely reorganized the agricultural agencies. The new structure requires further inprovement and tightening. It cannot be considered normal that the Russian Republic Ministries of Agriculture and State Farms and the majority of territory and province administrations and autonomous-republic Ministries of Agriculture are located in the cities and are thus remote from the collective and state farms and the research institutes. There have also been bureaucratic distortions in management of the state farms: More than 200 unnecessary trusts have been set up in the province and territory centers; these have a large administrative apparatus and have drawn experienced specialists from the state farms.

It should be admitted that the Party Central Committee's Bureau for the Russian Republic, the Council of Ministers of the republic and local Party agencies did not disclose these mistakes in good time. Only the intervention of the Party Central Committee helped to rectify the situation. The staffs of the administrations and trusts have been sharply reduced; the trusts themselves are being moved to large advanced state farms, and the heads of the trusts also now serve as directors of these state farms.

All agricultural agencies of the republic will soon be moved from city asphalt to rural expanses. The Ministry of Agriculture is already beginning to function at the Yakhromsky State Farm, and the Ministry of State Farms will move to the Dawn of Communism State Farm in Moscow Province. (Applause.) ...

It must be said that some executives are less concerned about obtaining high yields than about trying to get lower assignments. Apparently it does not matter to these people that the population will not receive an uninterrupted supply of certain food products; they seek an easy life. This, comrades, is a dangerous phenomenon. The people will not tolerate such leaders, as was the case, for example, with Comrade Butuzov, former Secretary of the Penza Province Party Committee. And are officials who at the beginning of the year trumpet their pledges on every possible occasion and give assurances of "fulfillment" and "overfulfillment," but whose words remain words, really any better? This cannot go on any longer—and it is time to understand this!

Unfortunately, it happens in the practice of Party work that a leader who has proved to be helpless and has failed in one place is moved to another, no less responsible post. Nikita Sergeyevich justly criticized us for this. ...

The Party Central Committee's Bureau for the Russian Republic is giving special attention to strengthening executive cadres. Many young, energetic, well-trained organizers have been promoted of late to replace weak officials who are behind life. More than one-third of the territory and province Party committee secretaries have been replaced this year. Most of the new comrades have an engineering-technical or agricultural education. ...

Akhundov

SPEECH BY COMRADE V. YU. AKHUNDOV, FIRST SECRETARY OF THE AZERBAIDZHAN COMMUNIST PARTY CENTRAL COMMITTEE. (Pravda, Oct. 21, p. 5. 3,500 words. Condensed text:) ... Comrades! Soviet Azerbaidzhan has traversed a glorious path of struggle and victories and has become—as V. I. Lenin dreamed of seeing it—a model republic for the peoples of the East. The achievements of Soviet Azerbaidzhan are striking not only in comparison with our immediate neighbors Iran and Turkey, which we have left far behind, but in comparison with the most highly developed capitalist countries. ...

Permit me now to cite some comparative figures on the status of women in America, which proclaimed the Declaration of Independence in 1776, and in the Azerbaidzhan Republic, which has existed since 1920. In the U.S. Congress 17 out of the 537 members are women; in the Azerbaidzhan Supreme Soviet 90 out of 325 Deputies are women. In 1958 7% of the doctors in the U.S.A. were women, whereas in the Azerbaidzhan Republic 67% were women. (Applause.) In the Azerbaidzhan Republic 44% of the teachers, including school principals, are women; this is undoubtedly many times more than in the U.S.A. and other capitalist countries. In 20 years the number of women in our republic with higher education has increased almost sixfold. ...

What we have achieved in the sphere of the emancipation of women in 41 years the U.S.A. has not been able to accomplish in 185 years. (Applause.)

The Azerbaidzhan people are well aware that they owe all their achievements, their joyful today and even more joyful tomorrow, to the wise Leninist Party of Communists and to Soviet rule, and to the fraternal help of all the peoples of our country, above all the great Russian people. (Applause.)

There is a saying among our people that goes as follows: "If your friend a Russian be, right and broad the road for thee." (Applause.)

Comrades! ... In the period since the 20th Party Congress output of oil in Azerbaidzhan has increased 22%, of gas 340%, of electric power 66%, cement 85%, slate 140% and steel pipe 190%. ...

There are shortcomings in the oil and chemical industries whose elimination depends on Union agencies. ...

In the matter of drilling, things do not fare satisfactorily in our republic. Oilworkers justly complain about the lag of material and technical facilities for deep and superdeep drilling. Yet the rich oil and oil-and-gas deposits of Azerbaidzhan lie at great depths. Drilling at great depths is on the agenda in other regions of the country also. The U.S.S.R. government recently adopted a very important resolution on developing drilling in our country. Implementation of this resolution will make it possible to eliminate the gap between the technical level of drilling equipment and the requirements of deep and superdeep drilling and will thereby substantially influence the growth of oil and gas extraction in Azerbaidzhan. ...

The output of our republic's chemical enterprises is to increase sixfold in the seven-year period, and by 1980 the chemical industry's share in the republic's total industrial output will rise to 25%. Naturally the new chemical enterprises being built in our republic should be examples of the latest word in Soviet and foreign equipment and technology. It should be noted, however, that the plans of individual design institutes for the chemical industry sometimes embody miscalculations both in the selection of technological processes and the equipment to be provided for them and also with respect to the full and integrated use of raw material. This was the case with an installation for the production of herbicides. It was just completed this year, and the organic chemistry institute is already drawing up a new technological plan, since the existing method causes a considerable corrosion of the apparatus and the pipelines. The Sumgait Petrochemical Combine now under construction will eventually be one of the largest chemical enterprises in the country. But already a substantial deficiency is evident in the plan in that only 20% of the petroleum raw material will be used at the combine for the needs of chemistry, while the remaining 80%, in the form of various fractions, will again go back into fuel. Yet these fractions could be used to obtain valuable products that find application in the artificial fiber, plastics and synthetic rubber industries.

It should be noted that the principle of integrated solution is not always observed in deciding the question of developing the chemical and oil-refining industries. It is known, for example,

that catalytic cracking yields the cheapest intermediary products for the chemical industry, above all for the production of rubber. This necessitates expanding the construction of catalytic cracking and pyrolysis installations in Azerbaidzhan. Unfortunately, these questions remain undecided. ...

The existing technology for the production of lubricating oils at Baku plants is becoming obsolete and even now cannot fully ensure the growing requirements with respect to quality of lubricating oils. Baku's oil refiners have worked out a complex of measures whose introduction will raise the quality of oils to the level of present-day demands. Among the measures for which we ask consideration, a large place belongs to the proposal to expand the production of admixtures and reagents.

Comrades! ... The lag of the republic's agriculture, especially animal husbandry and cotton growing, and the work of the Azerbaidzhan Party organization in this connection were justly and sharply criticized at plenary sessions of the Party Central Committee. This criticism helped the Party organization to assess the situation correctly and to direct the efforts of workers in the countryside into overcoming the existing lag in agriculture. We have achieved the first positive results. ... Last year the plans for the sale to the state of all basic farm products, with the exception of raw cotton, were fulfilled. ...

Thanks to the mass change-over to the new form of labor organization on the collective and state farms—the integrated mechanization of work in cotton farming and corn cultivation—expenditures of labor per centner of raw cotton dropped by one-half in two years, in the case of grain almost one-third and of corn more than two-thirds. ...

But the situation has been complicated by the worst drought in two decades. In the conditions of the capitalist system such a drought would be a national disaster, but here the population does not even feel it, because the Party Central Committee and the Soviet government have given the collective farms of our republic substantial help in the way of grain seed, credits and material resources. ...

A third of the cotton area has suffered greatly because of the shortage of irrigation water. This has created difficult conditions for cotton growing. As of Oct. 18, the collective and state farms had sold the state 55.63% of the raw cotton called for by the plan. ...

The loss of a large part of the winter grain and fodder crops has this year posed the task of obtaining high corn yields with particular sharpness. In zones supplied with water many collective farms and whole districts are obtaining a rich corn harvest. ...

Furtseva

SPEECH BY COMRADE YE. A. FURTSEVA, U.S.S.R. MINISTER OF CULTURE. (Pravda and Izvestia, Oct. 22, pp. 2-3. 7,000 words. Condensed text:) Comrade delegates! ... The enrichment of the national cultures is being fostered by the translation and extensive publication in all the republics of literary works produced in fraternal republics. For example, books and magazines are being published in our country in 89 languages of the peoples of the Soviet Union and in 47 foreign languages; in the past four years along, the peoples of the U.S.S.R. have more than doubled the translation and publication of one another's literary works. ...

Many theaters have begun to stage new operas, plays and ballets that have become favorites of the people. And it is particularly gratifying that plays on present-day themes should now form the basic repertoire. I shall cite just a few figures. Out of 1,114 Soviet plays staged in the country's theaters this year, 780, or more than 70%, are on present-day themes, that is, on the Soviet people's struggle to build a communist society in our country. (Applause.)

There have been substantial changes in the production of motion pictures. In the early 1950s the film studios turned out an average of six or seven pictures a year, whereas the number of feature films made last year alone came to more than 100; gifted young directors and actors, the future of Soviet cinema art, have developed at the studios. These days people in the most remote areas of the country see motion pictures. Movie attendance last year came to almost 4,000,000,000, not counting the enormous number of viewers who saw films on television. The network of projection units is growing. Completion of the seven-year-plan assignments in this sphere is running two years ahead of schedule. We now have a real chance of bringing the number of projection units up to between 118,000 and 120,000 as early as 1963, rather than by the end of the seven-year plan as scheduled. Some 3,000 movie houses seating 1,100,000 persons were built in the country in the period 1956-1961 alone. ...

Construction of rural cultural institutions has greatly increased. The rural localities currently have 115,000 clubs and Houses and Palaces of Culture, more than 100,000 libraries, some 85,000 projection units and hundreds of universities of culture. As Nikita Sergeyevich Khrushchev rightly said in the report of the Central Committee, we now have a great deal of work ahead of us in improving cultural services for the rural populace and accomplishing the bag tasks involved in eliminating essential distinctions between town and countryside. ...

The time has come for our artists, designers and master craftsmen in the applied arts to design highly artistic and original consumer goods of the very highest quality; Soviet people deserve this.

While speaking of the further development of all the professional arts, I should not neglect to mention the enormous development of amateur arts, which in recent years has taken on broad scope. Suffice it to say that there are now in existence some 600 amateur theaters (this is more than the number of professional theaters), which last year gave 22,000 performances; there are over 500,000 amateur groups and circles of various types in which more than 9,000,000 persons take part; 7,000 universities and schools of culture have been established; and there are about 1,000 amateur film studios. ...

Unfortunately, a good many literary works, plays and especially films are still produced that are far from adequate to the needs of the time, to the heightened requirements of the people, and that have been meeting with just criticism in the press, in letters from workers, and among the people.

The exacting Soviet audiences have been criticizing writers, playwrights, scenarists, film directors, composers and artists for these shortcomings.

What is the explanation for the fact that many mediocre and downright poor works still appear? Naturally, the reasons are many. The main one, however, is that some artists still have very feeble links with the life of the people and try to "get to know" that life, as they say, from a distance, from the sidelines But you won't see much from the sidelines, and if you do, you won't always understand what you see. ...

Our art should reflect the bright, life-affirming sides of our reality and at the same time implacably expose all that impedes our advance.

Life in socialist society is rich and many-faceted. The artist must study that life thoroughly, must be able to discern its new features, thoughtfully single out the phenomena and events that signify communist beginnings, generalize from them and hold them up as examples to be imitated. ...

An artist can study life only if he is intimately associated with the people he is writing about. And yet it must be said frankly that certain writers and artists still live in isolation from life. To be sure, an artist's ties with life do not depend solely on where he lives. But this factor does have more than a little importance. I am going to cite what are in my estimation highly important data indicating that we ought to think seriously about having our artistic intelligentsia reside closer to the places where material values are being created. For example, out of 5,200 writers, something like 4,000 live in the capitals of the Union republics. In the Russian Republic, for instance, 1,700 out of 2,700 writers live in Moscow and Leningrad. Nearly the entire Armenian Writers' Union is concentrated in Yerevan; only 15 out of 220 writers live in other cities and villages of the republic. In Latvia, 105 out of 116 of the re-

public's writers live in Riga, the capital.

The situation is roughly the same with respect to artists and composers. The question naturally arises: Should we then, launch a campaign to relocate writers and artists from the industrial centers to the localities? This is, of course, a very complicated and touchy matter. But it seems to us that it would not be a bad idea to appeal to our young artists to follow the lead of the young people who have set out from the country's industrial centers for the construction sites of communism, for the areas where the virgin lands are being developed— for the places where things are bursting with life. This would be useful for the writers and artists, and even more useful for the cause of our society. (Applause.) ...

I must cite instances of insincerity, lack of principle and mutual flattery to be encountered among the artistic intelligentsia. There is no point in denying that there are cases when a work receives many glowing comments during discussion at a meeting of an artistic or learned council, is called a wonderful production, a fine job, yet when it comes to a secret poll, lo and behold—not a single vote is cast "for" it. (Laughter.) The vote "against" has been unanimous. The people who had praised the work are naturally asked how this could have happened, and without even showing embarrassment they reply that they had expected that someone would surely vote for the work. That is, they had expected their unprincipled, improper attitude to a comrade's work to be covered up in that way. (Laughter. Applause.)

And in this connection we have very big demands to make of the critics. They are asked for a persistent effort to secure a high ideological-artistic level in works of art, to be unsparing in their treatment of any deviations from the principles of socialist realism.

One of the most important tasks of art scholars and critics is to wage an implacable struggle against ideological views inimical to us, to expose the reactionary nature of the art of the bourgeoisie, to administer a crushing rebuff to revisionists of every stripe and hue, vigorously support everything innovatory and resolutely oppose pseudo-innovation and formalism, all perversions in art. ...

Our friendly cooperation with the fraternal socialist countries in the cultural sphere has been growing year by year. Contacts with capitalist states are broadening. Suffice it to say that regular ties have now been established with 82 countries through the channels of the Ministry of Culture alone. I should like to mention in particular the development of cultural cooperation with the Asian and African countries that have set foot on the road of national independence. In 1960 alone, some 2,000 cultural figures made visits to 25 Asian and African countries.

There has also been considerable expansion of cultural ties and cooperation with Latin American countries. ...

There have been 39 international music competitions held in the last five years. Soviet performers took 27 first prizes and 35 second and third prizes at these competitions. (Applause.) This is evidence of the high standard of musical culture attained in our country.

Such forms of cooperation as motion picture festivals and national film weeks have been expanding vigorously in recent years.

Soviet films have emerged on the screens of the world and have won deserved success. The best Soviet films are being shown in 122 countries. "The Fate of a Man," the film adaptation of the work by Mikhail Alexandrovich Sholokhov, who is a delegate to our Congress, has been running for two years now in 85 countries. This film has been shown in 1,200 movie houses in Britain and 2,000 in France. With every passing year our literature and art will be exerting a still stronger influence on the development of cultural ties and the strengthening of friendship between peoples. (Applause.)

We note with satisfaction that the theater groups that have come to us from abroad have likewise been the object of enormous interest on the part of Soviet theatergoers and have met with a hearty and cordial reception from them.

We open our doors wide to our foreign guests. True, there have been some cases of guests who have abused our hospitality on the assumption that we would not notice their true purpose— to force alien ideas into our home. Everyone knows that Soviet people are hospitable, but it is naive to count on visiting us with such baggage. ...

Clearly visible from the height we have reached is the path
we have covered and the fearsome abyss into which we were
being pushed by the factionalists Molotov, Kaganovich, Malenkov,
Voroshilov, Bulganin, Pervukhin and Saburov, and Shepilov, who
joined them. The truth of the matter is that those were
perilous days for our party. And it is our great good fortune
that the June plenary session of the Central Committee should
have dealt a unanimous rebuff, which had the backing of our
whole party, to this anti-Party group, the members of which had
long since lost touch with the Party and the people and in their
secret hearts had lost faith in both the Party and the people.

The anti-Party group began fighting the new line long before
the June plenary session of the Central Committee. This was
an extended process. The factionalists opposed the re-estab-
lishment of Leninist norms because they themselves had at the
time been involved in their violation. They were against rehabilitation of innocent victims because they themselves were
to blame for the mass repression and gross infringements of
legality that had cost our people so tragic a price.

To get a clearer picture of the danger that this anti-Party
group represented, we must once again trace the positions they
took on some of the basic questions of domestic and foreign
policy of recent years. The comrades will recall the augmented
session of the Central Committee Presidium in 1954, which
was attended by all the Ministers of the Soviet Union and by
representatives of public organizations. At that time, on
Comrade Khrushchev's initiative, the Presidium was discussing
the question of amalgamating Moscow's construction organizations into a single system under the Chief Moscow Construction
Administration; heretofore these organizations had been
scattered among 60 departments. This amalgamation was essential if we were to get moving on housing construction and
establish an industrial base for construction work. Furthermore, the dispersal of construction work affected the distribution of housing accommodations, because in many instances the
departments had neglected to supervise this matter and permitted violations of the prescribed procedure. You should have
seen the fury with which Molotov opposed this proposal. What
arguments did he give? Only one, that the administration of
construction must not be concentrated in a single chief administration under the Moscow Soviet, but that all the departments
should concern themselves with this matter. Is any comment
needed?

At that time the amount of housing being built yearly in
Moscow was 500,000 square meters, while today the figure is
3,700,000 square meters, i.e., more than seven times as much.
And this reorganization in the construction field after all affected not only Moscow but Leningrad and Kiev, too, and for
that matter the whole country. This was a big issue of fundamental importance. It was a question of major reforms, of new
features that had to come into their own in the life of our state.

To continue, I would remind you that Molotov voiced his disagreement with the Party's new policy, with the measures the
Party had mapped for the development of agriculture, starting
with the overhauling of its planning and ending with the development of virgin and unused lands. ...

And finally, there was the question of reorganizing the
management of industry. The Central Committee spent a long
time in 1957 studying this acute matter, thoroughly and from
all sides. It was plain that the organizational forms of management then existing had begun to hamper the further development
of productive forces. The ministries had to be abolished and
economic regions formed. Conferences on this question were
held in the republics, provinces and cities. Then the Central
Committee of the C.P.S.U. convened an augmented conference
in which all members and candidate members of the Central
Committee's Presidium took part. At this conference no one,
not even Molotov, objected to the reorganization of the management of industry. The Presidium of the Central Committee
twice discussed the report that was to be submitted to the
plenary session of the Central Committee. There were no objections from Molotov on these occasions either. But the night
before the plenary session, at 3 a.m., the members of the
Central Committee's Presidium received from Molotov a half-
page note in which he informed the Presidium that he disap-
proved of the reorganization of industry, giving absolutely no
reasons and merely alleging that the time had not yet come for

such a reform in our country. Is there any need to comment on
this? Life has shown who was right.

Thus the problems involved in reorganizing the administration
of economic construction, problems of vital importance for our
state, were being successfully solved one after another, with
the support of the whole Party and of all the people, in spite of
the factionalists. It made them furious. They saw all this and
realized that life was casting them into the discard, but they
would not recognize, would not admit that they were in error or
draw the proper conclusions as to what they should do. On the
contrary, they proceeded to compound their mistakes.

There is one very important event which, to my mind, is
worth recalling in this connection. Not long before the June
plenary session of the Central Committee there was a meeting
of the Central Committee's Presidium, which was attended by
many members and candidate members of the present Presidium. I think that they can all clearly recall the situation at that
meeting. The meeting was discussing the complete rehabilitation, including rehabilitation in the Party, of persons who had
at one time been prominent in our army's leadership—Tukhachevsky, Yakir, Uborevich, Yegorov, Eideman, Kork and others.
So obvious was their innocence that even Molotov, Malenkov,
Kaganovich and others declared for their rehabilitation, although
they had had a hand in their tragic deaths. And at that point in
the discussion Nikita Sergeyevich very calmly but bluntly asked
them: "When were you right, then? When you voted to doom
them, and that doom was so tragically sealed, or now that you
are for completely rehabilitating them? Tell us, when were
you right?" This blunt and honest question infuriated and
flustered them. It had become plain from their conduct at that
meeting that they were afraid that the truth would come out,
that the flagrant violations of Soviet legality committed by them
would become known to the whole Party and to the people. And
at that point these dissidents resorted to conspiracy, with the
purpose of turning the Party back from the new policy of re-
establishing Leninist norms of Party life to the old practices of
the days of the cult of the individual. It was this that united
them.

Perhaps, comrades, there was no need for me to speak of
this in such detail. But it seems to me that after the 20th
Congress, the 22nd Congress is a Congress for rendering accounts, and that we must know and understand how difficult and
complicated the situation was in the Party leadership. The fate
of the new policy that our Central Committee had adopted for
guiding the Party and country was then being decided. And I can
say as a participant in the Congress, and I think I shall be
voicing your general opinion: How fortunate for our whole party,
how very fortunate for our Soviet people, that at this time the
Party Central Committee headed by our dear Nikita Sergeyevich
rose to the occasion and was able to rout the anti-Party group.
(Stormy, prolonged applause.) Our party's new policy had
triumphed! (Stormy, prolonged applause.) ...

Yefremov

SPEECH BY COMRADE L. N. YEFREMOV, FIRST SECRE-
TARY OF THE GORKY PROVINCE PARTY COMMITTEE.
(Pravda, Oct. 22, p. 3. 3,200 words. Excerpt:) ... A tremendous amount of credit is due the Central Committee for
having resolutely exposed and dealt a crushing ideological
defeat to the factionalist anti-Party group, which fiercely resisted implementation of urgent measures in all spheres of
economic and socio-political life and tried to swerve the Party
from the Leninist road. The bitter attacks made by Molotov,
Kaganovich, Malenkov, Voroshilov and the other members of
the anti-Party groups on the Party's Leninist policy reflected
their anxiety to escape personal responsibility for the mass
acts of repression against many Party and state officials. The
factionalists set themselves far-reaching goals. As we know,
in the grim period of the "Leningrad affair," which was
trumped up by Malenkov for purposes of provocation, a number
of Communists from Gorky were among the innocent victims
persecuted, and baseless political charges were brought against
the executive Party and Soviet bodies of the province; this
created a feeling of uncertainty in the Party organization and
hampered solution of very important problems in economic
construction and cultural development.

The Communists of our Party organization subscribe to the view expressed in the delegates' speeches that the anti-Party acts committed by Malenkov make him unworthy to remain in the ranks of our Leninist party. (Applause.) ...

Rasulov

SPEECH BY COMRADE D. RASULOV, FIRST SECRETARY OF THE TADZHIKISTAN COMMUNIST PARTY CENTRAL COMMITTEE. (Pravda, Oct. 22, pp. 4-5. 3,200 words. Excerpts:) Comrades! ... The agriculture of the Soviet Union was for a long time in a neglected state and its development was artificially held back. This had happened because Malenkov, who was at that time in charge of this vitally important branch of the economy, had no knowledge of agriculture and no desire to study it, was out of touch with the people and did not share their concerns. The Party had to make no small effort to overcome the lag in agriculture. I subscribe to the suggestions made in the delegates' speeches that Malenkov should incur more severe punishment for this. (Applause.) ...

Definite successes have been scored in agriculture, in the development of science and culture and in raising the living standard of the working people. But the republic's successes might have been far greater had not the Bureau of the Tadzhikistan Communist Party Central Committee committed major errors,* which, as we all know, were disclosed at the plenary session of the Tadzhikistan Communist Party Central Committee held in April of this year, in which Comrade F. R. Kozlov, member of the Presidium of the C.P.S.U. Central Committee and Secretary of the C.P.S.U. Central Committee, participated.

The Party organization made a correct political assessment of the cases of deception of the Party and state that had become common in the republic at the time and drew the necessary conclusions from this. The Communists and all the working people of Tadzhikistan express their deep appreciation to the Leninist Central Committee, to its Presidium and to Comrade Nikita Sergeyevich Khrushchev personally for their fatherly attention to the Party organization of Tadzhikistan and to the Tadzhik people, for having helped to expose and put a stop to the mistakes that were being committed. The Party organization has united even more solidly behind the Leninist Central Committee of the C.P.S.U. and is doing its best to rectify the situation as quickly as possible and to take fuller advantage of the big opportunities it has for the further development of the economy and culture of Tadzhikistan. And we are able to report to the Congress on some positive results that have been achieved. ...

I must tell you frankly, however, that the republic is still making poor use of its opportunities for accelerating the development of industry, construction, agriculture and other branches of the economy. ...

Accomplishment of the task of increasing the production of cotton and other farm products necessarily entails improving the provision of equipment, machinery and materials for the water-supply organizations, providing the collective and state farms with more effective means of combating crop pests and diseases and organizing the production of chemical weed-killers. The U.S.S.R. State Planning Committee must consider these matters and take decisions on them. ...

The construction of the Nurek and Rogun Hydroelectric Stations on the Vakhsh River opens up big opportunities for further development of the productive forces not only of Tadzhikistan but of all Central Asia. Construction of these hydroelectric stations will enable our republic to increase cotton production more than 100% and bring it up to 1,000,000 tons. Production of meat, milk and other agricultural products will also be substantially increased.

On the basis of cheap power from the Nurek, Rogun and other power plants and the availability of large resources of mineral raw materials, the chemical industry and nonferrous metallurgy will be rebuilt and undergo considerable development. We have submitted proposals in this connection, and they are now under consideration in the U.S.S.R. State Planning Committee and the State Economic Council.

The further development of Tadzhikistan's economy necessarily involves stepping up geological prospecting for gas and

oil; we are lagging substantially in this work. Our republic undoubtedly has rich reserves of oil and gas. But little has been done to survey them and hence they are not being utilized sufficiently in the economy. We ask that the U.S.S.R. State Planning Committee and the U.S.S.R. Ministry of Geology and Conservation of Mineral Resources consider our proposals and lend the republic assistance in geological surveying so that the oil and gas and nonferrous and rare metals that abound in Tadzhikistan can be harnessed more quickly in the service of the people. ...

Ovezov

SPEECH BY COMRADE B. OVEZOV, FIRST SECRETARY OF THE TURKMENISTAN COMMUNIST PARTY CENTRAL COMMITTEE. (Pravda, Oct. 22, p. 6. 3,400 words. Condensed text:) ... In the years of Soviet rule the face of Turkmenistan has changed beyond recognition. Industry in our republic has undergone extensive development, and a highly mechanized agriculture has been created. ... Our republic produces considerably more cotton than Iran and Afghanistan put together. (Applause.)

Turkmenistan has become a land of total literacy. This once backward outpost of tsarist Russia is now outstanding not only the countries of the Near and Middle East but such capitalist countries as the U.S.A., France and Italy in number of students per 1,000 population and in level of medical services. (Applause.) For example, we have 83 students per 10,000 population. This is twice as many as France and almost five times as many as Turkey. (Applause.) We have 17 doctors per 10,000 population, while the U.S.A. has 12, Great Britain 11 and France 11. (Applause.) ...

Through the development of new areas and the introduction of advanced technology, oil extraction in the first two years of the seven-year period increased more than 27% and the average daily output now exceeds 17,000 tons. In 1961 the output of oil in the republic will exceed 6,000,000 tons. The rates of growth are such that the seven-year plan will be fulfilled in 1963, and by the end of the seventh year the republic's oilworkers will be producing 10,000,000 tons of oil instead of 7,500,000 tons. (Applause.) ...

Turkmenistan's oil is distinguished for its high quality; a large variety of first-grade petroleum products for the market and valuable types of raw material for the chemical industry can be produced from it. Taking into account these possibilities, it is expedient to organize the production of plastics, artificial fiber, synthetic rubber, synthetic detergents and other petrochemical products in Turkmenistan. With the rapid development of oil extraction, the need arises of speeding expansion of the Krasnovodsk Oil Refinery and building new oil refineries in the eastern part of the republic. ...

On the basis of the raw material reserves of the Kara-Bogaz-Gol it is possible to organize the large-scale production of sulphates, chlorides, sodium, magnesium, bromine compounds and a number of fertilizers and other types of chemical products, as well as refractories and building materials. This wealth must be put at the service of the people more rapidly. The U.S.S.R. State Planning Committee must examine our proposals on this question. It is advisable to consider also the proposal for the construction in the next few years of a combine for the production of potassium fertilizers on the basis of the Gaurdak deposit. ...

The most urgent and complex problem in cotton growing continues to be completion of integrated mechanization, especially of harvesting. The existing pool of cotton-picking machines in the republic makes it possible to harvest only 10% of the crop. We have absolutely no machines for harvesting fine-fiber strains of cotton, whose share in gross cotton production this year amounts to 40%. Given our limited human resources, the lack of such machines will impede the further development of cotton growing. ...

Large-scale work is now going on in the republic to develop new lands. But we are already experiencing an acute shortage of equipment for leveling work and for cleaning the network of small irrigation channels. We have to deflect a great number of people for these jobs. In 1960, for example, 3,000,000 cubic meters of earthwork was done by hand in clearing small irrigation installations; this is more than one-third of the total volume of work. ...

The number of karakul sheep will almost double in the next few years, reaching 7,000,000. Karakul raising in our republic is based entirely on the use of range pastures in the Kara-Kum

---

*["Tadzhikistan Leaders Fired for Corruption and Faking," Current Digest of the Soviet Press, Vol. XIII, No. 15, pp. 9-12.]

desert. The economic development of these pastures is possible only if they are supplied with water, but in this matter we are encountering big difficulties, since the digging of wells and water hoisting are still not mechanized. About 6,000,000 hectares of pastureland has been developed in Turkmenistan in the years of the seven-year plan. We must develop many more millions of hectares, but now we will have to go into the very heart of the desert, overcoming the sand dunes and lack of water.

With the opening of the Kara-Kum Canal it has become possible to supply water to a part of the range pastures by building small pressure water pipelines. The U.S.S.R. State Planning Committee, the U.S.S.R. Ministry of Agriculture and the All-Union Farm Equipment Association must help the republic solve the urgent tasks in the accelerated development of karakul raising. ...

Mikoyan

SPEECH BY COMRADE A. I. MIKOYAN, FIRST VICE-CHAIR-MAN OF THE U.S.S.R. COUNCIL OF MINISTERS. (Pravda, Oct. 22, pp. 7-8; Izvestia, pp. 3-4. Complete Pravda text:) Comrade delegates! We, the members of the Central Committee, bear full responsibility for the activities of the Party Central Committee in the period that has gone by. I am in complete agreement with the Central Committee report and the report on the Party Program that have been delivered by Comrade Khrushchev. These reports reviewed the victories won by the Soviet people under the banner of Marxism-Leninism, adduced principled Leninist arguments for the main theses of the Program and shed light on the paths that the building of communist society is to take. These are fine results, this is a Program worthy of Communists, a great charter for mankind's bright future! (Applause.)

Comrades! The 20th Congress was a turning point in the life of our party and of the entire world Communist movement. The political course of that Congress and its theoretical instructions have already produced fine shoots. This has been proved by the historical experience of the past few years.

The ideological orientation of the 20th Congress was not something that manifested itself in the space of a day before the Congress or within the few days of its proceedings. It evolved over a span of two years preceding the Congress in the process of critical re-examination of certain ideological principles, reorganization of the practical work of the Party and the state, and the elimination of the harmful consequences of the cult of the individual.

Disagreements on basic questions of Party policy and practice had arisen within the Central Committee in this period. Molotov, Kaganovich, Malenkov and Voroshilov showed conservatism in their thinking and proved incapable of correctly assessing the postwar international and domestic situation, of comprehending the new line of conduct that was required of Marxist-Leninists. They rejected everything new and opposed the theses that were later advanced by the Central Committee at the 20th Congress of the C.P.S.U. The factionalist anti-Party group, of which Molotov became the chief ideologist, was later joined by Bulganin, Pervukhin, Saburov and Shepilov.

The members of the group fiercely resisted the restoration of Leninist norms of Party life and socialist legality and opposed the elimination of the harmful consequences of the cult of the individual, and they also opposed such urgent and vitally essential measures as the reorganization of state and economic administration, the reorganization of planning, especially in agriculture, the development and utilization of virgin lands, etc.

These differences with the conservative-dogmatic group were not differences on particular organizational or political points. No, they concerned the shaping of the Party's entire policy at the new stage of historical development, its general line.

V. I. Lenin indicated in his day that the reorganization of the Workers and Peasants' Inspection proposed in 1923 was not a simple organizational measure but had a bearing on all our work, our policy, our tactics, our strategy. It was a question at the time of ensuring the victory of socialism in the U.S.S.R. by maintaining working-class guidance of the peasantry.

Under today's conditions it was all the more a question not simply of organizational measures but of evolving a policy that would ensure the successful building of communism in our country and make it possible to prevent a world war.

How can the opposition of the conservative-dogmatic group be explained? Above all by the organic attachment of its members to the cult of the individual, which is alien to Marxism-Leninism, by their failure to understand that the country was entering a new stage of its development—the period of the full-scale building of communism, that the world socialist system was turning into the dominant factor in the evolution of mankind while the imperialist camp had lost its determining role in international relations. Indeed, just before the 20th Congress of the C.P.S.U. Molotov, in a report at a session of the U.S.S.R. Supreme Soviet, openly questioned whether a socialist society had been built in the U.S.S.R. His statement was: "Along with the Soviet Union, in which the foundations of socialist society have already been built, there are those people's democracies that have taken only the first, but extremely important, steps in the direction of socialism." According to Molotov, it appeared that, first, socialism had not yet been built in the U.S.S.R.; second, the first steps toward socialism were being taken by only some of the people's democracies; and, third, there were people's democracies in which even these steps had not been taken.

You yourselves appreciate that with premises like these there could be no thought of a plan for building communism.

Influenced by criticism in the Central Committee, Molotov was forced to excuse himself in the pages of the magazine Kommunist; he tried to reduce the issue to one of erroneous formulation. But it was not an erroneous formulation that was involved. If only the foundations of socialism had been built, it was clearly impossible to pose the question of transition to the full-scale building of communism. If only some of the people's democracies had taken the first steps in the direction of socialism, it meant that the world socialist system had not formed and there could be no talk, therefore, of its growing influence on the course of social development. This was a fundamentally wrong, non-Leninist assessment of the lineup of class and political forces in the world of today.

The result of his underestimating the forces of socialism and, consequently, overestimating the forces of imperialism was that Molotov made serious mistakes on questions of international development—on peaceful coexistence and the possibility of preventing a world war, and on the multiplicity of the forms of transition to socialism in various countries.

In general, Molotov rejects the line of peaceful coexistence, reducing the concept to nothing more than a state of peace, or rather the absence of war at a given moment, and denying the possibility of preventing a world war. In its substance this view approximates that of the foreign adversaries of peaceful coexistence, who interpret it as a variant of the "cold war," as a state of "armed peace."

This conception is at odds with the Leninist understanding of relations between the two systems and would have led to repudiating the broad development of economic relations between them and to the curtailment of contacts and cultural ties. Finally, it would to all intents and purposes have meant accepting the inevitability of war and abandoning the active quest for agreements aimed at reducing international tension and at disarmament. It is no accident, therefore, that he should reject the historic thesis of the 20th Party Congress on the possibility of preventing world war in this age.

He disputes the advisability of the personal meetings our Party and government leaders have been holding with leaders of the capitalist states, considering them a pure infatuation ascribable to excessive faith in personal contacts and talks. In defiance of this point of view, the Party undertook to broaden contacts between Soviet and foreign state and public organizations and figures. And experience has shown how right the Party was in these moves: I need only refer to the enormous political response to the meetings and speeches abroad of N. S. Khrushchev and other figures and to the great good they have done and continue to do. (Applause.)

Despite the differences, neither Molotov nor anyone else at the 20th Congress advanced his own particular point of view. They did not contest the political line of the Central Committee and voted along with all the rest.

The Central Committee thought that this would put an end to

the differences that had existed prior to the Congress. We assumed that unity had been established on the basic points of Party policy. It turned out afterwards, however, that this was far from the case. The stand that Molotov and others had taken at the Congress had been hypocritical. It is now clear that, knowing they would be isolated at the Congress if they came out openly against the new Congress theses advanced by the Central Committee, they chose different tactics for their struggle. These were tactics calculated to keep them from suffering a defeat at the Congress while enabling them at a later, more convenient time to try, using other means, to bring about a revision of the Party line.

As it turned out, the Congress had ended but the differences remained. But now they concerned the line of the 20th Congress, its decisions.

A sharp struggle against implementation of the decisions of the 20th Congress went on in the Central Committee for over a year. It was a question of whether the Party would take the path the Congress had condemned, the path that had been followed in the days of the cult of the individual, or would take the Leninist road. At a time when Comrade Khrushchev and others were busy working creatively to carry the decisions of the Congress into effect, these people were busy with just one thing—creating obstructions, hampering the activity of the Central Committee, winning over supporters from among the members of the Central Committee's Presidium and knocking together a group, doing it with utmost secrecy.

When the Party decided to abolish the industrial ministries and set up economic councils, and also to reorganize the Machine and Tractor Stations, the factionalists considered the moment had come for seizing power and changing the Party's policy by a coup at the top. They had held their peace at the Congress, but now, at their clandestine meetings, they began to hatch a plot against the Party. And then in June, 1957, the members of the group, having tallied the votes against the Party leadership that they could muster from the members of the Central Committee's Presidium, went over to the direct attack. But they miscalculated.

The plenary session of the Central Committee measured up to Leninist requirements and administered the anti-Party oppositionist group a crushing ideological and organizational defeat. (Applause.) The group's members made appropriate statements at the plenary session, and afterwards, a year to a year and a half later, wrote letters to the Central Committee in which they acknowledged and condemned their mistakes. Molotov was the only one who did not vote for the resolution of the Central Committee's plenary session or anywhere in any form repudiate his anti-Party activity or his views, which had inflicted great harm on the Party. What he had said in the primary organization about agreeing with the decision of the plenary session had been insincere, prompted by tactical considerations. To this day he clings bullheadedly to his conservative-dogmatic views.

The Central Committee consistently bases its activity on Leninist norms of Party life. This has shown itself in the fact that the fight against the conservative-dogmatic group was waged by the methods of inner-Party democracy, without resort to repressive state measures, as had been the case under the cult of the individual. But the victory of the anti-Party group would have led to reprisals against all the active supporters of the 20th Congress, by methods that the Party can never forget.

Had we not dealt a crushing ideological defeat to the conservative-dogmatic anti-Party group, we should not have been able to carry out the decisions of the 20th Congress and score the gigantic gains that have exalted our country and strengthened its might and authority on the world scene and that are ensuring success in the building of communism. (Stormy applause.) The Leninist spirit of innovation and dedication to principle have triumphed, the Leninist orientation has triumphed, the Leninist leadership of the Central Committee, headed by Comrade N. S. Khrushchev, has triumphed. The Party has arrived at its 22nd Congress united, monolithic and strong as never before. (Stormy, prolonged applause.)

Our Congress is discussing the new Program of the Communist Party of the Soviet Union. The decision to revise the Program was taken as far back as the 18th Party Congress.

We have no cause to regret that the Program was not drafted at that time and that we are discussing the new Program today, at the 22nd Congress. The Party could not have produced so scientifically sound a Program had it not done away with the cult of the individual and reinstated Leninist norms of inner-Party life, had it not creatively mapped the paths of communist construction.

It was essential that the Party provide answers to the fundamental questions raised both by the internal conditions in the country and by postwar world developments.

We can firmly state today that the 19th Party Congress was not ready to produce a new Party Program. It is now clear to all that the "Economic Problems of Socialism in the U.S.S.R." could not have constituted the basis for a new Program.

The Party had to overcome a number of erroneous notions about the transition to communism. One has but to recall that the prevailing view on the eve of the 19th Congress was that to achieve the transition to communism it was enough to ensure the continuous growth of production, convert collective farm property into public property, replace commodity circulation by a system of exchange of products between town and countryside, bring about the doubling of wages, and raise the cultural and technical level of the workers and peasants. This was an oversimplified conception.

The new Program of the C.P.S.U. puts the problem correctly: The most important thing for the victory of communism is to create the material and technical base of communist society and ensure communist abundance. It is a question not of the simple growth of social production but of raising the productive forces of our country to a qualitatively new and higher level, of creating the productive forces of communist society.

The question had been posed backwards. The creation of the material and technical base of communism had not even been advanced as the principal and decisive economic problem. On the contrary, it was the conversion of collective farm property into public property that was considered the most basic factor in the transition to communism.

It is a truism that communism presupposes a single form of public ownership. But one socialist form of ownership cannot be viewed as antithetical to the other. By virtue of special conditions the Virgin Land Territory is a territory of state farms, while in the agriculture of Krasnodar Territory, for example, the collective farm form of ownership prevails. But can anyone say on the strength of this fact which of these territories is "nearer" to communism? If one takes the position that the main thing in the building of communism is the elimination of collective farm ownership, one will inevitably be reduced to claiming that the Virgin Land Territory has already "entered" communism.

Collective farm ownership, far from inhibiting the development of the productive forces of socialist society, has the opposite effect: It facilitates our society's advance to communism. Such is the dialectics of development that the problem of creating a single form of communist property is solved specifically by the building of the material and technical base of communism. This is the basic link; by gripping it we can pull the whole chain representing the building of communist society and ensure the transformation of socialist relationships into communist ones.

The creation of the material and technical base of communism is the foundation of the Party's general line. The Party will pursue this line unswervingly.

Now to discuss some aspects of the problem of distribution in the transition to communism. We were told that to get to communism we had to raise the wages of workers and employees to at least twice what they were, if not more. This idea is incorrect if only because such a wage level falls far short of guaranteeing distribution according to need. As a matter of fact, the real incomes of Soviet workers, peasants and employees are already 60% higher than in 1950 and will be 130% higher by 1965. But we cannot by any means say that this will ensure the transition to communism.

This idea gave us the wrong orientation for future policy in the sphere of distribution; it would have prodded us into making wages the sole form of distribution. They held that everything should be paid for, and proposed—this was Molotov's demand—that apartment rents be raised, that work clothes now issued

free be paid for, that the charge for transport and public utilities be raised and that the students' stipend fund be reduced
and tuition fees introduced. In short, they were prodding us
into reducing the public consumption funds, and they denied that
these funds played a growing role in the transition to communism.

The Party has not taken this road. We cannot advance to
communism by adhering to a policy of distributing the social
product through wages alone. What we seek, after all, is to
create a communist way of life.

The new Program indicates that over the long-range period
covered by the general plan the citizens' requirements will be
met both through wages—the basic form of distribution—and
through the rapidly growing public consumption funds, which
must be so controlled that they do not conflict with the principle of material incentive and that they facilitate solution of a
number of major problems in the building of communism.

According to the estimates that have been made, by the end
of the 20-year period the role of the two forms in the distribution system will be approximately equal, and after that the
public consumption funds will begin to outweigh the other form.
This line allows of properly integrating socialist distribution
according to work with the policy of eliminating economic inequality, which we still have in our country.

Communist methods of distribution according to need cannot
possibly be introduced until we have attained a level of productivity that will ensure abundance. If the productive forces of
society have not matured sufficiently for communist distribution, attempts to introduce it will only result in retarding society's development, will force a retreat, a return to a mode of
distribution consistent with the level of productive forces that
has been attained. Only by exhausting the progressive role of
socialist principles can the complete affirmation of the principles of communism be achieved. Such is the dialectics of the
transition from socialism to communism.

Into the solution of what problems should the public funds be
directed?

First, the problems connected with population growth and the
maintenance of the rising generation. To accomplish this task,
society must gradually and in steadily increasing measure assume the cost of maintaining the rising generation until, under
communism, it shall have assumed this cost in full.

Second, communism is predicated on a high level of culture
and general education for the whole population. Consequently,
society must earmark larger and larger sums for education,
for schools and universities, for their construction and exemplary upkeep and for the utmost advancement of culture. It
goes without saying that expenditures on the advancement of
science, which has already become one of society's most important productive forces, must be sharply raised. Our scientists and our schoolteachers must do their very best to keep
our country in the lead in education and science! (Applause.)

Third, communism assumes the utmost concern for people's
health. The Program envisages substantial increases in public
expenditures on medical care, sanatoriums and rest homes,
boarding houses, tourist centers and the development of sports.

The achievement of an abundance of all the things man needs,
along with the strides made by medicine, will enable us to improve public health care considerably and focus our main efforts
on disease prevention and the total elimination of some of the
most serious illnesses and on extending the span of life. The
medical treatment of the ill will rise to a new level in all parts
of the country.

Our doctors and all workers on the medical front must so
improve public health care as to merit the hearty thanks of the
people! (Applause.)

Fourth, the most favorable possible conditions must be created for working members of society both at work and at home.
This means that we must, specifically, ensure that free meals
are introduced for working persons at enterprises and offices,
in city and countryside, and that every family is provided,
free of charge, with a comfortable modern apartment, public
utilities and transportation.

Fifth, our society must display a maximum of concern for
the aged. The humane character of communist society imposes
this responsibility.

These crucial problems of communist construction cannot be

solved without public consumption funds. Collective satisfaction
of a number of needs has become a matter of economic necessity in present-day society. Only communism, on whose
banner is inscribed "Everything for the benefit of man," is
engaged in solving this problem.

Another thesis with which the Party was unable to agree was
that the problems of distribution and circulation in the transition to
the full-scale building of communism are solved by the introduction of the exchange of products between town and countryside. There are still individual comrades who suggest that
commodity-money relations be abolished without delay. The
C.P.S.U. Central Committee has received letters to this effect in connection with the discussion of the draft Program.
Experience in our construction shows that the commodity-
money relations inherent in socialism will remain with us over
the entire period of transition to communism. As long as there
is control over the measure of labor and consumption there
will be money, and we must continue strengthening its stability.

The period of communist construction is not in any way a
period of curtailment of Soviet trade. Soviet trade will for a
long time to come remain the principal form of distribution
of consumer goods among the members of society, a most
sensitive instrument for studying growing and changing demand and a means of balancing production and consumption.
Soviet trade must therefore be expanded to the utmost, for
that is the only way in which we can develop the smoothly operating apparatus of distribution according to need that is required under communism.

A cult of fine and courteous "service" has been built up in
the capitalist countries. This "service" exists for the rich,
for people who have money, and its other side is turned
against the working people. It exists not for the sake of man
but in the name of profit. We must develop our own system for
providing Soviet people with excellent services, ensuring them
maximum conveniences and the very best satisfaction of their
material and cultural wants. Not only do we have an acute
need to overcome the lag in the technical facilities for trade
but we are in a position to do so—to increase the number of
stores and public dining rooms, to effect a sharp increase in
their technical equipment (various machines and automatic
devices; new designs for stores, public dining rooms, warehouses, freezing plants, etc.), to improve the organizational
forms and methods of trade and raise its standards. A certain
redistribution will have to be made in the balance of labor
forces, so as to increase the proportion accounted for by the
services sphere. We shall certainly do this.

Comrades, the main thing in the building of communist society is to create the material and technical base and to achieve
an abundance of all the goods we need. But the remolding of
man, of his thinking, his morality, his customs, character and
habits, must proceed at the same time that production relations are changing. What is involved is the molding of a man
who behaves like a Communist at work, in his private life
and in the use of his leisure, who has a feeling of dignity and of
respect for himself and for every member of society.

Lenin said: "We call communism the system under which
people become accustomed to discharging public duties without
any special machinery of compulsion, and work without pay for
the common good comes to be a universal phenomenon."
("Works," Fourth [Russian] Edition, Vol. XXX, pp. 260-261.)

Our goal must be for a communist social consciousness and
the principles of the moral code of the builder of communism
to become part of the very fiber of Soviet man, to become
habit, to become the normal standards of everyday life.

An enormous asset of the Party Program is that, in complete conformity with V. I. Lenin's instructions, the theoretical
principles governing the building of communist society are
linked inseparably in it with the 20-year plan for economic
development. Without a shred of fancy or utopian day-dream-
ing, the Program traces the concrete path along which the Soviet people will advance to communism. The Program will be
a guide to action; it summons the Soviet people to inspired
creative labor for the good of communism! (Applause.)

The Party Program further develops Lenin's theory of the
state. V. I. Lenin played an exceptionally great role in evolving the Marxist theory of the state. We must completely dis-
miss the claim, which was made at one time and which is far

from the truth, that Lenin merely defended Marx' and Engels' theory of the state against attacks by international opportunist groups but did not have time to elaborate and develop it further on the basis of our country's experience. The truth of the matter is that it was V. I. Lenin and none other who not only restored and upheld the Marxist teaching on the state but also evolved the theory of the socialist state on the basis of the experience of the Soviet regime.

Lenin declared the Soviet regime to be a form of dictatorship of the proletariat and defined the functions and tasks of the Soviet state. The formation of the first Soviet state in Russia and the emergence of new, Soviet agencies of government on the ruins of the tsarist state are linked most intimately with the name of the great Lenin.

This enormous work was particularly difficult not only because brand-new trails had to be blazed in all spheres but because Russia was a vast multinational state with extraordinarily complicated interrelations between nations. And we are indebted to Lenin for the very creation of the Union of Soviet Socialist Republics, for the choice of a socialist union of nations as the only sound organizational form. Right after the February Revolution, and particularly from 1919 on, he spoke of the need to form a Union of Soviet Republics. Lenin severely criticized and rejected the viewpoint of those who opposed the establishment of a union of independent national republics and proposed merely incorporating them in the Russian Republic on an autonomous basis. In a memorandum sent to the members of the Politburo in 1922, Lenin wrote that we consider ourselves equal with the Ukraine Republic and the others, and along with them, and on a level of equality with them, are joining a new union, a new federation, the Union of Soviet Republics. Lenin upheld the policy of establishing a union of equal and sovereign national republics.

But in the succeeding period a tendency to curb the rights of the Union republics began to manifest itself. Decision-making on many matters that were local in character or that concerned the republics was increasingly concentrated at the center, and the Union agencies became incredibly enlarged.

Now, as everyone knows, the rights of the republics and local agencies have been restored and broadened and many Union ministries have been eliminated. Economic councils, which Lenin said had a great future, have been established and have proved their viability. The Party is doing absolutely the right thing in strengthening them, giving them aid and support and confirming their importance in its Program.

None of these moves in the development of the state has been in any way detrimental to the political, economic and ideological unity of our state as a whole, as some conservative-minded figures had tried to frighten us into believing would happen. On the contrary, they have still further strengthened the unity of all our peoples in the great Union of republics, have resulted in heightened local initiative, the burgeoning of creative activity among the masses and the acceleration of our general advance.

Our Soviet society is stronger than ever and the friendship of the peoples of the U.S.S.R. is firm and indestructible! (Applause.)

Soviet culture, national in form and socialist in content, is in process of further flowering in the country, and at the same time the socialist nations are steadily drawing closer together. This process has two sides, both of them progressive in character. The Program contains the clear-cut and very sound statement that artificially prodding the nations to draw together, or checking this process, can do only harm. The development of the national cultures and economies of the national republics in combination with a policy of their rapprochement is one of the greatest motive forces on our way to communism.

Among the most important theoretical questions worked out and resolved by the Program, a question that is at the same time of the most vital practical importance, is the question of the dictatorship of the proletariat. The conclusion reached in the Program represents a new pronouncement by the Party, a serious contribution to the theory of Marxism-Leninism.

As we know, the dictatorship of the proletariat is called upon to suppress the resistance of the overthrown exploiting classes and to bring about their disappearance, to shift the peasants from small-scale commodity production to collective produc-

tion, to ensure the building of socialism and its complete and final victory, and to remold and re-educate the peasants, artisans, office workers and intelligentsia in a spirit of socialism and achieve the socialist unity of the people, so that workers, peasants and the intelligentsia become bearers of socialist production relations and exponents of communist spiritual aspirations.

The dictatorship of the proletariat has accomplished all these tasks that faced it. It was a necessity until such time as these tasks had been accomplished. It has ceased to be the necessary form of the state, inasmuch as these tasks have been accomplished in our country. The new conditions of our development have turned the state of the dictatorship of the proletariat into a state of the entire people.

It may be objected that the task of protecting socialism's achievements against any encroachments from without has remained. Yes, the task of defending the country does remain and will continue to exist. It will remain under communism, too, if imperialism is in existence. But it would be unwarranted to maintain that since the function of defending the country continues to exist, the dictatorship of the proletariat should be retained. The task of defending the country is a function intrinsic to the state in general, and it will be successfully discharged by the state of the entire people! (Applause.)

Leninists have always coordinated the development of the socialist state with the real needs of the new society. The development of the new state proceeds dialectically. "Forward development" from bourgeois democracy, wrote Lenin, "does not proceed simply, directly and smoothly toward greater and greater democracy, as liberal professors and petty-bourgeois opportunists portray the matter." ("Works," Fourth [Russian] Edition, Vol. XXV, p. 433.) Forward development from bourgeois democracy proceeds through the dictatorship of the proletariat, which brings a tremendous broadening of democracy for the working people but at the same time withdraws freedom from the exploiters in a number of ways. Democracy is broadened only after the exploiting classes have been eliminated. "Communism alone is able to offer really full democracy, and the fuller this democracy, the sooner will it become unnecessary and wither away by itself." (Ibid, pp. 434-435.)

With perfect justification the Program specifies that the comprehensive development and improvement of socialist democracy will be the principal trend in the evolution of the socialist state system in the period of communist construction. The Program contains a whole complex of measures that will operate to this effect. The Party itself is setting an example by further improving inner-Party democracy.

The Program states that the dictatorship of the working class ceases to be necessary before the state withers away. Our state has always fought both the opportunists, who have made use of the thesis of the withering away of the state to deny the need for socialist revolution and the dictatorship of the proletariat, and the revisionists, who have sought under cover of this thesis to weaken and undermine the socialist state.

Dogmatists may allege that in characterizing our state as a state of the entire people we are contradicting our teachers, who criticized the followers of Lassalle for the slogan of a "people's state." This criticism was quite correct, for what sort of people's state could be spoken of under capitalism, with society split into hostile classes? But it would be the sheerest dogmatism to transpose those conditions to our society, in which socialist unity of the people has been brought about and the state cannot but express the will of all the people in its actions.

The state of the entire people is elevating socialist democracy to a still higher level where more and more millions of society's members are participating in the administration of state and public affairs. From the socialist state system to the triumph of communist self-government—such will be the line of our development!

Comrades! In the past half-century the social development of mankind has been proceeding with unprecedented speed. "The cauldron of the sorceress History is boiling," as Marx said. The highroad for mankind today is socialism.

The Soviet people are building a communist society in the

fraternal family of the peoples of the socialist countries.

The welding of all the forces of socialism, of all the Communist and Workers' Parties, is the most important factor in our common advance. The Communist and Workers' Parties have placed a high assessment on our party's vanguard role in the international Communist movement and on the importance of the 20th Congress. Our party feels the moral support of the fraternal parties in all its work. (Applause.) Unfortunately, this does not apply to the leaders of the Albanian Party of Labor.

For many years the leaders of the Albanian Party of Labor on any and all occasions vowed their friendship with our party and the Soviet people and professed to support the decisions of the 20th Congress. But as recent events have shown, these vows and protestations of theirs were insincere. For more than a year now the Albanian leaders, having abruptly altered their political policy, have been waging a fight against the decisions of the 20th Congress of the C.P.S.U. and attacking our party and its Leninist Central Committee, headed by N. S. Khrushchev, and other Communist Parties. The actions of the Albanian leaders indicate that they are departing from internationalist positions and backsliding onto the path of nationalism.

Where nationalism and alienation from the socialist camp lead to is shown by the experience of Yugoslavia's revisionism, which is being given effect in practice and has found expression in concentrated form in the anti-Leninist program of the League of Communists of Yugoslavia. It would be worthwhile for the Albanian leaders to give this some thought.

The facts indicate that a deplorable situation has developed in the Albanian Party of Labor. Just how far Hoxha and Shehu have descended can be seen from the fact that they not only failed to publish the draft Program of the C.P.S.U. (this is, of course, their internal affair) but presented a distorted account of it in their press. What are we to make of this? Why, even The New York Times, as well as many other bourgeois organs, carried the draft Program in full. Even in Greece, Albania's neighbor, where bourgeois reactionaries are in power, progressive forces managed to have our Program published in a printing that was enormous for that country. But the Albanian people and the Albanian Communists are deprived of an opportunity to read this historic document. The Albanian leaders today see even the publication of the Program of the C.P.S.U. as a danger to them. The people have an expression for a situation of this kind: "How far can you go!"

Developments are showing that those who persist in revisionism and dogmatism arrive, even though from different directions, at one and the same thing—estrangement from Marxism-Leninism and from the socialist camp and the world Communist movement.

The Albanian leaders' disagreement with our party's Leninist policy as laid down by the 20th Congress is also to be explained by the fact that Enver Hoxha and Mehmet Shehu have long been cultivating in their party practices and methods that are incompatible with Marxism-Leninism. How Mehmet Shehu, for example, interprets the norms of Party life is plain from his statement at the recent Congress of the Albanian Party of Labor that anyone who disagreed with the leadership on a question would be (and I quote) "spat in the face, punched in the mouth and, if need be, have a bullet put into his brain."

Several prominent figures in the Albanian Party of Labor have only recently been expelled from the Party and subjected to repressive action: Liri Belishova, member of the Politburo, together with her husband, and Mago Como, member of the Central Committee and a government Minister (both of them were also deprived of their Deputies' credentials), and also Koco Tashko, veteran of the international Communist movement and the oldest member of the Albanian Party of Labor, who has been active since as far back as the Comintern days of the 1930s and who has never had a disagreement with the Party; until recently Enver Hoxha considered him his closest friend. Now he has been expelled from the Party. These people have been victimized merely because they did not wish to leave the tried and tested path of Albanian-Soviet friendship.

Albanian seamen who had been studying in our country recently returned home. In talks among themselves they voiced perplexity over what could have caused the sudden deterioration of relations between Albania and the U.S.S.R. Many of them landed in prison for this.

Albanian students who were studying in our country went home for their vacations, and afterwards many of them were not permitted by the Albanian authorities to continue their studies in the U.S.S.R. This naturally caused disgruntlement among them, and again many of the malcontents were subject to repressive action.

On the one hand the Albanian leaders persecute those who want to maintain friendship between our parties and peoples, and on the other hand they hold a Soviet-Albanian friendship month to deceive their people. This was in September.

It will be said that these are their internal affairs and must not be interfered in. But after all, the persecution and acts of repression are directed against Albanians who uphold the traditional friendship with the Soviet Union. And this is something that directly concerns us; we cannot remain indifferent in the matter, and are obliged to state our opinion.

The Albanian leaders are now extolling the cult of Stalin and seeking to use his name as a cover-up for actions that are intolerable to Leninism.

Can anyone really think that friendship between us is possible on the "basis"—if I may be excused for using the term—on which the Albanian leaders are now operating? No, they have to understand clearly that only by renouncing this course and taking positions that are mandatory for Communist parties can they count on the friendship of the Party of Lenin, the friendship of the Soviet people. This is the only way it can be! (Stormy, prolonged applause.)

Comrades! The Party Program contains a Leninist analysis of the national-liberation movement and correctly describes its prospects and tasks. The victory of the national-liberation revolutions is assessed as the most important development since the formation of the world socialist system. Comprehensive support for the anti-imperialist movement of liberation is the international duty of the socialist states.

Thanks specifically to the existence of the world socialist system, new opportunities—the paths of noncapitalist development—have opened up to the young national states.

The peoples of these countries do not want to follow the long and agonizing path of capitalist development. What this path, fraught with suffering for millions, has meant is strikingly illustrated by the history of the Latin American countries. It is a hundred or more years since the colonial yoke of Spain and the other European countries was thrown off by the insurgent peoples of Latin America, and a score of Latin American countries are formally independent states. But their development has proceeded along the capitalist path, with the domination of American imperialism as its distinguishing feature. And here is the result: In his speech to Congress shortly after becoming President of the United States, J. Kennedy was forced to state the harsh truth. He asserted that "in Latin America the rates of growth of the population already threaten to exceed the rates of economic growth, and in several areas of the continent the standard of living is actually falling." In other words, material resources per capita are steadily diminishing in Latin American countries, and life is growing steadily worse for the working people. This is virtually the death sentence for latter-day colonialism and an admission of where U.S. domination based on the notorious Monroe Doctrine has led.

Who is responsible for the economic backwardness and poverty of these countries? The Latin American people themselves? Are they really incapable of developing their economies? No, the point is that these peoples have fallen into the clutches of the American monopolies, which are plundering their wealth, strangling them economically, intruding into their domestic affairs and bribing and backing reactionary elements, above all the latifundistas, those medieval barbarians who are oppressing their peoples. The U.S. monopolies are blocking the development of national industry, above all processing industries. Reactionary elements are being artificially kept in power, which impedes social progress in the Latin American countries.

This means that having overthrown one group of colonialists, the peoples of Latin America fell under the sway of another—the American monopolies. Despite their surface attributes of independence, they are in effect under a foreign yoke. This is what is today called neocolonialism.

Kennedy talks of aid, of reforms, of development, while the

American monopolies, like a frightful octopus, squeeze these countries harder and harder.

Even the official data show that the influx of capital from the United States into the Latin American countries has amounted in the past 15 years to $6,500,000,000, while the profits taken out of them have come to almost $10,000,000,000. That's "aid" for you! This is barely concealed robbery, and in it lie the roots of the poverty of Latin America's working people. And the American rulers are not going to cure this malady with any "aid" poultices, because monopolies cannot change their nature, cannot stop robbing wherever they have penetrated.

Today revolutionary Cuba has taken the road of real liberation from the rule of the monopolies. It has driven out the latifundistas and other parasites on society and is building a socialist life. Under the leadership of Fidel Castro, hero of the revolution, and of his splendid comrades-in-arms, Cuba is taking seven-league strides in the development of the country—economic, social, cultural and political. (Applause.)

If Kennedy is such a champion of reform in the Latin American countries, and of their well-being, one would think he should rejoice at this, but he has declared virtual war on the little island of Cuba. Neocolonialism has removed its camouflage wrapping and revealed its true face, the face of the colonial robber. But times have changed, Messrs. Imperialists! Hands off revolutionary Cuba! (Prolonged, long-unabating applause.)

Actually, neocolonialism of the same kind threatens a number of countries in Africa and Asia, too.

The struggle of the peoples aimed at destroying all forms of colonialism meets with full support from the Soviet Union and the other socialist countries. But for the world socialist system there would not have been successful revolutions of national liberation, and the question of what paths should be taken by peoples that have won their freedom would not have arisen in all its magnitude.

The Soviet Union and the other socialist countries have come into the lives of these peoples bringing their just methods of maintaining economic ties on the basis of equality and their noble intentions of facilitating the advance of these peoples on the road of progress. We were taught this by the great Lenin. This is an example of proletarian internationalism in action under modern conditions. (Applause.)

The liberated countries will realize their opportunity for noncapitalist development by dint of an acute internal struggle, for the progressive and democratic forces in these countries will be opposed by both the world monopolies and the forces of internal reaction, to whom progress means death.

Is it any wonder that many of the statesmen and public figures of these countries, although they are not Marxists and sometimes even call themselves anti-Marxists, refuse to inscribe on their banners the slogan of development along the capitalist path? Capitalism has totally discredited itself in the eyes of the peoples. The peoples do not want to vegetate any longer in poverty and ignorance; they are seeking early deliverance from these things, and capitalism cannot give this to them. Hence the quest for new paths, new forms of development. We are convinced that they will find this road, and that it will be none other than the road of socialism. (Applause.)

Comrades, problems of foreign policy have occupied and will continue to occupy an important place in our party's activities. These problems cannot be separated from our domestic policy. What counts most for us is to ensure peaceful conditions for the building of a communist society.

The principle of peaceful coexistence embraces not only foreign policy but foreign economic relations. Lenin pointed out that there are "general economic relations involving the whole world," and that these relations are "a force greater than the desire, will or decision of any one of the hostile governments or classes." ("Works," Fourth [Russian] Edition, Vol. XXXIII, p. 129.)

These general world-wide economic relations continue to exist now that two world systems, the socialist and the capitalist, and consequently two world markets, two world economies, have come into being. Each of these markets and each of these economies is developing according to its own laws. But at the same time the two world markets are not shut off from one another by an impenetrable wall. Consequently the international division of labor remains, as does the world market con-

nected with it. The world market and world prices are not a fiction. Ignoring them could cause serious material harm in practice.

There is nothing more absurd than the bourgeois notion that the economic policy of socialism is a policy of autarky. American imperialism has tried to force a policy of autarky on us with its course of cutting off trade with the socialist world. But this course has come to nothing. Many of the capitalist countries have undertaken to develop mutually advantageous trade with the Soviet Union and the other socialist countries, and we are confident that this course will sooner or later be taken by the United States too.

The Soviet Union has become one of the world's greatest trading powers. The volume of our foreign trade is at present nearly ten times what it was in 1938, before the war. In the past ten years it has been growing at an average annual rate of 12.6%, which is even somewhat faster than the rate of growth of industrial output.

It is gratifying to see that this very year, when the volume of our foreign trade will amount to 10,500,000,000 rubles, we shall come very close to the level set for 1965; thus in terms of the rate of development, the seven-year plan for foreign trade will have been completed in approximately three years. (Applause.)

Our foreign trade and other forms of economic cooperation will continue to develop. According to the estimates of Soviet economists, the foreign trade of the U.S.S.R. may grow fourfold or more over the 20-year period. This will call for further improvements in planning and for a number of measures of an economic and organizational character. Broader use must be made of foreign trade as a factor for effecting economies in current outlays on production and in capital investment, with the object of speeding the development of particular industries. We must arrange for export goods to be produced in the most advisable locations, so that transport costs may be sharply reduced.

The Party has set itself the task of making Soviet products the finest in the world. This is especially important for the foreign market, where we are obliged to win out in competition. Nor should it be forgotten that our economic achievements are judged abroad by the quality of the goods we ship.

Peaceful coexistence is, further, an active and purposeful struggle to eliminate all seedbeds of war, to remove the most acute centers of conflicts fraught with war danger; it is the struggle for general disarmament. Today the absence of a German peace treaty has become one of the chief obstacles to ensuring a stable, lasting peace.

Adenauer is offended when parallels are drawn between the present trend in the Federal Republic of Germany and what happened in Germany under Hitler. But we judge by deeds, after all, and the policy of the F.R.G. does bear a great resemblance to Germany's policy before the second world war. It is based on militarism, revanchism and anticommunism.

For the third time in this century German militarism is making ready to unleash war in Central Europe, this time relying on the alliance of Western imperialist powers headed by the United States.

West Germany is a member of NATO, and this compounds the danger of the situation. The result of the automatic nature of existing allied obligations may be that the Bonn revanchists, having launched some military provocation, will drag the United States, Britain, France and other states into it; they are basing their main strategic plans on this.

We have time and again spoken of the urgent necessity of concluding a German peace treaty and of our wish to settle questions by agreement with the Western powers, to guarantee the existing borders of the G.D.R. and the F.R.G. on that basis, to normalize the West Berlin situation and to eliminate the breeding ground of war in Europe. But if we become convinced that the Western powers do not want a peace treaty with the two German states, we shall be compelled to conclude such a treaty with the G.D.R., and there is no force that could keep us from effecting this vitally essential peace settlement. (Stormy, prolonged applause.)

We cannot today neglect to mention what a great effort Comrade Khrushchev, head of the Soviet government, has made in upholding peace and in making clear to the Western countries the urgency of concluding a German peace treaty and our stand regarding the purpose and the substance of such a treaty. The fact that certain encouraging shifts have become apparent in the position of the West, and above all in public opinion in both the United States and the Western European countries, is in large measure attributable to this effort.

As you know, our Party and government delegation attended a celebration in the G.D.R. a few days ago. Personal contact with the German people and their leaders has provided most convincing evidence that peace, labor and socialism have firmly established themselves on this portion of German soil and that everything there breathes hatred for militarism and revanchism. (Stormy applause.)

It is truly fortunate for Europe that a German state of this kind—the G.D.R.—has at long last made its appearance, a state where the workers' and peasants' regime has blacked out the odious past and extends the hand of friendship and peaceful cooperation to all peoples! (Stormy, long-unabating applause.)

Comrades, 63 years have gone by since the founding of our party. Our Bolshevik party, reared by the great Lenin, has traversed a grand and arduous path, a glorious path, worthy of Communists. Its two Programs have been completed, and the accomplishment of each of them signified a whole epoch in the life not only of our party and country but of all mankind.

The Party brought our country Marxism, united it with the working-class movement, carried on and multiplied the deeds and the finest traditions of the whole preceding revolutionary movement in Russia. The prediction made by Marx and Engels came to pass—the center of the international working-class movement shifted to Russia at the turn of the century.

From that time to the present day, in the era of the emergence and successful development of the world socialist system, our party has held the communist banner high and is the acknowledged vanguard of the world Communist movement. (Applause.)

The Party, under the banner of Lenin, has today roused the entire people for the building of a communist society.

The new Program illumines for us the road to the already-near peaks of communism! The compass of history points to communism! (Stormy, prolonged applause.)

Suslov

SPEECH BY COMRADE M. A. SUSLOV, SECRETARY OF THE PARTY CENTRAL COMMITTEE. (Pravda, Oct. 23, pp. 4-5. 6,500 words. Condensed text:) ... The role of the Soviet Union in the international arena has grown to an unprecedented extent, and its influence on the liberation struggle of the working class and the working people throughout the world has increased. The stubborn and consistent struggle of the Party and the Soviet government against the threat of a new war of annihilation, against colonialism and imperialism and for the peaceful coexistence of states with different social systems, the disinterested assistance to peoples who have won or are striving for their national liberation, and constant concern for the further strengthening of the world socialist commonwealth have won our country enormous prestige among hundreds of millions of people in all parts of the globe.

We owe this above all to the fact that our Communist Party is profoundly faithful to the great teaching of Marxism-Leninism. Guided by the historic decisions of its 20th Congress, the Party has firmly and confidently pursued a Leninist domestic and foreign policy. In the first years after the 20th Congress the Party met with bitter opposition from the anti-Party group of Molotov, Kaganovich, Malenkov, Voroshilov, Bulganin and others, who tried to push the Party from the Leninist path and return it to the times of the cult of the individual. As is known, this contemptible group of factionalists, detached from the people, stubbornly opposed the implementation of such vitally important measures, warmly approved by all the Soviet people, as development of the virgin lands, reorganization of the management of industry and construction, development of inner-Party democracy, restoration of revolutionary legality and others. Many persons in this group were directly guilty of mass repressions against honest Communists in the period of the cult of the individual. In foreign policy the anti-Party group, especially Molotov, did everything possible to oppose the Central Committee's course of carrying out the principles of peaceful coexistence of states with different social systems and of ensuring a lasting peace. This factional activity could have done serious harm to the Party and the country. The Party ideologically routed and cast out the miserable clique of oppositionists. Life has fully overthrown their views and shown their utter bankruptcy. (Applause.) ...

The New Party Program—Great Document of Our Times.— ... The draft of the new Program retains full ideological continuity with the two previous Party Programs. Each of these documents naturally reflects the specific features of the given stage of our party's history.

The first Program, adopted in 1903 at the Second Congress of the Russian Social-Democratic Workers' Party, formulated the basic tasks of the workers' movement—overthrow of the tsarist autocracy, and then the carrying out of a socialist revolution and establishment of a dictatorship of the proletariat. At that time socialism was regarded only as the ultimate goal of the struggle.

The second Program was based on the victory of the October Revolution and the experience amassed in state, economic and cultural construction in the conditions of a dictatorship of the proletariat. In this Program socialism was advanced as the direct, immediate goal of the struggle. ...

At that time the experience of Soviet rule was completely inadequate to provide a comprehensive scientific description of communist society. This is why when Bukharin proposed giving a description of communism in the Program, V. I. Lenin categorically rejected his proposal. ...

The world-historic significance of the new Program is that for the first time in the entire history of mankind a plan, ways and means of building a communist society have been scientifically worked out. The draft of the new Program theoretically elucidates hitherto unexplored paths of the transition from socialism to communism, further develops major questions of Marxist-Leninist theory, gives a comprehensive description of communism and shows what its material and technical base and social relations will be and what the man of communism himself will be like. ...

The Communist and Workers' Parties of foreign countries have evaluated the draft of our Program as one of the most remarkable events in the history of the great victories of Marxism-Leninism. It has become for them a source of inspiration and support in the struggle. We Soviet Communists see in this a confirmation of the correctness of the policy of our party, a new expression of the ideological unity of the Communists of all countries on the basis of the principles of Marxism-Leninism and of their fidelity to the historic documents jointly adopted at conferences—the 1957 Declaration and the 1960 Statement. ...

In the conditions of warm approval of the draft Program by the working people of all countries, attention is drawn to the fact that in Albania the draft Program was published in abridged and distorted form. A distorted idea of the C.P.S.U.'s position on a number of fundamental questions has thereby been created. This unfriendly act of the Albanian leaders is no accident. Inflating in every way the cult of the individual in their party and country and grossly violating Leninist norms of Party life, they do not wish to reconcile themselves to the course being carried out by our party of overcoming the harmful consequences of the cult of the individual and restoring revolutionary legality. Today matters have reached a point in Albania where people who advocate preservation of friendship with the Soviet Union and the other socialist countries are dismissed from their posts and subjected to repressions. Yet only two years ago, at the 21st C.P.S.U. Congress, Enver Hoxha, First Secretary of the Central Committee of the Albanian Party of Labor, expressed to our Communist Party, the Soviet people and the Soviet government, and to Comrade N. S. Khrushchev personally, "the deepest gratitude for all they have done and are doing for the good and happiness of the small Albanian nation." How far have the Albanian leaders now departed from this, in defaming our party and its leadership in every way! At the same time, in their press they still continue hypocritically to paint a picture of friendship, trading on the good feelings of the Albanian people for the Soviet Union and our party.

Now the leaders of the Albanian Party of Labor's Central Committee have sent a letter. This letter, comrades, is a mixture of hypocrisy and slanderous insinuations. Permit me to tell the leaders of the Albanian Party of Labor: We are well aware where friendship is, and where hypocrisy. (Applause.)

Do the leaders of Albania realize what harm they are doing above all to the cause of the building of socialism in their country by undermining the foundation of friendship with the Communist Party of the Soviet Union and with the Soviet people and opposing themselves to the other fraternal parties on major questions of our times? Communist-internationalists cannot but be alarmed by the position taken by the leaders of the Albanian Party of Labor.

What was the reaction to the draft Program in foreign circles hostile to us?

In the imperialist countries there is, of course, no shortage of malicious attacks on the Program, of crooked falsification of it under the guise of criticism, of the cries, known to us even before the first five-year plans, of "mirage," "utopia," "fantasy," etc. Nevertheless, many of our opponents are compelled to admit the feasibility of the Party Program and are frightened by its great attractive force.

The American magazine Life bitterly complains that "the free world does not have a powerful operational group" for working out its own program capable of "attracting people to the ideas of the West." This is not the point, of course. In the U.S.A. and in other imperialist countries there are dozens of "operational" and "superoperational" groups of various sorts. But they are powerless to counterpose to the Program for building communism anything serious and convincing. No one is able to rehabilitate the misanthropic and obsolete capitalist system. (Applause.)

A few comments about the reaction of the Right Social Democrats to our Program. In general, as was to be expected, they are dragging behind bourgeois propaganda. Like the bourgeois politicians, they are most concerned about whether "Western democracy," i.e., the countries of monopoly capitalism, will be able to respond to the "Communist challenge" with a counterprogram capable of attracting people both in the West and, in particular, in the underdeveloped countries. In order to deceive the working people, the leaders of Social Democracy are also searching for a "convincing" anti-Communist counterprogram. Indeed: "Where the steed puts down his hoof, there rushes in the crab with its claw." For this purpose a congress of the Socialist International will convene in Rome soon. But all the attempts of the Right leaders of Social Democracy are in vain: Nothing can halt the triumphant march of the ideas of communism. (Stormy applause.)

The world discussion of the draft Party Program was at the same time like a court of history, which again placed with untold force before millions of people the question: "Who proved to be right—the Communists, who remained true to Marxism, or the Right Social Democrats, who long ago betrayed it?" As a result of the activity of the Communists, a mighty world socialist system has been created which is exerting an increasingly decisive influence on the entire course of world events. And what have the Right Social Democrats achieved? Many Right Socialist parties have come into and gone out of power, yet the omnipotence of monopoly capital and its oppression have not only been preserved but have grown stronger. As a matter of fact, this does not at all trouble the leaders of the Right Social Democrats. They are doing everything to adapt their parties not to struggle against monopoly capitalism but to serve it, to support it in every way, to combat the Communists and slander the socialist countries.

In recent years many Social Democratic parties have adopted new programs. However, they did not do so because they had fulfilled their previous programs—all their promises to the working people remained hollow talk—but in order to discard absolutely everything in them that was still reminiscent of Marxism, the class struggle and socialist revolution, and to adapt their policy and tactics even more to the defense of monopoly capital. Their new programs signify an actual rejection of socialism.

Formerly Social Democracy set the goal, at least formally, of socialization of ownership of the means of production. Now its new programs officially defend capitalist private property as "the foundation of democracy." "Our program and our ideal," states Ollenhauer, leader of the Social Democratic Party of Germany, "is a combination of private enterprise, private initiative and private property***with public control." It is quite obvious that this program does not contain a grain of socialism and that any bourgeois would sign it. It is not for nothing that the conservative British newspaper The Times wittily commented: "As a result of the adoption of the new program, Chancellor Adenauer won a victory at the Congress of the Social Democratic Party of Germany."

In the new Social Democratic programs the class struggle is declared to be an outdated concept. The supposedly utopian and harmful idea of liquidation of the bourgeois state is discarded. The slogan "Proletarians of all countries, unite!" is declared to be a "sinister offspring of the epoch of the first industrial revolution." The Social Democratic programs have replaced proletarian internationalism with "unification of Europe" and various cosmopolitan interstate combinations, which they count on as a means for "Western democracy" (i.e., for capitalism) to hold out in the competition with socialism.

The renunciation of socialism by the Right leaders of Social Democracy cannot but evoke and has already evoked serious dissatisfaction on the part of rank-and-file socialist workers in many parties. Along with passive protest, an active rebuff to the policy of the Right leaders is growing, as is the case, for example, in the British Labor Party, the French Socialist Party and others.

In criticizing Right Social Democracy from the positions of scientific socialism on behalf of the interests of the working class, universal progress and peace, we, as well as the Communists of all countries, pursue the aim of assisting the consolidation of all healthy progressive forces within the Social Democratic movement, which, if they were united, could lead this movement onto the class, revolutionary path.

Develop and Strengthen the Socialist System.— ... The experience of the Soviet Union and of the other socialist countries and the entire international revolutionary movement shows that the road to socialism lies only through socialist revolution and dictatorship of the proletariat. The preachings of the reformists and revisionists regarding other roads to socialism of one sort or another are deception of the working people. Also anti-Marxist is the conception of the Yugoslav revisionists, who demand a withering away of the socialist state almost immediately after victory of the proletarian revolution, which would disarm the proletariat in the face of its foreign and internal enemies and undermine its victory.

However, the working class is the only class in history that is not trying to perpetuate its political supremacy. It uses its dictatorship only to accomplish the tasks of building socialism.

The dictatorship of the proletariat is, consequently, a historically transient political institution linked with the accomplishment of definite historically conditioned tasks. After fulfilling its historical mission, it develops into a state of the entire people in which the working class, as the most advanced, organized force of Soviet society, continues to perform its leading role until classes disappear.

The state of the entire people is an important instrument in communist construction. Expressing the will of all the people, our state is called upon to organize the creation of the material and technical base of communism and the transformation of socialist relations into communist relations, to exercise control over the measure of work and consumption, to ensure a rise in the well-being of the working people, to safeguard the rights and freedoms of Soviet citizens, socialist law and order and socialist property, and to instill in the masses of the people conscious discipline and a communist attitude toward labor. At the same time it is called upon to ensure the reliable defense and security of the country, to develop fraternal cooperation with the socialist countries, to champion the cause of universal peace and to maintain normal relations with all countries. ...

The process of the withering away of the socialist state that is already under way cannot, however, be understood as transformation of the state into nothing. Communist society is not an anarchically formless and unorganized mass of people—as the ideologists of imperialism frequently write of it—but a highly organized and harmonious commonwealth of people of labor, distinguished for lofty communist awareness of their public duty and high discipline.

The process of the withering away of the state signifies the gradual transformation of agencies of state authority into agencies of public self-government through the further development of socialist democracy; this assumes the active participation of all citizens in administration of the state and management of economic and cultural construction and an improvement of the work of the state apparatus and a strengthening of public supervision over its activity.

The tasks of strengthening socialist legality increase in the period of the full-scale building of communism. In all its activity our state power uses persuasion on an ever-growing scale. But it does not follow that coercion will not be used also where this is necessary. It is known what enormous importance V. I. Lenin attached to the struggle against scoundrels, parasites and hooligans back in the early years of Soviet rule. He held that these enemies of socialism "must be brought under the special supervision of the entire population, they must be dealt with mercilessly for the least violation by them of the rules and laws of socialist society." ("Works" [in Russian], Vol. XXVI, p. 372.)

The total number of criminal manifestations in our country is steadily declining. This is understandable. In contrast to the capitalist states, where mass crime is inevitably engendered by the very nature of an exploiting society, in our country the rise in the material security, cultural level and social awareness of the working people creates all the conditions for eradicating crime. But it would be naive to count on simply letting matters take their own course in this respect and to tolerate unjustified liberalism, of which officials of our administrative agencies are frequently guilty. Utilizing all the necessary means of education and persuasion and the force of the community against violators of the law, the state of the entire people must also unwaveringly apply means of coercion—its punitive sword—against malicious and dangerous criminals, hooligans, plunderers of socialist property, loafers, parasites and other antisocial elements that hinder the people from building communism. (Applause.)

Rear the Man of Communist Society.— ... The Party's ideological work has tremendous importance in rearing the new man, in the common struggle for the victory of communism. The main thing in ideological work at the present stage, as the Program states, is education of all the working people in a spirit of lofty ideological conviction and devotion to communism and a communist attitude toward labor and the communal economy, complete elimination of the survivals of bourgeois views and morals, the all-round, harmonious development of the individual and the creation of a genuine wealth of spiritual culture. ...

Even in the course of the building of socialism our party did tremendous work in education of the masses. And we have a right to be proud of the wonderful fruits of this work. The leading people of our country already embody features of the man of the communist future. ...

Capitalism, with its principle "man is a wolf to man," has engendered egoism, money-grubbing, crookedness, parasitism, philistine indifference to the common cause, careerism and other detestable phenomena, which are still encountered as a heritage of the past in our life as well. In the course of building communism we must fully cleanse our society of all disgusting survivals of capitalism, rear every Soviet man in a spirit of lofty communist awareness, moral purity, industriousness, discipline and devotion to public interests.

The bourgeois ideologists and politicians and the opportunists, their agents in the workers' movement, slander the Communists, claiming that Communists deny morality and humanism. In actual fact, it is precisely communism that bears the loftiest principles of humanism and the most humane morality. Refuting the class egoistic morality of the exploiters, Communists counterpose to it their own morality—a just, humane and noble morality that expresses the interests and ideals of all working mankind. (Prolonged applause.)

Propaganda of the immortal ideas of Marxism-Leninism, their creative development and implementation, and system-

atic struggle against all manifestations of bourgeois ideology constitute a major task of the Party's ideological work.

Since the 20th Party Congress our ideological work has become more purposeful and effective, has embraced more and more millions of Soviet citizens and strengthened its ties with life. The measures carried out by the Central Committee to eliminate the consequences of the cult of the individual in political, ideological and cultural life and the restoration and consistent application of Leninist principles of Party leadership have opened up every opportunity for a mighty advance in ideological work. The working people's enormous interest in Marxist-Leninist theory contributes to this. Today tens of millions of Soviet people—Communists and non-Party people—are taking advantage of various forms of study to master political knowledge. In the academic year just past more than 19,000,000 persons studied in the Party education system alone. Party education, lecture propaganda, mass agitational work and the press and radio are developing on an ever broader scale and acquiring increasing importance in communist education. ...

Literature and art in our country have become a tremendous force in educating the people in a spirit of communist ideals, in molding the moral make-up and the entire structure of the thoughts and feelings of Soviet man. ...

Unfortunately, insipid and useless books and vapid and inartistic pictures and films still appear frequently in our country; these do not measure up to the high calling of Soviet art. And huge state sums are spent producing them. Although some of these works appear under mysterious titles, such as "Man From Nowhere" (stir in the hall), in ideological and artistic respects this film is clearly not from there, not from here. (Stir in the hall. Applause.) We know, too, where the funds vainly spent on the production of the film came from, how much (a great deal) was spent and where the funds went. Is it not time to stop the subsidizing of defective work in the field of art? (Applause.)

In order to show vividly and impressively the hero of our times, the man of large soul and ardent heart, the convinced builder of communism, the artist must know the depth of the people's life, always be together with the people and their vanguard—the Communist Party. (Applause.)

In the present historical period, when the competition of two world systems—socialism and capitalism—has acquired decisive importance, an implacable struggle against the philosophy and morality of the bourgeois world, which are outliving their age, becomes especially necessary.

Bourgeois ideology is experiencing an incurable crisis that reflects the general crisis of the capitalist system. This ideology has no future, since it is the ideology of a class that is departing from the historical scene. It is characterized by the deepest pessimism and fear of the future, distrust in science and in the forces and possibilities of man, mysticism and denial of progress, malicious anticommunism and defense of the system of hired slavery and oppression. This is why the complete bankruptcy of bourgeois ideology is inevitable. Millions of people abroad now see that only the communist ideology expresses the vital interests of the working masses, is deeply scientific and provides correct answers to the most burning questions of our times. In contrast to bourgeois ideology, our ideology is deeply optimistic, imbued with infinite faith in man and his happy future, and its victory is inevitable.

The Future Belongs to Communism.— ... In the period of the implementation of the new Program, in the period of the full-scale building of communism, the role of the Communist Party as the leading and organizing force of Soviet Society grows even greater. This is a law-governed process stemming from the unprecedented growth of the scope and complexity of the tasks of communist construction; the enormous growth of the political and labor activeness of the people and the enlistment of more and more millions of working people in administration of the state; the further development of all forms of socialist democracy; the increased role of public organizations in managing the affairs of society, and extension of the rights of the republics and local organizations; and the growing role of Marxist-Leninist science in the guidance of society and the grandeur of the tasks in educating the working people in a spirit of communism.

Only the Party—steeled in battles for the working people's interests, enjoying the boundless trust of its people, grown wise with tremendous experience, armed with revolutionary theory and therefore capable of profoundly disclosing the objective laws and scientifically outlining the paths and perspectives of the development of society, and possessing indestructible ideological and organizational solidarity—is capable of rallying and embodying the unity of all social strata of the population and all nations of the Soviet Union, of uniting and coordinating the diverse activities of state and public organizations and also of Union, republic and local bodies, and of rousing, organizing and concentrating the efforts, will and energy of all the Soviet people for accomplishing the great tasks of communist construction. The Communist Party of the Soviet Union, created and nurtured by the great Lenin, is precisely such a party. (Stormy applause.)

Only the Communist Party, guided by the fundamental interests of the entire Soviet people and the principles of proletarian internationalism, is capable, in the conditions of the complex international situation, of ensuring a correct foreign policy, developing fraternal ties with the Communist and Workers' Parties of the whole world, and doing everything necessary to strengthen the commonwealth of peoples of the socialist countries and solidarity and friendship among all peoples. ...

Kosygin

SPEECH BY COMRADE A. N. KOSYGIN, FIRST VICE-CHAIRMAN OF THE U.S.S.R. COUNCIL OF MINISTERS. (Pravda, Oct. 23, pp. 6-7; Izvestia, Oct. 24, pp. 4-5. 8,000 words. Condensed text:) Comrades! ... The crushing defeat of the anti-Party factionalist group composed of Molotov, Kaganovich, Malenkov, Voroshilov, Bulganin, Pervukhin, Saburov and Shepilov, who sought to turn the Party back to the old policy of the cult of the individual, to isolate the Party's guiding nucleus from the Party and from the people, has been of great importance for strengthening and consolidating the ranks of our party. They tried once again to violate the restored Leninist norms in Party life and government work and fought to preserve the old, obsolete economic policy in the spheres of agriculture and industry. The struggle against the anti-Party factionalist group was a struggle against the cult of the individual, with which all the members of the anti-Party group were infected.

Molotov and the other members of the anti-Party group considered themselves leaders of the Party for life and thought that the whole Party should do their bidding, rather than they the Party's bidding.

Molotov and the other members of the anti-Party group were strangers to everything new and progressive. They had so lost touch with life and practice that they challenged and were up in arms against every new proposal of value for developing the national economy.

This was in effect a line aimed at thwarting the Party's economic policy and the accelerated development of our economy.

They considered that the socialist style of economic administration was characterized purely and simply by centralization. The stand the members of the anti-Party group took on the solution of economic problems was often dictated not by economic or technical advisability but by considerations of personal prestige. They stifled any helpful initiative. This gave rise to intolerable conditions for work. These actions did tremendous harm to the national economy.

It is not because the anti-Party group constitutes a force at the present time, or a danger to our party in its work, that we are speaking about them at our Congress. Our party is stronger and more unified than ever. It is solidly united around its Central Committee headed by that stanch Leninist Nikita Sergeyevich Khrushchev. (Prolonged applause.) But we are doing this to show the Party and the people once again what the cult of the individual leads to, what irreparable harm the anti-Party group could have done the Party and the state. We want the lessons of history never to be forgotten.

We must and will do everything possible to see to it that from now on there is no place in our Party or our society for a cult of the individual, that its sprouts and roots are thoroughly destroyed.

Following the example of our party's fight for the unity of its ranks and for the purity of Leninist principles, the Party is educating its young cadres in a spirit of implacability toward any attempts to disrupt its unity. There should be no place in communist construction for a cult of the individual. (Stormy applause.) ...

Leninist standards of Party life are being flagrantly violated and the cult of the individual and arbitrary rule are thriving in the Albanian Party of Labor. Enver Hoxha and Mehmet Shehu have created an intolerable situation in the party, people are persecuted for any criticism and there is a reign of terror in the country.

The Albanian leaders have been giving a distorted presentation of the line of our party and its Leninist Central Committee and trying to blacken our foreign and domestic policy in the eyes of the Albanian people. They have practically barred access to Albania for Soviet publications and literature. This is being done with the object of concealing from the heroic Albanian people truthful information about our party's policy and about life in our country, and of misleading the masses of Albania.

We are criticizing the deviations from Marxism-Leninism by the leaders of the Albanian Party of Labor in the sharpest terms.

I am fully in accord with this assessment of the state of affairs in the Albanian Party of Labor and with the just criticism that has been leveled at the leaders of the Albanian Party of Labor by our party's delegates at our Congress and by representatives of the fraternal Communist and Workers' Parties. (Applause.) Our party will continue to follow Lenin's teaching and expose any distortions and departures from Marxism-Leninism with the utmost implacability. (Applause.)

Put Productive Capacity Into Operation More Quickly.— ... Our advantages in rates of economic development and in the character of the distribution of the national income enable us to channel major resources into increasing the accumulation fund while the consumption fund grows at the same time. More than one-fifth of the national income is being used for capital construction. ...

The state's capital investments this year are almost seven times larger than in 1940 and will amount to approximately 33,000,000,000 rubles.

The rate of growth of capital investments in our economy considerably exceeds the rate of growth of total capital investments in the U.S.A. Capital investments have increased 22% in the U.S.A. in the past ten years (in recent years the volume of capital investments has dropped somewhat). In the same period the volume of capital investments in our country has risen by more than 230%, and by 1959-1960 our investments in industry and agriculture exceeded the American investments in absolute magnitude. ...

According to the data of the census taken by the U.S.S.R. Council of Ministers' Central Statistical Administration, the value of the fixed capital of state and cooperative enterprises and organizations has trebled as compared with 1940 (despite the colossal devastation in the war period) and is 14 times as great as the value of the country's fixed capital at the start of the First Five-Year Plan. We have left all the European capitalist countries far behind in the absolute magnitude of fixed production capital.

Besides new capital construction, an effective means of rapidly increasing production capacity is the reconstruction and expansion of existing enterprises on a new technological basis. More than half the total capital investment is now being used for these purposes. ...

In the past ten years total capital investment has amounted to 229,000,000,000 rubles, and more than 8,000 industrial enterprises have been brought into operation, but plans call for almost three times as much to be invested in the national economy in the next ten years.

The draft Program contains the extremely important demand that capital investments be utilized in the most rational and economical fashion, that the greatest results be obtained with the least expenditure.

We have some successes to our credit in this area. For example, in the building of thermal power plants, transmission lines, cement plants, sugar refineries and several other kinds of industrial installations, capital investments per unit of production capacity are lower in our country than in the United States. In ferrous metallurgy, tire production and a number of other industries they are approximately at the U.S. level. But average per-unit capital investments are still high for industry as a whole, and for oil refineries and chemical and automobile plants they are approximately 50% higher than in the United States.

In a number of industries we are erecting large industrial installations within short periods of time. For example, it takes us less than a year to build the largest blast furnaces, six months to build large open-hearth furnaces and four or five months to build five-story large-panel houses. For the economy as a whole, however, the rate of capital construction is not yet adequate to present-day requirements. We are hampered by serious shortcomings in design work and the organization of construction, in material and technical supply and in the planning of capital projects.

The established norms for construction periods should be absolute law in the fixing of specific construction deadlines and volume of capital investments. Nonfulfillment by a republic or an economic council of its plan for putting capacity into operation should be looked upon as nonfulfillment of its over-all plan for economic development. ...

On instructions from the government, the U.S.S.R. State Economic Council and the U.S.S.R. State Planning Committee are working out standard optimal dimensions for enterprises so that we can build predominantly similar enterprises with the most advantageous capacity. This will make it possible to cut down sharply on design work and to effect enormous savings.

A large volume of new construction is in progress in newly settled areas. It is our duty to create good living and working conditions for the working people in these areas. It should be a rule that housing, stores and service and public catering enterprises be built at every new construction site before the construction of the enterprises gets fully under way.

Capital construction has now entered its most crucial period, and the success of the whole seven-year plan will essentially depend on the prompt commissioning of the entire complex of production capacity.

On the initiative of N. S. Khrushchev, the question of capital construction has been discussed in the Party Central Committee and the U.S.S.R. Council of Ministers and a special resolution has been adopted.

A new procedure is being introduced for the planning of capital construction. The volume of capital construction is henceforth to be closely coordinated with the supply of building materials and equipment. Earmarked capital investments and material resources should be concentrated in the first place on projects scheduled for early completion. Construction of new facilities may be initiated only after similar projects already begun have been fully provided with funds and material and technical resources. All these matters will largely be settled in the plan for 1962.

Special stress should be laid on making sure that capacity is commissioned as planned in the entire complex of interconnected industries. This must be carefully attended to; otherwise disproportions may arise in particular sectors of production, especially now that new industries are being set up on the basis of new sources of raw materials.

In order to heighten the responsibility of construction organizations for the prompt commissioning of production capacity, their activities should from now on be assessed not by the degree to which they have made use of funds allocated for capital construction but by the commissioning of completed installations, and this should be the basis for bonus payments to personnel.

In view of the large volume of capital construction work on projects due for early completion, it becomes especially important that they receive their full complements of equipment in good time.

Organizationally, these matters have already been settled. We have set up chief equipment-supply administrations under the U.S.S.R. State Planning Committee and the Union-republic State Planning Commissions, as well as under several of the ministries. The task of these administrations is to make sure that enterprises being built are completely equipped in good time. But their performance has so far been unsatisfactory. The U.S.S.R. State Planning Committee should make greater demands upon these agencies and heighten their responsibility for the efficient delivery of equipment to construction sites.

It is quite intolerable that defective machinery and equipment should sometimes be delivered to the construction sites. We must seriously reproach the management of even such large and advanced plants as the Podolsk Machine-Building Plant of the Moscow Province Economic Council, the Leningrad Metals Plant, the Elektrosila Plant and the Kharkov Turbogenerator Plant. Because of defects in power equipment delivered by these plants, 150,000- and 200,000-kw. generators at the Southern Urals and Nazarovo power plants have not yet gone into service, while at the Dnieper State Regional Power Plant there has been trouble with the equipment.

We must enlarge the installation organizations at the principal machine-building plants, and where there are no such organizations we must establish them, so that the installation of equipment at the construction sites is handled by these plants. Equipment installation will be the final stage, as it were, in the sequence of operations. It will heighten the responsibility of machine-building plants for the quality of the equipment and to a certain extent for its on-time delivery and start-up.

Another matter that should be looked into is the procedure used in paying the machine-building plants for equipment. It would appear advisable that equipment be paid for after it has been turned over for operation; bank credit could be made available for the plants to cover the period prior to delivery of the equipment.

More attention should be given to the installation organizations. They must be reinforced with highly trained engineers and workers, and arrangements must be made to give installation workers special training. ...

In order to provide enterprises and construction projects with a material stake in reducing the time and cost of construction and the volume of unfinished building, it would be advisable, by way of experiment, to go over from budget financing of capital investments to the extension of long-term credit. The practice of having the U.S.S.R. State Bank grant two- and three-year loans for modernization and improvement of operating equipment has fully justified itself. This procedure might be extended to cover reconstruction and expansion of existing enterprises. This would provide the builders with a greater incentive to speed up the commissioning of a unit under construction and to develop their own sources from which to make repayment of credit.

Builders must be provided with special truck transport for moving cement, concrete and reinforced concrete and with a sufficient number of large dump trucks for moving nonmetallic minerals; that is, transport facilities must be specialized.

Such truck factories as the ZIL, Gorky and Miass plants must strengthen their design bureaus so that they can concentrate on the design and production of up-to-date special-purpose trucks. This is important for almost all branches of the national economy. Production of such trucks, adapted for moving bulk loads, will ensure a sharp rise in the productivity of labor.

It is particularly important to make sure that the construction industry has the needed variety of metal types for production of reinforced concrete. Despite the significant increase in the production of reinforcing bars and other types of light rolled sections, the builders suffer a shortage of these items. And this is holding down the rate of construction.

The U.S.S.R. State Economic Council and the U.S.S.R. State Planning Committee are working out a program for increasing the output of the needed variety of metal types so that this important economic problem may be solved within a short time.

Improve the Organization of Socialist Production.—Comrades! ... Rational organization of production means in the first place making the very best use of production resources, which makes possible a substantial increase in output. We have registered good results in particular industries. For example, the increase in output in all branches of ferrous metallurgy in 1959-1960 was considerably greater than the increase in production capacity. In the cement industry, a 9,200,000-ton increase in production capacity over these same years was attended by a rise of more than 12,000,000 tons in the volume of production.

In the production of footwear, capacity for turning out 30,000,000 pairs was brought into operation, while output rose by 63,000,000 pairs. Unutilized reserves of this kind exist in all branches of the economy.

There are large unutilized reserves in the machine-building industry. At most machine-building plants machinery is in use for the equivalent of no more than 1.4 to 1.5 shifts. At enterprises spot-checked by the Central Statistical Administration, in the first two shifts only about half the stock of machine tools were working with a full load; furthermore, in the first shift every sixth tool was completely idle, and in the second shift every third tool. Not only the multipurpose equipment but also the single-purpose equipment, the special machine tools and machine-tool aggregates and the heavy forge-and-press machinery was greatly underloaded. Equipment downtime within the shifts is still great, amounting to 18% of total working time for particular machines.

Yet it is entirely feasible to increase the operating loads. At certain machine-building plants as much as 40% of the equipment downtime lasting a full shift and more than 50% of the downtime occurring within the shifts is caused by factors of an organizational character, chiefly the tardy supplying of materials and tardy feeding of billets and tools to the work places.

A very important role in the achievement of full utilization of equipment should be played by the broad extension of the practice of tending several machines at once, which will enable us to widen the work front and increase output without additional investment and without increasing the number of workers. Naturally, the simultaneous operation of several machines requires appropriate organizational and technical preparations—the rearrangement of equipment, its mechanical adaptation and the improvement of occupational skills. The system of material encouragement for persons operating several machines simultaneously should evidently be revised so as to provide them with greater incentive.

The technical improvement of socialist production calls for transition to new and superior labor organization. Enterprise directors must focus their attention on the efficient arrangement of the work place, the provision of normal lighting, the improvement of work hygiene, the introduction of advanced working methods, etc.—in a word, everything that is meant by the term scientific organization of labor, everything that lightens labor and raises its productivity.

The scientific solution of the entire complex of problems involved in organizing production at a modern, highly mechanized industrial enterprise is today an urgent task. Our scientific institutions—industrial and general economics institutes and design organizations—must accomplish this task. More attention must be given in educational institutions to studying problems of production organization. ...

The further improvement of production calls for the solution of a number of problems that go beyond the concerns of the economic region. This is attested by statements made in the press by economic executives—chairmen of economic councils (Comrades Sinitsyn, Lisnyak, Stepanov and many others), as well as by heads of committees and planning agencies and by scientists.

In the past few years the government has adopted decisions calling for further development of the machine tool and electrical equipment industries and of the production of diesel locomotives, construction and road-building machinery, compressors, castings, tools and metal products on the basis of the specialization and precise typing of enterprises.

The output of main-line diesel locomotives has almost doubled in the past two years as a result of the mastering of their specialized production.

But in a number of other branches of machine building specialization is proceeding too slowly. Existing foundry capacity is still inadequate to ensure production of the quantity of billets needed for the smooth operation of ma-

chine-building enterprises. Specialization has been slight in the lumber and wood-processing industries and in light industry. There have been cases of failure to observe the principle of specialization in the building of new plants and the operation of existing ones, which lessens the economic benefit of the specialization carried out.

Some 800,000 metal-cutting tools are scattered through the repair shops of various industrial enterprises. These tools are being used to make spare parts and components. In most cases these components are made individually without observance of technological requirements, and are too expensive.

It is obviously economically sounder to have repair work rationally centralized and to expand the specialized production of spare parts in the large economic regions or for several regions in a republic.

Several economic councils have done some work on setting up centralized enterprises to produce spare parts and components for equipment repair, centralizing repair facilities and improving the organization of auxiliary work. This initiative on the part of the economic councils certainly deserves favorable assessment. But the measures being taken by the economic councils do not solve the whole problem. Naturally, the economic councils are as a rule guided solely by their own needs. The problem of organizing the repair of basic equipment should therefore now be solved through the planning agencies, on a state-wide scale.

The plan for 1962 should provide for priority measures to specialize particular enterprises in the production of spare parts, while equipment now being used for the manufacture of spare parts should be employed to expand basic production.

A most important prerequisite of the progressive organization of production is the extensive introduction of standard specifications and the standardization of assemblies and components of articles and equipment and of technological processes. ...

Of enormous importance is the further improvement of our industry's qualitative indices, the production of highly efficient equipment and the lengthening of the life of machinery. We need but consider the production of diesel engines and motors. The increase in the amount of power available per worker depends largely upon the mass introduction of these engines. ...

But our diesels and motors still have too short a life, and therefore we have to produce excessive numbers of them in order to meet the needs of the economy. Increasing the life of diesels and motors must be made one of the major economic tasks.

The State Economic Council, the State Automation and Machine-Building Committee and the producer plants must study the complex of factors involved in increasing the life of diesels and motors, must try to develop new alloys and work to improve the quality of fuels and lubricants and of special additives, so that each new series of diesels and motors turned out has a longer life than the preceding one. This will yield the national economy enormous savings. Thought must be given to providing plant personnel with incentives to develop and manufacture diesels and motors with a longer life. ...

Shortcomings in the structure of the supply-and-marketing system, errors in planning and distribution, and in a number of cases unsupervised expenditure of materials create needless strain in the supply to enterprises and construction projects of certain raw and other materials and semimanufactured goods.

We must improve the coordination of planning and see to it that plans for production and construction are fully balanced with those for material and technical supply.

The improvement of norm-setting should be accomplished from the bottom up—from the enterprise and shop to the republic State Planning Commissions and the U.S.S.R. State Planning Committee.

The present norms for expenditure of materials are largely outdated. They should be flexible and must regularly be brought up to date, in keeping with the advance of technology and the development of new materials. ...

Zarobyan

SPEECH BY COMRADE YA. N. ZAROBYAN, FIRST SEC-

RETARY OF THE ARMENIAN COMMUNIST PARTY CEN-
TRAL COMMITTEE. (Pravda, Oct. 23, p. 8. 3,500 words.
Excerpts:) ... At present more than 1,000,000 Armenians live
in various capitalist countries, where they had to move to escape physical annihilation, primarily in the period of World
War I. While in Yerevan, Comrade N. S. Khrushchev met with
representatives of progressive Armenians abroad. Under the
indelible impression of this warm, cordial encounter and the
celebration of the republic's 40th anniversary, many progressive foreign Armenian newspapers gave truthful and enthusiastic testimonials to the achievements of Soviet Armenia. The
progressive newspaper Ararat, published in Beirut, stated:
"We can confirm that everything we saw is not a dream; it is
genuine, tangible reality."

The flowering of Soviet Armenia in the fraternal family of
peoples of the great Soviet Union is attracting like a magnet
the best sons and daughters of the Armenian people. The flow
of requests from Armenians living in capitalist countries has
greatly increased in recent years. These requests express an
ardent desire to leave the capitalist "paradise" and come to
their homeland, to Soviet Armenia. (Applause.) With the cooperation and considerable assistance of the Soviet government,
we have decided to organize, beginning in 1962, the gradual
return to the homeland of Armenians who have expressed a desire to come from foreign countries. We will do everything to
create the necessary conditions for their normal life and
creative labor. ...

The machines and equipment produced at enterprises in Soviet Armenia are exported to 37 countries of Europe, Asia and
Africa. The republic is giving other countries technical assistance; for example, it is helping the Iraqi Republic establish an electrical equipment industry.

Today Soviet Armenia is a country with complete electrification. Per capita power production in 1960 came to 1,478
kwh., i.e., more than in Italy, Japan, Denmark and other capitalist countries. (Prolonged applause.) I do not even mention
our neighbors on the other side of the Aras River, with whom
it is difficult to make any sort of comparison in terms of level
of development of productive forces. For example, in per
capita power output the Armenian Republic surpasses Turkey
15 times and Iran more than 32 times. (Applause.) ...

The number of students per 10,000 population in Soviet
Armenia is considerably higher than in Japan, France or Italy,
and is six times as high as in Turkey and 15 times as high as
in Iran. The number of pupils in all types of general-education
schools per 10,000 population is almost double the number in
Turkey and 150% higher than in Iran. (Applause.) ...

This year's drought ruined a large part of the grain and
fodder crops. The Party Central Committee and the Union
government gave considerable attention to the republic's
needs. Rural areas suffering from drought were given help in
the way of grain for food and fodder. Seed and cash loans were
given to the collective farms, and Rostov and Astrakhan Provinces, Krasnodar Territory and the Chechen-Ingush Autonomous Republic Assisted us with coarse fodder. ...

Speeches at this Congress have given an entirely correct evaluation of the schismatic, subversive active of the anti-Party
group, which tried to swerve the Party from the Leninist path
and return it to the old policy of the times of the cult of the
individual. It is not mere chance that Malenkov, one of the
participants in the anti-Party group, so zealously opposed the
elimination of the harmful consequences of the cult of the
individual. This bankrupt politico organized the slaughter not
only of cadres in the Leningrad and Belorussian Party organizations but also of executive cadres of the Armenian Communist Party. We consider correct the delegates' suggestion
that Malenkov is unworthy to be in the ranks of our great Party. (Applause.) ...

The recent Party conferences and the 22nd Congress of the
Armenian Communist Party were marked by unprecedented
activeness on the part of the Communists. On the basis of the
principles set forth in the drafts of the Party Program and
Statutes, there have been considerable replacements in the
memberships of the district and city committees, as well as of
the Central Committee of the Armenian Communist Party,
chiefly through the promotion to the executive Party bodies of
leading workers, collective farmers, specialists, scientific
personnel and young Party, Soviet and economic cadres who
have proved themselves in practical work. ...

There are many serious shortcomings and unresolved problems in the work of the Party organizations. A large number of
industrial enterprises are still not fulfilling plans in terms of
quantitative and technical-economic indices. There is a lag in
agriculture. The plan for industrial, housing and civic construction is not being met. These shortcomings are due to the
continuing inadequacy of Party-organizational and political-
educational work of Party organizations. ...

In 1961, the extraction of copper and molybdenum in the
republic comprised an insignificant percentage of existing
reserves of these useful minerals. And this when we annually
import a large quantity of copper for the country's needs,
spending valuta for this. However, for many years the construction of the very large Agarak Copper and Molybdenum
Combine, which could already be giving the country a large
quantity of copper and molybdenum concentrate, has essentially
been underestimated.

The U.S.S.R. State Planning Committee should study more
carefully the best variants for the economic use of local raw
material and ensure more purposeful and effective capital investments in the Union republics.

Finally, it must be noted that cases of nonfulfillment of plans
for the supply of complementary items have not yet disappeared
in our republic. This sometimes frustrates the work of a number of large industrial enterprises in our republic, which are
forced in turn to disrupt plans for deliveries to other economic regions. The reason for this lies not only in the slipshod
work of the respective departments of the U.S.S.R. State Planning Committee and the republic State Planning Commissions
but also in the violation of state discipline by a number of economic councils and their enterprises, such as the Odessa,
Penza, Saratov and certain other economic councils. ...

Polyansky

SPEECH BY COMRADE D. S. POLYANSKY, CHAIRMAN OF
THE RUSSIAN REPUBLIC COUNCIL OF MINISTERS. (Prav-
da, Oct. 24, pp. 2-3; Izvestia, Oct. 25. 6,500 words. Condensed
text:) Comrades! ... It has already been stated at the Congress
that the republic's industry is working successfully. The seven-
year plan is fulfilled ahead of schedule. The country will receive approximately 13,000,000 tons of steel, 10,000,000 tons of
rolled metal and 30,000,000 tons of oil above the established plan.
All this heartens us, but we must not rest content. For all our
successes, we must not close our eyes to the serious shortcomings that exist in the management of industry and construction.
These have been justly pointed out in the report of the Party
Central Committee and in the speeches of a number of delegates.
Many questions are decided in our republic extremely slowly,
organizational work is still poorly organized and the republic's
planning agencies make serious errors in working out the assignments for industry and construction. Production and construction plans are often not coordinated with plans for material and technical supply and cooperative deliveries. This
gives rise to unnecessary correspondence and "feverish activity" by all sorts of "expediters" and complicates the work of
enterprises and construction projects. ...

In this connection special attention should be given to proper
balance in planning and to the establishment of the necessary
reserves. Of course the shortcomings do not lie only in the
work of the planning agencies, in their miscalculations and
mistakes. Even carefully worked-out assignments can be
threatened with disruption if we do not achieve strictest observance of state discipline.

The task is to raise the activity of all our organizations to a
higher level—from the plants and economic councils to the
ministries and agencies, the State Planning Commission, the
All-Russian Economic Council and the Council of Ministers. A
thoughtful analysis of the work of every enterprise, construction project, economic council, ministry and agency will enable
us to disclose new unutilized potentials. At present it is especially important to judge work not only by how the plan is being fulfilled but also by how reserves for increased production

are being utilized, how new equipment and progressive technology are being introduced, and how quality of output is being improved. ...

More attention should be given to the development of ferrous metallurgy. Much work must be done to bring about a great improvement in the structure of metallurgical production, to increase the share of low-alloy steel and the output of heat-resistant and other kinds of metal and to expand the production of various rolled metal shapes. We will thereby save millions of tons of metal and achieve increased reliability of machines and structural parts.

The question of organizing the integrated use of resources is very acute. We lose a great deal in the so-called "dumps" of enterprises of ferrous and nonferrous metallurgy, and losses of natural and by-product petroleum gases are high. And how much wealth is lost in the lumber and wood-processing industry, how much timber is cut in our republic for nothing! Last year almost 300,000,000 cubic meters of wood was hauled out in the Russian Republic, and more than 100,000,000 cubic meters went to waste; processing of this waste would have yielded a large quantity of paper, cardboard, wood panels and chemical products.

Both republic and Union agencies must pay more attention to questions of the integrated use of resources if the national economy is not to continue to sustain unjustified losses.

Large reserves can be brought into play by increasing the number of shifts at enterprises. In the interests of accelerating tempos of communist construction it is necessary to utilize machinery, equipment and production facilities more productively. Can it be considered normal that at many machine-building plants only about half the total number of machine tools are used at full capacity? Here is a big reserve for increasing labor productivity and output. ...

The construction base lags seriously, and the funds allocated by some economic councils are not being used. At the same time, many local officials are striving with excessive zeal to obtain increased allocations for new projects and not paying sufficient attention to completing leading projects and those almost ready to go into operation. Cases of localism and even self-seeking, which are sometimes depicted as concern for the state's interests, are not rare. All this causes dispersal of funds, materials and manpower among many projects and slows down construction tempos. ...

The facts indicate that we lose a great deal from our inability to apply new and progressive developments rapidly in production. Factories are often spread out over too large an area and the advantages of consolidated buildings are not used. ...

It must be admitted that there are also serious shortcomings in selecting the orientation of capital work. I would like to cite one example in the coal industry. The advantages of strip coal mining are well known. The average monthly output per worker in underground mines is only one-fifth as much as in opencast mines, and the cost of a ton of coal is four times as great. Capital expenditures per ton of coal in the construction of underground mines are twice as high as in the construction of opencast mines. Yet in the Urals, Siberia and the Far East, which have favorable conditions for the strip method, few opencast mines are being built, while more than 100 underground mines are being built or modernized. This orientation in capital investments is clearly irrational. Therefore we shall now concentrate our efforts on developing strip coal mining.

There are large potentialities in the modernization and expansion of existing enterprises, about which Comrade Gaganova has just spoken, and in eliminating so-called bottlenecks. Full use is not yet being made of the potentialities. ...

Proceeding from the demands being made on agriculture, it must be frankly admitted that the results achieved are clearly inadequate and cannot satisfy us.

What is the difficulty here? Why is the republic still providing too few farm products? In recent years the Party and government have tripled capital investments in agriculture, the collective and state farms annually receive about 80,000 new tractors, 40,000 combines and much other equipment, and output of mineral fertilizers has increased. This has enabled many provinces to score notable gains. But we have many provinces that year after year fail to meet their pledges to the state and the Soviet people.

The major shortcomings in the agriculture of the Russian Federation have already been thoroughly and fairly discussed at the Congress. They are the result above all of poor management and organizational work on the part of republic and local agencies. Not all collective and state farms have been reinforced with good cadres, there are serious shortcomings in the organization of payment of labor, and equipment is not being used productively enough.

But the chief shortcoming, I should say, is the poor use of land. This applies to many regions, above all the Center and the Northwest and the Volga-Vyatka zone. These regions have up to 25,000,000 hectares of plowland, but it is being used poorly; very low yields are obtained, and only two to three poods of grain per hectare is sold to the state.

One feature is common to all regions—they all have zones in which the grass-crop system of farming has been introduced with special persistence. The question might arise: Why do officials of the Russian Federation speak so much about it? Because it is inflicting serious harm on the economy, impeding agricultural production and hindering progress. Under this system, about 40% of the plowland virtually lies idle. Formally it is considered to be under grasses, but the grass yield usually does not exceed ten to 12 centners per hectare. This amounts to only five or six centners of fodder units. ...

Who is to blame for the fact that the grass-crop system has been extended so widely and has become such a drag on us? Many are to blame, of course: the Academy of Agricultural Sciences, and the U.S.S.R. Ministry of Agriculture and those who headed it at that time. We executive officials of the republic are also to blame, because we did not quickly and decisively break the opposition of the grass-crop advocates.

I remind you that the most prominent progressive scientists of our country have long warned about the serious harm done by the grass-crop system. Back in the 1930s Academician D. N. Pryanishnikov spoke out sharply against it. Academician T. D. Lysenko has also sharply criticized the grass-crop system. ...

The Party Central Committee's Bureau for the Russian Republic and the republic Council of Ministers, jointly with province, territory and republic organizations, have worked out measures for improving the structure of sown areas. Next year it is planned, by reducing clean fallow and grasses and developing new land, to expand the area sown to grain crops by 6,000,000 hectares, including 3,500,000 hectares of grain legumes. Sowings of corn for grain will be increased to almost 4,000,000 hectares. This will make possible a considerable increase in output of grain and fodders.

The agricultural reserves of the Russian Federation are enormous. We can, and in the long run we must, produce 12,000,000,000 poods of grain a year—50% more than our entire country now produces—and sell the state 4,000,000,000 to 5,000,000,000 poods of grain annually. This is a difficult and complex task, but it is a realistic one.

What makes us confident that it is realistic?

First, in the future we plan to bring 25,000,000 hectares of land under cultivation and to obtain approximately 2,000,-000,000 poods more grain.

Second, it is planned to continue improving the structure of sown areas, to expand sowings of grain crops, grain legumes and corn by an additional 20,000,000 hectares. This will make it possible to increase the gross grain harvest by at least 2,200,000,000 poods a year.

Third—and most important—everything necessary will be done to increase the yields of all grain crops at least 100%. ...

In solving the grain problem, we bear in mind that it is indissolubly linked with the production of meat and milk. The grain problem cannot be detached from animal husbandry; these make up a single complex. In order to scale the planned heights for increasing output of livestock products, we must have a minimum of 450,000,000 tons of fodder units annually, including 50,000,000 tons of digestible protein. This means that at least 3,000 fodder units must be obtained per hectare of land, or roughly twice as much as at present. ...

It must be admitted that the work of the republic apparatus does not yet measure up to the new and growing demands. Herein lies one of the main reasons for the shortcomings in industry and agriculture that have been justly pointed out in the Party Central Committee's report and in the speeches of a number of delegates to the Congress. We are not satisfied with the work of the Russian Republic State Planning Commission and the All-Russian Economic Council, and we must admit that so far they have given little attention to improving their work. Some republic and local institutions clearly suffer from the disease of inflated staffs; this causes undoubted harm. The heads of these institutions interpret an increase in staffs as a battle won and a reduction in staffs as a severe defeat. ...

Unfortunately, we still have in our midst a highly tenacious category of people who constantly make a mess of things and yet for some reason remain numbered among the "responsible officials" year after year. Having once gotten on a certain approved list, they seem to have obtained a mandate for immortality in office. We ourselves are to blame for these abnormal conditions. ...

The Russian Republic Council of Ministers, as well as ministries and agencies of the Russian Federation, must pay considerably more attention to improving the work of local agencies of state and economic administration. This is especially necessary now, when the Party is raising the question of further extending their rights so that they may decide all questions of local significance. Considerable attention will be given to strengthening the district link, since it is here first of all that single democratic agencies will be formed for the management of all enterprises, institutions and organizations of district significance.

It must be assumed that it is precisely in the district centers that the initial agrarian-industrial associations, in which agriculture will be organically linked with the industrial processing of farm and livestock products, will arise as they become economically expedient.

The reorganization of the management of industry and construction on the basis of economic administrative regions has, as is known, fully justified itself. But the reorganization of management has not yet been carried through to the end. It cannot be considered normal, for example, that management of similar enterprises in provinces and territories is divided between the economic councils and agencies of local industry. Such divided management creates unnecessary difficulties in planning production and material and technical supply, leads to dispersal of cadres of specialists, complicates the introduction of advanced technology and increases production costs. ...

Local agencies and their leaders should clearly realize that the Party's policy of extending their independence in the decision of questions of state administration has nothing in common with the attempt to create self-sufficient economies on the local scale and to isolate them from one another. On the contrary, it is a matter of strengthening interdependence, eradicating local restrictiveness and enhancing the feeling of responsibility for the observance of state interests.

Councils for coordination and planning are now being set up in the major economic regions. ... The successful work of the councils will help transform the major regions into powerful complexes with many-branched economies. Eventually their role can become even more substantial. ...

Comrades! ... By restoring the Leninist principles of Party and state leadership of the country, the Central Committee awakened mighty new forces in the people. Only the anti-Party group of Molotov, Kaganovich, Malenkov, Voroshilov and others tried to impede this and opposed literally all measures of the Party on every major question of domestic and foreign policy. ...

It is necessary to speak in particular about Molotov. As is known, he opposed reorganization of the management of industry and construction, development of the virgin lands, improvement of planning methods and other measures of the Party that were dictated by life. It was characteristic that, in opposing the new steps of the Party and government, he offered no practical proposals. He feared everything new. He was also against the Party Central Committee's decision to change the practice of planning in agriculture. I recall the following incident. In the autumn of 1955, while in the Crimea during a vacation, Molotov decided—probably for the first time in many years—to visit a collective farm. He went to Krasnogvardeiskoye District. The purpose of his visit, it would appear, was to check on how the Party Central Committee's decision to change planning in agriculture worked. He wanted to confirm his own dogma in order to oppose the decision once again. Prior to this decision, all agricultural questions—for example, the question of how many hectares to plant to millet or some other crop—were decided in Moscow. And Molotov considered this correct. You will recall that at the time Nikita Sergeyevich proposed that this practice be abandoned; it was necessary, he

said, to turn over such questions of planning to the local areas. The local people know better; let them decide these questions. (Applause.)

When Molotov came to the collective farm, he asked Comrade Yegudin, the chairman of the farm, the following question: "How is the new planning system working on the farm?" Comrade Yegudin replied: "This was a wonderful decision. By adopting it the Central Committee untied our hands and gave us wings. We have now begun really to decide questions of agricultural development." (Applause.) And Molotov was obliged to say: "Oh! That means the Central Committee decision was right!"

The decision was indeed right, but after all Molotov was against it and sharply opposed its adoption. This dogmatist did not realize that the decision on planning had already been proved correct on the collective and state farms; he had stuck to his opinion in spite of everything.

Molotov was against the Party Central Committee's decisions on many other questions also, and he stubbornly defended incorrect positions in foreign policy. He opposed the Central Committee's efforts to get out of the blind alleys in foreign policy that had developed by that time as a result of Stalin's subjective approach to many international matters.

Being unable to interpret new phenomena of life correctly, he turned out to be completely under the sway of dogmatism. Considering himself a theoretician, the farther he went, the more he confused and confuses elementary Leninist propositions, and he even contradicts himself. If one speaks about people who are incapable of applying the Leninist teaching, this is true above all of Molotov. He long ago departed from creative Leninism and became a hopeless conservative.

It is also necessary to refer to Comrade Voroshilov's conduct as a participant in the anti-Party group. The Party Central Committee was very lenient with you, Comrade Voroshilov. After all, you played an active role in this group, although you do say that you were "confused by the devil." We don't believe the devil has anything to do with this. You wanted to cover up the traces of your participation in the repressions against completely innocent people, especially against the cadres of military leaders, repressions known to the whole country. As a member of the anti-Party group, and an active participant in it, Comrade Voroshilov behaved insolently, rudely and defiantly. At a critical moment he even refused to meet with members of the Party Central Committee who demanded the convening of a plenary session of the Central Committee. He forgot that he had been elected to the Presidium of the Central Committee and consequently could be deprived of this high trust. And how did he behave at the Central Committee plenary session? I will recall only one incident. When Kaganovich was accused of mass repressions in the Kuban, which were carried out on his instructions and with his personal participation, Voroshilov came to Kaganovich's defense; he jumped up from his seat and, shaking his fists, cried: "You are still young and we'll fix your brains." We then answered his remark: "Calm down, the Central Committee will look into the matter of whose brains should be fixed!" (Applause.) So, Comrade Voroshilov, don't pretend to be an innocent Ivan. You must bear full responsibility for your anti-Party deeds, like the anti-Party group. (Applause.) ...

Special importance attaches to the unity and solidarity of the countries of the world socialist system. Communism cannot be built in isolation. The report of the Party Central Committee provides a principled evaluation of the incorrect actions of the Albanian leaders. We delegates to the Congress fully share this evaluation, for it expresses the view of our entire party and of all Soviet people. (Prolonged applause.) ...

Speaking about the successes of our homeland and about the work of our party and its Central Committee, it is necessary to emphasize that in recent years the most important events in the life of the country and in the life of the Party, including the rout of the anti-Party group, have been indissolubly linked with the name of Nikita Sergeyevich Khrushchev! (Stormy, prolonged applause.) A man of great soul and inexhaustible energy, who has an excellent knowledge of life and draws new strength in contact with the people, Nikita Sergeyevich has won deep respect and great love from the broad masses! (Stormy, prolonged applause.)

The Soviet people and all progressive mankind link his name not only with the achievements of our homeland but also with the strengthening of the positions of the world socialist system, with the active struggle of the peoples for peace throughout the world. If today in the international arena the voice of the Soviet Union resounds as the voice of the mightiest power, this is to the tremendous credit of the Party Central Committee and to the tremendous credit of Nikita Sergeyevich Khrushchev personally! (Stormy, prolonged applause.) ...

Snieckus

SPEECH BY COMRADE A. J. SNIECKUS, FIRST SECRE-TARY OF THE LITHUANIAN COMMUNIST PARTY CENTRAL COMMITTEE. (Pravda, Oct. 24, pp. 3-4. 4,500 words. Excerpts:) ... Comrades! Thanks to the Leninist policy of the Communist Party, our young republic in the years of Soviet rule has come considerably closer to the most highly developed Soviet republics in level of economic development. ...

Soviet Lithuania's industrial output is almost twelve times the level of the prewar year of 1940. The republic's power base is becoming stronger. The Kaunas Hydroelectric Station went into operation ahead of schedule, and construction of the mighty Lithuanian Thermal Power Plant is proceeding successfully. In the first years of the seven-year period gross industrial output has risen almost 44%, that is, almost twice as much as the control figures stipulated. As early as this year industry will attain the level of production envisaged by the seven-year plan for 1963. ...

We drew serious practical conclusions from the criticism of our republic at the January plenary session of the Party Central Committee. The Party organization has adopted measures to increase grain production. This year's plan for grain deliveries to the state was fulfilled on the eve of the 22nd Party Congress.

In order to make better use of land, the area under clean fallow is being reduced and low-yield crops are being replaced with ones of higher yield. Legumes are being successfully grown this year. Special attention has been given to the cultivation of fodder legumes. ...

Sowings of corn have increased in the republic. Despite adverse climatic conditions this year, many collective and state farms obtained good corn yields. ...

In recent years 780,000 hectares have been drained in Soviet Lithuania, more than 200,000 of them by enclosed drainage. ...

The number of livestock in the republic has increased considerably in the period since the 20th Party Congress. We now have 32 head of cattle, including 20 cows, per 100 hectares of farm land. There are 64 pigs per 100 hectares of plowland.

In this same period the output of milk and meat has almost doubled. ...

In the period of the cult of the individual serious difficulties also developed in our republic, where Soviet rule was established comparatively recently. In the conditions of the class struggle that was waged in the years when the Lithuanian people had to break the resistance of the bourgeois-nationalist bands established by the Hitlerite occupiers and supported by the American-British intelligence services, the violation of socialist legality caused considerable harm. Taking unlawful actions against innocent people, the Beria adventurists tried to compromise the policy of the Soviet regime, made the struggle against traitors more difficult and sometimes thereby enabled the real enemies of the people and of socialism to evade responsibility. Violations of legality created great difficulties in our work of rallying the masses of the working people around the Party and the Soviet regime. The restoration of socialist legality by the Party had enormous positive importance for our republic. The resolutions of the 20th Congress condemning the cult of the individual set the sights of Party organizations on combating violations of Leninist norms of inner-Party life.

With the support of the broad Party circles, and under the leadership of the Party Central Committee, this struggle was waged successfully in our republic and yielded fruit. At the same time it would be incorrect to assert that it was easy. As often happens, people alien to the Party tried to use correct Party slogans in the interests of activity hostile to socialism.

The Party firmly pursued a Leninist national policy, adopted measures to extend the rights of the Union republics, while nationalist elements endeavored to supplant this policy with the preaching of localism and tried to mislead individual officials into discrimination on the basis of nationality in the matter of cadres.

The Party called for an end to the cult of the individual, while the nationalist elements strove to supplant criticism of the cult of the individual with criticism of Leninism and tried to cast doubt on the principles of democratic centralism, on the Party's policy in the countryside, collectivization.

In the difficult situation of these times certain mistakes were made in individual Party organizations of the republic. On the whole, however, the Lithuanian Communist Party, an integral part of the C.P.S.U. reared in internationalist traditions, stood firmly on the positions of Leninism and rallied even more closely around the Leninist Central Committee of the C.P.S.U. headed by Comrade N. S. Khrushchev. (Prolonged applause.) ...

The struggle to overcome bourgeois survivals is not only an ideological but a political struggle. The American imperialists and their servants—the Lithuanian bourgeois nationalists—are vainly trying to inflame nationalist prejudices for anti-Soviet purposes. The Vatican is also doing this, trying to exploit the influence the Catholic Church still has to some extent on individual groups of the population. ...

The Lithuanian people have become convinced from their own practical experience that friendship with the great Russian people and with all the peoples of our country is the guarantee of further rapid development of their economy and culture. The Lithuanian people will continue tirelessly to strengthen this fraternal friendship. ...

Comrades! ... Recently, in connection with Peace Week on the Baltic Sea, I had occasion to visit the German Democratic Republic. It was gratifying to see that the working people of the first worker-peasant state in the history of Germany—the German Democratic Republic—warmly welcome and support the Soviet Union's proposals on the German question. ...

Lithuania and neighboring Kaliningrad Province are on the extreme Western borders of the Soviet Union. We well understand our tasks in ensuring the firmness and inviolability of the state borders of the great socialist power. In conditions when the imperialists not only are not abandoning the arms race but are intensifying it, when they are sabotaging disarmament negotiations and increasing their armed forces, we are obliged to heighten our vigilance and to strengthen the country's defenses in every way. The working people of Soviet Lithuania unanimously support all the measures of the Soviet government aimed at further safeguarding the security of the Soviet Union.

The political figures abroad who sleep and dream about a return of the peoples of the Baltic area and other Soviet republics to the yoke of capitalism have not yet disappeared. Every year they organize a so-called Captive Nations Week. They include the Lithuanian people among these "captive nations." It is not to the imperialists' liking that Lithuania and the other Baltic republics have rid themselves of imperialistic rule and have ceased to be poverty-stricken outposts of capitalist Europe. ...

No, gentlemen, we say to the organizers of various "weeks" overseas that it is not we but the peoples of the capitalist countries who are still enslaved by imperialism. We Soviet people are unmoved by these "weeks." Would God the American people themselves were as free as we Lithuanians in the Soviet Union! (Applause.) ...

Usubaliyev

SPEECH BY COMRADE T. USUBALIYEV, FIRST SECRETARY OF THE KIRGIZ COMMUNIST PARTY CENTRAL COMMITTEE. (Pravda, Oct. 24, pp. 4-5. 2,700 words. Excerpts:) Comrade delegates! ... It is joyous to realize that our party, having decisively overcome the cult of the individual and routed the anti-Party group of factionalists who had detached themselves from life, has come to its 22nd Congress even stronger and rallied even more closely around the Leninist Central Committee headed by Comrade Nikita Sergeyevich Khrushchev. (Stormy applause.) ...

In tempos of industrial development Soviet Kirgizstan has far outstripped many capitalist countries of the West.

As for the capitalist countries of the East, such as Iran and Pakistan, the Kirgiz Republic has surpassed them manyfold in volume of output of major types of industrial production. ...

In Kirgizia there are now 80 students per 10,000 population. This is considerably more than in France, Belgium or Italy. ...

Since the beginning of the seven-year period gross industrial output has increased 31%. ...

Our successes are indisputable, but they would be even more substantial if it were not for the serious mistakes and short-comings permitted by us in the management of the economy. The republic's oil industry is lagging seriously, the power base is developing slowly and major shortcomings continue to exist in capital construction. ...

The Uch-Kurgan Hydroelectric Station is being built on the Naryn River; it will provide power not only for the southern part of our republic but for enterprises and collective and state farms of fraternal Uzbekistan. ...

The Naryn hydraulic system will be a mighty power base for the establishment in the republic and in adjacent regions of Uzbekistan and southern Kazakhstan of a whole series of large power-consuming enterprises for the production of mineral fertilizers and other chemicals.

In the Naryn system special importance attaches to construction of the Toktogul Hydroelectric Station, which was mentioned in Nikita Sergeyevich Khrushchev's report. This station will yield extremely cheap electric power, and the construction of a reservoir there with a capacity of more than 17,000,000,000 cubic meters will ensure water for existing fields in dry years and the irrigation of about 2,000,000 hectares of new land in the republics of Central Asia and in Kazakhstan. It is necessary to speed decision of the question of beginning construction of the Toktogul Hydroelectric Station.

Comrades! There are great prospects for the further development of agriculture in Kirgizia. At the January plenary session of the Party Central Committee the Kirgiz Communist Party Central Committee and the republic Council of Ministers were severely but justly criticized for unsatisfactory guidance of agriculture. We drew the necessary conclusions from this criticism. Kirgizia's collective and state farms worked out concrete measures and adopted higher socialist pledges for increasing the output of agricultural products. The output of meat, for example, will increase to 200,000 tons, of milk to 940,000 tons and of wool to 30,500 tons by the end of the seven-year period. ...

In order to achieve the planned level of output of livestock products, we must first of all achieve a rapid increase in the number of livestock. ...

We plan to expand the area under corn from 140,000 to 250,000 hectares; this will enable us to obtain more than 500,000 tons of grain and more than 6,000,000 tons of silage annually. Sowings of sugar beets for livestock fodder will also be increased considerably in our republic.

The capital investments for water-installation construction called for by the seven-year plan still cannot satisfy the the growing needs of Kirgizia's agriculture.

The further development of animal husbandry will largely depend on a fuller use of our rich mountain pastures, on which we obtain the cheapest meat and wool. The republic's Party organization must solve big tasks in further developing range pastures, especially in providing water for them and irrigating them. In the solution of these tasks we count on the assistance of the Union government. ...

Despite difficult climatic conditions, a good cotton harvest has been grown. As of today the working people of Kirgizstan have fulfilled their pledges for raw cotton deliveries by 86%. This is considerably more than on the same date last year. (Applause.)

Comrades! ... The Kirgiz people consider it their sacred duty tirelessly to strengthen and expand the indestructible friendship and economic and cultural ties with the fraternal peoples and to enrich the socialist content of their culture, constantly turning to such a mighty source as the culture of the great Russian people and the other fraternal peoples of our country. (Applause.)

The study of the Russian language has joined the Kirgiz people, like the other Soviet peoples, to the great culture of the Russian people and to world culture. (Applause.) The Russian language is the common language of intercourse among our nations; it is the language of progress, the language of cooperation, the language of wisdom, the language of friendship and brotherhood among all peoples of the Soviet Union. (Stormy applause.) ...

Ignatov

SPEECH BY COMRADE N. G. IGNATOV, VICE-CHAIRMAN OF THE U.S.S.R. COUNCIL OF MINISTERS. (Pravda, Oct. 25, pp. 3-4; Izvestia, p. 4. 5,500 words. Condensed text:)

Comrades! ... Carrying out the decisions of the January plenary session of the Party Central Committee, agricultural workers have this year scored a big victory: They have increased the gross yield and state purchases of grain. As of Oct. 20 the amount of grain purchased was 3,115,000,000 poods. The purchase of grain is continuing, and it cannot be doubted that the figure Comrade Khrushchev has named for purchases—approximately 3,300,000,000 poods of grain—will be met.

Our Party is giving day-by-day attention to further increasing the production of grain as the basis for the development of agriculture as a whole. It must be pointed out that there have been many obstacles in the way. The Party had to level serious criticism against the stereotyped use of the grass-crop rotation system of farming. Basic corrections had to be made in the structure of sown areas and priority given to the grain crops of the highest yield and greatest value—wheat, corn and legumes.

Quite a few people were slow to see the need for these measures. How much patient and intensive effort was required of the whole Party, and especially of Nikita Sergeyevich Khrushchev, to overcome the skepticism about, and at times outright opposition to, the introduction of corn plantings! There are still officials who cling to the old structure of sown areas, which includes many crops of little value and low yield. An enormous amount of work lies ahead in substantially extending plantings of corn and legumes, replacing clean fallow with green fallow, introducing second sowings and adopting other measures justified by the experience of leading workers. ...

The virgin lands are yielding more than 40% of our commodity grain. ...

Thanks to the virgin lands, our consumption of white bread has risen considerably. The state, appreciating the public demand for white bread of the best quality, has doubled the production of high-grade flour as compared with 1953, and more than 70% of the bread consumed by our people is now white wheat bread. (Applause.)

Grain exports have increased. The amount of grain sold over the past six years is 2,300,000,000 poods, two-thirds of which went to our friends, the countries in the socialist camp. (Applause.) ...

The state and the collective and state farms now have more seed for extending corn plantings than in any previous year. The task set by Comrade N. S. Khrushchev of increasing the gross grain harvest by replacing low-yield crops with high-yield ones—corn, peas and fodder beans—can thus be accomplished as early as 1962.

Comrades! A great deal of work has been done in carrying out the Party's decisions on strengthening the communal animal husbandry of the collective and state farms. Today the communal herds and flocks of the collective and state farms include more than 70% of all cattle, 53% of the cows, 74% of the pigs and 79% of the sheep. The collective and state farms have moved into the lead in the output of livestock products and their sale to the state.

The seven-year-plan control figures call for 20,310,000 tons of meant to be purchased in the first three years. Since the start of the seven-year-plan the collective and state farms have sold 21,000,000 tons, and before the year is out they will have sold at least 2,000,000 tons more under the terms of procurement contracts.

Milk purchases in the first three years of the seven-year-plan were set at 80,000,000 tons. Purchases since the start of the seven-year-plan have been 75,380,000 tons. Before the year's end the collective and state farms will have sold at least another 4,000,000 tons.

The seven-year-plan goals for egg purchases are also being met.

Retail trade has grown 50% in the past five years, and the physical volume of food sales has increased to the same extent. It follows from these data that the Soviet people have begun to eat better, to buy more milk, butter, eggs and other food products. We are cheered by these changes in the lives of Soviet people. They prove that for our party word and deed are never at variance, that it regards serving the people as its sacred duty.

These are good indices. But we are not yet fully meeting the public's demand for meat and certain other food and manufactured goods. To meet the people's growing needs more fully, the Party and government have decided to raise the production of consumer goods. ...

Comrades! The wonderful successes achieved by our country, which have been so glowingly described in the reports and the speeches by delegates to the Congress, have been made possible by the triumph of the Leninist course of the Party's policy, from which the factionalist group of Molotov, Kaganovich, Malenkov, Voroshilov, Bulganin, Pervukhin, Saburov and Shepilov tried to swerve the Party. They furiously resisted implementation of this course. This group of factionalists has now been rendered harmless. As our colloquial expression has it, the serpents have had their fangs pulled. Some of them are now crawling and others hissing, but none of them can bite any longer. If we talk about them, it is not because they constitute any danger to the Party but in order that the Party and the Soviet people will know the nature of these renegades who had lost touch with life and will know what they were out to do.

What aims had the anti-Party group set for itself? To render the Party leaderless, to change the membership of the Presidium when the Central Committee's back was turned, to seize the leadership of the Party, to turn the Party off the Leninist path and revive the practices that had obtained under the cult of the individual. Molotov, Kaganovich, Malenkov and Voroshilov were guided in this disgusting business not only by thirst for power but also by dread of being called to account for the unlawful and arbitrary acts they had committed, from which many innocent Party members and non-Party people had suffered.

After Comrade Khrushchev's truthful report to the 20th Congress on the cult of the individual, the Party learned about cases of the most flagrant violations of socialist legality, abuse of power and unjustified persecution. And when the Party set about eliminating the effects of the cult of the individual, the factionalists realized that the time would come sooner or later when they would have to answer for their villainous deeds. As you know from the speeches of the delegates to the Congress, the factionalists made long and painstaking preparations for accomplishing their designs; they gradually, one by one, recruited their supporters and with Jesuitical refinement created an intolerable situation in the work of the Presidium of the Central Committee. These were experienced plotters and double-dealers. They thought to lull the vigilance of the Party by voting in favor of the decisions of the 20th Congress; actually, they made every effort to thwart the implementation of those decisions. Everyone now knows that the anti-Party group always took its stand in opposition to any new questions Comrade Khrushchev might bring up, and these measures were put into effect only by dint of great effort.

It has already been mentioned here that when the question of developing the virgin lands was discussed, Molotov objected violently. He declared—these are his actual words—that the virgin lands were not a worthwhile project, that they did not justify the investment. Is there any need today, comrades, to prove the harmfulness and absurdity of these objections? Molotov arrogantly considered himself, and still considers himself, an expert on all aspects of international and domestic life. But it is a well-known fact that Molotov was and remains muddleheaded in his understanding of international relations and the country's internal development. He had a great many things all wrong on the question of ways and means of building communism in our country, in his assessment of the forces of socialism and imperialism, on the questions of the coexistence of states with different social systems, the possibility of preventing a world war, and the forms of transition to socialism in different countries. And no wonder. Molotov was and re-

mains a hopeless dogmatist who has lost all notion of reality. He was out of step with our Party.

As we know, when the anti-Party group had knocked together its so-called arithmetical majority in the Central Committee Presidium, it set about the practical realization of its plans to seize the leadership of the Party and the country. But its members made a big mistake; they forgot that, besides them, there was the Central Committee, whose members had implicit faith in Comrade Nikita Sergeyevich Khrushchev and stood with him for the consistent pursuit of the Leninist course mapped by the 20th Congress. (Applause.)

You have learned from the Central Committee's report that the members of the Central Committee who were in Moscow demanded that a plenary session of the Central Committee be called at once. They were vigorously supported by Comrade Khrushchev and other comrades who upheld the Leninist line. And the plenary session was called.

Let me tell you of a typical incident, which will give you a clearer idea of the true character of the factionalists and illustrate for you the extent to which the members of the anti-Party group, with their obsession for the mores of the cult of the individual, had lost touch with the Party and treated even members of the Central Committee with disdain.

The members of the Central Committee sent their representatives to the session of the Presidium with a statement on the need for convening a plenary session of the Central Committee. Let me read this statement to you:

"To the Presidium of the Central Committee: We, members of the C.P.S.U. Central Committee, have learned that the Central Committee Presidium is in continuous session. We are also aware that you are discussing the question of the leadership of the Central Committee and of the Secretariat. Matters of such importance for our whole party cannot be concealed from the members of the Plenum of the Central Committee. In view of this fact we, members of the C.P.S.U. Central Committee, urgently request that a plenary session of the Central Committee be called and this matter submitted to it for discussion. We, as members of the Central Committee, may not stand aloof from the question of our party's leadership."

When this request was reported to the Presidium, the factionalists kicked up a terrible fuss.

Comrades! It is not fitting that I recount to you from this lofty rostrum the vile things they said to the Central Committee's members when they arrived. And what do you think it was all about? Why, how dare the members of the Central Committee approach them?! Comrade Khrushchev and the other comrades who supported him flatly insisted that the members of the Central Committee be received. Then this so-called arithmetical majority—the factionalists—proposed that the members of the Central Committee be received not by the Presidium but by one of their supporters—Bulganin or Voroshilov. Seeing what this group was up to, Nikita Sergeyevich Khrushchev stated that he too would go to the meeting with the members of the Central Committee, and he stood his ground. And what a lucky thing that was for the fortunes of our party! (Stormy applause.)

N. S. Khrushchev.—They wanted to keep me from meeting with the members of the Central Committee, and they singled out Voroshilov for the job. I told them that the Plenum had elected me First Secretary of the Central Committee and no one could deprive me of the right to meet with the members of the Central Committee of the Communist Party. (Stormy applause.) It was the Plenum of the Central Committee that had elected me, and it should therefore be the Plenum that took the decision. It would be as the Plenum of the Central Committee decided. (Stormy applause.)

N. G. Ignatov.—Then the Presidium authorized Comrades Khrushchev and Mikoyan, as well as Voroshilov and Bulganin, to meet with the members of the Central Committee.

N. S. Khrushchev.—Two against two, as you see. (Stir in the hall.)

N. G. Ignatov.—As you see, the factionalists were unwilling to meet the members of the Central Committee, as Nikita Sergeyevich has told us so truthfully and vividly. More than that, instructions were given not to admit the members of the Central Committee to the Kremlin, and many of them had to use literally illegal means in making their way to where the

Central Committee's Presidium was in session. This is something unheard of, comrades, a disgrace!

Voices from the audience.—A disgrace!

N. G. Ignatov.—At the plenary session the members of the anti-Party group found themselves confronted with a Central Committee that was a monolithic wall. When they saw that the Plenum was unanimously behind Comrade Khrushchev in his principled fight to carry out the Leninist line, they began cravenly saying they were sorry, but one could not believe them. They had engaged in double-dealing before the plenary session and at the plenary session, and they did so after the plenary session. We became convinced of this, in particular, from the behavior of Molotov when our delegation was attending the 13th Congress of the Mongolian People's Revolutionary Party. Molotov was Ambassador to Mongolia at the time. At the request of the embassy's Party organization, he made a report on the June plenary session of the Central Committee and on other practical questions of the Central Committee's work. At that Party meeting it was demanded that Molotov say whether he accepted the decisions of the 20th Party Congress and was in agreement with the measures being implemented by the Central Committee. At the meeting Molotov replied that he was in agreement. But two days later, in a talk with a member of the delegation, he sought to convince him that the Machine and Tractor Stations should not be reorganized and the machinery sold to the collective farms (the plenary session was dealing with these matters at that very time), and that we should not be too hasty in carrying through other planned measures. This behavior on Molotov's part stamps him as a double-dealer.

Comrades! The struggle against the anti-Party group was a sharp one and involved fundamental principles. At issue was whether the Party would continue to follow its Leninist line or whether the Party and the country would go back to the days of the cult of the individual. That was the issue. I recall that many who took part in the plenary session felt that Molotov, Kaganovich and Malenkov could not possibly be allowed to remain in our party. I second the suggestions made from this rostrum by delegates to the 22nd Congress that Molotov, Kaganovich and Malenkov be expelled from the Party, and I consider these suggestions absolutely proper. (Applause.)

Comrades! The Leninist line of the Party laid down by the 20th Congress was supported by the fraternal Communist Parties of all countries. We Communists who are members of the Party of Lenin are cheered by this high assessment of the Party's work by our brothers in this common cause. But it now appears that the leaders of the Albanian Party of Labor were insincere when they said they fully supported our party's policy on all matters concerning the international Communist movement. Recently the Albanian leaders abruptly altered their political policy and began fighting the decisions of the 20th Congress of the C.P.S.U.; they have taken to attacking our party and its Leninist Central Committee and to slandering other Communist Parties as well. The delegates to our Congress and the representatives of the fraternal parties have been perfectly right in saying here that the Albanian leaders are departing from the general agreed-upon line of the entire world Communist movement on paramount problems of the day. It is to be regretted that the Albanian leaders should be harming the interests of the Albanian people with their conduct. We cannot hush this matter up, even if some people are displeased at our stating openly that the Albanian leaders are moving farther and farther away from internationalist positions and are sliding downhill to the path of nationalism. We cannot defer to anyone when Leninist principles are involved. ...

Malinovsky

SPEECH BY COMRADE R. YA. MALINOVSKY, U.S.S.R. MINISTER OF DEFENSE. (Pravda, Oct. 25, pp. 4-5; Izvestia, p. 5. 5,500 words. Condensed text:) Comrades! ... The plans the Party has mapped for the building of communism and the results that have already been achieved in fulfilling them are astounding in their grandeur and sweep. They vividly attest the superiority of the socialist system to the capitalist system, the invincible strength of communism. The capitalist world

has nothing to counter to the onward march of communism. Capitalism has no future; it has no ideas that could kindle enthusiasm in the peoples and win their allegiance. The history of the past few decades graphically confirms the Marxist-Leninist conclusion that the decrepit capitalist system is doomed and will inevitably fall. But in its death throes, outworn capitalism threatens mankind with frightful calamities. ...

U.S. President Kennedy declares his determination to protect vitally important interests in Berlin. But where is the United States and where is Berlin?! What vitally important interests can the United States of America have there?! Nevertheless, the U.S. President has increased the military budget by more than $6,000,000,000, i.e., 14%. He has promised by the end of 1964 to increase the number of Polaris-armed atomic submarines by 50%, to increase by 50% the number of strategic bombers on the runways and ready to take off 15 minutes after the alert; and to double the number of Minuteman missiles. He is increasing the numerical strength of the ground forces, bringing the production of rifles up from 9,000 to 44,000 a month, and increasing by 150% the troops for combating the guerrilla movement in oppressed countries. And all this is being done, as he puts it, "to achieve a balance with the Soviet Union."

Speaking in North Carolina on Oct. 12 of this year, President Kennedy was compelled to point out that the times had changed and that the United States was living through "extraordinary times. Angola and Algeria, Brazil and Bizerte, Syria and South Vietnam, Korea and Kuwait, the Dominican Republic, Berlin and the United Nations itself—these are all problems which 20 years ago we could not even have imagined. And all this in conditions when the two opposing powers are capable of destroying each other."

We agree with President Kennedy: Much has changed in 20 years, the times are different. If to the above we add other burning problems, for example the Congo, the Republic of South Africa, Cyprus, Iran, West Irian, Cuba, the Palestine question, the lynching of Negroes, chronic unemployment, and the impending U.S. deficit of more than $5,000,000,000, the outlook is indeed joyless for the American imperialists! (Applause.) ...

As a move in response to the intensified practical preparations for war being made by the Western countries with the "Berlin crisis" as the pretext, the Party Central Committee and the Soviet government were obliged to carry out a number of measures, which you know of, to strengthen the defense capacity and security of the U.S.S.R. The reduction of the armed forces that had been planned and was in process was temporarily halted; defense expenditures were increased somewhat; the regular demobilization from the army and navy to the reserve of noncommissioned officers and men who had completed their tour of active service was temporarily put off; nuclear weapons tests are being conducted.

Needless to say, a number of essential measures of a specific nature have been taken in the armed forces themselves in order to heighten their state of combat readiness. We are discharging our internationalist duty to the peoples of all countries by strengthening our defensive power. We have no intention of attacking anyone, but at the same time we are firm in stating that we shall destroy any aggressor who ignites the torch of a world war. (Stormy applause.) ...

The basic concrete tasks of the armed forces and the lines on which the military establishment will be developed in our country under present circumstances were clearly and expressively set forth in his historic report at the fourth session of the U.S.S.R. Supreme Soviet in 1960 by our Supreme Commander-in-Chief, Nikita Sergeyevich Khrushchev. (Stormy applause.) The report also contained a penetrating analysis of the nature of modern war; this analysis became the basis of Soviet military doctrine. One of the important tenets of that doctrine is that a world war, should it be loosed by the imperialist aggressors, would inevitably take the form of a nuclear-missile war, that is, a war in which the chief means of destruction would be nuclear weapons and the principal means of delivering them to the targets would be rockets. In view of this fact, war would start differently than in the past and be waged in a different way.

The use of atomic and thermonuclear weapons with unlimited possibilities for their delivery by rockets to any target in a matter of minutes makes it possible to achieve decisive military results at any distance, over a vast area, in the shortest space of time. The targets for crushing nuclear blows, besides groupings of the enemy's armed forces, will be industrial and vital centers and communications hubs—everything that sustains the war. The world war of the future, if not prevented, will assume an unprecedentedly destructive character. It will result in the deaths of hundreds of millions of people, and whole countries will be turned into lifeless, ash-covered deserts.

I must point out that the ruling circles of the West are also well aware of this, and they are therefore aiming to accomplish particular aggressive ends by waging local "small wars" using conventional weapons and tactical atomic weapons.

Although nuclear weapons will hold the decisive place in a future war, we are nevertheless coming to the conclusion that final victory over an aggressor can be achieved only through combined operations by all branches of the armed forces. We are therefore devoting due attention to the perfection of weapons of all types, teaching our forces how to use them skillfully and to achieve a decisive victory over the aggressor. (Applause.)

We also believe that under modern conditions any future war would be waged, despite the enormous losses, by mass, many-millions-strong armed forces.

The Presidium of the Party Central Committee and the Soviet government have called upon us to pay special attention to the initial phase of a possible war. The reason why this phase is important is that the very first massed nuclear blows can to an enormous extent predetermine the whole subsequent course of the war and result in such losses in the rear and in the armed forces that the people and country will find themselves in an exceptionally difficult situation.

A realistic assessment of the picture would lead one to believe that what the imperialists are preparing is a surprise nuclear attack on the U.S.S.R. and the socialist countries. Hence Soviet military doctrine regards it as the most important, the pre-eminent, the first-priority task of the armed forces to be in a state of constant readiness for effectively repulsing a surprise attack by the enemy and thwarting his criminal designs.

The point is that under present circumstances any armed conflict would inevitably develop into a global nuclear-missile war if the nuclear powers were drawn in. We are therefore compelled to prepare our armed forces, the country and the people as a whole to combat an aggressor first and foremost under conditions of nuclear warfare. ...

I should like now to remind you of certain facts. An official document of the U.S. Congress states that "in the initial phase of the war 263 thermonuclear strikes, each equivalent on the average to about 5,000,000 tons of TNT, may be made at the most important objectives in the United States." The Americans estimate that these blows would destroy 132 major military installations and many important industrial enterprises of various kinds, as well as 71 major cities. Furthermore, the total area of radioactive contamination would come to almost half the country's territory. As a result of all this, half the country's population would be nuclear casualties. According to estimates of the U.S. Public Health Service, the result of a nuclear blow at American cities would be that "out of a population of 188,000,000, the dead alone would number 53,000,000." In addition, a number of similar estimates are given for other countries. For example, they have figured that it will take no more than eight five-megaton nuclear warheads to knock out West Germany.

We are particularly astonished by the bellicose posture and military threats of Chancellor Adenauer and his war minister, Strauss. Or take the threats voiced in the British House of Commons in the name of the government by Conservative Party member Heath, Lord Privy Seal. What are these threats worth?

You must understand, madmen, that it would take really very few multimegaton nuclear bombs to wipe out your small and densely populated countries and kill you instantly in your lairs! (Stormy applause.)

On Oct. 21 of this year—quite recently, that is—U.S. Deputy Secretary of Defense Roswell Gilpatric addressed a meeting of the Business Council in Virginia, presumably not without President Kennedy's knowledge, and, brandishing the might of the United States, threatened us with force.

What is there to say to this latest threat, to this petty speech? Only one thing: The threat does not frighten us! (Stormy applause.)

We heartily approve the proposals of our party and government on the conclusion of a peace treaty with Germany, and we stand ready to carry out any task that may be assigned the armed forces. (Applause.) We warn our foes that if they force us to fight we shall have quite sufficient means to deal nuclear blows at a substantially greater number of the most varied objectives on the territory of any aggressor! (Applause.)

The American experts used as the unit for their estimates a warhead of only five megatons. But as you already know, we have nuclear warheads with yields ranging from 20 to 30 to 100 megatons, and our ballistic rockets have given such a splendid account of themselves that nobody can have any doubt as to their ability to lift these warheads and deliver them to any spot on the globe from which an attack might be made on the Soviet Union and the other socialist countries. (Stormy applause.)

In light of these more precise data, the American experts must obviously make fundamental corrections in their estimates with respect both to the yield of the nuclear warheads and to the number that the Soviet Union has at its disposal. Countries that make their territory available to the aggressor for military bases and missile sites should also give this some serious thought. These countries are small in size and have a high population density; the outbreak of a nuclear war would be the sheerest calamity for them.

I should now like to report to the Congress on the state of combat readiness of the armed forces of the Soviet Union. It is five and a half years since the 20th Party Congress. For our armed forces this has been a period filled with important events related to rearmament with new and up-to-date equipment and the extensive introduction of nuclear missiles in the forces. This has been truly a turning point in the development and build-up of our army and navy. On the basis primarily of the extensive introduction of these weapons, all the old branches, so to speak, of the armed forces have been greatly improved in the past few years. But what is most important is that on the initiative of Nikita Sergeyevich Khrushchev and by decision of the Party Central Committee and the Soviet government, a new branch of the armed forces has been established—the strategic rocket troops. These troops, comrades, are in a constant state of combat readiness. They already have sufficient numbers of launching installations and missiles with multimegaton warheads for us to be able, if the need arises, greatly to exceed the estimate of the American scientists and military men to which I have referred and to inflict a devastating defeat on the aggressor and the aggressor country. (Applause.)

I must stress that the establishment of the strategic rocket troops was attended by a reduction in the numerical strength of the armed forces as a whole. Where advisable, we have reduced the numerical strength of our forces, and especially of administrative staffs and service agencies; but at the same time we have substantially reinforced and are continuing to develop to the utmost another branch of the armed forces—the country's antiaircraft and antimissile defense troops. Our ground forces, air force and navy and our military air transport—which will play a very important role in a future war—have been fully supplied with up-to-date equipment.

The radical reorganization of the armed forces has made it necessary to revise the theory of the art of war and the regulations and manuals and to retrain personnel, especially officers and generals. The reorganization stage has now been basically completed. As a result, the might of the Soviet armed forces has grown immeasurably.

The Leninist Central Committee of our party headed by Nikita Sergeyevich Khrushchev has played the directing and organizing role in the reshaping of the armed forces. The Central Committee's sound policy on military equipment, the successes of industry and the outstanding advances of Soviet science and technology have made it possible in a relatively brief period to develop vast and qualitatively new material and technical facilities for arming the army and navy with modern combat equipment, above all missiles. (Applause.) ...

I must tell you that missile production has increased to such an extent in the past few years that we have not only a full supply but a large surplus of missiles of various types and purposes. (Applause.) All our rocket troops are now in excellent fighting trim. They are on constant alert and are capable of accomplishing any task entrusted to them. I might add that the practice firings held by the rocket troop in 1961 yielded conclusive results: Of the total firings of intermediate-range missiles, more than 90% were graded "excellent" or "good." (Applause.) As for intercontinental missiles, they have been performing all assignments without exception at a level of "excellent" or "good." It may seem strange, but the missiles hit their mark with greater accuracy at long range than at short. (Amused stir in the hall. Applause.) ...

I think the delegates to the Congress would be interested in knowing that the rocket troops at present have about 1,800 excellent units, and these men are highly expert at their job, expert at hitting any spot on the globe without a miss. (Stormy, prolonged applause.) ...

The ground forces have been reduced substantially of late. But their combat capabilities have greatly increased. They are able to carry on active military operations, involving great maneuverability, at unprecedented speeds and in enormous operational depth in conditions of the use of nuclear weapons by the enemy. The ground forces, especially in the border areas, are in a state of constant combat readiness. The main arms of the ground forces today are their rocket units and tactical echelons armed with nuclear and other missiles with ranges of from a few to many hundreds of kilometers. Combat-practice firing has confirmed the great fighting capabilities of these rocket troops: good accuracy in hitting the target, speed of on-the-march deployment for missile launching, ability to move great distances without losing combat efficiency.

Nor are we relaxing our attention to conventional arms, in particular artillery. The numerical strength of our motorized infantry division is considerably smaller than the strength of a division at the end of the last war. But on the other hand its firepower, not counting missiles, has more than quadrupled. (Applause.) And if we take tanks, there are more of them in our present-day motorized infantry divisions and tank divisions than in the mechanized and tank corps of the Great Patriotic War or in the corresponding divisions of any NATO country. ...

Marked progress has been made by our glorious parachute troops. Many of you observed their high proficiency and daring at this year's air show. These troops are well trained for parachute drops by day and night and from new types of planes. To give you an idea of the possible scale of such drops under present conditions, let me say that during training our military air transport alone dropped more than 100,000 parachutists, to say nothing of the personnel and cargo it transported. And these can also transport motor vehicles, artillery pieces and missiles. It is to be assumed that if the need arises our Civil Air Fleet, whose excellent capabilities you are all well aware of, will quickly come to the aid of the military air transport. Obviously, quite a few delegates came to the Congress on a TU-104, IL-18, AN-10 or some other of our wonderful planes. (Applause.)

The Party Central Committee has been and still is showing special concern for the country's antiaircraft and antimissile defense. The armament, as well as the troop organization, of the country's antiaircraft defense has changed radically in the period since the 20th Party Congress. The antiaircraft defense is today based mainly on the power of the antiaircraft rocket troops, which act in combination with the new fighter planes. The superiority of antiaircraft missiles to antiaircraft guns is strikingly indicated by the following fact. During the last war the antiaircraft artillery used an average of between 400 and 600 shells to destroy a single enemy plane. A modern plane, on the other hand, which has enormous speed and can fly twice as high as antiaircraft shells can reach, can be brought down by one or at most two missiles. I must report in particular that the problem of destroying missiles in flight has also been solved. (Stormy applause.)

The number of servicemen in the antiaircraft defense forces with excellent ratings in political and combat training has been growing and the number of excellent units increasing. As of the start of the Congress there were about 1,200 of these units. These are trusty sentinels guarding our cities against raids by today's carrion vultures. The echelons and units of the antiaircraft defense forces are on constant and vigilant duty. (Applause.)

In the period under review obsolete piston-engine military aircraft have been completely replaced in the air force by up-to-date jet planes, including supersonic long-range bombers. The rocket has replaced the cannon and machine gun in aircraft armament. In the past few years the speeds and ceilings of military aircraft have increased 50% to 150%. Missile-carrying planes capable of dealing long-range nuclear-missile strikes at an aggressor without entering his antiaircraft defense zone are being introduced in greater and greater numbers. This has greatly increased the military capabilities of our aviation.

Our air force, working in coordination with the country's antiaircraft defense forces, has heightened its readiness both to repulse an aggressor's air attack and, in joint operations with the strategic missile forces, to deliver powerful nuclear blows at him. This year's air show was very highly rated by the working people of our country.

There have been basic changes in our navy. Its power has grown and it has become a completely modern navy capable of accomplishing its assigned operational tasks far from our shores. The main arm of the navy is its submarines, designed for a variety of functions and incomparably more effective in nuclear-missile war than surface ships. Furthermore, we regard atomic submarines armed with powerful nuclear missiles as the basis of our submarine fleet. (Applause.)

The naval missile-carrying aircraft are to act in coordination with submarines in combat operations. Nikita Sergeyevich Khrushchev has reminded the mettlesome admirals of the West that today's military equipment makes it possible to bring vital centers under fire from submarine-launched ballistic and homing missiles and to destroy the naval vessels of any aggressor. I shall furthermore note that our missile submarines have learned to navigate well under Arctic ice and to take up precise positions for the launching of missiles, which is very important for sure strikes at land and water objectives. (Applause.)

Comrades! A great many military training exercises were held in 1961 both in our armed forces and jointly with the fraternal armies of the Warsaw Treaty countries. Primary attention in all these exercises was devoted to the study of nuclear missiles and other new military equipment and the waging of combat operations in conditions of the use by the aggressor of weapons of mass destruction.

The chief common task we have set for all our armed forces in the course of their combat and operational training is to study and master ways of effectively repulsing an aggressor's surprise nuclear attack and frustrating his aggressive designs by promptly dealing him a crushing blow. Stress was laid, furthermore, on conducting the exercises under conditions approximating the features of modern war, approximating the real situation that might arise in the initial phase of a war in the event of attack by an aggressor. New devices for directing the forces, including electronic computers, were used extensively in the exercises.

In view of the aggravated international situation, in the course of this year's inspections and exercises in the field we examined and checked up on echelons, units and formations of all branches of the armed forces. This made it possible to do a better job of uncovering shortcomings, providing the troops with concrete assistance on the spot and ascertaining in detail the real state of the armed forces' combat and mobilizational readiness.

All this enables me to report to the 22nd Party Congress, with full responsibility, that our armed forces are very well equipped at the present time and that their organizational structure and the level of their combat and operational training are fully adequate to the high demands of the Presidium of the Party Central Committee and to the needs of the present world situation. (Prolonged applause.) ...

It is significant that the proportion of Communists and Young Communist League members among officers, generals and admirals is almost 90%. (Applause.) One out of every four of them has a higher education.

The number of our engineers and technicians has been

steadily growing. In the rocket troops, for example, 72 out of every 100 officers are engineers or technicians. Nearly all officers on the regimental level and higher have had valuable combat experience gained in the battles of the Great Patriotic War. (Applause.) ...

We military men have a special grievance against the members of the anti-Party group. I see in this auditorium prominent military leaders who were innocently imprisoned. All army Communists unanimously and with special fervor approve the crushing defeat of the anti-Party group of Molotov, Malenkov, Kaganovich, Voroshilov, Bulganin, Pervukhin and Saburov and heartily thank the Central Committee of our party for its firm Leninist line in fighting the anti-Party group, and above all we thank Nikita Sergeyevich Khrushchev, that outstanding champion of the restoration of Leninist principles and norms in the guidance of the Party and state. (Prolonged applause.)

Former Minister of Defense Zhukov displayed adventurism and Bonapartist ambition for personal power. He spread his own cult of the individual in the army and followed a policy of curtailing and downgrading Party political work.

The Party Central Committee put a timely stop to this harmful activity and removed Zhukov from his position. In this connection a very important part was played in strengthening the army and navy by the decisions taken in 1957 by the October plenary session of the C.P.S.U. Central Committee; the session mapped measures for intensifying Party guidance of the armed forces and radically improving Party-political work in them. (Applause.) As a result of practical implementation of the resolution of the October plenary session and subsequent decisions of the C.P.S.U. Central Committee, Leninist principles have been fully restored in the guidance of the armed forces, the role of the political agencies and Party organizations in the forces has grown, the army's ties with the people have been strengthened and Party political work with personnel has improved considerably. Admission of the finest fighting men to the Party has resulted in sharply increased growth in Party ranks in the armed forces, and the number of Y.C.L. members has grown as well. At present Communists and Y.C.L. members make up 82% of the personnel of the armed forces. (Applause.) ...

The broadening and reinforcement of the ties maintained by army and navy Party organizations, political agencies and military councils with local Party, Soviet, Y.C.L. and trade union organizations is rendering the armed forces inestimable assistance in the patriotic education of fighting men and in helping the latter to acquire an even deeper appreciation and sense of their solid unity with the people. This joint work must be continued and improved. (Applause.) ...

Pavlov

SPEECH BY COMRADE S. P. PAVLOV, FIRST SECRETARY OF THE Y.C.L. CENTRAL COMMITTEE. (Pravda, Oct. 25, p. 5. 3,300 words. Condensed text:) Comrades! ... Since the 20th Party Congress the Leninist Young Communist League has traversed the path of a thorough reorganization and improvement of its methods of work and has grown ideologically and organizationally stronger. ...

It is known that in the period of the cult of the individual, and especially in its latter years, the Y.C.L. clearly lacked great and specific tasks that could really fire young people with enthusiasm. This is why the Party's call for undertaking the development of the virgin lands met with a wildly enthusiastic response from youth. More than 700,000 young patriots set out for the regions where the virgin lands were being opened up. But they were only a small part of those who responded heart and soul to the Party's call.

Soviet youth thereby demonstrated their devotion to our party, to the Central Committee and to that stanch Leninist, tireless fighter for the happiness of the peoples and for a bright future for youth, Nikita Sergeyevich Khrushchev. (Stormy applause.) The ardent participation of Soviet youth and of the people as a whole in the development of the virgin lands was also striking proof of the total untenability, groundlessness and bankruptcy of the views held by the wretched handful of factionalists. ...

The Y.C.L. reports to the Party today that all the concrete

commitments it made at its 13th Congress have been much more than fully discharged. (Stormy applause.) The Y.C.L. sent more than 1,200,000 of its members to crash construction projects in key branches of our industry. Dozens of blast and open-hearth furnaces and rolling mills, 54 chemical enterprises and nearly 20,000 km. of gas pipeline, railroads and electrified track were completed ahead of schedule with their help. ...

The years since the 20th Party Congress have been years in which young people have learned to love and respect the land and the manly and noble work of the grain grower and the livestock raiser. The greatest credit is due our party for the fact that youth today look upon the work of the peasant with entirely different eyes. More than 2,500,000 young men and women went to work in livestock sections alone on Y.C.L. passes. ...

The Y.C.L. is continuing to take an active part in the development of the virgin lands. In response to the appeal made by Nikita Sergeyevich Khrushchev, 11,000 skilled construction workers and more than 18,000 graduates of pedagogical, medical, agricultural and other higher schools went to Kazakhstan this year on Y.C.L. passes. ...

The fight for corn has this year become a test of political maturity for the Y.C.L. More than 500,000 young men and women, 130,000 youth teams and groups, raised 12,500,000 hectares of corn. ...

Nikita Sergeyevich Khrushchev summoned the country's young patriots to go to the taiga, the mountains and the deserts to help the Party harness the wealth of these regions in the service of the Soviet people. As always, our youth responded heartily to the Party's call. Literally in no time after Nikita Sergeyevich Khrushchev made his report, applications from young people started coming in to the Y.C.L. Central Committee and the Y.C.L. committees of Moscow, Leningrad, Kiev, Gorky, Sverdlovsk, Minsk and other cities. The stream of applications has been growing day by day. ...

Our young people, in their great wish to be of use to the nation, are not afraid of hardships. But there are objective hardships and there are those that are caused by the callousness, indifference and bureaucratic behavior of some economic executives. One can still encounter sorry excuses for managers who try to justify their heartless attitude to the elementary needs of the young workers by saying "I have a plan to meet," or "Others have had to endure worse." Incidentally, officials like these as a rule fail to meet the plan. It cannot be considered normal for economic executives to feel responsible solely for plan fulfillment. They must be equally responsible for providing young people with proper living and working conditions and recreational facilities. ...

Those who are in school today will be living in a communist society and managing its affairs. This is why inculcation of communist morality in the students, of eagerness to work and live like Communists, must hold a basic place in the work of the schools. But not enough advantage has thus far been taken of the big opportunities for this opened up by the Law on Strengthening Ties Between School and Life.* The pedagogical institutions are lagging somewhat behind life. The schools still have no concrete system for ideological and labor education as a single process. Generalized experience of this work is badly needed not only by the pedagogs but by the production personnel, those who handle the vocational training of the schoolchildren. The existing forms of political upbringing for pupils in many cases take no account of the children's heightened needs and interests and often amount to nothing more than the reading of newspapers aloud. A course on "Fundamentals of Political Knowledge" has so far been set up only on an experimental basis and in a small number of schools.

School problems are often settled by adults only. The children's initiative and enterprise are not being developed; the children's political organizations have not been given a heightened role, although after all there are 17,000,000 Young Pioneers in school today and more than 1,500,000 Y.C.L. members.

The formal instruction and upbringing of young people are being coupled in the best possible way in the boarding schools. Many enthusiastic teachers have, with the help and support of

---

*Current Digest of the Soviet Press, Vol. XI, No. 4, pp. 12-16.

the public at large, been taking good advantage of the possibilities offered by these schools. But not enough is being done
to disseminate the advanced experience of this truly Soviet
method of rearing schoolchildren. No wonder, then, that a
good deal of eccentric originality is tolerated in some of the
boarding schools and that there have been distortions of our
pedagogy. Here and there attempts are made to prescribe literally every step for the children. Instead of individual work with the pupils, the routine is here and there complicated by the introduction of all sorts of "regulations," "laws"
and "special rules of conduct." The children have hardly any
time left for the things they love to do, for reading a book,
listening to the radio, for games and songs.

In our judgment, the Russian Academy of Pedagogy, the ministries and pedagogical research institutions should devote far
more attention to the problems of the ideological upbringing of
schoolchildren. It would be of enormous benefit for the rearing of the rising generation if our labor veterans, scientists
and scholars, writers, actors, Soviet officials and public figures participated regularly rather than merely occasionally in
school activities. We believe such work should become a normal and honorable duty for the countless army of our Soviet
public.

We deeply appreciate the enormous contribution that our
pedagogical scholars have made to the development of the
Soviet schools. But I think it would do pedagogical science no
harm, would enrich it, if there were an influx of gifted young
people—schoolteachers and directors—into the scholars'
ranks. After all, today only four out of 65 corresponding members of the Russian Republic Academy of Pedagogy work in the
school system, while the average age of the members and
corresponding members of the Academy is over 65. ...

The Y.C.L. is intensifying its struggle against bourgeois
ideology. Fearing the attractive force of communist ideas,
the troubadours of the bourgeois world corrupt the minds of
their young generation by propagating the base aspirations of
the moneygrubbing property owner, by propagating egoism,
by advertising the philistine "joys" of life. Agence France-
Presse, succumbing to wishful thinking, recently alleged that
Soviet youth, too, are showing a steadily growing interest in
this way of life. Clearly, this could be written only by persons to whom it is not given to understand the minds and
hearts of our people. It is the young people themselves who
tell us about the real traits of Soviet youth, their true ideals.
Recently Komsomolskaya pravda took an extensive poll of its
readers, asking: "What do you think of your generation?"*
Young people were unanimous in stating their belief that the
chief distinguishing traits of the generation are patriotism,
devotion to the Party, belief in communism, diligence, courage and a feeling for the new. ...

Young people are sincerely happy when they make a new
friend of a book or film that tells an important truth about
Soviet people and has heroes in whom they want to believe and
whom they want to emulate.

They are therefore unwilling to accept works that are primarily concerned with the characters and actions of a wretched
little group of "scrofulous youth." It is an easy thing to relish
the adventures of the morally depraved, but it is not a noble
thing. This must not be done under the banner of the struggle
to educate man. It is a great pity that these strange tendencies
should have begun to manifest themselves most distinctly in
so respected a journal of the Writers' Union as Yunost
[Youth]. By the way, there is not a single educator or Y.C.L.
worker on the magazine's editorial board. We are at a loss
to understand the haste with which certain cinematographers
undertook to film the story "Mishka, Serega and I" or the novel
"Ticket to the Stars," which had been published in Yunost. I am
speaking of this because what young people need most is
works that will summon them to action, to creative labor, to
exploits, works that will inculcate readiness to battle for the
ideals of communism. (Applause.)

Comrades! The draft Program of the C.P.S.U. speaks of
the gradual transformation of the socialist state system into
public communist self-government. Technical-progress head-

*Current Digest of the Soviet Press, Vol. XIII, No. 2, pp. 32-
34; No. 15, pp. 15-21.

quarters, councils of young specialists, people's volunteers and
public design bureaus and laboratories have received permanent
"registration" in the everyday work and lives of young people.
There are 23,000 Y.C.L. headquarters and control posts functioning at the country's construction sites and enterprises.
These organizational forms are all helping young men and women
to develop the capacity for public self-government and for
economic management and are instilling in them a sense of
responsibility to the collective. True, young people sometimes
overdo things. For instance, when there was a delay in delivery of equipment from Britain, headquarters members at one
construction site rashly decided to send a Y.C.L. alarm signal
to Queen Elizabeth. (Stir in the hall. Laughter.) But the
majority of the aktivists refer to the right people for the solution of urgent problems. Many economic councils and ministries and the State Planning Committee have come to know the
Y.C.L. headquarters groups.

The principle of work on a voluntary, nonpaid basis is being
extensively applied in Y.C.L. committees, too. Since the 20th
Party Congress the number of paid staff workers in the district,
city and province Y.C.L. committees has been cut nearly 30%.
The Y.C.L. now has 5,600 nonpaid secretaries of district and
city committees, and tens of thousands of young men and women
are working on a voluntary basis in various permanent commissions of the Y.C.L. committees and on youth newspapers.
We realize the enormous future that volunteer work has in all
our activities, and it is our aim to have every young person,
while he is a member of the Leninist Young Communist League,
learn a volunteer occupation.

Comrades! The example of our country, the country that
is building communism, grips the minds and hearts of millions
of young people abroad. The attractive force of communist
ideas is also shown by the growing international contacts of
Soviet youth. We now have ties with 1,000 youth organizations.
This is three times as many as in 1956.

We can only rejoice at the way our ties with the youth of
Asian, African and Latin American countries have been developing and gaining strength. These ties are based on
genuinely disinterested friendship. A thousand young men
from Cuba have come to our country to spend a year studying
agricultural techniques and the Russian language, while 300
of our young specialists are coming along well in their work in
the fields of Cuba.

A World Youth Forum was held in Moscow this summer. And
once again young people representing the widest range of political orientations, and coming from 106 countries, heartily endorsed the peaceful foreign policy of the Soviet Union and the
countries of the socialist camp and the struggle of peoples and
of youth for national liberation.

Comrades! ... The history of the Y.C.L. is a history of loyal
service to the Party's cause. More than 75,000,000 persons
have received their first communist training in the ranks of
the Y.C.L., learned in our organization to fight for the Party's
cause and to translate its plans into reality. For a member of
the Y.C.L. there is no goal more noble than to merit the lofty
title of member of the Communist Party. We are proud that
more than 1,500,000 of the finest Y.C.L. members have joined
the great party of Lenin since the 20th Party Congress. (Applause.)..

The 19,000,000 members of the Leninist Young Communist
League and all Soviet youth will continue to be boundlessly devoted to the Party's cause and will unite even more closely
around its Leninist Central Committee. ...

Mukhitdinov

SPEECH BY COMRADE N. A. MUKHITDINOV, SECRETARY
OF THE PARTY CENTRAL COMMITTEE. (Pravda, Oct. 25,
pp. 6-7; Izvestia, Oct. 26, pp. 2-3. 6,000 words. Condensed
text:) ∴ I. Unity and Friendship of the Soviet Peoples—a Triumph of the Leninist National Policy.—In the sphere of national
relations the second Party program, adopted in 1919, set the
tasks of the international unity of the working people and the
establishment of the complete equality of all nations and the
creation of conditions for their firm and voluntary union. ...

Thus in adopting the third Program our party triumphantly
declares that it has brilliantly fulfilled the tasks in the sphere of
national relations advanced in the second Program. (Applause.)

The established and growing social homogeneity of Soviet nations multiplies their forces and strengthens mutual trust and fraternal cooperation among the peoples of the U.S.S.R. The new successes of the Leninist national policy scored in recent years are graphic evidence of this.

Representatives of the republics, speaking from this rostrum, are recounting vividly and convincingly the remarkable results of the work done by the Party organizations in the period under review.

What are the sources of these successes, and why is it precisely in recent years that they have been most substantial?

The primary reason is that since the historic 20th Congress the Party has ensured a decisive improvement in the style and methods of leadership and has raised the level of political and organizational activity of all links of the Party and state apparatus. This has been possible thanks to the resolute elimination of the harmful consequences of the Stalin cult and the restoration of Leninist norms of Party and state life and the principles of collective leadership.

As is known, the anti-Party group of Molotov, Kaganovich, Malenkov, Voroshilov, Bulganin, Pervukhin, Saburov and Shepilov bitterly opposed implementation of the decisions of the 20th Congress. They were ardent supporters of anti-Leninist methods and hoped to conceal their personal guilt for the persecution of honest people in the period of the cult of the individual.

The gross violations of the norms of Party democracy and revolutionary legality had a harmful effect not only on the work of central bodies but also on the life of the national republics. In some republics bankrupt people of the type of Bagirov, enjoying the protection of Malenkov, Kaganovich and Molotov and sometimes even on their direct instructions, acted arbitrarily and lawlessly. The representatives of the Central Asian, Transcaucasian and other republics present here at the Congress well remember how many devoted officials and representatives of the intelligentsia perished at that time in these republics.

Can it be forgotten that it was the 20th Congress that saved the lives and restored the honor of thousands of illegally repressed citizens of the Soviet Union! (Applause.)

Fiercely objecting to enhancement of the role and extension of the rights of the Union republics and the strengthening of their sovereignty and to the establishment of the economic councils, the factionalists did not simply cling to the old and outworn but in essence expressed mistrust in the cadres of the national republics.

The faulty methods of leadership of that period were also reflected in economic life. This can be shown from the example of cotton growing. In the cotton-growing republics there were serious violations of the practical proportions in the development of branches of the economy that had justified themselves in local conditions. While adopting the measures necessary to advance cotton growing, they incorrectly counterposed it to other branches of agriculture. The areas planted to cotton were expanded not only by developing new land but to a large extent by directly forcing out other valuable crops.

Although karakul raising was being successfully developed in the steppe zones, the possibilities for producing meat and milk on the cotton farms were underestimated. Furthermore, so-called theories of the mutual exclusiveness of cotton growing and productive animal husbandry had currency.

The one-sided development of agriculture in these republics in the long run also affected cotton growing itself. It was conducted by backward, conservative methods, and the requirements of science and technology and the experience of masters of high yields were ignored. ...

After the 20th Congress the Party thoroughly analyzed the state of affairs in the country, disclosed the shortcomings and mistakes and worked out means for the further economic development of each republic with due regard for its specific conditions, features and role in the national economy of the Soviet Union. With the full support and active participation of the people, the Party adopted a number of important organizational, economic and technical measures to develop agricultural production, which also had a direct bearing on cotton growing. Along with this, specific problems in advancing cotton farming were carefully examined and solved. ...

The results of the intensive work done by the Party and people are clear to see. In the past seven years the area under cotton in the country has increased by 400,000 hectares and the annual output of cotton by 800,000 tons. In the cotton republics the output of wool, meat and milk has increased 50% to 100%.

As the leaders of the cotton republics have assured us here, this year the state cotton plan will be fulfilled everywhere. This means that the highest yields and the largest harvest of cotton will be obtained in the country. ...

I want to stress that all the major measures for radically changing the structure, system and methods of cotton farming and for developing irrigation construction were proposed on the basis of a study and generalization of the experience of leading workers, and with due regard for the requirements of science and technology, by Comrade Nikita Sergeyevich Khrushchev personally. (Applause.)

Comrades! The Russian people have played and still play a decisive role in the successful implementation of the Party's national policy in our multinational country. The great Russian people—the first among equals—have by their revolutionary traditions and treasure stores of science and culture earned the love and deep respect of all the Soviet nations. (Applause.) It is not for nothing that the latter call the Russian people their older brother. (Applause.) ...

Lenin and the Bolshevik party founded by him worked out for the first time in mankind's history a national policy that accords with the interests of the masses of the working people and laid the basis for the great process of unification of nations.

The Communist Party of the Soviet Union and its Central Committee, led by Comrade N. S. Khrushchev, the continuer of Lenin's cause, are creatively developing and consistently applying the Marxist-Leninist teaching on the national question. (Applause.) ...

The Program attaches great importance to the integrated development and specialization of the economies of the Union republics. ...

All the preconditions have been created for a new advance in cotton growing in our country. It is necessary merely to utilize them correctly and skillfully and, as pointed out in the Central Committee report, to solve a number of urgent problems. It is a matter above all of completing the mechanization of labor-consuming operations. It cannot be tolerated that the machine harvesting of cotton is proceeding even less satisfactorily this year than last and as of Oct. 20 amounted to only 8%, although there was concentrated opening of the bolls and a great many new cotton-picking machines were available.

Selection and seed growing are seriously lagging, and a correct, rational crop structure has not yet been set up, a fact impeding the introduction of crop rotation and an increase in yields.

In irrigation farming there is waste in the use of water. The coefficient of its use now amounts to only 40% to 45%. Yet it is possible to double this figure merely through reinforcing the irrigation network and installing sluice gates and through correct organization of transport of the water and of irrigation itself. This would make it possible without large state investments to develop hundreds of thousands of hectares of new land and to prevent the bogging up and salinization of already irrigated fields.

In the cotton republics animal husbandry continues to be the most lagging sector. We must not rest satisfied with the first successes achieved. The leading collective farms, headed by such innovators as Comrades Tursunkulov and Khvan, have for many years been obtaining high, stable yields of corn and alfalfa, along with a large quantity of cotton. They are thereby setting an example of how it is possible on cotton farms to increase the output of meat and milk successfully and in a short period. However, the output of milk per 100 hectares of farmland in the republic as a whole is only one-fifteenth that of the collective farm of which Comrade Khvan is chairman. ...

The new stage in the development of national relations and the unprecedented advance in the economy and culture of the Union republics require increased attention by Party organizations to the internationalist education of cadres.

All grounds for nationalism and chauvinism have been completely eliminated in our country. But relapses of such survivals on the part of individuals have not yet been excluded. It is the duty of Communists to prevent and put a decisive end to any manifestations of chauvinism, national egoism and narrow-mindedness, and aspiration toward autarky and localism.

In a number of regions, provinces and republics some officials have engaged in report padding and have displayed conceit, immodesty and insincerity before the Party and state. It is necessary to draw serious conclusions from all this and to seal tightly all the cracks through which such alien ways penetrate to us.

***

Comrades! The historic successes of the Soviet Union and the socialist countries and their unity and solidarity sincerely gladden all honest people of the world. Against this background the anti-Marxist conduct of the present leaders of Albania stands out like a dirty spot.

You know that our Party and government delegation, headed by Comrade N. S. Khrushchev, visited Albania in May, 1959, at the invitation of the Central Committee of the Albanian Party of Labor. I, too, was a member of this delegation. I remember how in personal conversations and at well-attended meetings Hoxha, Shehu and other leaders of the Albanian Party of Labor swore friendship with the Soviet people and praised the successes of the foreign and domestic policy of the Soviet state and fully approved it. Yet today these same people, without a twinge of conscience, are denigrating the general line of our party and the decisions of the 20th Party Congress.

It is now obvious that when they spoke of eternal friendship and brotherhood, of the fact that the unity of the Albanian Party of Labor and the C.P.S.U. would exist as long as the Albanian mountains, they were double-dealing, deceiving the Albanian people and the Soviet people, concealing a stone behind their backs. Is this the morality of a Communist? Only dishonorable people for whom nothing is sacred can act in this way.

The Soviet government gave a great deal of disinterested aid and full support to the fraternal Albanian people so that Albania would become a flowering garden on the Adriatic and an example for the oppressed peoples. And after all this Hoxha and Shehu are slandering the Soviet Union and sowing hostility toward our party among the Albanian working people!

The Party Central Committee sincerely did everything it could to preserve unity on a principled basis. But the embittered nationalism and hostility of the present Albanian leaders is intensifying and manifesting itself in the crudest form.

The whole world is now living with the 22nd Party Congress. All progressive mankind is following its work with admiration, while the Albanian leaders are these days defaming our 22nd Congress and the new Party Program in a foul way. All this shows how deeply they have wallowed in the swamp of nationalism, how alien to them are the interests of the world Communist movement and of the Albanian people themselves.

Apostasy from Marxism-Leninism and betrayal of the principles of proletarian internationalism have never brought glory to anyone. Nor will they bring glory to the present Albanian leaders! (Applause.)

II. Collapse of the Colonial System of Imperialism. —Comrades! The unprecedented growth of the economic and military might of the Soviet state, its remarkable scientific and technical achievements and its successes in the sphere of national relations are of the greatest international importance, especially for peoples who are fighting for their freedom and independence.

We are living in an epoch when the colonial system of imperialism has collapsed. Speaking at the 20th Party Congress, Comrade N. S. Khrushchev said: "The complete abolition of the infamous system of colonialism has now been placed on the order of the day as one of the most acute and pressing problems." It is significant that it was from the rostrum of a Congress of our party that the ardent call to end colonialism forever was sounded.

In recent years many countries of Asia, Africa and Latin America have won political independence and emerged on the path of independent national development. Pursuing a policy of positive neutrality, they are playing an increasingly active role in international affairs, becoming an important factor in the world and building a new free life.

But the vestiges of colonialism and many of its severe consequences have not yet been eliminated. The colonialists are answering the just demands for independence on the part of the peoples of the oppressed countries with wars of annihilation, cruel terror and the ravishing of whole regions of Africa and other parts of the world. The peoples are become increasingly convinced from their own experience that imperialism never retreated and will not retreat from its political, economic and other positions voluntarily. ...

With its power and mighty prestige our state supports the great liberation revolution that has developed on the Asian, African and Latin American continents. It has officially proposed that the forthcoming year of 1962 be proclaimed the year of the complete and final liquidation of the colonial system. (Applause.) ...

The monopolies of the U.S.A. are the main bulwark of present-day colonialism. Relying on its military bases, the U.S.A. cynically interferes in the internal affairs of other peoples. It lords it over the aggressive NATO, CENTO and SEATO military blocs, which, along with their general orientation against the socialist countries, operate as agencies of collective colonialism.

The imperialist monopolies advertise in every way their "economic aid" to the underdeveloped countries. Who does not know what kind of "aid" this is? It is essentially nothing but economic expansion, a source of fabulous profits, and bears an openly militaristic, predatory character. It is not for nothing that one prominent Asian scholar compared American "aid" with honey that is offered to be licked through the glass of a jar. (Stir in the hall.)

The United States is also engaged in extensive ideological subversion against the Afro-Asian and Latin American countries. A special government body called the U.S. Information Agency has been set up for this purpose. The scope of this agency's subversive activity is indicated, for example, by the fact that it it has more than 12,000 agents in its service and operates 150 propaganda centers in 70 underdeveloped countries. It has now been decided to send to the support of the Information Agency the so-called Peace Corps—a fire brigade of preachers of the American way of life, which might correctly be called a corps of espionage, subversion and war.

The peoples are well aware that these latter-day preachers in no way differ from the former Western missionaries, about whose work they say in Africa: "When the whites came to us, they had the Bible and we had the land. Today the whites have the land and we have the Bible."

The monopolies of the U.S.A., Great Britain, France, the Federal Republic of Germany and the other imperialist countries are striving by every means to preserve the young sovereign states as their agrarian and raw material appendages, to keep them in the world capitalist system and to preserve their backwardness.

This is why the oppressed peoples have risen in resolute struggle against all forms of colonialism, old and new, open and concealed. The peoples of Asia, Africa and Latin America are fully determined to bury colonialism with all its attributes as quickly as possible. They are turning their gaze to that part of the world which by its very nature is the irreconcilable foe of colonialism—to the world of socialism. ...

In recent years there has been an unprecedented expansion of all-round cooperation between the Soviet Union and many young sovereign countries that economically are still underdeveloped. Whereas in 1954 the Soviet Union had intergovernmental economic agreements with only two underdeveloped countries, today it has agreements with 22 such countries. Our economic assistance at that time amounted to a few million rubles in the old currency; today it totals several billion rubles in the new currency.

With credits granted by the Soviet government on advantageous terms and on the basis of designs by our engineers and with their help, 380 industrial enterprises and other installations supplied with up-to-date Soviet equipment have been built or are under construction in these countries. They are playing an important role in creating and developing the national economies of these states.

Approximately 5,000 Soviet specialists are working selflessly in the countries that have won independence, at the invitation of their governments. Our people have every reason to be proud of the remarkable Soviet specialists, who are honorably fulfilling the noble mission of rendering selfless assistance to the peoples of friendly countries.

The Soviet Union engages in mutually advantageous bilateral trade relations with 35 Afro-Asian and Latin American states, and the volume of trade with them has increased eightfold in the past seven years.

Our country is also helping the young independent states to train highly skilled workers, engineers, agronomists and other specialists. More than 4,000 students from 74 countries of Asia, Africa and Latin America are now enrolled in the Lumumba University of Friendship of Peoples, Moscow State University and other higher educational institutions. (Applause.) ...

Comrades! The anticolonial revolutions have set in motion all classes and social strata of the countries that are seeking liberation. The steady growth of the working class and the rise in the political and national awareness of the masses are a significant fact in their life. This is reflected above all in the expansion of the ranks and the increased influence of the Communist and Workers' Parties, which now function in 48 countries of Asia, Africa and Latin America. ...

The imperialists are trying to undermine the national-liberation movement and to export counterrevolution under the false guise of anticommunism. We see today from the example of certain countries that anticommunism in effect leads to the restoration of reactionary regimes and is fraught with the danger of new imperialist ventures. But no anticommunist propaganda can shake the faith of millions of people in the bright ideals of communism. It is not chance that one prominent African political figure recently stated: "As a parched and thirsty land needs water, so Africa needs the ideas of scientific socialism." (Applause.) ...

III. The Schools Are a Reliable Assistant of the Party in Rearing the New Man. —Comrades! Our schools now have a major role to play in molding the new man of communist society. More than 50,000,000 persons—one out of every four citizens of the country—now engage in study in the Soviet Union; the higher educational institutions have an enrollment of 2,600,000 students, 20 times as many as before the revolution and more than double the number in the higher schools of all capitalist Europe. ...

The initiative in carrying out the reorganization of the schools and the working out of the basic principles of the law belong to Comrade N. S. Khrushchev personally. (Applause.)

The boarding schools, the establishment of which was warmly approved by Soviet people, are a new development in public education. Today there are more than 2,000 such schools with an enrollment of 700,000 children. But by the end of the seven-year period they will be able to admit 2,500,000 pupils.

The state does not spare funds to strengthen the schools' material and technical facilities. At the same time, education in our country has become the vital concern of all the working people. The remarkable initiative of the leading collective farms in the Ukraine, Uzbekistan, Moldavia and Bashkiria and in Belgorod, Kursk, Orenburg and many other provinces that are building schools and children's institutions with their own resources warrants every support and encouragement.

The draft Program calls for the further comprehensive development of public education. Universal compulsory secondary polytechnical education for all children of school age and at least an eighth-grade education for young people employed in the national economy are to be realized in the next decade. In the following decade the possibility will be created for all to obtain a complete secondary education, and for everyone who wishes it to obtain a higher or specialized secondary education.

Try to name just one bourgeois state that would set the task of assuring the entire population the opportunity of raising its general-educational, scientific and cultural level on such a scale. There were no such bourgeois states in the past and there are none today. Only our socialist state and our Marxist-Leninist party have for the first time in the history of mankind set such a noble task and are successfully carrying it out. (Applause.) ...

Enormous work has been done in our country in the training of teaching cadres. More than 100,000 young teachers are graduated annually from higher educational institutions. But the need for pedagogical cadres is rapidly growing. Therefore it is necessary to take measures now to increase admissions to higher pedagogical institutions and schools and to strengthen their material facilities.

Sensitivity and attention to the needs and requirements of teachers and to improving their housing and everyday living conditions, especially in rural areas, and concern for raising the ideological and political level and qualifications of teachers constitute a major duty of Party and Soviet agencies. ...

The Russian language is of fundamental importance in the further development of every socialist nation, the internationalist upbringing of the growing generation and completion of the cultural revolution in the country. ...

It is precisely in the Russian language that the Soviet nations acquired a powerful means for their development and for intercourse among the nations. This also explains the enormous and logical attraction to Russian both on the part of all Soviet peoples and in foreign countries. It is necessary to support this desire of the peoples in every way.

In the republics serious thought must be given to considerably improving the teaching of Russian in the schools, higher educational institutions and circles and over the radio, to issuing good textbooks and study and methodological aids, and to strengthening the corps of teachers. ...

Sholokhov

SPEECH BY COMRADE M. A. SHOLOKHOV, WRITER, ROSTOV PARTY ORGANIZATION. (Pravda, Oct. 25, pp. 7-8; Izvestia, p. 6. 4,500 words. Excerpts:) ... The speakers at the Congress have had a great deal to say about the factionalists, those who brazenly flouted the sacred ties of Party comradeship. New details of their criminal activities have been disclosed to us at this Congress. And the question spontaneously arises: How long are we going to find ourselves arm-in-arm in the Party's ranks with those who have done the Party so much irremediable harm? Are we not being too tolerant toward those who have on their consciences the deaths of thousands of loyal sons of the nation and the Party, the thousands of their kith and kin whose lives were destroyed?

Let the Congress—the supreme agency of the Party—pronounce its stern but just judgment on the factionalists and renegades. (Applause.) ...

I have little to add to what Comrade Furtseva has told you. She anticipated my speech, as it were, but still there are a few things that I think it necessary to dwell on. First of all, I want to say that we had long dreamed of having a Minister like Comrade Furtseva. And at last we have one. (Applause.) Our dear Yekaterina Alexeyevna has proved successful in every respect: She has done an excellent job of organizing her work, because she knows and loves it; she gives a charming appearance (applause), and is similarly charming in her handling of cultural figures. Meeting and talking with cultural figures, especially people in the arts, and not only that but guiding their work, is anything but an easy job, because these are all people of the most delicate feelings—to put it bluntly, spoiled and capricious people. (Applause.) If the smile you give one is not just so, the way you say hello to another not just so and the look you give a third not just so—you've given offense, and not just offense but mortal offense! Still, our Minister has been coping with all these matters and, as you see, coping well. And in the bargain more and more new talents of hers are coming to light, making us simply marvel and show our pleasure and astonishment. I'll tell you what I am referring to. When our Minister was speaking about the number of film-projection units in the country and the number of new amateur performing groups, everything went without a hitch for her, but just as soon as she began talking about the plays that are being written, her uncommon diplomatic flair manifested itself. Just look at the magnificent knight's move she made in resorting to the device of diplomatic silence.

I am not the Minister and am utterly lacking in diplomatic endowments, and so I feel like having a plain talk with Yekaterina Alexeyevna without passing things over in silence. All right, you say that out of 1,114 Soviet plays staged in the country's theaters, 780 are on present-day themes. You even figured out the percentage—more than 70%. What I want to ask is this: What percentage of these 70% will remain on the boards? If you don't mind, let's let the percentages be and move on to the absolute figures. God willing, out of these 780 plays 20 or 30, if that many, will last. (Applause.) And the second question: How many of these 20 or 30 plays will audiences remember? I am not referring grandiloquently to plays that will leave an indelible mark on the soul, but am simply asking how many will be remembered and make audiences think? Even fewer! It is the poor theatergoers who have to pay for the creative impotence of the playwrights. That's the whole trouble!

Figures and percentages, Comrade Furtseva, are tricky things and will, I'm afraid, let you down. (Applause.) A better place for these figures is somewhere in the Central Statistical Administration; they'll be more at home there than in art. (Laughter. Applause.)

Much the same thing is happening in fiction. A great many books come out which shortly afterwards head for "repulping," so to speak. The reason? You all know it. A natural gap is developing between the low caliber of the output and the high standards of the readers. But not everything is quite as bleak on the literary front as might appear at first superficial glance. Something is happening which, though not very noticeable to the readers, is very comforting: A whole galaxy of young and truly talented writers, who were previously known only from their short stories in the periodicals, are maturing and becoming very promising literary craftsmen. This is true not only of Russian literature but of all the national literatures. I am not going to recite names; they are quite familiar to the readers. But here is what I want to say: These writers need to be given every possible assistance, so that they have a chance to work a year or two without having to think about the future and without having to stop work on the big canvases that many of them have long since conceived and for which these writers, who know what they are doing, have already stored up real material.

The number of such people will be substantially increased if we help not only the writers of the capital cities but also the provincial writers, of whom there are very considerable numbers in the Writers' Union. ...

Comrade Furtseva cited some really shocking figures in her speech. Just think, out of 2,700 writers of the Russian Republic, 1,700 are permanent residents of just two cities, Moscow and Leningrad. And if to this we add those who make their homes in Voronezh, Rostov, Sverdlovsk and other privince centers, what is left for the rural localities?

A writer who writes about collective farmers or people on a state farm should, in my opinion, have a background in agriculture at least equal to that of a sector agronomist. (Stormy applause.) One who writes about a metallurgical plant, about factory workers, engineers and technicians, must have at least as good a knowledge of production as a highly skilled worker. One who devotes his work to our army absolutely must have as good a knowledge of war as Kuprin and Leo Tolstoy. ...

Our Minister, with oh-such-feminine courtesy, said that it would not be a bad idea to appeal to young artists to follow the example of our finest young people and head for the construction sites of communism. But ask her whether she herself believes that kind of appeal will meet with a hearty response. It's a safe bet that she does not. (Applause.) Some of the ones she's appealing to will go for a week's airing, to get a breath of ozone, and then start missing heated bathrooms and other blessings of city life (laughter, stormy applause) and in a flash be back in Moscow. (Applause.)

As for the young creators of "imperishable values" who live in the provinces, you won't bar them from coming into Moscow or the other big centers. They have been hearing about the triumph with which the literary evenings of our present-day fashionable boudoir poets have been coming off in Moscow, with a detail of mounted militia sure to be on hand and with the delirious shrieking of hysterical young stilyagi. They, too, would like to show off in incredibly narrow pants and unconscionably broad-shouldered jackets before easy-to-please girls. (General laughter. Applause.) They, too, would like to taste the fruits of fame. And so they make their way through thick

and thin to Moscow, like the faithful to Mecca. (Laughter. Applause.) There's no stopping them with any arguments or quarantines. As the saying goes, "walking or riding, crawling or climbing," they reach their goal. (Laughter. Applause.)

What is it to, say, Fedin, Leonov, Maxim Rylsky or me if some young girl walking along lets fall: "Take a look, dearie, that's so-and-so coming!" Our reaction is that "it doesn't have the hide it used to," as old pensioners say. (Loud, general laughter. Applause.) But a young fellow feels flattered. It may make you wince to hear your name taken in so familiar a manner, but it makes some young writers swoon. There is no need to take a patronizing attitude to this, but the nature of youngsters does have to be understood.

Many of you are sure to have seen peasants, in the past, sifting grain on a riddle, a large suspended sieve, cleaning the grain before sowing. The chaff, dust and tailings are borne off by the wind, while the full-bodied grain remains. It will be that way in literature: The grain will remain while the chaff is blown away. Life itself will shake the literary riddle, and the necessary process of winnowing will occür.

This, as I see it, is how matters stand as regards the young writers. But where those advanced in years are concerned, the situation is no better. How do you come off calling on some city dweller to go in his old age to the outlying districts he finds so forbidding? And for that matter, who needs him there, and for what? (Laughter. Applause.) I, personally, have long since given up any thought of getting writers to move closer to the people they write about. It's a lost cause! Let Comrade Furtseva get her share of bruises in this noble pursuit. I've had enough! (Loud burst of laughter. Applause.)

The hope has been voiced here at the Congress that we writers and people in the arts will continue to be kindly and sensible counselors to the Soviet people. But if a person is himself ignorant of life, it is hard for him to give advice. He might give advice that would make no sense at all. Really, how can a writer who is a typical urbanite, who had his last real look at the countryside 30 or 40 years ago and has long since lost all ties with the land, or who may never have had any such ties at all, give any advice on a production problem to, say, an experienced collective farm chairman or state farm director, people who know their jobs inside out? And when it comes to moral and ethical problems some of these people, unpretentious-looking fellows, can make some of the writers look like new-born babes. A writer who cannot tell whether a young growth is spring wheat or winter wheat and confuses oats with barley had better not offer unsolicited advice. ...

I realize that my speech is a bit on the dismal side, but I can't help myself: I am possessed by an accursed craving—I keep wanting to see more good books, and there are too few of them. So I get annoyed at myself and at others, and that does little good. Matters like these have to be settled above all collectively and without any special haste. ...

Be all this as it may, ours is an advanced literature, and advanced not only in its idea content. Our ties with foreign publishing houses have been growing stronger. Books by our writers are being brought out everywhere abroad. They are read more for their content than their form, because other countries are very much interested in our life, in our present-day reality.

But we Soviet writers have, I dare say, more complaints against foreign critics than against our own. If the majority of our critics know nothing of life, the foreign ones not only know nothing of it but have little insight into it. Often they have entirely unwarranted complaints to make against us. They claim our writing has a bias. Well, how would they have it?

Let's say that I'm writing about a soldier of ours, a man who is infinitely near and dear to me. How can I write ill of him?! He's mine, all mine, from his garrison cap to his puttees, and I try not to notice the pockmarks on his face, say, or certain flaws in his character. (Stormy applause.)

And if I do notice them, I shall try to write so that the reader comes to love him, taking him with these endearing pockmarks and the little flaws in his character. (Applause.) ...

I want to see a writer's hot blood boil when he writes, his face whiten with restrained hatred of the enemy when he writes about him; I want to see the writer laugh and cry with the hero he loves and holds dear. (Applause.)

N. S. Khrushchev.—That's right.

M. A. Sholokhov.—Only on these conditions will a real work of genuine art be created, and not a counterfeit. ...

There are many things we have to work for, and above all, it seems to me, to exert an influence on our youth. We have splendid young people. The country owes much to their youthful enthusiasm, their heroic labor. But there is a small segment of young people who are in spiritual turmoil, who seek romance in our heroic everyday working lives and do not find it. Yet it is within easy reach; they have only to stretch out their hands and to take a closer look at life. It is our duty to turn these young people away from alien influences and accustom them to labor and exploits in these arduous times of ours.

And this is not the only problem that faces our writers today and will face them tomorrow. The Soviet family, the moral makeup of the new man, the titanic labors of our people—these all clamor to be embodied in art, these all imperiously demand of us the production of big, expansive works. We people of art well understand all this and are aware of the full weight of responsibility we bear to the people and the Party. ...

Pelse

SPEECH BY COMRADE A. J. PELSE, FIRST SECRETARY OF THE LATVIAN COMMUNIST PARTY CENTRAL COMMITTEE. (Pravda, Oct. 26, p. 2. 3,300 words. Excerpts:) Comrade delegates! ... The conduct of the present leaders of the Albanian Party of Labor evokes a feeling of extreme surprise, regret and indignation. At the 20th C.P.S.U. Congress and, later, at their own Third Congress they sang the praises of our party, glorified it, but now, having left internationalist positions, they have found themselves in the swamp of militant nationalism and are slandering our Communist Party. Our Congress justifiably condemns the position of the Albanian leaders, which is hostile to Marxism-Leninism. ...

The vain attempts of the despicable handful of factionalists—Molotov, Malenkov, Kaganovich and others—who tried to swerve our party from the Leninist path appear pitiful and insignificant against the background of our great victories. Having failed once and for all, they have found themselves on the rubbish heap of history. This rubbish might justly be cast out of our Party home. (Applause.) ...

Comrade delegates! ... In 17 years of peaceful construction under the Soviet system the republic's industrial output has increased 12 times and the output of machine building and metalworking 80 times. This year Latvia's industry has produced each month as much as was produced in the entire prewar year of 1940. It is typical that in such a capitalist country as Sweden, which has not known war and its consequences, industrial output has increased only 120% in the past 22 years. ...

We can report to the 22nd Congress that this year Latvia's industry will give the homeland as much output as was planned for 1963. (Applause.) ...

In order to develop the radioelectronics industry as rapidly as possible and to increase the output of means of communication, we consider it extremely necessary to carry out specialization of the republic's radio equipment enterprises. It seems to us advisable to concentrate the productions of radio-phonographs and radios at the A.S. Popov Radio Plant in Riga; this will ensure the production of 1,200,000 sets a year, instead of the 605,000 now produced in the republic. At the same time, it is practical to build a specialized plant for the production of telephones. We will then be able to turn out as many as 2,500,000 telephones a year instead of the 1,000,000 envisaged by the seven-year plan.

Implementation of these measures will make it possible to specialize the well-known VEF [State Electrical Equipment] Plant in the production of large and special items of telephone equipment and to more than double the output called for in the seven-year-plan control figures. ...

The Murmansk, Kaliningrad, Lithuanian, Estonian, Latvian and other fleets now fish in the waters of the Atlantic. Each of them organizes its work completely separately, from operational exploration to delivery of the fish. Fishing vessels often lose valuable time waiting for their floating bases and in some cases have to go thousands of kilometers to deliver the fish to shore enterprises. ...

In order to make more rational use of the fishing fleet, floating bases and ports, ship repair enterprises and fish-processing plants and to improve the supplying of new fishing areas and their development, it is advisable to establish a chief administration for the fishing industry of the Northwest Basin of the Soviet Union. (Applause.) ...

The successes that have been achieved in the development of animal husbandry are the result of the unremitting attention of Party organizations to strengthening the fodder base. Taking into account Nikita Sergeyevich Khrushchev's advice given at the January plenary session of the Party Central Committee, the republic's collective and state farms this year planted almost 90,000 hectares of corn—350% more than in 1958. We can now report, Nikita Sergeyevich, that the workers in the Latvian countryside have really taken a liking to corn, and this crop is winning an increasingly firm place in the fodder balance. ...

Sowings of grain crops have been increased by more than 100,000 hectares and now amount to 42% of the total sown area. The area under oats has been considerably reduced. We realize, of course, that this does not fully solve the tasks confronting us, and we will continue to work persistently in this direction. ...

It is planned to drain 658,000 hectares of land in the republic in 1961-1965 and to develop 700,000 hectares that had formerly been taken out of cultivation; this will make possible a considerable increase in the output of grain, corn, coarse and succulent fodders, meat, milk, potatoes and vegetables. ...

A large number of Latvia's pedigreed cattle are shipped to other fraternal republics and some are exported. In the past few years alone the republic's collective and state farms have sold about 150,000 head of pedigreed and improved cattle. ...

In the near future Latvia could annually sell as many as 50,000 and more head of pedigreed and improved cattle of the brown Latvian breed. In this connection the question should be decided of including the pedigreed livestock delivered by the republic in the state plan for meat deliveries. Otherwise a large number of the pedigree livestock might be slaughtered. ...

Ilyichev

SPEECH BY COMRADE L. F. ILYICHEV, DIRECTOR OF THE PARTY CENTRAL COMMITTEE'S DEPARTMENT OF PROPAGANDA AND AGITATION FOR THE UNION REPUBLICS. (Pravda, Oct. 26, pp. 2-3; Izvestia, pp. 3-4. 5,000 words. Condensed text:) ... The cult of the individual had grave consequences for the ideological life of the Party and all ideological work. A situation formed where only one man in the Party had the right to the last word on all questions of theory. It is not surprising, therefore, that the works of Marx, Engels and Lenin were in effect belittled and that various propositions of Marxism-Leninism and even whole works were frequently evaluated extremely subjectively and arbitrarily.

The ideology of the cult of the individual is an anti-Leninist ideology. It is essentially destructive. Did it not lead to the dangerous divorce of theory from practice? In words—oaths of fidelity to Marxism-Leninism and appeals for the linking of theory and practice; in reality—narrow dogmatism and narrow-mindedness, intolerance of any fresh thought, any fresh word. In words—expansive statements about the role of the masses; in reality—subordination of the social sciences and all ideological work to a false goal, the extolling of a single individual.

It is no accident that for decades we had no works of real substance on political economy, philosophy and history. Suffice it to recall the history of the preparation of a textbook on political economy. A group of economists began work on the textbook back in April, 1937. It is known that more than ten variants of the textbook were created, but not one of them saw the light of day. Why? It turns out that the "Stalinist stage in the development of the political economy of Marxism" was poorly elucidated.

It became possible to create Marxist-Leninist works on basic aspects of the theory and history of the Party only after the consequences of the cult of the individual had been overcome. A number of valuable textbooks have been issued on

Party history, the fundamentals of Marxism-Leninism, philosophy and political economy. Publication of the multivolume history of the Civil War has been completed. Three volumes of the "History of the Great Patriotic War of the Soviet Union, 1941-1945" have come off the press. Work has begun on preparing a multivolume history of our party for publication.

Today it is difficult even to imagine how many obstacles were raised in the way of producing a scholarly biography of V. I. Lenin. Reminiscences of Lenin were not published. The pretext for this, of course, was the specious one that "mistakes might creep into" them. The old Bolsheviks attending this Congress know this well. The publication of their reminiscences of meetings with Lenin was virtually banned. Only recently has a biography been published that reveals the great importance of the life and work of our leader and teacher V. I. Lenin.

In the period of the cult of the individual it was uncomfortable, comrades, for vital theoretical thought; there was a suspicious attitude toward any attempt to look into the phenomena of life somehow in a new way, toward any attempt to understand new facts and draw new conclusions.

Presumably many of you will remember Comrade N. S. Khrushchev's article in a March, 1951, issue of Pravda on the urgent tasks of developing the collective farm countryside. The article contained new basic propositions on the development of agriculture; it boldly and openly raised painful questions of collective farm development and was permeated with deep humaneness and concern for the needs of the collective farm peasantry.

But this article brought down "wrath from on high." What happened? It seemed that Stalin "did not like" the article. He reacted to it very intolerantly and morbidly. I, who was editor-in-chief of Pravda at that time, was blamed for political immaturity. The very next day the editors were advised to publish a so-called "correction." This correction is worth repeating in full at the 22nd Party Congress.

"Editor's note: Correction of an error.

"Through an oversight of the editorial office, in printing Comrade N. S. Khrushchev's article 'On Building and Improvements on the Collective Farms' in yesterday's Pravda, an editorial note was omitted in which it was pointed out that Comrade N. S. Khrushchev's article was published as material for discussion. This statement is to correct this error."*

No, comrades, the article was absolutely correct, and was imbued with a spirit of Leninist creativity and concern for the flourishing of the collective farm system. There had of course been no thought of an editor's note. Therefore there had been no omission. What was "omitted" was simply common sense on the part of those who did not know life, were isolated from it and interpreted every creative thought as an insult, as an encroachment on their personal authority. (Prolonged applause.)

How did events develop subsequently?

The draft of a private letter of the Central Committee was prepared which in a raucous, extremely irritable tone literally annihilated the article. But Malenkov, the inspirer of this disgraceful document, overdid it. It was clear where the initiators of the document were leading the matter. Instead of proof, which of course did not exist, this entire so-called document consisted of outcries against the article, such as "condemn as anti-Marxist," "condemn as harmful," "condemn as erroneous," etc.

A simple question arose: Condemn what, and condemn it for what? After all, it was the Leninist principle of concern for people and for the development of socialist agriculture that was being condemned. The very idea of construction of production facilities and improvements on the collective farms was declared harmful for the entire cause of socialist construction, for expanded reproduction on the collective farms, for elimination of the essential distinctions between town and countryside, etc.

Life has refuted these unfounded, malicious attacks. The Central Committee rescinded the charge against the article published in Pravda as mistaken.

*[The article and correction were carried in The Current Digest of the Soviet Press, Vol. III, No. 7, pp. 13-16. The article proposed amalgamation of villages into "agro-cities."]

If today it is necessary to recall this, it is only to show how a wall was erected in the way of any fresh, creative thought springing from life and the requirements of the times. A genuinely creative atmosphere has now been established in our country. Any valuable initiative will find support from the Central Committee. This is the Leninist style, the Leninist spirit in work. (Stormy applause.)

The cult of the individual in the sphere of theory is in essence an attempt to solve theoretical problems by fiat, through administrative means. This is abuse of authority in the sphere of theory.

I shall cite still another example. This is a matter of gross arbitrariness in regard to a book that contained an attempt to analyze the Soviet Union's economy in the period of the Patriotic War—N. A. Voznesensky's book.

We shall not speak of the book's merits and defects; it has its errors and shortcomings. But it is known that the book contained new ideas and important conclusions about the development of the Soviet economy in a very important period for our homeland—the period of the Great Patriotic War. Stalin read this book with pencil in hand when it was still in manuscript form and made notations and even some insertions. Furthermore, it was awarded a Stalin Prize. People began studying the book, then suddenly it was withdrawn as anti-Marxist and antiscientific. The author's life ended tragically.

What had happened? What had happened was that to the dissatisfaction of the "god of theory," N. A. Voznesensky's book had become popular among economists and students. Some economists even zealously praised it, found in it something new and creative. This was enough to have the book withdrawn, thereby putting an end to the "elucidation" of theoretical truths in the sphere of Soviet economics and of the establishment of a political economy of socialism.

Is this how Vladimir Ilyich Lenin taught us to conduct theoretical work in the Party? No! Abuses of authority in the realm of theory are alien to Lenin. He knew how to defend passionately and develop Marxist theory and sharply criticize fundamental mistakes, and he carefully fostered what was sensible and good in the development of Marxist theory. (Stormy, prolonged applause.)

In the period of the cult of the individual completely inexplicable acts were committed whereby the names of prominent scholars were expunged from science. Such a fate, in particular, met the eminent Marxist historian and old Bolshevik M. N. Pokrovsky. There were many mistakes in his scholarly, as well as his political, work. This is true. But it is well known, after all, that he championed Marxism and made a big contribution to the elaboration of Soviet history. It is profoundly instructive to note how Vladimir Ilyich Lenin assessed the works of Pokrovsky, criticized him from principled, friendly positions and guided him.

On Dec. 5, 1920, Vladimir Ilyich Lenin wrote to M. N. Pokrovsky. Permit me to quote this remarkable letter:

"I highly congratulate you on your success: I was immensely pleased with your new book: 'Russian History in Briefest Outline.'" (I will say parenthetically that this very book was among those branded as anti-Marxist.—L. I.) "Original construction and exposition. Enormously interesting reading. In my judgment, it will have to be translated into European languages.

"I am going to venture one small observation," wrote V. I. Lenin. "For it to be a textbook (and it should become one), it must be supplemented with a chronological index. I shall explain what I have in mind; approximately this: (1) a column of chronological listings; (2) a column for bourgeois assessment (briefly); (3) a column for your, Marxist, assessment, with an index to the pages of your book.

"The students should know both your book and the index, so that superficiality is avoided, so that they know the facts, so that they learn to compare the old scholarship and the new." ("Works" [in Russian], Vol. XXXVI, p. 488).

Here you see how lovingly and exactly Vladimir Ilyich Lenin spoke with scholars. (Applause.)

Does Lenin's evaluation have anything to do with these grave charges made against M. N. Pokrovsky in the time of the cult of the individual? After all, comrades, he was declared to be the head of the anti-Marxist school in historiography, and all his works were inveighed against as a manifestation of vulgar sociologism, economic materialism and bourgeois historiography.

Theory and the social sciences could not develop fruitfully in the conditions of the cult of the individual. The question stood as follows: Will theory in the future march in step with life and illumine the path for practice or will it grow rigid? The Party decided this question at the 20th Congress in favor of the creative development of Marxism-Leninism. (Prolonged applause.)

The innovatory course of the Congress evoked the violent opposition of the anti-Party group of Molotov, Kaganovich, Malenkov, Shepilov and others. They opposed not only the restoration of Leninist principles in deciding political and economic questions. They proved to be unfeeling dogmatists in the solution of ideological and theoretical problems. How could they act otherwise, when they did not know life, themselves had not gone anywhere for decades and did not really know either theory or practice! Yet every one of them laid claim to the role of theoretician.

Molotov considered himself the chief "theoretician" among them. It is necessary to recall the events of 1957, when the anti-Party group shifted to an open attack on the Central Committee. Precisely at that time Molotov published the pretentious article "On Lenin" in the central press. The article deliberately represents the author as a "monopolist" on Leninism, a Leninist, a friend and companion-in-arms of our leader. The author was lecturing the Party on Leninism—and this at a time when Molotov had clearly broken with Leninism.

On April 18, 1960, Molotov sent the editors of the magazine Kommunist an article devoted to the 90th anniversary of V. I. Lenin. The article was entitled "On Vladimir Ilyich Lenin." Note that the article was written after the ideological, political and organizational rout of the anti-Party factionalist group. The editors did not publish the article. They were right in not publishing it, because it bore the stamp of a dogmatic position not only on many political and economic questions but also on questions of theory, a position condemned by the 20th Congress of our party. Not a single word was said in it about the subversive actions of the anti-Party factionalist group. It is as if it had never existed.

The article described the difficulties of 1921, caused by foreign intervention and the Civil War, in distorted fashion. It created the impression that the difficulties experienced by our country are also inevitable for other countries entering the path of socialist development.

The article revised the theses of the 20th Congress on questions of international relations. It underestimated the new balance of forces that had formed after the second world war, the increased might of the states in the socialist camp and above all of the Soviet Union, and the increased political activeness of the masses in the capitalist countries; it denied the real possibility of preventing a world war in our times.

In his article Molotov wrote of the February revolution: "It dealt a most powerful [silneishy] blow to world imperialism, a blow after which the affairs of imperialism, and not only in Russia, went downhill." Note—"the February revolution dealt a blow to imperialism." Yet it was the Great October Socialist Revolution and not the February revolution that dealt the chief blow. In his article Molotov, who tried to act as one of the chief theoreticians of the anti-Party factionalist group, did not say a single word about his attitude toward the correct decisions of the Central Committee of our party concerning the anti-Party factionalist group.

Take Kaganovich. His speeches as a rule abounded in elementary errors, but he, too, tried to picture himself as a theoretician. His zeal to extol the Stalin cult knew no bounds. It was he who pushed the proposal to introduce the concept "Stalinism" in place of Marxism-Leninism "to mark a new stage in theory." And the would-be economist Malenkov made the anti-Leninist assertion that the preponderant development of heavy industry was not obligatory. Fawning and playing the toady, Shepilov reached the point of outright and gross falsification of Marxism. He credited Stalin with discovering the law of the mandatory correspondence of production relations to the nature of production forces, although every student knows the name of the author of this law. Stalin was obliged

to state that not he but Marx had discovered this law.

The departure from creative Marxism-Leninism led the factionalist group to the adventuristic attempt to swerve the Party from the Leninist path.

To all who want to know what the Leninist laws of Party life and the laws of the conduct of the ideological struggle are, we can say: Look at the mode of actions of our party, the Central Committee and Nikita Sergeyevich Khrushchev with respect to the anti-Party group. After exposing and ideologically routing it, the Party, following the Leninist principles of the conduct of the ideological struggle, although it swept the members of the group from executive posts for severe crimes against the Party, nevertheless left them in the Party and gave them work, inasmuch as they had made statements admitting their mistakes.

What followed? Much time has passed. Life has had its say. Who can now doubt that the course worked out by the 20th Party Congress was and is the Leninist course! (Prolonged applause.)

Following this course, our homeland has achieved successes that chill the hearts of our enemies, successes that evoke joy and creative enthusiasm among our friends. If the people who still consider themselves members of the Party had even a grain of conscience left, they should have told the Party: "The years and life have shown that our position was profoundly harmful and erroneous, while the Party and its Leninist Central Committee have pursued the correct line and the country has achieved big successes."

But the Party did not hear any such thing. We have every reason to say that the factionalists did not realize the anti-Leninist essence of their views and their statements were false and hypocritical.

For me, a member of the Party and a delegate to the 22nd Congress, just as for the other comrades who have spoken here, there arises the question: Are the participants in the ideologically dethroned and organizationally routed anti-Party grouping worthy of the magnanimity shown by our party? No, they are not! (Applause.) He who took the path of behind-the-scenes intrigues and machinations against the Leninist Party and who persists in his mistakes must bear responsibility to the Party and the people. ...

It would be incorrect and harmful to confuse the authority of leaders with the cult of the individual.

Permit me to recall several important instructions of Lenin.

"Marxists," wrote V. I. Lenin, "cannot take the usual point of view of the intellectual-radical with his supposedly revolutionary abstractness: 'no authorities.'

"No. The working class, waging throughout the world a difficult and stubborn struggle for complete liberation, needs authorities***." ("Works" [in Russian], Vol. XI, p. 374.)

In another work Vladimir Ilyich Lenin pointed out: "Without a 'dozen' talented (and talents are not born by the hundreds), tested, professionally trained and long-schooled leaders, who have become a superbly well-knit group, no class can wage a stanch struggle in present-day society." ("Works" [in Russian], Vol. V, p. 430.)

An enormous service of the Party and the Central Committee headed by Nikita Sergeyevich Khrushchev is the rearing of true leaders of the Leninist type, skillful organizers of economic, political and cultural construction, selfless fighters for communism. The Central Committee constantly consults with the people and submits all major questions of economic and cultural construction for nationwide discussion.

In recent years our party has firmly abided by Lenin's instructions on the question of the authority of leaders and on the cult of the individual. The Party is doing everything to prevent the possibility of the appearance of a cult of the individual. But at the same time it has defended and will defend the authority of leaders who are genuinely devoted to the Party and people and give all their strength, knowledge and experience to the people and the great cause of the victory of communism. (Stormy applause.) ...

The Party builds its entire domestic and foreign policy on a strictly scientific basis; it opposes subjectivism in politics. It is the constant enrichment and the creative development of Marxist-Leninist theory that enable the Party to exercise truly scientific leadership of the life of Soviet society.

The present-day situation makes higher and qualitatively different demands on ideological workers.

What are these demands?

First, ideological work must in every way foster that great creative surge that the entire Party is now experiencing. Propaganda and agitation, the press and radio, television and cultural-enlightenment work, literature and art—the entire ideological front must be made a more active factor in transforming all sides of life of Soviet society on communist principles.

Second, our propaganda is called upon to generalize the processes of life boldly, to disclose their essence and theoretical meaning, to explain the scientific principles underlying the Party's practical work. Today it is especially important to disclose the historical logic of the great victories of our party and people, of the entire international Communist and workers' movement, and the profound logic of the inevitable fall of imperialism.

Third, it is necessary to intensify the struggle against pedantry and talmudism, for strengthening the ties of ideological work with life and increasing its effectiveness, which is manifested above all in concrete production results and growth of the labor and political activeness of the masses.

Detachment from life is our old misfortune. But the detachment of ideological work from life cannot be blamed solely on ideological workers. We still have Party and economic leaders who arrogantly say: "The ideas are yours—the work is ours."

Ideological education of the masses is the sacred duty of every Communist. ...

The tasks of ideological work are enormous, but our reserves, too, are great. They lie above all in drawing broad circles of the intelligentsia and all the working people into ideological work. What we call the development of public principles in our life contains inexhaustible opportunities for radical advances in ideological work. ...

Shvernik

SPEECH BY COMRADE N. M. SHVERNIK, CHAIRMAN OF THE PARTY CENTRAL COMMITTEE'S PARTY CONTROL COMMITTEE. (Pravda, Oct. 26, pp. 3-4; Izvestia, pp. 4-5. 4,500 words. Condensed text:) ... An enormous amount of work has been done since the 20th Congress to restore and develop Leninist norms of Party life, to eliminate the consequences of the cult of the individual and to strengthen socialist legality.

The Party Control Committee and local Party agencies have in this period reviewed the improper decisions expelling a large number of Communists from the Party, among them prominent Party workers and government figures who had in the past been brought to trial on groundless political charges. A close study of the materials and circumstances in the cases involving violation of Party principles and Soviet legality has re-emphasized the soundness of the conclusion drawn by the 20th Congress that the Stalin cult and the violations of collective leadership, inner-Party democracy and socialist legality that accompanied it did us great harm. Life itself has shown that the criticism of the mistakes and shortcomings born of the cult of the individual had to be precisely this kind of criticism—sharp and unreserved, as befits Leninists. This was the only way to get rid of the fetters that had been hobbling the ideological life of the Party and the creative activity of the masses; only thus could the road be cleared for progress. ...

In the course of the work done by the Party Control Committee to rehabilitate Communists condemned without reason, we constantly encountered the grievous consequences of the high-handed deeds and lawless acts perpetrated personally by Malenkov, Kaganovich and Molotov. It developed that in the period of the ascendancy of the cult of the individual, they had taken the lead in building up an atmosphere of suspicion and mistrust. Holding positions of authority, Malenkov, Kaganovich and Molotov committed the most flagrant violations of revolutionary legality and the Leninist norms of Party life. ...

It has now been established that Malenkov, bent on taking a leading position in the Party and the state, entered into close collusion with Yezhov and later on with Beria, and under the pretense of displaying "vigilance" arranged the mass fabrication of cases against Party and Soviet officials, who were charged with being enemies of the people. In so doing he resorted to the foulest devices: intrigues, frame-ups, lies.

When visiting Belorussia in 1937 Malenkov, working with Yezhov, concocted a story that there was a large anti-Soviet underground in the republic, allegedly headed by the Party and Soviet leadership. Pursuing this monstrous frame-up, Malenkov arranged for summary justice to be meted out to Belorussia's Party, Soviet, trade union and Young Communist League cadres. Comrade Mazurov has informed the delegates of these tragic facts in his speech. The Party Control Committee's investigations have fully confirmed Malenkov's criminal anti-Party activity in publicly dishonoring and destroying Belorussian Party and Soviet cadres. This blow at the republic's cadres had a grave effect on the entire socio-political and economic life of Belorussia, which had a special role to play in the defense of the Soviet state on the western borders.

That same year, using the same methods to frame people, Malenkov effected the destruction of devoted Party cadres in Armenia. On his way to Yerevan, Malenkov paid a call on Beria in Tbilisi and arranged with him the procedure for the so-called "inquiry" that was supposed to confirm their story that a widely ramified anti-Soviet organization existed in Armenia. The result of this frame-up was that, on Malenkov's personal instructions, almost the entire leadership of Armenia's Central Committee and Council of People's Commissars was illegally arrested. Malenkov personally interrogated the prisoners, using proscribed methods in the process.

Malenkov's trips to a number of provinces in the Russian Republic were equally ill-omened. Each trip was followed by the arrest of secretaries of province Party committees and many other officials.

Comrade Spiridonov, Secretary of the Leningrad Province Party Committee, was absolutely correct in what he said here. Malenkov bears a very substantial share of the blame for extremely flagrant violations of the Party Statutes and revolutionary legality committed with respect to the Leningrad Party organization in 1949 and 1952.

Equally great crimes against the Party and the Soviet people were committed by another member of the anti-Party group— Kaganovich. As early as October, 1934, while he was in Chelyabinsk, Kaganovich, in order to show that he was "ultra-vigilant," concerned himself with exposing the allegedly hostile activities of local officials. He introduced the proposal, which was meant to facilitate frame-ups, for instituting extrajudicial trials, in circumvention of the law, of persons brought up on political charges.

When Kaganovich visited Ivanovo, Yaroslavl and other provinces, he was responsible there also for extremely flagrant perversions of Party norms and Soviet laws. By means of blackmail and frame-ups he secured the arrest of many Party and Soviet officials. Kaganovich deceived the Party Central Committee by conveying to it information that he knew to be false regarding the existence of anti-Soviet organizations in the localities.

Kaganovich's assumption of the duties of People's Commissar of Transportation saw the beginning of mass arrests of railroad transport officials. He personally made groundless political accusations against innocent people and secured their arrest. Kaganovich tried to make Party and economic aktivists believe that disguised enemies of the people were operating in all sectors, and he demanded that the work of exposing them be broadened and intensified.

In his speech at a meeting of railroad aktivists on March 10, 1937, Kaganovich said: "I cannot name a single road or a single system where there has not been Trotskyite-Japanese sabotage.***Not only that, there is not a single branch of railroad transport in which these saboteurs have not turned up.***"

Under Kaganovich arrests of railroad officials were made by lists. His deputies, nearly all road chiefs and political-section chiefs, and other executive officials in transport were arrested without any grounds whatever. They have now been rehabilitated, many of them posthumously.

The Party Control Committee has in its possession 32 personal letters from Kaganovich to the N.K.V.D. demanding the arrest of 83 transport executives.

You can get a specific idea of the criminal ease with which Kaganovich brought unproved accusations against people from a letter of his to the N.K.V.D. dated Aug. 10, 1937. In this letter he demanded the arrest of ten officials holding positions of responsibility in the People's Commissariat of Transportation. Without the slightest grounds, for the sole reason that he, Kaganovich, thought their behavior suspicious, they were listed as spies and saboteurs. Their fates were as tragic as those of many others.

These actions of Kaganovich's were not an isolated occurrence. They represented his system, which he employed when he worked in railroad transport, when he was People's Commissar of Heavy Industry, and on his visits to province Party organizations.

Especially heavy blame for the violation of socialist legality must be laid at the doorstep of Molotov, who for a long time was Chairman of the Council of People's Commissars and in that capacity himself flouted Soviet laws in the most flagrant manner.

Thus in 1937, when the internal situation in the country was marked by great strides in economic construction and cultural development and by the strengthened moral and political unity of Soviet society, Molotov advanced "theoretical" arguments for the need to step up the effort against so-called "enemies of the people" and had a personal hand in the mass repressions. At the February-March, 1937, plenary session of the Central Committee, Molotov said: "The present subversive-sabotage organizations are especially dangerous in that these saboteurs, subversives and spies pretend to be Communists, ardent supporters of the Soviet regime."

Making cruel sport of those who sought to caution Stalin and Molotov against conjuring up all sorts of conspiracies and sabotage and espionage centers, Molotov called on the Party to annihilate the "enemies of the people" alleged to be hiding behind Party cards.

The documents show that it was under Molotov that so illegal a method as condemning people by lists was introduced. Molotov was well aware that this was in violation of the law. Nevertheless, exceeding his authority, he personally decided the fates of the people under arrest. Among those who suffered persecution with Molotov's sanction were many old Communists, prominent executive officials and well-known scientists and cultural figures. They have now been fully rehabilitated.

Here is an example of Molotov's inhuman attitude to the fate of people. In 1937 a professor who worked in the People's Commissariat of Foreign Affairs addressed an appeal to Molotov as the Chairman of the Council of People's Commissars. He wrote Molotov that his father had been arrested, obviously through a misunderstanding; he asked Molotov to intercede for his father. Instead of looking into this very human request, Molotov wrote a memorandum: "To Yezhov: Can it be that this professor is still in the People's Commissariat of Foreign Affairs and not in the N.K.V.D.?" Whereupon the writer of the letter was unlawfully arrested.

Here is still another example of Molotov's extreme cynicism. On a trip to the city of Prokopyevsk in 1934, the car in which he was riding went off the road, its right wheels landing in a ditch. None of the passengers was injured in any way. This episode subsequently provided grounds for a story about an "attempt" on Molotov's life, and a group of completely innocent people was sentenced for it. Who knew better than Molotov that in reality there had been no such attempt? But he had not a word to say in defense of these innocent people. That is what Molotov is like.

On the basis of many documents it has been established quite irrefutably that Malenkov, Kaganovich and Molotov committed the gravest misdeeds and did great harm to our party, the Soviet state and the Soviet people with their criminal anti-Party activities. They besmirched the lofty name of Communist and cannot remain in our party's ranks. (Prolonged applause.)...

It is significant that in the period of severe criticism of the mistakes made by Stalin and of the struggle against the anti-Party group of factionalists, Communists have one and all rallied even more solidly around the Central Committee headed by Comrade N. S. Khrushchev and have not allowed the members of that group, the conspirators, to impair the great Leninist unity of our party.

The restoration of Leninist norms of Party life, the ascendancy of the method of persuasion in educational work, the force of the Party collective's influence and the growing political consciousness of Party members are creating a situation where it is less and less often necessary to resort to the extreme penalty, expulsion from the Party. The number of expulsions has been dropping year by year. Fewer than half as many persons have been expelled from the Party in the five years since the 20th Congress as in the five years preceding the Congress.

In line with the decisions of the 20th Congress aimed at restoring Leninist norms of Party life and eliminating the consequences of the cult of the individual, serious shortcomings and mistakes that existed in the past in the work of the Party Control Committee and of the local Party bodies dealing with cases involving the personal affairs of Communists have now been eliminated. Evils such as the substitution of one-man decisions for collective decisions, preconceived opinions, undue suspicion in the handling of personal cases, discussion of personal cases in absentia in some instances and without proper verification of accusations leveled against Communists--evils that had taken root under the influence of the cult of the individual--have been done away with. The procedure called for by the Party Statues in dealing with personal cases of Communists has been fully restored.

In looking into appeals, the Party Control Committee has always been guided by the need to maintain purity and stanchness in the Party's ranks and has upheld the decisions of local Party bodies expelling persons who really had committed grave offenses that brought disgrace on the lofty name of Communist. These were persons who exploited their official positions for mercenary ends, were careless in their attitude to socialist property, were hard drinkers or behaved unworthily in their private lives. The Party has cleansed its ranks of such people and will continue vigorously to do so.

At the same time the Party Control Committee has reinstated in the Party Communists who had been expelled on unfounded charges and has mitigated Party penalties, confining itself to administering reprimands and pointing out the offenses committed.

In the period under review the Party Control Committee has looked into more than 70,000 appeals made by Communists against decisions of local Party agencies expelling them from the Party or imposing Party penalties. More than 15,000 persons have been reinstated in the Party. Among them are a large number of Communists expelled from the Party in the past on unfounded political charges.

It is gratifying to report to the 22nd Party Congress that in the past few years the Party Control Committee has not had to deal with cases in which Communists were called up before the Party on political charges. This testifies to the unity of our party's ranks and to the triumph of Leninist norms of Party life. (Applause.)

Comrades! ... It is well known how principled and severe the Party has been in its criticism of the antistate acts of hoodwinkers and careerists whose only concern was for their own ease and comfort. Those who have departed from Party principles have been duly rebuffed by the Party, which has not been deterred by their past services or the high positions they held. And rightly so. This should continue to be the case. Our party's strength lies in its being unafraid to expose shortcomings and in not allowing them to take root and spread.

Could one, for instance, have forgiven the acts committed by Comrade Voronin, ex-First Secretary of the Chelyabinsk City Party Committee, and Comrade Zakharov, chairman of the city executive committee, as well as some other officials in Chelyabinsk Province? In an effort to win cheap prestige for themselves and to make it seem that everything was going well, these executives added 36 unfinished apartment houses, which came to 15% of the yearly plan, to their figures on the fulfillment of the housing construction plan for the city of Chelyabinsk in 1960. In many of these houses the floors had not been laid or the walls plastered and the plumbing and heating systems had not been finished, and some of the houses even lacked roofs.

This antistate practice was roundly condemned by the Party Central Committee, and the persons who had undertaken to deceive the state were removed from their executive posts and called to account.

It is the duty of Party organizations to make the most exacting possible demands upon Communists with respect to their observance of state discipline and their efficient accomplishment of plans and assignments and execution of Party and government directives. Party control with the cooperation of the public at large must become an impassable wall blocking wastefulness and mismanagement, localism and the diversion of funds and materials for purposes not envisaged by the state plan.

To preserve the purity of the Party's ranks it is essential that an attitude of intolerance be shown to persons unworthy of the lofty name of member of the C.P.S.U. But every time the question of a Communist's Party membership comes up we must be strictly guided by the Statutes of the C.P.S.U., which call for maximum discretion and for painstaking probing of the validity of charges brought against a Party member. No Communist may be punished for nothing, without reason. (Applause.)

Comrades! ... We, the Party Control Committee, have been receiving a great many letters from working people in which they voice their concern to see shortcomings eliminated and the work of Party organizations in state institutions and industrial and agricultural enterprises improved. ...

Erroneous and occasionally bureaucratic attitudes to these letters must be vigorously rooted out. Unfortunately, such cases are still to be encountered in some institutions and organizations. No small part of the letters and referrals consists of complaints that can and should be settled locally, but because of the inconsiderate attitude shown to these letters people are forced to appeal to the top-level agencies.

Here and there Party organizations have failed to deal a prompt and sharp rebuff to those who suppress criticism and try to clamp down on persons who have criticized, who have sounded warnings. Let me tell you about one such case. A group of workers at a chemical plant in Kuibyshev Province wrote the Party Central Committee a letter telling about account padding, wasteful expenditure of funds, gross instances of administration by fiat and other irregularities at the plant.

A check-up showed the report to be correct. It was the duty of the Stavropol City Party Committee of Kuibyshev Province to take the action necessary to eliminate the shortcomings that had been brought to light. Some time passed and the Central Committee again began receiving complaints about the unsatisfactory state of affairs at this plant. The Party Control Committee made a check and discovered that instead of rectifying the mistakes Comrade Isyanov, the plant director, had persecuted, victimized, the authors of the letter for their criticism, firing them from their jobs on various pretexts. Nor did the Stavropol City Party Committee prove equal to the occasion: Its secretary, Comrade Parensky, came to the defense of those who had suppressed criticism.

The Party Control Committee has taken stern measures against those who were guilty of padding and of victimizing individuals for criticism.

The persecution and mistreatment of those who criticize, who sound warnings, can only be regarded as anti-Party acts. It is the duty of every executive to be attentive to the letters, referrals and complaints of the working people, to react quickly and effectively to any warning signal, to any critical comment. ...

Ponomarev

SPEECH BY COMRADE B. N. PONOMAREV, DIRECTOR OF THE PARTY CENTRAL COMMITTEE'S INTERNATIONAL DEPARTMENT. (Pravda, Oct. 26, pp. 4-5; Izvestia, pp. 5-6. 5,000 words. Condensed text:) ... Comrade N. S. Khrushchev and those comrades who have spoken in the discussion have shown what despicable, anti-Leninist positions were taken by the anti-Party group, what serious harm it could have done the cause of communism. The struggle proceeded around fundamental questions of the Party's line, including questions of ideology. The 20th Party Congress marked out the road to a radical improvement in the Party's ideological work. The Congress criticized the

Party history "Short Course" because it was permeated with the spirit of the Stalin cult, treated many fundamental questions incorrectly and belittled the role of V. I. Lenin, the Party and the masses. It was decided to create a scientific Marxist textbook on the history of the C.P.S.U. The necessary directives were worked out in order to give this book the correct, Leninist orientation. During discussion of the directives at a meeting of the Presidium of the Party Central Committee, Molotov and Kaganovich zealously, literally foaming at the mouth, opposed the very idea of producing a new textbook on Party history that would meet the requirements of Leninism. They thereby worked for the confirmation, contrary to the decisions of the 20th Congress, of the correctness of everything that had been done earlier, including the period 1937-1938. They also strove to see to it that Communists should continue to be reared on the basis of the "Short Course," which was imbued with the cult of the individual. Although they were rebuffed at the Presidium meeting, they continued their line. In April, 1957, not long before the anti-Party group acted openly, Molotov lauded the "Short Course" in the pages of the press without even mentioning the harmful consequences of the cult of the individual. Furthermore, he tried to erect his own type of "theoretical" basis for justifying the mistakes and lawlessness that characterized the period of the Stalin cult. In this article Molotov wrote: "We know that individual mistakes, and sometimes serious mistakes, are inevitable in solving such big and complex historical tasks. No one has or can have a guarantee on this score." In other words, Molotov tried to argue: "As it was under the cult of the individual, so it will continue to be." But the Party and its Central Committee said: "No, it must not and never again will be this way!" (Applause.) ...

Malenkov, Molotov and Kaganovich bear special responsibility for all the disgraceful, lawless actions against honest Communists, as has been discussed in detail by Comrade Shvernik, who exposed the whole picture of their shameful deeds. There is no room for them in the ranks of our Leninist party! (Applause.) ...

Comrades! ... Anticommunism is the ideology of misanthropy and war, of the exploitation, coercion and enslavement of man, of the destruction of democratic freedoms. Anticommunism permeates the policy and activity of the imperialist powers. It has become one of the chief weapons of the aggressive groupings—NATO, SEATO, CENTO. Thousands of special organizations have been formed to combat the ideas of communism. The reactionary ruling circles of the U.S.A. serve as the conductor of this shrill concert. The Hitlerites who haven't had their fill of defeat are in the same team with them. International reaction is giving special attention to inculcating a spirit of anticommunism in the armies of the imperialist military blocs. This is highly dangerous. We must not forget what bestialities and crimes were committed in Europe by the Hitlerite army, doped in its time with anticommunism and hatred for the Soviet and other peoples. ...

The Right leaders of Social Democracy occupy a disgraceful place in the ranks of the black army of anticommunism. Their conduct at present convincingly shows that anyone who chooses the road of anticommunism finds himself on the other side of the barricade of the workers' movement. Renegades of Brandt's ilk have fallen so low as to join up in the same ranks with Adenauer and his fascist entourage. Many of the Right Social Democratic leaders, like the liberal depicted by Saltykov-Shchedrin, at first begged the bourgeois government for "all possible" reforms, then for "at least something," and now they are "adapting to villainy." They are doing everything to induce Social Democracy to throw overboard the traditional socialist banners and slogans of the working class.

During the days of our Congress, which is outlining an inspired Program of struggle for communism, for the happiness of people and for peace, a regular congress of the Socialist International has convened in Rome. According to the intent of its organizers, that congress is to adopt a declaration to counterpose to the Statement of the Conference of Representatives of 81 Communist and Workers' Parties and to serve, as they put it, as a base for a "counterattack" on communism. The declaration they want to adopt, whose content has already been published in the foreign press, is permeated from beginning to end with an anticommunist and anti-Soviet spirit. The draft of this shameful document states that "the worst defects of capitalism have been eliminated" in Western Europe, the U.S.A. and Japan and that the North Atlantic Alliance is the bulwark of peace. This is no longer even reformism but open service to imperialism and the forces of war. ...

There is no doubt that the crisis Social Democracy is experiencing will deepen. Honest Social Democrats, true to the ideals of the working class and opposing collaboration with the bourgeoisie and complicity with the forces of war, will more and more come to the conclusion that the truth is on the side of the Communists and that unity is essential in the struggle for peace, against the dominance of the monopolies and for the vital interests of the working people. ...

After the 20th Congress the ideologists of the bourgeoisie and the revisionists who echoed them shouted about the "crisis" of communism. But these prophets again fell on their faces. The triumph of the Leninist principles of Party life led not to a weakening but to a strengthening of the international Communist movement. Since the 20th Congress the family of fraternal parties has grown by 12 Communist Parties and the total numerical strength of the international army of Communists by 7,000,000.

During the lifetime of Marx and Engels there were only 300 Communists in the world. Today there is hardly a country in Europe, Asia, America, Australia and Oceania where a Communist Party does not function. More and more Communist Parties are arising in long-suffering Africa. The total number of Communists in the whole world amounts to approximately 40,000,000. (Applause.) For the first time in history the Communist movement has assumed truly worldwide scope. ...

The Communist Parties are the hope of mankind. In the midst of corrupt and demoralizing capitalist society, the Communists represent the most selfless and most devoted fighters for the interests of the people. If it were not for the Communists, the future of the capitalist countries and of capitalist society as a whole would be extremely gloomy. But fortunately for the peoples, the Communist Parties are growing and becoming steeled and are pointing out to the broad masses the way of struggle for their interests. The world Communist movement has become the best organized, the most authoritative and the greatest force of our times. ...

On the basis of the ideas of the 20th Party Congress, new forms of cooperation and contacts between the fraternal parties have been found that accord with the new stage in the development of the Communist movement—bilateral and multilateral meetings and conferences and worldwide forums of Communists. The conferences held in Moscow in 1957 and 1960 and the Declaration and Statement worked out at them have played an outstanding role in strengthening and uniting the great army of Communists.

The leaders of one Party alone—the Albanian Party of Labor—have recently launched a disgraceful struggle against the policy of our party, against the positions of the entire international Communist movement and the documents worked out by it. They are opposing the line of the 20th Congress, which was approved by the international Communist movement and which has yielded such brilliant results, and the principles of proletarian internationalism; they are undermining the unity of the socialist camp. In their practice they are applying methods that have been condemned by the international Communist movement and that are inadmissible in the ranks of Marxist-Leninist parties. Beginning with loud, dogmatic statements to the effect that they alone are resolutely combating imperialism, they soon slipped into revisionist positions, repudiated in practice the basic tenets of the Declaration and the Statement, and counterposed their own narrowly nationalistic views to the common views of the Communist Parties.

Having made a sharp turnabout, the Albanian leaders are concentrating their chief fire on our party, resorting to the basest methods. As is known, the C.P.S.U. and the Soviet Union and the international army of Communists constitute the principal force in the struggle against imperialism. The Albanian leaders' claim to be the only true Marxists is ludicrous. One has to lose all sense of proportion to set oneself up as teacher of our Leninist party and the entire international Communist

movement. As the people say, "The hat doesn't fit." One should not overestimate the capabilities of the Albanian leaders, of course. Since the existence of our party, many people and groups have tried to counterpose the leadership of our party to the Party masses and the working people of the country. But all these attempts suffered failure. In our times the prestige of the Party and its Central Committee headed by Comrade N. S. Khrushchev is greater than ever before, both in the Land of Soviets and far beyond its borders. (Applause.) No one will ever succeed in undermining or weakening in the slightest the great prestige of the party of Lenin. (Applause.) ...

The accomplishment of the tasks outlined in the Program will make it possible:

first, to achieve an unprecedented strengthening of the positions of socialism in the international arena, to make the world socialist system a decisive factor in world development and thereby help to an ever-increasing extent to curb the forces of reaction and the imperialist exploitation of the working people;

second, to create, together with all our allies, such a preponderance of the forces of peace as will make it possible to paralyze in embryo any ventures of the aggressors and to exclude world war from the life of society forever, even if capitalism still remains in a number of countries;

third, to strengthen the base of the world liberation movement, to give ever-increasing help to states freeing themselves from colonialism in their movement along the road of independent development and social progress;

fourth, to show, by great deeds, by the example of the most perfect organization of society, by the flourishing of productive forces and by the creation of all the conditions for the happiness and well-being of man, the immeasurable superiority of communism over the antipopular system, capitalism, and to extol the ideas of communism and win to their side more and more hundreds of millions of the world's people. ...

Kirilenko

SPEECH BY COMRADE A. P. KIRILENKO, FIRST SECRETARY OF THE SVERDLOVSK PROVINCE PARTY COMMITTEE. (Pravda, Oct. 26, pp. 5-6; Izvestia, Oct. 27, pp. 2-3. 4,500 words. Excerpts:) ... Instances have already been cited at the Congress of the criminal activity of the members of the anti-Party group in Leningrad, the Ukraine, Belorussia and other places. I would like to say that many Party, Soviet and economic officials of Sverdlovsk Province were also subjected to mass repressions. Two successive province Party committees, the secretaries of city and district committees, and the heads of enterprises and higher educational institutions were almost all put out of action. Personnel of the Sverdlovsk Railroad suffered particularly severely. ...

We fully share the suggestion voiced at the Congress by a number of comrades that there is no room in the ranks of our Leninist party for Malenkov, Kaganovich and the ideological inspirer of the anti-Party grouping, as I would call him, Molotov. (Applause.) ...

Bodyul

SPEECH BY COMRADE I. I. BODYUL, FIRST SECRETARY OF THE MOLDAVIAN COMMUNIST PARTY CENTRAL COMMITTEE. (Pravda, Oct. 27, pp. 3-4. 4,000 words. Excerpts:) ... The delegates to the 22nd Congress from the Moldavian Communist Party support the suggestion that there is no room for Molotov, Malenkov and Kaganovich in our glorious Leninst party. (Applause.) ...

Last year I had occasion to visit Albania. Everywhere we saw tractors, automatic machines, machine tools and equipment from the Soviet Union, Czechoslovakia, Poland, Hungary and other fraternal socialist countries. Furthermore, all this had been supplied to Albania on advantageous credit terms or simply as a gift to the Albanian people. Many specialists from socialist countries were working amicably in the enterprises side by side with Albanian workers. The friendship of the Albanian and Soviet peoples was sealed with the blood of their best sons in the fight against fascism. And now all this that is sacred to the Albanian people is being defiled, soiled and slandered by Enver Hoxha and Mehmet Shehu. We cannot remain silent about this or conceal it from the Albanian people. To remain silent would mean to support the adventurism of the Albanian leaders and their departure from proletarian internationalism. The Albanian people are not indifferent to where their present leadership is taking them. It is the international-ist duty of all the fraternal parties to help the Albanian Party of Labor rectify the mistakes of its leadership and to prevent Albania's alienation from the socialist camp. (Applause.) ...

Comrade delegates! ... In the Moldavian Republic Russians, Ukrainians, Belorussians, Bulgars, Gagauz and the working people of other nationalities and peoples live and work side by side with Moldavians in an atmosphere of sincere friendship at factories and plants, in scientific institutions and in the state apparatus. ...

Since olden times the Moldavian people have gravitated toward Russia and the Russian people. Despite long isolation of a large part of the population from its motherland, the Moldavian people did not forget the Russian language and lovingly preserved common traditions. Today all Moldavians, from the humble to the great, understand Russian well, and an absolute majority of Moldavians are fluent in it. Thousands of Moldavian children willingly study Russian, and many young men and women are attending the higher education-al institutions of Moscow, Leningrad, Kiev and other cities. ...

The old-timers in the countryside remember what an enormous event the construction of one or two houses a year was in the pre-collective farm village; now about 50,000 dwellings have been built in the republic's villages in the past two years alone. This means that in two years one family in ten built a new house. ...

It should be admitted that the republic's Party organization has not yet succeeded in completely overcoming the lag of the fodder base. While having taken, on the whole correctly, the course of specialization of agriculture in the direction of ac-celerated development of viticulture, orchard growing and vegetable raising, we slackened attention to grain farming and animal husbandry. As a result the production of grain, and consequently of meat and milk, has grown slowly of late. In eliminating these shortcomings, we expanded sowings of the more productive crops, and this year we did not permit the use of corn for fodder before formation of the ears; we thereby laid in good silage and left almost 100,000 hectares of corn more to be harvested for dry grain than in 1960, although the area planted to this crop remained the same. ...

The implementation of these and other measures enabled the collective and state farms to obtain as much grain this year as the seven-year plan envisaged for 1964. (Applause.) In connection with this, we have revised the control figures of the seven-year plan and have called for an increase in grain output of 60%. ...

The growth of capacity in the food industry is lagging serious-ly behind output. Canneries, wineries and creameries are at present not ensuring the processing of all the products grown by the collective and state farms. A large part of the tomatoes, green peas, grapes and sunflowers remains on the farms and is not used rationally.

The possibilities for expanding production capacity at existing enterprises by replacing obsolete equipment are not being fully utilized. If equipment were available, it would be possible to set up canning shops at sugar refineries and to use the power facilities of these enterprises for producing hundreds of millions more cans of food products. We have submitted a proposal to the U.S.S.R. State Planning Committee for speeding up the rate of modernization, mechanization and automation of technological processes at canneries, wineries and other en-terprises and setting up canning shops at sugar refineries, and we ask the committee to support us.

Moldavia's collective and state farms have considerably greater potentialities for supplying the population of Moscow, Leningrad, the Urals and other industrial centers of the country with fruit, various table grapes and early vegetables in fresh form. The volume of products shipped out could be at least tripled in the next few years. Yet in the past few years the volume of grapes and fruit shipped out has increased hardly at all, while shipments of tomatoes, which can be shipped from Moldavia from June 20 to the end of October, have even de-clined. This is largely due to the fact that prices have not been adjusted and problems of prompt delivery of produce to the consumer have not been solved. This leads to huge losses, which in turn lessen the interest of collective and state farms in shipping out grapes, fresh vegetables and fruit. In our opinion, the U.S.S.R. State Planning Committee should study this question and work out measures that will make possible a considerable increase in the shipment from Moldavia of prod-ucts needed by the public. ...

Transport is a bottleneck in the republic's economy. The bulk of farm shipments in our republic consists of perishables—grapes, vegetables, fruit and volatile-oil raw material—which must be shipped in a short time. In addition, these shipments coincide in time with shipments of sunflowers, grain, sugar beets and other crops. Poor transportation facilities result in huge losses.

Because of the poor supply of chemical poisons, the collec-tive and state farms suffer enormous losses from diseases and pests in orchards and vineyards. The gross harvest of fruit and grapes could be increased 30% to 40% and their quality considerably improved just by protecting the crop from pests.

We ardently support the extensive program of irrigation work set forth in N. S. Khrushchev's report. The collective and state farms of Moldavia are able to allocate the necessary funds for financing the development of approximately 200,000 hectares of the most fertile floodlands. This requires earth-moving equip-ment which is in short supply in the republic. ...

Construction of a large power plant has begun in Moldavia on the decision of the U.S.S.R. government. When it is put into operation, the problem of supplying the economy with electric power will be solved. However, construction of this vitally important installation, as well as of the transmission lines, is proceeding slowly. There is a shortage of equipment and materials at the construction site. The U.S.S.R. Ministry of Power Plant Construction should give the builders help so that they can ensure opening of the plant on schedule. ...

Petrov

SPEECH BY COMRADE F. N. PETROV, PARTY MEMBER SINCE 1896, MOSCOW CITY PARTY ORGANIZATION. (Pravda, Oct. 27, pp. 5-6. 3,400 words. Excerpts:) ... I am confident that the 22nd Congress will approve with special satisfaction the activity of our Central Committee in re-storing Leninist norms of Party and state life. The Central Committee boldly disclosed the sores and ulcers engendered by the Stalin cult in order that the ways to which the anti-Party factionalist group so zealously clung might never again arise in our party. This group bears direct responsibility for the mass repressions against honest Party members, including the infamous persecution of many old Bolsheviks. (Applause.) ...

I would like to express deep satisfaction over Nikita Sergeyevich Khrushchev's announcement that the Party Central Committee has considered it necessary to add to the draft Party Program a special provision concerning conservation and the correct use of natural wealth. ...

This matter requires the creative cooperation of scientists and the broad masses, people of all generations, from Academicians to schoolchildren. It is necessary to establish people's universities and practical laboratories for the study, enrichment and integrated use of natural resources. ...

On the decision of the Party Central Committee, which is displaying enormous concern for the development of encyclo-pedia work in our country, publication of Soviet encyclopedias in various branches of knowledge—philosophy, history, geogra-phy, literature, physics, chemistry, economics and others—has now begun. It is already time to consider a new, third edition of the Large Soviet Encyclopedia. This should be the encyclopedia of the epoch of the full-scale building of communism (applause), at the basis of which, like a strong theoretical foundation, will stand the new Program of our party. (Applause.) The third edition of the Large Soviet Encyclopedia will reflect the latest level of contemporary scientific knowledge and the great social changes of our epoch, the epoch of the downfall of capitalism and the victory of communism. (Applause.) Soviet scholars and writers have sufficient forces to issue the new encyclopedia by the 50th anniversary of Soviet rule—the holiday of all freedom-loving mankind.

From the lofty rostrum of the Congress I would like to raise the question of a completely new, hitherto unknown publication—a World Encyclopedia of Communism. (Applause.) This publication should be produced with the forces of the Communist and Workers' Parties of all countries and the progressive scholars of the whole present-day world. ...

In present-day conditions, when the ideas of communism have a colossal force of attraction, a World Encyclopedia of Communism, issued in dozens of languages, will penetrate to every part of the globe. It will become an international encyclopedia of the peoples of the world, the cultural treasure store of all progressive mankind. (Applause.) ...

Gromyko

SPEECH BY COMRADE A. A. GROMYKO, U.S.S.R. MINISTER OF FOREIGN AFFAIRS. (Pravda, Oct. 26, pp. 6-7; Izvestia, Oct. 27, pp. 3-4. 6,500 words. Condensed text:) Comrades! ... In the period since the 20th Party Congress our Central Committee has done enormous work in uniting Party forces and exposing the renegades, the factionalists, who were trying to push the Party and the country off the Leninist path in both domestic and foreign policy. It is therefore quite natural that the Party Congress should address its first words of gratitude to the Central Committee and to that leading figure of our party and people who, marching in the front rank of the Communists, is holding the revolutionary banner of Leninism high and firm in his hands—the First Secretary of the Central Committee, Comrade Nikita Sergeyevich Khrushchev. (Applause.) ...

It can confidently be said that the danger of war would be many times as great as it is today, and mankind might already have been overtaken by a military catastrophe, but for the fact that peace has been safeguarded by the Soviet Union and the whole peace-loving socialist camp with its might and inexhaustible resources. (Applause.) ...

Never before has the foreign policy of the Soviet Union so forcefully demonstrated its superiority to the policy of the imperialist camp as it has since the 20th Congress, whose historic decisions expressed the Leninist line, the Leninist course.

More than 40 neutralist states today hold positions on basic international issues that coincide in the main with our positions, with the foreign policy of the socialist countries; they, like us, are committed to the line of peace and peaceful co-operation. (Applause.)

This is why India and Indonesia, Burma and Afghanistan ardently acclaimed the speeches Comrade N. S. Khrushchev made during his visits to those states.

This is why it was easy to see the signs of friendship in the eyes of the hundreds of thousands, the millions of Frenchmen who formed a veritable living corridor in the streets of the large cities and on the roads of France, hailing the head of the Soviet government. (Applause.)

This is why the American people at every step expressed their friendly feelings and respect for the head of the government of a great country to whose colossal economic, scientific and cultural achievements every honest American takes his hat off today. (Applause.)

Cuba, geographically distant but close to the hearts of Soviet citizens, has become one of the Soviet people's best friends. When great events erupted in little Cuba, the enemies of the Cuban people must have felt sure that the island was securely fenced off from the Soviet Union and the socialist camp by continents and oceans. But truth and the mutual feelings of friendship between people are stronger than any barriers. ...

Comrades, many words that originated in our country and many wonderful names, including those of our space heroes Gagarin and Titov, have come into the international political lexicon. But I have yet to meet a person abroad who, if he condemns war, has not had a kindly twinkle in his eyes when uttering three words: Moscow, Lenin, Khrushchev. (Applause.) ...

From the podium of the United Nations our country last year, through the lips of the head of the Soviet government, called upon governments and peoples to break the chains of colonialism and open wide the doors of independence and national freedom to the peoples who had borne these chains for many decades. We have cause to be proud that an overwhelming majority of states associated themselves with the ideas embodied in the Soviet government's proposals; all this brings nearer the final hour of colonial oppression. (Applause.)

The United Nations is a kind of mirror from which one can get an idea of the balance of forces in the international arena. True, that mirror often presents a distorted reflection. But dull rumbles from the great battle now under way on the main question of our time—peace or war—carry to the walls of U.N. headquarters, too.

If decisions that accord with the interests of the peoples are taken from time to time within its walls, this is primarily because words of truth are spoken from the U.N. podium by representatives of the socialist countries, even though not all these countries are today represented in the U.N. As is the case wherever the fight for peace is in progress, we constantly feel our friend and ally, the Chinese People's Republic, at our elbow in that organization. Regardless of whether or not the representatives of people's China are seated alongside us at the international conference table, our peoples are traveling the same road, and there is no power on earth that can disrupt the ranks of the socialist states. (Applause.) ...

All the issues that preoccupy our age, the opposition of two lines of international policy, were reflected as in a focus in N. S. Khrushchev's meeting in Vienna with U.S. President J. Kennedy. ...

Our party and all our people should know that at the conference table in Vienna the interests of the Soviet state and the whole socialist camp, the interests of all who want to erect a secure barrier against the unleashing of aggressive wars in Europe, the interests of peace between peoples were upheld with a revolutionary fervor, firmness and skill worthy of the party of the immortal Lenin, worthy of our people. (Applause.)

Vienna, Paris, Camp David and everything that is happening on the international scene warrant the statement that if there were a compass that could point to the direction from which peace comes and the direction from which comes the threat of war, the point of the needle indicating the pole of peace would unvaryingly turn toward the place where our Congress is now in session—toward the Kremlin. (Stormy applause.)

I think there is no need to specify the place and the hemisphere to which the other end of that compass needle would be drawn. (Stir in the hall.)

The situation in the world continues tense and unstable. Fresh reminders of this are the events in the Congo and in Laos, the colonial war in Algeria, the intervention in Cuba and the attack on Bizerte, and the ceaseless saber-rattling of the NATO powers. ...

Look at the direction in which West Germany is heading. Compare the policy being followed by the present-day leaders of the Federal Republic of Germany with Germany's policy in Hitler's time and you will see that the difference is slight, if it exists at all. ...

The industrial and financial monopolies that supported and guided the Hitlerite gang, generals who came out alive, Nazi judges and diplomats and high officials and politicians who went through the school of the Third Reich—these are the people who are today shaping the political countenance of West Germany. Once again the stacks of Ruhr plants are smoking day and night, those same plants that forged the weapons for Hitler's cutthroat hordes, and the territory of West Germany is covered with firing ranges, military airfields and barracks. What is the purpose of all these preparations? To what end have West German youth been assigned to Hitlerite generals and officers for training? They no longer make any particular bones about it in Bonn: It is to try to avenge themselves for the crushing defeat suffered in World War II. ...

If the West German revanchists should attempt to raise their hand against the Soviet Union and its friends, West Germany would become a cemetery in which there would probably not even be any grave-diggers left to clear away the wreckage of its war machine and to bury the ashes of those who had set that machine in motion. (Applause.) ...

The Soviet Union is entitled to present West Germany with a bill, which has still by no means been paid in full, for the misfortunes and destruction caused by the Hitlerite invaders on our soil, for the plundered national wealth and for the merciless exploitation of our people carried off to Germany in the war years. (Prolonged applause.)

The Soviet people can without any difficulty rouse in themselves a feeling of enmity and anger toward West Germany: They have but to think back on the crimes of the Hitlerite invaders. (Applause.)

But we want to hold our feelings in check; we do not want the past to cast a shadow on our relations with the German people, on whichever side of the Elbe they may be.

Still, let no one dare confuse the magnanimity characteristic of the Soviet people with a lack of determination to curb and punish an aggressor. ...

Every time the subject of the F.R.G. comes up, representatives of the Western powers try to reassure the Soviet Union by saying that since that state is making its military preparations within the framework of NATO, by virtue of this fact alone the West German militarists will never infringe upon the peace in Europe. Need one go into detail in stating that Soviet people cannot take this reasoning seriously? They know only too well the ways of German militarism. They are also quite aware of what NATO is: It is one of the most aggressive military blocs the Western powers have knocked together, and West Germany's participation has imparted to it an even more aggressive character.

Yet surprisingly enough, even Western European statesmen who show a capacity for clear thinking in their approach to some questions have continued right up to the present to develop "arguments" of this sort in justification of the arming of West Germany. I think I shall be revealing no great secret when I say that British Prime Minister Macmillan recently spoke to us in this vein.

Incidentally, in that same conversation, which proceeded on a friendly note, Mr. Macmillan voiced a number of opinions indicating a desire to seek a sensible solution to problems that concern both the Soviet Union and Britain. Recalling his talks with N. S. Khrushchev, particularly during his stay in Moscow in 1959, the British Prime Minister asked that these views be conveyed to the head of the Soviet government along with his very best wishes.

Western statesmen sometimes allege that in raising the question of the conclusion of a German peace treaty without delay, the Soviet Union is guided by a purely "theoretical concept." We heard this recently from U.S. Secretary of State Rusk.

No, for the Soviet state its security and the security of its allies' borders is not a question of theory but falls within the sphere of what Western statesmen, with reference to their own countries, call "vital interests." ...

If for certain figures in the West the German question is simply a "theoretical concept," for us it represents the millions of lives laid down by our compatriots for our country's freedom and for the liberation of Europe from fascist barbarism, it is a question of our security and the security of our allies. (Applause.) ...

As is indicated in the report of the Party Central Committee delivered by Comrade N. S. Khrushchev, we formed the impression after recent talks with U.S. and British statesmen that the Western powers showed a certain understanding of the situation and that they were inclined to seek a solution to the German problem and the question of West Berlin on a mutually acceptable basis. Yet things have been happening that are hard to reconcile with a desire to facilitate agreement. The question of the German peace treaty is being presented in the Western press on an altogether unrealistic plane. Is this the force of inertia or something else?

As everyone knows, our party's Central Committee and the Soviet government have been sparing no effort to find common ground with the Western powers on the question of concluding a German peace treaty. Our proposals on concluding a German peace treaty and on this basis normalizing the situation in West Berlin by converting it into a demilitarized free city are common knowledge. If, however, it should prove impossible to conclude a German peace treaty on an agreed basis, the Soviet Union, in company with many other countries, will sign a peace treaty with the German Democratic Republic. (Applause.)

Our country is doing everything possible, comrades, to de-

velop friendly relations with all states, big and small, near and distant. For understandable reasons, the Party Central Committee and the Soviet government have always given special attention to smoothing and broadening relations with the major powers of the West.

It was not the Soviet Union that advocated rupturing the ties that had come into being between it and the Western powers during the war years.

We are for the broadening of friendly relations with Britain, our comrade-in-arms in the struggle against Hitler Germany.

We are for the broadening of friendly relations with France and the French people; the peoples of our country felt their support, too, during World War II.

But while our country has been giving serious attention to smoothing and broadening relations with the major European powers, it attaches special importance to the state of relations between the two giants—the Soviet Union and the United States of America.

After all, if these two powers combined their efforts in safeguarding peace, who would dare to and who would be able to break it? No one. There is no such force in the world. No one doubts this simple truth, and this holds for people in the United States too. ...

The Democratic Party is now in power in the United States. President Kennedy is a representative of that party. Roosevelt, too, was a Democrat. It is presumably easier for the party most closely associated with the name of Roosevelt to revive the fine traditions of that great American in the matter of developing Soviet-American relations. We are convinced that the American people, too, would be grateful for such a change in U.S. foreign policy. It would be welcomed by all peoples. (Applause.)

This is why N. S. Khrushchev, in his message to J. Kennedy immediately after Kennedy's election to the presidency, voiced the hope that during Kennedy's term of office relations between the U.S.S.R. and the U.S.A. would get back to where they were under President Roosevelt. That was a stable and dependable state of relations. It is tested and leads only to peace.

In one of his recent talks with us, U.S. Secretary of State Rusk, expressing the U.S. government's viewpoint with regard to the situation that had developed in Europe and Germany, stated: "We all understand that N. S. Khrushchev and J. Kennedy would not like to go down in history as the statesmen who were presiding at a time of global catastrophe. The problem of security in the world is therefore of equal concern to the Soviet Union and the United States, as the world's two greatest powers."

This was a good, sensible statement. ... Rusk stated that he fully shared the Soviet government's aspirations for peace, and on behalf of the American government he expressed the hope that ways would be found to ensure world peace. We really are, he said, the two great powers, and the strongest. We do have allies, but much depends on what Washington and Moscow do.

This, too, is a sound judgment, and we can only welcome it if U.S. actions in the sphere of foreign policy have this orientation. (Applause.)

The statesmen of the Western powers sometimes claim that they are dismayed by the statements that the future belongs to communism and that capitalism is a doomed social system. They even say that this is the main factor hindering the normalization of Soviet-American relations. Such statements, unfortunately, are still today to be heard from the figures who are steering U.S. foreign policy.

Those words in the new Party Program and Comrade N. S. Khrushchev's report which reveal the inherent capabilities of our social system in all their grandeur will be stamped in gold letters in the history of our country. These words are our answer to the aforementioned reproaches from the statesmen of the capitalist world. In replying to these statesmen, Communists have said and continue to say: "Yes, communism is the future, and sentence has been pronounced on the capitalist social system, but it has been pronounced by history. This sentence bears the signature of history, not of the Kremlin."

We believe in the inexhaustible potentialities of our socialist system, believe that the dispute between socialism and capitalism will be settled in the arena of peaceful competition, peaceful coexistence. It is this line, this policy of peace, that is expressed in the new draft Program of the C.P.S.U. (Applause.)

One marvels at the reckless statements we sometimes hear, coming from the banks of the Rhine one moment, the next moment from the banks of the Seine, and the next from the Thames, that the West is not afraid even of atomic war. What heroes! The people who come out with statements of this kind are undaunted, you see, by the bottomless furnace of nuclear-missile war, but their knees shake at the prospect of concluding a German peace treaty.

What is most interesting is that the "heroes" who would have one believe that they do not dread nuclear war know themselves that this is just empty bravado. We, too, know that they are not telling the truth. And they in turn know that we've seen through them and are well aware that they are not telling the truth, and still there's no stopping them.

If their purpose is to gamble on making us nervous, our advice to them is to realize, at long last, that blackmail does not work on Soviet people, their nerves will not break. ...

Military men in the West, especially the higher-ups, continue to argue about whether it is possible to develop an ultimate weapon against which no defense can be found. This is the age-old dispute between the spear and the shield, the projectile and the armor, and it is for the military experts to settle. But such a weapon has long since been forged in the sphere of social relations and policy.

Our ultimate weapon in policy is not intercontinental missiles and nuclear bombs, although we should hold them in high esteem until general and complete disarmament has been brought about, since they serve the cause of peace well. Our ultimate weapon is the all-conquering Marxist-Leninist doctrine. With it, with this weapon, the older generation of our country's Communists stormed the Winter Palace in 1917. With this weapon our people, under the leadership of the great party of Lenin, will storm more and more new heights in building communism. (Applause.)

We Soviet people condemn capitalism and the ideology of capitalist society. We would always, at any international conference, be able to find strong language to describe the evils of capitalism with its exploitation of man by man. But in meeting with Western representatives at the conference table, we are invariably guided by the belief that questions relating to the ideological struggle should be divorced from relations between states. This is why our party, the C.P.S.U. Central Committee and the Soviet government, in pursuing our foreign policy, reject attempts to build relations between states on what divides them rather than what brings them together.

Only people who have long since lost faith in their own strength, in their social system, can base their policy on the inevitable solution of disputes and ideological difference by force of arms—in other words, on the inevitability of a military conflict. Capitalism must be in a pretty bad way if today certain of its leading figures who, presumably for want of someone better, are included among the architects of present-day bourgeois ideology go so far as to preach nuclear-missile war, urging that the salvation of the social system be sought in the annihilation of scores upon scores of millions of people.

The attention of the whole world is today riveted on the proceedings of our Congress. One has only to open any newspaper published abroad or tune in to any wave length on the radio to be thoroughly convinced that the 22nd Congress of the C.P.S.U. has burst commandingly into the lives and thoughts of the inhabitants of our planet. No cordon built by the cleverest of the master propagandists in the capitalist world can hold back the stream of powerful impulses flowing from the heart of our country to the hearts of all to whom the cause of peace is dear. (Applause.)

But some political figures and press organs in the West choose not to see the gigantic scope of our peaceful plans and deliberately pluck out of the materials of the Congress only those that testify to the strength of our armed forces. Not without ulterior motive, they are calling attention in particular to certain passages in Comrade R. Ya. Malinovsky's speech at the Congress.

But what follows from this speech? That our illustrious army possesses a formidable weapon that well serves the interests of safeguarding the security of the Soviet people and of our friends. This leads to an important conclusion one would think the statesmen of the major Western powers ought to draw: The thought of settling disputes by force of arms must be re-

nounced, threats must be renounced, and agreements must be reached on all outstanding issues.

To those who bear the responsibility for the present nuclear-missile race and who are today themselves frightened by the latest advances in Soviet military technology, we say: "Let us destroy the war machines of the states, carry out general and complete disarmament and close the chapter of the last war; your nerves can then relax and, most important, the threat of a new war will have been eliminated." (Applause.) ...

Satyukov

SPEECH BY COMRADE P. A. SATYUKOV, EDITOR-IN-CHIEF OF PRAVDA. (Pravda, Oct. 27, pp. 7-8; Izvestia, pp. 4-5. 4,500 words. Condensed text:) Comrade delegates! ... Great credit is due the Party Central Committee headed by that stanch Leninist Comrade N. S. Khrushchev for having shown deep devotion to principle, Bolshevik firmness, great courage and perseverance in carrying out the policy of the 20th Congress. It is precisely because of this courage, firmness and devotion to principle that the anti-Party group composed of Molotov, Kaganovich, Malenkov, Bulganin, Voroshilov, Pervukhin and Saburov, and Shepilov, who joined them, which tried to change the line of the 20th Party Congress, to turn the Party off the Leninist path and to retain and perpetuate the vicious methods of leadership that had obtained under the cult of the individual, was exposed and ideologically and organizationally routed. ...

How did they behave—these people who pretended to be disciples of Lenin and continuers of his work, who laid claim to the role of Party theorists and interpreters of Leninism? They became distraught and frightened. They should have gone to the masses, to the people, should have provided forthright and honest answers to the most acute and vitally important questions raised by life itself. They were afraid to do this. Having long since lost touch with the life of the Party and the people, these armchair politicos had forgotten how to talk to the people and could find no common tongue with the masses. This was why they tried to maintain, to freeze, the methods of leadership that had developed in the period of the Stalin cult. This was emulating a man who with their help and through their sycophantic zeal had set himself up as a kind of other-worldly divinity.

For years on end Stalin was silent, never going anywhere, never conversing with anyone; and it was not mere chance that he was silent. In the closing stage of his life he was more and more out of touch with the Party and people, did not know and did not want to know the things that preoccupied Soviet people, the things that agitated them. Is this not shown by the fact that in the complex and difficult period when the Party and people were busy rebuilding the war-ravaged economy, Stalin suddenly focused attention on problems of linguistics, on which there was a discussion in the Party press lasting several months? Were these really the problems then agitating the people and preoccupying the Party?

For years on end no Party Congresses or plenary sessions of the Central Committee were convened. The most active Party figures were unable, had not the right, to speak about the problems being raised by life itself. And if someone did try to broach such matters, he was rudely cut short. There has already been mention of the statements made on various aspects of economic construction by prominent figures in our party, and you know what repressive measures Stalin took against them.

The handful of factionalists, who had grown used to the musty atmosphere of the cult of the individual as swamp creatures grow used to the slime and mud, were up in arms against the Party's new line. What need, they asked, for these trips around the country, what was the point of all these conferences and meetings on collective farms, at construction projects and factories? Kaganovich went so far as cynically to call the trips being made by Party leaders to the localities needless "knocking about the country." We got along without them, he said, and we shall continue to do so. The Party dealt a crushing blow to these anti-Party views and these champions of the cult of the individual. (Applause.)

As has already been pointed out in the speeches of the Congress delegates, Molotov was the ideological inspirer of the anti-Party group. Having been one of the people chiefly to blame for the emergence of the Stalin cult and for blowing it up to inordinate proportions, he proved to be the most zealous opponent of the Party's policy aimed at exposing the cult of the individual and overcoming its consequences.

Until recently Molotov claimed a special standing in the Party, trying to set himself up as well-nigh the sole interpreter of Leninist doctrine. At every step he would arrogantly remind people that he had worked under Lenin.

Molotov did work under Lenin. But the plain truth of the matter is that he had no grounds for making excessive claims. As we know, in not one of Lenin's speeches or in his "Testament" addressed to the regular Party Congress in 1922 is Molotov mentioned at all among the prominent Party figures of the period. Nowhere and at no time did Lenin say anything about Molotov's "services in the area of theory," either. He said nothing because there were no such services. But Lenin did have something to say about Molotov's penchant for bureaucracy.

I should like in this connection to cite a document of Lenin's. It is a letter addressed to Molotov by Vladimir Ilyich in 1922 regarding the state of affairs in the sector for which Molotov was directly responsible as Secretary of the Central Committee in charge of matters of organization and cadres.

Here is what was said in the letter:

"After filling in the questionnaire or form of the latest census of members of the Russian Communist Party," writes Lenin, "I have come to the firm conclusion that the handling of statistical work in the Central Committee (and probably all registration-and-assignment work) is wretched.

"Either your person in charge of statistics is a fool, or somewhere in these 'departments' (if that is what these institutions attached to the Central Committee are called) there are fools and pedants occupying important positions and you, plainly, are too busy to keep an eye on things.

"1. The director of the Statistics Department must be fired.

"2. There must be a thorough shake-up in this and the registration-and-assignment department.

"Otherwise we ourselves ('while fighting bureaucracy') shall be breeding the most shameful and the stupidest bureaucracy under our very noses.

"The power of the Central Committee is immense. Its resources are gigantic. We have between 200,000 and 400,000 Party workers to whom we give assignments, and through [them] thousands upon thousands of non-Party people.

"And this gigantic communist task is being thoroughly bungled as a result of obtuse bureaucracy!"

This is how Vladimir Ilyich rated Molotov's work in the Central Committee post that had been entrusted to him: "***gigantic communist task is being thoroughly bungled as a result of obtuse bureaucracy!"

The partiality for bureaucracy that Lenin had noticed proved to be the determinant feature of all Molotov's work. He never did manage to make the grade as a political leader of the Leninist type, though he held high positions for a long time.

There is another document in which Molotov is characterized as a man given to cliquishness, demagogy and intrigue. It is a resolution of a Nizhny Novgorod Gubernia Party conference adopted in July, 1920, at a time when Molotov served for a short period as chairman of the Nizhny Novgorod Gubernia Executive Committee. The resolution states:

"Whereas in the case of the gubernia committee's report and especially in the discussion of candidacies for the new gubernia committee the old Party workers Comrades Molotov and Taganov, in defiance of all our party's traditions, agitated before the elections to the gubernia committee after all the lists had been made public but before the individuals had been personally discussed, in the course of which agitation they hurled a whole range of vague accusations of a general nature at gubernia and district officials in positions of responsibility, giving insulting nicknames to a dozen district officials and officials of the city committee and trying to vilify all the officials who made up the majority in the previous gubernia committee, with the object of clearing the way for a new grouping in the gubernia committee.

"Lack of proper tact," the resolution goes on to say, "and, most important, the factual groundlessness of the accusations

and completely inadmissible demagogy have forced the conference to censure the aforementioned comrades" (that is, Molotov and Taganov).

The documents are eloquent evidence that Molotov has long been noted for bureaucracy, a predilection for lifeless stereotype, haughtiness and contemptuousness toward rank-and-file workers and for his efforts to use not Party methods but the methods of cliques and schemers in his activities.

These two documents supplement the picture of Molotov, who later on, while occupying high office, did great harm to the Party and state with his improper actions and then slid down onto the path of factionalist anti-Party struggle. As chairman of the Council of People's Commissars between 1930 and 1941, Molotov abused his power. He is guilty of flagrant violations of revolutionary legality. Molotov's report on wrecking and sabotage delivered at the February-March, 1937, plenary session of the Central Committee, as well as Stalin's speech at that plenary session, served as the theoretical justification for the mass repressions against Party, state and economic cadres. And was it not Molotov who was responsible for the repressions against such prominent Party and state figures as Rudzutak and Chubar, vice-chairmen of the Council of People's Commissars, and of a number of honest Communists who held posts as People's Commissars?

As for Molotov's theoretical pretensions, much has already been said at the Congress about his confusion on major problems of domestic and foreign policy. This confusion is by no means innocuous. It shows a definite anti-Leninist tendency, and it continues to this day.

The delegates to the 22nd Congress should know that in October of this year, just before the Congress opened, Molotov sent a letter to the Central Committee. Without having a word to say about his subversive factionalist work against the Leninist Party and against the decisions of its 20th Congress, he tries afresh in this letter to pose as interpreter of Leninism and again attacked the Central Committee and the draft Program of the C.P.S.U.

True, something new has now made its appearance in Molotov's writings. He can now bring himself to criticize Stalin on the question of whether it is possible for communism to be victorious in a single country. But he does this in order to slander the new draft Program of the C.P.S.U. Molotov claims the new Program is antirevolutionary in spirit. This slanderous, shameful statement of Molotov's indicates that he has broken with the Party, has broken with Leninism. (Applause.)

Molotov declares in his letter that the draft Program fails, you see, to coordinate communist construction in the U.S.S.R. with the prospects for the revolutionary struggle of the working class in capitalist countries, with the prospects for socialist revolution on an international scale. And this at a time when the draft Program has been unanimously approved not only by our party and the Soviet people but by the international Communist movement.

Molotov goes so far as to make monstrous allegations that the draft Program sidesteps the difficulties in the struggle for communism and orients the Party and the people toward a continued advance to communism by the countries of the socialist commonwealth without revolutionary struggle. His contentions lead to the conclusion that it is impossible to continue the advance to communism without the most serious political conflicts with the imperialist countries, and hence without war.

We say to Molotov: No, the Communist Party of the Soviet Union has been and is doing everything possible to ensure peace for the Soviet people, the people who are building communism. (Stormy applause.) The Leninist principle of peaceful coexistence has been and remains our general line in foreign policy. This is plainly stated in the new Program, and the Party will pursue this line consistently. (Prolonged applause.)

Molotov has fallen so low as to come out openly against Lenin's clear-cut statements that the socialist state exerts its main revolutionary influence on the course of world events through its economic successes, through its example, through its triumphs in communist construction.

"We have said and continue to say: 'Socialism has the force of example,'" stated V. I. Lenin ("Works," Vol. XXXI, p. 426). In his report at the Tenth All-Russian Party Conference he spoke of the singular importance that questions of economic construction were acquiring for the Soviet land and said that we exerted our chief influence on international developments through our economic policy.

It is strange and monstrous to hear from a man who claims the role of interpreter of Leninism the contention that nowhere did Lenin ever speak of peaceful coexistence between states with different social systems. To say this is to contradict one of the most important of Lenin's theoretical propositions—his theory of the possibility of the victory of socialism in one separate country. If socialism has triumphed in one country, then that socialist country must inevitably coexist with the states of the other social system—the capitalist.

The statements on the existence of our Soviet republic side by side with capitalist countries that Lenin made in a report at the Ninth All-Russian Congress of Soviets in 1921 are common knowledge. We all know, too, the perfectly clear and definite answers that V. I. Lenin gave a correspondent of the American paper the New York Evening Journal in 1920 when asked about our aims in Europe and Asia: "Peaceful coexistence with the peoples, with the workers and peasants of all nations" ("Works," Vol. XXX, p. 340). V. I. Lenin spoke of a period "when socialist and capitalist states will exist side by side" ("Works," Vol. XXX, p. 21).

The question arises as to what Molotov has in mind in wanting to jostle us from the position of peaceful coexistence. He is trying to shove us onto the path of adventures, the path of war. The Party will not have this! This is not the teaching of Lenin, and we would not be Leninists if we heeded the Molotovs. (Stormy applause.)

Molotov maintains that there is pacifism and even revisionism in the draft Program. This is an odious libel on our Leninist party and its militant, revolutionary Marxist-Leninist Program, which all over the world has been called the Communist Manifesto of our time! (Applause.)

This letter of Molotov's is further convincing evidence that he holds obstinately to his anti-Leninist views. He does not care a rap about the colossal changes that have taken place in the world and refuses to see and take into account the extent to which the role of the world socialist system has grown. An incorrigible dogmatist, he fails to appreciate the revolutionary spirit of the Leninist doctrine, which requires that the real balance of forces be soberly appraised and that flexible, revolutionary strategy and tactics be followed at all times.

Only a person who has openly adopted anti-Leninist positions and broken with the international Communist movement could charge the new draft Program of the Party with pacifism and revisionism. Our Party unanimously endorses the draft of the new Leninist Program which the Central Committee has submitted to the 22nd Congress for consideration. It rejects the slanderous fabrications and attacks of an envenomed Molotov, who has grown politically blind, gone totally bankrupt and has exposed himself as a factionalist and plotter. People of this kind, who have taken to fighting the Leninist general line of the Party, have no place in our party's ranks! (Applause.)

I am not going to speak about the other members of the anti-Party group. I merely want to mention the particularly unseemly role of Shepilov, which is underscored by the very description of him as having "joined," as having fawned on the ringleaders of the anti-Party group. His character has been completely exposed as that of a careerist, political schemer and double-dealer. The following fact characterizes his make-up. In his desire to elbow his way to membership in the Academy, Shepilov decided, for purposes of self-advertisement, to publish under his own name a book on foreign policy in which he included notes and messages of the Soviet government as supposedly having been written by him.

Yesterday Comrade Ilyichev related how at the instance of Molotov and Malenkov a letter was drafted condemning a very important article in Pravda, written by Comrade N. S. Khrushchev, dealing with fundamental questions of collective farm development. Examination of the documents shows that this letter, anti-Party in nature and politically harmful, was drawn up at the instance of Molotov and Malenkov with the most zealous participation of Shepilov.

At a critical moment in the anti-Party struggle Shepilov counted an arithmetical majority in the Presidium of the Central Committee for the factionalist group, and he decided to curry favor with the conspirators through base and dirty intrigue and thereby further his career. For careerists of this kind, to whom nothing is sacred, who trim their sails to the wind, there is an apt folk saying: "Here leaping, there sidling, here crawling, there on all fours." Well, the careerist Shepilov crawled on all fours before the ringleaders of the anti-Party group. People of this sort must not be permitted within gun-shot of our great, sacred Party cause! Just think, it came out at the June plenary session of the Central Committee that Shepilov had a little notebook, a sort of conduct book containing the record of his vileness, in which he would jot down various bits of gossip about leading officials. He was a talebearer and tried to set the members of the Presidium quarreling among themselves, for which he was called a political prostitute at the plenary session.

While completely associating myself with the delegates who have said there is no room in the Party's ranks for the ringleaders of the anti-Party group, I think there is no room in the Party for the man who joined them, either! (Applause.)

Comrades! In the enormous work done by the Central Committee in restoring Leninist principles of leadership, a place of no small importance is held by the restoration of a wonderful Leninist tradition—the use of the press as a potent ideological weapon in the Party's hands, as collective propagandist, agitator and organizer in the struggle to carry out the Party line.

We are all well aware that at the time the Bolshevik Party was created Lenin attached prime importance to the existence of a general political Marxist newspaper. As a result of the elimination of the consequences of the cult of the individual, our press is now taking a worthy place in the life of society. The content of newspapers and magazines and the character of their work have changed, and their ideological and theoretical level has risen. They have come closer to the life of the people and have been treating the fundamental questions of communist construction more penetratingly and vividly. Work on a voluntary basis is becoming increasingly widespread in the press. The movement of worker- and peasant-correspondents is gaining in vigor and scope and numbers more than 5,000,000 persons in its ranks. ...

In the period since the 20th Congress the annual circulation of newspapers has increased by 20,000,000 copies and of magazines and other periodicals by 417,000,000 copies. The circulation of three central papers alone—Pravda, Izvestia and Komsomolskaya pravda—now stands at about 15,000,000 copies. When the Petersburg workers founded Pravda in May, 1912, it had a circulation of about 40,000. Today, at the time of its 50th anniversary, Pravda is printed in more than 6,000,000 copies and is the most widely sold daily paper in the world. The circulation of our newspapers and magazines could be considerably larger if our paper industry kept up with the rapid growth of the Soviet press. We Soviet press workers have serious complaints to make against the planning and economic agencies, which until very recently had not been giving the needed attention to the expansion of the paper and printing industries. ...

Semenov

SPEECH BY COMRADE N. N. SEMENOV, ACADEMICIAN AND CHAIRMAN OF THE BOARD OF THE ALL-UNION SOCIETY FOR THE DISSEMINATION OF POLITICAL AND SCIENTIFIC KNOWLEDGE. (Pravda, Oct. 27, p. 8. 4,500 words. Excerpts:) ... The Stalin cult, with its dogmatism and gross violations of socialist legality, was alien and hostile to Soviet scientists. After the 20th Party Congress Leninist traditions revived in our country with new force. They brought forth a tempestuous flood of creative initiative on the part of our people. Nikita Sergeyevich Khrushchev boldly and firmly stood and stands behind the correct Leninist cause, and we scientists, along with our entire people, are boundlessly grateful to him for this. (Applause.) Nikita Sergeyevich is a true friend and organizer of Soviet science. Thanks to his concern, there is now taking place in our country, just as in the 1920s, a surge of scientific creative endeavor, but on an incomparably vaster scale. ...

As we progress toward communism more and more people,

with the reduction in the length of the working day, will enthusiastically engage in scientific and technical creative work
in their leisure hours, since it gives man the highest enjoyment
and enables him to display his capabilities in the interests of
society. The time is not far off when this public "sector" of
science will determine its development no less than state scientific and scientific-technical institutes and laboratories. In
this connection, I propose that the last phrase of point "e" of
the first part of section five of the draft Program (p. 122) be formulated as follows: "People's leisure will be increasingly devoted to
public activities, cultural intercourse, mental and physical development and scientific, scientific-technical and artistic endeavor." ...

I propose that the 11th paragraph of the second part of the third
section of the draft Program be set forth as follows:

"Other public associations of the working people—unions of
writers, artists and journalists and cultural-enlightenment and
sports societies—will likewise be developed. The Party attaches special importance to disseminating knowledge and developing the scientific and technical creative work of the working people by means of such public organizations as the All-
Union Society for the Dissemination of Political and Scientific
Knowledge, scientific and scientific-technical societies and
organizations of rationalizers and inventors. The Party will
give these societies maximum attention and help." ...

Of course our scientific societies are still far from this
ideal. Much effort, attention and concern are required if in the
forthcoming 20-year period they are to form into qualitatively
new scientific societies that correspond with the communist
system. There exist for this all the objective possibilities and
prerequisites created by the Soviet socialist system. An example of this is the activity of the All-Union Society for the
Dissemination of Political and Scientific Knowledge. History
has not yet known such a public institution. In the 14-year
period of its work the All-Union Society has grown from a small detachment of scientists and cultural figures into a mass organization
of the Soviet intelligentsia. It has a membership of 1,200,000. ...

A tempestuous advance in the work of the society began after
the 20th Party Congress. The Party's profound and consistent
struggle against the cult of the individual and its consequences
and the sharp turn of propaganda toward life and toward the
practice of communist construction have helped to improve
the work of the All-Union Society: The public basis of its work
has expanded and the society's members have begun to approach
the propaganda of knowledge more creatively and, relying on
Leninist principles of ideological and propaganda work, to overcome dogmatism, pedantry and formalism in propaganda. ...

The development of the public basis of the work of the All-
Union Society is leading to an improvement in its organizational structure. Groups of society members at enterprises
and on collective farms now comprise its basic link. We now
have 75,000 such groups, two-thirds of them in the countryside. The groups unite the local intelligentsia and leading
workers and collective farmers and direct their efforts toward
the propaganda and creative application of scientific knowledge
in their collectives. Under the guidance of Party agencies,
they, as the initiating nucleus, organize the public scientific
movement of the broad masses of the working people.

Lecture propaganda, in which lecturers from the society's
local groups are playing an ever-increasing role, is steadily
expanding. Whereas in 1956 the society's members delivered
2,000,000 lectures, in 1960 they delivered 10,000,000 lectures.
At present 89% of all the lectures are given free of charge.
The transfer of lecture propaganda functions from the jurisdiction of the Ministry of Culture to the All-Union Society has
fully justified itself. The society has won wide popular recognation. ...

There is much that is positive and interesting in the work
of other scientific and scientific-technical societies. As is
known, 62 scientific-enlightenment, scientific and scientific-
technical societies uniting more than 5,000,000 persons now
function in our country. One can imagine what inexhaustible
forces this millions-strong army has for developing science
and technology. These forces will multiply if our scientists
and highly qualified specialists will daily guide and help this
army of people's creativity, and also learn something from it,
as Nikita Sergeyevich Khrushchev frequently points out.

Unfortunately, the many scientific and scientific-enlighten

ment organizations function separately, and in part duplicate
one another. Some of them are under the Central Council of
Trade Unions, others under the Ministry of Public Health, still
others under the Academy of Sciences, etc. The interagency
partitions that have formed and hardened prevent the employment of these organizations' forces and resources to the
maximum effectiveness, yet their aims and tasks are the same.
Frequently the same people are enlisted in the work of different societies.

Proceeding from the unity of the aims and tasks of all these
organizations, it seems to us expedient to merge the activity
of all scientific, scientific-technical and scientific-enlightenment organizations into a single mighty stream, into a single
public movement, into a united organization. The need for this
is all the more evident in the light of the fact that actual unification of primary cells of various scientific-enlightenment
and scientific-technical societies is already taking place locally
in many instances.

In our opinion, a federation or union of these societies could
become a rational form of unification. Such a federation would
make it possible to unite scientific forces and material resources, to improve the allocation of duties and to combine
the propaganda of knowledge better with the creative work of
the masses. Creation of a federation will also make it possible to raise the level of Party guidance of these organizations
in all links. ...

Kuusinen

SPEECH BY COMRADE O. V. KUUSINEN, SECRETARY OF
THE PARTY CENTRAL COMMITTEE. (Pravda, Oct. 27,
pp. 9-10; Izvestia, pp. 5-6. 5,000 words. Excerpts:)
Comrade delegates! Permit me to begin with the question of
the Program. After all, the new Party Program is our special
pride and the great joy of the entire Soviet people.

The Creative Nature of the New Program.—The need for a
new Program was felt in our party some time ago. I know that
back in the 1930s, on Stalin's initiative, two attempts were made
to draft a new Program. But these attempts were not really
serious, and they yielded such pitiful results that Stalin did not
even deem it necessary to acquaint the members of the Politburo with the written drafts.

But even if a draft Program had been prepared most carefully
at that time, the Party still would not have had a document comparable to the present draft Program. It is clear why—because
at that time the necessary prerequisites did not exist for
creating a program for the building of a communist society.

What were these prerequisites?

First, we needed that exceptionally important turn in policy
that was made by the Party, beginning with the reorganization
of the management of the national economy, the development
of the virgin lands and the elimination of the consequences of the
cult of the individual. This new political course was, as is
known, confirmed by the 20th Party Congress and further developed at the 21st Congress, which marked our country's
emergence into the period of the full-scale building of communism.

Second, it was necessary that the drafting of the new Program be guided by a Marxist-Leninist who would combine
creative boldness and farsightedness with an ardent desire to
improve production and achieve scientific-technical progress
in all spheres of life; who would be distinguished by lofty adherence to principle, an ability not to lose sight for a minute
of the ultimate goal of historical progress and at the same
time never to be detached from existing realities; who would
know the life of the working people as well as his own, believe
in the people and sensitively reflect their concerns and aspirations.

Considering all this, it will become clear how important it
was that the working out of the new Party Program was directly
supervised by such a leader of the Leninist type as Comrade
Nikita Sergeyevich Khrushchev. (Stormy applause.) ...

The portions of the new Program concerning the diversity
of paths of the transition of various countries to socialism, the
more or less simultaneous entry of the socialist countries into
communism, the nature of the present-day epoch and the distinctive features of the new stage of the general crisis of capitalism, and the possibility of a noncapitalist path of development

for the countries of Asia and Africa that have won their freedom have been greeted in the fraternal Marxist-Leninist parties with full approval. ...

The Question of War and Peace.— ... Nowhere has the process of development of state-monopoly capitalism, the process of the subordination of the state apparatus to the magnates of big capital, gone so far as in the U.S.A. And nowhere is this power seized by the monopolies being used so unrestrainedly for the purpose of further enriching the big corporations at the expense of the people and for extending their sway over other countries.

It is no accident that it is precisely in the epoch of state-monopoly capitalism that the claim to "leadership of the world," or to put it more simply, to world domination, matured in the United States.

Of course, the bosses of American "big business," accustomed to operating behind the scenes, do not make public their specific plans for seizing spheres of influence in the capitalist world. They prefer to act under another guise—of "anti-communism." But this, as is known, is not a very original invention. After all, the former contender for world domination—Hitlerite Germany—also began by declaring itself the "savior" of the world from communism. ...

The American imperialists cannot but realize that a war against the countries of the socialist camp is an extremely risky undertaking for them. At the same time, they calculate, not without reason, that under the noise of "combating communism" it is easier for them to extend their tentacles into many capitalist countries.

In the colonial and dependent countries the banner of "anti-communism" is being used to combat the national-liberation movement and preserve colonial oppression. In the countries of Asia and Africa that have won their freedom, "anticommunism" is a weapon for undermining their national independence and drawing these countries, if possible, into military blocs organized by the American imperialists. ...

The Hornets' Nest of Warmongers.— ... For more than ten years now the organizers of NATO have been hoodwinking gullible people by depicting their aggressive bloc as a "defense alliance." They are helped in this by the apostles of "anti-communism" from among the Right Social Democrats, such as Gaitskell, Willy Brandt and others. But even the most zealous myrmidons of NATO realize what indignation and resistance an aggressive war against the socialist countries would arouse among the people. Therefore the NATO leaders are preparing to lay the blame for starting a war on the Soviet Union. It has become known that NATO has a plan for so-called "psychological war." This plan states that in starting a war against the U.S.S.R. it is necessary above all to convince the peoples of the West that the countries of the West have become the victims of Soviet attack.

What insolence! The Soviet Union is constantly waging a persistent struggle for the preservation of peace. Even broad bourgeois circles are compelled to acknowledge that the Soviet Union does not intend to attack anyone. ... But in any event the fact is that the NATO system has proved to be highly convenient for American expansion. With its help the United States, like a battering ram, has broken open the gates of the capitalist countries of Western Europe to the penetration of American capital. It is not by chance that it is precisely Western Europe, above all Great Britain, that has been deluged in the postwar years with private investments by U.S. corporations. But the main thing is that the NATO system enables the financial bosses of America to present their expansion under the guise of a "collective policy" of the so-called "free world." ...

We are far from regarding the entire present-day bourgeoisie as something unitary and homogeneous. ... One trend is belligerent and aggressive. It is supported by the most frantic circles of the imperialist bourgeoisie, which count on the force of arms to mend the shaky affairs of world capitalism. The other trend is a moderately sober one, supported by the circles of the bourgeoisie that realize the danger for capitalism itself of a new war, and that are prepared to accept in some form the principle of peaceful coexistence.

In essence, the entire postwar policy of the imperialist states reflects the contradictions and conflict of these two trends of different groups of the bourgeoisie. In practice the bourgeois governments most frequently take the course of compromise between the demands of the two extreme flanks of the bourgeois camp. This compromise is none other than the policy of supporting international tension whenever the pressure of the masses is not strong enough to force the ruling circles to agree to a relaxation of tension.

It is clear, however, that artificial support of tension is fraught with mortal danger for the cause of peace. It creates an atmosphere in which war could easily explode. In the imperialist countries there is no shortage of bellicose elements who are capable of losing their composure and self-control. Those who fan tension risk falling into the situation of the ill-starred sorcerer who could not cope with the supernatural forces summoned up by his incantations.

Yes, the utmost vigilance is necessary in the struggle to defend peace against the imperialist aggressors. It is also necessary to strengthen the defense might of the socialist state. The prime internationalist duty of our Soviet state is to be a reliable and mighty bulwark of peace, a bulwark on whose firmness other peace-loving peoples can boldly rely. (Applause.)

On Economic Competition Between the Two Systems.—In our times a gigantic political struggle of the peoples to curb the bellicose imperialists is developing throughout the world. Increasingly substantial successes can be expected from this popular movement.

At the same time, the victory of the cause of peace depends to a decisive extent on the successes of the socialist countries in their economic competition with capitalism, above all the competition between the Soviet Union and the U.S.A.

The greater our economic might and the more graphically socialism demonstrates its superiority to the capitalist system, the more hopeless will be the position of the warmongers. ...

Today twice as many apartments are being built per 1000 persons in the Soviet Union as in the U.S.A. Why should not the American government respond to this "challenge" to double the volume of housing construction in its country? True, this would require, according to the calculations of economists, $14,500,000,000. But this sum is less than one-third of the U.S. military budget. If this money were taken from the spendthrifts in the Pentagon, the United States could share with the Soviet Union the first and second places in volume of housing construction.

Or another example. Expenditures on rent, medical care and taxes now devour at least 34% of the American worker's earnings. Why should not the United States try to catch up with the Soviet Union in this sphere as well? After all, in order to ease the position of the working people a little bit, it would suffice to cut the military budget by only a few billion dollars.

Speaking seriously, of course, this is not to be expected from the ruling circles of the United States. They prefer to economize not on the arms race but on social services for the working people. By this reckless policy of theirs they are speeding the shattering of the foundations of the capitalist system.

On Unity of the Party and International Solidarity. — ... In the course of my long life I have many times had the opportunity to participate in the Party's struggle against various kinds of opposition factions — Trotskyites, Zinovievites, Bukharinites and others. Usually each of these factions began the struggle against the Party by proclaiming political differences. But it soon became clear that the main thing for them was not political arguments but seizing power. They always placed their own personal ambition and striving for power above the cause of the working class, the cause of socialism and communism.

This feature was also characteristic of the latest anti-Party group. Of course, the members of this group also had political motives for their factionalist activity: They opposed everything new and creative in the Party's policy, they were against eliminating the consequences of the cult of the individual, and so on. In general they rebelled against the Leninist line of Party leadership. But even at the very beginning it came to light that the chief aspiration of this group was to remove Comrade Nikita Sergeyevich Khrushchev, continuer of the cause of Lenin, from the Presidium of the Central Committee and to take full leadership into their own hands.

The factionalists of 1957, as distinguished from the previous anti-Party groups, did not even have any written political platform. Molotov apparently noticed this "omission" only later. This is why he has recently engaged in writing notes that unscrupulously distort the Leninist line of the Party Central Committee and basely slander the political position of Comrade Khrushchev. In essence, Molotov is trying to concoct a kind of sectarian platform for his further anti-Party profiteering. He apparently has decided to stir up the waters in order to try later on to catch a fish in these muddy waters. Perhaps the bait will be swallowed by some bony sprat (laughter) if not here in home reservoirs, then at least somewhere in foreign waters. (Stir in the hall. Laughter.)

It seems to me—and I think that you too, comrade delegates, are of the same opinion—that our Leninist Party has no need for such an incorrigible and malicious political profiteer in its ranks. (Applause.) ...

As internationalists who consider ourselves bound to defend the international solidarity of the Communist movement, we cannot ignore the schismatic activity of the leadership of the Albanian Party of Labor.

It must be said that even in 1960 the Albanian leaders aroused general indignation at meetings of representatives of the fraternal parties by their slanderous sallies against the C.P.S.U. and Comrade Khrushchev.

The Central Committee of our party tried many times to reach agreement with the Albanian leaders. But they behaved downright defiantly, not wishing even to hear of any agreement. Then the arrests of Albanian citizens who spoke out for friendship with the U.S.S.R. began in Albania, as well as the expulsion of Soviet specialists who had come to the country at the invitation of the Albanian government. In order to arouse ill feelings toward the Soviet Union among the people, the Albanian leaders began to circulate foul rumors to the effect that the U.S.S.R. was supporting Greek claims to the southern areas of Albania or to the effect that the U.S.S.R. had stopped supplying grain to Albania. How low one had to fall to invent such monstrous stories!

Only schismatics who have set themselves the aim of undermining the friendship of the Albanian and Soviet peoples and in general sowing dissension in the family of socialist countries could behave this way.

The Albanian leaders themselves claim that they are nevertheless opponents of imperialism. In words this may be so, but their deeds only play into the hands of the imperialists. After all, the imperialists seek nothing so much as a split in the socialist camp. What are we to do—encourage such conduct, ignore it at our Congress, or even pat the slanderers and schismatics on the back?

This would mean rejecting our duty to defend the international solidarity of the socialist camp. (Applause.) Our friendly feelings for the fraternal Albanian people remain unchanged, and it distresses us that, because of a few leaders who have strayed from the internationalist path, misfortune has befallen these people. ...

Shelepin

SPEECH BY COMRADE A. N. SHELEPIN, CHAIRMAN OF THE U.S.S.R. COUNCIL OF MINISTERS' STATE SECURITY COMMITTEE. (Pravda, Oct. 27, p. 10; 4500 words; Izvestia, Oct. 28, p. 3. Condensed text:) ... The ideologists of imperialism, who today speak in the name of anticommunism, openly proclaim that the subversive activity of their intelligence services must play a prominent part in the struggle for world domination. The ruling circles of the imperialist powers are making active and cynical use of intelligence agencies in their foreign policy, imparting to it an ever more sinister and provocational character.

Medieval "cloak and dagger" methods, adjusted to make use of electronics and cybernetics, are once again being resorted to. These methods are above all characteristic of American intelligence, which, acting as a tool of the monopolies and meddling grossly and brazenly in the internal affairs of other countries, is completely exposing the reactionary policy of the United States and its role as international gendarme.

The Pentagon and the Central Intelligence Agency are becoming less and less accountable to the American Congress and President for their actions. In its domestic and foreign policies the U.S. government is adhering ever more blindly to the adventurist course of these agencies.

Whatever tense aspects of the international situation we consider—the conspiracy against the legitimate government of Cambodia, events in the Congo, the actions of the insurgents in Laos, the insurrection of the "ultras" in Algeria, the infiltration of the U-2 spy plane into the territory of the U.S.S.R., the intervention against revolutionary Cuba, the resignation of President Quadros of Brazil, and the provocations in West Berlin—everywhere the traces of the U.S. Central Intelligence Agency are clearly to be seen.

The governments of the U.S.A. and other Western powers are extending all-round assistance to the government of the Federal Republic of Germany in its militarization of the country. The intelligence agencies of those states have turned West Berlin into a center of espionage and sabotage activity against the socialist countries. Some 4,000 agents of the Western powers have been caught in the territory of the German Democratic Republic in the past 18 months alone. Government agencies of the Western countries have worked out a special plan, which has been given the name "Live Oak." This plan—which, being doomed, it would be more accurate to call not "Live Oak" but "Living Corpse"—is directed against the G.D.R. and envisages, should the situation grow aggravated, the engineering of uprisings, sabotage, fires and other provocations.

It may be asked how U.S. intelligence manages to have such ramified tentacles. The answer is quite simple: The American government spends huge sums on it—$3,000,000,000 a year. The Central Intelligence Agency has a staff numbering more than 40,000 people. The State Department, which has more than 32,000 people on its Washington and overseas staffs, also employs a considerable number of intelligence people.

The imperialist intelligence agencies are directing their activities primarily against the Soviet Union and the other socialist countries. Infiltrating their agents into our country, they are making wide use of our ever-broadening international ties, especially tourist contacts, for espionage and the collection of intelligence data. Having no social base among the Soviet people for subversive activity, they try to influence individual politically and morally unstable citizens of ours in an anti-Soviet spirit and to recruit them as agents; they resort to all sorts of stratagems and provocations and carry on subversive activity on the ideological front.

Appreciating all this, the agencies of the State Security Committee are concentrating their main efforts on exposing and firmly suppressing the activities of hostile intelligence agencies. The greater the vigilance of the Soviet people, the more actively they assist the security agencies, the more resolutely and relentlessly our whole public takes action against cases of political carelessness, complacency and gullibility—and we still, unfortunately, have quite a few such cases—the more successful will this effort be.

It is the sacred duty of Soviet people to safeguard Party, state and military secrets. It goes without saying, comrades, that spy mania, which breeds suspicion and mistrust among people, must not be tolerated in our ranks. ...

Some comrades may think that the unmasking of the anti-Party group was a simple and easy matter. Comrades, this is not the case. It was a sharp, principled and difficult fight that was waged against the anti-Party group. ...

Numerous documents in our possession prove irrefutably that the members of the anti-Party group were guilty of illegal mass repressions against many Party, Soviet and Young Communist League workers and military people and bear direct personal responsibility for their physical destruction.

Stalin and his intimates Molotov and Kaganovich used the murder of Sergei Mironovich Kirov as an excuse for organizing reprisals against people who were objectionable to them, prominent state figures.

This was the time when the emergency criminal laws were adopted that made it possible to expose to public dishonor and to exterminate honest leaders who were devoted to the Party and the people. A whole series of extrajudiciary bodies made their appearance in this period. It has been established that the proposal for instituting them was personally drafted by Kaganovich. The draft of this document, in his writing, is in the archives.

Flagrantly abusing their high positions in the Party and state, Molotov, Kaganovich and Malenkov sealed the fates of many people with a stroke of the pen. One is simply amazed at the criminal thoughtlessness with which all this was done.

I want to give the delegates a few more facts to supplement what has already been said at our Congress. In November, 1937, Stalin, Molotov and Kaganovich sanctioned the arraignment (their signatures are preserved on this document) before a court of the Military Collegium of a large group of comrades from the ranks of prominent Party, state and military workers. Most of them were shot. Those innocently shot and posthumously rehabilitated include such prominent Party and state figures as Comrades Postyshev, Kossior, Eikhe, Rudzutak and Chubar; People's Commissar of Justice Krylenko; Unshlikht, Secretary of the U.S.S.R. Central Executive Committee; People's Commissar of Education Bubnov, and others.

The brutal attitude that was shown to people, to executive comrades who found themselves under investigation, is evidenced by a number of cynical notations written by Stalin, Kaganovich, Molotov, Malenkov and Voroshilov on letters and petitions from the prisoners. Yakir, for example, a former commander of a military district, had sent a letter to Stalin assuring him of his complete innocence.

Here is what he wrote: "****I am the honest fighting man, devoted to the Party, state and people, that I have been for many years. My entire conscious life has been spent working selflessly and honestly in full view of the Party and its leaders. ***Every word I say is honest, and I shall die with words of love for you, the Party and the country, with boundless faith in the victory of communism."

Stalin wrote on this letter: "Scoundrel and prostitute." Voroshilov added "A perfectly accurate description," Molotov put his name to this and Kaganovich appended: "For the traitor, scum and***(next comes a scurrilous, obscene word) one punishment—the death sentence."

The day before he was shot, Yakir sent Voroshilov the following letter: "To K. Ye. Voroshilov. I ask you, in memory of my many years of honest service in the Red Army in the past, to give instructions that my family, helpless and quite innocent, shall be looked after and given assistance. I have addressed the same plea to N. I. Yezhov. Yakir, June 9, 1937."

On this letter from a man with whom he had worked for many years, who as he well knew had time and again looked death in the face while defending the Soviet regime, Voroshilov wrote his conclusion: "In general I doubt the honesty of a dishonest person. K. Voroshilov. June 10, 1937."

Isn't it a good thing that Comrade Voroshilov saw his mistakes in time!

In June, 1937, an official of the U.S.S.R. State Planning Commission sent a letter to Stalin alleging that G. I. Lomov (Oppokov), a member of the Bureau of the U.S.S.R. Council of People's Commissars' Soviet Control Commission, had been on friendly terms with Rykov and Bukharin. Stalin wrote on this letter the instructions: "To Comrade Molotov. What to do?" Molotov wrote: "I'm for arresting this scum Lomov immediately. V. Molotov." A few days later Lomov was arrested, charged with membership in a Right Opportunist organization, and shot. He has now been rehabilitated. Who was Lomov? He had been a Party member since 1903, was elected to the first Council of People's Commissars as People's Commissar of Justice, then served as vice-chairman of the Supreme Economic Council, vice-chairman of the State Planning Commission, and was elected to the Central Committee of the All-Union Communist Party (Bolsheviks) at the Sixth, Seventh, 14th, 15th and 16th Party Congresses.

Molotov gave his sanction for the arrest of Kabakov, First Secretary of the Urals Province Party Committee; Ukhanov, People's Commissar of Light Industry; Krutov, Chairman of the Far Eastern Territory Executive Committee, and many, many other comrades.

And after all this Molotov calls himself a Leninist! This is blasphemy against the name and memory of Lenin! This is not what Lenin taught, and he never acted this way toward his class comrades and comrades-in-arms. (Prolonged applause.)

It has been established on the basis of documentary evidence

that Kaganovich, before the court sittings on various cases had come to an end, would personally edit the draft sentences and arbitrarily insert changes that suited him, such as the allegation that acts of terrorism had been planned against his person.

As has already been stated here, Malenkov has on his conscience the so-called "Leningrad Case," which brought grievous tragedy into the families of many Communists of that glorious city so dear to us. For careerist ends, Malenkov by means of intrigue compromised Comrade Kuznetsov, former Secretary of the Party Central Committee; Comrade Voznesensky, member of the Politburo, and other prominent Party workers.

Crying out to Malenkov's conscience is the memory of a number of workers of the Armenian Party and Soviet apparatus who were arrested on his instructions in connection with the murder of Comrade Khandzhyan, First Secretary of the Armenian Party Central Committee, who, as it later developed, had been killed in his office by Beria personally. By thus destroying quite innocent people, Malenkov helped his associate Beria to cover up his crime.

This is how inhumanly, comrades, the members of the anti-Party group for years, right up to the time the inveterate enemy Beria was exposed, settled the fates of innocent people. You sometimes wonder how these people can calmly walk the earth, how they can get a quiet night's sleep. They should be haunted by nightmares, they should hear the sobs and curses of the mothers, wives and children of comrades who perished innocently.

Comrades! I want to tell you about still another case. In the June days of 1957, when the factionalists had gone over to an open attack on the Central Committee, Bulganin, abusing his official position, posted his bodyguard in the Kremlin and stationed additional guards—who allowed no one in without his instructions—at the government building in which the Presidium of the C.P.S.U. Central Committee was holding its session. This shows that the conspirators were prepared to take the most extreme steps to achieve their filthy purposes.

Happily for us, the Central Committee saw the danger of the anti-Party group in time and rendered it harmless. (Prolonged applause.)

I must declare at this Congress, with a full sense of responsibility for the statement, that several members of the anti-Party group, and above all Molotov, have thus far failed to draw the proper conclusions from this grim lesson, are behaving badly, double-dealing with the Party and holding to their old views.

The time has therefore come for the Party Central Committee's Party Control Committee to consider calling the members of the anti-Party group to the strictest account. And in this matter I fully support the proposals made by the delegates who have spoken before me. (Applause.)

Comrades! The unanimous condemnation of the anti-Party group at our Congress has provoked an anti-Soviet clamor in the West, above all in the Western press. In an effort to mislead public opinion and divert the attention of the world public from what is most important, decisive and basic in the work of our Congress—our party's magnificent Program—the bourgeois papers are now alleging the existence of a "hidden internal threat," "internal difficulties," a "crack in the Reds' monolithic structure," some sort of "opposition group in the present leadership," are saying that "the fresh condemnation of the anti-Party group is intended to warn the excessively hotheaded," and so on and so forth.

Bourgeois commentators of all stripes and hues and the circles they represent are indulging in wishful thinking. This is truly a case of the hungry fox dreaming of chickens! But we must disappoint the bourgeois propagandists.

The anti-Party group is not being talked about at our Congress because it represents a danger to the Party today. It does not! The members of the anti-Party group are political corpses, who, far from representing any danger, do not even represent a shadow of a danger. We are talking about these factionalists with the purpose of once more laying bare their true complexion, of once more underlining the full extent of their nothingness as compared with the greatness of what the Party and people have accomplished since the 20th Congress, with the truly breathtaking horizons being opened up to us by the magnificent new Program of the C.P.S.U.! (Prolonged applause.) ...

Comrades! We are pleased to report to the Congress today

that perversions in the work of the state security agencies and violations of socialist legality have been completely eliminated. The decisive measures of the Party Central Committee and the Soviet government have put an end to this, and for good. (Prolonged applause.)

The state security agencies have been reorganized, have been cut down substantially, relieved of functions not proper to them and purged of careerist elements. The Party has assigned a large contingent of Party, Soviet and Y.C.L. workers to positions in them. The State Security Committee and its local agencies now have well-trained, competent cadres who are supremely devoted to the Party and people and are capable of successfully handling the complicated task of safeguarding our state security. The entire activity of the agencies of the State Security Committee is now under the continual supervision of the Party and government and is founded on complete trust in Soviet people and on respect for their rights and dignity.

Today no one can be adjudged guilty of committing a crime and punished other than by sentence of a court. Inviolability of the person in conformity with the U.S.S.R. Constitution is most rigorously safeguarded in our country, not in word but in deed. (Prolonged applause.)

The Party has restored true Leninist style and methods of work in the state security agencies. The Chekists derive their support from the people and have close links with the working people and the Soviet public at large. The state security agencies are no longer the frightening specter that enemies—Beria and his aides—sought to make them not very long ago but are truly people's—in the literal sense of the word—political agencies of our party. An exceptionally big role is being played in the activities of the agencies of the State Security Committee by the Party organizations, which have taken a worthy and fitting place in all our work. The Chekists can now look the Party and Soviet people in the eye with a clear conscience. (Applause.)

What is fundamentally new in the work of the state security agencies is that, along with intensifying their efforts to deal with hostile intelligence agents, they have begun extensively applying preventive and educational measures in the case of Soviet citizens who commit politically improper acts, sometimes bordering on crime, without any hostile intent but simply out of political immaturity or thoughtlessness. This, as I see it, is one of the forms of participation by agencies of the State Security Committee in the exercise of the socialist state's educational functions. (Applause.)

Needless to say, the actions of spies and other enemies of the Soviet state will continue to be punished with all the severity of our laws. (Prolonged applause.) ...

Comrades! Our juridical science has to a certain extent played a part in the restoration of legality. But our legal scholars are still far removed from reality, from the practical work of the state agencies. Many students of the law show conservatism, and for years on end carry on empty discussions on such problems as, for example, whether or not a homemade dagger is a cold weapon (stir in the hall), and other similar questions.

Instead of working to solve problems of vital importance, many of our students of the law are doing work on such topics as, for example, the state systems of Monaco, San Marino and the principality of Liechtenstein, "Family Law in Feudal Greece" and other such subjects.

Meanwhile our laws currently in force contain a number of provisions that have long since become obsolete, and there are problems that call for really thorough theoretical exploration. Take, for instance, the existing Russian Federation Civil Code. It states that every citizen of the Russian Federation has the right to set up industrial and commercial enterprises and to establish corporations and concessions. Several articles in this code give their blessing to the right of private ownership and the right to the use of hired labor. And this, comrades, at a time when we are setting foot on the threshold of a communist society. (Applause.)

Meanwhile, certain urgent questions growing out of the times are not covered by the law. For instance, it seems to me time the law provided penalties for manifestations of bureaucracy. Indeed, a man is brought to justice in our country for stealing ten rubles. And it is right that he should be. Yet we do not bring to trial bureaucrats who are guilty of shelving valuable rationalization proposals and inventions for years, who prevent

and impede the introduction of new equipment and technology into industry, or who are to blame for the fact that extremely important Party and government decisions are sometimes not carried out.

But it is not only a question of material loss. Bureaucracy seriously impairs communist education, engenders an unwholesome attitude in some Soviet people and weakens their will and drive. It is essential, therefore, that bureaucrats be punished most severely, and that arrangements be made for show trials in these cases. (Applause.)

In our time, when the Soviet people are engaged in the practical solution of the task of building communism, the actions of hooligans, thieves, loafers, bribe-takers and slanderers should be classed as grave crimes. (Prolonged applause.)

Soviet laws are the most humane in the world, but their humaneness should extend only to honest workers, while the laws should be stern in the case of parasitic elements, all who sponge off the people—for persons in this category are our internal enemy. (Applause.)

Comrades! The major shortcomings in the science of law, its departure from compelling, down-to-earth problems, are not a matter of chance. The point is that there has developed in jurisprudence a kind of cult of Vyshinsky, whose "theoretical" studies, particularly in defining the concept of law, were based on the well-known and erroneous thesis that as we advanced to communism the class struggle would sharpen, which must entail intensification of repression and of other measures of coercion. Law as defined by Vyshinsky amounted to nothing more than measures of coercion, and its educational role was completely dismissed, while the "theory" he developed that the confession of the accused was conclusive proof in cases of state crimes in effect justified the mass instances of arbitrariness in court and investigatory practice at the time.

Evidently these "theoretical" studies are to this day a heavy weight on many of our legal scholars.

It has become a matter of urgent necessity, therefore, to take a close look at the situation in jurisprudence and get the scholars to concentrate on those problems of state and law that are of greatest importance under present conditions. Perhaps the facilities of the scattered legal research institutions should be drawn upon to set up one authoritative research center which would be brought into the closest possible contact with life and practice (Applause.) ...

Shkolnikov

SPEECH BY COMRADE A.M. SHKOLNIKOV, FIRST SECRETARY OF THE STALINGRAD PROVINCE PARTY COMMITTEE. (Pravda, Oct. 28, pp. 2-3. 2,600 words. Excerpt:) ... It is horrible even to think about the ruinous path onto which the factionalists Molotov, Kaganovich, Malenkov, Voroshilov and their accomplices were pushing us. It must be said outright: If the anti-Party group had succeeded in seizing power in the Party and country, the methods of leadership that prevailed in the period of the cult of the individual, with all their severe consequences, would have again been revived. Our great happiness is that the Party Central Committee promptly exposed and disarmed the anti-Party group, which dared encroach on the unity of our party and its leaders headed by Nikita Sergeyevich Khrushchev, firmly standing on Leninist positions! (Applause.)

One cannot but be indignant at Voroshilov's reaction to the completely just statements by the delegates to our Congress, who are giving a correct political evaluation of the schismatic actions of the anti-Party group, including Voroshilov, an active participant in this group. Despite the grave crimes committed by Voroshilov, the Party Central Committee acted very humanely and magnanimously by leaving him in the Central Committee, and in that period also in the Presidium of the Central Committee. Voroshilov should thank the Central Committee, bow his head before the Party and ask its forgiveness for his crimes. (Applause.) As for Molotov, Kaganovich and Malenkov, they should be immediately expelled from the Party. There is no room for them in our Leninist Party. (Applause.) ...

Pospelov

SPEECH BY COMRADE P.N. POSPELOV, DIRECTOR OF THE PARTY CENTRAL COMMITTEE'S INSTITUTE OF

MARXISM-LENINISM. (Pravda, Oct. 28, pp. 4-5; Izvestia, pp. 3-4. 3,600 words. Condensed text:) ... Soviet society has shown graphically and tangibly that socialism has truly gigantic forces and that mankind has now passed to a new stage of development that affords unusually brilliant possibilities.

And at this greatest turning point in history there have appeared miserable renegades, falsely calling themselves Marxists, who are trying to oppose our Program with anti-Leninist, unworthy and slanderous attacks. These are the Albanian leaders and the chief ideologist of the schismatic anti-Party group, Molotov.

The anti-Party attacks by Molotov against our Program have already been discussed yesterday and today. I would like to dwell on this matter in somewhat more detail. It is known that at the 20th Congress Molotov voted for all the decisions of the Congress. Later, however, he took the course of revising and denying these decisions, approved not only by our party but also by the highly authoritative conferences of the fraternal parties in 1957 and 1960.

Molotov, showing himself to be an unprincipled double-dealer, began opposing not only condemnation of the Stalin cult, not only the Party's policy of eliminating the consequences of the cult of the individual and developing socialist democracy. Molotov opposed the major fundamental proposition of the 20th Party Congress concerning the possibility of averting a new world war in the present epoch. ...

He especially dislikes the way the Program poses the question of the winning over of new hundreds upon hundreds of millions of people to the side of communism—"not through war with other countries but by the example of a more perfect organization of society." It turns out, according to Molotov, that it is precisely through war that we must win over hundreds of millions of people to the side of communism! But this is precisely what our enemies want to impute to us; it is the same "big lie" about the Soviet Union's supposed intentions of promoting the spread of communism to other countries by means of war rather than by force of example that is spread by imperialist propaganda.

In opposing the basic propositions of our Program, based on the major instructions of Vladimir Ilyich Lenin, Molotov is opposing Lenin and breaking with the great Leninist teaching.

Permit me to remind you of Lenin's programmatic instructions, valid for many decades, concerning the question of peaceful coexistence and concerning the fact that socialism has the force of example and will exert its chief influence on the development of the international revolution, on the minds and hearts of peoples of a country, through the successes of its economic construction. Even the first Soviet Decree on Peace contained a powerful appeal to the peoples to put an end to the imperialist war and laid the basis for the peace-loving foreign policy of the socialist state.

After the young Soviet Republic routed the campaign of the 14 imperialist states and defended its existence in the heroic struggle against the hordes of interventionists and White Guards, Lenin unswervingly defended the possibility and necessity of peaceful coexistence of states with different social systems.

Lenin believed—and this can be confirmed by a number of his pronouncements in 1920 and later—that the contradiction between the two systems, the socialist and the capitalist, can and should be resolved not by means of arms, not through war, but by peaceful economic competition, in the course of which socialism would necessarily demonstrate its complete superiority to capitalism. ...

The prophetic words of our great teacher Lenin have come true. And how the influence of our economic successes on the entire course of the historical development of mankind has multiplied now that the world's first country of socialism has become hundreds, thousands of times stronger than in 1921! ...

Molotov does not want to understand this. This is no longer simply dogmatism or ignorance, because surely Molotov could not have forgotten altogether Lenin's great, immortal, crystal-clear instructions. This is a direct thrust at the fundamental propositions of Leninism; it is stupid, factionalist stubbornness, the desire to counterpose at all costs his own rotten, anti-Leninist, factionalist line to the Party's Leninist course.

But there is, after all, a limit to the patience and generosity of the Party: Surely our great Party cannot tolerate in its ranks renegades and schismatics who impudently oppose the major propositions of Leninism, the Leninist course of our party and the great new Program of our party, this now generally recognized Manifesto of the Communist Party of our epoch. Many delegates to the Congress were right in saying that Molotov, Malenkov and Kaganovich cannot be members of our great Leninist party. There is no doubt that the 22nd Congress will unanimously approve the proposal of a number of delegations to exclude these schismatics and factionalists from the Party's ranks. (Applause.) They should be held responsible both for their criminal actions during the period of the Stalin cult and for the attempt to counterpose their own anti-Party, anti-Leninist line, dangerous and harmful to the cause of communism, to the Party's Leninist course!

Some might ask: How could Molotov, a veteran political figure, descend to such shameful political depths?

Our party and its Leninist Central Committee highly value and respect the old members of the Party. The 22nd Congress has vividly demonstrated this. (Applause.) But one must not forget Lenin's well-known remarks to the effect that a Party record in itself affords no guarantee against theoretical and political mistakes. In April, 1917, Lenin spoke indignantly of those so-called "old Bolsheviks" who "more than once played a sorry role in the history of our party, thoughtlessly repeating the memorized formula instead of studying what is unique in the new, living reality."

It is among politicians of this type, stubbornly repeating memorized formulas instead of studying what is unique in the new, living reality, that Molotov belonged and belongs.

I would like to say a few words about the behavior of the Albanian leaders. On behalf of the Central Committee, Comrade Andropov and I attended the Fourth Congress of the Albanian Party of Labor as members of our delegation. The Congress made a painful impression both on us and on the delegations of the fraternal parties. The Congress became a rowdy, noisy, importunate demonstration of the cult of the individual alien to Marxism-Leninism, a demonstration of incredible self-adulation of the Albanian Party of Labor, which supposedly never had made and never would make any mistakes. Yet all Marxist-Leninists should have known Lenin's words on this question: "What applies to individuals applies, with corresponding adjustments, to policy and parties. He is not wise who makes no mistakes. There are and can be no such people. He is wise who makes mistakes that are not very essential and who knows how to rectify them easily and quickly." (Applause.)

The Albanian leaders are slipping more and more toward the most thoroughgoing nationalism, grossly trampling upon the principles of proletarian internationalism and friendship of peoples, and departing more and more from Leninism. Our party has patiently done everything to facilitate the Albanian leaders' return to the path of Party spirit and Party friendship with the C.P.S.U. For example, during the last Congress of the Albanian Party of Labor we encountered a number of glaring instances of direct anti-Soviet attacks by prominent Albanian officials, instances of a humiliating, hostile attitude toward our specialists, geologists and Soviet seamen. On behalf of the Central Committee, we handed the Albanian leaders the following protest and warning on Feb. 20, 1961:

"The Central Committee of our party considers that such instances not only impede the development and strengthening of Albanian-Soviet friendship but also run counter to the interests of the entire socialist camp.

"If these abnormal phenomena are not stopped in good time, they may entail highly serious consequences," our statement said. Do you think this warning brought the Albanian leaders to their senses? No, after this they further intensified their behind-the-scenes, anti-Leninist activity, hostile to the Soviet Union, at the same time hypocritically declaring their alleged friendship with the Soviet people and the C.P.S.U. At the 22nd Congress this hypocritical, double-dealing position of the Albanian leaders has been rightly condemned by our party and representatives of the fraternal parties who spoke from this rostrum. (Applause.) We hope that the Albanian Communists and the Albanian people will draw the appropriate conclusions from this fact and will in the end understand into what a dangerous antirevolutionary swamp they are being dragged by the misguided Albanian leaders.

Comrades! ... Thanks to the Party's concern, the Institute of

Marxism-Leninism has collected the originals and photostats of about 6,000 documents relating to K. Marx and F. Engels and more than 30,000 documents relating to V. I. Lenin. This colossal and priceless ideological wealth is more and more becoming the possession of the people, more and more deeply penetrating the consciousness of the working people.

The institute is reorganizing its work in conformity with the Party Central Committee's instructions on intensifying scientific research on topical problems of Marxist-Leninist theory. Publication of the "History of the Civil War in the U.S.S.R." in five volumes was completed in 1960. Extensive work is under way on the creation of the history of the Great Patriotic War.

Three volumes of the "History of the Great Patriotic War" have now been published and have been received favorably by the Soviet public and press. These volumes provide a comprehensive treatment of the world-historic exploit of the Soviet people, who saved mankind from the threat of fascist enslavement, the exploit of our party, the inspirer and organizer of the great victories of the socialist state over fascism. (Applause.) The Central Committee's main instruction guiding the chief editorial board and the directors of the Institute of Marxism-Leninism in preparing this fundamental work has been to create a history of the Great Patriotic War on the basis of documentary materials. We are carrying out this instruction strictly. Suffice it to say that in preparing the three volumes already published a study was made of more than 4,000 Party and state documents, tens of thousands of documents of the Soviet Army and various agencies and organizations, an enormous amount of Soviet and foreign literature and the memoirs of participants in the war, and many hundreds of consultations were held with direct participants in decisive battles of the Great Patriotic War. The fourth and fifth volumes of "History of the Great Patriotic War" will be published in 1962 and the sixth and final volume in 1963. ...

Upon the decision of the Party Central Committee, the Institute of Marxism-Leninism has begun work on a multivolume history of the C.P.S.U. The Central Committee has approved the chief editorial board for the multivolume Party history and the editorial boards of each of the six volumes. The basic lines of this historical work have been worked out. We expect to issue the first volume in 1963, by the 60th anniversary of the Second Party Congress, which laid the foundations of our great Leninist party. ...

Adzhubei

SPEECH BY COMRADE A. I. ADZHUBEI, EDITOR-IN-CHIEF OF IZVESTIA. (Pravda, Oct. 28, pp. 5-6; Izvestia, pp. 4-5. 4,500 words. words. Condensed text:) ... Recently some Soviet journalists, myself among them, had a talk with President Kennedy. Just think, comrades. The President of the United States—such a wealthy and, I should say, still haughty power—was with pencil in hand figuring out when we would pull ahead of it. If someone had told the American Presidents of the 1920s that their successors would, as early as the 1960s, be totaling up the balance for an economic competition with the Soviet Union and be concerned that that same Russia which at one time they had not even reckoned with as a world factor was going to catch up with the United States and surpass it, such a person would have been contemptuously called a visionary, to say the least. Yet for Kennedy this is no longer a fantasy; it is a worry, and what a worry! (Prolonged applause.)

For us as Communists, comrades, the days this Congress has been meeting have not only meant a great deal of serious, solid work but have also been a joyous celebration, a celebration that none of us will ever forget. But our party has in it people who are not pleased with either our Congress or our strides. That is correct. I'm not wrong about this—they are not pleased! I have in mind the contemptible renegades, the factionalists. They have Party cards in their pockets, but not a grain of Party spirit to their name. I can see them—this one working desultorily, that one retired on a pension—sitting at home sputtering over our 22nd Congress. From this rostrum they have once more been thoroughly discredited. We now see, too, that they have not accepted the 20th Congress, and we now know from Molotov's letter that they do not accept the 22nd Party Congress either.

The factionalists are not simply unprincipled philistines; they take anti-Leninist positions. The most rancorous of them is Molotov. He is attacking the Party for its work all along the line, which includes foreign policy. Anastas Ivanovich Mikoyan has already said in his speech that Molotov is against contacts between our statesmen and Party figures and foreign political figures, is against trips to foreign countries. Holier-than-thou in his "orthodoxy," Molotov warns: "Look out, beware of contacts, they're dangerous, don't make concessions to the world of capitalism."

What can we say to this? Contacts with figures of the capitalist world are a rather complicated, now and then unpleasant, and in some cases simply distasteful undertaking. (Stir in the hall.) Self-isolation is a much easier position. One can, of course, imagine that things actually are in the world as you've invented them in your mind. But the most ordinary people, to say nothing of diplomats, know that this is not so, know that the world has many outstanding problems and unresolved disputes.

To be a Leninist, you must roll up your sleeves and work hard to uphold the validity of your viewpoint. But if you are afraid even to show yourself, if you're not sure of yourself and are capable only of droning out a speech composed of generalities, what sort of fighter for the interests of the Soviet state, the interests of the Party, are you?

Self-isolation is easy. Contacts are harder. But it is contacts that our people need. As for the slanderous prating about "concessions," the best answer is furnished by the numerous testimonies of both our friends and our ill-wishers that the trips abroad made by Party and state figures always result in gains for the Soviet Union, and its international prestige has risen to an unrivaled height. (Stormy, prolonged applause.) ...

In company with journalist colleagues, I was in the United States the times Nikita Sergeyevich Khrushchev was there. These trips were a model of the Leninist blending of firmness and flexibility in the conduct of foreign policy. Nikita Sergeyevich used the same language when he spoke with ordinary Americans, with the President and with representatives of business circles—the language of the Communist. (Stormy applause.) It was his sincerity, straightforwardness and frankness, the total lack of any inclination to, so to speak, tailor his remarks to the audience, that won over the sympathies of millions of Americans, and others as well! (Prolonged applause.)

Two thousand American businessmen came to the Waldorf-Astoria in New York (the city's most sumptuous hotel) for a get-together with the head of the Soviet government in the lavishly gilt ballroom; people fought for tickets to get in. Contacts with people of this kind are, from the standpoint of orthodox squeamishness, something seditious. But these are the people who run the greatest capitalist state in the world; we must talk to them, we have to have dealings with them. Some of these gentlemen had cold looks in their eyes, the eyes of others showed malice and of others good will—because there are people there, too, who appreciate that we are all living on the same planet. White-gloved lackeys scurried about noiselessly; there was a glow of candles. All in all, the atmosphere was frankly not to our taste.

Suddenly, some people starting hissing and catcalling while Comrade Khrushchev was speaking. How does a Communist respond in a case like this?

"Gentlemen," said Nikita Sergeyevich calmly, "since you invited me, I ask you to listen carefully to what I have to say. If you don't want to, nothing says I have to speak. I have not come to the United States as a suppliant. I represent the great Soviet state, the great people that made the Great October Revolution. And no shouted interruptions of yours, gentlemen, can drown out what our great people have achieved, what they have accomplished and what they want to accomplish." (Stormy applause.)

That was really blunt talking, face to face! That was really fighting for our great cause. Here was flexibility blended with firmness!

I recall a day shortly before the 15th session of the General Assembly began its proceedings. The scene was the building on New York's Park Avenue in which the Soviet representatives were housed. You had the impression that it was besieged by at least a division. This was all done on the specious pretext of protecting the Soviet delegation. Well, on this particular day cars bearing the red Soviet flag headed for Harlem, the Negro section, which in the sight of "respectable" American society is inhabited by the outcasts of this world and where it is indecent for "whites" to show themselves.

As you know, the American authorities, who are envenomed against revolutionary Cuba, denied Fidel Castro and his delegation hospitality. Fidel Castro found quarters in a Harlem hotel. And that was where Comrade N. S. Khrushchev drove. When the head of the Soviet government embraced Fidel Castro, we journalists saw tears come to the eyes of this bearded man of iron who feared neither bullet nor bomb and had for years fought in the mountains and swamps. He said: It's very important that the Soviet Union should be embracing Cuba here in the United States. If you only knew how important. This means more than diplomatic recognition. We thank the Soviet Union for it! (Stormy, prolonged applause.)

It is for this that we must cross oceans, comrades! There are hungry people in the world, there are wars raging, French boys and Algerian patriots are dying, mothers are weeping. If we are to be able to give the Cuban people our warm support, if we are to tell the truth about peace, about the anxieties and hopes of the peoples, we need contacts, trips. But some people who consider themselves old hands in politics seem not to understand this. Let these political figures—or rather, political bankrupts—ask our Cuban friends whether or not such contacts are needed?! (Applause.)

The ruling circles of the United States had grown accustomed to look upon the United Nations as their private domain. A nauseating atmosphere of showy solemnity and so-called classic parliamentarism had reigned there for years. The Soviet delegation dispelled this deadly boredom and gave the Western political figures firmly to understand that they would not be able to boss things there forever. To show their attitude to the gentry who devote themselves to deceiving the people, and to shatter the hypocritical stillness, the Soviet delegations and the delegations of the other socialist countries used obstructionist tactics whenever lying, provocative speeches, insulting to the dignity of the socialist camp, the colonies and the states now winning their freedom, were heard from the rostrum of the United Nations. When the fists of the delegates from the socialist camp tired of thumping on the tables in sign of protest, other ways were found to bridle the pharisees and liars.

It may have shocked the ladylike diplomats of the Western world, but it was just great to see Comrade N. S. Khrushchev, when a Western diplomat was once delivering one of these provocative speeches, take off his shoe and start pounding on the table with it. (Stormy applause. Laughter.) It was immediately made plain to all that we were absolutely opposed to such speeches, that we did not want to listen to them! What was more, Nikita Sergeyevich Khrushchev held the shoe in such a position (the delegation seated in front of ours was fascist Spain's) that the tip almost poked Franco's representative in the neck, but not quite. Diplomatic flexibility was shown in this case! (Laughter, stormy applause.) ...

If we linked together the kilometers covered by Nikita Sergeyevich and other Party and state leaders on their trips, we should surely find that they girdle the globe many times over. But the number of kilometers is not the point. We journalists are eyewitnesses, so to speak, chroniclers of events. We have seen millions of people (without exaggeration, millions) come from little villages, come down from the mountains riding oxen and camels, or walking, sometimes hungry and barefoot, to meet Soviet delegations so that they might learn the truth about the happy Land of Soviets.

And if there are people who are displeased, nay, infuriated by the triumph of the trips made abroad by Soviet leaders, these people are our enemies. The Westerners most hostile to us would be happy, would congratulate one another, were a policy of self-isolation to prevail in our country. But it has long been known that if your enemy is in a rage, it means you're right! (Applause.)

Comrades! The short phrase "personal contacts and trips" conceals hard work, work that can frankly be called grueling, on occasion leaving no time for either sleep or rest, work that demands constant concentration, ingenuity, and skill in bringing all the force of argument to bear. It also demands, if you will, personal courage.

When the "Baltika" was on its way to America "unidentified"

submarines hovered close by the vessel at a spot in the Atlantic. When Comrade A. I. Mikoyan was returning from the U.S.A., two of the plane's engines caught fire for "reasons unknown." When Comrade L. I. Brezhnev was making his flight to Africa, an "unidentified" French military aircraft opened fire on the plane "by mistake." Mistake, indeed! No, these are not tourist junkets! These trips are made on the people's behalf and in the people's interest! (Applause.)

Naturally it's easier to stay at home, to sit in your office twirling a globe in front of you and determining the picture of world developments from it, and to substitute pencraft for sharp, face-to-face political discussion.

No, the Party has not taken that road and will not take it. We shall avail ourselves of every opportunity to uphold the national interests of the Soviet Union and to champion world peace, which all peoples yearn for. (Stormy applause.)

With your permission, comrades, I should like to dwell, if only briefly, on a matter that has to do with our internal life. ... I want to talk about relationships between people, about the treatment of people, the consideration shown them.

How many examples could be cited, moving enough to bring tears, of the consideration and concern shown by Soviet people for their comrades both in the line of duty and simply out of their obligations as human beings. ...

But how many letters still come to our editorial office, and to other institutions in Moscow and elsewhere, that it makes you ill to read. A legless invalid wants to exchange a third-floor apartment for one on the ground floor. For months he's given the runaround, although a man living on the ground floor of the same building would be glad to move to the third. ...

Or take the railwayman Fedorov, who had been awarded the Order of Lenin for irreproachable work. He had a few months to go before retiring on a pension. But because he had displeased someone as a "faultfinder" he was not allowed to finish his time and was dismissed. He then began appealing to one place and another—to the Volga Railroad Administration and to the Ministry of Transportation. (The stack of letters is huge.) At last someone in Moscow who had given a letter of his a careful reading sent it to the Stalingrad City Party Committee. We made a special inquiry to learn how much time it had taken to look into the case. A few minutes, and the man had been reinstated in his job!

Why couldn't this have been done right away; why wear a man's nerves to a frazzle? After all, Nikita Sergeyevich Khrushchev correctly noted in his report that the productivity of labor depends in large measure on how well organized things are in our everyday life. This, too, can be said: In the final analysis the productivity of labor also depends on how good a man's spirits are! (Stormy applause.)

I want at once to put in this qualification: I am not talking about the "professional" complainers who want to "get" something they are not entitled to, to get it dishonestly, who want to spoil life for others. Such people must be put in their place! We are not talking about them, however. We are talking about a heartless, thoughtless attitude to people. ...

Lack of sympathy for people, indifference to them are not indictable offenses. But they are indictable before the bar of our, communist, opinion. They are indictable before the bar of Soviet conscience, communist conscience. While we are building our splendid communist edifice and firmly establishing the principles of the moral code in our Program, we must do our utmost to make sure that our life is free of these echoes of the old world. ...

Kucherenko

SPEECH BY COMRADE V. A. KUCHERENKO, PRESIDENT OF THE U.S.S.R. ACADEMY OF CONSTRUCTION AND ARCHITECTURE. (Pravda, Oct. 28, pp. 6-7. 2,800 words. Excerpts:) ... The cities of capitalism are disintegrating. It is not for nothing that the prominent American architect Saarinen called his book "The Development, Growth, Decay and Death of Cities."*

---

*[The book referred to would appear to be Eliel Saarinen's "The City: Its Growth, Its Decay and Its Future."—Trans.]

The 17 countries of capitalist Europe and the U.S.A. built 3,218,000 apartments in 1955 and 3,269,000 apartments in 1960. Thus in five years the annual volume of apartment construction in these countries increased only 1.6%. In 1955 the Soviet Union built about 1,500,000 apartments and in 1960 approximately 3,000,000 apartments—that is, in this same period the volume of apartment construction in our country almost doubled. ...

Today the Soviet urban developer is thought of not as a narrow planner and even less as a mere designer of buildings but as an active participant in the planning and construction of a new way of life. Builders and architects now have all the possibilities for this, for in the period since 1954 a sharp turn has taken place in architecture under the direction of Nikita Sergeyevich Khrushchev, a turn toward mass construction and industrialization of construction, toward an architecture that meets the people's urgent needs.

The struggle, under the Party's leadership, against excesses in architecture was at the same time a struggle against the harmful line in architecture, which was a kind of reflection of the cult of the individual. Kaganovich pursued this line in Moscow, crudely implanting false architectural solutions, as in the case of the Theater of the Soviet Army and certain tall buildings and apartment houses on the main thoroughfares of Moscow. The negative examples of architectural practice in the capital were widely disseminated in the country in this period, impeding the industrialization of construction and deflecting attention from the needs of mass construction for the people. ...

The construction of large residential complexes in the form of microboroughs and of entire residential areas is being more and more widely developed in our country, and in the near future this will become the basic form of residential development in the Soviet Union. It is precisely this form of residential construction that can create the best conditions for developing the personal, community and cultural life of the population.

Yet today there are still substantial shortcomings in this matter. First and foremost, these include the lack of balance between the construction of residential buildings and the construction of service premises and mass public institutions. There is no need to prove that these shortcomings in the construction of residential complexes sharply reduce living conveniences for the people and deprive them for a long time of often urgently needed everyday services. ...

The task of personnel in construction science and of designers now is to base the technology of housing construction combines on architectural and structural solutions of residential and public buildings that will satisfy the requirements of the future and to overcome existing shortcomings in standard designs for large-panel apartment houses more rapidly and ensure their high quality and durability. ...

Beshchev

SPEECH BY COMRADE B. P. BESHCHEV, U.S.S.R. MINISTER OF TRANSPORTATION. (Pravda, Oct. 28, p. 7. 2,900 words. Condensed text:) ... The assignments stipulated in the control figures for basic indices of the seven-year plan—growth of freight movement, increase in labor productivity and reduction in shipping costs—are being met ahead of time. In 1961 freight movement by rail reached 1,570,000,000,000 ton-km.; this is almost double the freight movement on railroads in the U.S.A. (Applause.) ...

I deem it necessary to tell of the criminal activity in railroad transport of one of the participants in the anti-Party group—Kaganovich. His style of work consisted of continuous insulting shouts and threats and every kind of humiliation of human dignity. He surrounded himself with toadies who engaged in informing and denunciations; this created an unbearable situation in work. Passing himself off as a great expert in railroad matters, Kaganovich absolutely refused to tolerate any opposition, even in the solution of purely technical problems.

To further his personal career and establish his own cult in transport, Kaganovich devised the so-called "theory of counter-revolutionary limit-setting on output," with the help of which he organized the mass destruction of engineering and technical cadres. In a short period of time most of the directors of railroads and of the railroads' political departments and many

executive officials of the central apparatus and lines were dismissed from their jobs and later arrested, as Comrade Shvernik has told you in his speech. All this caused great harm and impeded the technical development of railroad transport.

When our country began developing the virgin lands and the question sharply arose of providing housing for the first virgin-land settlers who went to the steppes of Kazakhstan and the Altai, the railwaymen considered it necessary to convert 15,000 old-type closed freight cars into field wagons at enterprises of the Ministry of Transportation. But the former Transport Bureau, headed by Kaganovich, sharply protested. Furthermore, Kaganovich accused the Ministry of Transportation of antistate practices, and of squandering rolling stock. Only after the personal intervention of Nikita Sergeyevich Khrushchev and his incisive criticism of Kaganovich's incorrect actions was the question decided favorably.

Today, when electric and diesel locomotives account for half the freight movement by rail, as against 14.1% in 1955, and when within the next few years no trains at all will be drawn by steam locomotives, how pitiful and ridiculous seems Kaganovich's statement in 1954 at an aktiv meeting of railroad workers in the Kremlin: "I am for the steam locomotive; I am against those who dream that the steam locomotive will disappear from our country."

Contrary to this "prognosis," if you will excuse the term, the production of steam locomotives was soon entirely halted by decision of the Party Central Committee and the Soviet government, and we began introducing new, progressive types of locomotives at a rapid rate. (Applause.) Electrification of the Moscow-Baikal Railroad, which is approximately 5,500 km. in length—the world's largest railroad and the line carrying the most freight—was completed on the eve of the 22nd Party Congress, and today a freight train travels this distance in three days less than with steam traction. (Applause.)

The effect of the shift in traction grows greater with every year. As a result of the introduction of electric and diesel locomotives, shipping costs fell by 2,500,000,000 rubles in 1956-1961, and more than 170,000,000 tons of coal was made available to the national economy for other uses. The reduction in rail shipment costs has created the necessary conditions for reducing freight shipment charges by approximately 20% in the near future. ...

The use of progressive types of traction has brought into being fundamentally new methods of organization of train movement that make possible far better use of rolling stock. Whereas every locomotive used to have a brigade attached to it and stood idle a long time at its turnaround point (and the distance between turnaround points amounted to only 70 to 120 km.), now the locomotive travels up to 1,000 km. without being uncoupled from the train, with a change of brigades on the way. The average 24-hour run of electric and diesel locomotives in 1961 was 50% higher than in 1955. With the former methods of operation, it would require an additional 500 powerful electric or diesel locomotives to handle this year's volume of shipments.

The extensive introduction of new equipment, constant improvement of methods of organization of shipments and development of the creative initiative and activeness of railroad workers have made it possible to increase labor productivity 56% in the past six years. The growth in volume of freight shipments and passenger transportation in this period has been achieved with hardly any increase in the number of personnel. ...

In connection with the sharp rise in oil output in the country, it is very urgent to speed the development of pipelines, by which oil and oil products can be transported almost one-third as cheaply as by rail.

Broad use will be made of highway transport in the country's economy. Many little-used, unprofitable spur lines have been retained from the previous system of departmental subordination, when each enterprise tried to provide its own transportation facilities. There are about 5,000 railroad spur lines in the country with a length of one kilometer or less, on which approximately one to two cars are loaded and unloaded a day. If these lines were dismantled and if trucks were used to deliver this freight from the railroad stations, it would be possible to free roughly 350,000 tons of metal and reduce shipping costs.

Cargo movement by river transport must be increased through bulk shipments. Such shipments should be considerably less costly. Very unfortunately, for certain types of freight they now cost the state more than railroad shipments.

The correct distribution of shipments among the various forms of transportation, along with rationalization of economic ties in the country, will contribute to a considerable reduction in transport expenditures in the national economy, which now total approximately 20,000,000,000 rubles a year. Since the reorganization of the management of industry and construction the average length of rail freight hauls has decreased by 25 km., and 300,000,000 rubles has been saved as a result. ...

The draft Party Program provides for the mass electrification of transport. By the end of the current ten-year period more than 45,000 km. of railroad line will operate on electric traction, and in the following ten years electrification of basic heavily used lines of the network will be completed.

Before us stands the task of utilizing the capital funds allocated for electrification of the railroads sensibly and economically. The progressive system of electric traction on alternating current, under which the expenditure of nonferrous metals is reduced by half and cost of work is greatly lowered, will be predominantly used. Along with continued technical re-equipment of the existing network, the need arises of stepping up the rate of new railroad construction.

Locomotive plants should more rapidly organize the series production of new types of electric rolling stock using alternating current, in particular more powerful main-line electric locomotives and electric units with semiconductor rectifiers, and also diesel locomotives and diesel trains with hydraulic transmission, the production of which yields large savings of copper.

It is very important to increase the production of roller bearings for new railroad car building and modernization of existing cars. Equipment of cars with these bearings will increase the speed of trains, save the national economy 12,000 tons of lead and 250,000 tons of lubricating oils annually, and reduce the expenditure of fuel and electric power for railroad traction approximately 10%. ...

Gribachev

SPEECH BY COMRADE N. M. GRIBACHEV, WRITER AND EDITOR-IN-CHIEF OF THE MAGAZINE SOVETSKY SOYUZ [THE SOVIET UNION]. (Pravda, Oct. 28, pp. 8-9; Izvestia, pp. 5-6. 2,800 words. Condensed text:) ... Here is how America's President Kennedy, a millionaire by birth, uses art and culture for his purposes. Taking advantage of the German problem to rattle the saber, he appeals. in his hostility to communism, for saving the "moral values of the free world" from us, the Communists. This is said with bombast and arrogance. What are these values, though? If, from his lofty perch of authority, the President were to descend to Broadway, that pompous advertisement for Americanism, he would see much that is instructive. He would see counters with books on whose jackets glint numberless knives and pistols, the blood runs thick and corpses rot. He would see film epics in which engagements between gangsters and the police rage on a battlefront scale; horror films in which, as a tribute to the Dark Ages, the heroes are ghosts and vampires; and burlesque films in which women only half-dressed as it is take off the last stitch. A henchman of Hitler's once said: "When I hear the word 'culture' I reach for my gun." Is it not this psychology, this religion of savages, that is served by "moral values" of this sort?

Of course, this cesspit aspect is not all there is to American life; of course, genuinely gifted people and distinguished cultural figures blaze up and shine even in the twilight of bourgeois culture. But their lives are full of vicissitudes, and their works appear in pitifully small editions, while vulgarity and cynicism are produced on a conveyer-belt basis and blanket the country.

Can a government that keeps true art enchained and encourages these floods of filth, this mass spiritual poisoning—can such a government lay claim to being the savior of culture? The only thing one can say to this is, "Physician, heal thyself!"

No, the real homeland of contemporary culture is socialism, the Soviet land. It is we who lead the world in the output of books; the works of Mark Twain are published in larger and more complete editions in our country than in America, the works of Balzac in larger editions than in France and those

of Shakespeare and Dickens than in England. And the day will come—perhaps it is not far off now—when the peoples of the present-day capitalist West will tender us, the people of socialism, their deepest thanks for thus honoring their true spiritual riches and keeping them alive for the living. (Stormy applause.) ...

Today we face not lesser but perhaps even greater tasks. Events have quickened their pace, man and the world have grown more complicated, the laws of development have rendered many esthetic formulas obsolete, the level of education and hence the demands of the readers have risen immeasurably. We shall have to work hard and do much searching, although the ultimate goal has been clearly and incisively formulated in the Party Program and N. S. Khrushchev's reports, to record our great life with artistic truth, to create the images of our contemporaries, who are boldly building a new society, refashioning the world and storming the heavens. (Stormy applause.)

Our present literary forces, reinforced with new talent, are capable of accomplishing this. A few years ago, it is true, our literature was fever-racked, because a small group of writers had swallowed the undisguised bait of the Western fishers of souls. Demands were put forward at that time, and sometimes by Communists, for a revision of the Party line in literature, for the elimination of the Party's influence on literature; there were even demands that everything written, however it was written, be published, and without editing, since, as one of the proponents of this view put it "the writer has the right to ravings." On the whole, this was the literary metastasis of revisionism. The Central Committee of the C.P.S.U., and in particular Nikita Sergeyevich Khrushchev, with his explosive polemic temperament and his wonderful restraint and good sense in practical matters, gave our literature quick and effective help. The storm that swept over us one summer day washed away the rubbish, freshened the air and was followed by fine weather.* (Prolonged applause.)

The general ideological health of our literature is normal today. But the passage of time has made certain improvements a matter of urgency. In the first place, in criticism. Some of our critics, having slept through reveille, still harbor in their bosoms the grudge of narrow group interests. And although this is dangerous and degrading for themselves most of all, literature, too, is none the better for it. And in the second place, most of the older critics have gone off into literary scholarship, while the labors of the young ones often boil down to mere descriptive reviews; since a practical esthetic is at present poorly developed, they pass hit-or-miss judgments, quite often lauding what has never merited praise—philistine melodrama, pseudo-innovation, vulgar sentimentality. It is the vagueness of the critics' premises and their inability to make of a critical judgment an instrument for influencing art and educating the public that above all explain the appearance of a great many dull, insignificant works. For what you encourage is what you get. The lame theory even exists that there are no petty themes, there is only deficient skill. But Leo Tolstoy, back in his day, derided writers who did not aspire to great generalizations, writing of them: "A muzhik comes along, they describe a muzhik; a pig wallows, they describe it, etc. But is this art? Where is the inspiring thought that makes truly great works immortal?" The stop signal for petty themes and mere copying of life, and the green light for works in which our new man lives, creates, struggles, loves and hates at white heat—it is criticism that must press the switch! To achieve this we must on the one hand create an atmosphere of public respect for our critics, and on the other hand we must call upon them for work that is objective, inspired, and intelligent in both substance and form.

The problem of youth has generated much passion. But when the Young Communist League Central Committee had a frank talk recently with young poets, it was clearly evident that the

*[The reference is to remarks made by Khrushchev at a reception of writers and artists in May, 1957; Current Digest of the Soviet Press, Vol. IX, No. 35, pp. 3-10. These were later described by him at a meeting of intellectuals in July, 1960, as a summer storm; Current Digest of the Soviet Press, Vol. XIII, No. 17, p. 3.]

overwhelming majority of them are prepared to invest their energies in the common effort of construction. The talk to the effect that young people have some sort of special orientation benefits only the philistines and was started by them, but in the view of many serious writers it is being fanned and exaggerated by the irresponsibility of Literaturnaya gazeta, which has been giving too little attention to the national literatures and has been dealing poorly with esthetic problems, while on the other hand it has been regularly engaging in unsavory sensations. (Applause.)

It is time to stop playing up the little brawls that are started by persons of no great intellect, and at the same time to stop harping on the subject of narrow trousers—which, by the way, are being worn by most of the men here. (Amused stir in the hall. Applause.) It would be more helpful to explain to young writers that mere verbal eccentricities and boudoir lyrics will earn them neither honor nor glory among the people. And for that matter, it would not be amiss to take a serious look at the problem of innovation; some examples of such innovation could be new only for those who have not read the poems of Khlebnikov and Tsvetayeva carefully and have not properly digested Hemingway and Remarque. Other innovations are for all the world like square wheels—they look original enough, but take a ride and they'll shake the soul out of you. (Laughter. Applause.) There are costs of another sort that our poetry is having to pay. An American schoolboy, confused on an examination, said that there are three kinds of poetry—dramatic, lyric and epidemic. (Laughter. Applause.) It seems to me that the numberless high-flown poems in celebration of holidays and drives are taking on the character of just such epidemic poetry. Their language is tinselly, their rhymes are forced, there is hardly a drop of feeling in them and the ideas are cribbed from an article published a few days back. Editors just dote on these poems—why, the article brought a response! —but they leave the readers cold. (Applause.) We are for drawing upon all fruitful traditions and we are for searchings in the area of depictive devices, but we also want to see those searchings soberly weighted against the serious touchstones of art. We are for all types of poetry, including publicistic and political poetry, but it must be poetry, not soulless, mindless twaddle. (Applause.)

It is time our literature was disencumbered of its heavy schedule of meetings, which is having a desiccating effect on it. Here is how the matter stands in the Moscow writers' organization. It has six sections which hold meetings—fiction, poetry, translation, criticism, drama and children's literature; the six bureaus of these sections hold meetings; the six Party organizations of these six sections hold Party meetings; the Moscow organization as a whole holds meetings; the board of that organization holds plenary sessions; the presidium of the board holds meetings; there are gatherings of the Party organization as a whole and meetings of the Party committee. And here are figures that come from the Party committee itself: about 70 meetings a month and about 40 writers' club activities.

Where, then, are people to find time for thought, for writing? (Applause.)

It would be far better if, for example, instead of this helter-skelter, magazines, publishing houses, newspapers, theaters and film studios were to have writers' groups set up under them, with Communist writers registered at those same places, closer to actual work on their manuscripts and to public activities. And let these groups compete to bring honor to their magazines, newspapers, film studios, and so forth. (Applause.) By the way, the designers and physicists have no special Party organizations, you know, and their business is none the worse for it: They have already gone into space! (Amused stir in the hall. Applause.) ...

Tvardovsky

SPEECH BY COMRADE A. T. TVARDOVSKY, WRITER AND EDITOR-IN-CHIEF OF THE MAGAZINE NOVY MIR. (Pravda, Oct. 29, p. 7. 5,000 words. Excerpts:) ... The years since our party's 20th Congress have been years of a creative upsurge

among the masses, of fruitful labor. For Soviet literature this has been a period of spiritual renewal, as it were, of deliverance from a certain constraint or confinement imposed on it by the well-known antihumane features associated with the cult of the individual. Suffice it to say that in this period, in company with the thousands of people to whom the Party, having dethroned the cult of the individual, restored honor and life, many of our fellow writers have regained their literary reputations and their place in the history of Soviet literature. (Applause.) ...

For many of us, making the serious and highly complicated ideological turn that has marked the period since the 20th Congress has not been an easy or simple matter. ... The difficulties that this shift in the minds and sentiments of our literary people inevitably entailed have been surmounted. But some vestigial forms, as they say, of the thinking peculiar to the days of the cult of the individual, of habits in the actual practice of literature, in writing, in the methods of portraying our reality, are still to be encountered. This must be talked about in all frankness, without mincing words. ...

Wherein lies the basic defect in our literature, to be seen today with particular clarity in the light of the full content and message of our 22nd Congress? It lies in its holding back, its incomplete depiction of the manifold processes under way in life, of the various sides of life and of the problems it is raising—in plain terms, its lack of depth and truth in dealing with life. ...

How often does our exacting reader, having finished a book devoted to a particular sector of reality with which he is on terms of practical familiarity—how often does he mentally turn to the writer, reproachfully and deploringly: "What are you trying to tell me here? I know more about all this than you do, and you either don't know much or you know but are holding something back, have sidestepped it because your courage failed you." This is a terrible indictment of a book, and one that quite often is delivered not only mentally but in the form of a letter to the author or a public statement at a readers' conference or on some other occasion. And it should be noted that our advanced reader is not hypercritical; he is prepared to forgive the writer an occasional technical or factual inaccuracy in the details of a portrayal (provided, of course, it is not too striking), but he has an organic inability to tolerate untruth in what really counts, in what is essential. ...

Yes, the lack in many of our books is first of all a lack of the truth of life, a wariness on the author's part as to what is permissible and what is not—i.e., mistrust of the reader. "I'm smart," the writer thinks, "I understand everything, but he might suddenly misunderstand something and stop fulfilling the plan." All this is nothing but a concession to the tactics and customs of those years in our development that were marked in general by a spirit of mistrust and suspicion, a spirit especially deadly to art. Mistrust of the reader is a grave sin, and one that is certain to leave its mark on the quality of a book and to rob it of its power to influence the human heart. ...

The reader is acutely in need of the whole truth about life. Evasiveness and dissembling in a writer sicken him. Nikita Sergeyevich frankly says, for example, that the cup of plenty without which communism is unthinkable is not yet full, but it will be full—we all believe this. But if an artist or journalist assures the reader that at this very moment the cup is brimful or even overflowing, this can provoke nothing but irritation and a sneer in the reader. The essential contact between writer and reader is broken, and this is irreparable. We must not resort to this, we must not fight shy of showing difficulties. This is essential not only in the direct furtherance of our great work of construction but also because it involves the emotional, the psychological side of the Soviet toiler, the builder of a new life. ...

In our writings, while reciting the labor deeds of our marvelous soldiers, the people, we often have not a word to say about the privations and hardships they are enduring on their great march. We wound their pride, the rightful pride of people who are coping with difficulties and marching unswervingly toward their high, chosen goal. But we should be reinforcing this feeling of pride in them, paying tribute to their courage, stamina, patience, high-minded unselfishness and readiness to make sacrifices when the need arises. (Applause.) And this we can do only by a thoroughly honest, true-to-life portrayal of the labors and exploits of our people, without varnishing and without any crafty smoothing over of contradictions. I think this is precisely what we are committed to by the lines in the Program that speak of the need for strengthening literature's ties with life and for portraying the many sides of our reality truthfully and with high artistry.

The cult of the individual is gone, but its inertia, its vestigial echoes are still in evidence, unfortunately, in literature and in our press generally. One cannot help, for example, regarding as such vestigial components of the cult of the individual the note of intemperate bragging that now and then erupts in our press and the wish to see only the Sundays in life, the red-letter days, and to lose sight, as it were, of all the working days of the week, filled with labor, cares and needs. ...

Writers have been called the Party's right-hand helpers. This is a lofty title and one that imposes great responsibility, but it can be understood in different ways. Some think that to be the Party's helper means to provide the accompaniment to well-known Party tenets and economic and production tasks set by the Party, to illustrate them with "the means of artistic depiction." How this looks in practice is roughly as follows: "The bright rays of the setting sun still gilded the tops of the birches on the farmstead of the Road to Communism Collective Farm when milkmaid Grunya, after reckoning the possibilities, decided to milk so-and-so many liters above the pledges she had made." (Laughter. Applause.) It may not look so primitive in all cases, of course, but in essence the illustrative method strips down to just this sort of "artistic rendering." The flimsiness of the method is obvious.

It's a different story when a writer's keen and searching eye has discerned something important in life, something new that may not even have been mentioned in Party documents or Pravda editorials, and he comes out honestly and boldly, from a Party position, with his observations, with his ideas and even his conclusions. That's being a real helper of the Party. (Applause.)

Recall Valentin Ovechkin's sketch "District Working Days," published on the eve of the September, 1953, plenary session of the Party Central Committee, the impact it had on the readers and the fine service it performed. In it the author, showing great knowledge of his subject, broached the question of the deplorable management of the collective farms in those years. It was a serious and helpful statement, and the reader assessed it according to its deserts.

But the Party and our society as a whole expect more from literature than just this kind of immediate practical testimony on the country's economic life, its production life. These expectations and demands are considerably broader; they cover the spiritual life of our people, all their joys and sorrows, cares and wishes, not only in their working lives but in their home life, in the relationships of the family, of love and of fatherhood and motherhood—they cover, in short, the full complexity of life as it is. ...

I quite agree with Comrade Furtseva that it would be a good thing to urge some writers, young ones especially, to spend some time "out in the world," as they say, and in the case of certain of them, perhaps even to see for themselves that loaves of bread do not grow in the Gorky Street delicatessen but come into being under somewhat different circumstances.

That's all very well, but the geography of a writer's residence in and of itself is not crucial. (Applause.) After all, one can live, say, at Yerofey Pavlovich Station—there is such a place in the Far East—or even in a skin tent somewhere in Chukotka and still lead an ivory-tower life. ...

I was born and grew up in the country; for many years I lived "in the provinces," so to speak, and I am simply unable to write without every so often going out there. But the conception of Moscow as a kind of Babylon, full of all sorts of temptations and supreme vanities, and as the antithesis, as it were, to the righteous life seems to me hardly valid. As though Moscow were not the center of the country's political and cultural life, were not one of the most important sectors of our construction, as though it did not provide wonderful and extremely rich material for studying life in all its most intricate interweavings. We are very badly in need, incidentally, of a novel, and perhaps several novels, in which our Moscow would be pictured—socialist and communist Moscow, all its strata

and from all angles, as Balzac pictured Paris at the time of the bourgeoisie's ascent to power.

People are perplexed, similarly, when the theme of the present day in literature comes to be discussed. Who among us is against the present-day theme? There are none such, but it is understood to mean different things. Some comrades are inclined to limit the concept of the contemporary to this year, or even the past six months. What has happened since the January plenary session is contemporary, while what happened before it is by now the remote past, and they say, if an artist turns to last year's events for his material, this is lagging behind life. To be sure, these opinions are not couched in just these terms, but some people tend to interpret themes of the day as essentially meaning just this, and in their struggle to keep up with the calendar they tend to lower their standards with respect to the excellence of idea content and artistry, the quality of their works. Thus the reader's interests are often openly slighted, and the book market receives half-baked works that are incapable of affecting minds deeply and that on occasion simply compromise the contemporary theme.

This is to say nothing of the fact that every day and year, each period of the nearly half-century of our development, constitutes an imperishable value, is of worldwide interest and can successfully serve as an object to be portrayed in art. ...

A few words about the contemporary hero of our literature. It seems to me a big shortcoming in the portrayal of the contemporary hero in literature that although this hero is usually shown more or less correctly as far as his actions and judgments are concerned, although he embodies all the virtues he is supposed to have, he is often lacking in one simple indispensable quality—human charm, the charm of a generous heart, of goodness, nobility, love of people, all the things that endear our favorite fictional heroes to us.

Sometimes you read a book and get to know its protagonist; the author tries his best to present him as a model person, and from all indications he really is such: He knows his job, he overfulfills his plan, he knows how to organize people, to place them properly, etc. But picture having occasion to travel with him to Vladivostok in the same compartment: It's something you would not wish to do, it would be dull, you find the thought distasteful. Our favorite heroes, on the other hand, we usually seem to project from the pages of a book or the stage of a theater into the circle of our immediate friends; we feel their presence, live with them and are prepared to find ourselves not only in the same train compartment with them but, should it turn out that way, in the same foxhole, under fire, at a moment of danger and of the sternest testing of our spirit. (Applause.) ...

While the arguments go on about what the contemporary hero in literature should be like, in real life and in his work he behaves as he actually is, without regard to what he is supposed to be like according to the prescriptions and conceptions of some of our critics and writers. He raises grain, fattens herds, smelts metal, erects giant dams, teaches children, treats the sick, explores outer space—in a word, he is busy with the real work of a present day pointed into the future.

What sort of a person is he, what does he look like, how old is he? We need not go far to find out. Let us take a look at our Congress: Here they are, the contemporary heroes of all vocations, positions and titles—from the Minister and the general to the miner and the milkmaid, from the machine operator and the builder to the Academician and the Cosmonaut. Every one of them a book, and what a splendid, stirring book! (Applause.)

But although there are about five thousand of the country's heroes here, does this represent all of them? No, it can safely be said that if there are thousands of them here, there are tens and hundreds of thousands, millions more of them outside the walls of this vast auditorium.

And our writers, artists and cinematographers have all this wealth of human types and characters at their disposal. Our finest and most gifted colleagues in the bourgeois world could not in the past and cannot now even dream of such opportunities. ...

There are still in our reality phenomena that counteract our advance and that our literature must expose, as the Program states. This is a task, of course, for all genres and forms of literature.

But there is one potent weapon above all that we should not neglect in this struggle—the weapon of laughter. Here, once again, one cannot help speaking of the imprint of moroseness, of a certain unsmiling quality, that has remained from the time when we were frequently in no mood for laughter, as they say. But here too, incidentally, we have an extremely rich classical literary tradition—Griboyedov, Gogol, Herzen, Saltykov-Shchedrin, Chekhov. The objection may be raised that their satire drew its characters and accusatory inspiration from the sea of social monstrosities and contrasts that was the old Russian reality of serfdom and the bourgeoisie. But one mustn't think that human folly, egoism, small-mindedness, conceit and that direct inheritance from the past, bureaucracy in its various forms and modifications, at once disappear of themselves with the elimination of social contrasts.

And finally, besides angry, sarcastic and unforgiving laughter, there is the laughter of joy, of friendly well-wishing, of gay and unoffending mischievousness. Far from fading, the need for this kind of laughter becomes still greater in man as he advances on the road to happiness. I feel like saying "Make way for laughter!" except that it sounds so terribly serious. ...

Other Speakers

[In the interests of space, speeches by those listed below have been omitted from this chapter. Translations of their speeches may be found in The Current Digest of the Soviet Press, Vol. XIII, Nos. 48-52, and Vol. XIV, Nos. 1-6.

[October 19.—P. N. Demichev, First Secretary, Moscow City Party Committee.

[October 20.—M. V. Keldysh, President, U.S.S.R. Academy of Sciences; I. G. Kabin, First Secretary, Estonian Communist Party Central Committee.

[October 21.—V. V. Grishin, Chairman, Central Council of Trade Unions; A. V. Gitalov, tractor brigade leader at 20th Party Congress Collective Farm, Kirovograd Province; M. I. Rozhneva, assistant foreman at Kupavna Fine Fabric Mill, Moscow Province Party organization; G. I. Vorobyev, First Secretary, Krasnodar Territory Party Committee.

[October 23.—V. I. Gaganova, brigade leader at Vyshny Volochek Cotton Combine, Kalinin Party organization; A. P. Shitikov, First Secretary, Khabarovsk Territory Party Committee; V. M. Kavun, Chairman of Stalin Collective Farm, Bershad District, Vinnitsa Party organization.

[October 24.—V. V. Grachev, chairman of collective farm at village of Kalinovka, Kursk Party organization; G. G. Abramov, First Secretary, Moscow Province Party Committee.

[October 25.—V. A. Smirnov, assembly worker at Sergo Ordzhonikidze Baltic Shipyard, Leningrad Party organization; V. V. Krotov, Director, Urals Machine-Building Plant, Sverdlovsk Party organization; Z. N. Nuriyev, First Secretary, Bashkir Province Party Committee; A. A. Kolchik, brigade leader at mine of Chistyakovo Anthracite Trust, Stalino Party organization; I. A. Kairov, President, Russian Republic Academy of Pedagogy.

[October 26.—V. E. Dymshits, First Vice-Chairman, U.S.S.R. State Planning Committee; F. A. Tabeyev, First Secretary, Tatar Province Party Committee; G. A. Nalivaiko, Director, Altai Agricultural Research Institute; G. S. Titov, U.S.S.R. Cosmonaut, Moscow Province Party organization.

[October 27.—M. T. Yefremov, First Secretary, Chelyabinsk Province Party Committee; I. T. Novikov, U.S.S.R. Minister of Power Plant Construction; B. V. Ioganson, President, U.S.S.R. Academy of Arts; M. A. Olshansky, U.S.S.R. Minister of Agriculture; A. Ye. Korneichuk, writer and Vice-Chairman of Soviet Peace Committee.]

IX. KHRUSHCHEV: CONCLUDING REMARKS

CONCLUDING REMARKS BY COMRADE N. S. KHRUSHCHEV, FIRST SECRETARY OF THE PARTY CENTRAL COMMITTEE, AT 22ND PARTY CONGRESS OCT. 27, 1961. (Pravda and Izvestia, Oct. 29, pp. 1-3. Complete text:) Comrade delegates! The discussion of the report of the Party Central Committee and the report on the program of the Communist Party of the Soviet Union, which has proceeded on a high political plane, has come to an end. Many delegates to the Congress have spoken from this rostrum. What may be said about these speeches? I think you will agree with me that every one of them can be called a kind of report, an accounting to the Party. Everyone who has mounted this rostrum has spoken of the most exciting and the most essential things that have been accomplished and that remain to be accomplished. These speeches have been pervaded with unshakable faith in the triumph of communism. (Prolonged applause.)

The speakers have unanimously endorsed both our Central Committee's political line and practical activities and our party's draft Program—the program for building communism. The 22nd Congress has been a most striking demonstration of the unity of our Leninist party and of the solidarity of all the Soviet people in their support of it. (Applause.)

The whole content of its proceedings has confirmed the unshakable allegiance of the 22nd Congress to the Party line that was framed by the 20th Congress. (Applause.) It has now become even more abundantly clear that the 20th Congress, by clearing away all the aftergrowth of the period of the cult of the individual, opened a new chapter in the history of our party and had a wholesome effect on the development of our country and of the entire world Communist and workers' movement. (Applause.)

The focus of attention at our Congress is the Party Program—the program for building a communist society. All the delegates to the Congress who have spoken from this rostrum have not only approved the draft Program submitted by the Central Committee but have discussed in businesslike fashion concrete practical ways of translating it into reality. They have expressed firm confidence that the new Program will be successfully implemented, that Soviet people are prepared to do their utmost to carry out our party's third Program as successfully as they carried out its first and second Programs. (Prolonged applause.)

The strength and the vitality of our Program derive from the devoted labor of Soviet people. What joy and pride one feels listening to the speeches of such wonderful innovators as Valentina Gaganova, Alexander Kolchik, Maria Rozhneva, Vasily Kavun, Vasily Smirnov, Alexander Gitalov and many others. How much initiative, resourcefulness, knowledge and perseverance in labor have our leading workers been showing in the performance of their duty to the homeland and to the people. The millions of such innovators are the flower and pride of our Soviet society. (Applause.)

It is extremely important today that at every plant, factory and construction project, on every collective and state farm, the efforts of all working people be directed toward fulfillment and overfulfillment of production plans. The higher productivity and quality are, the more values will be created; and the more values there are, the more rapidly will the Soviet people stride toward the great goal—the building of a communist society. (Applause.)

Speeches have been made at the Congress by representatives of all the republics and many of the territories and provinces of our country—Party and Soviet officials, leading workers in industry and agriculture—our wonderful beacons, as they are called figuratively; the Congress has heard from scientists and scholars, writers and workers in the arts, and representatives of our glorious armed forces.

The delegates have given their views on the basic problems of communist construction. They have spoken of the ways and means of building the material and technical base of communism; of urgent matters relating to the work of industry and the further development of agriculture; of the prospects for still greater progress in science, culture, education, art and literature in our country; on the tasks involved in molding the man of the new communist society. All these questions have been dealt with in thoroughgoing and comprehensive fashion at the Congress. Today, at the 22nd Congress, we see even more clearly that the building of communism has become the practical task of the Party, the cause of the whole Soviet people. (Applause.)

The delegates' speeches have been marked by a high level of principle, businesslike content and intolerance of shortcomings. The comrades have rightly called attention to the need for comprehensive development of the productive forces of Soviet society, for improving the planning and organization of production and methods of economic management, and for making proper use of the reserves of industry and agriculture. They have made suggestions that in substance aim at obtaining maximum economic results with minimum expenditures of labor.

Important problems entailed in further improving the management of the national economy have come up in the discussion of the Central Committee's report and of the draft Program. The Congress has shown that the Party is unanimous in approving the measures that the Central Committee and the government have carried through in this field in the past few years. In particular, the establishment of the economic regions and the organization in amalgamated economic regions of councils for coordinating and planning the work of the economic councils have found general support.

The measures that the Party Central Committee and the government have carried out in agriculture in the past few years have met with the unanimous approval of the delegates to the Congress.

We have heard a good many brilliant and cogent speeches here. The suggestions that have been placed before the Congress on various matters relating to the advancement of the economy, science and culture and to the working conditions and everyday lives of Soviet people deserve all possible support. It is difficult even to enumerate all the valuable suggestions that have been put forward in the course of the discussion.

Comrade Keldysh rightly emphasized, for example, the necessity of undertaking the organization of joint scientific institutions in the economic regions and the Union republics.

Comrade Rozhneva raised the question of eliminating night shifts for women. This is a big problem. As you yourselves realize, to solve it completely will require time and the necessary conditions. The Central Committee and the government will take the matter up and do everything possible to solve this problem. (Applause.)

Comrade Gitalov rightly underscored the need for really

broad dissemination of the results of experience in the integrated mechanization of agricultural work.

A number of other important suggestions have been put before the Congress in the course of the discussion. The implementation of these proposals will undoubtedly facilitate the successful accomplishment of the tasks facing us. The Central Committee, the Council of Ministers and local Party and Soviet agencies should study all these suggestions carefully and take the required action.

Comrades! Present at our Congress are delegations from nearly all the Communist and Workers' Parties of the world. The speeches made from this rostrum by our dear guests and the messages of greeting received by the Congress from fraternal parties have reflected the great unity that exists in the ranks of the world Communist movement and have once again demonstrated that the Leninist policy of our party is approved and supported by all Marxist-Leninist parties. (Prolonged applause.)

On behalf of the Congress, on behalf of our whole party and the Soviet people, let me express our deep and heartfelt appreciation to the Communist and Workers' Parties of the world for their high appraisal of the activities of the Communist Party of the Soviet Union and of its role in the international Communist and workers' movement for their confidence and wishes of success in translating our new Program into reality. (Stormy applause.)

Let me assure you, our dear foreign comrades and brothers, that in the future as well the Communist Party of the Soviet Union will carry high the great banner of Marxism-Leninism and with still greater energy will build communism, which will see the reign of Peace, Labor, Freedom, Equality, Brotherhood and Happiness for all peoples. (Prolonged applause.)

The speeches delivered at our Congress by the leaders of the Communist and Workers' Parties of the countries in the socialist camp have shown that the fraternal parties are unanimously committed to the Declaration of 1957 and the Statement of 1960. The socialist camp has once more demonstrated the monolithic solidarity of its ranks and the growth and cohesion of the forces of world socialism. (Applause.)

The presence at the 22nd Congress of delegations from 80 Marxist-Leninist parties and their speeches here have reflected the mighty upsurgence of the international Communist and workers' movement and of the movement of national liberation and the inviolable allegiance of the Communists of all lands to the principles of proletarian internationalism bequeathed to us by Marx, Engels and Lenin. (Prolonged applause.) We all rejoice to see the forces of champions of the people's happiness, of peace and social progress, of communism gaining strength and becoming steeled in all corners of the globe! (Applause.)

On behalf of our Congress, comrades, let me heartily thank the representatives of the democratic national parties of the independent African states of Guinea, the Republic of Ghana and the Republic of Mali. These parties are not Communist, but we are glad that they accepted our invitation and have sent their delegations to the 22nd Congress. Representatives of these parties are attending our Congress and can see and hear the things that the Communists are engaged in, the tasks they are setting themselves.

We ask these delegations, when they return home, to convey to their parties and peoples the very best wishes from our Congress and from the Soviet people. (Prolonged applause.) The whole Soviet population wishes great success and prosperity to the sovereign African states that have taken or are taking the road of independent economic and political development. (Applause.)

Comrades! In their speeches at the Congress the delegates have expressed approval of the Soviet government's foreign policy. The matters brought up in the Central Committee's report and the report on our party's Program are also being discussed outside the walls of this auditorium. Furthermore, not only our friends but our adversaries as well are participating in the discussion. They too are having their say about the foreign and domestic policies of our party and are assessing them from their own class standpoints.

The successes of the Soviet Union and all the socialist countries have a great attractive force. Like the sunrise, they illumine the right road for other peoples, the road that will lead them in the briefest historic period to the victory of the most equitable of social systems.

Appreciating this, the imperialists would like to stay our swift progress. It is this that explains the aggressive character of the policy pursued by the ruling circles of the United States, Britain, France, West Germany and other imperialist powers. Their policy is being shaped not in the interests of peace and of tranquility for people but in the interests of profits for the monopolists, in the interests of maintaining the domination of the imperialists. To this end they seek to heighten tension in international relations and are obstructing the peaceful settlement of urgent international problems.

Let us take, for instance, the problem of doing away with the vestiges of the second world war in Europe. Further procrastination in solving it is fraught with grave consequences for the cause of peace.

The Soviet Union has long proposed concluding a German peace treaty and on that basis normalizing the situation in West Berlin and eliminating the occupation regime there. The Soviet Union wishes to create conditions for peaceful coexistence in Central Europe.

What could be more just than this aim? Are we threatening anyone, or seeking to take anything away from the West? We are not. With the signing of a peace treaty, relations among the states of Europe will be normalized and the peoples will be in a better position to develop neighborly relations.

But in response to our peace-loving proposals the Western powers have openly threatened to take up arms against us.

The Western powers are now condescendingly "explaining" that the Soviet Union may, if you please, conclude a peace treaty with the German Democratic Republic, but that it does not have the right to repudiate commitments entered into by the victorious allies at the time of Hitlerite Germany's defeat.

What commitments are they talking about? Perhaps the commitments to eradicate German militarism and revanchism, which the Soviet government is really making an effort to do, and which the allies committed themselves to do at the end of the second world war? No, they are not talking about the commitments that we and the Western powers jointly assumed at Yalta and Potsdam, and which they have long since sacrificed to NATO's military plans. By threatening war they want to force us to perpetuate U.S., British and French occupation rights in West Berlin.

What need have they of these rights today, one may ask, more than 16 years after the end of the war? The Western powers would have us believe that they need these rights "to safeguard the freedom" of West Berlin. But no one is seeking to encroach on West Berlin's freedom—neither the Soviet Union, nor the German Democratic Republic, nor the other socialist countries.

The Western powers speak of "freedom" but what they mean by this is the occupation of West Berlin. They want to keep their armed forces there and to maintain centers for intelligence activities, which is to say that they want to go on using West Berlin for hostile subversive activities against the German Democratic Republic, against the Soviet Union, against all the socialist countries. This is their real objective, and it is for the sake of this objective that they cling to their outdated occupation rights. And they would like us to abet them in this in the bargain!

They want us to act as traffic controllers and guarantee uninterrupted transportation of their military goods, spies and saboteurs to West Berlin for subversive activities against us and our allies.

What do these gentlemen take us for? Can they really have come to believe that they can do anything they like, that they can get us to act contrary to our vital interests, contrary to the interests of world peace and security?

It is time, high time, they grasped the simple truth that the Soviet Union and the socialist camp as a whole can today be talked to only from a position of reason, not from a position of strength. (Prolonged applause.) And reason and justice are on our side, not theirs.

No sane person will understand, or agree, that the Western powers have some sort of legal or moral right to attack us in retaliation for the signing of a German peace treaty and the termination of the occupation regime in West Berlin. Millions of Americans, Britons and Frenchmen—and people of all other nations—will roundly curse those who dare to start a war over the conclusion of a German peace treaty! (Applause.)

The policy of the Western powers on the German question is governed not by the interests of peace but first and foremost by the interests of the militarist and revanchist forces of West Germany. The chief demon behind this policy is Chancellor Adenauer.

The aggressive militarist circles make no secret of their hatred for the Soviet state and for our peaceful foreign policy. This does not surprise us a bit. We cannot expect the imperialists ever to like our social system. But whatever feelings they may harbor about socialism, let them renounce hope of ever imposing their capitalist ways on the socialist countries. (Applause.) We can once more say to them today: Don't take leave of your senses, gentlemen; don't try to test the strength and stability of our system. (Prolonged applause.) In the past, as we know, enemies have made more than one such attempt, and everyone is aware of how these attempts ended. (Applause.)

As was noted in the Central Committee's report, the Soviet government holds that if the Western powers show a willingness to settle the German problem, the matter of a deadline will not be so important. We shall not then insist on the signing of a treaty before Dec. 31. We are not superstitious people, and we believe that both the figures 31 and 13 can be lucky. (Stir in the hall. Applause.) What counts most is not the particular date but a businesslike and honest settlement of the question. We want the Western powers to recognize the necessity of doing away with the vestiges of the second world war for the sake of preserving peace on earth, in the interest of all countries, in the interest of all humanity. (Applause.)

We stand ready to meet with representatives of the Western countries, to exchange views with them, so that the groundwork may be laid for fruitful negotiations. But it is essential that real preparations be made for the negotiations, and that there be a desire to reach an agreement, so that mutually acceptable solutions to the problems involved in eliminating the vestiges of the second world war may be found through round-table talks in which all the interested countries participate.

But the Soviet Union will not stand for the holding of talks merely for the sake of holding talks, will not stand for letting the representatives of the Western countries take advantage of them to delay a peace settlement in Europe. If anyone is pinning his hopes on this, let him know beforehand that such hopes are not to be realized. This is our position. We have held to it, and we shall continue to hold to it firmly. (Prolonged applause.)

Bourgeois propaganda has recently been making a big fuss over the nuclear tests that the Soviet Union has been forced to resume. This clamor became quite hysterical after it was announced at the Congress that testing of a 50-megaton nuclear weapon was scheduled. Voices are being heard alleging that these tests are immoral.

Strange logic! When the United States first developed the atom bomb, it considered itself legally and morally justified in dropping it on the defenseless people of Hiroshima and Nagasaki. This was an act of wanton cruelty for which there was no slightest military necessity. Hundreds of thousands of women, children and old people were burned to death by those atomic explosions. And this was done merely to strike fear into peoples and make them bow to the might of the U.S.A. Certain American politicians took pride in this mass murder and, strange as it may seem, still do to this day.

Not one government or President of the United States since the war has declared that these were immoral acts. Why not? Because they are guided by the morality of imperialism, according to which might makes right. They thought their monopoly in nuclear weapons would enable them to establish world domination.

But within a short time the Soviet Union had developed a powerful thermonuclear weapon and thereby put an end to the monopoly of the United States of America in this field. (Prolonged applause.)

When we launched the first satellites into outer space, when Soviet ships blazed the first trails in space, and when Comrades Gagarin and Titov accomplished their unparalleled flights around the earth, the whole world perceived that the Soviet Union had left the United States far behind in important fields of science and technology. Even President J. Kennedy has been forced to admit that the United States is confronted with a difficult task in

overtaking the Soviet Union in this area. As you see, the word "overtake" has now made its appearance in the vocabulary of Americans, too. (Stir in the hall. Applause.)

I have repeatedly said that the Soviet Union is going to catch up with the United States in corn production. The Americans have received this somewhat skeptically. But it is easier to catch up in corn production than in the conquest of space. There the task is far more complicated! (Stir in the hall. Applause.) The facts show that the situation has changed substantially in favor of socialism.

But while the President of the United States speaks of the need to overtake the Soviet Union, U.S. Secretary of State Rusk continues to call for a "position of strength" policy. A few days ago he said: "Mr. Khrushchev should know that we"—i.e., the United States—"are strong." He let it be understood that the Western powers mean to continue talking to us "from a position of strength." It turns out that the right hand does not know what the left hand is doing.

No, the thinking of some Western political figures is clearly pointed in the wrong direction. If we are bent on making peace more than just a lull, a breathing space between wars, we must create a situation in which the possibility of starting a war would be permanently ruled out.

The Soviet Union is far from desirous of dictating its will and terms to other states. Even though we have achieved unquestionable superiority in nuclear missiles, we have proposed general and complete disarmament and the destruction of nuclear weapons under the strictest international control. More than that, the Soviet Union unilaterally carried out a substantial reduction of its armed forces, dismantled its military bases abroad and put through a number of other measures along the same lines.

As we know, the United States, Britain and France not only failed to follow the Soviet Union's lead but have lately stepped up the arms race and have begun to increase their forces and to conduct military maneuvers close to our borders. They have begun openly threatening us with war over the German peace treaty.

In the face of direct threats and the danger of a war, the Soviet Union was forced to take the measures necessary for strengthening our defense capacity, for protecting the Soviet people and the peoples of the whole great commonwealth of socialist countries.

We were confronted with the necessity of perfecting our thermonuclear weapons and testing new types of these weapons. This decision of the Soviet government's, taken in a setting of seriously aggravated international tension, met with understanding from all who hold peace dear and who will not close their eyes to the dangerous intrigues of the enemies of peace. (Prolonged applause.)

In taking this decision the Soviet government did, of course, appreciate that not everyone would immediately understand why we had been forced to resume testing. And actually there are even some fair-minded people who have expressed anxiety about the aftereffects of the nuclear explosions that are being staged. I have received letters and telegrams from some of them. We have no reason to doubt the sincerity of these people; they fear that nuclear blasts may poison the atmosphere.

To them we say: Esteemed friends, esteemed sirs! The peoples of the socialist countries would like nothing better than to see the skies of our planet clear and bright. What we live and work for is to build a radiant future for the peoples, to turn the earth into a flowering garden. We have children, grandchildren and even great-grandchildren, just as you have. We are concerned not only for their present but for their future as well. The fact is that our scientists are doing everything necessary to reduce the harmful effects of the tests to a minimum.

But we cannot refrain from conducting these tests at a time when the imperialists of the United States, Britain, France and West Germany are preparing to destroy not only the gains of socialism but the peoples of our countries. They not only pose the threat of poisoning the atmosphere, after all; they want to take the lives of millions of people.

In the face of a real threat to our security, the Soviet people could not forgo measures to strengthen the defense capability of the Soviet Union and of the commonwealth of socialist countries as a whole. We would be unworthy leaders if we failed to perfect all the means of defense necessary for the security of the Soviet state. (Prolonged applause.)

It is truly regrettable that some fair-minded people abroad have so far been unable to find their bearings in the complicated international situation. Imperialist propaganda has been exploiting the humane feelings of these people to prevent us, through them, from perfecting essential means of defense and to make it easier for the imperialists to prepare for a new war against us.

In strengthening the defenses of the Soviet Union we are acting not only in our own interests but in the interests of all peace-loving peoples, of all mankind. When the enemies of peace threaten us with force they must be and will be countered with force, and more impressive force, too. (Stormy applause.) Anyone who is still unable to understand this today will certainly understand it tomorrow.

We once again point out to the leaders of the United States, Britain, France, West Germany and other countries that the most sensible thing would be to discard the "position of strength" policy and the "cold war" policy. (Applause.) A realistic policy of peaceful coexistence must be pursued in international affairs. (Applause.)

And this means having to reckon with the tangible fact that side by side with the capitalist world on our planet, developing successfully and growing stronger year by year, are the countries in the world socialist system. To be blind to this fact, to fail to reckon with it, would in our times be simply ridiculous and shortsighted.

The imperialists are not happy to see the socialist countries growing and developing. They would like to hold us in check, to lecture us, as they would children, on how best to order our lives. After all, the imperialists consider the Soviet regime an illegitimate child. And they are quite unable to accept the fact that we have today grown up to the point where we are not only learning from others but have a good deal to teach them. Here too, as you see, there are contradictions between the old and the new. Naturally, we cannot and are not going to live as the imperialists would like us to. And they're not pleased about it. They threaten to take a stick to us, as it were. But if they come at us with a stick, we'll let them have it with a whole broom! (Stormy applause.)

But seriously speaking, the most sensible thing for states with different systems would be to coexist peacefully and foster neighborly relations. Being neighbors, after all, is not like being husband and wife, not choosing one another by mutual consent. Countries do not elect to be neighbors; it does not depend on our desires. Our country, for example, has as its neighbor in the south present-day Iran, whose rulers pursue a policy that is anything but neighborly. If it were up to us, we would probably pick a more agreeable neighbor. I think that the rulers of Iran would also prefer to have a different neighbor. But history has worked things out so that our countries find themselves side by side, neighbors. And there is nothing to be done about it. We must reckon with the actual situation. One must not interfere in the affairs of neighbors, or allow them to interfere in one's own affairs. (Applause.)

I would like to elaborate somewhat on a matter of great theoretical and political importance—the question of the characteristics of present-day imperialism and of the peaceful co-existence of states with different social systems.

The peaceful coexistence of states with different social and political systems is the paramount problem of the day. There exist on the globe states comprising two distinct world systems— the socialist and the capitalist. For all the power of modern science, it is impossible to cut the globe up into parts and allot a definite area to each of these systems, put space between them so to speak. So the coexistence of states with different social and political systems is a historical fact.

A sharp struggle is under way between the two social systems, a contest to see which is the better system, which of them provides more benefits for people. How should the contest between these two systems be resolved—by war, or in peaceful economic competition? Unless one proposes that issues that arise in relations between states be settled through military conflicts, one must accept the peaceful coexistence of states with different systems. The socio-political system in each state is the internal affair of the people of that state, and the

peoples themselves must decide this question, and do decide it, as they choose.

Some people attack us, accusing us of oversimplifying or softening the picture when in assessing the international situation we underline the need for peaceful coexistence in present-day circumstances. We are told that those who lay stress on peaceful coexistence somehow underestimate the nature of imperialism and even end up contradicting Lenin's assessment of imperialism.

Vladimir Ilyich Lenin's classical definition of imperialism is well known. This definition of Lenin's discloses the reactionary and aggressive nature of imperialism as the final stage of capitalism. Imperialism is inseparably linked with wars, with the struggle for the division and redivision of the world, for enslaving people and bringing them under the rule of monopoly capital. It is capable of any adventurous undertaking.

This appraisal of the nature of imperialism retains full validity today. Far from disavowing it, our party reaffirms it and is guided by it in all its policy, in its working out of the strategy and tactics of revolutionary struggle. This is impressively shown in the draft of our party's new Program. At the same time the Party is obliged, if it hews to creative Marxism, to take into account the great changes that have occurred in the world since Lenin gave his analysis of imperialism.

We are living through a period in which there are two world systems, a period in which the world socialist system is developing rapidly and the time is not far off when it will surpass the world capitalist system in the production of material wealth. As for science and culture, the countries in the world socialist system have already greatly surpassed the capitalist countries in a number of fields. At present the world socialist system is mightier than the imperialist countries militarily as well.

This being the case, it cannot be maintained that nothing has happened, that nothing has changed in the world in the past few decades. Only people who are out of touch with life, who are blind to the great changes that have occurred in the balance of forces in the world arena, can maintain this.

It is a fact that the essence of imperialism, its aggressive nature, has not changed. But the possibilities open to it today are no longer what they were in the period when it exercised undivided sway. The situation today is such that imperialism cannot dictate its will to all, or pursue its aggressive policy unimpeded.

Standing in the way of the imperialists' predatory aspirations to redivide the world and enslave other peoples are the invincible forces of the world socialist system, and above all of the Soviet Union. (Prolonged applause.) These forces are curbing the wolfish appetites of the imperialists. Hundreds of millions of people in the peace-loving countries are working for peace; all the peoples, in fact, are calling for peace. This is the main thing. This must be understood. (Applause.)

To make my thought clearer, let me cite an illustration. The tiger is a beast of prey and remains such until death. But it is a known fact that the tiger will never attack the elephant. Why not? Elephant meat, after all, is presumably no less savory than the meat of any other animal, and the tiger would probably not mind feasting on it. But it is afraid to attack the elephant because the elephant is stronger than the tiger. If a frenzied tiger does attack an elephant, it is sure to be killed. The elephant will trample it to death. (Stir in the hall. Applause.)

In films about life in Africa and Asia you are certain to have seen kings, princes, rajahs and other notables hunting tigers on elephants. They do this because they know that hunting the tiger this way is not dangerous. And to continue the comparison, it should be said that the Soviet Union and the countries in the socialist camp are today too strong for the imperialists, more so than the elephant is for the tiger. (Stir in the hall. Applause.)

Roughly the same situation holds for imperialism: Today the imperialists are compelled—not so much by their reasonableness as by the instinct of self-preservation, if it can be put that way—to face up to their inability to squeeze, rob and enslave all others with impunity. Imperialism is being forced to reckon with the mighty forces that today block its way. The imperialists realize that if they unleash a world war, the imperialist system so hated by the people will inevitably perish in it. (Prolonged applause.)

The world socialist system has today grown mightier than ever. It already takes in more than a third of mankind, and its forces are growing swiftly; it is the great bulwark of world peace. (Applause.) Under present circumstances the principle of the peaceful coexistence of states with different social systems assumes vital importance.

The only people who fail to see this are the hopeless dogmatists who, having learned by rote general formulas on imperialism, stubbornly turn away from life. This continues to be the position of the diehard Molotov. He and his like fail to appreciate the changes in the world situation, the new developments in life. They have not kept up with the times and have long since become a drag, a needless burden. (Applause.)

***

Comrades! The Central Committee's report and also speeches by delegates to the Congress have referred to the erroneous position of the leaders of the Albanian Party of Labor, who have taken the path of combating the line of our party's 20th Congress and undermining the foundations of friendship with the Soviet Union and other socialist countries.

The representatives of the fraternal parties have declared in their speeches that they share our alarm over the state of affairs in the Albanian Party of Labor and roundly condemn the dangerous actions of its leaders, which are prejudicing the fundamental interests of the Albanian people and the solidarity of the entire socialist commonwealth. The speeches by delegates and by representatives of the fraternal parties are convincing evidence that our party's Central Committee was absolutely correct in reporting to the Congress, openly and as a matter of principle, on the abnormal state of Soviet-Albanian relations.

We were obliged to do this because our repeated attempts to normalize relations with the Albanian Party of Labor have unfortunately borne no fruit. I should like to emphasize that the Central Committee of our party has shown a maximum of patience and has done everything in its power to restore good relations between our parties.

The members of the Presidium of the Central Committee of the C.P.S.U. have tried time and again to get together with the Albanian leaders and discuss the issues that have arisen. Back in August, 1960, we twice proposed a meeting to the Albanian leaders, but they avoided it. They were equally persistent in declining to have talks with us at the time of the Moscow conference of fraternal parties in November, 1960.

When, at the insistence of the Central Committee of the C.P.S.U., such a meeting did take place, Enver Hoxha and Mehmet Shehu disrupted it and moved on to actions that can only be described as provocative. The leaders of the Albanian Party of Labor made a deliberate show of walking out on the November conference, indicating their refusal to defer to the collective opinion of the fraternal parties. To our subsequent suggestions that we meet, exchange views and resolve our differences they again responded with a rude refusal, and they stepped up their campaign of attacks and slander against our party and its Central Committee.

There are no expedients that the leaders of the Albanian Party of Labor shrink from using in their efforts to hide from their people the truth about what our party and people are doing. Albania is the only country in the socialist camp in which the draft Program of the C.P.S.U. was not published in full. The Albanian press carried only sections of the draft, deliberately creating a distorted impression of our party's activities. This fact speaks for itself. After all, even communism's adversaries were unable to pass over our Program in silence.

We can understand why the Albanian leaders are concealing the C.P.S.U. Program from their party and people. They fear the truth like the plague. The Party Program is something sacred for us, our lodestar in the building of communism.

Had they published it in full, the working people of Albania would have been able to tell truth from slander, would have seen that all our party's activities, all its plans accord with the vital interests of the peoples, including the interests of the Albanian people, who are friendly to us. (Prolonged applause.)

Our great party has more than once been subjected to bitter and filthy attacks from open and covert enemies of commu-

nism. But it must be said outright that we do not recall an instance in which anyone shifted with such dizzying speed from protestations and vows of eternal friendship to unbridled anti-Soviet slander as the Albanian leaders have done.

Presumably they expect in this way to lay the groundwork for earning handouts from the imperialists. The imperialists are always willing to pay thirty pieces of silver to those who cause a split in the ranks of the Communists. But pieces of silver have never brought anyone anything but dishonor and shame. (Applause.)

Clearly, the Central Committee of our party could not fail to tell the Congress the whole truth about the reprehensible stand taken by the leadership of the Albanian Party of Labor. Had we not done so, they would have gone on claiming that the Central Committee of the Communist Party of the Soviet Union was afraid to let the Party know of its differences with the leadership of the Albanian Party of Labor. Our party and the Soviet people should know how the Albanian leaders have been acting. And let the Congress, which is empowered to speak for the whole Party, state its attitude to this matter, pronounce its authoritative opinion.

It has been emphasized at our Congress that we are prepared to normalize relations with the Albanian Party of Labor on the basis of Marxist-Leninist principles. How have the Albanian leaders responded to this? They have lashed out at our party and its Central Committee with a blatant, mud-slinging statement.

Comrade Chou En-lai, head of the delegation of the Communist Party of China, voiced concern in his speech over our having openly raised the issue of Albanian-Soviet relations at the Congress. As far as we can see, his statement primarily reflects alarm lest the present state of our relations with the Albanian Party of Labor affect the solidarity of the socialist camp.

We share the anxiety of our Chinese friends and appreciate their concern for the strengthening of unity. If the Chinese comrades wish to apply their efforts to normalizing the Albanian Party of Labor's relations with the fraternal parties, it is doubtful whether there is anyone better able to facilitate accomplishment of this purpose than the Communist Party of China. This would really redound to the benefit of the Albanian Party of Labor and accord with the interests of the entire commonwealth of socialist countries. (Prolonged applause.)

It is true, of course, that Communists should so frame their inter-Party relations as not to provide the enemy with the slightest opening. But unfortunately the Albanian leaders have grossly flouted this requirement. For a long time now they have been openly attacking the line of the 20th Congress, providing the bourgeois press with food for all sorts of speculation. It is they, the Albanian leaders, who have been shouting from the rooftops about having a position of their own, views of their own that differ from the views of our party and the other fraternal parties. This showed clearly at the Fourth Congress of the Albanian Party of Labor, and has been particularly clear of late.

Why did the Albanian leaders launch a campaign against the decisions of our party's 20th Congress? What treason do they see in them?

Above all, the resolute condemnation of the Stalin cult and its harmful consequences is not to the liking of the Albanian leaders. They are displeased that we should have resolutely denounced the arbitrary rule, the abuse of power from which many innocent people suffered, among them eminent representatives of the old guard who had been with Lenin in building the world's first proletarian state. The Albanian leaders cannot refer without vexation and rancor to the fact that we have put an end for good to the situation where one man at his own pleasure arbitrarily decided all-important questions relating to the life of our party and country. (Prolonged applause.)

Stalin is no longer among the living, but we have thought it necessary to denounce the disgraceful methods of leadership that flourished in the setting of the Stalin cult. Our party is doing everything possible to prevent phenomena of this sort from ever again recurring.

One would have supposed that the Leninist line of the 20th Party Congress, which was supported by the fraternal parties, would have met with support from the leadership of the Albanian Party of Labor too, since the cult of the individual is incompatible with Marxism-Leninism. Actually, the Albanian leaders heaped encomiums on the Stalin cult and launched a violent campaign against the decisions of the 20th Party Congress, in an effort to make the socialist countries swerve from this sound course. This, naturally, was no accident. All that was reprehensible in our country in the period of the cult of the individual is manifested in its worst form in the Albanian Party of Labor. It is now an open secret that the Albanian leaders remain in power by resorting to force and arbitrary rule.

For a long time now there has existed in the Albanian Party of Labor an abnormal, evil situation in which any person objectionable to the leadership is liable to meet with cruel persecution.

Where today are the Albanian Communists who built the Party, who fought the Italian and German fascist invaders? Nearly all of them are victims of the bloody misdeeds of Mehmet Shehu and Enver Hoxha.

The Central Committee of the C.P.S.U. has received more than one letter from Albanian Communists appealing to us to restrain the Albanian leaders from dealing savagely with the finest sons and daughters of the Albanian Party of Labor. The delegates to the Congress can form their own idea of the Albanian leaders' moral complexion by having a look at some of these letters.

The Albanian leaders reproach us with meddling in the internal affairs of the Albanian Party of Labor. I should like to tell you what form this so-called meddling took.

A few years ago the Central Committee of the C.P.S.U. interceded with the Albanian leaders over the fate of Liri Gega, a former member of the Politburo of the Central Committee of the Albanian Party of Labor, who had been sentenced to death along with her husband. This woman had for a number of years been a member of leading bodies of the Albanian Party of Labor and had taken part in the Albanian people's struggle for liberation. In approaching the Albanian leaders at the time, we were guided by considerations of humanity, by anxiety to prevent the shooting of a woman, and a pregnant woman at that. We felt and still feel that as a fraternal party we had a right to state our opinion in the matter. After all, even in the blackest days of rampant reaction, the tsarist satraps, who tortured revolutionaries, scrupled to execute pregnant women. And here, in a socialist country, they had sentenced to death, and they executed, a woman who was about to become a mother, they had shown altogether unwarranted cruelty. (Stir in the hall. Shouts: "Shame! Shame!")

People of integrity today incur punishment in Albania just for daring to come out for Soviet-Albanian friendship, which the Albanian leaders are fond of talking about in such high-sounding and florid terms.

Comrades Liri Belishova and Koco Tashko, prominent figures in the Albanian Party of Labor, were not only expelled from the Party's Central Committee but are now being called enemies of the Party and the people. And all this merely because Liri Belishova and Koco Tashko had the courage honestly and openly to voice their disagreement with the policy of the Albanian leaders and took a stand for Albanian solidarity with the Soviet Union and the other socialist countries.

People who today advocate friendship with the Soviet Union, with the C.P.S.U., are regarded by the Albanian leaders as enemies.

How is all this to be squared with the vows and protestations of friendly feelings for the C.P.S.U. and the Soviet Union that have been heard from Shehu and Hoxha? It is obvious that all their spouting about friendship is nothing but hypocrisy and deception.

This is the atmosphere that prevails in the Albanian Party of Labor, and this is why the Albanian leaders oppose the Leninist line of the 20th Party Congress. After all, to put an end to the cult of the individual would in effect mean that Shehu, Hoxha and others would have to give up their key positions in the Party and government. And this they do not want to do. But we are certain the time will come when the Albanian Communists and the Albanian people will have their say, and then the Albanian leaders will have to answer for the harm they have done their country, their people and the cause of socialist construction in Albania. (Stormy, prolonged applause.)

Comrades! Our party will continue to combat revisionists of all shades as it has in the past. Steadfastly conforming to the principles of the Declaration and the Statement of the conferences of Marxist-Leninist parties, we have exposed and shall continue unremittingly to expose the revisionism that has found expression in the program of the Yugoslav League of Communists. We shall also constantly combat dogmatism and all other deviations from Marxism-Leninism. (Applause.)

***

Comrades! The 22nd Congress can be called with perfect justice a congress of monolithic unity of the Leninist party and of complete unanimity and solidarity. Our enemies are terrified by the growing unity of our ranks. They are placing hope in the fact that our Congress has devoted considerable attention to discussing the harmful consequences of the cult of the individual, as well as to the definitive exposure of the anti-Party factionalist group. But these sterile attempts of the enemies of communism are in vain; they will gain nothing from them.

The difference between the Marxist-Leninist parties and all other political parties is that the Communists, without wavering, boldly expose and eliminate shortcomings and defects in their work. Criticism, even of the sharpest type, helps our forward movement. This is a sign of the strength of the Communist Party, testimony to its inflexible faith in its cause. (Prolonged applause.)

Many comrades who have spoken here have angrily condemned the anti-Party subversive activity of the handful of factionalists led by Molotov, Kaganovich and Malenkov. Our whole party and the entire people have rejected these schismatics who opposed everything new and who wished to restore the defective methods that reigned under the cult of the individual. They wanted to return to those days, so difficult for our party and our country, when no one was ensured against arbitrariness and repressions. Yes, Molotov and the others wanted precisely that.

We resolutely reject such methods of leadership, if they may be so called. We stand and we shall continue to stand firmly on the position that inner-Party affairs must be solved on the basis of Leninist norms, on the basis of the methods of persuasion and broad democracy. (Applause.) The Party's strongest weapon is its ideology, the great teaching of Marxism-Leninism, which has brought many glorious victories to the Party, to the Soviet people and to the whole international Communist movement. (Prolonged applause.)

Is it possible for different opinions to appear in the Party at various periods of its activity, especially during transitional stages? Yes, it is possible. What should be done, then, with those who express their own opinion, different from that of others? Our stand is for the application in such cases not of repressions but of Leninist methods of persuasion and explanation.

Let me recall the following episode from the history of our party. On the eve of October, in the decisive days when the question was whether the Great Socialist Revolution was or was not to be, Zinoviev and Kamenev spoke out in the press against the armed uprising contemplated by the Party and revealed the plans of the Central Committee of the party of Bolsheviks to its enemies. This was a betrayal of the cause of the revolution.

Vladimir Ilyich Lenin unmasked Zinoviev and Kamenev and demanded their expulsion from the Party. The subsequent development of the revolution fully confirmed the correctness of Lenin's policy of armed uprising. When Zinoviev and Kamenev later declared that they had been in error and admitted their guilt, Lenin showed great magnanimity toward them and himself raised the question of reinstating them in the Party leadership.

Vladimir Ilyich firmly pursued a course of developing inner-Party democracy. He based himself on the broad masses of Communists and non-Party people.

In the years following Lenin's death, the Leninist norms of Party life were grossly distorted in the conditions of the Stalin cult. Stalin elevated limitations on inner-Party and Soviet democracy to the status of norms of inner-Party and state life. He crudely flouted the Leninist principles of leadership and permitted arbitrariness and abuses of power.

Stalin could look at a comrade sitting at the same table with him and say: "Your eyes are shifty today," after which it could be assumed that the comrade whose eyes were supposedly shifty was under suspicion.

Comrade delegates! I wish to tell the Congress how the anti-Party group reacted to the proposal that the question of abuses of power in the period of the cult of the individual be placed before the 20th Party Congress.

Molotov, Kaganovich, Malenkov, Voroshilov and others categorically objected to this proposal. In answer to their objections they were told that if they continued to oppose the raising of this question, the delegates to the Party Congress would be asked to decide the matter. We had no doubt that the Congress would favor discussion of the question. Only then did they agree, and the question of the cult of the individual was presented to the 20th Party Congress. But even after the Congress, the factionalists continued their struggle and obstructed in every possible way the clarification of the question of abuses of power, fearing that their role as accomplices in the mass repressions would come to light.

The mass repressions began after the murder of Kirov. A great deal of effort is still necessary to determine fully who was guilty of his death. The more deeply we study the materials relating to Kirov's death, the more questions arise. It is noteworthy that Kirov's assassin had previously been twice arrested by the Chekists near the Smolny, and that weapons had been found on him. But both times, upon someone's instructions, he had been released. And this man was in the Smolny, armed, in the very corridor along which Kirov usually passed. And for some reason or other it happened that at the moment of the murder the chief of Kirov's bodyguard had fallen far behind S. M. Kirov, although his instructions forbade him to be so far away from the person he was guarding.

The following fact is also very strange. When the chief of Kirov's bodyguard was being driven to the interrogation—and he was to have been questioned by Stalin, Molotov and Voroshilov—on the way, as the driver of the vehicle later said, an accident was deliberately staged by those who were to bring the chief of the bodyguard to the interrogation. They reported that the chief of the bodyguard had died in the accident, although actually he had been killed by the persons escorting him.

Thus the man who guarded Kirov was killed. Then those who had killed him were shot. This was apparently not an accident but a premeditated crime. Who could have committed it? A thorough study of this complex case is now under way.

It was found that the driver of the vehicle that was carrying the chief of S. M. Kirov's bodyguard to the interrogation is alive. He has said that as they were riding to the interrogation an NKVD man was sitting with him in the cab. The vehicle was a truck. (It is strange, of course, that this man was being driven to the interrogation in a truck, as if in this case no other vehicle could be found for the purpose. It seems that everything had been thought out in advance, down to the smallest detail.) Two other NKVD men were in the back of the truck with the chief of Kirov's bodyguard.

The driver went on to say that as they were driving down the street the man sitting next to him suddenly grabbed the wheel out of his hands and steered the truck directly at a house. The driver grabbed the steering wheel back and straightened out the truck, and they merely sideswiped the wall of the building. Later he was told that the chief of Kirov's bodyguard had been killed in this accident.

Why was he killed while none of the persons accompanying him was even injured? Why were both these NKVD men who were escorting the chief of Kirov's bodyguard later themselves shot? This means that someone had to have them killed in order to cover up all traces.

There are still many, a great many, unclarified circumstances in this and other similar cases.

Comrades! It is our duty to make a thorough and comprehensive study of all such cases rising out of the abuse of power. Time will pass, we shall die, we are all mortal, but as long as we continue to work we can and must find out many things and tell the truth to the Party and the people. We are obliged to do everything possible to establish the truth now, for the greater the length of time that separates us from these events, the more difficult will it become to re-establish the truth. It is now too late to bring the dead back to life, as the saying goes. But it is necessary that all this be recorded truthfully in the history of the Party. This must be done so that phenomena of this sort can never be repeated in the future. (Stormy, prolonged applause.)

You can imagine how difficult it was to solve these questions when the Presidium of the Central Committee included people who had themselves been guilty of abuses of power, of mass repressions. They stubbornly resisted all measures aimed at exposing the cult of the individual and then opened up a struggle against the Central Committee, wishing to change the composition of its leadership, to change the Leninist Party policy, the course laid down by the 20th Congress.

Naturally, they did not want to investigate cases of this sort. You have heard Comrade Shelepin's speech. He told the Congress many things, but needless to say he told by no means all that has now come to light. Thousands of completely innocent people perished, and each person is a whole story. Many Party, government and military figures perished.

Of course, those people in the Presidium of the Central Committee who had been responsible for violations of legality and mass repressions resisted in every possible way the exposure of arbitrary acts in the period of the cult of the individual, and then they launched an anti-Party factionalist struggle against the leadership of the Central Committee, concentrating their fire primarily against me personally, as First Secretary of the Central Committee, inasmuch as it had fallen to me in the line of duty to raise these questions. It was necessary to accept blows and to reply to these blows. (Stormy, prolonged applause.)

The participants in the anti-Party factionalist group hoped to seize leadership in the Party and the country and to remove the comrades who were exposing the criminal actions committed in the period of the cult of the individual. The anti-Party group wanted to place Molotov in the leadership. Then, of course, there would have been no exposures of these abuses of power.

Even after the 20th Congress had condemned the cult of the individual, the anti-Party group did all in its power to prevent the exposure from going any further. Molotov said that in large matters there may be bad things and good. He justified the actions that had taken place in the period of the cult of the individual and claimed that such actions are possible and that their repetition in the future is possible. Such was the course of the anti-Party factionalist group. This is not a simple aberration. It is a calculated, criminal and adventurist position. They wanted to divert the Party and the country from the Leninist path, they wanted to return to the policy and methods of leadership of the period of the cult of the individual. But they miscalculated. The Central Committee, our whole party and the entire Soviet people administered a decisive rebuff to the anti-Party group and exposed and smashed the factionalists. (Stormy, prolonged applause.)

People have spoken here with pain about many innocent victims among outstanding Party and government figures.

Such outstanding military commanders as Tukhachevsky, Yakir, Uborevich, Kork, Yegorov, Eideman and others fell victim to the mass repressions. They had been worthy people of our army, especially Tukhachevsky, Yakir and Uborevich, who had been brilliant military leaders. Later Blyukher and other outstanding military commanders fell victim to the repressions.

A rather curious report once cropped up in the foreign press to the effect that Hitler, in preparing the attack on our country, planted through his intelligence service a faked document indicating that Comrades Yakir and Tukhachevsky and others were agents of the German general staff. This "document," allegedly secret, fell into the hands of President Benes of Czechoslovakia, who, apparently guided by good intentions, forwarded it to Stalin. Yakir, Tukhachevsky and other comrades were arrested and then killed.

Many splendid commanders and political officials of the Red Army were executed. Here among the delegates there are comrades—I do not wish to name them so as not to cause them pain—who spent many years in prison. They were being "persuaded"—persuaded by quite definite techniques—that they were either German or British or some other kind of spies. And several of them "confessed." Even in cases when such people were told that the accusation of espionage had been withdrawn, they themselves insisted on their previous testimony, because they believed it was better to stand on their false testimony in order to put an end as quickly as possible to the torment and to die as quickly as possible.

That is the meaning of the cult of the individual! That was the meaning of the actions of Molotov and the others who wanted to restore the vicious practices of the period of the cult of the individual. It was to this that the anti-Party group wanted to return the Party; this is precisely the reason why the struggle against them was so bitter and difficult. Everyone understood what it meant.

I knew Comrade Yakir well. I knew Tukhachevsky too, but not as well as Yakir. In 1961, during a conference in Alma-Ata, his son, who works in Kazakhstan, came to see me. He asked me about his father. What could I tell him? When we investigated these cases in the Presidium of the Central Committee and received a report that neither Tukhachevsky nor Yakir nor Uborevich had been guilty of any crime against the Party and the state, we asked Molotov, Kaganovich and Voroshilov:

"Are you for rehabilitating them?"

"Yes, we are for it," they answered.

"But it was you who executed these people," we told them indignantly. "When were you acting according to you conscience, then or now?"

But they did not answer this question. And they will not answer it. You have heard the notations they wrote on letters received by Stalin. What can they say?

In his speech to the Congress, Comrade Shelepin has told you how these finest representatives of the Communist Party in the Red Army were killed. He also read Comrade Yakir's letter to Stalin and the recommendations on this letter. It should be said that at one time Yakir was highly esteemed by Stalin.

It may be added that when Yakir was shot he exclaimed: "Long live the Party, long live Stalin!"

He had so much faith in the Party, so much faith in Stalin that he never permitted himself the thought that a deliberate injustice was being committed. He believed that certain enemies had found their way into the NKVD agencies.

When Stalin was told how Yakir had behaved before his death, he cursed Yakir.

Let us recall Sergo Ordzhonikidze. I attended Ordzhonikidze's funeral. I believed what was said at the time, that he had died suddenly, because we knew he had a weak heart. Much later, after the war, I learned quite by accident that he had committed suicide. Sergo's brother had been arrested and shot. Comrade Ordzhonikidze saw that he could no longer work with Stalin, although previously he had been one of his closest friends. Ordzhonikidze held a high Party post. Lenin had known and valued him, but circumstances had become such that Ordzhonikidze could no longer work normally, and in order to avoid clashing with Stalin and sharing the responsibility for his abuse of power, he decided to take his life.

The fate of Alyosha Svanidze, the brother of Stalin's first wife, who was less well known to the broad circles of our party, was also tragic. He had been an old Bolshevik, but Beria made it appear, through all kinds of machinations, that Svanidze had been planted near Stalin by the German intelligence service, although he was a very close friend of Stalin's. And Svanidze was shot. Before the execution, Svanidze was told that Stalin had said that if he asked for forgiveness he would be pardoned. When Stalin's words were repeated to Svanidze, he asked: "What am I supposed to ask forgiveness for? I have committed no crime." He was shot. After Svanidze's death, Stalin said: "See how proud he is: He died without asking forgiveness." It never occurred to him that Svanidze had been above all an honest man.

Thus many completely innocent people perished.

That is what the cult of the individual means. That is why we cannot show the slightest tolerance toward abuses of power.

Comrades! The Presidium of the Congress has received letters from old Bolsheviks in which they write that in the period of the cult of the individual outstanding Party and state figures, such loyal Leninists as Comrades Chubar, Kosior, Rudzutak, Postyshev, Eikhe, Voznesensky, Kuznetsov and others, died guiltless.

The comrades propose that the memory of the outstanding Party and state figures who fell victim to completely unjustified repressions in the period of the cult of the individual be perpetuated.

We believe this proposal to be a proper one. (Stormy, prolonged applause.) It would be advisable to charge the Central Committee that will be elected by the 22nd Party Congress with deciding this question positively. Perhaps a monument should be erected in Moscow to the memory of the comrades who fell victim to arbitrary rule. (Applause.)

In the conditions of the cult of the individual the Party was deprived of normal life. People who usurp power cease being accountable to the Party, they escape from under its control. Herein is the greatest danger of the cult of the individual.

The situation in the Party must always be such that every leader is accountable to the Party and its agencies, and the Party can replace any leader when it considers this necessary. (Applause.)

Now, since the 20th Congress, Leninist principles of Party life and collective leadership have been restored in the Party. The new Party Program and Statutes give legal force to propositions that restore the Leninist norms of Party life and preclude the possibility of relapses into the cult of the individual.

The 20th Congress of our party condemned the cult of the individual, restored justice and demanded that the distortions that had taken place be eliminated. The Party Central Committee adopted resolute measures to prevent a return to arbitrariness and lawlessness. The anti-Party group of Molotov, Kaganovich, Malenkov and others resisted in every possible way the implementation of these measures.

The factionalists undertook an attempt to seize the leadership and to steer the Party away from the Leninist path. They prepared reprisals against those who defended the course set by the 20th Congress. When the anti-Party group was smashed, its participants expected that they would be treated in the same way they had dealt with people at the time of the cult of the individual and in the way they hoped to deal with those who favored the restoration of Leninist norms of Party life.

I had a typical conversation with Kaganovich. This was two days after the end of the June plenary session of the Party Central Committee, which expelled the anti-Party group from the Central Committee. Kaganovich called me on the telephone and said:

"Comrade Khrushchev, I have known you for many years. I ask you not to let them treat me in the vindictive way people were treated under Stalin."

And Kaganovich knew how people had been treated because he himself had been a participant in these reprisals.

I answered him:

"Comrade Kaganovich! Your words once more confirm the methods you intended to use to achieve your disgusting ends. You wanted to return the country to the state of affairs that existed under the cult of the individual, you wanted to indulge in reprisals against people. And you measure other people by your own yardstick. But you are mistaken. We firmly observe and we shall adhere to Leninist principles. You will be given a job," I said to Kaganovich, "you will be able to work and live in tranquility if you labor honestly, as all Soviet people labor."

Such is the conversation I had with Kaganovich. This conversation shows that when the factionalists failed, they thought they would be dealt with in the same way they intended to deal with the Party cadres if they had succeeded in realizing their wicked designs. But we Communists-Leninists cannot embark on the path of abuse of power. We stand firmly on Party, Leninist positions, we believe in the strength and unity of our party and in the solidarity of the people around the Party. (Stormy applause.)

Many delegates have referred with indignation in their speeches to the participants in the anti-Party group and have cited instances of their criminal actions. This indignation is understandable and justified.

I want to talk particularly about Comrade Voroshilov. He has been approaching me and telling me about his tribulations. His state of mind is understandable, of course. But we are political leaders and we cannot be guided by feelings alone. Feelings may differ, and they can be deceptive. Here at the Congress Voroshilov listens to the criticism directed against him and walks around like a beaten man. But you should have seen him at the time when the anti-Party group raised its hand against the Party. Then Voroshilov was a man of action; he came forth, if not on horseback, at least in his full regalia, in battle dress, so to speak.

The anti-Party group used Comrade Voroshilov in its struggle against the Central Committee. It is no accident that the factionalists singled out Voroshilov to meet with the Central Committee members who were working to convene a plenary session of the Central Committee. The anti-Party group calculated that with his prestige Voroshilov could influence the Central Committee members and shake their resolve in the struggle against the anti-Party group. The anti-Party group also named Bulganin for the meeting with the Central Committee members. But Bulganin did not enjoy the same prestige as Voroshilov. They placed great hopes on Voroshilov, as one of the oldest Party leaders. But this too was of no help to the factionalists.

The question arises: How did Comrade Voroshilov get into this group? Some comrades know about the strained personal relations between Voroshilov and Molotov, between Voroshilov and Kaganovich and between Malenkov and Voroshilov.

And yet, despite these relations, they nevertheless joined forces. Why, on what basis? Because after the 20th Congress they were afraid of further exposures of their illegal actions in the period of the cult of the individual, they were afraid they would have to answer to the Party. It is known, after all, that all the abuses of that time were committed not only with their support but with their active participation. Fear of responsibility and a desire to restore the state of affairs that existed in the period of the cult of the individual—these are what united the participants in the anti-Party group despite the personal animosity they felt toward one another.

Comrade Voroshilov committed grave errors. But I believe, comrades, that he must be treated differently than the other active participants in the anti-Party group—than Molotov, Kaganovich and Malenkov, for instance. It must be said that in the course of the bitter struggle with the factionalists during the early part of the June plenary session of the Central Committee, when Comrade Voroshilov saw the monolithic unity of the Central Committee members in the struggle against the anti-Party group, he apparently became aware that he had gone too far. Voroshilov understood that he had joined with men who were fighting against the Party, and he condemned the actions of the anti-Party group and admitted his mistakes. He thereby in some measure helped the Central Committee. We cannot underestimate this step on his part, comrades, because at the time this was a support for the Party.

The name of Kliment Yefremovich Voroshilov is widely known among the people. Therefore his participation in the anti-Party group along with Molotov, Kaganovich, Malenkov and the others strengthened this group, as it were, and made a certain impression on people inexperienced in politics. By leaving this group, Comrade Voroshilov helped the Central Committee in its struggle against the factionalists. Let us answer him in kind for this good deed and make his situation easier. (Prolonged applause.)

Comrade Voroshilov has been sharply criticized; this criticism was just, for he committed grave mistakes and Communists cannot forget them. But I believe that our approach to Comrade Voroshilov should be considerate, that we should show magnanimity. I believe that he sincerely condemns his actions and repents them. (Applause.)

Kliment Yefremovich Voroshilov has lived many years and has done much good for our party and people. I want to say that when the Central Committee considered Comrade Voroshilov's request that he be relieved of the duties of Chairman of the Presidium of the U.S.S.R. Supreme Soviet for reasons of health, the members of the Central Committee, despite the mistakes he had committed, spoke warmly about him. In May, 1960, in recognition of his services to the Party and the state, the Presidium of the Supreme Soviet awarded Kliment Yefremovich Voroshilov the title Hero of Socialist Labor. (Applause.)

I believe that Kliment Yefremovich will, together with us, actively fight for the cause of our party. (Stormy applause.)

***

Comrades! The 22nd Congress has confirmed with full force that the course of the 20th Party Congress, the course of the restoration and further development of Leninist norms of Party and state life, the course of raising the leading role of the Party and the creative activeness of the popular masses, is the only correct course. The 22nd Congress is confirming this beneficial course. The Party Program and Statutes and the resolutions of the Congress set forth new guarantees against relapses into the cult of the individual. The role of the Party as

Voroshilov's Statement

STATEMENT TO THE 22ND CONGRESS OF THE COMMUNIST PARTY OF THE SOVIET UNION. (Pravda and Izvestia, Oct. 29, p. 6. Complete text:) Dear comrade delegates! Being unable, for reasons of health, to speak at this historic 22nd Congress of our great Leninist party, I consider it my Party duty to state the following:

1. I wholly and fully subscribe to all the propositions of the Central Committee's report to the 22nd Party Congress and the report "On the Program of the Communist Party of the Soviet Union," delivered at this Congress by Comrade N. S. Khrushchev, First Secretary of the Party Central Committee.

2. The draft of the new Party Program is a document of the greatest significance. It is the credo both of our party and of the entire Soviet people. It is a guiding beacon for all progressive forces of the world and for all mankind in its onward march toward communism—the bright future of all the peoples of our planet.

3. The Central Committee's report to the 22nd Party Congress, delivered by Comrade N. S. Khrushchev, contains a just appraisal of the factionalist activity of the anti-Party group of Molotov, Kaganovich, Malenkov, Bulganin and others, and my name is mentioned among the factionalists.

Yes, I admitted and admit that at the beginning of the struggle against this group I supported certain erroneous, harmful statements by some of its members, but I had no idea of its factionalist activities until their true face was exposed and they themselves admitted their factionalist activity in the course of examination of the conduct of these "cliquists" at the June, 1957, plenary session of the Party Central Committee. After this I immediately stated that I had never known about this, had never joined any group and had never had any dealings or associations with this sort of people.

Having deeply realized the enormous harm that could have been done our party and country by the anti-Party group of Molotov, Kaganovich, Malenkov and others, I resolutely condemn its factionalist activity, which was aimed at diverting the Party from the Leninist path. I fully understand the gravity of the mistake I made when I supported the harmful statements of the members of the anti-Party group.

4. My attitude toward our Leninist party, toward its executive bodies and toward its policy in all domestic and foreign policy questions was clearly and definitely set forth in my speeches at the 20th and 21st Party Congresses. This attitude is determined by my deep devotion to the interests of the Party and the people, and I have no other interests but these. I am in full accord with the important work done by the Party to restore the Leninist norms of Party life and eliminate the violations of revolutionary legality of the period of the cult of the individual, and I deeply regret that in this situation I, too, made mistakes.

5. Throughout my 58 years in the ranks of our glorious Communist Party I have never, nowhere and under no circumstances, retreated from the Statute and Program requirements and norms for the members of our party, have never betrayed the great principles of Marxism-Leninism, have never participated and will never participate in anti-Party—whatever they may be called—groupings.—K. VOROSHILOV, delegate to the 22nd Party Congress and Party member since 1903. Oct. 26, 1961.

the great inspiring and organizing force in the building of communism is rising higher still.

I would like to say a few words about the following question. In many speeches at the Congress, and not infrequently in our press as well, when mention is made of the activity of our party's Central Committee a certain special emphasis is placed on me personally, and my role in carrying out major Party and government measures is underlined.

I understand the kind feelings guiding these comrades. Allow me, however, to emphasize emphatically that everything that is said about me should be said about the Central Committee of our Leninist party and about the Presidium of the Central Committee. (Stormy, prolonged applause.) Not one major measure, not one responsible pronouncement has been carried out upon anyone's personal directive; they have all been the result of collective deliberation and collective decision. (Stormy applause.) And this concluding speech, too, has been considered and approved by the executive collective. (Prolonged applause.) Our great strength, comrades, lies in collective leadership, in collegial decisions on all questions of principle. (Stormy applause.)

No matter what abilities this or that leader may possess, no matter what contributions he may make to the cause, he cannot achieve true and lasting success without the support of the collective, without the most active participation of the whole Party and of the broad popular masses in the implementation of adopted measures. This must be clearly understood and constantly borne in mind by all. (Applause.)

Communist leaders are strong through the activity of the masses they lead. If they correctly understand and express the interests of the Party, the interests of the people, if they struggle for these interests without sparing their strength, their energy and even their life, if they are inseparable from the Party in great matters and in small, just as the Party is inseparable from the people, such leaders will always be supported by the Party and the people. And the cause for which such a leader fights will inevitably triumph. (Prolonged applause.)

Of course, one must possess the qualities necessary for the struggle for the cause of the Party and for the vital interests of the people. After all, our ideological opponents, our enemies concentrate their fire in the first place against those leaders who, rallying the aktiv and through the aktiv the whole people around the executive agencies, guide the cause along the only correct, Leninist path.

Here at the Congress much has been said, for instance, about the furious energy displayed by the anti-Party factionalists Molotov, Kaganovich, Malenkov and others against the Leninist Party Central Committee and against me personally. Speaking against the course set forth by the 20th Congress, the schismatics concentrated their main fire against Khrushchev, who did not suit them. Why against Khrushchev? Well, because Khrushchev had been promoted by the will of the Party to the post of First Secretary of the Central Committee. The factionalists badly miscalculated. The Party smashed them both ideologically and organizationally. (Stormy applause.)

The Central Committee of our party has displayed an exceptionally high political maturity and a truly Leninist understanding of the situation. It is characteristic that literally not one member or candidate member of the Central Committee and not one member of the Inspection Commission supported the miserable handful of schismatics. (Prolonged applause.)

While resolutely pronouncing themselves opposed to all the disgusting phenomena of the cult of the individual, Marxist-Leninists have always recognized and will continue to recognize the authority of leaders.

But it would be incorrect to single out this or that leader, to set him apart from the executive collective or to exalt him inordinately. This is contrary to the principles of Marxism-Leninism. It is known with what impatience Marx, Engels and Lenin spoke out against those who eulogized their contributions. Yet it is difficult to overestimate the great role of the founders of scientific communism Marx, Engels and Lenin and their contributions to the working class and to all mankind. (Prolonged applause.)

Feelings of self-praise and any special emphasis on or excessive exaggeration of the role of individual leaders are utterly alien to true Marxist-Leninists. They find it simply insulting when someone tries obtrusively to set them apart, to isolate them from the executive nucleus of comrades. (Stormy applause.)

We Communists highly value and support the authority of correct and mature leadership. We must safeguard the authority of the leaders who are recognized by the Party and the people. But each leader must also understand the other side of the matter—never to plume himself on his position, to remember that in holding this or that post he is merely fulfilling the will of the Party and the will of the people, who may have invested the greatest power in him but never lose control over him. (Applause.) The leader who forgets this pays heavily for his mistake. I would add that he will pay while he is alive, or even after his death the people will not forgive him, as has happened with the condemnation of the cult of Stalin. (Applause.) A person who forgets that he is obliged to fulfill the will of the Party and of the people cannot, properly speaking, be called a true leader; there must be no such "leaders" either in the Party or in the state apparatus. (Applause.)

Of course, for many reasons great power is concentrated in the hands of the man who holds an executive post. A leader advanced by the Party and the people must not abuse his power. In the reports to the Congress you have heard about the measures that we have implemented and that we shall carry out in order that a revival of the ugly phenomena of the cult of the individual may never recur in the future. But there is one thing that no statutory provision can prescribe: The collective of leaders must thoroughly understand that a situation must not be permitted to arise whereby any authority, even the most deserving one, can cease to heed the opinions of those who have advanced him. (Applause.)

It is wrong, comrades, it is simply impossible to permit the inception and development of instances when the merited prestige of an individual may assume forms in which he fancies that everything is permissible to him and that he no longer has need of the collective. In such a case this individual may stop listening to the voices of other comrades who have been advanced to leadership, just as he was, and may begin suppressing them. Our great teacher V. I. Lenin resolutely fought against this, and the Party paid too dear a price for not heeding his wise counsel in good time.

So let us be worthy disciples of Lenin in this important matter. (Stormy, prolonged applause.)

*** *** ***

Comrades! For more than 100 years a struggle has been under way between two ideologies—the ideology of the working class, which is expressed in the Marxist theory of scientific communism, and the ideology of the exploiting classes, the bourgeois ideology.

With the appearance of the teaching of Marx and Engels the working class, the most revolutionary class, acquired a powerful ideological weapon in the struggle for its emancipation, for the revolutionary transformation of society, for the dictatorship of the proletariat.

In the early days the ideas of scientific communism were understood only by the most progressive intelligentsia and the advanced part of the working class. The path of development of revolutionary consciousness was not an easy one. The dissemination and assimilation of the new ideas met with great difficulties, because these ideas called for a revolutionary struggle to destroy the capitalist system, the system of brutal exploitation.

This struggle demanded sacrifices and privations, it called for exploits in the name of the future that was to be built on the ruins of capitalism. It was a call for a harsh revolutionary class struggle, and such a struggle could be waged only by courageous people who had developed in themselves a hatred of the exploiting system and were filled with confidence in the inevitable victory of the working class. This path was chosen by the best of the best, by the revolutionaries of the revolutionaries, and they won, after overcoming incredible difficulties. (Applause.)

It was the great good fortune of the working class of our country that more than half a century ago the Party created by Vladimir Ilyich Lenin assumed the leadership of its revolutionary struggle. At the Second Congress the Party adopted its first Program, which was worked out with the active participation of Lenin. The chief task posed in this Program was the overthrow of the rule of the capitalists and landholders and the establishment of the rule of the working class, of the toiling people.

Under the banner of the great ideas of Marxism, the working people of Russia achieved the socialist revolution in October, 1917, and took power into their own hands.

But having seized power, the working people also received the legacy of an economy destroyed by the world war. They had to overcome great difficulties and privations and make many sacrifices. They had to repel the attacks of the foreign interventionists, suppress counterrevolution at home, create an industry, put the ruined and neglected agriculture back on its feet, restore transportation, organize trade and overcome chaos and famine. The working class was called on to show a clear understanding of the need to work selflessly for the sake of the morrow, for the sake of the future.

This was an extremely complex and difficult task, but a noble one. Enthusiasm for the struggle for its realization could be evoked only among people who were ready to make sacrifices today in order to create a better future for their children and grandchildren.

After the establishment of the dictatorship of the proletariat our party adopted its second Program, the program for the construction of socialism, of which Lenin was the author. The great result of the implementation of this Program was the complete and final victory of socialism in our country, which became a country with a powerful industry, a large-scale agriculture and an advanced science and technology.

Now, comrades, we have entered the third state of the great struggle. We are adopting the third Program of the Leninist party, the program for the construction of communism. How far have we advanced, how different are present-day conditions from those in which the second Party Program was adopted, to say nothing of the first!

The socialist economy has gained such strength and possesses so much energy that from the summits we have now reached we can openly challenge the most powerful capitalist country, the United States of America, to peaceful economic competition.

The struggle of the two ideologies is now of a completely different nature than at the dawn of Marxism. The ideas of scientific communism have seized the masses and have become a great material force. They have become embodied in life, and the material and technical base of the new society is being created by the labor of the peoples. The struggle has shifted from the purely ideological sphere to the sphere of material production.

Now not only the most advanced section of society but entire peoples of our country and of other socialist countries are waging a struggle for the realization of the great ideals of communism. The Soviet Union is now both literally and figuratively storming the skies, and in putting into effect the ideas of communism is demonstrating the superiority of the socialist system over capitalism. (Stormy applause.)

Socialism is today not merely an idea for the sake of which the Party calls on the working people to fight. Socialism has become a reality. We say: Look at the Soviet Union and at the socialist countries, and you will see what the working people and all laboring people can do when they hold power and are putting into effect the ideas of scientific communism. See what they have achieved in a short period of history! Their successes and their example exert a powerful influence on the masses of working people, on the peoples of the whole world. (Applause.)

Socialism no longer lies somewhere in the future but is today bringing great material and spiritual benefits to the peoples who have set out on the path of building a new life. The example of the countries of socialism is becoming ever more attractive to the working people of all countries. The ideas of communism are spreading ever more widely and deeply, are inspiring hundreds of millions of people to become makers of history.

The powerful and increasingly rapid movement toward communism will sweep away everything that stands in the path to the cherished goal—the building of the most just society on earth. (Prolonged applause.) This is not a struggle of some against others to legalize their domination over them; this is struggle against oppression, against slavery, against exploitation, a struggle for the happiness of all. We firmly believe that the time will come when the children and grandchildren of those who today do not understand and do not accept communism will live under communism. (Stormy applause.)

***

Comrades! The tasks that the 22nd Congress sets before the Party and the people are truly vast. Enormous efforts on the part of the whole Party and of the entire people will be required to make our majestic Program a reality. But we have everything necessary for carrying out this Program. (Applause.)

The task is now, without losing a single day, to direct all our efforts, all the seething, inexhaustible energy of our people, into the accomplishment of the practical tasks of building communism. (Applause.)

The Program has been unanimously approved by the Congress. It is now a matter of getting to work, with all the passion characteristic of Bolsheviks, to embody it in life. (Applause.)

Our Congress is a splendid testimonial to the readiness and resolve of the Party and of the entire Soviet people to achieve the great goal—the building of communism in our country. And there can be no doubt whatsoever that communism will be built in the Soviet Union—such is the will of the Party, the will of the people! (Stormy, prolonged applause.)

When the 22nd Congress ends, the delegates will depart to all corners of our great homeland. They will be armed with the program for building a communist society. Our goals are clear, the paths have been charted. It is not in some distant future but today that we shall embark on the practical realization of the Program. (Prolonged applause.)

Comrades! Never have our forces, the forces of world socialism, been as powerful as now. The new Program opens up before the Party and the people the brightest and most thrilling perspectives. The sun of communism is rising over our country! We shall do everything to hasten, with our selfless labor, the dawn of that day when this sun will shed its light on the vast expanses of our wonderful homeland! We shall devote all our forces, all our Bolshevik energy to the cause of the triumph of communism! (Stormy applause.)

Under the leadership of the glorious Leninist party—forward to the victory of communism! (Stormy, long-continued applause growing into an ovation. All rise. Shouts in the hall: "Hail to our Communist Party!" "Glory to the Soviet people!" "Hail to communism!" "Hail to the friendship of the peoples!" "Glory to the fraternal parties!" Shouts in foreign tongues from representatives of fraternal parties abroad acclaiming the C.P.S.U., acclaiming the peoples of the U.S.S.R. Mighty shouts of "Hurrah!" roll through the hall.)

X. KOZLOV: REPORT ON THE PARTY STATUTES

ON CHANGES IN THE STATUTES OF THE COMMUNIST PARTY OF THE SOVIET UNION.–Report by Comrade F. R. Kozlov, Secretary of the Party Central Committee, Oct. 28, 1961. (Pravda and Izvestia, Oct. 29, pp. 4-6. 13,000 words. Condensed text:) Comrades! ... The Program of the Communist Party of the Soviet Union is the fruit of the collective creative thought of the whole Party and of its Leninist Central Committee headed by Comrade N. S. Khrushchev. His creative approach to theory, his close contact with life and his ability to give correct expression to the fundamental interests of the people stamp Comrade N. S. Khrushchev as a true Leninist, as an outstanding political figure and Marxist-Leninist theorist. (Stormy applause.) ...

Comrades! The question of changes in the Statutes of the C.P.S.U. has been submitted to the 22nd Congress for consideration. The Statutes of the Party are the basic law governing its internal life. They determine the norms of inner-Party life, the organizational principles of the Party's structure and the methods of its practical activity. ...

The great Lenin taught us that every time the Party is confronted with new tasks, it should work out organizational forms, rules and norms for its internal life that are in accordance with the historical conditions of its activity and that will ensure accomplishment of these tasks. These were the principles by which the Central Committee was guided in working out the draft Statutes of the C.P.S.U. that have been submitted to this Congress for consideration.

The Statutes currently in effect were adopted, as everyone knows, in 1952 at the 19th Party Congress, at which the report "Changes in the Statutes of the All-Union Communist Party (of Bolsheviks)" was delivered by Comrade N. S. Khrushchev. The basic Leninist organizational principles of the structure and work of the Party embodied in the existing Statutes remain immutable. The draft Statutes being presented to the 22nd Congress for consideration develop these principles. They proceed entirely from the requirements of the new Program of the C.P.S.U. and reflect the very great changes that have occurred in the life of the country and the Party in the years that have gone by and the needs entailed in our further development.

The Communist Party of the Soviet Union has in these years increased numerically and grown stronger ideologically and organizationally. Having overcome the consequences of the cult of J. V. Stalin, the Party has fully restored the Leninist norms of Party life and the principle of collective leadership and has united even more closely around the Leninist Central Committee. The role of the Party as the guiding and directing force of the Soviet people has been enhanced. The Party has been enriched with new experience in the political leadership of the masses. Never has the Leninist unity of the Party's ranks been as solid and indestructible as it is today. (Prolonged applause.) ...

All the changes in and additions to the Party Statutes are called upon to raise the Party's organizational work to the level of the great tasks of communist construction outlined by the new Program of the C.P.S.U. The indestructible ideological and organizational solidarity of the Party is the most important source of its invincibility. (Prolonged applause.)

The Building of Communism and Enhancement of the Title of Party Member.—Comrades! In present conditions the role of every Communist and his responsibility to the Party and people have been immeasurably enhanced, as has the title of Party member. "It is the duty of a Communist," states the Program, "by his entire behavior in production, in public and in private life to be a model in the struggle for the development and strengthening of communist relations and to observe the principles and norms of communist morality."

Proceeding from these propositions of the Program, the draft Statutes define the basic duties and rights of a Communist and state the organizational rules governing the procedure for admission to and expulsion from the C.P.S.U.

The question of Party membership is one of the fundamental questions of Party construction. The Party's successful fulfillment of its responsible role as vanguard of the Soviet people, its strength and its militancy depend above all on its membership. The Party will continue to reinforce its ranks from among the most socially conscious and active members of our society, to preserve the title of Communist in its purity and hold it high.

Art. 1 of the draft Statutes reads:

"Any citizen of the Soviet Union who accepts the Party Program and Statutes, takes an active part in communist construction, works in one of the Party organizations, carries out Party decisions and pays membership dues may be a member of the C.P.S.U."

The Leninist principle of Party membership is fully preserved in this article. What is new in the definition is that Party membership is open to any citizen who "takes an active part in communist construction." This requirement is in line with the new conditions in the life of the Party; it is a major criterion for deciding who is worthy of the title of member of the C.P.S.U. in the period of the full-scale building of communist society. (Applause.)

Communism makes man's life secure, joyful and happy. But for all the springs of public wealth to yield abundantly, labor for the good of society must become a prime necessity of life for all Soviet people. This is why the duties of a Party member that relate to social labor, to production, to the creation of the material and technical base of communism are moved to the forefront in the draft Statutes of the C.P.S.U.

A Party member must exemplify the communist attitude to labor, must raise labor productivity, take the initiative in all that is new and support and propagate all that is advanced and progressive. The Communist is called on to master technology, to improve his qualifications and to take an active part in economic and cultural construction. The degree of a Communist's political maturity and dedication to the great cause of Marxism-Leninism can be determined above all by the way in which he discharges this duty. (Applause.)

The Soviet people are marching in the vanguard of the revolutionary transformation of human society. Their world view is the most advanced theory of our time—Marxism-Leninism. While working tirelessly to perfect his knowledge of that theory and being guided by it in his everyday activity, the Communist is obliged to be an active propagator of the Marxist-Leninist teaching among the masses of the working people. A high degree of social consciousness among Soviet people is the decisive precondition of their creative activity and of the development and consolidation of communist forms of labor and new communist social relations.

We know, however, that survivals of the past in people's consciousness and behavior have not yet been completely eradicated in our society. These survivals show themselves in the disdainful attitude of some people toward work, in their desire to sponge off society, in private-property tendencies, in improper behavior at work and at home and in religious prejudices. These things are all constantly being bolstered by bourgeois propaganda, which works its way into our country through various channels and exerts a harmful influence on individual Soviet citizens.

It is the duty of a Communist to contribute unremittingly to the molding and education of the man of communist society, to wage a determined struggle against all manifestations of bourgeois ideology, against the vestiges of private-property psychology and other survivals of the past, to be a model in observing the rules of communist morality, and always and in all things to place public interests above personal interests.

Comrades! For a Marxist-Leninist party in power there is no surer and more reliable method of improving its work, training cadres, eliminating shortcomings and rectifying mistakes than the tried and tested method of criticism and self-criticism.

When an official stops seeing his own shortcomings and mistakes and is uncritical in appraising the results of his work, he becomes conceited and complacent, lives in the past and loses perspective. When his shortcomings and mistakes are pointed out to such an official, he treats the remarks of his comrades in a manner unbecoming a member of the Party and all too often takes the course of suppressing criticism.

There are cases where certain conceited leaders consider even an appeal for criticism to be an infringement on their authority. For instance, Comrade Gasparyan, former First Secretary of the Artashat District Committee of the Communist Party of Armenia, ordered an issue of the district newspaper to be withdrawn and destroyed for the sole reason that it carried an editorial that in the most general terms called upon the delegates to a district Party conference to criticize shortcomings in the work of the district Party committee. Gasparyan felt that this appeal undermined his personal authority as district committee secretary. But what sort of Party leader is this? This is not a leader but a sheer misfortune! (Stir in the hall.)

The Party Statutes to be adopted by the Congress are called upon to arm Communists for combating intolerable occurrences of this sort. One of the paramount duties of a Party member is to develop criticism and self-criticism and to combat ostentation, conceit, complacency, bureaucracy and localism.

A Communist is called upon to rebuff firmly any attempts to suppress criticism and to resist any actions detrimental to the Party and the state. We must everywhere establish conditions that will enable a Party member to exercise freely the right to criticize any Communist regardless of the position he holds. The draft Party Statutes not only proclaim this right for a Party member but guarantee it. "Persons guilty of suppressing criticism or persecuting anyone for criticism," says the draft, "must be held to strict Party responsibility, up to and including expulsion from the ranks of the C.P.S.U."

Our party exists for the people and regards serving the people as its supreme mission, the whole point of its activity. The Party is at every turn guided by Lenin's instructions that it not only teach the masses but learn from them as well, that it study and utilize the experience of the masses. It is the duty of a Communist to explain the policy of the Party to the masses, to help strengthen and broaden the Party's ties with the people, to be tactful and considerate with people and to respond promptly to the wants and needs of the working people. The strengthening of the Party's unbreakable ties with the masses of the working people is an essential requirement for successfully translating the great plans for communist construction into reality. (Applause.)

The draft Statutes consider the education of Soviet people in a spirit of proletarian internationalism and socialist patriotism to be one of the most important duties of a Party member. A Communist must combat survivals of nationalism and chauvinism, must contribute by word and deed to strengthening the friendship of the peoples of the U.S.S.R. and the fraternal ties of the Soviet people with the peoples of the countries in the social-

ist camp and the proletarians and working people of all countries. (Applause.)

The strength and invincibility of our party lie in the unity and indestructible monolithic solidarity of its ranks, in conscious iron discipline. It is the duty of a Party member to defend the ideological and organizational unity of the Party in every way, to display vigilance, and to safeguard the Party against the infiltration of persons unworthy of the lofty title of Communist.

Be truthful and honest, observe Party and state discipline strictly, and serve your people faithfully—this is what the Party demands of every Communist and of any Party leader.

Unfortunately, we still come across officials who forget this indisputable truth and who take the course of deceiving the Party and state.

Take, for instance, the former leaders of the Tadzhik Party organization—Uldzhabayev, Dodkhudoyev and Obnosov. Having proved incapable of insuring the further development of the republic's economy, cotton growing in the first place, they resorted to anti-Party acts that to all intents and purposes constituted fraud. To conceal their political bankruptcy and at the same time make it appear that they were marching in step with life, these sorry excuses for leaders went in for hoodwinking and account padding. The republic was failing to meet the state plan for cotton procurements, but its leaders, having lost all shame and conscience, reported that the plan had been met ahead of schedule. They implanted servility and toadyism in the organization, trod inner-Party democracy underfoot and violated state laws.

It must be pointed out that the Party organization of Tadzhikistan proved equal to the situation. After investigating the state of affairs in the republic, with the help of the Central Committee of the C.P.S.U., it denounced the anti-Party behavior of the former leaders, and, as you know, a plenary session of the Central Committee of the Communist Party of Tadzhikistan dismissed them from their positions and expelled them from the Party.

The Party Statutes make it incumbent on a Communist to oppose any actions detrimental to the Party and the state, to adhere to principle at all times and in all things and to show Bolshevik intolerance of deception, falsehood and hypocrisy.

Our party is flesh of the flesh of its great people. It is strong by virtue of its links with the people, its loyalty to the people and its thorough understanding of their interests. The people will not stand for deception and untruth! Only that Communist, only that Party leader who is honest and truthful is respected by the masses. Only such a leader works boldly and confidently. He does not fear just criticism of his actions but on the contrary regards criticism as help and support from the masses. (Applause.)

Thus the duties of a Party member as set forth in the draft Statutes derive from the need to heighten the responsibility of every Communist for our great cause. The Party member's clear understanding of his duties under the Statutes and his comprehensive exercise of the broad rights envisaged by the Statutes should ensure the further development of the initiative and independent activity of Communists and heighten the militancy of all Party organizations.

Comrades! In the period since the 20th Congress the Party has substantially reinforced its ranks with advanced workers, collective farmers and representatives of the intelligentsia. Party organizations have begun to concern themselves more closely with the growth and regulation of the ranks of the C.P.S.U.

This does not mean, however, that there are no shortcomings in the way we handle admissions to the Party. Quite often Party organizations fail to observe the principle of individual selection; they show an interest in the work reference of a comrade who has applied for admission, which is as it should be, but know little about his public activities or his behavior in the family, in his private life.

The Statutes of the C.P.S.U. are being supplemented with a number of provisions that should still further increase the responsibility of Party organizations for admissions to the Party, for observing the principle of individual selection of the most socially conscious and advanced people in Soviet society for membership in the C.P.S.U. The Party organizations must be required to show greater concern for the education and ideological molding of youthful Communists and candidates for Party membership.

The clause permitting the extension of the probationary period for candidate members has been dropped from the draft Statutes. This measure was introduced after the 19th Party Congress. The reason for its introduction was that there were many candidate members in the Party whose probationary period had expired: At that time the Party had more than 300,000 persons who had been candidates for over five years. At present the Party has some 10,000 candidate members whose probationary period has lasted two or three years.

The lengthening of the period of probation has unquestionably played a positive role. However, as the above data show, there is no further need for this. Moreover, the leaders of some Party organizations, wrongly interpreting the right to prolong the probationary period, did little in the way of preparing candidate members to join the Party within one year's time. The draft Statutes envisage a different procedure. If in the period of his probation the candidate for Party membership has not proved himself and because of his personal qualifications cannot be admitted into the Party, the Party organization adopts a resolution refusing him admission to Party membership. The probationary period should actually serve as a school for preparing candidates for full membership in the C.P.S.U.

The invigoration of ideological life in the Party, the strengthening of Party discipline and the heightening of political consciousness among Communists have brought about a sharp decline in the number of expulsions from the C.P.S.U. in recent years. Our position will continue to be that expulsion from the Party, the highest Party penalty, should be resorted to only in the case of people who are really unworthy of being in the Party

In order to set up guarantees against unwarranted application of the highest Party penalty and to heighten the responsibility of Party organizations for the fortunes of their members, a new provision has been introduced in the draft Statutes: The decision of a primary organization to expel a member from the Party shall be considered carried only if at least two-thirds, rather than a simple majority, of the Party members present at the meeting vote for it.

The primary Party organizations are granted the right to discuss calling to account and imposing penalties upon Communists elected to district, city, region, province or territory Party committees or to the Central Committees of the Union-republic Communist Parties, as well as members of the respective auditing commissions.

All matters bearing on the fate of a Party member must be looked into closely. But at the same time there must be no lowering of the standards expected of Communists. Party organizations should show intolerance and take a principled stand in dealing with those who by their behavior and actions do the Party harm.

The Further Development of Inner-Party Democracy.—The draft Statutes consistently uphold the idea that the extension of democracy in Party life is an essential requirement for further invigorating the activeness and initiative of all the Party's organizations and for involving all Communists in vigorous, creative Party work. In the organization of its internal life the Party must serve as a model in working out the very best forms of communist public self-government.

The Party's organizational structure is firmly based on the Leninist principle of democratic centralism, which harmoniously combines a high degree of organization and the strictest discipline with the broadest inner-Party democracy. The draft Statutes elaborate this inviolable Leninist principle of Party construction on the basis of the experience accumulated by the Party.

Of extraordinary importance is the thesis contained in the draft Statutes that collective leadership is the highest principle of Party leadership, a principle that guarantees the Party and all its bodies against unilateral, subjective decisions and actions. Only collective leadership creates the conditions under which the activeness and initiative of Communists can develop and ensures the proper training of cadres. Needless to say, collective leadership in no way lessens the personal responsibility of a Party worker for matters entrusted to him, for the execution of collectively adopted decisions.

Leninist standards of Party life, the principle of collective

leadership and the systematic turnover of the membership of Party agencies preclude excessive concentration of power in the hands of individual officials and the chance that the collective will lose control over their actions, and they ensure a broad influx of fresh forces into executive Party bodies and the proper combination of old and young cadres. (Applause.)

In conformity with the Program of the C.P.S.U., the draft Statutes call for the periodic turnover of the membership of Party committees and for continuity of leadership.

It is contemplated that at all regular elections of the C.P.S.U. Central Committee and its Presidium, not less than one-fourth of their membership shall be newly elected; in the case of the Central Committees of the Union-republic Communist Parties and of territory and province Party committees, not less than one-third; and in the case of region, city and district Party committees and the committees and bureaus of primary Party organizations, one-half. The need to introduce these important new provisions is demonstrated profoundly and comprehensively in Nikita Sergeyevich Khrushchev's report on the draft Program of the C.P.S.U.

It must be said, comrades, that we have all that is required for carrying out this provision. The Party's cadres have increased numerically and grown stronger ideologically and politically. Thousands upon thousands of Communists are swelling the ranks of the Party aktiv year after year. In actuality, the regular turnover of the membership of executive Party bodies has become the rule in recent years.

Let me cite some data. In the last elections, 45% of the members of the Central Committees of the Union-republic Communist Parties and of territory and province Party committees were newly elected, and in the case of city and district committees the figure was 40%. Turnover of the membership of executive bodies must become a norm of Party life. This process has therefore been embodied in the Program and Statutes and is being made a law of Party life. (Applause.)

Previously, in many Party bodies a certain number of the executive officials served a very long time without being replaced. The draft Statutes preclude this possibility. They specify that members of the Presidium of the Central Committee of the C.P.S.U. shall not, as a rule, be elected for more than three successive terms. Similarly, members of the Central Committees of the Union-republic Communist Parties and of territory, province, region, city and district Party committees and committees and bureaus of Party organizations may not be elected for more than three terms. Secretaries of primary Party organizations may not be elected for more than two consecutive terms.

The wisdom of this system of elections to Party bodies is plain. New people, Party workers who are developing and are full of initiative, should steadily be moving into positions of leadership. At the same time firm steps must be taken to rid the executive bodies of the Party of persons who have been in office much too long, who have come to believe themselves irreplaceable, have stopped growing and, though they cannot cope with the tasks assigned them, cling tenaciously to executive positions.

Take, for instance, Comrade Dolgatov, former secretary of the Sergokala District Party Committee in the Dagestan Autonomous Republic. Having in his conceit come to believe himself irreplaceable, he began ignoring the opinions of the Party organization. When, in response to warnings from the Communists, the question of his work was brought up at a plenary session of the district committee, Dolgatov declared: "No tsar ever surrendered power voluntarily, and I have no intention of surrendering mine without a fight." (Laughter in the hall.) The Communists of the district fired the presumptuous bureaucrat from his position as secretary of the district committee. (Applause.)

But it is not only on the district level that we see "leaders" of this sort in action. For example Comrade Kosov, former first secretary of the Tyumen Province Party Committee, decided that for him "no holds were barred." He took to abusing his authority and breaking socialist laws. Kosov was removed from the position of province committee secretary and severely punished.

The proposed procedure for systematic turnover of the membership of Party bodies, ensuring as it does an influx of fresh forces into leadership and continuity of leadership, is at the same time aimed against people who have grown conceited and who violate the norms of inner-Party life, as well as against weak-willed workers lacking initiative, who, as the saying goes, "have nothing to boast of, being all thumbs."

It should be pointed out that the principle of systematic turn-over of the membership of Party bodies is closely bound up with the principle of continuity of leadership. By no means does it deny the importance of the role played by experienced Party workers who enjoy high prestige. Without a more or less stable group of leaders it is not possible to ensure continuity in leadership, the transmission of accumulated experience. The draft Statutes therefore provide that particular Party leaders, particular Party officials may, by virtue of their recognized authority and the high order of their political and organizational abilities, be elected to executive bodies for a longer period. In such cases, however, for the candidate in question to be elected he must receive at least three-fourths of the votes cast by secret ballot.

During the discussion of the draft Statutes, the opinion was voiced that the possibility of electing particular Party officials to executive Party bodies for longer periods than envisaged by the draft Statutes should apply only to the C.P.S.U. Central Committee and its Presidium. One cannot agree with this suggestion. Suppose a secretary of a primary Party organiza-tion who has served two successive terms as a member of the district Party committee is elected second secretary of the district committee during his third term. He proves himself an able worker, deserving of promotion to the position of first secretary. However, he may not be elected a member of the district committee for a fourth time unless provision is made in the Statutes for extending the tenure of an authoritative, able Communist on an elective Party body. We must not obstruct the natural development and promotion of competent, enterprising and energetic Party workers.

Every Party worker in a position of leadership must in all his actions set an example of service to the people, must be a model for all Communists and non-Party people. (Applause.) The higher the position a Communist holds in the Party, the higher the degree of his responsibility. This is specifically under-scored in the draft Statutes of the C.P.S.U. through the introduc-tion of the following provision:

"A member or candidate member of the Central Committee of the C.P.S.U. must by his entire activity justify the high trust placed in him by the Party. If a member or candidate member of the Central Committee of the C.P.S.U. has sullied his honor and dignity, he cannot remain a member of the Central Com-mittee."

This provision of the draft Statutes shows what high demands our party makes upon those entrusted with membership in its militant Leninist general staff. (Prolonged applause.)

The draft Statutes envisage a change in the procedure for determining the results of balloting in elections to Party bodies Under the provision now in force, candidates who receive a larger number of votes than the others running for office, and the votes of more than one-half of the participants in the meet-ing, conference or Congress, are considered elected to the Party body.

The practical effect of this, quite often, is that a Party worker who may be experienced and valuable and who has been voted for by an absolute majority is rejected because some three to five votes have been cast against him. This is altogether out of keeping with the policy of all-round development of inner-Party democracy, since it permits an insignificant minority to impose its will on the absolute majority.

The draft Statutes therefore provide that any candidate who receives the votes of more than one-half of the participants in the meeting, conference or Congress is considered elected.

It may be objected that with this kind of voting the member-ship of a Party body may in certain cases prove somewhat larger than contemplated. There may indeed be such cases. But the draft Statutes do not specify the number of persons on elective Party bodies. A meeting of a Party organization, a conference or a Congress is entitled to decide for itself how many there shall be in its executive body. It goes without saying that the membership of a Party body should not be unduly large. However, all the details involved in the election of Party bodies

must be settled, as before, by appropriate instructions from the Central Committee of the C.P.S.U.

Another stipulation of the draft Statutes that is consistent with the further development of inner-Party democracy is the duty of Party bodies to keep Party organizations regularly informed about their work. This will help to strengthen ties between the Party's executive bodies and the masses and to reinforce control by the Party community, by all Communists, over the activities of their elective agencies.

The Party is strong by virtue of the activeness of its mem-bers. The Communist not only carries out the decisions of higher Party bodies but participates personally, as far as possible, in the framing of those decisions. We must therefore make sure that every opportunity exists for free and business-like discussion of questions of Party policy and for holding discussions on disputed or insufficiently clear questions, both in individual organizations and in the Party as a whole. This has been reflected in the draft Statutes.

An important feature of the draft Statutes is that they enhance the role of local Party bodies, broaden the sphere of their initi-ative and independent action in the accomplishment of the eco-nomic and political tasks facing the province, territory or republic.

It must at the same time be made clear that the C.P.S.U. is not a federation of parties or Party committees. It is a central-ized organization. The Communist Parties of the Union repub-lics and the territory and province organizations are parts of a single whole—the Communist Party of the Soviet Union. (Pro-longed applause.) The strict subordination of the individual Party organizations to the center and of lower organizations to higher ones is an absolute requirement for the Party's success-ful fulfillment of its historic tasks.

The Party is resolute in combating all manifestations of localism, all attempts to approach problems of Party policy from a parochial standpoint, as phenomena and tendencies that are alien to the Marxist-Leninist Party spirit. Lenin stressed that "refusal to submit to the leadership of the centers amounts to refusal to be in the Party, amounts to wrecking the Party."

Centralism is not inconsistent with inner-Party democracy. It assumes the utmost development of local initiative and creative activeness and a high degree of conscious discipline. Democratic centralism ensures the unity of the Party's will and actions and gives the Party mobility, enabling it to re-form its ranks rapidly as the situation changes, to concentrate the efforts of the whole Party on accomplishing the historic tasks of communist construction. (Applause.)

The C.P.S.U. unites in its ranks on a voluntary basis the advanced, most socially conscious members of Soviet society. Freedom of opinion, freedom to discuss any matters pertaining to the policy and the practical activities of the Party is a norm of Party life. The more important the question, the greater, as a rule, should be the number of Communists who participate in discussing it. And it is only natural that a diversity of opinions should be expressed in the process. From the exchange of opinions a single, correct point of view is evolved, which is then confirmed in a Party decision binding on all.

Needless to say, we cannot allow the Party to be drawn into a sterile discussion at the whim of some small group of con-fused or immature persons, or tolerate the undertaking by par-ticular anti-Party elements of actions that tend to undermine Party unity. The Party is not justified in excluding from its arsenal weapons that can be used in the struggle for the ideolog-ical and organizational unity of its ranks. (Prolonged ap-plause.) The Statutes therefore retain guarantees against attempts by an insignificant minority to impose its will on the majority, against attempts to form factionalist groups and attempts to split the Party.

During the discussion of the draft Statutes the following questions were asked: Does not the monolithic unity of the C.P.S.U. and of Soviet society as a whole exclude the possibili-ty of any divisive activity within the Party's ranks? Under present circumstances, need the Statutes contain any formal guarantees against factionalism and clique activity?

Yes, comrades, such guarantees are needed.

To be sure, there is no social base left in Soviet society that could feed opportunistic currents in the Party. But the sources of ideological waverings on the part of particular individuals or groups have not yet been entirely eliminated. Some persons may fall under the influence of bourgeois propaganda from the outside. Others, having failed to comprehend the dialectics of society's development and having turned, in Comrade N. S. Khrushchev's wonderful expression, into dying embers, will have nothing to do with anything new and go on clinging to old dogmas that have been toppled by life.

We all know how fiercely the factionalist anti-Party groups that included Molotov, Kaganovich, Malenkov, Voroshilov, Bulganin, Pervukhin and Saburov and that was joined by Shepilov sought to resist implementation of the Leninist line laid down by the 20th Party Congress.

The members of this group betrayed the Leninist principles of Party life. They were intent on carrying out their anti-Party designs at any cost, and they descended to the point of organizing secret gatherings and hatching plans to seize the leadership of the Party and country and alter the Party's policy. Molotov and the others wanted a return to the days, so painful for our party and country, when the reprehensible methods and actions spawned by the cult of the individual held sway and when no one was safe from arbitrary and repressive acts. They ignored the fact that the Leninist line that our party had adopted at the 20th Congress had been warmly endorsed by the entire Party, by the whole Soviet people and by the fraternal Marxist-Leninist parties. (Applause.)

It is quite clear that the factionalist group that sought to impose its anti-Party, anti-Leninist views on the Party might have seriously prejudiced the cause of communist construction.

I fully agree with Comrade N. S. Khrushchev that had these renegades won out they would have stopped at nothing to accomplish their nefarious purposes and would have made short shrift of honorable, wholly innocent people. It is our great good fortune, comrades, that the anti-Party group was rendered harmless and that we have been able, by adhering strictly to the Leninist line, to effect mighty changes in the country and to lift the prestige of our party and the Soviet state on the international scene to an unprecedented height. (Prolonged applause.)

In the struggle against the anti-Party factionalist group, in the defense of the Leninist policy of our party, the First Secretary of our party's Central Committee, Nikita Sergeyevich Khrushchev, displayed Bolshevik firmness and dedication to principle. (Applause.) The whole Central Committee rallied around Comrade Khrushchev. In this complicated situation the Central Committee of our party held firm to Marxism-Leninism, resolutely and unsparingly exposed the factionalist anti-Party group and thoroughly smashed it. (Applause.) These actions of the C.P.S.U. Central Committee and of Comrade N. S. Khrushchev met with the approval of the entire Party and the whole Soviet people. (Stormy, prolonged applause.)

From this lofty rostrum of the 22nd Congress many delegates have wrathfully condemned the unsavory deeds of the anti-Party group as a whole and of its individual members.

Facts have been disclosed and set forth attesting that Molotov, Kaganovich and Malenkov had a hand in the destruction of many altogether innocent people, including prominent Party figures and statesmen, and that by their careerist policy and their departure from Marxism-Leninism they contributed to the establishment and flourishing of the cult of the individual.

The facts show that even now the organizers of the anti-Party group are still endeavoring to uphold their pernicious views. Molotov has been showing particular zeal in this respect. He has even gone so far as to describe the new Program of the C.P.S.U. as antirevolutionary in spirit. It means nothing to Molotov that in the general discussion of the Program it met with universal approval from the Party and the people and from the fraternal Marxist-Leninist parties, or that all honorable people on earth are calling it the Communist Manifesto of our times. This declaration of Molotov's is in effect a challenge to our whole party and to the 22nd Congress of the C.P.S.U., which has given its unanimous approval to the new Program. I share the opinion of the delegates who have spoken here that Molotov, Kaganovich and Malenkov should be called to strict account before the Party and the people for all their anti-Party, criminal acts.

The anti-Party group, above all Molotov, Kaganovich and Malenkov, opposed with all their might the effort to undo the consequences of the cult of the individual. They feared they would be called upon to answer for the abuses of power perpe-

trated in the period of the Stalin cult.

The violation of Lenin's behests by Stalin, the abuse of power and the mass repressions of blameless Soviet citizens have been condemned by our party and by the whole Soviet people. (Prolonged applause.)

Comrades! In the Central Committee's report to the Congress and yesterday in his concluding remarks, Nikita Sergeyevich Khrushchev stated that recently, without any cause on the part of the Communist Party of the Soviet Union or its leadership, the leaders of the Albanian Party of Labor have abruptly altered their political policy and taken the course of sharply impairing relations with our party, with the Soviet Union and with other socialist countries. The actions of the leaders of the Albanian Party of Labor, above all Mehmet Shehu and Enver Hoxha, plainly show what can happen when there are relapses into the cult of the individual, when Leninist principles of Party leadership are violated and antidemocratic practices are implanted in a party and a country.

The Albanian leaders have forgotten what the help and support of the Soviet Union and the other socialist countries have meant for their country. While continuing to talk hypocritically about Soviet-Albanian friendship, they have in reality been going back on that friendship and persecuting the true friends of the Soviet Union. The Albanian leaders have in their actions gone so far as to openly attack our party and its Leninist Central Committee and the leadership of the fraternal parties of the socialist countries. The leaders of the Albanian Party of Labor for their part masquerade as all but the sole consistent Marxist-Leninists. Actually, however, they have been resurrecting in their party and country all that was reprehensible in our country in the period when the cult of the individual held sway, and they are holding on to power through resort to force and arbitrary action.

The pernicious policy of the Albanian leaders may result in divorcing Albania from the socialist camp and isolating the Albanian Party of Labor politically in the ranks of the international Communist movement. This kind of anti-Leninist course may at the same time seriously prejudice socialist construction in Albania, construction that has cost that country's heroic people such exertion and labor, and may impair the country's position in the international arena.

The Moscow conference of representatives of Communist and Workers' Parties held in November, 1960, set down in its Statement: "A resolute defense of the unity of the international Communist movement on the basis of the principles of Marxism-Leninism and proletarian internationalism and the prevention of any actions that could undermine that unity are necessary conditions for victory in the struggle for national independence, democracy and peace, for the successful accomplishment of the tasks of socialist revolution and of the building of socialism and communism. Violation of these principles would lead to a weakening of the forces of communism."

This historic Statement, as everyone knows, bears the signature of the Albanian Party of Labor. Yet all the recent actions of its leaders indicate that they have begun to depart from the agreed general line of the international Communist movement on the major problems of the day. What is more, the leadership of the Albanian Party of Labor turned down repeated moves by the Central Committee of the C.P.S.U. and other fraternal parties to iron out the differences that had arisen. The Albanian leaders responded by rudely rebuffing these moves, and went over to what were in effect provocative actions.

What was the Central Committee to do in a situation when numerous attempts at persuading the Albanian leaders to renounce their sectarian activities had been made without success and, through the fault of those leaders, their disastrous policy of departure from the principles of proletarian internationalism had become known to our ideological adversaries? It is obvious that in this situation, principled censure of the Albanian leaders' anti-Leninist behavior and an open appeal to seek ways of ironing out the differences that had arisen was the only correct, serious Marxist-Leninist approach to this matter. (Prolonged applause.) This is why, in its report to the Congress, the Central Committee has told the whole truth about the reprehensible stand of the leaders of the Albanian Party of Labor.

Comrade N. S. Khrushchev has related facts showing that Mehmet Shehu, Enver Hoxha and other Albanian leaders have in the past few days, even while the 22nd Party Congress has been proceeding with its work, committed acts indicating that they are drifting still farther toward nationalism and sectarianism, moving still farther away from the agreed line of the international Communist movement, and have taken to leveling outright slander against the C.P.S.U. and its Central Committee and to deceiving their party and their people. Why, it is nothing short of a disgrace, comrades, that the Albanian leaders should regard as their enemies all who today advocate friendship with the Soviet Union!

We must state emphatically that the genuine unity of the fraternal Communist and Workers' Parties is possible only if it is based on commitment to Marxist-Leninist principle, and not on ignoring the pernicious line of the Albanian leaders. (Applause.) In this case to take the line of hushing things up is to encourage people to continue their wrong, anti-Leninist acts. Our party cannot take that course. (Prolonged applause.)

We Soviet Communists will go on resolutely exposing all renegades from Leninism, all revisionists and dogmatists. The cause of socialist revolution, the cause of Marx and Lenin, is a great cause. And the fight for the purity of the Marxist-Leninist teaching, for its creative development and for ideological unity in the ranks of the entire world Communist movement is the sacred duty of every Soviet Communist, and our whole Leninist party. (Stormy, prolonged applause.)

The Growing Role of the Party's Local Bodies and Primary Organizations.—Comrades! The policy of the Party is being translated into reality by the labor of millions of Soviet people. Under the leadership of the Party, of its local bodies and primary organizations at factories and plants, on collective and state farms, in scientific institutes and in institutions, the Soviet people are enthusiastically pursuing the enormous tasks of communist construction.

The most important thing in the activities of district, city, region, province and territory organizations of the Party and the Union-republic Communist Parties and their executive bodies is to carry out the policy of the Party, to organize the implementation of the decisions of Party Congress and directives of the C.P.S.U. Central Committee. This general task is given specific form in the draft Statutes in a list of the basic duties of the Party's local organizations and their executive bodies.

The most important of these duties are the all-round development of industrial and agricultural production and work for a steady rise in the living standard and cultural level of the working people. Party bodies can ensure the fulfillment of these duties by raising the level of political and organizational work among the masses, improving the selection and training of cadres and intensifying guidance of state and public organizations.

Selecting and placing executive cadres and instilling in them a spirit of communist ideology and a high sense of responsibility to the Party and people for the work entrusted to them—this is the central task in the organizational work of the Party, its local bodies and primary organizations.

The Party organizations have done a great deal of work in the matter of improving the selection, placement and education of cadres, and it has produced positive results. The overwhelming majority of the Party's cadres possess the requisite knowledge and organizational experience. More than nine-tenths of the secretaries of province and territory Party committees and Central Committees of the Union-republic Communist Parties and almost three-fourths of the secretaries of the city and district Party committees have a higher education. In the past five years the number of secretaries of district and city committees who have a higher education has more than trebled. The number of engineers, economists, agronomists, zootechnicians and other specialists among the Party's executive cadres has been increasing year by year.

This being the case, it is particularly intolerable that some sectors of Party, Soviet, economic and cultural construction should still quite often be directed by people who lack the required knowledge or who are simply poorly trained. There is one reason for this—inattention to the selection, placement and education of cadres.

In the selection and placement of cadres, Party bodies sometimes fill vacant positions mechanically, by hastily promoting personnel, rather than following a carefully thought-out policy

dictated by the needs of the situation. Here is one example. It was necessary to choose a director for the Building Materials Machinery Plant in the city of Kuibyshev. How did they go about it? The economic council telephoned the province Party committee, and it was decided, without looking into the matter thoroughly, to promote to the position Comrade Kuroyedov, a shop superintendent at one of the plants. No one was disturbed by the fact that a short time previously Kuroyedov had been exposed for account padding and hoodwinking, for which he had been called to Party and administrative account. It should come as no surprise that after Kuroyedov became director of the plant he indulged in padding on an even bigger scale, with the result that it soon became necessary to remove him. It is characteristic, however, that in relieving Kuroyedov of his position as director, neither the economic council nor the Kuibyshev City Party Committee could muster the courage to admit its mistake and state outright that he was being dismissed from his job for hoodwinking. As a cover for all this they fell back on the ambiguous, "elastic" formula: "Released in connection with transfer to other work." (Stir in the hall.)

It is surely clear that this incorrect practice breeds irresponsibility and new mistakes in the selection and promotion of personnel.

Party committees must be highly exacting in the demands they make upon cadres. It is their duty to work patiently with people and to educate them in a spirit of high-mindedness and adherence to principle. But there are still Party committees that know no other means of exerting any influence on personnel than threats and administrative action. Was not this style of leadership typical, for instance, of the Kardymovo District Committee of Smolensk Province? Within a brief period 32 collective farm chairmen were replaced in the district. At a district Party conference one of the collective farm chairmen offered a figurative characterization of such methods of "leadership." "The district committee," he said, "managed the collective farms from a position of strength and keeping personnel on the brink of incurring a strict Party reprimand or being expelled from the Party." (Laughter in the hall.)

We must put an end to this treatment of cadres. It runs counter to the Party's policy of further promoting inner-Party democracy. The Statutes of the C.P.S.U. point the efforts of Party bodies toward further improving work with cadres, heightening the accountability of Party workers to the Party and people and improving the methods of Party leadership.

Important measures have been carried out in the past few years for broadening the rights of local Soviet and economic agencies. In planning, in the management of industry and agriculture and in the employment of financial and material resources, the restrictions that had cramped local initiative and independent action have been lifted. Conditions have thereby been made more conducive to efficient utilization of the resources of provinces, territories and republics. Today the local Party committees also have broad rights in deciding questions of Party organization.

This policy of developing socialist democracy has had a favorable effect on the activities of local bodies. The responsibility of Party organizations for the condition of the management of state and public affairs has unquestionably grown. This does not, however, mean that Party committees should supplant Soviet and economic agencies, should take on functions proper to these agencies.

Unfortunately, Party committees are still to be encountered that concern themselves with matters that might well be handled by other agencies. This is evident from the fact that certain Party and Soviet agencies have been adopting a good many joint resolutions on matters of secondary importance. Was it after all really necessary that the Buryat Province Party Committee and the republic's Council of Ministers adopt a joint resolution on the utilization of natural thickets of sea buckthorn in Selenga District? This sort of practice implants irresponsibility and teaches Soviet and economic cadres to solicit decisions from Party agencies on the slightest pretext.

State and economic agencies must be released from petty tutelage. This requirement is reflected in the following provision of the draft Statutes of the C.P.S.U.: "Party organizations do not supplant Soviet, trade union, cooperative or other public organizations of the working people and must not permit a merging of the functions of Party and other agencies or unnecessary parallelism in work."

Strict observance of these requirements of the Statutes will enable Party agencies to concentrate on vigorous organizational work with the masses. It is necessary to draw the working people more actively into the administration of state and public affairs, to improve the selection, placement and education of cadres, and to organize effective supervision and verification of fulfillment; these matters are treated exhaustively in the Central Committee's report to the Congress.

The development of voluntary, unpaid participation in Party work has been of vast importance for improving the work of local Party organizations. The diversity and scope that it has already assumed can be judged from the following data. Non-staff instructors, lecturers and members of various permanent commissions of the district, city, region, province and territory Party committees and of the Central Committees of the Union-republic Communist Parties now number more than 230,000 persons. More than 600,000 Communists serve on the commissions of the primary Party organizations for supervising the work of management. Thousands of political education centers, Party study rooms and libraries have been established and are operating successfully on a voluntary basis in Party organizations for supervising the work of management. Thousands of political education centers, Party study rooms and libraries have been established and are operating successfully on a voluntary basis in Party organizations, and this is also true of the nonstaff editorial boards and departments in the press. The Party commissions that have been set up under the borough committees of Moscow and Leningrad, also on a voluntary basis, for preliminary consideration of matters pertaining to admission to the Party and to personal affairs are one of the new organizational forms for enlisting the efforts of the aktiv. These commissions are doing a useful job. A close look should be taken at their work; their experience should be studied and thought should be given to its wider application.

What we need is a reduction of the apparatus of the Party agencies and an increase in the ranks of the Party aktiv. The Party agencies, says Nikita Sergeyevich Khrushchev, should have more and more commissions, departments, instructors and secretaries of district and city committees working on an unpaid basis.

Comrades! The basic Party link, the place where the Communist is molded as a high-principled, socially conscious and active fighter, is the primary Party organization. Nothing can replace the schooling that the Communist receives in the Party collective. The primary organizations carry on their work in the very thick of the masses. It is through the primary Party organizations that the Party actually exercises its leadership of the masses and puts its policy and decisions into effect.

In the past few years the primary Party organizations have grown in strength and increased in numbers. There are at present some 300,000 primary organizations in the Party. The section on the primary Party organizations in the draft Statutes has been substantially reworked, in the light of the tasks set by the Party Program and in view of the greater demands that are being made upon all sectors of Party work.

The chief things at the center of attention of the primary Party organizations today are the struggle to create the material and technical base of communism, the development of communist social relations and problems of the communist education of the working people. (Applause.)

The primary organization, state the draft Statutes, acts as the organizer of the working people in carrying out routine tasks of communist construction and heads socialist competition for the fulfillment of state plans and pledges of the working people. One of its most important tasks is to mobilize the masses for disclosing and making better use of the internal reserves of enterprises and collective farms and for widely introducing in production the achievements of science and technology and the experience of leading workers. The primary organizations are asked to work for the strengthening of labor discipline and for a steady rise in labor productivity and an improvement in the quality of output and to show concern for protecting and increasing public wealth at enterprises and state and collective farms.

The primary organizations of industrial and trade enterprises and state and collective farms possess a powerful and effective instrument for the successful accomplishment of these tasks—the right to supervise the work of the administration. The draft Statutes now grant this right also to the primary organizations of design bureaus and research institutes directly connected with production.

The primary organization helps the working people to develop skills in the administration of state and public affairs and, through the broad development of criticism and self-criticism, combats manifestations of bureaucracy and localism and violations of state discipline. It is a duty of the primary organization to work hard to enhance the vanguard role of Communists in the sphere of labor and in socio-political and economic life and to improve agitation and propaganda work among the masses.

Comrades! The Communist Party, exponent of the Soviet people's finest aspirations, is the standard-bearer of communist morality. On its banner are inscribed the highest and brightest ideals. The Party will be able to accomplish its great tasks only if it educates all its members and all Soviet people in a spirit of communist morality, deep social consciousness and ideological commitment, diligence and discipline, and dedication to public interests. An enormous role will be played in this by the moral code of the builder of communism, formulated in the Program of the C.P.S.U. and included in the Statutes. This code will become the standard of behavior for a Party member, a tuning-fork, so to speak, that the Communist himself and the Party organization will use to compare and gauge the moral qualities of Party comrades. (Prolonged applause.)

Thus all the provisions in the draft Statutes affecting primary organizations are intended to enhance their role still further and make them more active and militant in working to accomplish the great tasks of communist construction.

In the period of the full-scale building of communism the Soviets, trade unions, cooperatives and other mass organizations of the working people play a heightened role. Through them the Party will continue broadening and strengthening its ties with the masses, will consult the people on major aspects of its policy and will draw all the working people on a broader scale into the administration of state and public affairs. The draft Statutes emphasize that the Party exercises leadership of the mass organizations through the Party groups in them, by promoting the independent initiative and vigorous activity of the masses as the essential requirement for the gradual transition from the socialist state organization to communist public self-government.

The task of Party groups in non-Party organizations is to heighten the Party's all-round influence and give effect to its policy among non-Party people, to strengthen Party and state discipline, to combat bureaucracy and to check on the execution of Party and state directives.

The Young Communist League is growing in importance. The Party looks upon young people as a great constructive and creative force in the effort of the Soviet people to achieve communism, and upon the Y.C.L. as a public organization of young people which displays independent initiative and is the Party's active helper and reserve. (Applause.) The Y.C.L. is called upon to help the Party rear young people in a spirit of communism, to involve them in the building of the new society, to produce a generation of well-rounded people, people who will be living, working and administering the affairs of society under communism.

The Communist Party regards as its sacred duty concern for strengthening the U.S.S.R.'s defense capacity; the Party considers its leadership to be the keystone in the development and organization of the armed forces. The draft Statutes declare that the Party organizations of the Soviet Army are guided in their work by the Program and Statutes of the C.P.S.U. The basic tasks of Party organizations in the armed forces are set forth in the draft Statutes. They contain the very important statement that the guidance of Party work in the armed forces is effected by the Central Committee through the Chief Political Administration of the Soviet Army and Navy, which functions as a department of the Central Committee of the C.P.S.U.

Results of the Discussion of the Draft Statutes of the C.P.S.U.— Comrades! The draft Statutes have been widely discussed at meetings of primary Party organizations, at district, city, region, province and territory Party conferences and at Congresses of the Union-republic Communist Parties, with the participation of more than 9,000,000 Communists. More than 1,500,000 persons spoke in the discussions that followed the reports on the draft Statutes. Party bodies and the editorial offices of newspapers and magazines received more than 120,000 letters containing various comments on and additions to the draft Statutes.

We have good grounds for saying that the whole of the Party, all Communists, took part in discussing the draft Statutes of the C.P.S.U. The draft Statutes met with unanimous approval at all Party meetings, conferences and Congresses without exception. (Prolonged applause.)

The extremely active participation in the discussion of the draft Statutes and the comments and suggestions for changes and additions that were made indicate that the army of Communists of the Soviet Union, many millions strong, is imbued with concern for further strengthening the Party's ranks, heightening its militancy and still further improving its organization, and augmenting the role of every Party organization and every Communist in making a reality of the historic blueprints in the new Program.

The suggestions and comments of the Communists touch on many aspects of the further development of the Party, the promotion of inner-Party democracy, Leninist standards and principles of Party life, membership in the Party and the duties and rights of the Communist.

The suggestions received can be broken down into three groups.

The first group covers those that supplement or develop particular provisions of the draft Statutes. They include suggestions that more emphasis be given to the need for constantly improving the forms and methods of Party work, promoting inner-Party democracy and raising the level of the leadership of the masses. These suggestions were all given careful study by the Central Committee, and appropriate additions and more precise formulations have been introduced, in generalized form, in the text of the draft Statutes that has been passed out to the delegates.

I think it necessary to pause briefly on several of these suggestions.

In the course of the discussion many Communists expressed the wish that in the period between conferences and Congresses local Party committees would keep Party organizations more extensively informed about their work. These wishes accord with the Party's insistence on greater control by the Party rank and file over the work of elective bodies. This is a sound suggestion and is reflected in the draft Statutes.

Many think it essential to include in the Statutes a provision to the effect that every Communist has the duty of helping in every way to strengthen the defense might of the U.S.S.R. and to wage a tireless struggle for peace. Everyone knows that our party regards the defense of the socialist homeland and the strengthening of the U.S.S.R.'s defenses as the sacred duty of the Party and of the Soviet people as a whole, as an essential condition for the preservation and consolidation of peace all over the world, and regards the struggle for peace among nations as its paramount task. (Applause.) Due attention has been given to this thesis, too, in the draft Statutes.

It is further suggested that there be written into the Statutes the obligation of the Communist to be an active atheist and propagator of the scientific materialist world view. This suggestion merits attention. Religious prejudices and superstitions tenaciously persist and are still prevalent among a certain section of the population. Who but the Communist has the duty of explaining the antiscientific nature of religious ideas?

Besides the suggestions and additions described above, corrections of an editorial nature were also suggested when the draft was discussed, corrections aimed at improving particular formulations in the draft Statutes. Some of these corrections have been accepted and appropriate changes made in the draft.

The second group of suggestions, additions and comments includes those primarily intended to spell out in greater detail, or to expand, particular provisions already set down in the draft Statutes of the C.P.S.U.

It is suggested, for example, that the range of a Communist's duties be considerably broadened. But if many of these suggestions were to be accepted, it would mean including in the Statutes the important and the less important, the essential and the nonessential. We think this should not be done. The question of what the Party demands of a Communist in the period of the full-scale building of a communist society is answered fully and extensively in the list of duties of a Party member formulated in the draft Statutes.

It has also been suggested that the new Statutes retain the numerous statements that failure by a Party member to fulfill a particular duty listed in the Statutes is incompatible with continued membership in the Party. But the draft Statutes do contain special articles that specify the accountability of a Communist for nonfulfillment or violation of requirements under the Statutes. This is quite sufficient.

Many comments and additions were submitted on the questions of admission to the Party and probationary candidacy. Some people suggest tightening the requirements for persons joining the Party: increasing the period of probation for candidates to two years and the period of membership for Communists making recommendations to five years; conducting admissions to the Party by secret ballot; requiring that persons seeking admission to the Party submit recommendations from collectives of workers and employees, trade union organizations, etc. Others, conversely, think it necessary to relax the present rules for admission to the C.P.S.U., for example to accept Y.C.L. members into the Party without the probationary candidacy; to shorten the probationary period to six months; and to reduce the number of recommendations required.

In our opinion, the procedure that the draft Statutes envisage for admission to the C.P.S.U. is in keeping with the present phase of our party's development and should not be changed. (Applause.)

Quite a few suggestions relate to problems of communist morality. Wishes were expressed that the Statutes might be more detailed in defining the duty of Party organizations to combat manifestations of private-property psychology, strivings for personal enrichment and the antisocial behavior of some Communists. The draft Statutes make suitable provision with respect to what is demanded of Party members in the section on the duties of a Communist and in the moral code of the builder of communism. The draft underscores the duty of a Party member to be intolerant of injustice, parasitism, dishonesty and money-grubbing. In general, the Party's position on the question of the Communist's moral complexion has been dealt with comprehensively in the reports by Comrade N. S. Khrushchev at our Congress, and all Party organizations will be guided unswervingly by the points made in those reports. (Prolonged applause.)

The third group covers suggestions and additions that fail to take account of the conditions under which the Party operates today.

It has been suggested, for example, that secretaries of district, city, province and territory Party committees and the Central Committees of the Union-republic Communist Parties be elected not at plenary sessions but directly at conferences and Congresses, and secretaries of Party bureaus at Party meetings. But if these suggestions were accepted and the secretaries of Party bureaus and committees were elected directly at meetings and conferences, it would mean that the secretaries would be vested with greater powers than the other members of the bureau or committee and set above the bureau or committee. This suggestion conflicts with the principle of collective leadership, and its acceptance would be inexpedient. (Applause.)

Nor can there be agreement with the proposal that the secret ballot be replaced with a show of hands in elections to Party bodies. Those who advance this proposal give as their reason that open voting does more than the secret ballot to cultivate in Party members a spirit of adherence to principle and encourages the development of criticism. This argument is unconvincing. Secret balloting is preceded, as everyone knows, by an open discussion of the nominations to the Party body. Every Party member has an unrestricted right to criticize and to challenge any candidate. Consequently, every opportunity exists for principled discussion of the merits and shortcomings of the nominees and hence for fostering in Communists a spirit of adherence to Party principles. The repudiation of the secret ballot would signify a step back in the evolution of inner-Party democracy, an abridgment and restriction of the Party member's right to the free and independent expression of his will. (Applause.)

I must also pause to consider the proposal that the institution of candidate membership in the Party be abolished. The argument advanced in support of this suggestion is that the political and cultural level of the people has risen substantially, that the primary Party organizations work in the very midst of the masses and can therefore acquaint themselves with the merits of every working person who desires to join the Party, without resorting to the probationary period for candidates.

The Communist is a man in the vanguard of Soviet society, he is an example for non-Party people. The probationary candidacy is the most important means of checking on whether a person seeking admission to the Party stands ready to fulfill the honorable and complex duties of a Communist. It is in the Party organization, in work performed jointly with members of the Party, that the qualifications of the future Party member are thoroughly revealed. To give up the probationary candidacy would mean lowering the standards for persons coming into the Party.

Suggestions were submitted that the Statutes provide for the revival of periodic Party purges. As we know, the Party deemed it necessary as far back as its 18th Congress to renounce the mass purges. The resolution of that Congress stated: "The method of mass purges, which was introduced at the beginning of the New Economic Policy, in a period when capitalist elements were reviving, to safeguard the Party against infiltration of its ranks by persons corrupted in connection with NEP, has lost its validity for the present situation, when the capitalist elements have been liquidated."

Since that time 22 years have elapsed. Socialism has triumphed fully and conclusively in the country, and the U.S.S.R. has entered the period of the full-scale building of communism. Is there any need, under the circumstances, to revive the Party purges?

The purges were necessary in a setting of acute class struggle in the country. Today, in the period of the full-scale building of communism, when indestructible moral and political unity of the whole people has been established in the country, there is no need for a measure of this kind. So strong is the Party ideologically and organizationally that persons who violate the Program and Statutes can be cleared out of its ranks without purges. (Prolonged applause.)

There are also suggestions and additions that, although well taken, are not specifically relevant to the Statutes. They are primarily concerned with the organization and conduct of report-and-election meetings and Party conferences, with determining the results of balloting, and other matters of this kind. As I have already stated, these suggestions and comments should be taken into consideration when the appropriate instructions of the C.P.S.U. Central Committee are worked out.

Finally, during the discussion of the draft Statutes Communists and non-Party people had a good many critical comments to make respecting the work of the local Party bodies. They pointed to specific shortcomings in the way these bodies handle their organizational and political work, to particular instances of violation of Leninist norms of Party life, to an improper attitude toward criticism and to distortions of the Party line in the selection of cadres. The Central Committees of the Union-republic Communist Parties and territory and province Party committees should closely examine all the critical comments and specific suggestions made by Communists with reference to local Party bodies and take appropriate steps to eliminate the shortcomings.

***

Comrades! The reports delivered by Comrade N. S. Khrushchev—the Central Committee's report and the report on the Party's draft Program—and the Program of the C.P.S.U., which the Congress has unanimously and most enthusiastically approved, open up broad new horizons to the Party and to the whole Soviet people. Our road to the great goal—communism—has now been outlined with the utmost clarity and scientific authenticity. (Applause.) ...

The Statutes of the C.P.S.U. to be adopted by the 22nd Party Congress will help all Party organizations and all Communists to determine their place in the common effort and to work with redoubled energy for the practical implementation of the decisions of the Congress. "The organizational principles laid down in the Statutes," Comrade N. S. Khrushchev has said, "should ensure successful accomplishment of the Program and strengthen the solidarity and unity of the Party—the Soviet people's fighting vanguard in the struggle for communism!" (Prolonged applause.)

XI. DISCUSSION OF KOZLOV'S REPORT

Kazanets

SPEECH BY COMRADE I. P. KAZANETS, SECOND SECRE-
TARY OF THE UKRAINE COMMUNIST PARTY CENTRAL
COMMITTEE. (Pravda, Oct. 29, p. 9.2,500 words. Excerpts:)
Today 10,000 nonsalaried instructors, 157 nonstaff departments and 1,940 public councils and commissions for various
questions of Party guidance are functioning in the Party committees of our republic. More than 55,000 Communists have
been enlisted in active Party work on a volunteer basis through
these forms alone. This is four times as many as the total
number of paid personnel in Party agencies.

Approximately 20,000 Party control commissions have now
been set up in primary Party organizations of the Ukraine in
accordance with the Party Central Committee's decisions.
These have a membership of more than 90,000 Communists.
As the two years' experience of work of these commissions
has shown, they have fully justified themselves and are an effective form of Party control of the work of management.
These commissions should be given legal status in the new
Party Statutes....

Comrade delegates! ... The principle of systematic renewal
of the membership of Party agencies and continuity of leadership advanced in the draft Statutes has been unanimously approved. Application of this principle will make it possible to
enlist fresh forces in active work and to rear new cadres. In
elections held in our republic there was a turnover of more
than 40% in the memberships of province city and district
Party committees. However, many district and city committee
secretaries, secretaries of Party organizations and Communists who spoke think that the tenure in office of secretaries
of primary Party organizations should not be limited to two
terms, i.e., to two years. This is especially important for
large Party organizations that have Party committees.

Take the Party committee at the Azov Steel Plant in Zhdanov, for example. This enterprise is spread over a large
area, and the plant's apartment houses, dormitories, educational combines and other services are located in various
parts of the city. A large number of Communists work in
them, and the total number of Communists at the plant is
2,200, united in 55 shop Party organizations, 46 of which have
the rights of primary organizations. There are 105 Party
groups at the plant. Consequently the secretary of such a
Party committee needs considerable time to familiarize himself with people and with production and to acquire the experience of Party work. A secretary has hardly acquired the
necessary experience before it is time for new elections.
Therefore perhaps the tenure in office of secretaries of large
Party organizations, at least, should be set at three terms.
(Applause.)

Comrades! In his report Comrade F. R. Kozlov spoke of
the proposal of many Communists to the effect that in the
period between reports local Party committees keep Party
units informed about their work. We fully support this. This
practice of reports has recommended itself in Party organizations in the Ukraine. In Lvov Province last year, for
example, all 36 city and district Party committees acquainted
the primary Party organizations with their work. Fifty thousand Communists attended the meetings held for this purpose,
and about 10,000 spoke. ...

Many proposals were made at Party meetings and conferences and at the Congress of the Ukraine Communist Party
concerning the necessity of granting city and district Party
committees the right of final decision on the question of expelling Communists from the Party. After all, they have final
decision on questions of Party admission and thereby bear full
responsibility to the Party for its qualitative composition.
Then why not give them the right of final decision on expulsion
from the Party, particularly since the draft Statutes provide
that persons excluded from the Party who do not agree with
the decision of the city or district Party committee may appeal to higher Party agencies, right up to the Party Central
Committee? (Applause.) This will help to strengthen Party
discipline and enhance the responsibility of city and district
Party committees for the purity of Party ranks. ...

Yegorychev

SPEECH BY COMRADE N. G. YEGORYCHEV, SECOND
SECRETARY OF THE MOSCOW CITY PARTY COMMITTEE.
(Pravda, Oct. 29, pp. 9-10. 2,700 words. Excerpts:) Comrade
delegates! ... At conferences and meetings the Communists
and all the working people of Moscow are unanimously expressing their indignation over the actions of the anti-Party
group, supporting the proposal of many delegates concerning
the expulsion of Molotov, Malenkov and Kaganovich from the
Party and condemning the schismatic actions of the leaders of
the Albanian Party of Labor. (Applause.)

The delegates to the Congress from the Moscow City Party
organization unanimously and warmly approve Nikita Sergeyevich Khrushchev's proposal that a monument be erected in
Moscow commemorating the remarkable Party and state
workers who were lost during the time of the Stalin cult. (Stormy
applause.) They perished as steadfast, faithful fighters of the
Leninist Party, fighters for the victory of socialism and communism in our country.

Great anger fills the heart as one listens to the speeches at
the Congress exposing the monstrous crimes against the Party
and the people committed by the despicable group of political
adventurists during the time of the cult of the individual. A
bitter lump rises in your throat when you hear of the physical
and mental sufferings the courageous fighters of the Party had
to endure. And how proud you are in the realization that the
Party even in those gloomy days succeeded in preserving the
purity of its ranks and its devotion to Leninism and that it
found in itself great forces to mercilessly expose the group of
pitiful intriguers and cast them on the dump of history. ...

Moscow has considerably expanded its boundaries. The city's
population has risen from 5,000,000 to 6,000,000. The city
Party organization has increased its ranks by 177,000 persons
since the 20th Congress and now numbers 586,000 Communists.
The number of administrative boroughs has been reduced from
25 to 17 and the number of staff employees in the boroughs by
15%. Today Moscow's boroughs have a population of up to
500,000, and a borough Party organization unites up to 40,000
Communists in its ranks. ...

The public principle in Party work has received wide dissemination in the Moscow City Party organization, just as it
has in the Ukraine. More than 6,000 Party commissions have

been set up in Moscow to exercise rights of supervision over the activity of management, and 34,000 Communists have been elected to them.

More than 1,000 nonsalaried instructors now function in the 17 Moscow boroughs—twice as many as the total number of salaried instructors. ...

Considerable work is being done by the nonstaff Party commissions for the preliminary consideration of matters pertaining to Party admission and to the personal cases of Communists, which have been established with the permission of the Party Central Committee in all Moscow boroughs.

Realizing the great importance of further expanding the public principle, the Moscow City Committee and the borough Party committees have begun to search for more and more new forms of enlisting Communists in Party work. Thus a permanent commission for urban development (which includes prominent architects, builders, artists, economists and industrial personnel); a commission for ideological work, called upon to enlist the public widely in the communist education of the working people; and a headquarters of people's volunteer detachments, which organizes and directs the work of more than 150,000 people's volunteers, have been set up under the city Party committee.

Technical-economic councils, councils of production innovators, propaganda and the introduction of advanced experience, methodological councils for Party-organizational questions, Party control inspection commissions and others have been formed in the borough Party committees. In setting up these commissions and councils, we have proceeded from the needs of life, the practice of Party work, from the urgent tasks that face us.

Public principles have been most widely disseminated in ideological work. More than 1,000 political-education study rooms and methodological councils and 207 people's universities are functioning on a public basis in Moscow, and nonstaff departments have been set up in Party committees and the editorial boards of city and factory newspapers. ...

Until recently mass political work among the working people at their place of residence was poorly organized in our city. After the small housing administrations in the city were replaced by large housing offices, we set up Party organizations in the housing sectors subordinate to them; these united 25,000 nonworking Communists. The Deputies in a housing sector united in Deputy groups and set up councils for work among the population. More than 50,000 aktivists work in the sector and apartment house committees. These measures have made it possible considerably to enliven mass political work at places of residence and to establish supervision by the working people over the use of housing and to enlist all the people in participation in urban improvement. More than a million Muscovites were taking part in this work on the eve of the Congress. ...

Thus since the 20th Party Congress more than 100,000 Communists of Moscow have been enlisted on a voluntary basis in participation in new forms of Party work. The development of public principles has enabled us to draw virtually all Communists into active Party and community life.

The public principle has also been widely developed in the work of all Soviet agencies, trade unions, the Y.C.L. and other mass organizations.

Sometimes one hears objections to this practice: Are Party agencies not being depersonalized? Is their leading role not declining? Aren't too many different commissions and councils springing up, and aren't they being set up artificially?

We have been persuaded of the correctness of this practice, since the more firmly the Party is linked with the masses, the stronger it becomes and the more successfully do its affairs proceed. ...

If certain new forms do turn out to be impracticable, they will quickly disappear; on the other hand, everything useful, everything that proceeds from life will grow stronger and will contribute to a further rise in the level of Party work. ...

Tolstikov

SPEECH BY COMRADE V. S. TOLSTIKOV, SECOND SECRETARY OF THE LENINGRAD PROVINCE PARTY COM-

MITTEE. (Pravda, Oct. 29, p. 10. 2,600 words. Excerpts:) ... A large group of young workers, specialists in various branches of the national economy, has been advanced to Party, Soviet and economic work. About 90% of the persons included in the nomenklatura [list of persons entitled to executive-rank appointments and nominations.—Trans.] of the province Party committee have a higher or incomplete higher education. Out of 115 secretaries of district and borough Party committees of Leningrad and the province, 110 have a higher or incomplete higher education, and 73 of them are specialists in industry and agriculture. Seventy secretaries of district and borough Party committees are under 40 years of age; 23 are women, and five of these are first secretaries. ...

Since the 20th Congress the Leningrad Party organization has grown by more than 68,000 persons. At the same time the paid Party apparatus has been reduced by 20%. On the other hand, more than 800 nonsalaried instructors have been enlisted in active work in the district borough and city Party committees and the province Party committee. ...

Permit me to mention the work of the nonstaff Party commissions for preliminary consideration of matters pertaining to admission to the Party and to the personal affairs of Communists about which Comrade F. R. Kozlov spoke in his report. ...

The activity of these commissions has enabled Party committee workers to devote considerably more time to direct organizational work in primary Party organizations. ...

We propose that regulations governing these commissions be worked out. ...

Comrades! ... The draft of the Party Statutes calls for the transfer of a Party member to the status of candidate member as a measure of punishment for Communists. It seems to us that this penalty might be incorrectly interpreted by some Communists. Indeed, becoming a candidate for Party membership is a joyous, outstanding and festive event in a person's life, a significant landmark on his path in life. This is understandable. After all, the person has become a candidate for membership in the great Leninist party of Communists. At the same time, the draft Statutes call for imposing transfer to the status of candidate member as a penalty for a Communist who has not justified the Party's trust. This would mean that the Party candidates will include people who have been accepted as candidates and who consider it a high honor to work in one of the Party's organizations, and also persons who have been proved unworthy of bearing the lofty title of Party member. This, in our opinion, demeans the title of candidate member of the Party and disparages its importance as the last stage before admission to Party membership. (Applause.)

Therefore we propose that the provision concerning the transfer of a Communist from the status of member to that of candidate member of the Party as a penalty be excluded from the draft of the Statutes, particularly since the draft provides an ample number of other penalties; moreover, this measure of punishment is applied very rarely. (Applause.) ...

Golikov

SPEECH BY COMRADE F. I. GOLIKOV, DIRECTOR OF THE CHIEF POLITICAL ADMINISTRATION OF THE SOVIET ARMY AND NAVY. (Pravda, Oct. 30, p. 3. 3,400 words. Condensed text:) Comrade delegates! ... In the struggle for the Leninist line of the Party, the struggle against the consequences of the cult of the individual and against the anti-Party group of factionalists—Molotov, Malenkov, Kaganovich and the others—the Communists of the Soviet Army and Navy have at all times been the steadfast support of our Leninist Central Committee. They are its monolithic support today, and such they will continue to be. (Applause.) ...

The opinion voiced by Congress delegates that there is no room in the Party for the leaders of the anti-Party group I consider to be very well-founded, and I second it.

Military people well know the enormous losses suffered by the army and navy in the period of mass repressive and arbitrary acts against Party and state cadres. The gravity of the losses was the greater in that they were suffered on the eve of the most formidable military trials for our nation, party and army, in the struggle against German fascism and its satellites. And I want to emphasize that the Communists in the armed forces highly appreciate and ardently approve the dedication to principle, the wisdom and the courage of the Central Committee in boldly telling the Party and people the Leninist truth about Stalin, his cult and the painful consequences of that cult.

The October, 1957, plenary session was an expression of the Central Committee's firm Leninist line in its work and holds a special place in the life of our armed forces. The dangerous anti-Party line and the Bonapartist policy actively pursued by ex-Minister of Defense Zhukov were nipped in the bud by the decisions of that plenary session.

How serious the situation was can be seen from the extent to which the role of the military councils, political agencies and Party organizations had been undermined and vitiated; absolutely all Party criticism of shortcomings in the behavior and performance of Communist commanders of all grades was forbidden in the army; the Party basis of one-man leadership was thrown overboard; arrogance, rudeness, arbitrariness and intimidation were rife in the treatment of subordinates; dissension between commanding officers and political workers was cultivated. Party life and the work of the political agencies were administered by fiat and were reduced to purely educational activity. The Chief Political Administration was slighted and downgraded. "Unter-Pribisheyev"* methods were permitted in military research. Attempts were made to evade, in one way or another, control by the Central Committee, to undermine the influence of the Party and to cut the army and navy off from the Party and the people. A Zhukov cult was implanted. There was a growing drift to unlimited authority in the army and the country.

The report at the October plenary session by Comrade M. A. Suslov, Secretary of the Party Central Committee, emphasized in this regard that we were dealing in this case not with isolated mistakes but with a system of mistakes, with a definite line followed by the former Minister of Defense, with his tendency to regard the Soviet Armed Forces as his private domain, with a line that was leading to dangerous isolation of the armed forces from the Party, that was tending to keep the Central Committee out of decision-making on crucial matters connected with the life of the army and navy. ...

The decisions of the plenary session made possible a radical improvement in the situation in the army, the prompt reinstatement of Leninist Party principles in the guidance of the armed forces, a strengthening of the role and importance of Party organizations, political agencies and military councils, the effective reinforcement of one-man leadership on a Party basis, a heightening of the role of the public and an intensification of Party influence on all aspects of life in the forces.

On the basis of the decisions of the plenary session, the Central Committee introduced new Regulations on Military Councils and Political Agencies as well as instructions to Party and Young Communist League organizations, and Party committees were established in regiments and on ships, in military schools and research institutes, at headquarters of military districts and in the central apparatus of the Ministry of Defense. Party organizations in battalions and divisions were granted the rights of primary Party organizations. A bureau was set up in the Chief Political Administration as an agency for collective decision-making on all major questions having to do with Party political work, and it is functioning successfully.

As a result of the measures taken by the Party Central Committee, the Party organizations have grown ideologically and organizationally stronger and their vigor and militancy in the accomplishment of all major tasks have increased markedly. There has been an intensified influx of the finest fighting men into the ranks of our party, while the principle of individual selection has been strictly observed. Almost two and a half times as many servicemen have been admitted into the Party since the October plenary session of the Party Central Committee as in the same period of time preceding the plenary session.

The Party stratum among the officers has grown. In so important a category of officers as company and battery commanders it has reached 90% for the armed forces as a whole and even more in a number of military districts. At the same time the proportion of Communists among privates, sergeants

---

*["Warrant Officer Pribisheyev"—a petty tyrant in a Chekhov story.—Trans.]

and sergeant-majors has grown enormously in our Party organizations.

The number of primary Party organizations in the army and navy, counting those in battalions and divisions, has doubled since the October plenary session of the Party Central Committee. As of Jan. 1, 1958, there were Party groups in only 40% of the companies and units equivalent to them, whereas today we have Party organizations, or at the very least Party groups, in 93% of the total number of such units.

The Leninist Young Communist League is a powerful force in the army and navy. The Party stratum in the army and navy Y.C.L. has more than quadrupled since the 20th Party Congress. Thanks to improved Party guidance, the work of the Y.C.L. organizations has grown more interesting and meaningful. They have been initiating many important patriotic undertakings. I should like to note that the Y.C.L. Central Committee has been devoting ever-increasing attention to Y.C.L. work in the armed forces. ...

We must promote the public principle more extensively in Party-political work. This is a matter of the vigorous introduction of many measures envisaged by the draft Party Statutes, taking due account of the conditions obtaining in the army and navy.

One of the most important principles underlying the organization of the Soviet Armed Forces is one-man leadership. Present-day conditions and military weapons call for particularly firm and precise control of troops, for rapid, well-coordinated and resolute operations, for daring, initiative and independence on the part of commanders of all grades, for readiness on the part of every commanding officer to assume full responsibility for the accomplishment of assigned tasks, and for unquestioning execution of orders by subordinates, and all this can be achieved only with one-man leadership.

In our Soviet conception, one-man leadership demands that every commanding officer approach the task assigned him with the interests of the Party and state in mind, that he be able to implement the policy of the Communist Party firmly and consistently, relying on the Party organizations and the forces of the public in all his work. ...

Persons in positions of one-man leadership today enjoy vastly greater authority in the Party and as commanders than they did before the October plenary session of the Party Central Committee. Suffice it to say that the number of Communists from among commanding officers of units and ships who have been elected to Party committees in the armed forces as a whole is 23 times as great today as it was in 1937.

The cadres of political workers are in many ways more mature and experienced; nine-tenths of them today have a higher or secondary military education. Many commanding officers are successfully holding responsible political posts in the armed forces, and many political workers are confidently commanding units large and small. All this fundamentally promotes the consolidation of forces and the strengthening of unity in the activities of all our military cadres. ...

The Soviet Army has everything it needs for ideological-educational work: 800 evening universities of Marxism-Leninism and Party schools, thousands of clubs, including hundreds of officers' clubs, dozens of museums and theaters; the resources of our libraries amount to more than 80,000,000 books. The magazines Kommunist Vooruzhennykh Sil [Communist of the Armed Forces] and Sovetsky voin [Soviet Fighting Man] and the newspaper Krasnaya zvezda are mass publications. The Military Publishing House is one of the largest in the U.S.S.R.

There are more than 400 universities of culture, 650 lecture bureaus and schools of culture, 250 amateur film studios, many amateur people's theaters, dozens of literary groups with 2,500 beginning writers, and a large number of other creative groups.

Our army's Alexandrov Song and Dance Company is well known to the peoples of many countries.

The Soviet Army is an army with a high level of spiritual culture. Close friendship between fighting men and cultural workers has become a fine and firm tradition. Since the October plenary session of the Party Central Committee, cultural patronage in the armed forces has taken on especially broad scope.

It is a very good thing that more works on military, patriotic themes have lately begun to appear in literature, music, the graphic and plastic arts and the motion pictures. But there is no hiding the fact that in some works Soviet military service has been portrayed in a contrived and distorted fashion, without any knowledge of the subject or proper understanding of the Party principles underlying the organization of the armed forces, or that there are sometimes even elements of pacifism. The men of our army and navy are at times portrayed without objectivity, as spiritually impoverished, and the principles laid down in the manuals with respect to military routine, strictness, discipline, and the commander's honor and authority are dealt with from premises that are erroneous and inadmissible.

Unfortunately, Literaturnaya gazeta has not been considerate of the servicemen's views on these matters, and it could, after all, play a big role in rectifying the shortcomings noted.

In the light of the tasks we face, we think it very important to step up our efforts in educating Soviet fighting men and Soviet youth as a whole in the rich revolutionary and fighting traditions of our great party, our people and their armed forces. We need to intensify the work we are doing to expose pernicious bourgeois ideology and, in particular, the falsifiers of the history of the last war, who are using every means in their effort to belittle the great exploit of the Soviet people.

"Historians" of this kind would do well to recall the words of former U.S. Secretary of State Stettinius: "***The American people should not forget that they were on the verge of disaster in 1942. Had the Soviet Union not held its front, the Germans would have been able to conquer Britain. They would also have been in a position to seize Africa and then establish bridgeheads in Latin America."

But the matter by no means ends with falsifiers among historians. Mention should be made, I think, of the height of cynicism, the supreme insult to the memory of millions of people who died heroically in the struggle with fascism, in a statement made by U. S. Vice-President Johnson. Only recently, on Aug. 20, he made bold to say the following in West Berlin, having the German revanchists in mind: "The Western powers—the U.S.A., France and Britain—have never had better or more courageous allies."

But no one and nothing can detract from the greatness of the Soviet people's exploit and victories! (Prolonged applause.)...

I should like to underscore the very important role being played in the thorough scholarly treatment of the past war by the fundamental work being published by decision of our party— "The History of the Great Patriotic War of the Soviet Union, 1941-1945."...

The Soviet Army is a real school of active builders of communism. People who have been through the stern school of military life are toiling selflessly in all corners of our boundless homeland. Last year alone more than 200,000 volunteers demobilized from the army went to work at the crash construction projects of communism. With the reduction in the size of the army and navy, many thousands of officers and a number of generals who were transferred to the reserve or retired entered the sphere of material production.

The draft Party Statutes stress that every member of the C.P.S.U. has the duty of helping in every possible way to strengthen the defensive might of the U.S.S.R. In this connection I should like to note the great importance of the mass defense work being done with the public, with youth below the military age and reservists. All organizations must continue seriously improving this work and giving the utmost support to the Voluntary Society for Cooperation With the Army, Air Force and Navy, which has now grown into a mighty, mass organization. ...

Kolchina

SPEECH BY COMRADE O. P. KOLCHINA, SECOND SECRETARY OF THE MOSCOW PROVINCE PARTY COMMITTEE. (Pravda, Oct. 30, p. 4. 2,800 words. Excerpt:) ... We take great satisfaction in endorsing the provision in the draft Party Statutes calling for Party organizations to be kept regularly informed of the activities of higher Party agencies.

With reference to the additions made to the draft Party Statutes, I should like to dwell on the following matter. As Comrade Kozlov's report indicates (and this is reflected in the draft of the Statutes that has been passed out to the delegates), the Party Central Committee proposes the inclusion in the

Statutes of an article making it the duty of Communists to wage a vigorous struggle against religious prejudices. This is right and timely. We cannot draw comfort merely from the fact that the majority of working people have turned away from religion. We cannot help noting that individuals among us, including young people, are still being caught in the snares of the clergy and sectarians, who have stepped up their activity of late. At the same time, some Party organizations have relaxed their drive on religious prejudices and have not been doing much work with people on an individual basis.

There are serious complaints to register against the lecture associations, including the All-Union Society for the Dissemination of Political and Scientific Knowledge. Having largely drained dry the many old forms of antireligious propaganda that had come into being back in the early years of the Soviet regime, they have been timid in their quest for new forms and new methods of work and have gradually lost their staffs of antireligious propagandists. It should be added that, owing to complacency and unconcern, some of our comrades are by their actions willy-nilly creating for the clergy conditions conducive to the revival of religious beliefs and to the observance of religious holidays. We are at a loss, in particular, to understand the attitude of executives in the Ministry of Trade, who sanction the sale of church candles in the stores and, before Easter, of the sweet Easter loaves, diffidently calling them "spring cakes." (Stir in the hall.) ...

[After the speeches on the Statutes by Chernyshev and Basov, which were omitted for reasons of space, the Congress interrupted the discussion of Kozlov's report to hear statements on the removal of Stalin's body from the Mausoleum in Red Square.]

Speeches on the Mausoleum

STATEMENTS BY DELEGATIONS OF LENINGRAD PROVINCE AND MOSCOW CITY PARTY ORGANIZATIONS AND GEORGIAN AND UKRAINE COMMUNIST PARTIES. (Pravda, Oct. 31, pp. 1-2; Izvestia, pp. 2-3. 3,500 words. Condensed text:) Speech by Comrade I. V. Spiridonov, Leningrad Province Organization.—Comrades! In their speeches many delegates have cited instances of arbitrariness and lawlessness perpetrated in the period of the Stalin cult.

The Leningrad Party organization suffered particularly large losses of Party, Soviet, economic and other personnel as a result of the unjustified repressions that befell Leningrad after the murder of Sergei Mironovich Kirov.

For a period of four years there was an uninterrupted wave of repressions in Leningrad against honest and completely innocent people. Promotion to a responsible post often amounted to a step toward the brink of a precipice. Many people were annihilated without a trial and investigation on the basis of false, hastily fabricated charges. Not only officials themselves but also their families were subjected to repressions, even absolutely innocent children, whose lives were thus broken from the very beginning.

Both the repressions of 1935-1937 and the repressions of the postwar period of 1949-1950 were carried out either on Stalin's direct instructions or with his knowledge and approval. What enormous damage was done the country by this annihilation of cadres, which became possible only in the conditions of the unrestrained dominance of the Stalin cult in all spheres of life!

The harm of the cult of the individual was by no means confined to the annihilation of Leninist cadres, people reared and educated under the direct leadership of Vladimir Ilyich Lenin.

The great and frequently unjustified harm of the cult of the individual in various spheres of economic, political and ideological life has been disclosed with sufficient fullness at both the 20th and the present Congresses.

The Leningrad Party organization unanimously condemned the Stalin cult and approved the measures aimed at eliminating its harmful consequences, as did the entire Party. Even in the course of discussing the results of the 20th Party Congress, many Party meetings and gatherings of the working people of Leningrad adopted decisions to the effect that the presence of Comrade Stalin's body in the Vladimir Ilyich Lenin Mausoleum, next to the body of the great leader and teacher of the world's working class, the founder of our glorious party and of the world's first proletarian state, was incompatible with the lawless actions abetted by Stalin. (Shouts in the hall: "Right!" Stormy applause.)

The life and name of the great Lenin may with full grounds be called Justice with a capital J. (Stormy, prolonged applause.) It cannot be tolerated that beside Vladimir Ilyich Lenin, to whom not only the working people of our country but all honest people of the whole world come to pay homage—that beside him there lies a man who has stained his name with great injustice. (Shouts in the hall; "Right!" Applause.)

To the question of why the 20th Party Congress and the Party Central Committee did not adopt a decision to move Stalin's remains we replied at the time that this was not the most important thing, that the most important thing was to condemn the cult of the individual and to restore Leninist norms of Party life and the principles of collective leadership. Now that many other instances of lawlessness and injustice perpetrated both by Stalin himself and by the participants in the anti-Party group—Molotov, Kaganovich and Malenkov—have become known to the Congress delegates, to the entire Party and the entire people, the question of moving Stalin's body from the Vladimir Ilyich Lenin Mausoleum is being raised once again and even more persistently by Communists and non-Party members. (Applause.)

Our delegation has received the resolutions of the meetings of the working people of the Kirov Plant (the former Putilov Plant) in Leningrad and the Neva Lenin Machine-Building Plant—where our teacher and leader spoke many times—in which the Leningraders propose that Stalin's remains be moved to another place. (Shouts in the hall: "Right!" Stormy applause.)

The Leningrad delegation to this Congress joins its voice to this proposal. On behalf of the Leningrad Party organization and the working people of Leningrad, I submit for the consideration of the 22nd Congress the proposal that Stalin's remains be moved from the Vladimir Ilyich Lenin Mausoleum to another place, and that this be done as soon as possible. (Shouts in the hall: "Right!" Stormy, prolonged applause.)

Speech by Comrade P. N. Demichev, Moscow City Party Organization.— ... Comrades! There is much that makes the Communists of Moscow and Leningrad kin. Muscovites were pained by the destruction of the Leningrad aktiv by Stalin and Malenkov. Many prominent Party, Soviet and economic workers of the Moscow organization also perished innocently. And we know that our Leningrad comrades were likewise pained by this.

Our entire party and all our people are severely condemning the lawlessness and arbitrariness that reigned in the period of the cult of the individual. Muscovites speak with anger of the anti-Party group and fully support the proposals of the Congress delegates that the miserable renegades Molotov, Malenkov and Kaganovich be expelled from the ranks of our Leninist party. (Applause.)

Since the 20th Congress, and especially now, demands have been made at Party aktiv meetings and gatherings of the working people in both Moscow and Leningrad that the sarcophagus with J. V. Stalin's coffin be removed from the Mausoleum. To leave it there would be blasphemy. (Shouts in the hall: "Right!" Stormy applause.)...

The proposal of the Leningrad comrades is also the proposal of the Communists and all the working people of our capital. (Stormy applause.) We are confident that it will be supported by all the delegates to the 22nd Party Congress. ...

Speech by Comrade G. D. Dzhavakhishvili, Georgian Communist Party.—Comrades. ... A proper assessment has been made at the Congress of the anti-Party group of Molotov, Malenkov, Kaganovich and others who tried for their own base purposes to seize leadership of the Party and restore the methods, so hostile to Leninism, of the period of the cult of the individual. The situation that developed in the country in connection with the cult of the individual gave rise to lawlessness and arbitrariness. Many prominent leaders of the Party and state became victims of this arbitrariness; their names have been mentioned at the Congress.

Many adventurers took advantage of the atmosphere of lawlessness and arbitrariness and perpetrated their foul deeds. The members of the Central Committee and many comrades know what great harm was done to the Party organization of Georgia. As a result of this arbitrariness, the prominent figures Mamia Orakhelashvili, Secretary of the Transcaucasus Territory Party Committee; Mikha Kakhiani, Shalva Yeliava, Levan Gogoberidze, Soso Buachidze, Lakoba, Kartvelishvili, and many other others perished innocently. These comrades have been posthumously rehabilitated.

Everyone knows of the provocational cases, such as the Mingrelia case and others, that were fabricated against Party leaders. All these are hard and bitter facts, comrades. But the Party Central Committee, in the name of justice, in the name of our Leninist truth and in the interests of our triumphant onward progress, could not and cannot do otherwise than tell the people the whole truth honestly and frankly, so that this will never happen again in the history of our glorious party. (Applause.)

The Georgian Party organization fully approves and supports the proposals of the Leningrad and Moscow delegations on moving Stalin's remains from the Mausoleum to another place. (Applause.) ...

Speech by Comrade D. A. Lazurkina, Party Member Since 1902, Leningrad Party Organization.—Comrade delegates! I wholly and fully support the proposals of Comrade Spiridonov and other comrades who have spoken here on removing Stalin's body from the Lenin Mausoleum. (Stormy applause.)

In the days of my youth I began my work under the leadership of Vladimir Ilyich Lenin, learned from him and carried out his instructions. (Applause.) ...

And then, comrades, in 1937 I was to share the lot of many. I had an executive post in the Leningrad Province Party Committee and, of course, was also arrested. When they arrested me and when the prison doors closed behind me (this was not the first time that had closed; I was imprisoned and exiled many times in tsarist days), I felt such a horror, not for myself but for the Party. I could not understand why old Bolsheviks were being arrested. Why? This "why?" was so agonizing, so incomprehensible. I explained to myself that something horrible, obviously sabotage, had taken place in the Party. And this gave me no rest.

Not for a minute—either when I sat in prison for two and a half years or when I was sent to a camp, and later exiled (I spent 17 years in exile)—not once did I blame Stalin. I always fought for Stalin, who was assailed by the prisoners, the exiles and the camp inmates. I would say: "No, it is not possible that Stalin would have permitted what is happening in the Party. This cannot be!" They would argue with me, some would become angry with me, but I stood firm. I had high esteem for Stalin, I knew that he had done great service before 1934, and I defended him.

Comrades! And then I returned completely rehabilitated. I arrived just at the time when the 20th Party Congress was in session. This was the first time I learned the hard truth about Stalin. And now at the 22nd Congress, as I hear about the disclosed evil deeds and crimes that were committed in the Party with Stalin's knowledge, I wholly and fully endorse the proposal for the removal of Stalin's remains from the Mausoleum.

The great evil caused by Stalin consists not only in the fact that many of our best people perished, not only in the fact that arbitrary actions were committed and innocent people were shot and imprisoned without trial. This was not all. The entire atmosphere that was created in the Party at that time was totally at variance with the spirit of Lenin. It was out of harmony with the spirit of Lenin.

I shall recall only one example that characterizes that atmosphere. In May, 1937, Comrade Zhdanov was Secretary of the Leningrad Province Party Committee. He assembled us executive workers in the province committee and said: "Two enemies—Chudov and Kadatsky—have been exposed in our ranks, in the Leningrad organization. They have been arrested in Moscow." We could not say a word. It was as if our tongues had frozen. But when this meeting was over and Zhdanov was leaving the room, I said to him: "Comrade Zhdanov, I don't know Chudov. He hasn't been in our Leningrad organization long. But I vouch for Kadatsky. He has been a Party member since 1913. I have known him for many years. He is an honest member of the Party. He fought all the oppositionists. This is incredible! It must be verified." Zhdanov looked at me with his cruel eyes and said: "Lazurkina, stop this talk, otherwise it will end badly for you." But I never stopped to think whether it would end well or badly for me when I stood up for the truth. I only thought about whether it was good for the Party or not. (Stormy, prolonged applause.)

Under Lenin an atmosphere of friendship, comradeship and mutual faith, support and assistance prevailed in the Party. I recall the years in the underground. When we were arrested, we accepted the accusations without thought in order to protect the organization, to divert the blow from the comrades who had not yet been arrested, to save the underground literature and printshops.

And what was the atmosphere in 1937? Fear, which was uncharacteristic of us Leninists, prevailed. People slandered one another, they lost their faith, they even slandered themselves. Lists of innocent people who were to be arrested were drawn up. We were beaten so that we would slander others. We were given these lists and forced to sign them. They promised to release us and threatened: "If you don't sign, we'll torture you!" But many stood fast; they kept their Bolshevik hearts and never signed anything! (Prolonged applause.)

We fought to the end. We did not believe there could be such arbitrariness in our Leninist party. We wrote, wrote endlessly. If one were to look through the files of my letters, he could count volumes. I wrote endlessly to Stalin. I wrote to others also, and I wrote to the Party control body. But unfortunately, even our Party control was not at the proper level at the time; it yielded to the common fear and also refused to consider our cases.

Such was the atmosphere created by the cult of the individual. And we must root out the remnants of it! It is good that the 20th Party Congress raised this question. It is good that the 22nd Party Congress is uprooting these remnants.

I think that our wonderful Vladimir Ilyich, the most human of humans, should not lie beside someone who, although he did service in the past, before 1934, cannot be next to Lenin.

N. S. Khrushchev.—Right! (Stormy, prolonged applause.)

D. A. Lazurkina.—Comrades! ... The only reason I survived is that Ilyich was in my heart, and I sought his advice, as it were. (Applause.) Yesterday I asked Ilyich for advice, and it was as if he stood before me alive and said: "I do not like being next to Stalin, who inflicted so much harm on the Party." (Stormy, prolonged applause.)

Speech by Comrade N. V. Podgorny, Ukraine Communist Party.—Comrades! The delegation of the Ukraine Communist Party wholly and fully supports the proposals submitted by the delegates of the Leningrad and Moscow Party organizations and the Georgian Communist Party. (Stormy applause.) This is the unanimous opinion of all the Communists of the Ukraine and of all the Ukrainian people. (Stormy, prolonged applause.) ...

Back in 1956 the Communists and working people of the Soviet Ukraine, like those of the other republics, after familiarizing themselves with the materials of the 20th Party Congress, voiced the opinion that Stalin's remains cannot lie in the V. I. Lenin Mausoleum, a place sacred to the Soviet people and all working people of the world. (Shouts in the hall: "Right!" Stormy applause.) But far from everything was yet known at that time. ...

Discussing the materials of the 22nd Party Congress at numerous meetings and gatherings, the Communists and working people of our country vigorously demand that the organizers of the monstrous crimes—Molotov, Kaganovich and Malenkov—be severely punished. The participants in the meetings consider it inadmissible that the body of Stalin, with whose name is linked so much evil caused to our party, the country and the Soviet people, should lie beside our leader and teacher, the great Lenin, the banner of all the victories of communism. (Applause.)

We cannot but heed these entirely correct demands of the Communists and the working people of our entire country. The time has come to restore histroical justice! (Applause.)

Comrades! Permit me on behalf of the Leningrad and Moscow delegations and the delegations of the Ukraine and Georgian Communist Parties to submit for your consideration the following draft resolution of the 22nd Party Congress:

"The 22nd Congress of the Communist Party of the Soviet Union resolves:

"1. Henceforth to call the Mausoleum in Red Square at the Kremlin Wall, established to perpetuate the memory of Vladimir Ilyich Lenin, the immortal founder of the Communist Party and Soviet state, the leader and teacher of the working people of the whole world: THE VLADIMIR ILYICH LENIN MAUSOLEUM. (Stormy, prolonged applause.)

"2. To recognize as unsuitable the continued retention in the Mausoleum of the sarcophagus with J. V. Stalin's coffin, since the serious violations by Stalin of Lenin's behests, the abuses of power, the mass repressions against honest Soviet people and other actions in the period of the cult of the individual make it impossible to leave the coffin with his body in the V. I. Lenin Mausoleum." (Stormy, prolonged applause.)

Rodionov

SPEECH BY COMRADE N. N. RODIONOV, SECOND SECRETARY OF THE KAZAKHSTAN COMMUNIST PARTY CENTRAL COMMITTEE. (Pravda, Oct. 31, pp. 3-4. 3,000 words. Excerpts:) Comrade delegates! ... The participants in the anti-Party group have been called dogmatists. This is correct. But what they tried to do in June, 1957, was not dogmatism. It was banditry, it was robbery in broad daylight. And for robbery it is necessary to answer with the full severity of the law. ...

Voroshilov has been elected to the presidium of the Congress. He sits at the same table with Comrade Khrushchev. Only the Leninist party can display such lofty humanism and magnanimity. The humanism and magnanimity of the Party Central Committee are brilliantly reflected in Nikita Sergeyevich Khrushchev's concluding remarks. The Congress shares this magnanimity. But we all want Comrade Voroshilov to understand and evaluate this as pardon granted him by the Party and not as an underestimation of his sins. Comrade Voroshilov was in the same den with the anti-Party beast, and he did not stray in there by accident, as he has tried to make out in his statement to the Congress. One can err on certain particular questions, although even this is not good, but one cannot err when it is a matter of the fate of the Party and its honor. (Applause.)

Of course Comrade Voroshilov is an old man, and one does not want to hurt him. But we are all well aware that if the anti-Party group had gained the upper hand in June, 1957, they would not have reckoned with either age or past services, and many and many delegates to the Congress would have been missing from this hall today. Cruel new repressions would have befallen our party, and many devoted Communists would have been thrown in prison and destroyed. A victory of the anti-Party group promised terrible calamities. This is why we delegates to the 22nd Congress, expressing the will of the entire 10,000,-000-strong Party, say again and again: Thank you, a big thank you to Nikita Sergeyevich Khrushchev for the great courage he has displayed in defending the interests of the Party. We say thank you to the members of the Central Committee, who rallied around Nikita Sergeyevich and followed him. The Party knows that where Comrade Khrushchev is, there is truth and progress, life and happiness. (Stormy applause.) ...

Since the 20th Congress big changes have taken place in the life of the Kazakhstan Party organization, just as they have in the life of the entire Party. In these years the Kazakhstan Communist Party has grown by almost 100,000; it has been enriched by the new experience of political leadership.....

Among the varied forms of Party work that have arisen in recent years, the commissions of primary Party organizations for exercising the right of supervision over the economic activity of management have acquired great importance everywhere. In the Party organizations of our republic there are more than 6,000 such commissions, staffed by more than 25,000 Communists. The new forms of Party control have firmly entered life and have fully justified themselves. ...

More than 1,7000 unsalaried instructors now work in the republic's Party commissions. ...

The provision of the Party Statutes concerning the regular turnover of a definite part of the membership of all elective Party bodies with retention of continuity of leadership is meeting with the universal approval of Communists. ...

The elections of local Party bodies held on the eve of the 22nd Congress confirmed the vitality of this provision. There was a 46% turnover in the membership of the republic's city and district committees and a 50% turnover in the province committees. Fresh new forces of the Party have come to leadership. ...

The Party Central Committee's resolution on establishing Party committees at collective and state farms has played an important role in strengthening the primary Party organizations. In 1959 there were 53 Party committees in Kazakhstan and in 1961 there are 482. The formation of new Party committees and the expansion of the network of shop Party organizations and Party groups has increased Party influence among the masses even more and has created the conditions for better management of the economy. ...

Serdyuk

SPEECH BY COMRADE Z. T. SERDYUK, FIRST VICE-CHAIRMAN OF THE PARTY CENTRAL COMMITTEE'S PARTY CONTROL COMMITTEE. (Pravda, Oct. 31, pp. 5-6. 3,200 words. Condensed text:) ... When the Party at its 20th Congress dethroned the Stalin cult and it came to light that during Stalin's lifetime reprisals had been organized against people objectionable to him, prominent Party and state figures, the Central Committee did not yet know the facts about the personal participation of Molotov, Kaganovich and Malenkov in the mass repressions. I recall that Molotov was even appointed chairman of a commission to investigate violations of socialist legality committed in the past. But here, too, Molotov did everything possible to conceal the truth from the Party. This had its logic—the logic of the criminal who cannot be a judge of his own crimes. Indeed, how could Molotov take from the archives the lists of persons innocently arrested and shot and report to the Central Committee that it was he who had sanctioned both the arrests and the shootings?!

This, comrades, is not a fabrication, not a slander against Molotov, who has the impudence to call himself a Marxist-Leninist. There are countless accusatory documents, any one of which can serve as a stern indictment. Here is one such document. Yezhov wrote:

"Comrade Stalin.

"I am sending for your approval four lists of persons to be tried by the Military Collegium:

"List No. 1 (general).

"List No. 2 (former military personnel).

"List No. 3 (former personnel of the N.K.V.D. [People's Commissariat of Internal Affairs].)

"List No. 4 (wives of enemies of the people).

"I request sanction to convict all in the first degree.—Yezhov."

It should be stated that a first-degree conviction meant death by shooting.

The lists were examined by Stalin and Molotov, and on each of them is the notation:

"Approve. J. Stalin.

"V. Molotov."

In his concluding remarks Comrade N. S. Khrushchev spoke of the great importance of an elucidation of all the circumstances of the murder of S. M. Kirov, the event that set off the mass repressions. Investigation of this case has not yet been completed, but highly important facts can be gleaned even from existing materials. For example, on the day of the murder (which at that time had not yet been investigated, of course), upon Stalin's instructions from Leningrad, a law was adopted on an accelerated, simplified and conclusive examination of political cases. This was immediately followed by a wave of arrests and political trials. It is as if they had been waiting for this pretext in order, by deceiving the Party, to launch anti-Leninist, anti-Party methods of struggle to maintain a leading position in the Party and state. This and much else must be carefully studied. As Comrade N. S. Khrushchev said, this is our duty to the Party and the people! This must and will be done!

I would also like to call attention to the following: How did it happen that the secretaries of many province Party committees who were known as honest people devoted to the cause of the Party suddenly turn out to be enemies of the people? Here is how. Kaganovich went to Ivanovo and once there

immediately sent a telegram to Stalin in Moscow:

"First acquaintance" (note: first acquaintance!—Z. S.) "with the materials shows that province committee secretary Yepanechnikov must be arrested at once. It is also necessary to arrest Mikhailov, head of the province committee's propaganda department."

A second telegram followed:

"Acquaintance with the situation shows that Right-Trotskyist sabotage has assumed wide scope here—in industry, agriculture, supply, trade, public health services, education and Party-political work. The apparatuses of province institutions and the province Party committee are deeply infected."

You see how little it took for Kaganovich to come to a place, look around, and slander and rout the cadres of a whole province. And it was not from one province alone that Kaganovich and Malenkov sent such telegrams. They fanned a struggle against imaginary enemies of the people in many places and sowed distrust and suspicion everywhere. Molotov, Kaganovich and Malenkov grossly violated both the norms of Soviet law and the provisions of the Party Statutes, which are sacred to every Communist. After this, what binds them to the Party and what grounds have they for remaining in the ranks of our Leninist party? Delegates have given a firm reply to this question from this rostrum, and they have been unanimously supported by all the delegates to the 22nd Congress of the Communist Party of the Soviet Union. (Stormy applause.)

It is characteristic that Molotov, Malenkov and Kaganovich worked to the full of their capacities in massacring personnel, putting a great deal of energy into this dirty work. Yet how incompetent and helpless they proved to be when it was a matter of the national economy, when useful advice and businesslike proposals were expected from them.

Take Malenkov. Without having visited the countryside for decades, having no knowledge of its needs, he stifled any initiative on the part of the masses. It was he who in a report to the 19th Party Congress forced through the thesis on forbidding the collective farms to produce brick, tile and other building materials. This agrarian, if I may so call him, who took charge of agriculture at that time, considered such activity an obstacle to the development of collective farm production.

In his speech Comrade Ilyichev mentioned Comrade N. S. Khrushchev's article "On Building and Improvements on the Collective Farms," published in Pravda in 1951, and the reaction that it evoked among the dogmatists who were detached from life. But in fact, Comrade N. S. Khrushchev's article contained extremely valuable ideas and recommendations. Even at that time Nikita Sergeyevich spoke of the fact that "in large artels there is an opportunity to organize building crews, to set up enterprises producing building materials—brick, tile, etc.—to hire skilled labor and to develop construction of buildings for cultural and everyday needs and farm structures, and likewise to undertake the building of homes for farm members on a large scale." What Comrade Khrushchev spoke of ten years ago is now being done on a large scale for the benefit of agricultural production and for the good of the collective farm peasantry. It is such new and fresh ideas that they tried to silence and proscribe!

In this connection I recall the following incident. Shortly after the 19th Party Congress a district Party committee official visited the collective farmers of the Victory Collective Farm in Tiraspol District of the Moldavian Republic. On seeing that the farmers were building a shop for the production of tile, he flew at the chairman:

"What are you doing? Didn't you read Malenkov's report to the 19th Congress?"

"I did read the report," answered the chairman, "but you can't cover a cow shed with a report. For this you need tile."...

Comrades! Our people, under the leadership of their glorious party, have achieved big successes. These gladden and inspire all Soviet people. But V. I. Lenin taught the Party not to tolerate conceit and complacency but to disclose mistakes and shortcomings in work boldly and overcome them decisively. This is why the question of Party, state and public control from top to bottom and from bottom to top now assumes prime importance. The sense of responsibility of every leader, every Communist, for the work entrusted to him should be increased more than ever. ...

It must be pointed out, comrades, that there are still people among us who do not know how to save the people's ruble. Enormous funds are sometimes spent on the construction and repair of installations that are of far from primary importance. We have, for example, organizations that are engaged in restoring buildings of historical and cultural value. They are doing a very useful thing, of course, in preserving architectural monuments for posterity. But because of absence of control, favorable conditions have formed in a number of these organizations for wastefulness, for the expenditure of funds and materials at the whim of individual architects. In the Moscow Restoration Studio alone, expenditures—chiefly for the repair and restoration of churches, big and little—amounted to 50,000,000 rubles (in the old currency) in the past three years, including 25,000,000 rubles out of allocations for the capital repair of housing. Indeed, one might think that our restorers had set the aim of restoring the appearance of old Moscow, in which, as the saying went at the time, there were "40 times 40 churches"! In some cases the churches are literally rebuilt anew according to the architect's fancy, and even with a claim to a certain architectual priority. ...

We must improve in every way the organization of control and of checkup on fulfillment, without permitting red tape, bureaucracy and formal indifference to the exposure and elimination of shortcomings. And such phenomena are still encountered, unfortunately. Let me cite an example. In July, 1961, Izvestia published an article entitled "Crooks With Seniority." The article correctly reported the poor state of affairs in the selection and training of personnel in certain trade organizations of the Moscow Railroad Station Restaurant Trust. It is impossible, and indeed unnecessary, to list these and similar facts here, but I want to call attention to the impermissible indifference with which certain officials of the Russian Republic Ministry of Trade regard the shortcomings. For instance, they did not react at all to the just statements of the press and have done nothing in practical terms to eliminate the shortcomings disclosed. ...

A gratifying sign of the times is that the working people not only report shortcomings to Party and Soviet agencies but, utilizing the force of public control, themselves participate in checkups and in the elimination of shortcomings. The sharp edge of Party and public control is being directed against grabbers and moneygrubbers, swindlers and schemers—these and other people who like to profit at the expense of the state. Cases of economic accumulation by some people and their private-property impulses are receiving a sharp rebuff.

An analysis of the personal cases examined by the Party Central Committee's Party Control Committee shows that persons of this category even turn up in the ranks of our Leninist party. The Communists do right when they resolutely cut off such elements. At the same time, some Party organizations do not react promptly to manifestations of private-property aspirations on the part of certain individuals and thus do not prevent them from committing serious misdemeanors. The work of educating members and candidates of the Party in the spirit of communist morality must be intensified in every way. ...

In the molding of a Communist chief place is given to ideological work, to practical participation in the struggle for the Party line. But measures of Party influence must play an auxiliary role and be applied only in exceptional cases. It is incorrect when, instead of thoughtful educational work, severe penalties are applied to Communists, right down to expulsion from the Party, without special need or without sufficient grounds. Sometimes Communists are called to Party accountability without a thorough checkup on the charges brought against them. There are cases where they are deprived of the possibility of giving personal explanations. As a result, erroneous decisions are taken. The following data testify to this. In 1960 district and city Party committees rescinded one-fifth of the decisions of primary Party organizations concerning expulsion from the Party, while the province and territory committees and the Central Committees of the Union-Republic Communist Parties, in turn, rescinded more than one-fourth of the decisions of district and city committees on expulsion from the Party One can hardly agree, therefore, to the proposals that the district and city Party committees be granted the right of final decision on questions concerning expulsion of Communists from the Party. This would probably be a premature measure. The provision of the present Statutes ensures correct decision of this question. ...

Vecherova

SPEECH BY COMRADE YU. M. VECHEROVA, LOOM OPERATOR AT SOLIDARITY FACTORY IN SAVINO, IVANOVO PARTY ORGANIZATION. (Pravda, Oct. 31, p. 6. 2,000 words. Excerpt:) ... In our republic people still remember, nor will they ever forget, the especially grave and foul crimes committed in 1937 by Kaganovich. The Communists call his visit to the city of Ivanovo in 1937 "the black tornado." At that time he accused the entire Party organization, which had great revolutionary traditions, of supposedly standing aloof, of being off to the side of the high road. At a plenary session of the province committee he pinned the label of enemy of the people on the majority of executive officials without any grounds. As a result, many honest Communists were arrested. Our delegation, expressing the will of the entire province Party organization, wholly and fully supports the suggestion that there is no room for Molotov, Kaganovich and Malenkov in the ranks of our party. (Applause.) ...

Goryachev

SPEECH BY COMRADE F. S. GORYACHEV, FIRST SECRETARY OF THE NOVOSIBIRSK PROVINCE PARTY COMMITTEE. (Pravda, Oct. 31, pp. 6-7. 2,600 words. Excerpts:) ... It must be recognized, said Comrade N. S. Khrushchev at the 19th Congress, that a great evil in many Party, Soviet and economic organizations is an incorrect approach to the selection of cadres, selection not on the basis of job qualifications and political considerations but on the basis of friendship, personal loyalties, local allegiance or kinship. This observation has real significance today too. One could cite many examples of persons who, having failed in their jobs and been dismissed, are given favorable references and are shifted to another post of equivalent status, sometimes even at a higher salary. ...

In this connection, it is advisable, in our opinion, to set forth the relevant section of the Statutes as follows:

"Communists are obligated undeviatingly to carry out the Party's instructions concerning the correct selection of cadres on the basis of their political and work qualifications. The leaders of organizations bear personal responsibility for violation of these instructions, i.e., for the selection of cadres on the basis of friendship, kinship or personal loyalties." ...

Art. 52 of the draft Statutes provides for the establishment of permanent and temporary commissions for various questions of Party work in region, city and district Party committees. But it should be borne in mind that at enterprises and in scientific institutions there are now a large number of Party organizations numbering 1,500 to 1,800 Communists with a Party committee at their head. Therefore it is advisable to formulate this article of the Statutes as follows:

"The region, city or district committee or the Party committee of a large Party organization has unsalaried instructors, sets up permanent or temporary commissions for various questions of Party work and employs other forms of enlisting Communists in the work of the Party committee as a public duty." ...

The time has obviously come to expand the work of Party commissions under province and territory committees, which are now predominantly engaged in the examination of appeals against Party penalties. It is necessary that these commissions help Party organizations disclose shortcomings and mistakes in the work of individual leaders and check more vigorously on the warnings of Communists and non-Party members concerning shortcomings in the work of organizations, enterprises, institutions and collective and state farms. Active work by these commissions and expansion of their functions will make it possible to enlist the working people more widely in the struggle to eliminate shortcomings and will help to improve the investigation of complaints and petitions and to intensify the struggle against bureaucracy and red tape. ...

Kochetov

SPEECH BY COMRADE V. A. KOCHETOV, WRITER AND EDITOR-IN-CHIEF OF THE MAGAZINE OKTYABR. (Pravda, Oct. 31, p. 8. 3,200 words. Condensed text:) Dear comrade delegates! ... The Central Committee report states: "The

Party's premise is that art is called upon to educate people first and foremost on the basis of positive models in life, to educate people in the spirit of communism." This is not the first time that the Party has told us this. It was very well expressed by Nikita Sergeyevich in 1957, and later at the Third Writers' Congress in 1959. We heard a timely reminder also at the government reception last summer. The Party and its Central Committee always remember us and always show a paternal concern for the ideological health of our writers' organization. And one could enumerate many books published in these years, books centered around positive heroes, heroes truly of our times—leading workers, leading scientists, collective farmers, Party workers and men of the Soviet Army.

The truth also compels us to admit that among writers there are still the dismal compilers of memoirs, who spend more time looking backward than into the present or the future and who because of their distorted vision dig about in the dump heaps of their errant memories with a zeal worthy of better application, in order to unearth long-decayed literary corpses and present them as something still viable. The people in such cases say: From each its own—from the apple tree an apple, and from the fir tree a cone.

The truth also compels us to say that in the literary milieu, in poetry—and in prose as well—there are also chicks, barely covered with yellow down, who are dying to look like formidable fighting cocks.

The numbers of both types can be counted on the fingers of one hand, and it is not their dreary, monotonous notes that make the music of Soviet literature. Our literature is great, many-sided and colorful; it attracts our reader and the foreign reader both by its form and by the wealth of its ideas. This has been well put in Nikita Sergeyevich's report. Viewing all the Union republics, all the territories and provinces of the country, through the eyes of this literature shows a picture by no means disheartening.

After the 20th Party Congress, when breaking the resistance of the dogmatists and factionalists—the unrestrained incense bearers of the cult of the individual—the wind of revolutionary, Leninist transformations refreshed the whole of public life in our country and thereby, of course, also the atmosphere in literature and art—in these years tens of hundreds of books were created about our contemporaries and about our heroic times. ...

To tell the truth, it is the leadership of the U.S.S.R. Writers' Union that should have told the Congress about the state of our literary affairs. But sad though it may be, it has lost—you can see yourselves—its combat readiness, to use military language, and stands in need of decisive reorganization.

It could have spoken of many things if it had not consigned the main questions of our ideological and creative life to oblivion. ...

Nikita Sergeyevich once decisively rejected the epithet "embellisher" with which the estheticizing critics attempted to stigmatize writers who joyfully, proudly following the dictates of their hearts, devoted their pens to serving the cause of the Party. This is no longer applied to them today. Thank you very much for your help, for your support, Nikita Sergeyevich! On the other hand, the esthetes have thought up something new, or, more accurately, they have dragged out of the arsenal something old: They either say nothing about works objectionable to them, or they speak about them with supercilious contempt, or they simply recommend that they be classified as inartistic. A novel about virgin-landers is "inartistic." A novel about the deeds and thoughts of the Stavropol collective farmers who wanted to reorganize their village in a new way "does not deserve attention, is narrow and shallow." A novel about the metalworkers of the Urals "smells of coke and pig iron," whereas it should at least have smelled of tea-rose petals.

The same judgment, by the way, was once passed on Nikolai Ostrovsky's "How the Steel Was Tempered," on Furmanov's novel "Chapayev" and on many other wonderful works. But life has judged them differently than these wretched critics: These militant books are still alive and fighting today, while the "tea roses" have faded long ago.

Such connoisseurs of art and judges of literature prefer to consider artistic the published result of digging about in human squabbles, in the trifles of everyday life, in maladjust-

ments and messes. Furthermore, without a twinge of conscience, they point to the great literature and the great art of the past: There is art for you, this is what is meant by art.

What is true is true: The art of the 19th and certain other centuries was mighty. But who can say that it fed on the refuse, on the waste of human existence!

All-vanquishing and all-conquering love, a feeling of lofty patriotism, incorruptible loyalty, readiness for self-sacrifice, fortitude and courage, strength and skill, intellect, friendship, the striving for lofty ideals—these are the things that inspired the great masters of the word, the brush and the chisel of the past and the things they glorified in man. Of course they also told the world about ugliness, about outrages, baseness, treachery, cowardice, perfidy and corruption. But they spoke of these things in order that, set next to them, the beauty of man might tower even higher, in order that man's beauty might be contrasted to the uglinesses and might flower even more vividly in the cruel and tireless struggle against them. Great literature and great art have always striven to open wide to man the horizons of the future, to instill courage in him, to lend him wings, and never to use their influence to make man feel small, pitiful and helpless, to compel him to abandon the struggle for his ideals, to fold his hands passively and, hanging his head, to surrender to the current of the times and events.

From the first hour of its existence Soviet literature inherited these features from classical Russian and world literature. Socialist realism has never rejected criticism of shortcomings. Socialist realism views life in all its complexity, in all its contradictions, in its implacable struggle for the new, which was born of the old and the doomed. One-sided, preponderant depiction of shortcomings alone narrows the writer's horizons, impoverishes his world and conceals from him the beauty of man and of life. It makes the artist one-eyed.

We can understand some of the writers of the capitalist world. They are the children and citizens of their society, of the life in which their world outlook is shaped. The world of such artists is not a wide one. It is indeed no bigger than a throw rug—or, more accurately, than the bed in which the actions of countless Western novels, stories, plays and films take place.

Comrades! If the world of capital had Yury Gagarin, German Titov, Valentina Gaganova, Tursunoi Akhunova, Alexander Gitalov and hundreds of thousands of people of daily labor exploits, would not its most talented writers consign the whole of their bedroom-and-brandy literary rubbish to the garbage heap? Would not their hearts be fired with real inspiration? I am sure that if they are real artists—and there are quite a few real artists among them—they will envy us. They will envy us for the abundance, the wealth, the beauty of human lives, characters and deeds at the disposal of us Soviet writers. (Applause.)

Yes, our good fortune is that we have something to write about. And we shall write about our heroic times, about our folk-toilers, the builders of communism.

There are some who think that if one writes about the present, about our heroes, he must perforce do so hurriedly, colorlessly, photographically. But Balzac wrote about his times, and did he write colorlessly? Turgenev wrote about the most burning problems of his times, and do not his fine books still live today? And Mayakovsky! The pulse of his times throbbed in every line of his verse. Or can one say that the words cited by Nikita Sergeyevich these days sound outdated and colorless: "Let us live to be a hundred without growing old!" These words have become even more contemporary. Indeed, the average longevity in our country is approaching a hundred years. ...

The theory of "distance" is an unsound one. Who, if not we in works of literature and art, will tell our contemporaries, our descendants, especially the young people, and our friends abroad about the epoch in which we have the good fortune to live, about the great party of Lenin, which is rebuilding the world in a revolutionary way?!

Comrade Ye. A. Furtseva's speech contained a thesis about which I would like to say a few words, although it has already been discussed. Comrade Furtseva said that, very unfortunately, poor films and poor books, which arouse the just indignation of audiences and readers, appear in our country from time to time.

This is so. Alongside excellent films and literary works there is also a great deal of trash. I completely agree with you, Yekaterina Alexeyevna, that this is due to the fact that some of our writers and scenarists do not know the present-day life of the people.

But I do not think such ignorance of life is due solely to the fact that the authors of poor books and scripts live in Moscow or in the capitals of the Union republics. (Stir in the hall.) You can transfer a writer to a Cossack village in the Kuban, to a distant Siberian village, to Bratsk, Magnitogorsk—wherever you like, into the very thick of life, it would seem—and he will still go on writing about the times of Martha the Mayoress of Novgorod, about adulteries and divorces, about whatever he likes, only not about the workers of the Kuban, Siberia or Bratsk, not about their exciting, vivid, ardent deeds.

On the other hand, you plant another writer right here in the Kremlin, in the Granitovaya Palace, or even higher up, in the decorated chambers of the boyars, and, surrounded by antiquities, he will still write about the people who are plowing up the virgin land, about workers, engineers, scientists, about the heroes of our time. And he will write well!

Where a writer lives is not unimportant, of course. But even more important than where he lives is how he lives, what moves him, what attracts him, what he thinks about and to what he has given his heart. (Stir in the hall, applause.)

I would say that the worst films and books do not simply spring from ignorance of the life of our people but most often result when some of us try to depict life in the manner in which it is depicted in the bourgeois West, when formalist effect-seeking is put to the fore in the theater, films, books and paintings, when, not out of ignorance but fully aware of where we are going, we depart from the truth of our life, from the method of socialist realism, when we concentrate on details and fail to see behind them the main, heroic element in the lives of the people.

Our ideological opponent reacts to such failures and mistakes with almost lightning speed. If a film is in the Western spirit, if a book has a wrong twist, if a painting has been slapped to-gether, the bourgeois press bursts into tempestuous praise and cheers: Now this is real art! Even gold medals and all sorts of prizes may be forthcoming; laurel wreaths are woven.

But if a writer or artist hews firmly to the positions of Party spirit, don't expect any praise; expect only every kind of vituperation.

But the abuse of the enemy, as Lenin taught, is the best praise. When the enemy praises and offers prizes, one cannot help but wonder and be on one's guard: Apparently you must have gone wrong somewhere. (Applause.)

If we are faithful to the method of socialist realism, if we are faithful to the principles of Party spirit and folk quality—and we have no intention of deviating from them in our creative work—failures and mistakes will not be likely. It is more likely that Soviet artists will have more and more successes in literature, the theater, films, painting and music. ...

Other Speakers

[In the interests of space, speeches by those listed below have been omitted from this chapter. Translations of their speeches may be found in The Current Digest of the Soviet Press, Vol. XIV, No. 7.

[October 28.—S. K. Toka, First Secretary, Tuva Province Party Committee; V. Ye. Chernyshev, First Secretary, Maritime Territory Party Committee; A. V. Basov, First Secretary, Rostov Province Party Committee.

[October 30.—A. V. Georgiyev, First Secretary, Altai Territory Party Committee; A. I. Shibayev, First Secretary, Saratov Province Party Committee; P. A. Leonov, First Secretary, Sakhalin Province Party Committee; S. N. Shchetinin, First Secretary, Irkutsk Province Party Committee; V. I. Gubanov, secretary of Party committee, Victory Collective Farm, Stavropol Territory Party organization.]

XII. THE CONGRESS RESOLUTIONS

Resolutions Commission

RESOLUTION OF THE 22ND CONGRESS OF THE COMMUNIST PARTY OF THE SOVIET UNION ON THE REPORT OF THE PARTY CENTRAL COMMITTEE (Adopted Unanimously Oct. 27, 1961). (Pravda and Izvestia, Oct. 28, p. 1. Complete text:) Having heard and discussed the report by Comrade N. S. Khrushchev, First Secretary of the Party Central Committee, on the work of the Party Central Committee, the 22nd Congress of the Communist Party of the Soviet Union resolves:

To approve wholly and fully the political line and practical work of the Central Committee of the Communist Party of the Soviet Union in the sphere of domestic and foreign policy. To approve the conclusions and proposals contained in the report of the Party Central Committee.

***

The 22nd Congress adopted a decision to form a Commission for Preparing the Draft of a Detailed Resolution of the 22nd Party Congress on the Report of the Party Central Committee and for Considering Amendments and Additions to the Draft Party Program consisting of the following [in Russian alphabetical order except for Khrushchev's name]: N. S. Khrushchev (chairman), G. G. Abramov, A. I. Adzhubei, Yu. V. Andropov, A. B. Aristov, V. Yu. Akhundov, A. V. Basov, B. P. Beshchev, I. I. Bodyul, L. I. Brezhnev, G. I. Vorobyev, G. I. Voronov, V. I. Gaganova, K. I. Galanshin, A. V. Gitalov, A. V. Georgiyev, V. V. Grishin, I. A. Grishmanov, A. A. Gromyko, P. N. Demichev, L. N. Yefremov, M. T. Yefremov, Ya. N. Zarobyan, N. G. Ignatov, L. F. Ilyichev, V. M. Kavun, I. A. Kairov, J. E. Kalnberzins, I. V. Kapitonov, V. A. Karlov, M. V. Keldysh, A. P. Kirilenko, T. Ya. Kiselev, F. R. Kozlov, A. A. Kokarev, A. A. Kolchik, A. N. Kosygin, A. Ye. Korneichuk, D. S. Korotchenko, V. V. Krotov, F. D. Kulakov, D. A. Kunayev, O. V. Kuusinen, J. G. Kabin, K. T. Mazurov, R. Ya. Malinovsky, T. K. Malbakhov, S. I. Manyakin, V. P. Mzhavanadze, A. I. Mikoyan, L. G. Monashev, A. S. Murysev, N. A. Mukhitdinov, V. N. Novikov, I. T. Novikov, Z. N. Nuriyev, B. Ovezov, M. A. Olshansky, N. N. Organov, S. P. Pavlov, A. J. Pelse, F. N. Petrov, N. V. Podgorny, D. S. Polyansky, B. N. Ponomarev, P. N. Pospelov, D. Rasulov, Sh. R. Rashidov, M. I. Rozhneva, R. A. Rudenko, A. P. Rudakov, K. N. Rudnev, P. A. Satyukov, N. N. Semenov, V. A. Smirnov, A. J. Snieckus, T. I. Sokolov, I. V. Spiridonov, M. A. Suslov, D. F. Ustinov, T. Usubaliyev, P. N. Fedoseyev, Ye. A. Furtseva, V. Ye. Chernyshev, N. M. Shvernik, A. N. Shelepin, P. Ye. Shelest, A. P. Shitikov, A. M. Shkolnikov, M. A. Sholokhov, V. V. Shcherbitsky and S. N. Shchetinin.

Party Statutes Commission

COMMISSION FOR CONSIDERATION OF AMENDMENTS AND ADDITIONS TO THE DRAFT PARTY STATUTES. (Pravda and Izvestia, Oct. 31, p. 1. Complete text:) The 22nd Congress adopted a decision to form a Commission for Consideration of Amendments and Additions to the Draft Party Statutes consisting of the following [in Russian alphabetical order except for Kozlov's name]: F. R. Kozlov (chairman), A. B. Aristov, L. I. Brezhnev, S. Z. Borisov, Ye. I. Bugayev, G. I. Voronov, F. I. Golikov, A. F. Gorkin, F. S. Goryachev, K. N. Grishin, I. S.

Grushetsky, A. D. Danialov, N. G. Yegorychev, G. S. Zolotukhin, N. G. Ignatov, N. F. Ignatov, I. P. Kazanets, A. A. Kandrenkov, A. P. Kirilenko, A. V. Kovalenko, O. P. Kolchina, N. S. Konovalov, A. N. Kosygin, M. K. Krakhmalev, O. V. Kuusinen, L. I. Lubennikov, K. T. Mazurov, V. P. Mzhavanadze, A. I. Mikoyan, N. A. Mukhitdinov, N. V. Podgorny, M. A. Polekhin, D. S. Polyansky, G. I. Popov, S. O. Pritytsky, S. T. Puzikov, N. N. Rodionov, Z. T. Serdyuk, I. P. Skulkov, M. S. Solomentsev, F. A. Surganov, M. A. Suslov, F. A. Tabeyev, V. N. Titov, F. Ye. Titov, S. K. Toka, V. S. Tolstikov, Ye. A. Furtseva, S. D. Khitrov, N. S. Khrushchev, N. M. Shvernik, V. M. Churayev and A. I. Shibayev.

On Lenin Mausoleum

RESOLUTION OF THE 22ND PARTY CONGRESS ON THE VLADIMIR ILYICH LENIN MAUSOLEUM. (Pravda and Izvestia, Oct. 31, p. 1. Complete text:) The 22nd Congress of the Communist Party of the Soviet Union resolves:

1. Henceforth to call the Mausoleum in Red Square at the Kremlin Wall, established to perpetuate the memory of Vladimir Ilyich Lenin, the immortal founder of the Communist Party and Soviet state, the leader and teacher of the working people of the whole world: THE VLADIMIR ILYICH LENIN MAUSOLEUM.

2. To recognize as unsuitable the continued retention in the Mausoleum of the sarcophagus with J. V. Stalin's coffin, since the serious violations by Stalin of Lenin's behests, the abuses of power, the mass repressions against honest Soviet people and other actions in the period of the cult of the individual make it impossible to leave the coffin with his body in the V. I. Lenin Mausoleum.

On Central Committee Report

RESOLUTION OF THE 22ND PARTY CONGRESS ON THE REPORT OF THE PARTY CENTRAL COMMITTEE (Adopted Unanimously Oct. 31, 1961). (Pravda and Izvestia, Nov. 1, pp. 3-4. Complete text:) The 22nd Congress of the Communist Party of the Soviet Union has convened at a time when our homeland has entered the period of full-scale construction of a communist society, when socialism has become firmly established in the people's democracies and the forces of progress and peace are growing at a tempestuous pace all over the world.

The years since the 20th Congress of the C.P.S.U. have been of exceptionally great importance in the life of our party, of the Soviet people and of all mankind. Pursuing the Leninist general line, the Party mobilized all the working people to accomplish the tasks of communist construction along the whole wide front of great projects. A major milestone on the road of the U.S.S.R.'s advance to communism was the extraordinary 21st Congress of the C.P.S.U., which adopted the seven-year plan for the development of the national economy.

It is with great satisfaction that the 22nd Party Congress reviews the world-historic victories of the Soviet people. The Land of Soviets has traveled a path of heroic struggle and is today in the full flower of its creative forces. The might of the Soviet Union has grown still greater, and its international prestige, as champion of the cause of peace and progress, the friendship of peoples and the happiness of mankind, has risen immeasurably.

The whole course of events confirms the soundness of our party's theoretical conclusions and political line. The policy of the 20th Congress, which was dictated by life itself, by concern for the people's welfare, and was pervaded with a spirit of revolutionary Leninist creativity, has fully triumphed.

Having heard and discussed the report by Comrade N. S. Khrushchev, First Secretary of the Central Committee, on the work of the Party Central Committee, the 22nd Congress of the Communist Party of the Soviet Union resolves:

That the political policy and practical activities of the Party Central Committee in the spheres of domestic and foreign policy be wholly approved. That the conclusions and proposals contained in the report of the Party Central Committee be approved.

I.—The 22nd Congress notes that the determinative feature of the present international situation is the further growth of the forces of socialism, democracy and peace all over the world. Life has confirmed the soundness of our party's foreign policy line aimed at preventing war and consolidating peace. This line accords with the fundamental interests of the Soviet people and has met with support from the peace-loving forces in all countries. The Congress has highly assessed the consistency, flexibility and initiative of this foreign policy and fully approves the measures being taken by the Central Committee and the Soviet government to strengthen political, economic and cultural ties with all states.

The fact that war has been successfully averted and that the Soviet people and the peoples of other countries have been able to enjoy the blessings of a peaceful life must be regarded as the main result of the work done by the Party and its Central Committee in building up the might of the Soviet state and carrying out the Leninist foreign policy, as a result of the work done by the fraternal parties of the socialist countries and of the invigoration of peace-loving forces in all countries.

The Soviet Union, the Chinese People's Republic and all the countries in the world socialist system are confidently pursuing the path of socialist and communist construction. Relying on their increased power, and with the support of peace-loving forces all over the world, the socialist countries have prevented the imperialists from pushing the world off the rails of peaceful economic competition between the two systems onto the path of global catastrophe. The peaceful competition of the two opposing social systems, which is the pivot of present-day international life, has entered the decisive phase. The policy of friendship and peace among peoples is winning ever greater acceptance and support and is prevailing over the imperialist policy of aggression and war.

The world socialist system is developing successfully, gaining strength and becoming the determinant factor in the progress of human society. The Soviet Union has entered the period of the full-scale building of communism; most of the people's democracies have done away with their mixed economic structures and are completing the building of socialism; the peoples' living standards are rising steadily; fraternal cooperation and mutual aid among the socialist states are expanding. The Congress ardently acclaims the signal gains of the fraternal parties and peoples of the socialist countries and wishes them glorious new victories.

The 22nd Congress approves the policy of the Central Committee and the Soviet government aimed at steadily intensifying economic, political and cultural cooperation between the socialist states based on the principles of proletarian internationalism, equality and comradely mutual assistance. The Congress makes special note of the great and fruitful work being done by the Central Committee to expand and strengthen cooperation between the C.P.S.U. and the fraternal Communist and Workers' Parties on the basis of Marxism-Leninism and in the interest of the unity and solidarity of the international Communist movement. The Congress flatly rejects as unfounded and slanderous the attacks on the Communist Party of the Soviet Union and its Leninist Central Committee by the leaders of the Albanian Party of Labor. The actions of the Albanian leaders are at variance with the Declaration and Statement of the 1957 and 1960 Conferences of Representatives of Communist and Workers' Parties and can only be considered as being divisive, aimed at undermining the friendship and solidarity of the socialist countries, and as playing into the hands of imperial-

ism. The Congress expresses the hope that the Albanian leaders, if they hold the interests of their people dear and really want friendship with the C.P.S.U. and with all the fraternal parties, will renounce their erroneous views and return to the path of unity and cooperation with all the socialist countries and with the international Communist movement.

Further consolidation of the unity of the socialist camp and the heightening of its power and defensive capacity remain one of the most important tasks. The coordination of efforts in the development of the economy of each socialist country with the common efforts to consolidate and expand economic cooperation and mutual assistance—this is the path of continued prosperity and progress for all the countries of the socialist commonwealth, of the world socialist economy.

The achievements of the socialist countries are exerting a growing all-round influence on the peoples of the nonsocialist countries, revolutionizing and accelerating the advance of all mankind on the path of progress. Today it is not imperialism but socialism that is determining the main trend of the world's development.

The conclusion reached by the 20th Congress on the inevitable deepening of the general crisis of capitalism has been fully borne out. A further weakening of the economic, political and ideological positions of imperialism has occurred in the years gone by, its basic contradictions have become still sharper, and the revolutionary struggle of the working class and the democratic and national-liberation movement of the peoples have taken on vast scope. The capitalist system is ever increasingly discrediting itself in the eyes of the peoples as a system of brutal exploitation of the working people, of national and colonial oppression, of the arms race and annihilating wars.

Under the mighty blows of the national-liberation movement the colonial system has virtually fallen apart. The imperialist forces, above all American imperialism—the pillar of world reaction and international gendarme—are striving to hold on to their positions by employing new and subtler forms of colonial enslavement. But as a result of historical experience the peoples of the colonies are becoming more and more convinced that only final liberation from all forms of economic and political dependence, only the noncapitalist path of development can lead their countries to true freedom, prosperity and happiness.

In the teeth of prophesies by imperialism's ideologists and their right-wing socialist and revisionist stooges, the class struggle in the capitalist countries is not tapering off but is acquiring ever greater scope and assuming an ever more acute character. The peasant and general democratic movements are gathering momentum along with the revolutionary action of the working class. Unification of all the forces opposing imperialism and the decisive defeat of the ideology and practice of anticommunism and reformism are becoming an imperative need.

The entire course of social development and the unceasing buildup of forces taking a stand for socialism and against imperialism confirm the soundness of the conclusion reached by the 20th Congress on the diversity of forms of transition to socialism in various countries. This conclusion, endorsed by the international Communist movement, was embodied and amplified in the Declaration of 1957 and the Statement of 1960 adopted at the conference of Marxist-Leninist parties.

The Marxist-Leninist parties are spearheading the struggle of the working class and of all working people in their countries to bring about a socialist revolution and establish the dictatorship of the proletariat in one form or another.

The forms and paths of development that the socialist revolution takes will depend on the specific relationship of class forces in the particular country, on the organization and maturity of the working class and its vanguard, and on the extent of resistance from the ruling class. No matter what the form in which the dictatorship of the proletariat is established, it will always signify the broadening of democracy and the transition from formal, bourgeois democracy to real democracy, democracy for the working people. The working class and its vanguard, the Marxist-Leninist party, seek to accomplish the socialist revolution by peaceful means. Realization of this possibility would accord with the interests of the working class and the people as a whole, the national interests of the entire country.

In the present situation in a number of capitalist countries, the working class headed by its vanguard is in a position, through a workers' and people's front and other possible methods of bringing various parties and public organizations into agreement and political cooperation, to unite the majority of the people, win power in the state without a civil war and achieve the transfer of basic means of production to the people.

By relying on the majority of the people and firmly rebuffing opportunist elements who are unable to forsake the policy of conciliation with the capitalists and landlords, the working class has a chance to defeat the reactionary, antipopular forces, win a secure majority in parliament, turn parliament from a tool that serves the class interests of the bourgeoisie into a tool that serves the working people, launch a broad mass struggle outside of parliament, break the resistance of the reactionary forces and establish the conditions needed for peaceful accomplishment of a socialist revolution. All this will be possible only given the broad and continuous expansion of class struggle by the worker and peasant masses and the middle urban strata against big monopoly capital, against reaction, and for thoroughgoing social reforms, peace and socialism. In a situation where the exploiting classes resort to force against the people, another possibility must be borne in mind—the nonpeaceful transition to socialism. It is a teaching of Leninism, confirmed by historical experience, that ruling classes do not yield power voluntarily. How fierce the class struggle is under these conditions and the forms it takes will depend not so much on the proletariat as on the vigor with which the reactionary circles resist the will of the overwhelming majority of the people, on whether these circles use force at one or another stage of the struggle for socialism.

Communism has become the most influential political force of our time. There is today no country with a more or less well developed workers' liberation movement in which the influence of the Communists—the most consistent, stalwart and courageous champions of the peoples' interests—is not felt. The historic 1957 and 1960 Conferences of Representatives of Communist and Workers' Parties and the documents framed by those conferences have been of tremendous importance for the further consolidation of the ranks of the international Communist movement. The Congress places a high assessment on and fully approves the work of the C.P.S.U. delegation at the Conferences of Representatives of Communist and Workers' Parties.

An implacable and consistent fight on two fronts—against revisionism, as the main danger, and against dogmatism and sectarianism—is of decisive importance for the triumph of Marxism-Leninism. The C.P.S.U. sees it as its internationalist duty to strengthen the monolithic solidarity of the international Communist movement in every possible way and to wage a struggle against all who try to weaken the unity of the Communists of all countries. It is necessary to continue exposing the theory and practice of latter-day revisionism, which has found its most concentrated expression in the program of the Yugoslav League of Communists.

The question of war and peace has been and remains the burning issue of the day, one that agitates all mankind.

The events of recent years have confirmed the soundness of the conclusion reached by the 20th and 21st Congresses that in this age wars between states are not inevitable, that they can be prevented. Today the powerful forces safeguarding the peace possess all the means necessary for bridling the imperialist warmongers. The world socialist system is becoming an ever more dependable shield protecting not only the peoples of the socialist countries but all mankind against the military adventures of imperialism. The steadily growing power of the Soviet Union and the other socialist countries is an important guarantee of world peace.

Fighting for peace side by side with the socialist states are the Asian, African and Latin American countries that have won their freedom from colonial oppression, as well as the working class and all the working people of the capitalist states; the movement of peace partisans is growing all over the world. The people are the decisive force in the fight for peace. The greater the might of the socialist camp and the more vigorously the fight for peace is pressed in the capitalist countries themselves, the harder for the imperialists to loose a new world war. The struggle of the socialist countries and of all peace-loving forces against preparations for a new war is the main content of contemporary world politics.

As a result of the fundamental shift in favor of socialism in the balance of forces in the world arena, the policy of the peaceful coexistence of states with different social systems has acquired an even firmer foundation. The principle of the peaceful coexistence of states with different social systems, which was enunciated by V. I. Lenin and constitutes the basis of the Soviet Union's foreign policy, has won broad recognition as the way to preserve peace and prevent a new world war. Under present circumstances there is a prospect of ensuring peaceful coexistence over the entire period within which the social and political problems today dividing mankind should find their solution. The situation is so developing that even before the complete victory of socialism on earth, while capitalism remains in part of the world, it will actually be possible to exclude world war from the life of society.

At the same time, it must be remembered that the foreign policy of the imperialist states is shaped by the class interests of monopoly capital, in which aggression and war are organically inherent. As long as imperialism lasts, there will be soil for aggressive wars. International imperialism, American imperialism above all, represents the chief danger to world peace. It is making preparations for the most ghastly crime against mankind—a thermonuclear world war. The imperialists have created a dangerous situation in the center of Europe, threatening war in response to the proposal of the Soviet Union and other peace-loving countries that an end be put to the vestiges of the second world war, a German peace treaty concluded and the status of West Berlin normalized. The forces of reaction have time and again placed world peace in jeopardy in recent years, and they have not ceased their attempts to exacerbate the international situation and bring mankind to the brink of war. A higher degree of vigilance than ever is today demanded of the peoples.

The Congress considers the measures taken by the Central Committee and the Soviet government for further strengthening our homeland's defense capacity to be timely, sound and necessary. As long as imperialist aggressors exist, we must be on the alert, keep our powder dry and improve the defenses of the socialist countries, their armed forces.

The consolidation of peace calls for the solution, without delay and on the basis of the principles of peaceful coexistence, of fundamental international problems, first and foremost: general and complete disarmament with the strictest international control; the final elimination of colonial oppression in all its forms and manifestations and the furnishing of tangible and effective aid to peoples who have recently won their independence; elimination of the vestiges of the second world war, and a peace settlement with Germany; restoration of the legitimate rights of the Chinese People's Republic in the United Nations; fundamental improvement of the machinery of the United Nations; and the development of businesslike relations between states and of economic and cultural ties among all countries.

The Communist Party of the Soviet Union will do everything necessary to preserve and consolidate peace and friendship between peoples in the name of the triumph of the high ideals of social progress and the happiness of the peoples.

The 22nd Congress of the C.P.S.U. considers it necessary to continue to:

—steadily and consistently implement the principle of the peaceful coexistence of states with different social systems as the general foreign policy line of the Soviet Union;

—unflaggingly strengthen the unity of the socialist countries on the basis of fraternal cooperation and mutual aid and contribute to reinforcing the might of the world socialist system;

—develop and deepen cooperation with all forces fighting for world peace;

—strengthen proletarian solidarity with the working class and working people of the whole world and extend the utmost support to peoples fighting for their liberation from imperialist and colonial oppression and for the consolidation of their independence;

—still further expand international business ties, mutually advantageous economic cooperation and trade with all countries;

—pursue a vigorous and flexible foreign policy, working for

the settlement of urgent world problems through negotiation, expose the intrigues and maneuvers of the imperialist war-mongers, and strengthen world peace.

II.—The Congress notes with satisfaction that in the period under review steadfast implementation of the internal policy laid down by the 20th Congress has resulted in important successes in the development of all branches of the economy. Industry and agriculture have been making rapid strides, the economic might and defense capacity of our nation have been still further reinforced, and the material and spiritual needs of Soviet people have begun to be satisfied more fully. The work of creating the material and technical base for commu-nism has been put on a firm footing.

The paramount feature of the period since the 20th Congress has been the acceleration of the pace of communist construction.

Industrial production has increased almost 80% in the last six years. The seven-year-plan is being successfully fulfilled. Instead of the 8.3% slated for the first three years of the seven-year plan, the average annual increase in industrial output has actually been 10%. Major new reserves have been uncovered in the socialist economy and brought into play, which has made possible production of approximately 19,000,000,000 rubles' worth of industrial output over and above the assignments for the first three years of the seven-year plan. A great deal of work has been done on the technological re-equipping of all spheres of material production. Thousands of new types of machines, machine tools, apparatuses, instruments and means of automation have been developed.

The Congress notes that thanks to the unflagging concern of the Party and the government and to the dedicated labor of the Soviet people, the rearmament of the Soviet Army with nuclear missiles has been fully completed. In the hands of our people mighty weapons serve as a secure defense of socialist gains and further the consolidation of world peace.

Since the 20th Congress there have been substantial qualita-tive changes in industry, construction and transport. The struc-ture of the fuel balance has been radically improved; power engineering has been shifted to a new technical base; there has been a considerable speed-up in the development of the chemi-cal industry and the technological renovation of all forms of transport. The Party and government have taken steps to de-velop light industry and the food industry, and the production of consumer goods has been increased; this is already having a salutary effect in raising the living standard of Soviet people, and as time goes on its effect will be still greater.

As a result of the outfitting of construction projects with new equipment and the extensive use of precast reinforced concrete, capital construction has taken on unprecedented scope. In the years 1956-1961 capital investments in the national economy came to 156,000,000,000 rubles; this exceeds the volume of investments in all the years of the Soviet regime's existence up to the 20th Congress. Some 6,000 new state enterprises were brought into operation, among them the world's largest hydroelectric stations, metallurgical, chemical and machine-building plants and textile combines; extensive advantage is being taken of a highly economical and effective way of building up production capacity—the reconstruction and expansion of existing enterprises.

The program mapped by the Party for accelerated develop-ment of productive forces in the eastern regions of the country is being steadily translated into reality. On the basis of rich water-power resources and cheap coal, mighty electric power stations are being erected, extremely rich deposits of iron ore and natural gas are being exploited, good progress is being made in the establishment of a third metallurgical base, non-ferrous metallurgy and the chemical, machine-building and construction industries are being developed, and new cities and industrial centers are arising.

The Congress fully approves the reorganization of the manage-ment of industry and construction effected by the Central Com-mittee and the Soviet government. This revolutionary and vitally essential measure broke down the departmental parti-tions that had become a brake on the further development of the country's productive forces, heightened the role of the Union republics and of local Party, Soviet and economic agencies in economic and cultural development, and unleashed the creative initiative of the masses. Reorganization of the management

of industry and construction has resulted in better and more efficient operations in all branches of the national economy and fuller exploitation of production reserves.

The task of overtaking and surpassing the most highly devel-oped capitalist countries in per capita output is being success-fully solved. The Soviet Union has already outdistanced the most highly developed capitalist country—the United States of America—not only in rates of growth but in absolute annual increase in production. The U.S.S.R. is now mining more iron ore and coal and producing more coke, precast reinforced con-crete, mainline electric and diesel locomotives, lumber, woolen fabrics, butter, sugar, fish and a number of other goods and foodstuffs than the U.S.A.

Completion of the seven-year plan will bring the economy of the Soviet Union to a point where it will take but little time to outstrip the U.S.A. in per capita output as well. This will represent the world-historic victory of socialism over capital-ism.

The Congress notes the great work done by the Central Com-mittee in improving agriculture. As a result of the effects of the war and of mistakes and shortcomings tolerated in the management of agriculture in the past, the country found itself in difficulties. The low level of farm production could have held back the development of the Soviet economy and seriously af-fected the well-being of the people.

Having uncovered the reasons for the lag in agriculture, the Central Committee drew up and put into effect urgent measures aimed at the further expansion of agricultural production. With the active participation of all the people, the Party strengthened the material and technical base of the collective and state farms, carried through the reorganization of the Machine and Tractor Stations, elevated the role of the state farms in communist construction, introduced a new procedure for the planning of agricultural production, reinstated the Leninist principle of material incentive for collective farmers and state farm workers to increase the output of farm products, reinforced the collec-tive and state farms with executive cadres and specialists, reorganized the work of the agricultural agencies and height-ened the role of science in agriculture.

An outstanding part in increasing the production of grain and developing agriculture as a whole was played by the plowing up of virgin and idle lands, which now account for more than 40% of the total grain procurements in the country. The plowing up of the virgin lands was a great labor feat of the Soviet people that will be remembered forever!

The measures taken by the Party to achieve an agricultural advance have already yielded solid results and these results will be still more substantial as time goes on. In five years the gross output of agriculture has risen 43% compared with the preceding five-year period. The state had earlier been purchasing only about 2,000,000,000 poods of grain annually, whereas in recent years its purchases have come to 3,000,-000,000 poods and more. Purchases of other farm products have risen substantially. Fundamental changes have been brought about in the development of animal husbandry, which for years had been in a state of neglect. The number of cattle on the collective and state farms has increased 68% and of pigs 150% in the past five years; procurements of animal products have greatly increased.

Noting the great importance of the resolutions of the January (1961) plenary session of the Party Central Committee con-demning smugness and complacency and the slackening of at-tention to agriculture in a number of provinces and republics, as a result of which the rates of growth of production of grain, meat and milk in 1959 and 1960 had dropped and were lagging behind the seven-year-plan targets, the Congress fully approves the concrete measures worked out by the Central Committee for further increasing the output of farm products. As this year's preliminary returns show, these measures have pro-duced positive results. The collective and state farms have increased the production of grain. The state will purchase considerably more grain this year than last. There have also been increases in the production of cotton, sugar beets, sun-flowers and other crops. The number of livestock has risen, and production and purchases of animal products have in-creased. Nevertheless, the rates of growth of meat and milk production are still far short of meeting the necessary level.

On the basis of the experience they have gained, the collective and state farms must now take a big new stride forward and fulfill the seven-year-plan assignments. Revision of the crop structure by the collective and state farms and the substitution of higher-yield crops, primarily corn and legumes, for ones of lower yield are of especially great importance in the solution of agriculture's urgent problems. The reserves of agriculture must continue to be exploited with the utmost persistence, with a view to accomplishing one of the most important tasks of communist construction—the creation of an abundance of agricultural products for the people.

The Party organizations and the working people of the Russian Federation, the Ukraine and Kazakhstan have worked out long-range plans for sharp increases in grain production.

—The Russian Federation has set itself the goal of bringing the production of grain up to 12,000,000,000 poods and of purchases to between 4,000,000,000 and 5,000,000,000 poods;

—the Ukraine Republic, to bring production to 3,800,000,000 poods and purchases to 1,500,000,000 poods;

—the Kazakh Republic, to bring production up to 3,500,000,000 poods and purchases to more than 2,000,000,000 poods.

The Congress approves the initiative of the Party and Soviet organizations and all the agricultural workers of the Russian Federation, the Ukraine and Kazakhstan, and wishes them success in attaining the levels they have mapped.

The material well-being of the working people has been rising steadily. On the basis of the growth of the U.S.S.R.'s national income, the real incomes of workers and employees (calculated per working person) have increased 27% in five years and the incomes of collective farmers 33%. Retail turnover in state and cooperative trade has risen by more than 50%. All workers and employees have been transferred to a seven- or six-hour working day. The adjustment of wages is being completed and their level has been raised, especially for workers and employees in the low-paid categories, while excesses in the pay of workers in several categories have been eliminated. Pension arrangements have been improved and the average old-age pensions more than doubled. Abolition of taxes paid by the public began in 1960. Public funds are playing a steadily greater role in raising the people's living standard. Payments and benefits received by the public from these funds came to 24,500,000,000 rubles in 1960, as against 4,200,000,000 rubles in 1940, and they will increase by the end of the seven-year plan to 40,000,000,000 rubles. The state housing construction program mapped for 1956-1960 was completed; more housing was erected in the five years than in the previous 15 years, and some 50,000,000 persons received new living quarters.

The period between the 20th and 22nd Congresses was marked by outstanding achievements by Soviet science and culture. A brilliant new age in the evolution of man's scientific knowledge was ushered in by the Soviet Union's victories in the exploration of outer space and the unrivalled flights of history's first cosmonauts, Yury Gagarin and German Titov. Soviet scientists registered significant advances in the peaceful uses of atomic energy, in cybernetics and the development of high-speed computers, in the chemistry of polymers, in the development of automation and remote control, radio engineering and electronics, in the social sciences and in other fields of science and technology.

The Congress regards as correct the measures taken to reorganize public education and strengthen the ties between school and life, to set up boarding schools and extended-day groups, to develop the system of correspondence and evening education, and to produce highly qualified specialists for all spheres of economic and cultural development.

The past few years have seen the production of a number of significant works of literature and art which truthfully reflect our reality and show the character traits of the new people, the builders of communism.

The development of productive forces and the increase in the material and spiritual wealth of Soviet society have been the basis for a steady improvement of socialist social relations. The Congress approves the policy of further strengthening the public and collective farm-cooperative forms of socialist property and bringing them closer together, of consistent application of the principle of material incentive, of developing socialist democracy, of bringing the cultures of the Soviet

socialist nations into closer association and achieving their mutual enrichment in all spheres, of reinforcing the moral and political unity of our society, and of actively molding communist principles in the labor, daily life and thinking of Soviet people.

The great gains scored by our nation under the Party's leadership gladden Soviet people and instill in them confidence that in the future our country will advance on the road to communism even more successfully and rapidly. Our party, true to Leninism, never tolerates conceit and complacency, sees not only the successes but the shortcomings as well in the activities of Party, Soviet and economic agencies, and concentrates on the accomplishment of tasks undone. All energies must be directed toward achieving still more rapid economic growth, improving the people's well-being and strengthening the might of the Soviet state. The more vigorously everything new and advanced is supported and the more widely it is adopted in production, and the more sharply shortcomings are exposed and the more quickly they are eliminated, the more successfully will the tasks confronting us be accomplished. The cause of communist construction is the great cause of millions, the cause of all the people.

The Congress instructs the Central Committee to continue to direct the energies of the Party and the people toward speeding the pace of communist construction, and to take even fuller advantage of the vast inner reserves possessed by all branches of the socialist economy.

The attention of the Party and the people should be centered on the accomplishment of the following key tasks above all:

—to insure fulfillment and overfulfillment of the seven-year-plan assignments, which will be of decisive importance for the creation of the material and technical base of communism and for our victory in the peaceful economic competition with capitalism. Heavy industry, above all power, metallurgy, the chemical, machine-building and fuel industries and the construction industry, must continue to be developed at a stepped-up pace. The Congress charges all Party organizations with mobilizing the working people for the effort to meet the seven-year-plan assignments with their upward adjustments. It shall be considered essential that everything possible be done to expand the output of consumer goods. Funds accumulated as a result of the overfulfillment of plan assignments by industry shall be channeled principally into agriculture, light industry and the food industry;

—on the basis of continuing technological progress, to work for maximum growth of labor productivity in industry, construction, agriculture and transport. Raising the productivity of labor is a matter of cardinal importance where the policy and practice of communist construction are concerned, an absolute requirement for improving the people's well-being, for creating an abundance of material goods and cultural benefits for the working people;

—to insistently improve organizational work in the management of the economy, and to arrange matters in such a way as to ensure the greatest increase in output with the least expenditures. To accomplish this it is essential to choose the most progressive and economically profitable lines of development for the branches of industry; to improve specialization and cooperation; to mechanize and automate production processes on an integrated basis; to speed the application of the latest scientific and technical advances and of progressive technology and innovations in the sphere of production; to make better use of the inner reserves of economic regions and enterprises and construction projects; to tighten state discipline in all sections of the economic apparatus and wage a relentless struggle against mismanagement, wastefulness, inertia and conservatism. The reduction of the cost and improvement of the quality of output, frugality and economy in all things, and the heightening of profitability and enlargement of socialist accumulations should become law for every Soviet enterprise in its operations;

—to drastically improve the planning and organization of capital construction, sharply heighten the effectiveness of capital investments, and put a stop to the antistate, localist practice of scattering funds, material and technical resources and manpower. Special attention should continue to be given to developing the productive forces of the eastern regions, to exploiting their natural resources and utilizing them in integrated fashion;

—to manage agriculture concretely and competently, persistently promote the adoption of scientific advances and progressive methods, make better use of the land, introduce a more efficient crop structure, widely introduce corn, peas, fodder beans and other high-yield crops, sharply increase the collection and improve the use of fertilizers, improve the quality of farm work and on this basis bring about a significant rise in yields and gross harvests of grain and other farm crops and a systematic increase in the number of livestock and the output of animal products. The Congress considers it an urgent task to intensify the mechanization and electrification of agriculture, fully satisfy the needs of collective and state farms for modern equipment, and increase the production of mineral and organic fertilizers, as well as herbicides and other chemicals for combating weeds and plant diseases and pests. A rise in labor productivity and a reduction of production costs must be ensured on the basis of integrated mechanization. A most important principle of communist construction in the countryside is the production of maximum output with minimum expenditures of labor. In the next few years purchases of grain are to be brought up to 4,200,000,000 poods, of meat to 13,000,000 tons and of milk to 50,000,000 tons a year, and production of sugar beets, cotton, flax, potatoes, vegetables, fruit, tea and other agricultural products is to be increased substantially. The development of agriculture is a cause of the whole Party and of all the Soviet people;

—to ensure a steady rise in the people's standard of living on the basis of the continued growth of industrial and agricultural production. The Congress considers it essential that further measures be taken to shorten the working day and week and to abolish taxes paid by the people; that the wage adjustment for workers in all categories be completed; that housing construction be carried out at a faster pace and its quality improved and cost reduced; that construction of service facilities, nurseries and kindergartens be speeded; that the pension system and the organization of trade, public catering, and medical and everyday services for the public be improved; and that there be constant improvement of public education at all levels;

—to carry out purposeful scientific research, and to open the doors of science more widely to young people. The Congress sets before Soviet scientists as their paramount task the attaining of a level of development of Soviet science that will enable it to win leading positions in all the main fields of world science and technology;

—to develop the literature and art of socialist realism, raise their ideological and artistic level and strengthen their ties with the practice of communist construction, with the lives of the people;

—to maintain at the necessary level and strengthen in every possible way the defense capacity of our homeland, the bulwark of world peace, to perfect the armament of the Soviet Army, raise the level of combat and ideological-political training of its personnel, heighten our people's vigilance, and securely safeguard the constructive labor and peaceful life of the Soviet people, the builders of communism;

—to develop and improve socialist social relations: to strengthen the public and collective farm-cooperative forms of socialist property; properly combine material and moral incentives to labor; broaden participation by the masses in the administration of all the country's affairs; strengthen the friendship of the peoples; and in every possible way encourage the aspiration of Soviet people to work and live like Communists.

The creation of the material and technical base of communism, the development of socialist social relations and the molding of the man of communist society—these are the paramount tasks in the sphere of domestic policy facing the Party in the period of the full-scale building of communism.

III.—Our country's successes in the spheres of foreign and domestic policy are the result of the heroic labor of the Soviet people and the enormous organizational and educational activity of the Communist Party, the result of consistent adherence to its Leninist line, which was given profound and creative expression in the historic decisions of the 20th Party Congress. The Party has still further strengthened its ties with the people. As a result of the victory of socialism in the U.S.S.R. and the consolidation of the unity of Soviet society, the Communist

Party, which came into being as a party of the working class, has become a party of the entire people and has extended its guiding influence to all aspects of society's life. The Communist Party arrived at its 22nd Congress solidly united, full of creative energy and with indomitable will to march forward under the banner of Marxism-Leninism to the complete triumph of communism.

The Congress notes that a most important aspect of the Party's work in the period under review was the restoration and further development of Leninist norms of Party life and principles of collective leadership at all levels of the Party and state.

The open and bold condemnation of the cult of J. V. Stalin by the Party and its Central Committee were of enormous importance for the building of socialism and communism and for the entire international Communist movement. The Party has told the people the whole truth about the abuses of power in the period of the cult of the individual and has vigorously condemned the mistakes and perversions and the methods alien to the spirit of Leninism that were spawned under the cult of the individual. The Party has castigated the cult, overcome the perversions and mistakes of the past and is persistently carrying into effect measures that will entirely preclude a repetition of mistakes of this kind in the future. These measures have found expression in the Program and Statutes of the Party.

The 22nd Congress wholly approves the great and fruitful work done by the Central Committee in reinstating and promoting Leninist principles in all spheres of Party, state and ideological work; this has given the Party and people ample scope for creative initiative, has facilitated the broadening and strengthening of the Party's ties with the masses and has heightened its combat efficiency.

The Congress considers quite correct and fully approves the decisive measures taken by the Central Committee in exposing and administering a crushing ideological defeat to the anti-Party group made up of Molotov, Kaganovich, Malenkov, Bulganin, Pervukhin and Saburov, and Shepilov, who joined them, which took a stand against the Leninist policy laid down by the 20th Congress, resisted implementation of measures aimed at overcoming the cult of the individual and its consequences, and sought to maintain forms and methods of leadership that had discredited themselves and to retard the evolution of the new in our life. Serious mistakes were committed during the factionalist struggle of the anti-Party group by Comrade Voroshilov, who took his stand with this group against the Leninist line of the Party. In the course of the June plenary session of the Central Committee, Comrade Voroshilov admitted his mistakes and condemned the factionalist acts of the anti-Party group; to some extent this facilitated exposure of the anti-Party renegades. Having cast aside the unprincipled factionalists, plotters and careerists, the Party closed ranks still more tightly, strengthened its ties with the people and mobilized all its forces for the successful implementation of its general line.

In the name of the whole Party, the 22nd Congress indignantly condemns the subversive anti-Party factionalist activity as incompatible with the Leninist principle of Party unity. Those who take the path of factionalist struggle, backstage intrigue and machination directed against the Leninist line of the Party, against its unity, act against the interests of their people, the interests of communist construction. Expressing the will of all Communists, the Congress declares that the Party will continue steadfastly implementing the Leninist law calling for preservation of the unity and purity of the Party's ranks and implacably combating all manifestations of cliquishness and factionalism.

The restoration and development of Leninist principles of collective leadership have been of particular importance for the Party and the Soviet state. Regular convocation of Party Congresses, plenary sessions of the Central Committee and all elective bodies in the Party, nationwide discussion of major problems of state, economic and Party development, and extensive consultation with workers in various branches of the economy and fields of culture have become the norm in Party and state life. All major questions of domestic and foreign policy have been widely discussed in our party and are the expression of its collective intelligence and experience.

The unbreakable ties between the Party and the people are strikingly manifested in the growth of the Party's ranks, the constant influx of fresh forces into the Party. In the period under review the numerical strength of the Party has increased by 2,500,000 persons, and today it stands at nearly 10,000,000 Communists.

The 22nd Congress instructs the Central Committee to continue to strengthen the unity of the Party, to fight for the purity of its Marxist-Leninist world view, to reinforce the Party's ranks with advanced people from the working class, collective farm peasantry and intelligentsia, and to raise still higher the title of Communist—active, stanch and politically conscious fighter for the happiness of the people, for communism.

The Congress notes that in the past few years the Party has made a decisive shift to concrete guidance of the national economy. The Central Committee has turned the attention of Party organizations and executive cadres to the fulfillment of national economic plans, the mobilization of our economy's reserves, and the study and broad dissemination of progressive experience, and has taught proper economic management on the basis of concrete positive examples. The Congress emphasizes that the effectiveness of the Party's guidance lies in its ability to organize and direct the efforts of the masses toward the accomplishment of the principal tasks, in the art of integrating the talents, knowledge and experience of many people for the accomplishment of great undertakings. Ever mindful of Lenin's statements that the Party is strong by virtue of the awareness and activeness of the masses, we must work still more vigorously to heighten the communist awareness and political activeness of the working people, uniting them even more closely around the Party.

The Congress calls particular attention to the need for improving work with cadres, to their selection and education, to the proper combination of old, experienced officials and young, energetic organizers who know their jobs well. There should be no room in executive work for people who have lagged behind, grown conceited and lost touch with life, who are lacking in ideals and principles. The Party is waging and will continue to wage an implacable struggle against persons who commit breaches of Party and state discipline and who take the path of deceiving the Party and state, and against bootlickers, adulators, hoodwinkers and bureaucrats. Criticism and self-criticism—our sharpest weapon—must be developed to the full in the struggle against shortcomings.

The Congress attaches great importance to the principle of turnover in elective bodies, which will afford new opportunities for broad application of the creative energies of the Party and the people in the furtherance of communist construction. The regular turnover of elective bodies should become an inviolable rule of Party, state and public life in our country.

The best school for the training and political molding of cadres is life, practical activity. The traits of a Party and state leader of the Leninist type are formed in the struggle to carry out the Party line, in practical work, in the accomplishment of the concrete tasks of communist construction. More vigor must be displayed in drawing the great body of aktivists into work on a voluntary, unpaid basis in Party bodies.

Party, state and public control over the proper organization of matters, over the precise fulfillment of the requirements of the Party Program and Statutes and of directives and instructions of the Party and the Soviet government by every official in whatever post, is taking on paramount importance under present circumstances. The system of control is an effective means of improving the guidance of communist construction on the basis of genuinely democratic principles; it is a dependable weapon in the struggle against bureaucracy and red tape, and a school of communist education for the masses.

To intensify control over and inspection of actual performance, it is essential to institute a strict procedure for reporting by local Party agencies to higher Party agencies and to the Communist rank and file on fulfillment of Party decisions. The 22nd Congress instructs the Central Committee to devise effective measures for improving and perfecting Party, state and public control.

The Congress attaches great importance to the activities of mass working people's organizations—the Soviets, trade unions, Young Communist League and cooperatives. Now that communist self-government is continually broadening, the role of these organizations in the life of socialist society is steadily growing.

It is essential to heighten still further the role of the Soviets in guiding economic construction and cultural development and in drawing the masses into the administration of the socialist state. The further extension of Soviet democracy is a most important prerequisite for the gradual transition to communist public self-government.

The Party will do its utmost to promote intensification of the trade unions' activities in the management of the economy, the organization of Communist Labor competition, the instruction of the masses in the administration of socialist production and public affairs, and the heightening of the communist awareness of the working people. Constant attention to man, his labor, education, home life, health and leisure, represents an important task of the trade unions.

Our Party sets a high assessment on the activities of its militant helpmate—the Leninist Young Communist League. The chief task of the Y.C.L. is to rear young men and women on the heroic traditions of revolutionary struggle, on examples of the selfless labor of workers, collective farmers and the intelligentsia, and on the great ideas of Marxism-Leninism, and to prepare stalwart, highly educated young builders of communism who love work. Ahead for youth is the exploitation of new mineral wealth and the building of factories, plants, mines, state farms, institutions of science and art, and new cities. The future belongs to them; it is they who are to build and perfect the communist society.

Further improvement and intensification of ideological work constitutes one of the Party's chief tasks and a most important prerequisite for success in all its practical activity. In the interests of communist construction it is essential that the communist education of the working people, above all the young generation, be central in the activities of every Party organization and of the Soviet public as a whole.

The principal directions that ideological work must take under present-day circumstances are: propaganda of the Marxist-Leninist doctrine and the development of a scientific outlook in all members of society; a struggle against the survivals of capitalism in the thinking of people and against the influence of hostile bourgeois ideology; the education of the working people in a spirit of the noble ethical principles embodied in the moral code of the builders of communism; and the molding of well-rounded members of communist society. The preparation of the individual for labor and the inculcation of love and respect for labor as a prime vital need constitutes the essence, the heart, of all the work of communist education.

The most important thing in ideological work at the present time is to explain the Party Program thoroughly, to arm the working people of Soviet society with the great plan of struggle for the victory of communism, to mobilize all the working people for the translation of the new Party Program into reality. All the Party's means of exerting ideological influence on the masses—propaganda, agitation, the press, radio, television, motion pictures, cultural and educational work, literature and art—must be subordinated to the accomplishment of this task.

Ideological work is a most important means to the accomplishment of the tasks of communist construction. It must foster the growth of the political and labor activeness of Soviet people and of their communist awareness. Thorough study by Party and state cadres of Marxist-Leninist theory and of the world-historic experience of the Communist Party and the Soviet people in their struggle for the triumph of socialism and communism, the heightening of the level of educational work and intensification of its influence on the lives and labors of the people remains one of the Party's most important tasks in its propagandist and ideological work. It must be guided by a most important Party principle—the unity of ideological and organizational work.

The extent and importance of the theoretical work of the Party and its Central Committee have grown greatly in the last few years. Waging a struggle on two fronts—against revisionism, as the main danger, and against the dogmatic stultification of revolutionary theory—the Party has firmly defended and creatively developed the doctrine of Marxism-Leninism. The period in the Party's life under review has been marked by the creative solution of major theoretical problems in the building of communism in our country and of pressing problems of the international Communist movement. The 22nd Congress unanimously and with great satisfaction approves the Party Central Committee's fruitful theoretical work, which has found its fullest expression in our party's new Program.

The Congress underscores the need to continue holding high and keeping pure the all-conquering banner of Marxism-Leninism and to develop and enrich the theory with new conclusions and theses generalizing the experience of communist construction. Guided by the Leninist principle of the unity of theory and practice, the Party must regard the defense and creative development of Marxism-Leninism as a most important duty.

The 22nd Congress sets all Party organizations the following tasks in the area of organizational and ideological work:

—to continue heightening the Party's role in the building of communism, strengthening its ties with the masses of working people, providing all sectors of communist construction with concrete guidance, heightening the level of organization and businesslike efficiency in their work, and fostering the initiative and political and labor activeness of the masses;

—to observe and develop Leninist norms of Party life and the principles of collective leadership, to improve the selection, placement and education of cadres, to heighten the responsibility of Party agencies and their officials to the Party, to intensify the activeness of Communists, their participation in the framing and implementation of the Party's policy, and to promote inner-Party democracy, criticism and self-criticism;

—to heighten the role of the Soviets, the trade unions and the Y.C.L. in communist construction and in the Marxist-Leninist education of the masses;

—to improve Party, state and public control and mold it into genuinely popular control of the activities of all state and public organizations and officials;

—to widen the scope and raise the level of ideological work, solve new problems advanced by life, and educate Soviet people in a spirit of loyalty to Marxism-Leninism and irreconcilability to any manifestations of bourgeois ideology;

—to expand fraternal ties with all Communist and Workers' Parties and, in company with them, wage a determined struggle for the purity of Marxism-Leninism and against revisionism, dogmatism and sectarianism, and to strengthen the unity of the whole international Communist and workers' movement.

In the course of the discussion of the draft Program and Statutes of the C.P.S.U. at Party meetings, conferences and Congresses of the Union-republic Communist Parties, at meetings of working people, in the press, and in letters sent in to the Central Committee and to local Party bodies, Communists and non-Party working people had many practical suggestions and comments to offer on economic and cultural development, on improving the people's standard of living and services for them, and on eliminating the shortcomings in the work of Party, Soviet, economic, trade union and Y.C.L. organizations and various institutions.

The Congress instructs the Central Committees of the Union-republic Communist Parties and the territory and province Party committees to look into all the comments and suggestions that were forthcoming in the course of the discussion of the draft Program and Statutes, to take measures to eliminate shortcomings, and to report on these measures to plenary sessions of Party committees, to conferences, and to the Central Committee of the C.P.S.U.

***

The world-historic victories in the building of socialism and communism in our country are recognized by all mankind. They represent the magnificent results of the heroic labor and selfless struggle of the Leninist Party and the Soviet people, the triumph of the ideas of Marxism-Leninism.

The great vitality of the Marxist-Leninist doctrine has never been as fully revealed as today, when socialism has completely and finally triumphed in the Soviet Union and is winning victories in the people's democracies, and when the international Communist, workers', democratic and national-liberation movements are growing at a tempestuous pace. Under the influence of the successes of the international Communist movement, colossal social changes, the most profound revolutionary transformations, are and will be taking place in the world.

The 22nd Congress of the Communist Party of the Soviet Union appeals to Communists and Young Communists and to every Soviet individual to participate actively in the effort to complete the program of communist construction. The Congress is imbued with unshakable confidence that the workers, collective farmers and Soviet intelligentsia will spare no effort to translate the great communist ideals into reality.

In the name of the ten million Communists, and expressing the will of all the Soviet people, the 22nd Congress declares:

The Communist Party of the Soviet Union will continue to carry high the triumphant banner of Marxism-Leninism, will fulfill its internationalist duty to the working people of all countries and devote all its energies to working for the people's interests, for the achievement of the great historical goal—the building of a communist society.

The Party solemnly proclaims: the present generation of Soviet people will live under communism!

Other Resolutions

[The Congress also resolved unanimously to approve the following: the report of the Central Inspection Commission (Oct. 27); the Party Program (Oct. 31); and (Oct. 31) the Party Statutes.]

XII. OFFICIALS ELECTED

Who's Who of the Central Committee†

MEMBERS

1. G[rigory] G[rigoryevich] ABRAMOV.* [First Secretary of Moscow Province Party Committee since July 7, 1960. Member of C.C.'s Bureau for the Russian Republic since Oct. 31, 1961.]

2. P[yotr] A[ndreyevich] ABRASIMOV.* [First Secretary of Smolensk Province Party Committee since Feb. 11, 1961. Ambassador to Poland from Oct. 3, 1957, to Feb. 6, 1961, and prior to that Minister-Counselor to China.]

3. A[lexei] I[vanovich] ADZHUBEI.* [Editor-in-Chief of Izvestia since May, 1959. Secretary of Journalists' Union. Formerly Editor-in-Chief of Komsomolskaya pravda.]

4. Y[ury] V[ladimirovich] ANDROPOV.* [Director of a department of C.C. since May, 1957. Formerly Ambassador to Hungary.]

5. A[verky] B[orisovich] ARISTOV. [Ambassador to Poland since Feb. 2, 1961. Until his present appointment, member of C.C.'s Bureau for the Russian Republic. He was also a member of C.C.'s Presidium until Oct. 31, 1961, and Secretary of C.C. until May 4, 1960.]

6. S[ergei] A[lexandrovich] AFANASYEV.* [Chairman of All-Russian Economic Council and Vice-Chairman of Russian Republic Council of Ministers since June 4, 1961. Formerly Chairman of Leningrad Economic Council.]

7. V[eli] Yu[sufovich] AKHUNDOV.* [First Secretary of Azerbaidzhan Communist Party C.C. since July 11, 1959.]

8. I[van] Kh[ristoforovich] BAGRAMYAN.† [Marshal of the Soviet Union. Deputy Minister of Defense and Commander of Rear Services. Formerly head of Voroshilov Military Academy.]

9. A[lexander] V[asilyevich] BASOV.* [First Secretary of Rostov Province Party Committee since June 15, 1960. Formerly Chairman of Rostov Province Executive Committee.]

10. I[van] A[lexandrovich] BENEDIKTOV. [Ambassador to India since April 21, 1959. Formerly Russian Republic Minister of Agriculture.]

11. B[oris] P[avlovich] BESHCHEV. [Minister of Transportation since 1948.]

12. S[ergei] S[emyonovich] BIRYUZOV.† [Marshal of the Soviet Union. Deputy Minister of Defense and Commander-in-Chief of Antiaircraft Defense Forces.]

13. I[van] I[vanovich] BODYUL.* [First Secretary of Moldavian Communist Party C.C. since May 29, 1960, and prior to that its Second Secretary.]

14. L[eonid] I[lyich] BREZHNEV. [Member of C.C.'s

---

†[The list of Central Committee members and candidate members is published as it appeared in Pravda and Izvestia, Nov. 1, p. 2; the order follows the Russian alphabet. Given names, patronymics and positions as of May 1, 1962, have been added by the translator and appear in brackets. The names of new members and new candidate members have been marked with asterisks, and the names of members promoted from candidate membership and of candidate members dropped from full membership have been marked with daggers.]

Presidium since June 29, 1957. Chairman of Supreme Soviet Presidium since May 7, 1960.]

15. K[onstantin] A[ndreyevich] VERSHININ.* [Chief Marshal of Aviation. Deputy Minister of Defense and Commander-in-Chief of Air Forces since 1957.]

16. A[lexander] P[etrovich] VOLKOV. [Chairman of State Committee on Labor and Wages since June 9, 1956.]

17. G[eorgy] I[vanovich] VOROBYEV.* [First Secretary of Krasnodar Territory Party Committee since June 10, 1960. Formerly Director of C.C.'s Agriculture Department for the Russian Republic.]

18. G[ennady] I[vanovich] VORONOV. [Member of C.C.'s Presidium and First Vice-Chairman of C.C.'s Bureau for the Russian Republic since Oct. 31, 1961. Formerly candidate member of Presidium from Jan. 18, 1961, and prior to that First Secretary of Orenburg Province Party Committee.]

19. F[eodosy] D[enisovich] VORONOV.† [Present position unknown. Formerly Chairman of Chelyabinsk Economic Council, and prior to that Director of Magnitogorsk Metallugical Combine.]

20. V[alentina] I[vanovna] GAGANOVA.* [Brigade leader at Vyshny Volochek Cotton Combine, Kalinin Province.]

21. A[nton] I[vanovich] GAYEVOI. [Secretary of Ukraine Communist Party C.C. since May 21, 1961. Formerly First Secretary of Dnepropetrovsk Province Party Committee.]

22. K[onstantin] I[vanovich] GALANSHIN.* [First Secretary of Perm Province Party Committee since Feb. 20, 1960.]

23. V[asily] F[yodorovich] GARBUZOV.* [Minister of Finance since May 16, 1960.]

24. A[lexander] V[asilyevich] GEORGIYEV.* [First Secretary of Altai Province Party Committee since March 18, 1961.]

25. F[ilipp] I[vanovich] GOLIKOV.* [Marshal of the Soviet Union. Director of Chief Political Administration of Soviet Army and Navy since January, 1958.]

26. S[ergei] G[eorgiyevich] GORSHKOV.† [Admiral. First Deputy Minister of Defense and Commander-in-Chief of Navy since 1956.]

27. F[yodor] S[tepanovich] GORYACHEV. [First Secretary of Novosibirsk Province Party Committee since February, 1959. Formerly First Secretary of Kalinin Province Party Committee.]

28. A[ndrei] A[ntonovich] GRECHKO.† [Marshal of the Soviet Union. First Deputy Minister of Defense since 1956 and Commander-in-Chief of Armed Forces of Warsaw Pact Countries since July 24, 1960. Formerly Commander-in-Chief of Ground Forces.]

29. V[iktor] V[asilyevich] GRISHIN. [Chairman of Central Council of Trade Unions since March 16, 1956. Candidate member of C.C.'s Presidium since Jan. 18, 1961.]

30. K[onstantin] N[ikolayevich] GRISHIN.† [First Secretary of Ryazan Province Party Committee since Oct. 3, 1960. Formerly First Secretary of Vladimir Province Party Committee.]

31. I[van] A[lexandrovich] GRISHMANOV.* [Chairman of State Committee on Construction Affairs since Jan. 26, 1961. Formerly Director of C.C.'s Construction Department.]

32. A[ndrei] A[ndreyevich] GROMYKO. [Minister of Foreign Affairs since Feb. 15, 1957.]

33. I[van] S[amoilovich] GRUSHETSKY.* [First Secretary of Lvov Province Party Committee since Feb. 11, 1961.]

Formerly First Secretary of Volhynia Province Party Committee.]

34. A[bdurakhman] D[anialovich] DANIALOV. [First Secretary of Dagestan Province Party Committee since 1949.]

35. S[alken] DAULENOV.* [Chairman of Kazakh Republic Council of Ministers since Jan. 25, 1961.]

36. P[yotr] V[asilyevich] DEMENTYEV. [Chairman of State Committee on Aviation Technology since Dec. 15, 1957.]

37. P[yotr] N[ilovich] DEMICHEV.* [Secretary of C.C. since Oct. 31, 1961. First Secretary of Moscow City Party Committee since July 7, 1960.]

38. G[eorgy] A[polinaryevich] DENISOV. [Ambassador to Bulgaria since May 25, 1960. Formerly Director of C.C.'s Agriculture Department for the Union Republics, and prior to that First Secretary of Saratov Province Party Committee.]

39. G[ivi] D[mitriyevich] DZHAVAKHISHVILI. [Chairman of Georgian Republic Council of Ministers since Sept. 22, 1953.]

40. N[ikolai] A[lexandrovich] DYGAI.† [Chairman of Moscow City Executive Committee since Sept. 2, 1961. Formerly USSR Minister without portfolio.]

41. V[eniamin] E[mmanuilovich] DYMSHITS.* [First Vice-Chairman of State Planning Committee.]

42. N[ikolai] G[rigoryevich] YEGORYCHEV.* [Second Secretary of Moscow City Party Committee since Feb. 26, 1961.]

43. V[yacheslav] P[etrovich] YELYUTIN.† [Minister of Higher and Specialized Secondary Education since June 22, 1959. Formerly Minister of Higher Education.]

44. G[eorgy] V[asilyevich] YENYUTIN. [Chairman of State Control Commission (known as Soviet Control Commission prior to Aug. 15, 1961) since Dec. 12, 1957.]

45. V. V. YERMILOV.* [Fitter in Red Proletarian Plant, Moscow.]

46. L[eonid] N[ikolayevich] YEFREMOV. [First Secretary of Gorky Province Party Committee since September, 1958. Member of C.C.'s Bureau for the Russian Republic.]

47. M[ikhail] T[imofeyevich] YEFREMOV. [First Secretary of Chelyabinsk Province Party Committee since March 18, 1961. Formerly Director of Department of Party Agencies for the Russian Republic, and prior to that First Secretary of Kuibyshev Province Party Committee.]

48. I[van] K[uzmich] ZHEGALIN. [Ambassador to Rumania since Nov. 27, 1960. Formerly First Secretary of Stalingrad Province Party Committee.]

49. Ya[kov] N[ikitovich] ZAROBYAN.* [First Secretary of Armenian Communist Party C.C. since Dec. 29, 1960.]

50. A[lexander] F[yodorovich] ZASYADKO.* [Vice-Chairman of Council of Ministers since March 31, 1958. Chairman of State Scientific-Economic Council since April 22, 1960. Formerly Vice-Chairman of State Planning Committee.]

51. M[atvei] V[asilyevich] ZAKHAROV.* [Marshal of the Soviet Union. First Deputy Minister of Defense and Chief of General Staff of Army and Navy since April, 1960. Formerly Commander-in-Chief of Soviet Forces in East Germany.]

52. V[alerian] A[lexandrovich] ZORIN.† [Permanent Representative to the United Nations since Sept. 25, 1960. Deputy Minister of Foreign Affairs since July 17, 1956.]

53. O[lga] I[lyinichna] IVASHCHENKO.† [Secretary of Ukraine Communist Party C.C. since 1954.]

54. N[ikolai] G[rigoryevich] IGNATOV. [Vice-Chairman of Council of Ministers since May 4, 1960. Chairman of State Procurements Committee since Feb. 26, 1961. Until Oct. 31, 1961, member of C.C.'s Presidium and Bureau for the Russian Republic, and until May 4, 1960, Secretary of C.C.]

55. N[ikolai] F[yodorovich] IGNATOV. [First Secretary of Orel Province Party Committee since Jan. 14, 1960. Until March 3, 1959, Chairman of Moscow Province Executive Committee.]

56. L[eonid] F[yodorovich] ILYICHEV.* [Secretary of C.C. since Oct. 31, 1961. Formerly Director of C.C.'s Agitation and Propaganda Department for the Union Republics.]

57. V[asily] M[ikhailovich] KAVUN.* [Chairman of 22nd Party Congress Collective Farm, Bershad District, Vinnitsa Province.]

58. I[van] P[avlovich] KAZANETS.† [Second Secretary of Ukraine Communist Party C.C. since Feb. 20, 1960. Formerly First Secretary of Stalino Province Party Committee.]

59. V[alery] D[mitriyevich] KALMYKOV.† [Chairman of State Radioelectronics Committee since Dec. 14, 1957.]

60. J[anis] E[duardovich] KALNBERZINS. [Chairman of Latvian Republic Supreme Soviet Presidium since Nov. 27, 1959. Prior to that First Secretary of Latvian Communist Party C.C., and until Oct. 31, 1961, candidate member of C.C.'s Presidium.]

61. I[van] V[asilyevich] KAPITONOV. [First Secretary of Ivanovo Province Party Committee since Sept. 23, 1959. Formerly First Secretary of Moscow Province Party Committee.]

62. M[stislav] V[sevolodovich] KELDYSH.* [President of Academy of Sciences since May 19, 1961, and prior to that its Vice-President. Mathematician.]

63. A[ndrei] P[avlovich] KIRILENKO. [First Secretary of Sverdlovsk Province Party Committee since Dec. 13, 1955. Member of C.C.'s Bureau for the Russian Republic since Feb. 28, 1956. Until Oct. 31, 1961, candidate member of C.C.'s Presidium.]

64. I[van] I[vanovich] KISELEV.* [Director of Gorky Automobile Plant.]

65. T[ikhon] Ya[kovlevich] KISELEV.* [Chairman of Belorussian Republic Council of Ministers since April 9, 1959. Formerly Second Secretary of Belorussian Communist Party C.C.]

66. V[asily] K[onstantinovich] KLIMENKO. [Chairman of Ukraine Republic Council of Trade Unions since March 19, 1961. Formerly First Secretary of Lugansk Province Party Committee.]

67. A[lexander] V[lasovich] KOVALENKO.* [First Secretary of Belgorod Province Party Committee since Dec. 14, 1960. Formerly Chairman of Belgorod Province Executive Committee.]

68. Ye[vgeny] F[yodorovich] KOZHEVNIKOV.* [Minister of Transport Construction since Sept. 6, 1954.]

69. F[rol] R[omanovich] KOZLOV. [Member of C.C.'s Presidium since June 29, 1957, and Secretary of C.C. since May 4, 1960.]

70. A[lexander] A[kimovich] KOKAREV.* [First Secretary of Krasnoyarsk Territory Party Committee since February, 1958.]

71. V[asily] G[rigoryevich] KOMYAKHOV.† [First Secretary of Poltava Province Party Committee since Jan. 3, 1961. Formerly First Secretary of Crimea Province Party Committee.]

72. I[van] S[tepanovich] KONEV. [Marshal of the Soviet Union. Commander-in-Chief of Soviet Forces in East Germany. Formerly Commander-in-Chief of Armed Forces of Warsaw Pact Countries.]

73. N[ikolai] S[emyonovich] KONOVALOV.* [First Secretary of Kaliningrad Province Party Committee since July 25, 1961.]

74. A[lexander] Ye[vdokimovich] KORNEICHUK. [Writer and playwright. Member of Board and Secretary of Writers' Union. Vice-Chairman of Soviet Committee for Defense of Peace and member of World Peace Council Presidium. Chairman of Ukraine Republic Supreme Soviet.]

75. D[emyan] S[ergeyevich] KOROTCHENKO. [Chairman of Ukraine Republic Supreme Soviet Presidium since 1954. Until Oct. 31, 1961, candidate member of C.C.'s Presidium.]

76. N[ikolai] G[avrilovich] KORYTKOV.* [First Secretary of Kalinin Province Party Committee since Sept. 29, 1960.]

77. A[natoly] I[vanovich] KOSTOUSOV.† [Chairman of State Automation and Machine-Building Committee since Feb. 28, 1959. Formerly Chairman of Moscow Province Economic Council.]

78. A[lexei] N[ikolayevich] KOSYGIN. [Member of C.C.'s Presidium since May 4, 1960, when he was promoted from candidate member. First Vice-Chairman of Council of Ministers since May 4, 1960. Until that date, Chairman of State Planning Committee.]

79. M[ikhail] K[onstantinovich] KRAKHMALEV.† [First Secretary of Bryansk Province Party Committee since Dec. 13, 1960. Formerly First Secretary of Belgorod Province Party Committee.]

80. A[lexei] G[eorgiyevich] KRYLOV.* [Director of Likhachev Automobile Plant, Moscow, since 1958.]

81. N[ikolai] I[vanovich] KRYLOV.* [General of the Army.

Commander of Moscow Military District. Formerly Commander of Leningrad Military District.]

82. V[asily] V[asilyevich] KUZNETSOV. [First Deputy Minister of Foreign Affairs since March 22, 1955.]

83. F[yodor] D[avidovich] KULAKOV.* [First Secretary of Stavropol Territory Party Committee since June 25, 1960. Formerly Russian Republic Minister of Grain Products.]

84. D[inmukhamed] A[khmedovich] KUNAYEV. [First Secretary of Kazakhstan Communist Party C.C. since Jan. 20, 1960. Prior to that, Chairman of Kazakh Republic Council of Ministers.]

85. R[akhmankul] KURBANOV.* [Chairman of Uzbek Republic Council of Ministers since Sept. 27, 1961. Formerly First Secretary of Andizhan Province Party Committee.]

86. O[tto] V[ilgelmovich] KUUSINEN. [Secretary of C.C. and member of its Presidium since June 29, 1957.]

87. V[ladimir] A[lexeyevich] KUCHERENKO. [President of Academy of Construction and Architecture since Jan. 26, 1961. Until then, Chairman of State Committee on Construction Affairs.]

88. P[avel] S[ergeyevich] KUCHUMOV.* [Chairman of All-Union Farm Machinery Association since its establishment on Feb. 20, 1961. Formerly Deputy Minister of Agriculture.]

89. I[van] G[ustavovich] KABIN. [First Secretary of Estonian Communist Party C.C. since April 9, 1950.]

90. M[ikhail] A[vksenteyevich] LESECHKO.* [Chairman of U.S.S.R. Council of Ministers' Commission for Foreign Economic Affairs since April 25, 1962. Previously First Vice-Chairman of State Planning Committee.]

91. P[yotr] F[adeyevich] LOMAKO.† [Vice-Chairman of C.C.'s Bureau for the Russian Republic since Oct. 31, 1961. Formerly Chairman of Krasnoyarsk Economic Council.]

92. L[eonid] I[gnatyevich] LUBENNIKOV. [First Secretary of Kemerovo Province Party Committee since Feb. 13, 1960.]

93. A[lexander] P[avlovich] LYASHKO.* [First Secretary of Donetsk (Stalino) Province Party Committee since Feb. 19, 1960.]

94. K[irill] T[rofimovich] MAZUROV. [First Secretary of Belorussian Communist Party C.C. since July 29, 1956. Candidate member of C.C.'s Presidium since June 29, 1957.]

95. R[odion] Y[akovlevich] MALINOVSKY. [Marshal of the Soviet Union. Minister of Defense since Oct. 26, 1957.]

96. N[ikolai] F[yodorovich] MANUKOVSKY.* [Brigade leader at Kirov Collective Farm, Novaya Usman District, Voronezh Province.]

97. S[ergei] I[osifovich] MANYAKIN.* [First Secretary of Omsk Province Party Committee.]

98. V[asily] P[avlovich] MZHAVANADZE. [First Secretary of Georgian Communist Party C.C. since September, 1953. Candidate member of C.C.'s Presidium since June 29, 1957.]

99. A[nastas] I[vanovich] MIKOYAN. [First Vice-Chairman of Council of Ministers since Feb. 28, 1955. Member of C.C.'s Presidium since 1935.]

100. N[ikolai] A[lexandrovich] MIKHAILOV. [Ambassador to Indonesia since July 1, 1960. Until May 4, 1960, Minister of Culture.]

101. L[eonid] G[avrilovich] MONASHEV.* [First Secretary of Kursk Province Party Committee since October, 1958.]

102. K[irill] S[emyonovich] MOSKALENKO. [Marshal of the Soviet Union. Deputy Minister of Defense and Commander-in-Chief of Rocket Troops since Oct. 25, 1960. Formerly Commander of Moscow Military District.]

103. A[lexander] S[ergeyevich] MURYSEV.* [First Secretary of Kuibyshev Province Party Committee since Dec. 30, 1959.]

104. N[uritdin] A[kramovich] MUKHITDINOV. [Present position unknown. (According to N.Y. Times, rumored to be Vice-Chairman of Central Union of Consumers' Cooperatives.) From Dec. 17, 1957, to Oct. 31, 1961, Secretary of C.C. and member of its Presidium.]

105. Ya[dgar] S[adykovna] NASRIDDINOVA. [Chairman of Uzbek Republic Supreme Soviet Presidium since March 25, 1959. Formerly Vice-Chairman of Uzbek Republic Council of Ministers.]

106. T[atyana] N[ikolayevna] NIKOLAYEVA.* [Secretary of Central Council of Trade Unions since March 28, 1959.]

107. V[ladimir] N[ikolayevich] NOVIKOV.* [Vice-Chairman of Council of Ministers and Chairman of State Planning Committee since May 4, 1960.]

108. I[gnaty] T[rofimovich] NOVIKOV.* [Minister of Power Plant Construction since Jan. 3, 1959.]

109. Z[ia] N[uriyevich] NURIYEV.* [First Secretary of Bashkir Province Party Committee since June 15, 1957.]

110. B[alysh] OVEZOV.* [First Secretary of Turkmenistan Communist Party C.C. since June 13, 1960. Until then Chairman of Turkmenian Republic Council of Ministers.]

111. N[ikolai] N[ikolayevich] ORGANOV. [Chairman of Russian Republic Supreme Soviet Presidium since Nov. 27, 1959. Member of C.C.'s Bureau for the Russian Republic since Oct. 31, 1961.]

112. S[ergei] P[avlovich] PAVLOV.* [First Secretary of Young Communist League C.C. since March 25, 1959.]

113. N[ikolai] S[emyonovich] PATOLICHEV. [Minister of Foreign Trade since Aug. 27, 1958.]

114. N[ikolai] M[ikhailovich] PEGOV. [Ambassador to Iran since Aug. 17, 1956.]

115. A[rvids] J[anovich] PELSE.* [First Secretary of Latvian Communist Party C.C. since Nov. 24, 1959.]

116. N[ikolai] V[iktorovich] PODGORNY. [First Secretary of Ukraine Communist Party C.C. since Dec. 26, 1957. Member of C.C.'s Presidium since May 4, 1960.]

117. D[mitry] S[tepanovich] POLYANSKY. [Chairman of Russian Republic Council of Ministers since April 1, 1958. Member of C.C.'s Presidium since May 4, 1960. Member of C.C.'s Bureau for the Russian Republic since April, 1958.]

118. B[oris] N[ikolayevich] PONOMAREV. [Secretary of C.C. since Oct. 31, 1961. Formerly Director of C.C.'s International Department.]

119. N[ina] V[asilyevna] POPOVA.† [Chairman of Presidium of Union of Soviet Societies for Friendship and Cultural Ties With Foreign Countries since Feb. 18, 1958. Chairman of Committee of Soviet Women since 1945.]

120. P[yotr] N[ikolayevich] POSPELOV. [Director of C.C.'s Institute of Marxism-Leninism. Until Oct. 31, 1961, candidate member of C.C.'s Presidium and member of C.C.'s Bureau for the Russian Republic, and until May 4, 1960, Secretary of C.C.]

121. S[ergei] O[sipovich] PRITYTSKY.* [First Secretary of Minsk Province Party Committee since Feb. 5, 1960. Formerly First Secretary of Molodechno Province Party Committee.]

122. A[lexander] M[ikhailovich] PUZANOV. [Ambassador to North Korea since Feb. 22, 1957.]

123. K[onstantin] G[eorgiyevich] PYSIN. [Minister of Agriculture since April 26, 1962. First Deputy Minister of Agriculture, March 16, 1961—April 26, 1962. Formerly First Secretary of Altai Territory Party Committee.]

124. D[zhabar] RASULOV.* [First Secretary of Tadzhikistan Communist Party C.C. since April 16, 1961.]

125. Sh[araf] R[ashidovich] RASHIDOV.† [First Secretary of Uzbekistan Communist Party since March 14, 1959. Candidate member of C.C.'s Presidium since Oct. 31, 1961. Formerly Chairman of Uzbek Republic Supreme Soviet Presidium.]

126. P[yotr] A[kimovich] ROZENKO.* [Vice-Chairman of Ukraine Republic Council of Ministers and Chairman of Ukraine State Planning Commission since April 17, 1959.]

127. R[oman] A[ndreyevich] RUDENKO.† [U.S.S.R. Prosecutor General since June 29, 1953.]

128. K[onstantin] N[ikolayevich] RUDNEV.* [Vice-Chairman of Council of Ministers and Chairman of State Committee for Coordinating Scientific Research since June 10, 1961. Formerly Chairman of State Committee on Defense Technology.]

129. A[lexei] M[atveyevich] RUMYANTSEV. [Editor-in-Chief of Problems of Peace and Socialism, organ of Communist and Workers' Parties, since 1958.]

130. V[asily] M[ikhailovich] RYABIKOV.† [First Vice-Chairman of State Planning Committee since June 18, 1961. Formerly Chairman of All-Russian Economic Council and Vice-Chairman of Russian Republic Council of Ministers.]

131. P[avel] A[lexeyevich] SATYUKOV.* [Editor-in-Chief of Pravda since 1956. Chairman of Board of Journalists' Union since Nov. 14, 1959.]

132. I[van] S[emyonovich] SENIN.† [First Vice-Chairman of Ukraine Republic Council of Ministers since Sept. 12, 1953.]

133. Z[inovy] T[imofeyevich] SERDYUK. [First Vice-Chairman of Party Control Committee since May 29, 1960. Formerly First Secretary of Moldavian Communist Party C.C.]

134. M[ikhail] S[afronovich] SINITSA.* [First Secretary of

Odessa Province Party Committee since Feb. 9, 1961. Formerly First Secretary of Kiev City Party Committee.]

135. V[ladimir] V[ladimirovich] SKRYABIN.* [First Secretary of Zaporozhye Province Party Committee since Dec. 19, 1957.]

136. Ye[fim] P[avlovich] SLAVSKY.* [Minister of Medium Machine Building since July 24, 1957.]

137. L[eonid] V[asilyevich] SMIRNOV.* [Chairman of State Committee on Defense Technology since June 10, 1961.]

138. A[ntanas] J[uosovich] SNIECKUS. [First Secretary of Lithuanian Communist Party since 1940.]

139. N[ikolai] A[lexandrovich] SOBOL.* [First Secretary of Kharkov Province Party Committee since March 1, 1961. Formerly Chairman of Kharkov Economic Council.]

140. T[ikhon] I[vanovich] SOKOLOV.† [First Secretary of Virgin Land Territory Party Committee since Dec. 28, 1960, and Secretary of Kazakhstan Communist Party C.C. since Jan. 20, 1960. Formerly First Secretary of Perm Province Party Committee.]

141. L[eonid] N[ikolayevich] SOLOVYEV.† [Secretary of Central Council of Trade Unions since March 28, 1959.]

142. M[ikhail] S[ergeyevich] SOLOMENTSEV.* [First Secretary of Karaganda Province Party Committee since Oct. 22, 1959.]

143. I[van] V[asilyevich] SPIRIDONOV.* [Secretary of C.C., Oct. 31, 1961, to April 26, 1962. Chairman of Council of Union of Supreme Soviet from April 26, 1962. First Secretary of Leningrad Province Party Committee, Dec. 25, 1957, to May 3, 1962.]

144. S[ergei] A[lexandrovich] STEPANOV.† [Chairman of Sverdlovsk Economic Council since 1957. Formerly Minister of Transport Machine Building.]

145. F[yodor] A[nisimovich] SURGANOV.† [Second Secretary of Belorussian Communist Party C.C. since April 10, 1959.]

146. M[ikhail] A[ndreyevich] SUSLOV. [Member of C.C.'s Presidium since July, 1955, and Secretary of C.C. since 1947.]

147. F[ikryat] A[khmedzhanovich] TABEYEV.* [First Secretary of Tatar Province Party Committee since 1961.]

148. V[italy] N[ikolayevich] TITOV. [Director of C.C.'s Department of Party Agencies for the Union Republics. Until March 1, 1961, First Secretary of Kharkov Province Party Committee.]

149. F[yodor] Ye[gorovich] TITOV. [Second Secretary of Uzbekistan Communist Party C.C. since Sept. 11, 1959. Previously First Secretary of Ivanovo Province Party Committee.]

150. V[asily] S[ergeyevich] TOLSTIKOV.* [First Secretary of Leningrad Province Party Committee since May 3, 1962. Formerly Second Secretary of Leningrad Province Party Committee.]

151. N[ikita] P[avlovich] TOLUBEYEV.* [First Secretary of Dnepropetrovsk Province Party Committee since May 25, 1961.]

152. D[mitry] F[yodorovich] USTINOV. [Vice-Chairman of Council of Ministers since Dec. 14, 1957. Formerly Minister of Defense Industry.]

153. T[urdakun] USUBALIYEV.* [First Secretary of Kirgiz Communist Party C.C. since May 10, 1961.]

154. P[yotr] N[ikolayevich] FEDOSEYEV.* [Director of Academy of Sciences' Philosophy Institute since 1955.]

155. V[italy] A[lexeyevich] FOKIN.* [Admiral. Commander of Pacific Fleet. Formerly Chief of Naval Staff and Deputy Commander-in-Chief of Navy.]

156. Ye[katerina] A[lexeyevna] FURTSEVA. [Minister of Culture since May 4, 1960. Until Oct. 31, 1961, member of C.C.'s Presidium, and until May 4, 1960, Secretary of C.C.]

157. N[ikita] S[ergeyevich] KHRUSHCHEV. [First Secretary of C.C. since September, 1953. Member of C.C.'s Presidium since March, 1939. Chairman of Council of Ministers since March 28, 1958. Chairman of C.C.'s Bureau for the Russian Republic since Feb. 28, 1956.]

158. S[tepan] V[asilyevich] CHERVONENKO.* [Ambassador to China since Oct. 14, 1959. Formerly Secretary of Ukraine Communist Party C.C.]

159. V[asily] Ye[fimovich] CHERNYSHEV. [First Secretary of Maritime Territory Party Committee since May 8, 1959.]

160. V[asily] I[vanovich] CHUIKOV.† [Marshal of the Soviet Union. First Deputy Minister of Defense and Commander-in-Chief of Ground Forces since April, 1960. Formerly Commander of Kiev Military District.]

161. V[iktor] M[ikhailovich] CHURAYEV.† [Member of C.C.'s Bureau for the Russian Republic since Oct. 31, 1961. Formerly Director of C.C.'s Department of Party Agencies for the Union Republics.]

162. N[ikolai] M[ikhailovich] SHVERNIK. [Member of C.C.'s Presidium since June 29, 1957. Chairman of Party Control Committee since Feb. 26, 1956.]

163. V[ladimir] V[asilyevich] SHEVCHENKO.* [First Secretary of Lugansk Province Party Committee since March 20, 1961.]

164. A[lexander] N[ikolayevich] SHELEPIN. [Secretary of C.C. since Oct. 31, 1961. From Dec. 25, 1958 to Nov. 13, 1961, Chairman of Committee on State Security.]

165. P[yotr] Ye[fimovich] SHELEST.* [First Secretary of Kiev Province Party Committee since Feb. 1, 1957.]

166. A[lexei] I[vanovich] SHIBAYEV.* [First Secretary of Saratov Province Party Committee since Dec. 29, 1959.]

167. A[lexei] P[avlovich] SHITIKOV.* [First Secretary of Khabarovsk Province Party Committee since Feb. 21, 1957.]

168. A[lexei] M[ikhailovich] SHKOLNIKOV. [First Secretary of Volgograd (Stalingrad) Province Party Committee since Nov. 26, 1960. Formerly First Secretary of Voronezh Province Party Committee.]

169. M[ikhail] A[lexandrovich] SHOLOKHOV.* [Writer. Member of Board of Writers' Union. Member of Academy of Sciences.]

170. V[iktor] A[lexandrovich] SHURYGIN.* [First Secretary of Orenburg Province Party Committee since Jan. 26, 1961.]

171. V[ladimir] V[asilyevich] SHCHERBITSKY.* [Chairman of Ukraine Republic Council of Ministers since Feb. 27, 1961. Candidate member of C.C.'s Presidium since Oct. 31, 1961. Formerly Secretary of Ukraine Communist Party C.C.]

172. S[emyon] N[ikolayevich] SHCHETININ.* [First Secretary of Irkutsk Province Party Committee since May 4, 1957.]

173. I[van] Kh[aritanovich] YUNAK.* [First Secretary of Tula Province Party Committee since July 17, 1961. Formerly Chairman of Dnepropetrovsk Province Executive Committee.]

174. I[van] I[gnatyevich] YAKUBOVSKY.* [Colonel General. Deputy Commander-in-Chief of Soviet Forces in East Germany. Formerly Commander-in-Chief of that command.]

175. M[ikhail] A[lexeyevich] YASNOV. [First Vice-Chairman of Russian Republic Council of Ministers since Dec. 18, 1957. Member of C.C.'s Bureau for the Russian Republic since Feb. 28, 1956.]

CANDIDATES (ALTERNATES)

1. M[alik] ABDURAZAKOV.* [First Secretary of Tashkent Province Party Committee since Feb. 15, 1961. Formerly Secretary of Uzbekistan Communist Party C.C.]

2. A[bdy] A[nnaliyevich] ANNALIYEV.* [Chairman of Turkmenian Republic Council of Ministers since June 13, 1960.]

3. A[lexei] K[onstantinovich] ANTONOV.* [Chairman of Leningrad Economic Council since June, 1961. Formerly its Vice-Chairman.]

4. V[asily] I[vanovich] ANTONOV.* [First Secretary of Astrakhan Province Party Committee since April 18, 1961. Formerly First Secretary of Karachai-Cherkess Province Party Committee.]

5. Sh[mavon] M[inasovich] ARUSHANYAN.* [Chairman of Armenian Republic Supreme Soviet Presidium since April 22, 1954.]

6. Ye[vgeny] I[vanovich] AFANASENKO.* [Russian Republic Minister of Education since March 28, 1956.]

7. P[avel] Ya[kovlevich] AFANASYEV.* [First Secretary of Magadan Province Party Committee since Feb. 13, 1958. Formerly Chairman of Magadan Province Executive Committee.]

8. V[ladimir] N[ikolayevich] BAZOVSKY.* [First Secretary of Novgorod Province Party Committee.]

9. V[iktor] G[eorgiyevich] BAKAYEV.* [Minister of Merchant Marine since Sept. 27, 1954.]

10. P[avel] F[yodorovich] BATITSKY.* [Colonel General. Commander of Antiaircraft Defense Forces of Moscow Military District since 1956.]

11. M[asymkhan] BEISEBAYEV.* [First Secretary of Alma-Ata Province Party Committee since Feb. 1, 1958.]

12. A[lexander] F[ilippovich] BORISOV.* [Chairman of Chelyabinsk Economic Council. Formerly Vice-Chairman of All-Russian Economic Council.]

13. S[emyon] Z[akharovich] BORISOV. [First Secretary of Yakut Province Party Committee since 1951.]

14. A[lexander] P[ankratovich] BOCHKAREV.* [Chairman of Saratov Province Executive Committee since 1956.]

15. K[onstantin] I[vanovich] BREKHOV.* [Chairman of Moscow Province Economic Council since 1959.]

16. N[ikita] D[mitriyevich] BUBNOVSKY. [Secretary of Ukraine Communist Party C.C. since March 26, 1954. Formerly First Secretary of Vinnitsa Province Party Committee.]

17. S[emyon] M[ikhailovich] BUDENNY. [Marshal of the Soviet Union. Member of Supreme Soviet Presidium.]

18. A[lexander] A[lexandrovich] BULGAKOV.* [Secretary of Central Council of Trade Unions since March 28, 1959.]

19. B[oris] Ye[vstafeyevich] BUTOMA.* [Chairman of State Shipbuilding Committee since Dec. 14, 1957.]

20. A[lexander] S[emyonovich] BUKHAROV.* [Vice-Chairman of Russian Republic Council of Ministers since July 6, 1960. Formerly Secretary of Moscow Province Party Committee.]

21. S[ergei] S[ergeyevich] VARENTSOV.* [Chief Marshal of Artillery. Commander of Artillery since 1955.]

22. A[lexei] F[edoseyevich] VATCHENKO.* [First Secretary of Khmelnitsky Province Party Committee since May 18, 1959.]

23. P. A. VORONINA.* [Second Secretary of Bauman Borough Party Committee, Moscow.]

24. M[ikhail] A[lexandrovich] GAVRILOV.* [Second Secretary of Kirgiz Communist Party C.C. since May 9, 1961.]

25. K[onstantin] M[ikhailovich] GERASIMOV.* [Vice-Chairman of Russian Republic Council of Ministers and Chairman of Russian Republic State Planning Commission since May, 1960.]

26. A[ndrei] L[avrentyevich] GETMAN.* [Colonel General. Commander of Carpathian Military District.]

27. N[ikolai] M[atveyevich] GRIBACHEV.* [Editor-in-Chief of Sovetsky Soyuz since 1950. Secretary of Board of Writers' Union.]

28. I[van] S[tepanovich] GUSTOV.* [First Secretary of Pskov Province Party Committee since April 19, 1961. Formerly its Second Secretary.]

29. G[eorgy] Ya[kovlevich] DENISOV.* [First Secretary of Murmansk Province Party Committee since 1957.]

30. A[lexander] F[ilippovich] DIORDITSA.* [Chairman of Moldavian Republic Council of Ministers since Jan. 23, 1958. Formerly its Vice-Chairman.]

31. Ye[vgenia] A[lexeyevna] DOLINYUK.* [Team leader on 22nd Party Congress Collective Farm, Melnitsa-Podolskaya District, Ternopol Province.]

32. A[natoly] S[emyonovich] DRYGIN.* [First Secretary of Vologda Province Party Committee since 1960. Formerly First Vice-Chairman of Leningrad Province Executive Committee.]

33. V[asily] S[emyonovich] YEMELYANOV.* [Present position unknown. Until Feb. 15, 1962, Chairman of State Atomic Energy Committee from its creation on June 3, 1960. Prior to that, Director of Chief Administration for Peaceful Uses of Atomic Energy.]

34. A[lexei] A[lexeyevich] YEPISHEV. [Ambassador to Yugoslavia since Nov. 27, 1960. Formerly Ambassador to Rumania from Aug. 13, 1955.]

35. A[ndrei] I[vanovich] YEREMENKO. [Marshal of the Soviet Union. Deputy Commander-in-Chief of Armed Forces of Warsaw Pact Countries. Formerly Commander of Northern Caucasus Military District.]

36. L[ev] B[orisovich] YERMIN.* [First Secretary of Penza Province Party Committee.]

37. V[ladimir] F[yodorovich] ZHIGALIN.* [Chairman of Moscow City Economic Council since January, 1960. Formerly its Vice-Chairman.]

38. M[arina] I. ZHURAVLEVA.* [Secretary of Young Communist League C.C. since March 24, 1959.]

39. M. Ye. ZAKHAROV.* [Lathe operator at Polotsk Plant, Vitebsk Province.]

40. G[rigory] S[ergeyevich] ZOLOTUKHIN. [First Secretary of Tambov Province Party Committee since 1956.]

41. V[asily] P[etrovich] ZOTOV. [Vice-Chairman of State Planning Committee since 1957. Formerly Minister of Food Products Industry.]

42. A[lexander] V[enediktovich] IVASHCHENKO.* [First Secretary of Nikolayev Province Party Committee.]

43. M[amed] A[bdul ogly] ISKENDEROV.* [Chairman of Azerbaidzhan Republic Supreme Soviet Presidium. Formerly Chairman of Azerbaidzhan Republic Council of Ministers.]

44. S[emyon] M[atveyevich] ISLYUKOV. [First Secretary of Chuvash Province Party Committee since 1957. Formerly Chairman of Chuvash Autonomous Republic Council of Ministers.]

45. A[lexander] A[kimovich] ISHKOV. [Director of State Planning Committee's Fishing Industry Department since 1957. Formerly Minister of Fishing Industry.]

46. M[ikhail] I[lyich] KAZAKOV.* [General of the Army. Commander of Leningrad Military District.]

47. I[van] A[ndreyevich] KAIROV.* [President of Russian Republic Academy of Pedagogy.]

48. S[tepan] V[lasovich] KALCHENKO.* [Chairman of Altai Territory Executive Committee since June 22, 1960. Formerly Russian Republic Minister of Agriculture.]

49. A[ndrei] A[ndreyevich] KANDRENKOV.* [First Secretary of Kaluga Province Party Committee since August, 1961. Formerly its Second Secretary.]

50. V[ladimir] A[lexeyevich] KARLOV.* [Director of C.C.'s Agriculture Department for the Union Republics. Until Sept. 29, 1960, First Secretary of Kalinin Province Party Committee.]

51. A[bdulakhad] KAKHAROV.* [Chairman of Tadzhik Republic Council of Ministers since April 16, 1961.]

52. V[ladimir] A[lexeyevich] KIRILLIN.* [Director of C.C.'s Department of Science, Higher Educational Institutions and Schools for the Union Republics since 1955.]

53. V[alter] I[vanovich] KLAUSON.* [Chairman of Estonian Republic Council of Ministers since October, 1961. Formerly its First Vice-Chairman from 1954.]

54. A. P. KLIMOV. [Chairman of Board of Central Union of Consumers' Cooperatives.]

55. I[van] G[rigoryevich] KOVAL.* [Second Secretary of Tadzhikistan Communist Party C.C. since April 15, 1961.]

56. P[avel] V[asilyevich] KOVANOV.* [Second Secretary of Georgian Communist Party C.C. since Sept. 8, 1956.]

57. N. F. KOZINETS.* [Position unknown.]

58. V[asily] I[vanovich] KOZLOV. [Chairman of Belorussian Supreme Soviet Presidium since 1948.]

59. P[avel] P[antelyevich] KOZYR.* [First Secretary of Vinnitsa Province Party Committee since September, 1955.]

60. F[yodor] S[tepanovich] KOLOMIYETS.* [Chairman of Krasnodar Territory Executive Committee. Formerly Secretary of Krasnodar Territory Party Committee.]

61. O[lga] P[avlovna] KOLCHINA. [Second Secretary of Moscow Province Party Committee since July 6, 1960.]

62. V[asily] I[vanovich] KONOTOP.* [Chairman of Moscow Province Executive Committee since March 10, 1959. Formerly Second Secretary of Moscow Province Party Committee from 1957.]

63. L[eonid] R[omanovich] KORNIYETS. [First Vice-Chairman of State Procurements Committee since Feb. 26, 1961. Formerly Chairman of State Grain Products Committee from November, 1958.]

64. A[lexei] K[irillovich] KORTUNOV.* [Director of Chief Gas Industry Administration since 1957.]

65. A[nton] Ye[rvandovich] KOCHINYAN.* [Chairman of Armenian Republic Council of Ministers since November, 1952.]

66. P[yotr] K[irillovich] KOSHEVOI.* [Colonel General. Commander of Kiev Military District.]

67. V[iktor] V[asilyevich] KROTOV.* [Director of Urals Heavy Machine-Building Plant.]

68. A[nton] S[avvich] KUZMICH.* [Chairman of Ukraine Economic Council since March 29, 1961. Formerly its First Vice-Chairman.]

69. P[avel] N[ikolayevich] KUMYKIN. [Deputy Minister of Foreign Trade since 1953.]

70. S[ergei] V[ladimirovich] KURASHOV.* [Minister of Health since Jan. 11, 1959. Formerly Russian Republic Minister of Health.]

71. M[ikhail] A[lexeyevich] LAVRENTYEV.* [Vice-President of Academy of Sciences and Chairman of its Siberian Division. Mathematician.]

72. P[avel] A[rtemovich] LEONOV.* [First Secretary of Sakhalin Province Party Committee.]

73. F[yodor] I[vanovich] LOSHCHENKOV.* [First Secretary of Yaroslavl Province Party Committee since June 17, 1961. Formerly First Secretary of Novosibirsk City Party Committee.]

74. L[ydia] P[avlovna] LYKOVA. [Second Secretary of Smolensk Province Party Committee. Formerly Second Secretary of Ivanovo Province Party Committee.]

75. I[van] K[ondratyevich] LUTAK.* [First Secretary of Crimea Province Party Committee since Jan. 6, 1961. Formerly Chairman of Cherkassy Province Executive Committee.]

76. T[imbora] K[ubatiyevich] MALBAKHOV.* [First Secretary of Kabardino-Balkar Province Party Committee since 1957.]

77. N[ikolai] Ya[kovlevich] MAMAI.* [Brigade leader at Sukhodol Mine No. 1, Krasnodon Coal Trust, Lugansk Province.]

78. B[olot] MAMBETOV.* [Chairman of Kirgiz Republic Council of Ministers since May 9, 1961. Formerly Kirgiz Republic Minister of Water Resources.]

79. I[van] T[ikhonovich] MARCHENKO.† [First Secretary of Tomsk Province Party Committee since 1960. Formerly Second Secretary of Moscow City Party Committee from 1954.]

80. P[yotr] M[ironovich] MASHEROV.* [Secretary of Belorussian Communist Party C.C. since April 9, 1959. Formerly First Secretary of Brest Province Party Committee from 1956.]

81. N[ikolai] A[fanasyevich] MELNIKOV.* [Second Secretary of Moldavian Communist Party C.C. since May 29, 1960.]

82. M[ikhail] A[lexeyevich] MENSHIKOV. [Russian Republic Minister of Foreign Affairs. Until Jan. 3, 1962, Ambassador to U.S.A.]

83. M[irzamakhamud] M[irzarakhmanovich] MUSAKHANOV.* [Secretary of Uzbekistan Communist Party C.C. since 1961. Formerly Secretary of Central Council of Trade Unions, and prior to that, Chairman of Uzbek Republic State Planning Commission.]

84. A[lexei] A[lexandrovich] MUURISEPP. [Chairman of Estonian Republic Supreme Soviet Presidium since Oct. 12, 1961. Formerly Chairman of Estonian Republic Council of Ministers from 1951.]

85. K[onstantin] K[uzmich] NIKOLAYEV.* [Chairman of Sverdlovsk Province Executive Committee since 1949.]

86. K[onstantin] A[lexandrovich] NOVIKOV.* [First Secretary of Archangel Province Party Committee since November, 1960. Formerly Chairman of Archangel Province Executive Committee.]

87. M[ikhail] A[lexandrovich] OLSHANSKY.* [Minister of Agriculture, Dec. 29, 1960 to April 26, 1962. President of Academy of Agricultural Sciences as of April 5, 1962.]

88. G[eorgy] M[ikhailovich] ORLOV. [Chairman of State Committee for Lumber, Pulp-and-Paper and Wood-Processing Industries and Forestry since Jan. 22, 1962. Formerly First Vice-Chairman of State Planning Committee.]

89. G[eorgy] I[vanovich] OSIPOV.* [First Secretary of Mordvinian Province Party Committee since 1958. Formerly First Secretary of Komi Province Party Committee.]

90. G[eorgy] S[ergeyevich] PAVLOV.* [First Secretary of Mari Province Party Committee since 1958.]

91. J[ustas] I[gnovich] PALECKIS. [Chairman of Lithuanian Republic Supreme Soviet Presidium since 1940.]

92. B[oris] Ye[vgenyevich] PATON.* [President of Ukraine Republic Academy of Sciences since Feb. 27, 1962. Prior to that, Director of Ukraine Republic Academy of Sciences' Ye. O. Paton Electric Welding Institute.]

93. J[an] V[oldemarovich] PEIVE.* [Chairman of Latvian Republic Council of Ministers, Nov. 26, 1959 to April 26, 1962. Formerly its First Vice-Chairman.]

94. V[alentin] A[ntonovich] PENKOVSKY.* [General of the Army. Commander of Belorussian Military District. Formerly Commander of Far Eastern Military District.]

95. B[oris] F[yodorovich] PETUKHOV.* [First Secretary of Kirov Province Party Committee. Formerly Chairman of Krasnodar Territory Executive Committee.]

96. M[ikhail] A[lexandrovich] PIMENOV.* [Second Secretary of Turkmenistan Communist Party C.C. since June 13, 1960.]

97. I[ssa] A[lexandrovich] PLIYEV.* [Colonel General.

Commander of Northern Caucasus Military District.]

98. M[ikhail] A[rsentyevich] POLEKHIN.* [Director of C.C.'s Department of Party Agencies for the Russian Republic. Formerly its Assistant Director.]

99. D[mitry] A[lexeyevich] POLIKARPOV.* [Director of C.C.'s Department of Culture since 1956.]

100. V[asily] I. POLYAKOV.* [Editor-in-Chief of Selskaya zhizn. Formerly Pravda's editor in charge of agricultural affairs.]

101. I[van] Ye[vteyevich] POLYAKOV.* [First Secretary of Gomel Province Party Committee since December, 1957. Formerly Chairman of Gomel Province Executive Committee.]

102. M[ikhail] A[lexandrovich] PONOMAREV.* [First Secretary of Vladimir Province Party Committee since Aug. 10, 1961. Formerly First Secretary of Kalmyk Province Party Committee.]

103. G[eorgy] I[vanovich] POPOV.* [First Secretary of Leningrad City Party Committee since Jan. 11, 1960. Formerly Second Secretary of Leningrad Province Party Committee.]

104. S[ergei] O[sipovich] POSTOVALOV. [Present position unknown. Until August 1961, First Secretary of Kaluga Province Party Committee.]

105. M[ikhail] M[oiseyevich] PRIVALOV.* [Senior foreman at Kuzmetsk Metallurgical Combine, Kemerovo Province.]

106. N[ikolai] D[emyanovich] PSURTSEV.* [Minister of Communications since 1948.]

107. S[ergei] T[imofeyevich] PUZIKOV.* [First Secretary of Lipetsk Province Party Committee since Nov. 21, 1960. Formerly Chairman of Rostov Province Executive Committee.]

108. G[eorgy] M[aximovich] PUSHKIN.* [Deputy Minister of Foreign Affairs since March 13, 1959. Formerly Ambassador to East Germany.]

109. N[ikolai] N[ikolayevich] RODIONOV.* [Second Secretary of Kazakhstan Communist Party C.C. since Jan. 20, 1960. Formerly First Secretary of Leningrad City Party Committee.]

110. K[onstantin] K[onstantinovich] ROKOSSOVSKY.* [Marshal of the Soviet Union. Deputy Minister of Defense.]

111. A[lexei] V[ladimirovich] ROMANOV.* [Member of C.C.'s Bureau for the Russian Republic. Formerly Assistant Director of C.C.'s Propaganda and Agitation Department for the Union Republics.]

112. A[lexander] P[etrovich] RUDAKOV. [Director of C.C.'s Heavy Industry Department since 1957.]

113. S[ergei] I[gnatyevich] RUDENKO.* [Marshal of Aviation. Chief of General Staff and First Deputy Commander-in-Chief of Air Force.]

114. Ye[vgeny] Ya[kovlevich] SAVITSKY.* [Marshal of Aviation. Deputy Commander-in-Chief of Air Force.]

115. V[adim] A[rkadyevich] SAYUSHEV.* [Secretary of Young Communist League C.C. Formerly First Secretary of Leningrad Province Y.C.L. Committee.]

116. V[alentin] A[lexandrovich] SEMENOV.* [Director of Volgograd Tractor Plant.]

117. I[van] M[ikhailovich] SEMENOV.* [Chairman of New Life Collective Farm, Shchekino District, Tula Province.]

118. N[ikolai] N[ikolayevich] SEMENOV.* [Chairman of Board of All-Union Society for the Dissemination of Political and Scientific Knowledge since Jan. 28, 1960. Director of Academy of Science's Physical Chemistry Institute.]

119. V[ladimir] Ye[fimovich] SEMICHASTNY. [Chairman of State Security Committee since Nov. 13, 1961. Formerly Second Secretary of Azerbaidzhan Communist Party C.C. from Aug. 11, 1959. Prior to that, Director of C.C.'s Department of Party Agencies for the Union Republics from April, 1959. Previously First Secretary of Young Communist League C.C.]

120. I. D. SERBIN.* [Director of a department of C.C.]

121. G[ennady] F[yodorovich] SIZOV. [First Secretary of Kurgan Province Party Committee since 1955.]

122. S[emyon] A[ndreyevich] SKACHKOV.* [Chairman of State Committee on Foreign Economic Relations since Feb. 20, 1958. Formerly Chairman of Kharkov Economic Council.]

123. A[natoly] A[ndryanovich] SKOCHILOV.* [First Secretary of Ulyanovsk Province Party Committee since Aug. 7, 1961. Formerly Secretary of Tatar Province Party Committee.]

124. I[gor] P[etrovich] SKULKOV. [First Secretary of Udmurt Province Party Committee since 1959. Formerly Chairman of Russian Republic Soviet Control Commission.]

125. A[lexander] I[vanovich] SMIRNOV.* [First Secretary of Chita Province Party Committee. Formerly Chairman of Chita Province Executive Committee.]

126. V[asily] A. SMIRNOV.* [Assembly worker at Sergo Ordzhonikidze Baltic Shipyard, Leningrad.]

127. N[ikolai] I[vanovich] SMIRNOV.* [Vice-Chairman of State Planning Committee since 1961. Formerly Chairman of Leningrad Province Executive Committee from 1957.]

128. N[ikolai] I[vanovich] SMIRNOV. [Chairman of Leningrad City Executive Committee since 1954.]

129. V[asily] D[anilovich] SOKOLOVSKY.† [Marshal of the Soviet Union. Formerly Chief of General Staff of Army and Navy.]

130. V[ladimir] P[etrovich] SOTNIKOV.* [Russian Republic Minister of Agriculture since Feb. 2, 1961. Formerly Chief Scientific Secretary of Academy of Agricultural Sciences.]

131. V. P. STEPANOV.* [Editor-in-Chief of Kommunist. Formerly Assistant Editor-in-Chief of Pravda.]

132. N[ikolai] I[vanovich] STROKIN. [Vice-Chairman of State Planning Committee since 1957.]

133. A[lexander] I[vanovich] STRUYEV.† [Vice-Chairman of the Russian Republic Council of Ministers since May 29, 1958.]

134. A[ndrei] T[rofimovich] STUCHENKO.* [Colonel General. Commander of Transcaucasian Military District. Formerly Commander of Northern Group of Forces.]

135. V[ladimir] A[lexandrovich] SUDETS.* [Marshal of Aviation. Commander of Strategic Air Force.]

136. A[lexei] A[lexandrovich] SURKOV. [Secretary of Board of Writers' Union since May 25, 1959. Formerly its First Secretary. Member of Presidium of Soviet Committee for Defense of Peace.]

137. A[lexander] M[ikhailovich] TARASOV.* [Chairman of Belorussian Economic Council since Sept. 12, 1958. Formerly Director of Minsk Tractor Plant.]

138. A[lexander] T[rifonovich] TVARDOVSKY.* [Poet. Editor-in-Chief of Novy mir since 1958. Secretary of Board of Writers' Union.]

139. V[adim] S. TIKUNOV.* [Russian Republic Minister of Internal Affairs since July 26, 1961. Formerly Vice-Chairman of State Security Committee.]

140. S[emyon] K[onstantinovich] TIMOSHENKO. [Marshal of the Soviet Union. Chairman of Presidium of Soviet Committee of War Veterans. Formerly Commander of Belorussian Military District.]

141. N[ikolai] A[lexandrovich] TIKHONOV.* [Vice-Chairman of State Scientific-Economic Council.]

142. S[alchak] K[albakhorekovich] TOKA. [First Secretary of Tuva Province Party Committee since 1946.]

143. V[iktor] S[tepanovich] FEDOROV.* [Chairman of State Chemistry Committee since Sept. 19, 1958. Formerly Chairman of Bashkir Economic Council.]

144. V[asily] R[odionovich] FILIPPOV.* [First Secretary of Buryat Province Party Committee since 1960. Formerly Chairman of Buryat Autonomous Republic Council of Ministers.]

145. N[ikolai] P[avlovich] FIRYUBIN. [Deputy Minister of Foreign Affairs since Sept. 29, 1957. Formerly Ambassador to Yugoslavia.]

146. L[eonid] Ya[kovlevich] FLORENTYEV. [First Secretary of Kostroma Province Party Committee since 1956.]

147. G[eorgy] P. FRANTSOV.* [Rector of Academy of Social Sciences under C. C. Chairman of Soviet Sociological Association. Vice-Chairman of All-Union Society for the Dissemination of Political and Scientific Knowledge.]

148. V. S. FROLOV.* [Director of C.C.'s Machine-Building Department.]

149. S[tepan] D[mitriyevich] KHITROV.* [First Secretary of Voronezh Province Party Committee since Nov. 26, 1960.]

150. N[ormakhonmadi] D[zurayevich] KHUDAIBERDIYEV.* [First Secretary of Surkhan-Darya Province Party Committee since 1961. Formerly Vice-Chairman of Uzbek Republic Council of Ministers.]

151. A[ndrei] T[rofimovich] CHABANENKO.* [Admiral. Commander of Northern Fleet.]

152. A[lexander] I[vanovich] SHOKIN.* [Chairman of State Electronics Committee since March 17, 1961. Formerly First Vice-Chairman of State Radioelectronics Committee.]

153. M[otejus] J[uozovich] SUMAUSKAS. [Chairman of Lithuanian Republic Council of Ministers since Jan. 15, 1956. Formerly Second Secretary of Lithuanian Communist Party C.C.]

154. B[oris] Ye[vdokimovich] SHCHERBINA.* [First Secretary of Tyumen Province Party Committee since May 6, 1961. Formerly Second Secretary of Irkutsk Province Party Committee.]

155. I[smail] YUSUPOV.* [Secretary of Kazakhstan Communist Party C.C. since Oct. 26, 1959. Formerly First Secretary of South Kazakhstan Province Party Committee.]

Central Inspection Commission

COMPOSITION OF THE C.P.S.U. CENTRAL INSPECTION COMMISSION ELECTED BY THE 22ND PARTY CONGRESS. (Pravda and Izvestia, Nov. 1, p. 2. Complete text, in Russian alphabetical order:)

1. A. A. Abdrazyakov	34. V. Ye. Lobanok
2. V. P. Abyzov	35. V. N. Malin
3. O. M. Bagdasaryan	36. N. V. Martynov
4. N. Bairamov	37. N. R. Mironov
5. S. A. Baskakov	38. Z. V. Mironova
6. A. P. Boikova	39. P. I. Morozov
7. Ye. I. Bugayev	40. V. P. Moskovsky
8. G. Ye. Burkatskaya	41. N. A. Muravyeva
9. S. A. Vinogradov	42. M. A. Orlov
10. I. M. Vladychenko	43. A. S. Panyushkin
11. A. F. Gorkin	44. I. S. Pankin
12. B. B. Gorodovikov	45. P. F. Pigalev
13. D. P. Goryunov	46. V. A. Podzerko
14. M. P. Gribkov	47. B. V. Popov
15. R. F. Dementyeva	48. A. A. Prokofyev
16. S. M. Dzhafarov	49. V. F. Promyslov
17. G. S. Dzotsenidze	50. M. Rakhmatov
18. A. G. Dmitrin	51. V. S. Semenov
19. V. I. Drozdenko	52. I. I. Senkin
20. A. G. Yegorov	53. V. A. Serov
21. P. M. Yelistratov	54. N. S. Skripko
22. G. A. Zhukov	55. V. I. Smirnov
23. F. Z. Zagafuranov	56. V. I. Snastin
24. M. V. Zimyanin	57. A. A. Soldatov
25. B. Ye. Kabaloyev	58. V. N. Starovsky
26. Ya. I. Kabkov	59. V. I. Stepakov
27. I. S. Koditsa	60. A. S. Trofimov
28. G. I. Kozlov	61. T. N. Khrennikov
29. V. A. Kochetov	62. Ye. T. Cherednichenko
30. S. A. Krasovsky	63. I. Sharipov
31. Ya. G. Kreizer	64. I. V. Shikin
32. T. Kulatov	65. G. T. Shuisky
33. M. V. Kulikova	

IN THE CENTRAL INSPECTION COMMISSION OF THE COMMUNIST PARTY OF THE SOVIET UNION. (Pravda and Izvestia, Nov. 1, p. 2. Complete text:) A meeting of the Central Inspection Commission of the Communist Party of the Soviet Union was held Oct. 31, 1961.

The Central Inspection Commission elected Comrade N. A. Muravyeva Chairman of the Commission.

Presidium and Secretariat

COMMUNIQUE ON PLENARY SESSION OF THE CENTRAL COMMITTEE OF THE COMMUNIST PARTY OF THE SOVIET UNION. (Pravda and Izvestia, Nov. 1, p. 2. Complete text:) A plenary session of the Party Central Committee, elected by the 22nd Party Congress, was held Oct. 31, 1961.

The plenary session elected the Presidium of the C.P.S.U. Central Committee as follows:

Members of the Presidium: Comrades L. I. Brezhnev, G. I. Voronov, F. R. Kozlov, A. N. Kosygin, O. V. Kuusinen, A. I. Mikoyan, N. V. Podgorny, D. S. Polyansky, M. A. Suslov, N. S. Khrushchev and N. M. Shvernik.

Candidates for membership in the Presidium: Comrades V. V. Grishin, Sh. R. Rashidov, K. T. Mazurov, V. P. Mzhavanadze and V. V. Shcherbitsky.

The plenary session elected the Secretariat of the C.P.S.U. Central Committee as follows: Comrades N. S. Khrushchev, First Secretary of the Party Central Committee, F. R. Kozlov, P. N. Demichev, L. F. Ilyichev, O. V. Kuusinen, B. N. Ponomarev, I. V. Spiridonov, M. A. Suslov and A. N. Shelepin.

The plenary session elected Comrade N. M. Shvernik Chairman of the Party Central Committee's Party Control Committee and Comrade Z. T. Serdyuk First Vice-Chairman of the Party Control Committee.

Bureau for the Russian Republic

PARTY CENTRAL COMMITTEE'S BUREAU FOR THE RUSSIAN REPUBLIC. (Pravda and Izvestia, Nov. 1, p. 2. Complete text:) The Presidium of the Party Central Committee approved the Party Central Committee's Bureau for the Russian Republic as follows:

Comrade N. S. Khrushchev—Chairman.

Comrade G. I. Voronov—First Vice-Chairman; Comrade P. F. Lomako—Vice-Chairman.

Members of the Bureau: Comrades G. G. Abramov, L. N. Yefremov, A. P. Kirilenko, N. N. Organov, D. S. Polyansky, A. V. Romanov, V. M. Churayev and M. A. Yasnov.

XIV. KHRUSHCHEV: SPEECH AT THE CLOSING

SPEECH BY COMRADE N. S. KHRUSHCHEV AT CLOSING OF 22ND PARTY CONGRESS. (Pravda and Izvestia, Nov. 1, p. 1. Complete text:) Dear comrades! The work of the 22nd Congress is finished. We have come to the end of the agenda. The Congress has adopted a resolution on the report of the Central Committee, has adopted the new Party Program and Party Statutes, has approved the report of the Party's Central Inspection Commission and has elected the executive bodies of the Party.

It can be said with full justification that the 22nd Congress marks a major stage in the life of our party and the country, in the struggle for the triumph of communism. (Stormy applause.)

The path to be followed in the struggle to build a communist society was scientifically charted by the great teachers of the working class Marx, Engels and Lenin. Our immortal leader Vladimir Ilyich Lenin created the revolutionary party of Bolsheviks, which led the working class, the working people to the victory of the Great October Socialist Revolution. After October our party assumed the name Communist. This meant that its goal was the building of communism. The Communists, all working people, had firm faith in Lenin, in the Party. But to many people then communism seemed a dream, attractive, desirable, but very distant.

Since then we have traveled a very long road. The Soviet people have built socialism, have carried out majestic transformations in the country's economic, political and state life, and have set out on the high road of communist construction.

In adopting the new Program, the 22nd Congress has proclaimed before all mankind that the peoples of the Soviet Union, led by the Communist Party and guided by the teachings of Marxism-Leninism, carry high the banner of struggle for the building of a communist society in our country. The building of a communist society has become a practical task of the Party and the people. (Applause.)

The establishment of communism requires a firm material base and an abundance of material and spiritual goods. This cannot be achieved through incantations and appeals. Communism can be built by labor, labor and only by the labor of millions. (Prolonged applause.)

Comrades! The Congress has received tens of thousands of telegrams and letters with warm greetings and wishes for fruitful work by the Party Congress. More than 10,000 reports have been received from workers' collectives, collective farmers, state farm workers and workers in science, culture and the arts on the fulfillment of pledges assumed in honor of the 22nd Party Congress.

Permit me, in the name of the delegates to the Congress, to express heartfelt gratitude to all the collectives and all the comrades who have sent their greetings to the 22nd Congress and to wish them new and great successes in labor. (Stormy applause.)

In the name of the delegates to the Congress, in the name of our party and the Soviet people, permit me to express once more warm gratitude to the fraternal Marxist-Leninist parties for their participation in the work of the Congress and for their kind wishes. (Prolonged applause.) We assure our friends that the Leninist Party will continue to carry high the banner of communism, the banner of proletarian internationalism. (Prolonged applause.)

We cordially thank the representatives of the democratic national parties of the independent states of Africa for their warm greetings to our Congress. (Stormy applause.) We support and we shall continue to support the struggle of peoples for their freedom and independence, against colonial slavery. (Stormy applause.)

We shall strengthen friendship among all peoples, undeviatingly apply the Leninist principle of peaceful coexistence, fight for peace throughout the world. (Stormy applause.)

Armed with the new Program, our people will rally still more closely around the Party, under the banner of Marxism-Leninism. (Stormy, prolonged applause.)

Our goals are clear, the tasks are set.

To work, comrades! For new victories of communism! (Stormy, prolonged applause, turning into an ovation. All rise.)

***

Permit me to declare the 22nd Congress of the Communist Party of the Soviet Union closed.

(Stormy ovation. The delegates to the Congress and the guests sing the Party hymn "The International" with enormous enthusiasm. After the singing of the hymn, the ovation breaks out with renewed vigor and lasts several minutes. From all corners of the hall are heard congratulatory shouts: "Hurrah for the 22nd Party Congress!"—"Hurrah for the Leninist party!"—"Glory to the Leninist party!" "Hail to the Leninist Party Program! Hurrah!" "Hurrah for the fraternal Marxist-Leninist parties!" "Hurrah for the socialist camp!" "Hail to the Leninist Central Committee! Hurrah!" "Hurrah for the Soviet people!" "Viva Cuba!" The hall resounds: "Leninism-Communism!" "Leninism—Communism. Hurrah!" "Friendship of peoples!" "Friendship of peoples!" "Peace!" "Hurrah!"

(Comrade Khrushchev proclaims: "Hurrah for the fraternal Marxist-Leninist parties!" Again ovations thunder out and congratulatory shouts are heard in honor of the international Communist and workers' movement and in honor of Marxism-Leninism.

("Long live the peoples fighting for their freedom and independence, against the oppression of colonialism and imperialism! Hurrah!" Thousands of delegates and guests to the Congress warmly welcome the representatives of the peoples of Asia, Africa and Latin America who are fighting for their freedom and independence.

(The foreign guests offer toasts in honor of the Soviet Union, in honor of the great party of Lenin; in honor of the unity and brotherhood of peoples in their struggle for peace and a bright future.

(It was a powerful and stirring demonstration of the unity and solidarity of the great Leninist Party, of its readiness to put into effect its new Program, the program of building communism.)

INDEX